# The Great Ideas

Detail of *Triumph of St. Thomas Aquinas,* fresco by Andrea da Firenze.
In the Spanish Chapel of Santa Maria Novella, Florence.

# The Great Ideas Today

# 1974

*Encyclopædia Britannica, Inc.*

Chicago • London • Toronto • Geneva • Sydney • Tokyo • Manila • Johannesburg • Seoul

# The Great Ideas Today 1974

Printed in the U.S.A. Library of Congress Catalog Number: 61-65561
International Standard Book Number: 0-85229-299-6

*Distributed to the trade by* Praeger Publishers, Inc., New York, Washington

# Contents

# A NOTE ON REFERENCE STYLE

In the following pages, passages in *Great Books of the Western World* are referred to by the initials '*GBWW*,' followed by volume, page number, and page section. Thus, '*GBWW*, Vol. 39, p. 210b' refers to page 210 in Adam Smith's *The Wealth of Nations*, which is Volume 39 in *Great Books of the Western World*. The small letter 'b' indicates the page section. In books printed in single column, 'a' and 'b' refer to the upper and lower halves of the page. In books printed in double column, 'a' and 'b' refer to the upper and lower halves of the left column, 'c' and 'd' to the upper and lower halves of the right column. For example, 'Vol. 53, p. 210b' refers to the lower half of page 210, since Volume 53, James's *Principles of Psychology,* is printed in single column. On the other hand, 'Vol. 7, p. 210b' refers to the lower left quarter of the page, since Volume 7, Plato's *Dialogues,* is printed in double column.

*Gateway to the Great Books* is referred to by the initials '*GGB*,' followed by volume and page number. Thus, '*GGB*, Vol. 10, pp. 39-57' refers to pages 39 through 57 of Volume 10 of *Gateway to the Great Books,* which is James's essay, "The Will to Believe."

*The Great Ideas Today* is referred to by the initials '*GIT*,' followed by the year and page number. Thus '*GIT* 1968, p. 510' refers to page 510 of the 1968 edition of *The Great Ideas Today*.

# PART ONE

# A Symposium
# on Tradition

# Introduction

In 1970 *The Great Ideas Today* held a symposium on the idea of revolution, it being thought that, as this idea had at the time gained fresh currency and power in human affairs, there was reason to examine it to see how well we understood it. This year we take up the idea of tradition, not because it too has gained currency and power, but because it has not—because, on the contrary, as the idea of revolution has waxed in importance, the idea of tradition seems to have waned, to have grown dim, as if the thing it represented were enfeebled and might disappear or otherwise be lost from human life.

Of course it cannot be lost, and will not disappear. In a passage in the *Physics* that is often quoted by Aquinas, Aristotle remarks that man is begotten of both man and the sun.* We can take this to mean that, if we wish to understand what man is, we must look to his own work as well as to the work of nature. The work of nature is a matter of heredity, transmitted by our genetic endowment. The work of man is a matter of culture and comes to us in, and through, tradition. It provides us with, among other things, the language we use, the alphabet in which we write, the number system with which we count, the written record of what men have learned, unwritten customs and practices, the forms with which we exchange greetings and farewells, the food we eat and the times at which we eat it, the games we play, and the prayers and rituals with which we worship. Implicit, unstated, most of this is, like our genetic makeup, simply part of what we are. We could not do without it if we wanted to, and in most cases we do not want to.

There are, however, certain human activities, such as the arts, sciences, and learned professions, in which the role or influence of tradition, if not simply a matter of choice, yet is explicit, formalized, and subject to a measure of control beyond what is possible in daily life. In such activities, the extent to which we allow the past to be preserved indicates the degree to which we approve of it and wish it to survive. It could therefore be significant if changes of method or attitude had occurred in these activities—changes that might suggest that "tradition," or "the tradition," or "the idea of tradition" had indeed suffered a decline or was at least peculiarly vulnerable in our time. Hence the editors of *The Great Ideas Today* thought it worthwhile to arrange a discussion of the ways in which the various disciplines and professions make use of their pasts, to note the differences among them in this respect, and to see if such changes were reported.

As sometimes happens on such occasions, the results are inconclusive. On the one hand, it is clear that in certain interesting and important respects these learned activities *have* changed recently, and can no longer regard themselves as they used to do or entertain the same expectations. On the other hand, it is not maintained that we are on the threshold of a dramatic (if temporary) eclipse of tradition such as occurred with the advent of the Romantic movement at the end of the eighteenth century, or a revival of the idea, suggested by the influence of such a figure as T. S. Eliot, which may be said to have occurred, more briefly and with slighter effect, in the twentieth.

The contributors to the symposium are Yves Congar, who speaks for theology, and in particular of Catholic theology; Harry Kalven, Jr., who represents the law; Frank Kermode, who was responsible for the arts; Theodosius Dobzhansky, who writes as a scientist of science; and J. H. Plumb, who was asked to say something about the special interest in tradition—that is to say, in the part of the past that somehow remains present —that any historian inevitably has.

---

* *Physics* 2. 2. 194b.

# Tradition in Theology

## Yves Congar

It is an indication of the stature of Yves Congar among contemporary theologians that, closely identified as he has been with the ecumenical movement that culminated in the Second Vatican Council, and an advocate as he is of the "openness" of the Church in the modern world, he also seemed the best person to whom the editors of *The Great Ideas Today* could apply for an account of religious tradition (his account is only and specifically of Catholic tradition) as part of this symposium. Such a choice was dictated in part by the fact that Father Congar has written an important book on the subject, translated into English as *Tradition and Traditions* (1966), among numerous other works of great erudition and wide influence that he has published. He is the author also of *A History of Theology* and other writings intended for a larger audience.

Born in Sedan, France, in 1904, Father Congar was educated at the Institut Catholique in Paris from 1921 to 1924, and was ordained a priest of the Dominican Order in 1930. From 1931 to 1954 he was professor of fundamental theology and ecclesiology at the Dominican House of Studies, Le Saulchoir. He lives and writes now at the Dominican Convent Monastery of Saint Jacques, Paris.

Every science puts its questions in terms of the latest that has been achieved. For science, truth, or at least a greater truth, lies ahead, not behind. The case of Galileo provides an eloquent example of this. But scientists can make new discoveries only by starting from what they have received. To willingly ignore or suppress the past would amount to cutting off the branch on which one is seated. As the Polish philosopher Leszek Kolakowski declared at a recent "International Meeting of Geneva," to do so would destroy the very possibility of the future. In short, we are inheritors.

Among the sciences, theology occupies a special position. It is, in fact, the scientific cultivation of faith, the form that faith takes within a reason based on philosophy, philology, and history, the means by which the believer uses the resources of his culture and his reason to understand his faith, to interpret it, to organize it intellectually, and put it into dialogue with the questions that the world is facing. Faith addresses itself to that which is called Revelation, that is, to the sequence of facts and words attested by the Scriptures, in which God has taken the initiative within the history of the world to draw man to communion with him in his covenant of grace. Christianity is a historical religion, a religion that has been "instituted," in a theological sense, which is not exactly the sense given that term by Joachim Wach, author of *The Sociology of Religion* and other works. It has proposed to us a belief that certain facts once occurred that offered a definitive covenant destined for all men. There was *one* Abraham, *one* exodus from Egypt, *one* Moses, *one* covenant on Sinai, *one* history of the Jewish people with its prophets and psalms. There was *one* John the Baptist, *one* Mary of Nazareth, *one* Jesus Christ, God-with-us. There was *one* confession of Peter, *one* Last Supper, *one* Resurrection, *one* Pentecost. All this, along with other facts and words, constitutes "the faith which has been once and for all entrusted to the saints,"[1] of which *The Letter of Jude* speaks.

It can be said of every man that he is an inheritor and of every scientist that he has predecessors. But this is true in a stricter and more specific sense of the Christian, because of his faith, and hence of theology, which is the scientific state of the faith. The theologian does not have to discover his data; he receives it from tradition, that is, by transmission. He enters into a

---

Translated from the French by Otto Bird.

series that has at its origin a moment that must be called *constituent* or *instituting,* as distinguished from the series itself, which is *constituted* or *instituted.*

Such being the statute of Christianity and of theology, one cannot subscribe purely and simply to the statement of the biologist Jean Rostand:

> *I am unable to accept a "revelation" claiming to have been made to our ancestors in the far past of our history. This kind of tradition may be respected and may have had a large role in our moral past, but I cannot agree to accept it as a certitude from which to begin. As I see it, the only valid beliefs are those that are repeatable at any time by the intelligence so that they can be formed de novo in the mind of a man today, starting afresh from materials furnished by science or by free reflection. . . . It is impossible for me to believe in a Truth that is behind us. The only truth I believe is one that is discovered slowly, gradually, painfully, and that imperceptibly grows each day.*[2]

We would agree with this text so far as it concerns scientific truths offered to the investigation and even to the discovery of reason. But not so far as it concerns truths of faith that have issued from the initiative and revelation of God. Of course, to refuse it or find it impossible to believe are attitudes that are possible. We respect them without sharing them. The believer, hence too the theologian, receives from tradition (by transmission) the faith that he professes, the Eucharist that he celebrates, the structure of the church to which he belongs.

Nevertheless, even for the theologian, there is some truth in what Rostand says. For although he receives his faith and the plan of his life from the initiative of a revelation made in the past, the theologian is seeking a truth that, in a certain sense, still remains to be found today and tomorrow. And this is so because of the very nature of tradition. This does not consist in a purely material repetition of the same thing, on the ground that it requires a reception. Transmission and reception are two moments of one and the same process. A completely mechanical transmission, a purely material repetition, would ruin the reality of the transmission; if nothing were truly received, nothing would be truly transmitted.

The history of the missions provides a striking illustration of this. When Constantine-Cyril and his brother Methodius undertook the evangelization of the Slavs of Moravia, they encountered adversaries who refused to allow the use of the Slavic tongue on the ground of the pseudoprinciple that there were only three sacred languages, Hebrew, Greek, and Latin. This incident shows how a completely material "tradition"—material in the sense of being limited to certain languages—would have been contrary to the real transmission of the Eucharist, as if this could not be suitably received in any other tongue. Fortunately, Pope John VIII approved the use of Slavic, first for preaching and then even for the celebration of the sacred mysteries (879–880). From that day to the present, the same history has been repeated in every missionary situation. Serious studies have shown that catechetical instruction imported as such from Europe to black Africa without any creative innovation runs the risk of transmitting nothing at all. So with other cultural and historical situations. The introduction of confessionals in the churches in the sixteenth century led to a renewal in the practice of the sacrament of penance; today it seems that confessionals have become an obstacle, and something different must be found.

Tradition contains as an essential note a reference to its origin: it transmits something without creating freely and de novo, as Rostand says. It is a communication. In Roman Law, *tradere, traditio* signified the intention, from one side, of transferring an object, and, from the other side, that of acquiring it. For example, one would hand over a field or a house by exchanging symbolically a clod of earth or a key. These are cases that involve material goods. But in the case of spiritual goods, the one who transmits does so by communicating his wealth without alienating or losing it. Thus a teacher transmits his knowledge by enabling the student to share in what he gives him, without thereby losing it himself. This is still more true in the case of Christianity. For Christianity is precisely a communion, and a communion with a universal vocation, in the gift made once for all that was described above. The unity, catholicity, and sanctity of the church are "apostolic." Thus the apostle John could write:

> *Something which has existed since the beginning, that we have heard, and we have seen with our own eyes; that we have watched and touched with our hands: the Word, who is life—this is our subject. That life was made visible: we saw it and we are giving our testimony, telling you of the eternal life which was with the Father and has been made visible to us. What we have seen and heard we are telling you so that you too may be in union with us, as we are in union with the Father and with his Son Jesus Christ.*[3]

That is a reality, unique and identical, of the faith that must be shared by a multitude across space and time. Hence, the importance of a faithful transmission, without alteration, and of the note of apostolicity.

But the faith must be communicated and received across space and time. There it meets a variety of men and of cultures, a perpetual renewal of questions, a succession of human creations of which the mind is so fertile. The Church of the *constituting* period could indeed fix the faith of the Church of the *constituted* period, that is, of the history of the people of God for however long it should last. But its task was not that of merely repeating a lesson. If no more than that had been done, the Scriptures would not have been translated, as they have been, until they exist today in more than three thousand languages. For that, the message had to be understood in the spoken language, where *language* designates not only a vocabulary and a syntax but also the expression of a culture, of a certain historical situation with its own questions and its own answers. Much is made today of hermeneutics, and, doubtless, there is sometimes the danger that personal problems tend to replace the message. Yet

Each church has its own unique ceremonies for "the celebration of the sacred mysteries." First Communion in a Roman Catholic church gives substance to the idea that "Christianity is precisely a communion, and a communion with a universal vocation . . . the believer . . . receives from tradition . . . the faith that he professes."

hermeneutics fulfills a necessary function: not only that of understanding the text exegetically, namely of what Paul, Luke, or John meant, but also that of rereading it personally so as to apply it to our lives and to the questions that are asked today. John did not foresee Arius, and yet he had to reply to him by the hermeneutics of Athanasius. Paul did not foresee Pelagius, and yet he had to respond to him by the intelligence of Augustine. Neither Paul nor John foresaw Marx, nor with them did Luke foresee Freud, nor did Matthew foresee the problems of war and of economic development. It remains for us to obtain from these original witnesses a word that is faithful to them at the same time that it applies to what is always being put forward, unforeseeably, by history, since that is the cloth the word (in this sense) is made of.

In brief, faith and the Church have been constituted, but they must always assure their fidelity by creating new expressions and new forms of that which makes their identity. The preservation of this identity calls for much more than its material repetition. What is required is a criticism of forms that have become obsolete and the creation of new responses.

The gift God made to his people, making them his people in the history of the world, did not cease with the gift of his word (*parole*). It includes the gift of his Spirit after the Incarnation of the Word (*Verbe*), the communication of his Spirit at Pentecost as a consequence of Easter. The Word (*Verbe*) is the precise form of the word (*parole*), which unrolls in the history (including the thought) of Israel from Abraham to Jesus. Through this history, which is significant as such, even in its most human aspects, the word (*parole*) established and disclosed the structure of the religious relation of covenant. The Word (*Verbe*) of God, become man in Jesus, renewed this relation and gave it a structure conforming to a new and definitive covenant: the revelation of the Father and of the appeal to us to become children of God, baptism, Eucharist, the mission of the Twelve. The Word is a form and a certain defined structure, although in the Gospel it is so only in a very large way. The Spirit is breath, impulsion, life. There seems to be a constant in the action of God, who first constructs according to a certain form or structure, and then gives animation and movement.[4]

The Spirit was given to the primitive institution of the Apostolate to teach, to recall, to actualize all that Jesus had said (John 14 : 26), to "lead you to the complete truth. . . and tell you of the things to come" (John 16 : 13). Thus the Spirit ceaselessly carries forward into history what the Word (*Verbe*) has revealed or posited once and for all. It is characterized as having been "spoken by the prophets." This means that it assures at once both what was delivered once for all and the identity of that which is transmitted and that lives in history. Technically, it is said to be the transcendent subject of tradition, always active in advance in the unknown of history. It is also said that the Church is constructed on an apostolic foundation that is at the same time prophetic.[5] The martyr Polycarp, bishop of Smyrna in 156, is called "the apostolic and prophetic doctor," which ex-

Above, a circumcision ceremony in Tanzania; facing page, a baptism. *"A reality, unique and identical, of the faith . . . must be shared by a multitude across space and time. Hence, the importance of a faithful transmission, without alteration, and of the note of apostolicity. . . . What we have called 'the traditions' belong . . . to the practical order: customs, local rites, devotions, particular forms of discipline and observance."*

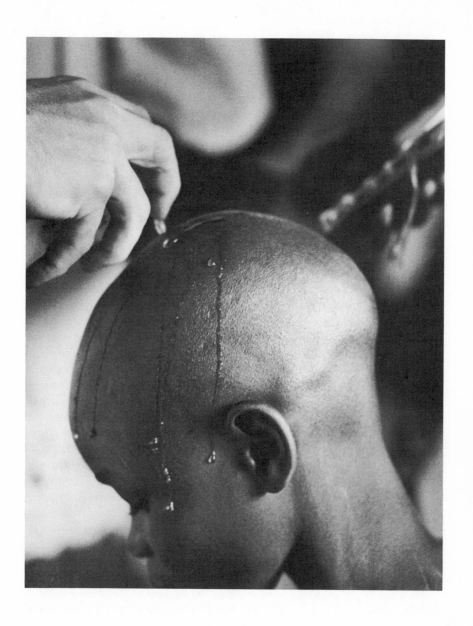

presses his character as both a faithful witness or bearer of the tradition completely posited at one time and as a summons to the mission of the time in which he lived.[6]

We have spoken of "history"; with that term, a second sense of "tradition" has begun to appear. Tradition is not simply the transmission of what has been given once and for all in the constituent moment; it is also that which develops in history through the use of new resources in response to new questions and as a result of reception in new historicocultural conditions. In theological terminology it is said that an ecclesiastical tradition is one that carries on the apostolic tradition. In fact, the two must be distinguished, as they long have been. Yet they must not be separated. For the apostolic tradition reaches us only as borne by the Church, and as read and understood in the Church, and the ecclesiastical tradition is only a deployment of that which has been received from the apostles. But whereas the apostles had the benefit of the charisms of founders and a grace of inspiration and of revelation, the Church for its historical life has only an "assistance" of the Spirit, which does not have the same guarantees.

Given the facts with which we are concerned, how have things developed? Christians at every epoch have thought and expressed their faith. Sometimes they did so simply to communicate with other Christians for edification: such are the letters of Ignatius of Antioch, about the year 110. Or the aim was to defend the Christian cause before the authorities or public opinion, as the Apologists of the second century did. But soon it was thought necessary to oppose errors, such as those of Gnosticism, as Saint Irenaeus did about 180, or to refute heresies. And, finally, the faith was proclaimed in order to instruct the people, both in schools, as Clement and Origen did at Alexandria, and by preaching, which usually consisted of a commentary on the Scriptures. When one consults a chronological tableau showing, decade by decade, the literary activity of Christian writers,[7] one is struck as by a massive fact how, after the relative scarcity of names in the second and third centuries, the columns suddenly begin to fill up between the middle of the fourth and the mid-fifth centuries. Names and works crowd the page, the greatest names and the most decisive works: Athanasius (d. 373), Basil (d. 379), Gregory of Nazianzus (d. ca. 390), Gregory of Nyssa (d. 394), Ambrose (d. 397), John Chrysostom (d. 407), Jerome (d. 420), Augustine (d. 430), Cyril of Alexandria (d. 444), Leo the Great (d. 461). Such are the principal geniuses who were also churchmen and saints and who are called "the Fathers."

They lived and worked at a time when the Church confronted a difficult but decisive situation. In an empire that had become Christian, they faced the temptation of complacency towards power and of compromises with a pagan culture whose tradition was still strong. At the same time, errors of some subtlety had begun to appear in the theology of the Trinity and of Christ. This was the moment at which the Church fixed the bases of its doctrine, of its discipline (in the canons of the councils), and the forms of

*"Tradition is the educational milieu that forms the sensibility and mind at a deeper and more vital level than that of theory. . . . A teacher transmits his knowledge by enabling the student to share in what he gives him, without thereby losing it himself."*

its liturgy. The "Fathers" merit that title because they contributed powerfully to give the Church its face and its temperament. They engendered the faith for us. When we profess the divinity of Jesus, we do so thanks to Saint Athanasius; the divinity of the Holy Spirit, thanks to Saint Basil; the divine maternity of Mary, thanks to Saint Cyril. Without them, we would not be all that we are; the Church would not be all that it is.

That great epoch was for the Church a little like what a classical period is for a culture. But history did not stop with the fifth century any more than it stopped for French culture with the death of Bossuet. New questions continued to arise and new resources entered into the great current of theology. Let us cite only, in the east, Maximus the Confessor (d. 662) and John Damascene (d. 749), in the west, Saint Gregory the Great (d. 604), Saint Bernard (d. 1153), the great scholastics Thomas Aquinas and Bonaventure (both d. 1274), the Council of Trent (1545–63). Those are some of the great names, some of the peaks. There was also the life of all the Christian people, which Saint Paul describes as a letter written by the Spirit (2 Cor. 3 : 3). This life created and preserved customs that can be called traditions, particularly in their devotions. For many centuries such life remained, from lack of instruction and of knowledge, in the situation of a minority, subservient. More recently, however, worldwide social conditions have had their repercussion upon liturgical, canonical, and religious structures, and even upon doctrinal representations. On any hypothesis, today the experience of the faithful determines large sectors of Christian thought. As an example, there is the theology of liberation in South America, with its opening to socialism.

All this history has resulted in constituting a sort of treasure. Much, certainly, has been forgotten. But the Church is anything but amnesiac. Rome is a unique city: it has preserved something, often noble and beautiful, from each generation. The Church has done the same. Newman did not forget Thomas Aquinas, nor did Thomas forget Augustine, Basil, or Athanasius. Devotions have been added to the essential liturgy. The whole constitutes a treasure accumulated through the centuries. All that is called "tradition," even though many traditions are mixed in it.

The Commission on Faith and Order of the World Council of Churches established a commission in 1954, with one section in Europe and one in the United States, charged with studying "tradition and the traditions." This work reached its conclusion in the Conference of Montreal in July 1963. The two terms were not used there in exactly the sense that we have been using them. "Tradition" was taken as the transmission of the Gospel and the Apostolic Kerygma, that is, the good news of Jesus Christ and the economy of salvation of which he is the center. By "the traditions" was understood the form in which each confession or denomination has expressed and still presents that message. Our study has been located within the catholicism of east and west, so that we have been understanding by "tradition" the continuity of the great doctrinal current that issued from Apostolic Jerusalem and was enriched through centuries in which it traversed many different socio-historical-cultural conditions. What we have called "the traditions" belong rather to the practical order: customs, local rites, devotions, particular forms of discipline and observance. Tradition in the sense that we mean is a large river that has received in its course many tributaries and carries a little of all. Even the most venerated Fathers of the Church have maintained positions that we should criticize and abandon: Irenaeus professed millenarianism; Augustine hardened the affirmation of "original sin"; several Fathers taught the damnation of the nonbaptized, including even catechumens. This great river, marvelously deep and rich, indeed carries a little of all. It needs discernment, even a filter, one might say. But who will operate this, and how?

Who? The church. How? By its life. It is the Church in the unity and fullness of its communion that recognizes the faith. This Church is not a simple association established by human initiative. It is a people called together and assembled by its ministers and structured upon a sacramental basis. It is entirely animated, down to each one of its communicants, according to the condition and for the sake of its mission. That is why one recognizes in the Church an ordained ministry that exercises a public authority. For a little more than a century one has spoken of its "magisterium." This intervenes with the power corresponding to its mission to evaluate the authenticity and value of the various contributions of the tradition. But it cannot be isolated from the Christian people and their experience, nor can we attribute to it an autonomy in teaching the meaning of the deposit of Revelation. The "magisterium" witnesses, transmits, evaluates, but it does not have the creativity of a source.

Having shown what tradition is and specified its status, we must now ask what theology does with it, how it uses it.

Before theology is a product—a literary product occupying sections BJ to BX in the Library of Congress—it is the work of a man, or of a woman, but in either case it is, more precisely, the work of a believer. If a person were to take certain dogmatic propositions as principles and, without believing them, construct new conclusions and organize them into a system, the result would not be theology any more than the mimicry of a parrot is a human language. There is no theology without faith. First of all the theologian is one of the faithful. Hence his first act with regard to tradition is to be nourished by it. He meets it and practices it as, incorporated in the liturgy, in certain attitudes toward life, in practices, in art, in sensibility, it forms the Christian, and more precisely the Catholic, consensus. To the extent that it is legitimate to distinguish between instruction and education —without opposing them, however—it can be said that tradition is the educational milieu that forms the sensibility and mind at a deeper and more vital level than that of theory. How did I become a man for whom lying is a horror? Certainly not from lectures on morals, thanks be to God, but because I grew up in an environment from which lying was banned, so that love of truth came along with life, with games and festivals, with stories and concrete examples. Max Scheler has well expressed this in his analysis of the way in which models, as distinct from leaders, act upon us:

> *The second vehicle for the active influence of models is called tradition. Tradition holds a place midway between heredity and the mode of reception proper to learning and education by the act of "understanding." It is communicated automatically, vitally. It consists in receiving a certain mentality and certain ways of wanting and judging things by means of contagion and mechanical imitation of the manifestations of daily life. In short, in tradition—and this is its essential note—I do not know what I receive, and I take the will of another as my own will; I make no judgment of its value before receiving it, I do not choose it. One thinks that he has himself perceived that which is transmitted, and himself has judged it. Long before education and the conscious effort to teach by influence have laid hold of the child, the broad lines of his future destiny have already been sketched in him by his actions and by all the things that he has lived through before understanding their meaning.*[8]

Certain expressions in this text may seem to suggest the Freudian superego. In fact, in Christianity more than in any social order, we have been *preceded*. It is a question of *entering into* a communion; the Gospel speaks of "entering the kingdom." But it is a spiritual thing and must be ratified by life.

But whereas one of the faithful may do this simply by living it, the theologian must do so by making clear in a critical way the value of what he has received. Theology, as we have seen, is an effort to understand, express, and organize the content of the faith with the help of the scientific means at our disposal. The distinction between two moments in this process has become classic: "auditus fidei" (hearing the faith) and "intellectus fidei" (understanding the faith): the moment of information and the moment of elaboration, taking possession of the data, interpreting and organizing it. It is customary to speak of positive theology and speculative theology. Yet the two are certainly not separable; in any case, the second is not separable from the first, and it is the first in which we are interested.

The theologian turns to the monuments or witnesses of the tradition; he seeks out the places where it can be found. This fact has given rise to the expression "theological places" (Melchior Cano, d. 1560). The questions concerning these are rather complicated, and there is a whole "theological criteriology" that seeks to determine precisely their value and the conditions for employing them. The principal "theological places" are the following:

First, in a class by itself, are the canonical Scriptures, that is, those that the Catholic church recognizes as normative. Some fifty of the Jewish writings were left outside of the Old Testament, and fifty others were not included in the New Testament. The Bible is considered to be "inspired," and hence is for faith and theology not only an inexhaustible and invaluable source of knowledge but also an absolute and sovereign norm — *"norma normans, non normata,"* — a norm that provides a rule for everything else and is not itself ruled by anything superior to it. The "magisterium" itself is subject to it, for although the "magisterium" provides a rule for the faithful in the sense that it can judge the interpretations that individuals make of the Scriptures, that does not give it a position of superiority or of independence with respect to the written word of God; interventions of the "magisterium" in this realm have, fortunately, been very rare. Through the pains and difficulties of the complex biblical sciences (archaeology, geography, history, philology, etc.) the theologian endeavors to acquire an authentic and deep knowledge of the biblical data, a work that is for him a source of incomparable joy.

One may find it surprising that we have located the Scriptures within tradition. It has been customary to distinguish those two things and, if not to oppose them, at least to place one outside the other. Did not the Second Vatican Council, in 1962, have a debate on the "two sources"? That is true, but: first, the council explicitly put aside this way of speaking and treated

"It is not a matter of dogma . . . that the Church holds to tradition to the exclusion of Scripture, or to Scripture to the exclusion of tradition. . . . The Second Vatican Council, in 1962, . . . treated Scripture and tradition simply as two ways by which the Church comes to a fuller knowledge of the saving truth."

Scripture and tradition simply as two ways by which the Church comes to a fuller knowledge of the saving truth. In fact, it is not a matter of dogma either that the Church holds to tradition to the exclusion of Scripture, or to Scripture to the exclusion of tradition (beginning with the canon of the Scriptures—that is, the list of works admitted as inspired). Second, we will endeavor to make more precise how the theologian works with his "donné." The Scripture itself forms the principal part of this "donné" at the documentary level. It provides a norm, at least negative, for every other expression of tradition, both of the "donné" as well as of the "constructed." And what an inexhaustible fountain it is!

We have already mentioned the Fathers. They were assiduous commentators on the Scripture. Confronting the first heresies that attacked the basis of the faith, the Fathers centered their thought upon the essential. They introduced little by way of particular researches and arguments in their teaching; they never ceased to consider the whole of faith in the unity that it derives from its center, namely the Christian mystery, and from its end, our assimilation to God. That is why, in considering always the whole and the center, the Fathers always kept them present in considering any part. They did not speak of Christ without speaking of the Church, nor of baptism or the Eucharist without showing the totality of the mystery of our redemption and of our union with God. For them, everything is consonant, everything converges. For this reason the Fathers are privileged witnesses of the tradition. In them one breathes its very spirit and is impregnated with it. The benefit that the theologian can derive from them far surpasses anything that he can get from any other text or argument: from them one obtains an education in the *sensus catholicus,* much as one learns his native language from intimacy with the greatest writers of its history.

The same can be said of a fervent practice of the liturgy, which is "the Tradition itself at the highest degree of power and solemnity" (Guéranger), "the great teacher of the Church" (Pius XI). In its celebration the whole content of the faith is presented to us by joining together marvelously in ritual and sensible language a treasure of texts and of words. It has been said (by Pie Duployé) that "we derive greater if slower nourishment from things themselves than we do from their explanation,"[9] and, if a personal note is allowed, I would say that I owe to the practice of the sacred liturgy at least half of my understanding of the Christian mysteries.

We frequently have the illusion that the centuries of the past were calm and half empty, whereas ours is disturbed by many questions. The questions have varied according to the state of the culture, but questions there have always been. In politics, the powerful have always resorted to force. In the field that is our concern, men have always exercised their reason. That has often precipitated a crisis. In matters of doctrine, concepts are applied that betray one aspect of it; one value is privileged to the detriment of others and the balance of the whole is disturbed. Thus have appeared what the Church, through the voice of its pastors and especially of its councils, has called heresies: the Gnosticism of the second century (a syncretist reconstruction of a religious universe), Arius in the theology of the Trinity in the fourth century, Eutyches in Christology in the fifth century, Pelagius on grace. Later, there were the difficult problems relating to predestination and the real presence of Christ in the Eucharist. In the sixteenth century the Reformation put in question the entire edifice of medieval Latin catholicism. Moreover, every time that new means of research emerged, there was a crisis from the side of the "traditionalists." One need mention only Abelard at the beginning of the twelfth century, with his proposal to explain everything; the invasion of theological teaching around 1220 by the dialectical method and Aristotelian philosophy; the explosion of humanism and textual criticism and printing in the sixteenth century; the introduction of comparative studies in the eighteenth century; the victorious rise in the nineteenth of history and of critical methods, not to mention the awakening of the conscience of the masses. The "magisterium" has intervened every time, first under the form of councils of bishops, then, since the sixteenth century, by the voice of the popes. As a result there is a mass of authoritative documents, rather diverse, but imposing themselves upon the consideration of the theologian and even upon his acceptance: dogmatic formulas of the councils, professions of faith, condemnations, lists of propositions, encyclicals, and so forth. All these enter also into the great river of tradition, providing the "donné" that the theologian must take into account and even with which he must begin in doing his proper work. As the river carries materials of very different value, the theologian must apply a sanely critical hermeneutic to it: he will not treat as on the same level the dogmatic definition of the Council of Chalcedon and the *Syllabus* of Pius IX, both of which are historical remains, but different in weight and import.

Such, at least, was the recognized status of theological work up until recently. It is always valid. Today, however, at least in France, theologians begin more often with a global consideration of the faith and of questions posed by the surrounding culture, questions that are philosophical, political, pastoral, and so on. Others, such as Karl Rahner, begin with the positive conclusions of the faith and proceed by a conceptual analysis to elaboration of a philosophical kind. Theology no longer presents the unity it formerly showed, but although more dispersed, it remains just as active. Its task has always been to actualize the Christian "donné" as, received from its origins, that "donné" has been developed through the centuries, in a cultural situation that changes from generation to generation. Theology is a rereading, made in a new light with the eyes of a new generation, of a life that is first of all a reality experienced by each people and each generation, and that has produced in the course of time a multitude of its own expressions that each generation takes up as its heritage and attempts to make its own, to hand on still further enriched. We would willingly make our own the formula of Rabbi Safran of Geneva: "To read the past in terms of the present and the present in terms of the past." Maurice Blondel, for his part, wrote in 1904: "Tradition anticipates the future and helps to enlighten it by the very effort that it makes to remain faithful to the past." And the Orthodox theologian Paul Evdokimov wrote: "In a paradoxical way, thanks to the Witness that remains, Tradition is an agreement with the future that one finds in the past. . . . 'The Spirit has spoken by the prophets,' and it is from this prophetic dimension of the Church that it draws *from behind*, in Christ, what it announces *as ahead*."[10] That is how the theologian is nourished by tradition, in applying it to the present and carrying it forward, thereby transmitting it to a new generation that will continue the work.

---

[1] All translations from the Bible are taken from *The Jerusalem Bible* (Garden City, N.Y.: Doubleday & Co., 1966).

[2] *Ce que je crois* (Paris: Editions Bernard Grasset, 1953), pp. 15–16.

[3] 1 John 1 : 1–3.

[4] See Gen. 2 : 7 for the example of Adam; look at Ezek. 37 : 5–10, for the prophecy of the dry bones.

[5] Cf. Eph. 2 : 20 and 3 : 5 (where the article is not repeated before the word *prophets* so as to refer to the "holy apostles" themselves).

[6] *Martyrium Polycarpi* 16. 2.

[7] Cf. the *Synopsis Scriptorum Ecclesiae Antiquae* of Gervais Dumeige (Uccle, Belgium: W. Rousseau, 1956).

[8] *Vorbilder und Führer*, translated into French as *Le Saint, le Génie, le Héros* (Lyon: Editions Vitte, 1958), p. 56.

[9] In *La Maison-Dieu*, no. 10 (1947), pp. 43–46.

[10] *L'Orthodoxie* (Paris: Delachaux et Niestlé, 1959), p. 196.

# Tradition in Law

## Harry Kalven, Jr.

Harry Kalven, Jr., who appeared in last year's *Great Ideas Today* as coauthor with Walter Blum of an essay on taxation, is Harry A. Bigelow professor of law at the University of Chicago. He is a graduate of that university, from which he received his law degree in 1938, and where he joined the law faculty in 1945. His major fields of teaching have been torts and constitutional law, and for over a decade he was director of the Jury Project, an interdisciplinary study of a legal institution.

Among his books are: *The Uneasy Case for Progressive Taxation* (1953) with Walter Blum; *The Negro and the First Amendment* (1965); *The American Jury* (1966) with Hans Zeisel; and *Cases and Materials on Torts* (2d edition, 1969) with Charles O. Gregory. He has also published widely in legal journals.

At present he is working on a book having to do with freedom of speech and the press that will be a study of how the Supreme Court has elaborated the rule so briefly articulated in the First Amendment.

He is a member of the American Academy of Arts and Letters and was a Guggenheim fellow in 1970.

The question of the role of tradition in law poses an engaging challenge to the lawyer to look at his field freshly. Law depends much on a variety of continuities with the past; yet tradition is not a term it uses consciously in describing and understanding itself. Law does find congenial other terms that are closely, if subtly, related—role, profession, custom, institution, craft, history, practice, values, usage, precedent—but it is clear that we cannot proceed by reporting directly what the law has had to say about tradition.

We will not struggle over the troublesome problem of definition. For our modest purposes it will be a sufficient marking out of an idea to specify the passing on or handing down of a corpus of writings and practices to the next generations that is venerable, finite, respected, mulled over, and that exerts a control on the present. Tradition in this loose sense will include the unwritten as well as written and that which is unconsciously received as well as that received with full awareness.

There are then, we find, three senses in which the law responds to tradition in an important way. We shall use them to frame this essay. First, there is tradition in the sense of the unwritten complement of a legal order, the aspect the anthropologist or sociologist is most likely to call attention to; then there is the obvious sense—the use of the precedent of past decisions as a control on future decisions, the aspect the lawyer himself is most likely to be attentive to; finally, there is the difficult sense in which precedent and, in a way, practices embody values that transcend technical limits, an aspect perhaps associated most often with constitutional law.

I

Before exploring these points of legal contact with tradition, it is appropriate to note that the courts may draw on the unwritten traditions of the people as a source or clue for decision. Sometimes the court will do so in construing a statute. The formula is that since the legislature was familiar with the traditions of the society, it cannot be taken to have intended a meaning that would be inconsistent with those traditions, unless it very explicitly says so. A classic example is found in the World War I opinion of Judge Learned Hand in *Masses Publishing Co.* v. *Patten*, the first important

American free speech case. It involved editorials, poems, and cartoons in the old radical magazine *The Masses,* all of which were bitterly antiwar. The postmaster general had excluded the magazine from the mails on the ground that these materials violated the Espionage Act of 1917 because they would "cause" insubordination in the armed forces by generating disaffection and discontent in the public with the war. Judge Hand conceded that this was likely to be true, but argued that to construe "cause" so broadly would entail the suppression of all hostile criticism in time of war, and would "contradict the normal assumption of democratic government that the suppression of hostile criticism does not turn on the justice of its substance or the decency and propriety of its temper." He then made his appeal to tradition: "Assuming that the power to repress such opinion may rest in Congress in the throes of a struggle for the very existence of the state, its exercise is so contrary to the use and wont of our people that only the clearest expression of such a power justifies the conclusion that it was intended."[1]

A somewhat different example of a deep appeal to the traditions of a free people is found in an opinion some forty years ago by Justice Roberts. The case involved testing the constitutionality of an effort by a municipality to ban all distribution of leaflets in public places in order to prevent littering. Justice Roberts, infused with the customs of the people, perceived the streets and parks as constituting a public forum to which access could not be denied except for weighty reasons. He thus finds traditional practice useful in construing the Constitution itself. He states: "Wherever the title of streets and parks may rest, they have immemorially been held in trust for the use of the public and time out of mind, have been used for purposes of assembly, communicating thoughts between citizens, and discussing public questions. Such use of the streets and public places has, from ancient times, been a part of the privileges, immunities, rights, and liberties of citizens."[2]

II

Tradition as an unwritten complement of law touches it almost everywhere. We begin with the continuity stemming from law when viewed as a profession. There is the remarkable uniformity of style in the professional legal education, which pursues now a century later the so-called Langdell "case-method" of teaching law discovered and promulgated by a Harvard dean back in 1870. It is a method that has no true counterpart elsewhere in the university world—in its emphasis on concrete instances, its careful exegesis of texts, drawn largely from the opinions of appellate courts, and in its eschewing lectures for the Socratic method of discussion, even in large classes. Generations of young law teachers and law students have shown signs of rebelling against the case method, but it survives, and in most cases slowly earns begrudging admiration. This is possibly the most

*"There is what might be called the tradition that the law student must literally saturate himself in legal culture once he embarks on law study so that for a period of three years his intellectual energy is fully taken up with law."*

accessible instance of tradition's potency in law: law teachers tend to teach as they were taught, and the tradition is literally passed. Then, too, there is what might be called the tradition that the law student must literally saturate himself in legal culture once he embarks on law study so that for a period of three years his intellectual energy is fully taken up with law. Sociologists, who have occasionally been in residence in law schools, have observed that legal education has its features that resemble rites of passage.

There are traditions of the profession itself—aspirations to service, skill, loyalty, fiduciary trust, and courage and independence in defense of the unpopular—that warrant speaking of the practice of law as a profession and not a trade or business. These arguably have become more rhetoric than vital tradition today; the public dismay at the role and prevalence of lawyers in the Watergate affair can be read as, among other things, a measure of a departure from tradition. But lawyers would still speak of certain actions as "in the finest tradition of the bar" and would still tend to recall together Hughes's defense of the Socialist leaders in 1920, Frankfurter's public intervention on behalf of Sacco-Vanzetti, Willkie's representation of William Schneiderman in the Supreme Court when he was threatened with deportation for Communist ties, or Williams's defense of Senator Joe McCarthy in the censure proceedings in the Senate.

Then there are local practices among lawyers, particularly with respect to matters of procedure, that take on over time the status of local or regional traditions. For example, in our studies of the jury, Hans Zeisel and I discovered that the frequency of waiving jury trial for judge trial in felony cases varied greatly over the country, ranging from roughly 75 percent of all cases in states like Wisconsin and Connecticut to about 5 percent in states like Minnesota and Utah. We concluded, "The chief determinant in the decision whether or not to waive the jury in a criminal case is simply regional custom."[3] Presumably, lawyers tend to adopt the habits of older lawyers under whom they came into law practice. The example is an interesting one; it is a subtradition within the generic tradition that jury trial is a safeguard for the accused.

The jury example suggests another series of continuities predicated this time on the law viewed as an institution. Several important characteristics of the American jury, for example, depend on unwritten practices that have continued over time and may now appear almost unalterable. Among these are that the jury has twelve members, that it decides by unanimous vote, that the taking of notes by jurors during the trial is generally forbidden, that the judge's instructions to the jury on the law may come after closing argument by lawyers rather than before it, that jurors may not ask questions during the trial, that a jury elects its own foreman, that it deliberates in secrecy, and so on. Undoubtedly, all institutions acquire such marginal unwritten characteristics over time, but what may set the law apart is that on occasion it is called upon to arbitrate, as it were, the boundaries of its tradition. In recent years the United States Supreme Court has passed upon whether it is constitutionally compatible with a right to jury trial to alter the size of the jury or the unanimity requirement.

The jury instance is matched for American society by the example of the electoral college. It is an institution written into the body of the original Constitution and qualified by the Twelfth Amendment. It deals with a matter of the highest importance—the election of the president of the United States. Yet its key characteristics are defined not by the constitutional texts but rather by tradition. It was intended that the electors be an elitist group of representatives who would serve not so much to choose the president as to nominate leading candidates who, lacking a majority of electoral votes, would then be elected by the members of the House of Representatives voting by states. The electoral college became almost at once what we know today: a scheme in which the electors themselves cease to have any discretionary role and any significance as persons, but one in which the president is elected by a unit vote by states, with all the electoral votes of a state going to the candidate who receives the largest popular vote. Although nothing legally binds the elector to cast his vote as directed, there have been in the two centuries of the scheme only a handful of faithless electors. The power comes from the force of the tradition and the expectations it has generated in political parties and the public as to how the role will be performed.

The most intriguing instances of unwritten tradition encrusting institutions in law are, not unexpectedly, found with the judge and his role. I single out two features for comment: first, the special etiquette accorded judges, and, second, the expectation that the judge give public reasons for his decision.

A few years ago the trial in Chicago of the so-called Chicago Seven before Judge Julius Hoffman for conspiring to violate the federal antiriot statute in connection with the 1968 Democratic National Convention made us aware that the courtroom had become a last citadel of etiquette in contemporary society. The trial lasted five months; because of the almost chemical interaction of this particular judge and these particular defendants, it supplied a national news story daily. It ended with Judge Hoffman coming down heavily on the side of etiquette, and sentencing the various defendants and their counsel to jail on 175 separate contempts of court. The example is a complex one, with undertones of civil disobedience in the defendants' behavior. A rounded account of it is not possible here, but it put to the bench and bar a genuine question as to the extent to which courtroom etiquette was functional for a rational orderly trial and the extent to which it was simply the etiquette of another day that had been passed on to an impolite, impatient age. One of the defendants, David Dellinger, had accused Judge Hoffman during the trial of being more concerned with "decorum than with justice."

The distinctive thing is again not so much the special manners in a courtroom—addressing the judge as "your honor," rising when he enters, not interrupting him, etc.—but that reflexively the law is called upon to arbitrate the limits of its tradition. The contempt citations were upset on appeal. On retrial late in 1973 before another judge, some of the defendants were found guilty of contempt, vindicating the cause of etiquette, but no sanctions other than censure were imposed, and the vast majority of the items in Judge Hoffman's inventory were discarded. A tension between justice, aggressive defense in cases with political overtones, and the unwritten tradition of high decorum in the courtroom continues.

Various practices of American appellate courts exhibit this force of unwritten traditions, such as that opinions are not delivered seriatim by each justice as in the English bench but as "a committee" opinion for the court; that there is a privilege of justices who disagree with the majority opinion to file dissenting opinions seeking to impeach it, which are published with and preserved alongside the "official" majority opinion, a remarkable example of tolerance for public dissent on serious issues. But the most important tradition is that appellate judges give reasons for their decisions and that their reasons be public reasons. The requirement goes to the heart of the judicial process as a ceremony of reason.

It should not be taken for granted that public officials always support

Some recent trials have raised "a genuine question as to the extent to which courtroom etiquette was functional for a rational orderly trial and the extent to which it was simply the etiquette of another day that had been passed on to an impolite, impatient age."

their action with reasons. The executive and the legislature often may not; trial courts rarely do; and the jury never does.

What I wish to highlight is not the giving of reasons, but that not all reasons are acceptable. The judge must give an impersonal public reason; he may not say that the defendant was Jewish or the plaintiff Republican. There are, to be sure, dangers in this tradition, as many have pointed out. It may limit the realism of the court; it may invite pieties and rationalizations; it may conceal the "real" reasons for decision; it may affect not how the court decides but simply how it talks. But the countervalues have carried the day, and the tradition is a sturdy one. The tradition in its interplay of public reason and "real" reason accounts for much of the fascination of law study.

One example, drawn from a field of special interest to me, must suffice. In 1964 the Supreme Court was faced with a libel judgment of $500,000 entered by the Alabama courts against the *New York Times* for publishing an editorial advertisement on behalf of Martin Luther King, Jr., and the civil rights movement. On a tortured technical construction, it was read to have defamed and damaged the reputation in his community of the police commissioner in Montgomery, Alabama. The case thus bristled with real-politik. The Supreme Court, however, under the tradition had to find public reasons for upsetting the judgment; the centuries-old law of libel had been thought compatible with the free speech guarantees of the First

Amendment. The Court revised substantially its interpretation of the First Amendment, finding its "central meaning" in the idea that there should be no offense of seditious libel. Writing enthusiastically a decade ago about the outcome in the case, *New York Times* v. *Sullivan*,[4] I put it this way:

> *My thesis is that the Court, compelled by the political realities of the case to decide it in favor of the* Times, *yet equally compelled to seek high ground in justifying its result, wrote an opinion that may prove to be the best and most important it has ever produced in the realm of freedom of speech.*[5]

### III

The great instance of the law's relationship to tradition is the use of precedent in the common law. The predominant characteristic of legal argument is the obligation to "connect it up" with the past. The careful preservation of the written records of prior decisions and opinions of appellate courts, the careful indexing and analysis of them, and the careful arguing from them in present controversies must constitute an unparalleled dependence on a written tradition to control present action. What is especially distinctive is the degree of control. In theory, precedent does not merely inform or advise present judgment; under the principle of *stare decisis* it controls and dictates it. Professional legal education consists principally of the study of precedents; commercial legal publications consist principally of digesting, indexing, and collating precedents; scholarly commentary consists principally of analysis and criticism of precedent and the discovery of new patterns in it; lawyer's argument consists principally of citation to precedent and inferences from it; judicial opinions consist principally of justifications derived from precedent. This is equivalent to saying that in law present controversies are quite literally arbitrated by tradition.

It seems impossible to overstate the law's dependence on this written tradition. It is no accident that Karl Llewellyn's study of appellate judging, the final work of his long career as a leader of the realist school in jurisprudence, was entitled *The Common Law Tradition*[6] and was dedicated: "To the undying succession of the Great Commercial Judges whose work across the centuries has given living body, toughness and inspiration to the Grand Tradition of the Common Law."

Yet so summary a sketch of the dependence on precedent does oversimplify, if not overstate, the hold of tradition, and calls for several qualifications and corrections. The common law is itself no longer at the center of the American legal enterprise. There has in the past century been enormous growth on three fronts all outside common law tradition: the ever increasing domain and salience of constitutional adjudication; the momentum of legislation at state and federal levels so that statutes increasingly preempt what was once common law; and, finally, the growth of a vast network of administrative agencies regulating aspects of American life.

The school desegregation decision is a sufficient example of the first, the no-fault auto-insurance legislation of the second, and the Federal Communications Commission of the third. It is beyond the scope of this essay to attempt a summation of the relative shares of these kinds of law in the legal enterprise as a whole or to venture an account of the varying role that precedent plays in each of them. It retains, of course, some role, but that role is not so dominant nor is the hold of the past so distinctive. From this perspective, one major distinguishing characteristic of legislation is that it is lawmaking that may sever ties with tradition and break completely with the past. The legislators, however, somewhat like the scientists, may find that they have inherited ways of thought that are not so easily discarded. Lawyers are fond of quoting Maitland's epigram about older procedural rules, forms of action, which were abolished, but which "continue to rule us from the grave."

Moreover, the account thus far has advisedly concealed from view the sense of mystery about precedent at common law. There has been endless fascination with the logical puzzle of just how a decision in individual case A can control a decision in a somewhat different individual case B. There is no fire left in the old controversy over whether judges make law or find it. Edward Levi spoke of "reasoning by analogy"; Karl Llewellyn, of "leeways" and "reckonability"; H. L. A. Hart, of "open textured rules." There has also been in more recent decades the realists' curiosity as to whether, as a matter of human behavior, precedent is ever the real reason for a decision. My mature hunch is that being obedient to precedent is like riding a bicycle: it is much easier to do it than to describe it.

Viewing these matters from the standpoint of tradition brings us back to the puzzle of delimiting the term. It seems easy and appropriate to talk of precedent as the passing on of a written tradition. Yet it is widely perceived today that the common law process was but one of the ways of making law. We do not see tradition in the same sense in the other ways of making law. No one, I think, would find it profitable to talk of the continuity of a statute, which had remained in force unamended and unrepealed for, say, fifty years, as a tradition. The United States Constitution may fall somewhere in between; after almost two centuries it is more a living tradition than simply a written text passed on from generation to generation. But reference to the Constitution underscores how difficult it is to say in law where tradition leaves off and some other form of continuity begins. A constitution is an organizational blueprint for the distribution of power and function in the governance of society. It is the source of the continuity of legal institutions upon which legitimation crucially depends. It is important that law be made and enforced in the traditional ways by the traditional institutions. One source of contemporary unease about impeachment is that we have no tradition of use to appeal to. But does it foster insight to speak of the presidency, the Senate, the Supreme Court as traditions?

The most splendid thing about the common law as tradition is its capacity for growth, change, and self-correction. The law has a fine metaphor for the process; it speaks of the "law working itself pure." Perhaps this is a necessary characteristic of any vital tradition or any tradition subject to continuous reexamination and study. In any event, the purifying of the tradition is so recurring a phenomenon in law as in itself to be a tradition. Examples are abundant. New York for seventy-five years had an odd rule governing damage caused by the use of explosives as in blasting operations. If the damage to the plaintiff was caused by debris hurled onto his property, the blaster was held, as the law put it, strictly liable; that is, liable without the need to prove that the blasting operation was carried on in a flawed fashion. If, however, the damage was caused simply by concussion, the injured plaintiff in order to recover damages had to prove that the blasting was done negligently. The distinction was viewed as artificial and trivial, an echo of a long-abandoned conceptualization from fifteenth-century pleading in trespass and trespass on the case. It was rejected in the majority of other American states. Nevertheless, it was often applied, and survived in New York until 1969. In the case that upset the rule, Chief Justice Stanley Fuld of the New York Court of Appeal, after noting at the outset of his opinion that the rule stemmed from the 1893 decision in the *Booth*[7] case, stated explicitly: "We are now asked to reconsider that rule." He then reviewed its reception elsewhere in the United States and went on to discover that the 1893 *Booth* rule itself had been out of line with the New York cases:

> *We need not rely solely, however, upon out-of-state decisions in order to attain our result. Not only has the rationale of the* Booth *case . . . been overwhelmingly rejected elsewhere, but it appears to be fundamentally inconsistent with earlier cases in our own court which had held, long before* Booth *was decided, that a party was absolutely liable for damages to neighboring property caused by explosions.*[8]

The example is instructive in several respects. If possible, a court will alter the tradition by returning to its older, and purer, form. Thus, although a change is being made, it is done in a fashion that is highly respectful to the power of tradition. Moreover, it indicates the modest limits within which the common law struggles for consistency. Strict liability was itself out of line with the long dominant principle at common law for determining liability, the negligence principle. All Justice Fuld attempted was to iron out the small inconsistency between rules for debris and for air-wave damage. He did not trouble over the larger inconsistency between negligence liability for activity generally and strict liability for blasting. Only small inconsistencies are the hobgoblin of the law. And even then, it may take a century to iron them out.

Two other very recent instances, one involving death and the other, life, clamor for attention. A famous anomaly in the common law is the rule that there was no redress for the wrongful death of another, a result attributable to a misplaced philosophic view that human life was beyond price and to a mistake by Lord Ellenborough in a decision in England in 1808. The rule was, in all American states and England, altered over time by the passage of statutes creating a cause of action for money damages for wrongful death. Once the statutes were on the books it was no great practical matter what the common law had been. But recently, the Massachusetts court was faced with a technical problem involving the statute of limitations. To escape the bar of the statute it elected to reexamine the status of wrongful death at common law. Again the court found it appropriate to correct the tradition, relying largely on the total consensus for 150 years reflected in the wrongful death statutes everywhere. "We are convinced," said the court, "that the law in this Commonwealth has also evolved to the point where it may now be held that the right to recovery for wrongful death is of common law origin, and we so hold."

The final example, which seems to come straight out of news of the day, concerns that which has been called "wrongful life." May the failure to guarantee contraception be regarded as a tortious wrong when birth results? The case involved a sterilization operation performed on a mother of four. It was performed imperfectly with the consequence that a fifth child was born. The lawsuit was for damages from the unwanted pregnancy and birth. The Delaware court, with only modest hesitation, decided in favor of the plaintiff, even to the extent of allowing damages for the pain and suffering of the pregnancy. Here the court was filling in a gap in the tradition rather than altering the tradition. There was not, strictly speaking, a tradition on this precise point; the question had never been raised. It became possible to ask it only because of changes in the society's attitudes toward birth control. The legal tradition, although it links the society securely to the prudential judgments of the past, is capable of interstitial growth and change as the values of the society change. Moreover, the instant case fitted easily into traditional notions of medical malpractice; it stated a complaint for a negligently performed operation. The change, although astonishing, was handled so as to seem incremental.

The common law thus abounds in examples of a tradition that changes. The puzzle is: If tradition changes, can it still be thought of as tradition? The puzzle perplexes American legal scholars today and has been especially salient in the controversy over the performance of the "Warren Court." As far as I can see, the uneasy resolution lies in the tempo of the change. If the process is speeded up and the patterns of precedent are redrawn at short intervals, then whatever the surface rhetoric, there has been a change in kind. The obligation to tradition has been dissolved. To rephrase the Chinese proverb, the wisdom of the common law was to make law slowly.

A footnote on the common law as written tradition: We have spoken only of cases and judicial opinions, not of books and commentaries. There is no doubt that the hold of books as a written tradition has changed for lawyers over the past three centuries. I have recently read a study of American lawyers and judges during the era of slavery. Their arguments over slavery reflected education in a given intellectual tradition in which the writings of Coke, Hale, Hawkins, Pufendorf, Grotius, Montesquieu, Viner, and the Bible itself loomed large, and in which Blackstone's *Commentaries* were central. To a lesser extent this could be said of the great treatises of the nineteenth century such as Kent, Cooley, and Story. But today their influence has all but evaporated, and an educated American lawyer may well never have had occasion to open Blackstone. The great treatises in particular fields of modern times, such as Wigmore in Evidence, Williston and Corbin in Contracts, or the American Law Institute *Restatements*, are respected and frequented but simply as secondary commentary, largely indistinguishable from the abundant other commentary in lesser books and innumerable journal articles. The written tradition of law, contemporary American law, is imbedded in the original authoritative data itself, the cases, statutes, and constitutions.

## IV

We come then to the last sense of tradition in law. It is a difficult sense to capture; yet there are areas of law where the precedents taken as a whole, rather than in logical, precise, vertical sequences, carry a compulsion and inspiration that goes beyond literal holdings. It is here that the lawyer may find resonance in T. S. Eliot's essay *Tradition and the Individual Talent*. Eliot's advice to the poet to inform and discipline his individual talent with the tradition of English poetry is not unlike Justice Frankfurter's advice to his fellow justices on how to discipline and inform their "individual talent" in a great case. In 1951 in *Dennis* v. *United States* the Supreme Court was called upon to pass on the compatibility with the First Amendment of the conviction of leaders of the Communist party for the crime, as the law so tortuously put it, of conspiring to organize the party to teach and advocate the overthrow of any government in the United States by force or violence. In brief, did the convictions of the Communist leaders involve an abridgment of freedom of speech? Politically and legally it appeared at the moment as a great case. The appeal had followed a nine-month trial, and it exacted some 100 pages of serious opinion writing from the justices. To resolve a question of this magnitude, implicating values of this rank, required, according to Justice Frankfurter, resistance to "immediate overwhelming interest which appeals to the feelings and distorts the judgment."

He went on:

> *Unless we are to compromise judicial impartiality and subject these defendants to the risk of an* ad hoc *judgment influenced by the impregnating atmosphere*

*of the times, the constitutionality of their conviction must be determined by principles established in cases decided in more tranquil periods. If those decisions are to be used as a guide and not as an argument, it is important to view them as a whole, and to distrust the easy generalizations to which some of them lend themselves.*[9]

As the passage may make evident, Justice Frankfurter was launching an opinion that would affirm the constitutionality of the convictions. Although I think Justice Frankfurter, after taking the corpus of precedent as a whole, still reached the wrong result in the case before him, he displayed the right stance toward the tradition.

Interestingly enough, it was again Justice Frankfurter, in the same term of court in another great controversy over Communism and Communist front organizations—the case involved the so-called Attorney General's List of subversive organizations—who best articulated the sense in which legal tradition can transmit a concept or norm that transcends precedent. He is speaking in praise of the idea of "due process of law":

*The requirement of "due process" is not a fair-weather or timid assurance. It must be respected in periods of calm and in times of trouble; it protects aliens as well as citizens. But "due process," unlike some legal rules, is not a technical conception with a fixed content unrelated to time, place and circumstances. Expressing as it does in its ultimate analysis respect enforced by law for that feeling of just treatment which has been evolved through centuries of Anglo-American constitutional history and civilization, "due process" cannot be imprisoned within the treacherous limits of any formula. Representing a profound attitude of fairness between man and man, and more particularly between the individual and government, "due process" is compounded of history, reason, the past course of decisions, and stout confidence in the strength of the democratic faith which we profess."*[10]

There is matter for another essay in the question of why it is Justice Frankfurter, whose performance as a justice has not been uniformly admired, who proves to be the sensitive and eloquent spokesman for the role of tradition in constitutional law. Suffice it here to note that he has been the justice who most articulately struggled with the dilemmas of judicial restraint.

Another example of tradition as inspiration centers today on developments in the last fifty years of the First Amendment. Llewellyn's toast to the commercial judges who fashioned the common law tradition could well be raised to Hand, Brandeis, Holmes, Hughes, Roberts, Black, Douglas, Harlan, and Brennan, whose work over the past half-century has given "living body, toughness, and inspiration" to what is now for me the worthiest tradition in American law, the tradition of freedom of speech, press, and political action.

## V

This has been a provincial account of tradition and law limited by the accident that my knowledge is of the Anglo-American system. Arguably, continental codes, canon law, Chinese law, primitive law, Roman law, or Soviet law would each exhibit a tradition of different strengths. But it is unlikely in the extreme that one intimately acquainted with those legal orders would be unable to trace in them the steadying, conserving, but not deadening pressures of tradition. In the end the effectiveness of law as a strategy of control lies in its combining the selective use of force with a moral tradition of obedience to law. It is respect for the past that gives law in an orderly society its crucial aura of legitimation. And it is tradition, too, that may best explain how a society can hope to have a government of laws and not of men.

---

[1] Masses Publishing Co. v. Patten, 244 Fed. 535 (S.D.N.Y. 1917).

[2] Hague v. Committee for Industrial Organization, 307 U.S. 496 (1939).

[3] *The American Jury* (Boston: Little, Brown & Co., 1966), p. 24.

[4] New York Times v. Sullivan, 376 U.S. 254 (1964).

[5] "The New York Times Case: A Note on 'The Central Meaning of the First Amendment,'" *Supreme Court Review* (1964), pp. 193–94.

[6] *The Common Law Tradition* (Boston: Little, Brown & Co., 1960).

[7] Booth v. Rome Railroad Co., 140 N.Y. 267 (1893).

[8] Spano v. Perini, 25 N.Y. 2d11 (1969).

[9] Dennis v. United States, 341 U.S. 494 (1951).

[10] Joint Anti-Fascist Refugee Committee v. McGrath, 341 U.S. 123, 162–63 (1951).

# Tradition in the Arts

## Frank Kermode

Photograph by Jill Krementz

Frank Kermode is a respected and influential figure in contemporary English studies. Educated at Liverpool University, from which he received his degree in 1940, he taught at Durham and Reading before going to Manchester, where he was appointed John Edward Taylor professor of English literature (1958–65). He has since been Winterstoke professor of English at the University of Bristol (1965–67) and Lord Northcliffe professor of modern English literature at University College, London (1967–74), and has just been made King Edward VII professor of English at Cambridge.

Professor Kermode is the author of *The Romantic Image* (1957), *Puzzles and Epiphanies* (1962), and *The Sense of an Ending* (1967), as well as studies of Donne, Milton, and Wallace Stevens. A book called *The Classic*, based on the T. S. Eliot memorial lectures given at Canterbury, is forthcoming.

A contributor to *Partisan Review*, the *New York Review of Books*, the *New Statesman*, and other well-known periodicals, Professor Kermode was coeditor of *Encounter* in 1966–67. He is the editor also of *The Tempest* in the Arden Shakespeare, and of the series called Modern Masters published by the Viking Press.

There is a spiritual community binding together the living and the dead; the good, the brave and the wise, of all ages. We would not be rejected from that community." So Wordsworth in his pamphlet on *The Convention of Cintra* (1809). The sentiment was earlier familiar to readers of Burke, and later to readers of W. H. Auden, who gave it equal solemnity. Wordsworth and Auden, as it happens, were both poets who had professed, but later abjured, faith in a revolutionary future, a sharp severance between the future and the past. And among the illiterate, who are less able to examine the past and its constraints, there are also millennial aspirations—blueprints of a future that shall be free of those constraints; but even in these aspirations the past continues to exercise its power, to assert the existence of old habits of thought, old psychological and cultural patterns.

"To treat the dead as entirely dead would show a lack of affection, and should not be done; to treat them as if they were entirely alive would show a lack of wisdom, and should not be done." This judicious observation was not made by a modern thinker, conscious of a need for balance between the demands of the past and those of the present; it occurs in the *Li Chi*, a Chinese work of about 200 B.C. For the Chinese the "spiritual community binding the living and the dead" was more than a matter of piety; it was a political force. The ruler assumed powers to ennoble or degrade a man's ancestors, and so lengthen or shorten their posthumous lives and dignities. But the effect of this was of course felt by the living. Confucius himself was not very interested in the supernatural; he recommended the careful observance of traditional rites, including ancestor worship, for the good of the living community, which would benefit from the civilized ritual of the cult of the dead. That is also the spirit of the *Li Chi*, which recognizes both the pastness and the presentness of the past.

Tradition is to preliterate and illiterate societies what history is to the literate. Unblemished truth was habitually ascribed to a remote original condition; it could be maintained, as a necessary component of the culture, by correct oral transmission. In time it might be written down, whereupon it would be the subject of learned commentary, and of accommodation to the needs of a society that had necessarily suffered historical change; but the word preceded the writing, and the old oral tradition is often held to be purer than the later tradition of the commentators. For this reason the

Jewish historian Josephus distinguished between the *paradosis pateron* (the tradition of the fathers) and the legalisms of the Pharisees.

Paradosis ($\pi\alpha\rho\acute{\alpha}\delta\sigma\sigma\iota\varsigma$) is rendered in Latin as *traditio,* which may be translated as both "handing over" and "handing down." The early fathers of the Church used the word in the first of these senses to mean the deliverance to the faithful of the divine revelation, the work of the apostles and evangelists. But what was then handed over must subsequently be handed down, and that was the work of the Church. As time went on this second sense bred difficulties; it had to be defended against protest, and given more dogmatic definition. It is not too much to say that in the ecclesiastical arguments about tradition we find the best model for the difficulties that attend its use in later and more worldly literary contexts.

The argument about the relation of Scripture and tradition anticipates, from the moment of its origin, hermeneutic problems that became apparent only much later in secular scholarship. The earliest *traditio* ("handing over") was of course oral, and preceded the documents called Scripture. These were inspired but they were also sometimes obscure, and from the time of Tertullian (late second and early third century A.D.) it was held that the Bible must be expounded by reference to a rule of faith that was continuous with the original teaching only because the Church had accurately preserved it. On the other hand, the only way to prove that tradition orthodox was by reference to the Scripture. So, as Henry Chadwick observes, "the argument is . . . circular: the tradition of Church teaching must be proved orthodox by biblical revelation; yet doubtful books are admitted to the New Testament canon because they are orthodox by the standards of Church tradition, and only the tradition can ensure that the interpretation of Scripture is sound."[1]

Tertullian came to think of tradition and Scripture as independent but complementary sources of revelation, and the Roman church has continued in this opinion, citing the words of St. Paul: "Keep the ordinances, as I delivered them to you" (1 Cor. 11 : 2), and "Hold the traditions which ye have been taught, whether by word, or our epistle" (2 Thess. 2 : 15). The tradition was appealed to whenever heresy threatened; and the responsibility for its preservation became a political matter, as for example in the dispute as to whether final authority rested with the papacy or with the general council, an issue that continually divided pope and emperor.

It was heresy that compelled the Church to stricter definitions of tradition, and these were promulgated at the Council of Trent (1545–63). Among all the issues controverted between the Protestants and Rome, this was the one that touched the authority of the Church most closely; for if Scripture was alone sufficient, the institution that preserved and derived its authority from tradition was dispensable. Consequently, the council laid down, in April 1546, that the Christian truth and discipline "are contained in written books and in unwritten traditions, which were received by the Apostles from the lips of Christ himself, or, by the same Apostles, at the

"The struggle between parents and children grows more obvious and intense; yet the gap between them is the gap across which the spark of tradition must leap."

dictation of the Holy Spirit, and were handed on and have come down to us . . . preserved by unbroken succession in the Catholic Church."[2] Scripture and tradition were accordingly to be reverenced alike. To believe otherwise was to allow that the first generation of Christians had no authoritative rule of faith, and also that it had taken fifteen centuries for the preeminence of Scripture to become evident, and then in such a way that this knowledge became a source not of unity but of schism.

Sociologically as well as ecclesiastically, the Tridentine ruling is of much interest. The heretical outbreaks of the Waldenses and Wycliffites in the thirteenth and fourteenth centuries had already caused theologians to deny that charity or grace was essential to the just exercise of authority; it was desirable, certainly, but not necessary; to argue the contrary would render the whole ecclesiastical hierarchy unstable and encourage charismatic heretics.[3] Now the tradition required that it be upheld by an infallible institution; and as the power of councils waned (there was none between Trent and Vatican I in 1869), infallibility came more and more to be vested in the pope himself, until Pius IX, who was responsible for the definition of papal infallibility in 1870, was capable of saying "*I* am the tradition."

We might see this as a characteristic rejection of the charismatic by the institutional, or a persistence in what Weber called "routinization of charisma," or as what some of his dissident successors think of as a diffusion through an institution of its original charismatic force; this last comes closest to the view of the Roman Catholic church, which is of course that the Holy Spirit inheres in it, and has kept the true tradition unbroken. But the forces of reform were also compelled, by the instability of charismatic succession, to institutionalize, and to do so (since there was no absolute control over scriptural interpretation) in a great variety of ways. These I cannot here describe; only two points can be made. First, the need for acceptable interpretations of Scripture was so acute that scholars such as Flacius (*Clavis scripturae,* 1567) took the first steps toward something like a modern biblical criticism; and this involved the evolution of a new attitude to history as well as to textual provenance. Secondly, Western Christendom was finally split up into sects, each claiming a different means of access to the primitive Christian truths. In short, the nature of tradition was henceforth a matter for perpetual dispute; and so there were instituted new senses of the historical past. The sixteenth-century argument about tradition may therefore be taken as a model of the modern dispute between those who speak for the past as they institutionalize it and those who charismatically ignore or attempt to abolish the past; and it also signifies the historical origin of the modern debate, which may question the validity of any tradition, or at any rate the claim of any particular group or institution to transmit, interpret, and enforce acceptance of one version.

At that time our civilization began to develop in ways unknown to others, indeed to become unique. Weber explained this development as proceeding from the Protestant ethic. "Those material and technical pre-conditions," says his expositor Herbert Luethy, "on which Europe started to build her civilisation after the late Middle Ages, existed equally or even more richly in other high cultures . . . yet in no other case did they cause a similar leap from the mérely static to the irresistibly dynamic."[4] And Weber feared that what he called "rationalisation"—the substitution of rational action for compliance with inherited prerational social norms—would "disenchant" the world, perhaps had already done so. To ignore *mos maiorum* (the custom of our ancestors) is to give the society a dynamic that others, maintaining a traditional respect for tradition, must lack; but it is also to lose some or all of what they keep. The solution of the judicious Chinese—to show affection and wisdom at once—is harder to achieve in a "modern society." And the problem is complicated by the necessary restructuring of the past that comes about when there is no central tradition about which all other nongenetically transmitted information groups itself. We who lack interest in the mores of our ancestors (or even argue that they are irrelevant, because subject to different historical conditioning) must have either many pasts or no past at all, many sources of authority or none at all. This explains, in part, the flight of a Wordsworth or an Auden, or of many another, from charismatic millennialism to an institution (in both cases the Church of England) that offered a more moderate traditionalism than the Roman church; but it also explains the attractiveness, to generations of modern intellectuals, of the latter institution.

In politics it is conservatism that offers the comforts of a stable tradition. What is is right because it *is*, and because "it preserves continuity with the past and with the values of our dead forefathers. . . . The authority of existing forms of society must therefore be upheld and preserved, an authority seen as deriving, in Burke's famous words, from 'a partnership between those who are living, those who are dead, and those who are to be born.' . . . conservatism as an ideology is essentially traditionalism become conscious of itself."[5] It is founded on a quite different notion of history from any held by the parties of the Left. These may be anarchist, dedicated to the supersession or destruction of the past, to revolution for its own sake; or chiliast, expecting a millennial condition from which all history represents either a monstrous deviation or a complicated approach; or gradualist. There are, paradoxically, many *traditions* of the Left (for even anarchism has a history). But insofar as the status quo is rejected, the view of the past implied must be schismatic; and this is true of even the most gradualist of political reform movements.

Perhaps the "nuclear" political unit, the family, resisted antitraditionalist interpretation longest, though one would need to qualify that statement by reference, for example, to the history within our society of schismatic "communes" and other eschatological sects, who may hold wives and children in common. And in any case the "rationalisation" of the family is at least as old as this century; or, as it might be better put, customs once identified with nature are now seen, in the light of anthropology and psychoanalysis, as specifically cultural. Freud's insistence on oedipal conflict, and the development of the superego as the guarantee of civilization, was the cardinal lesson. He contrasts the behavior of childish people who will gratify themselves in any way provided they cannot be found out with those in whom "authority has been internalized by the development of a superego."[6] Thus authority, once externally exercised by the father (and indirectly, through him, by one's ancestral traditions), becomes a part of the personality. It is, for Freud, a sad situation, for the authority of the superego is not such that it can also offer the rewards that go with obedience to a father and with the renunciation of satisfactions forbidden by him, the rewards being love and guiltlessness.

The fact well recognized by Freud that the child's superego is likely to be based on the parents' accounts for the strength and continuity of moral systems.[7] Analysts in the Freudian tradition have developed the concept and given it a more complex relationship, both to various stages of the individual's life and to the effect upon the superego of changing cultural conditions. It now seems to many that the transmission across generations of an ancestral superego, however modified, has grown less and less a matter of course. They feel that nongenetic information is no longer transmitted as it used to be (in times when the structure of authority in the family was less controverted) and are aware of an intergenerational conflict that they often regard as untraditional. The historical uniqueness of this situation is undoubtedly exaggerated, but acuteness must in some measure be due to the "rationalizations" of what Erikson calls "the psychoanalytic enlightenment" that sought to replace "age-old repression" with "enlightened judgment."[8] It is true that the dynamic processes within our society change it ever faster, so that whereas everybody still belongs to a family, his adjustment to the culture is a different task from that of his parents, and *mos maiorum* is in general a less useful guide. The parents often know this, too, and assert the traditional sanctions more hesitatingly.

In any case, the family is changing. More frequent divorce, television, increased mobility both physical and social progressively alter it, and neither parents nor children can benefit as easily as before from the old appeal to custom. Because they are rooted in the earliest stages of life, the old unconscious struggles go on as before; and it is to those struggles that such relatively new techniques as family therapy have to address themselves. Those who speak of "the politics of the family" regard it as a miniature of the oppressive state, with the children as underprivileged citizens. If anything, familial conflicts have intensified, partly because of rehousing policies that break up neighborhoods and exile grandparents, whose role in previous generations was most important, not only because they provided a link with old forms of authority and with a lost tradition of family life but because, as everybody knows, the grandparent-child relationship is free of many of the tensions that exist between father and son, so that behind the recent and unacceptable past there was another less threatening, not requiring to be destroyed.

Thus the struggle between parents and children grows more obvious and intense; yet the gap between them is the gap across which the spark of tradition must leap. For tradition is cultural; it has to do with that which cannot be transmitted genetically from one generation to another; it is nongenetic and consists of information that can "in principle be lost, and in one generation."[9] Some of this information is secured by institutions, as, in principle, the Church of Rome preserves the original tradition; or as the law, slowly adapting itself to rapid cultural changes, hands on its qualifications of past statutes or judgments. Here are continuities, bureaucratically ensured, that will survive all but the total collapse of that more fragile institution, the family, though they are in so many ways committed to its protection.

So far I have been writing about the maintenance of tradition—and about schismatic antitraditionalism—in the contexts of religion, sociology, and analytic psychology. But this I have done as a necessary prelude to speaking of the exemplary case of the arts. It is impossible, I think, to divorce this from the other issues I have spoken of. The history of an art is the history of an institution. Heresy and revolution, as they occur in such histories, have the same typology as in the history of religion; and an art, like a church or a society or a language, would die of incommunication if it contrived to abolish its past. There are claims to the contrary, but how quickly we accommodate them into our continuities! A militant protestantism, which seeks access to original truth (a primitive church, a primitive art stripped of the sophistications laid on it by centuries during which a false authority claimed total possession of its tradition), is active also in the arts: thus the poet's proposed return to a language spoken by men, the painter's abjuration of perspective and other illusionisms, are primitivisms on the protestant model. Such heresies divide the institution into sects, and it is easy enough to argue that what Weber said of the history of our religions and our society applies also to its arts, in which a heretical dynamism produces ever more new movements, and a situation in which there is always a great need to change, to *go ahead*. Wyndham Lewis deplored this competition in *aheadofness*, and others have remarked its ill-effect on young artists, who are obliged to establish their novelties almost before they have understood what the old art was.

Yet even in this situation tradition asserts itself, as we may see by citing some familiar instances. One of the crucial dates of art history is 1907, the date of Picasso's *Demoiselles d'Avignon*. We know that this work, the first cubist painting, emerged from sketches intended to issue in a picture of quite a different kind: probably of a man entering a brothel carrying a skull. Yet the end product was the extraordinary work from which so much of the modern tradition, with its abolition of established methods of pictorial representation, is held to derive. Matisse thought it was a hoax. We can see, from our point of vantage, that behind it there is a whole history: impressionist color techniques, the powerful impulses of Cézanne, of Negro masks, of African fetishes.[10] We see the truth of Ortega y Gasset's remark, that in a culture that has chosen "futurism" rather than the hierocratic traditionalisms of Egypt, Byzantium, or the Orient, new styles grow out of antagonisms to traditional styles, which therefore have a negative influence;[11] but we see also that the increasingly complex dialogue between artist and spectator that forms part of the history of the institution of Western art could bring it to a point where traditional skills and language had to be challenged, and a whole new view of the past, and of original truth, had to be sought.

If Matisse was shocked by Picasso's painting, we need not be surprised that the Parisian audience at the first night of *Le Sacre du printemps*, doubtless adherents of conventions they identified with tradition, thought Stravinsky's music a hoax and an insult, nor that T. S. Eliot, who admired it, heard in it the sound of modern traffic, of horns and motors. Now we may watch the ballet with excitement and pleasure, observe the "period" primitivism of decor and dance, and respond to the brilliance of the orchestra without for a moment thinking the music unintelligible or for that matter confusing the sounds we hear with the noise outside the theater. What we do not feel is insult, the flouting of a cherished past. And Stravinsky later gave us cause to label him a "neoclassicist," a cultivator of that tradition, or of parts of it, that he was believed to have desecrated.

Eliot himself supplies a third familiar instance. Before and after he wrote *The Waste Land*—a poem that defies conventions of narrative sequence and traditional exposition—he was elaborating a theory of tradition that, he held, must be worked for, since its orderly transmission had been interrupted, but that placed the individual sensibility of the modern artist in a vital relationship with all past art that was not in itself heretical, which partook of an original and timeless truth.

So three crucial works of art, all of them on the face of it representing a breach with tradition, assume that tradition, in some form, as necessary to their substance; their novelty lies in a breach with the recent, rather than the remoter past; they may be said to represent to us what tradition must be in a culture that prefers change to submissiveness.

What, then, of more strident manifestations of "abolitionism"? The twentieth-century history of the arts is full of manifestos, full of avant-gardes—an expression that, even as late as Baudelaire, had a purely military sense but later was fully appropriated by the arts. On so vast a subject, an essay as brief as this one can say little. But we may again briefly consider some instances, such as futurism, Dada, the "anti-traditionalist" enterprise of Guillaume Apollinaire. All, as it happens, are associated in some way with the First World War. The futurist Marinetti proclaimed the supremacy of the machine, the death of nineteenth-century humanitarian hypoc-

Picasso's *Demoiselles d'Avignon*, 1907 (facing page), now considered the first cubist painting, encompasses many traditions, including Negro masks (above). *"Traditional skills and language had to be challenged, and a whole new view of the past, and of original truth, had to be sought."*

risy, a total break with the past and its meanings. For a time his disgust with the past and enthusiasm for a technological future unrelated to it seemed attractive, but his achievement belongs to the history of advertising rather than of art. Apollinaire, a better poet, took up futurism as he did almost all new movements; a publicist of cubism, he also produced a manifesto called *L'Antitradition futuriste*, in which he cursed traditional art and order and blessed only living artists, including himself. Because they were good artists, they demonstrated that he had a genuine sense of the tradition by becoming part of it.

Dada is perhaps a more difficult matter, more destructive and desperate, though in its way also Utopian. Its influence belongs in part to social rather than art history. Yet in urging us to be rid of false reverence, and indeed to be rid of Art, it invites us to cleanse our perceptions, to discover the truth of our activity when, because we think of it as a piece of art, we

look at an object as if it were different from others; and this is that quest for original truth in which all heresies begin. A desperate reaction against the previously unthinkable horrors to which our culture, its idea and its practice of order, had brought us, gave the dadaists, as it has since given other rebels, a specially abolitionist tone. "Is it conceivable," asked Ortega, "that modern Western man bears a rankling grudge against his own historical essence?"[12] Dada, of all the movements of modern art, came nearest to justifying a positive answer. Yet even its direct descendant, surrealism, which had a more positive stance and established strong psychoanalytical and political connections, means less to us than the artists—Eliot, Stravinsky—who came to an understanding with tradition.

One of the largest claims for modernism as schismatic—it is founded on Picasso, Dada, and the others—is that it depends on the abandonment of illusion: a modern picture offers itself as a picture, a modern text as

Craftsmen and artisans of all countries (above and the following pages) keep alive the artistic tradition of their culture. *"It appears that a relation to the history of art is a precondition of being an artist, and such a relation implies an acceptance, or*

*choice, of tradition. Every artist seeks to achieve something new, . . . but the best have recognized that without tradition there simply is no art, and their works are testimony to the effort they make to discover tradition in its full original purity."*

necessarily opaque writing, not a fake transparency through which one sees a reassuringly settled "reality." The latest version of this claim—it amounts to a rejection of a supposedly traditional illusionism—is made in the work of the French "structuralist" avant-garde, which repeats, in its publicity as well as in its theory, the same errors. For, as Leo Steinberg has demonstrated for painting and as one could as forcefully establish for literary texts, there is no such break of continuity as the propagandists suppose. It is true that the demand of the modern arts on the interpretative cooperation of reader and spectator is more overt and more urgent, and that modern works draw attention to themselves as artifacts, incomplete without that cooperation, more insistently than the works they are held to supersede. But, as Steinberg remarks, it is "a provincialism" to suppose that there has been a schismatic change, for "What is constant is art's concern with itself, the interest that painters have in questioning their operation."[13] And this holds true for the other arts; only the questions are now asked in a new tone, and less submissively.

What we are seeing is in fact less an abolition than a multiplication of traditions as more of the past becomes available and history makes neglected parts more interesting. A young man dressed in leather wears a Marilyn Monroe button. He was only a child when Marilyn Monroe died, but she is part of a past he can accept, of a new tradition that he supposes may connect him to a primitive truth. A boy who could play Beethoven well abandons him for rock, and within months he is looking for something more than the brief excitement of the "single," seeking in rock the kind of music that will give him the pleasures of structure, of inventive play within rules inherited from the music he has, for the time, consigned to the past.

It has been argued that every artist must, in his own way, submit to the past—after a more or less bitter rebellion—for without this acknowledgment of the father, which is tradition, the child cannot renounce those satisfactions that must be renounced in order that he shall have the rewards of obedience. Whether this is true or not, it appears that a relation to the history of art is a precondition of being an artist, and such a relation implies an acceptance, or choice, of tradition. Every artist seeks to achieve something new, and we need not expect him to think much about the Burkeian community with the dead, much less to display a Chinese wisdom. His task may perhaps be expressed as that of distinguishing, from where he stands, between custom and tradition, as the old Anglicans did— custom being the dead hand of the past, imposing an authority that turns out on inspection to be spurious, merely conventional; and tradition, the conveyor of original truth. In a modern society such distinctions are hard to establish and harder to maintain, and the consequence is what Marxists, in their way highly traditionalist, call a riot of decadence. Certainly it is a situation beset with difficulties; certainly it is easy to be deceived into producing or accepting novelties of no value, to squander one's inheritance.

But the best have recognized that without tradition there simply is no art, and their works are testimony to the effort they make to discover tradition in its full original purity.

---

[1] Henry Chadwick, *The Pelican History of the Church*, vol. 1, *The Early Church* (Harmondsworth, Eng.: Penguin Books, 1967), p. 45.

[2] *Documents of the Christian Church*, selected and edited by Henry Bettenson (London: Oxford University Press, 1943), p. 365. Some took an even more extreme view and placed tradition above Scripture, believing that "the doctrines of faith were now so cleared that we ought no more to learn them out of Scripture" (*The Historie of the Councel of Trent*, written in Italian by Pietro Soave Polano [Fra Paolo Sarpi] and faithfully translated into English by Nathanael Brent [London, 1620], pp. 158–59). For a comparison between the Tridentine definitions and the contemporary effort to clarify the tradition of Aristotle, see my "Modern Poetry and Tradition," *Yearbook of Comparative and General Literature*, 14 (1965): 5–15.

[3] See Gerson's strictures on the heretics in John B. Morrall, *Gerson and the Great Schism* (Manchester: Manchester University Press, 1960), p. 101.

[4] Herbert Luethy, "Once Again: Calvinism and Capitalism," *Encounter* 22, no. 1 (January 1964): 26–32; reprinted in *Max Weber*, ed. Dennis Wrong (Englewood Cliffs, N.J.: Prentice-Hall, 1970), p. 126.

[5] *Max Weber*, p. 42.

[6] Sigmund Freud, *Civilisation and Its Discontents*, trans. Joan Rivière, 3d ed. (London: The Hogarth Press, 1946), p. 108; *GBWW*, Vol. 54, p. 792.

[7] See Heinz Hartmann and Rudolph M. Loewenstein, "Notes on the Superego," in *Psychological Issues* 4, no. 2, monograph 14 (New York: International Universities Press, 1964): pp. 144–81.

[8] Erik H. Erikson, *Identity, Youth, and Crisis* (New York: W. W. Norton & Co., 1968), p. 37.

[9] P. B. Medawar, *The Uniqueness of the Individual* (London: Methuen & Co., 1957), p. 141.

[10] For a brilliant study of Picasso's personal and historical situation see E. H. Gombrich, "Psycho-Analysis and the History of Art," in *Meditations on a Hobby Horse* (London: Phaidon Press, 1963), pp. 30–44.

[11] *The Dehumanization of Art* (Princeton, N.J.: Princeton University Press, 1968), p. 43.

[12] Ibid., p. 45.

[13] Leo Steinberg, *Other Criteria* (New York: Oxford University Press, 1972), p. 77.

# Advancement and Obsolescence in Science

## Theodosius Dobzhansky

One of the great figures in the science of genetics, known particularly for his formulation of the role of genetics in the origin of species, Theodosius Dobzhansky has held many academic positions and received numerous academic and public honors and awards in a career that has lasted for more than half a century. Born in Nemirov, Russia, in 1900, he graduated from the University of Kiev, where he subsequently taught zoology, in 1921, and was a lecturer in genetics at the University of Leningrad from 1924 to 1927. In the latter year he came to the United States, of which he became a citizen in 1937, and where he has been, in succession, professor of genetics at the California Institute of Technology (1936–40); professor of zoology at Columbia University, New York City (1940–62); professor at the Rockefeller University, New York City (1962–71); and, since 1971, professor of genetics at the University of California, Davis.

Of his books, *Mankind Evolving* (1962) was described by George Gaylord Simpson as "the most interesting . . . the most judicious scientific treatise that has ever been written on the nature of man." He is the author also of *Genetics and the Origin of Species* (1937; 3d edition, 1951), and *Evolution, Genetics, and Man* (1955).

A member of the National Academy of Sciences and of the American Philosophical Society, Professor Dobzhansky has at various times been president of the Genetics Society of America, the American Society of Zoologists, the Teilhard de Chardin Association, and the Behavior Genetics Association. He was awarded the 1964 National Medal of Science by the president of the United States.

Science is cumulative knowledge. Each generation of scientists works to add to the treasury assembled by its predecessors. A discovery made today may not be significant or even comprehensible by itself, but it will make sense in conjunction with what was known before. Indeed, this will usually have been necessary to its achievement. Newton could not have done his work without Copernicus, Galileo, and Kepler. Einstein could not have done what he did without Newton. Of course, new discoveries may change the meaning of prior knowledge. Old hypotheses may be invalidated, old theories discarded. Yet many new discoveries are clearly based upon older ones even when they show these to have been inexact or incorrect. Some interpretations given by Aristotle to his observations seem naive to modern scientists. Aristotle's science is obsolete. It would be silly to set him at naught, however. The works of Aristotle were extremely powerful stimuli of intellectual life for many centuries.

Other disciplines do not show this cumulative character, at least to the same degree. In literature or music, the productions of one era are not the necessary conditions of later ones. Nor are they ever superseded. We probably enjoy Bach and Beethoven today as much as their contemporaries did. Bach and Beethoven are not obsolete. Shakespeare and Dostoevsky have at least as much appeal to us as do the works of our contemporaries. Shakespeare and Dostoevsky are in no sense obsolete. Their writings are timeless. They deal with human problems that have existed and will exist, we may suppose, forever.

Because science is cumulative, it transcends individual accomplishments. In the modern era, particularly, important advances are often based on results obtained by hundreds, even thousands, of research workers. These researchers get their salaries, but gain few prizes and honorific titles. Their names are known only within a more or less narrow circle of specialists, and are soon forgotten or at best embalmed in scientific bibliographies. Yet without the efforts of such rank-and-file scientists, the work of those with great names, winners of Nobel Prizes and such, would be impossible. We do not find this dependence in the great men of other fields. Had Dostoevsky died in his Siberian prison, or had Tolstoy perished from a stray bullet, *The Brothers Karamazov* and *War and Peace* would simply not exist. These masterpieces were contributions that only Dostoevsky or Tolstoy could have made. In contrast, had Darwin not traveled on the *Beagle* and become instead a country doctor or parson, something like *The Origin of Species** would doubtless have appeared. The data on which Darwin relied had been collected by countless other workers, without whose researches Darwin could not have propounded his theory, and with which, another than himself could have done what he did. In point of fact, one of Darwin's contemporaries, Alfred Russel Wallace, outlined a theory of evolution by natural selection independently of and simultaneously with Darwin; had Darwin not been born, we would have "Wallaceism" instead of "Darwinism." The work of Gregor Mendel, largely unnoticed in his lifetime, was repeated after his death, independently and simultaneously, by three investigators in three different countries—Correns in Germany, de Vries in Holland, Tschermak in Austria—who did not know what he had done.

The cumulative and collective aspects of the scientific enterprise make it more sensitive than other human endeavors are to historical developments. A scientific discovery may be made prematurely, or it may be inordinately delayed. Mendel's work is an example of prematurity. That it was forgotten for three and a half decades after it was written up is only partly explained by the fact that it was published in an obscure provincial journal, the last place likely to inspire further researches by a competent contemporary. After all, some competent people read Mendel, yet failed to perceive the significance of what they read. We shall forever be in doubt as to what would have happened had Mendel sent his work to Darwin. Quite possibly, not even Darwin would have understood it. On the other hand, while there have probably always been persons capable of understanding the mechanisms of sexual reproduction, these remained mysterious until the seventeenth century when the invention of the microscope made possible the discovery of the sex cells. Once a microscope became available, the Dutch pioneer biologist Leeuwenhoek and his student Hamm could examine, as they did, the seminal fluids of several animals, including man. In 1675 Leeuwenhoek and Hamm saw in these fluids the squirming spermatozoa. Leeuwenhoek sent a communication describing his discovery to the Royal Society in London, saying that its publication might be withheld if the topic were found to be offensive. Fortunately it was not so considered. A little later, egg cells were discovered by another Dutch biologist, de Graaf. Advances in the understanding of sexual reproduction became rapid thereafter, though until that time almost no progress had been made since Aristotle, who, for lack of the ability to perceive the small objects involved, had arrived at what seem to us some mighty strange ideas on the subject.

Because science is cumulative knowledge, old discoveries are as important as recent ones. In a sense they are more important, since they can be seen to have been the points of departure for all that has followed. (Of

---

* *GBWW*, Vol. 49, pp. 1–251.

course I mean old discoveries that have been validated, such as are apt to be described in the introductory chapters of textbooks and the initial lectures of science courses.) To be sure, a modern student gets his information more easily from secondary sources than from any direct report of these discoveries. Take again the topic of sexual reproduction. Must a student start with Leeuwenhoek's description of the "animalcules" in the seminal fluid? A modern textbook or manual has much better drawings and photographs of the spermatozoa of different animals, including man. Some textbooks, perhaps ill-advisedly, do not even mention the name of the original discoverer of the spermatozoa. A student is still less likely to begin his study of astronomy reading the classical work of Copernicus *On the Revolutions of the Heavenly Spheres.** In the first place, the work is rather too long; moreover, Copernicus assumed that the planetary orbits are circular rather than elliptical, and this made his computations very imprecise. It is after one becomes familiar with the fundamentals of modern astronomy that it is fascinating as well as instructive to see what Copernicus was able to accomplish with the inadequate observational data at hand.

We seem to be facing a contradiction. The discoveries of scientific classics are basic: one must know about them, but not necessarily know how and by whom they were made. Thus some as a rule mediocre but still competent scientists are callously disdainful toward the history of their own science. The history of science, they say, is mainly of interest to scientists in their dotage. Indeed, a former colleague of mine, then a young professor, proudly declared that he had no interest in reading anything written more than five years before. Fortunately, this attitude is uncommon. It is generally accepted that one does not really understand a scientific problem unless one knows at least in rough outline how it came to be formulated.

Perhaps the reason why some scientists are uninterested in the history of their field is that it does, as we have seen, imply obsolescence. This is no merely abstract concern of the scientific investigator. While every scientific advance makes previous knowledge to that extent obsolete, it also implies the eventual obsolescence of the new discovery. In that sense, the scientist is always working to make obsolete his own achievement. The more significant his discovery is, the more rapidly is the obsolescence likely to overtake him. An important idea or finding attracts the attention of many other scientists. The idea is elaborated and tested with the aid of more precise instruments and perhaps a variety of materials beyond the range of the original experiment. The results of the new tests may be more adequate and more impressive than were those of the original ones. The idea, or a theory growing out of it, may be reformulated in a more satisfactory fashion, and not only may become better known than the discovery that led to it but may be associated with a different name!

In these terms it is not hard to see why an investigator, who could be elated to see the advancement in science generated by his work, often seems moved by sentiments of the opposite kind. Scientists are human, and many of them are jealous of their colleagues. Unfortunately, they often show the fact in undignified fashion. Priority squabbles are among the saddest and most futile episodes that blacken the memories of otherwise admirable scientists. Men as great as Newton and Leibniz engaged in this folly. What does it matter now, long after their deaths, which of them was first to invent the calculus? Both of them invented it, largely independently. And nobody at present learns that branch of mathematics from the original works of either Newton or Leibniz, there being hundreds of textbooks that are better for the purpose, even though written by mathematicians of far lesser distinction. Not that this detracts anything from the glory of Newton and Leibniz. Only if mankind were to relapse into barbarism could their contributions to mathematics and science be forgotten.

The one consolation the investigator has is the fact that even the contributions of rank-and-file scientists tend to be preserved, are seldom lost, become part of the storehouse of human knowledge. They do, that is, if they are not rendered obsolete in the manner just indicated. Suppose you have measured a physical constant, determined the distance to some star, collected fossils in a geological formation, or described a new species of animal or plant. You publish an account of your work in a scientific periodical. The volume of the periodical is perused by colleagues in the same specialty and comes eventually to rest on the shelf of some library. Will anyone read it fifty or a hundred years from now? Yes, this may happen; scientists sometimes have to pore over the dusty volumes of old periodicals. More likely, your findings will make a paragraph, perhaps only a line, in some fat compendium volume. But they will survive. Of course, they sometimes remain hidden in their place of preservation. Scientists find it easier to consult summaries and compendiums than to read original papers. Even if these are looked for, they may not be found. Often enough a scientist undertakes the study of a problem unaware that it has been solved years earlier. He may eventually stumble on the forgotten work and acknowledge that what he has achieved is only the confirmation of earlier researches. That is what happened in the case of Mendel. Mendel's work could have remained undiscovered indefinitely. As scientific advances usually end in obsolescence, so the not uncommon fate of scientific investigators is oblivion. But these results are less certain in science than in other human affairs, which are not cumulative in the same way, and in which the individual achievement, not being part of any larger enterprise, will, unless it is genuinely distinguished in its own right, be quickly and utterly forgotten.

The most interesting part of the history of science and the chief reason to study it is, of course, the work of the great figures in the field. It is not only the results of their investigations that repay examination. One can

---

* *GBWW*, Vol. 16, pp. 505–838.

learn from them how to formulate problems with skill and artistry, how to plan experiments, how to assemble observations in significant patterns. None of this can be done without facts, certainly, and these can be gathered only by many minds and many hands. But science does more than collect facts; it makes sense of them. Great scientists are virtuosi of the art of discovering the meaning of what otherwise might seem barren observations. An idea that is born and grows in the mind of a great scientist ties together disjointed facts, inferences, and hypotheses to shape a theory that is intellectually satisfying and even beautiful. So it was with Mendel, whose experiments on crossing varieties of peas were in themselves not unlike the experiments of several of his predecessors, who had worked on other species of plants; what Mendel brought to the subject was an insight that made his own experiments reveal how biological heredity is transmitted from parents to offspring. Again, the idea of evolution was not new when Darwin wrote *The Origin of Species*. What Darwin did was to examine critically a great mass of observations, his own and those of other biologists, in the light of an idea that others had not perceived. When T. H. Huxley, who became Darwin's most effective advocate, saw the result, he reproached himself: how stupid he was not to have seen what Darwin made so clear! His self-reproach was unnecessary. Great ideas often seem simple and self-evident, but only after somebody has explained them to us. Then, how interesting they become! The act of insight is among the most exciting and pleasurable experiences a scientist can have, when he recognizes what all the time was there to be seen, and yet he did not see it.

It should not be imagined, of course, that great ideas in science are revealed at once, and that they do, or do not, immediately thereafter become obsolete. Even though the germ of an idea may come suddenly, it must grow and develop. Then it may become the nucleus of a theory that makes sense of a multitude of facts, and that serves to guide others as well as the original investigator in the search for further related facts. The theory of evolution by natural selection is a case in point.

Evolution postulates that the state of the world we observe now has emerged from very different states. In general, the farther back in time we look, the more unlike the present these past states were; slow and imposing as the process is, moreover, the difference between past and present is becoming greater all the time. Evolution is not only a historical event; it is ongoing. The causes that underlie it are still in operation, and, in principle at least, can be made the subject of observation and experiment.

In the widest sense, the term evolution is applicable to cosmic or inorganic, to biological or organic, and to human or cultural development. Cosmic evolution has been going on for somewhere between ten and fifteen billion years, biological for perhaps four billion years, human for a mere two or three million years. The causes that bring about these three kinds of evolution are quite distinct; two of the kinds, the biological and the human, have taken place, so far as we know, exclusively on the planet earth. Yet some philosophers see the three evolutions as parts of a single creative enterprise.

Some historians find germs of evolutionary ideas in the creation myths of various peoples, or in the speculations of ancient Greek philosophers. Whether or not these myths and speculations, often couched in poetic imagery, can be regarded as coming anywhere near to what evolution means in our terms is questionable. Even Herodotus and Thucydides, the ancient Greek historians, while giving well-reasoned, accurate, and critical accounts of events, never put them in the perspective of a developmental process taking mankind from one state to another. Perhaps such a perspective can be seen in the Judeo-Christian world view, which envisages history as a sequence of happenings, from the Creation to Redemption and finally to the Kingdom of God. If so, how ironic it is that the opposition to evolutionary theory in recent times has come mainly from religious circles! In the eighteenth century, the Age of Enlightenment, mankind was conceived to have developed from a primitive state to one that promised eventual perfection. Condorcet, waiting to be executed by revolutionary terrorists, gave an explicit statement of this view in 1793. The evolutionary origin of the sun and the planetary system was postulated late in the eighteenth and early in the nineteenth centuries by Kant and Laplace. The theory of uniformitarianism, according to which the evolution of mountains and seas has been brought about by the same cosmic forces, which are held to be still in operation, stems mainly from Lyell, whose *Principles of Geology* appeared in 1830.

Evolution in the biological sense, the theory that life itself evolves, is the keystone of evolutionary science. Its discovery came last, after cosmic and cultural evolution had been accepted. Although several great thinkers, from Descartes to Buffon, toyed with the underlying idea, it was Lamarck who became the first explicit evolutionist, beginning with publication of his *Philosophie Zoologique* in 1809. His greatness has never been properly recognized, at least not outside France. That is probably so because the term *Lamarckism* has for long been used to indicate only a part of Lamarck's theory, the part that asserts that characteristics acquired during the lifetime of an individual can be inherited, and that is now generally regarded as erroneous. This notion was not original with Lamarck, however, whose main insight, a brilliant one, was that the whole living world is the product of an evolutionary development.

In 1858 and 1859 appeared the works of Darwin and Wallace. From then on, evolution became the great unifying idea in biology. Darwin and Wallace not only affirmed that evolution occurs but also gave a convincing explanation of its main causes. Though they assumed—mistakenly, as we now know—the inheritance of acquired traits as a subsidiary factor, they identified natural selection as the chief source of evolutionary change. This identification has been borne out by biological research during the century and more that has elapsed since their time, though our present concept is not simply taken over from Darwin's writings but has undergone important modifications.

Darwin deduced his concept of natural selection from Malthus's earlier idea of overpopulation, which led him to stress the struggle for existence, survival of the fit, and the death of the unfit. There is no doubt that overpopulation, struggle, and differential mortality occur in nature. But they are not of the essence. Darwin himself said that he intended the word *struggle* to mean something more general than violence or combat. Yet this was the sense in which the term was mostly taken during the nineteenth century and even through much of the twentieth, when evolutionary fitness was equated with brawn, aggressiveness, and competition. According to the current concept of natural selection, the fittest are simply those who have a greater number of surviving progeny, or who have them at an earlier age, not those who excel in the use of force. Vigorous health, physical strength, and long life increase fitness as Darwin—or at least the nineteenth century—understood it only if they further the reproductive process. When food and other resources needed for survival and reproduction are plentiful, mortality may for a time be reduced. In some organisms, most or even the entire progeny may survive in some generations, as happens among humans in certain countries, owing to modern medicine and hygiene. Does this mean that natural selection no longer operates among mankind in these countries? Not necessarily. Natural selection is still taking place in the sense that the carriers of some genetic endowments within the population produce more progeny than do those of other genetic variants. Or again, suppose that in a human population every woman has the same number of children, will this do away with natural selection? Again, not necessarily. If some people would marry and have children at an earlier age than others, selection would still operate, providing that those who married early were in some ways genetically different from those who did so later.

It is not an underestimate of Darwin's greatness to say that he left many basic problems of evolutionary biology unsolved. One such problem was the source of hereditary variation. For natural selection to operate, the parents who leave the greater number of surviving progeny must differ in their genetic makeup from those who leave few or no progeny. Darwin correctly inferred that this is what really happens, but he did not know why it happens. The answer had to wait almost half a century for the emergence of the science of genetics. Mutations—changes of hereditary constitution—were studied first by de Vries in evening primroses (*Oenothera*), then by the school of T. H. Morgan working with *Drosophila* flies, and later by molecular biologists. It was established that mutant genes are inherited according to the laws discovered by Mendel in 1866 and rediscovered by de Vries, Correns, and Tschermak in 1900. Such genes accumulate among the countless constellations of genes that sexual reproduction generates in any population. If some of these genes enhance the Darwinian fitness of their carriers, natural selection will increase their frequency in the population and will eventually make them its adaptive norm. Mutational changes in the genes most commonly occur through the substitution of single nucleotides in the DNA molecules composing the genes. That in turn leads to alteration of single amino acids in the proteins coded by the mutated genes. The end result is a change in the character of the species.

In *The Origin of Species*, which appeared in 1859, Darwin confined himself to biology. Only at the end of the book did he remark that with the acceptance of his theory, "light will be thrown on the origin of man and his history."* Darwin's forbearance, or timidity, failed to protect him from the attacks of traditionalists. His "light" aroused their anger. Finally, in 1871, Darwin clearly spelled out in *The Descent of Man*† that mankind, like all other biological species, is a product of evolutionary development. Our remote ancestors were animals, not men, and the more unlike ourselves they were, the farther back we look. The great evolutionary idea became as pivotal in anthropology as in biology. And evolutionary anthropology has not stood still since Darwin, any more than evolutionary biology has.

The first task facing Darwin and his successors was to adduce incontrovertible evidence of man's evolutionary origins. Comparative morphology and anatomy show that the human species is related most closely to the anthropoid apes, somewhat less closely to monkeys, still less to other mammals. In Darwin's time, almost nothing was known about man's fossil ancestors and collateral relatives. Human and prehuman fossils are comparatively rare and usually fragmentary. Yet the interest and importance of knowing mankind's biological antecedents is so great that paleontologists and prehistorians have, especially in recent decades, unearthed so much material that the story of mankind's evolutionary ascent is becoming quite well documented. In the nineteenth and early twentieth centuries paleoanthropologists were eager to find "the missing link," a form intermediate between man and apes. At present, so many "links" have been found that one can ponder a more ambitious task: tracing out where and when the various evolutionary changes were taking place. This does not mean that a complete series of hominids and humanoids is known from, say, mid-Tertiary times to the present. Much remains to be discovered. However, we do know some of the benchmarks in man's evolutionary history—the australopithecines, the pithecanthropines (*Homo erectus*), the Neanderthal, and modern races of *Homo sapiens*.

From Darwin's time until perhaps a quarter of a century ago, it was necessary to prove that mankind is like other biological species. This task

---

* *GBWW*, Vol. 49, p. 243.
† *GBWW*, Vol. 49, pp. 253–597.

has been successfully accomplished. Now a different, and in a sense antipodal, problem has moved to the fore. This is to establish the evolutionary uniqueness of man. In several ways, mankind is a singular, quite extraordinary product of the evolutionary process. Biological evolution has transcended itself giving rise to man, as inorganic evolution did in giving rise to life. All organisms evolve and become adapted to their environments by changing their genes to fit these environments. Mankind evolves chiefly, though not exclusively, by making its environments fit its genes. A single example will suffice as an illustration. Animals adapt to cold climates by growing warm fur, or by winter dormancy, or by genetically fixed drives to migrate to warmer climates. Man adapts to cold by dressing in warm garments and building heated dwellings. Like all other biological species, mankind has a biological heredity transmitted by Mendelian genes. Mankind has also a cultural heredity, transmitted by instruction and learning. In this transmission, symbolic languages, which are also unique to man, play key roles.

Culture is not inherited through genes. It is acquired, by every person for himself, through contacts with other people, who may or may not be biological relatives. Difficult and controversial questions arise concerning the interrelationships of the biological and cultural "heredities." What are the causes of the variations in the expression of cultural characteristics among humans? At one extreme are those who think that the biological evolution of mankind had been completed when culture first appeared, that all humans have essentially the same genetic endowments, and that the domain of culture is wholly separate from biology. At the opposite pole is the view that race, class, and individual cultural differences originate in the genes. The scientific controversy over these matters is all too often linked with political convictions and biases of the exponents of the different views. But a few very general statements may appropriately be made here about the whole question.

It is certain that a human genetic endowment is requisite for acquisition of any human culture. It is also certain that no two persons (so-called identical twins excepted) have the same genes. Every nonpathological human genetic endowment confers upon its carriers the capacity to acquire a culture, but the genes do not predetermine which one of the many existing cultures is to be acquired. An analogous situation is found with human language: human genes are required for learning a human language, but they do not decide which language will be learned, still less what a person will say when he learns it. Natural selection has always favored in mankind the development of educability, i.e., of a capacity to learn what a given culture makes necessary in its members, to profit by experience, and to modify and adjust one's behavior in the light of circumstances. Educability is a fundamental trait of the species *Homo sapiens*. It is what makes human behavior different from that of nonhuman animals. And yet this trait is individually variable. Some individuals learn more easily and successfully certain things, and other individuals other things. Every individual is unique and unrepeatable; people are not interchangeable.

Science has been called "the endless frontier." The more we know, the better we realize that our knowledge is a little island in the midst of an ocean of ignorance. There will always be plenty of problems to invite study, thought, and research. Yet from time to time some people conjecture that a branch of science is essentially complete. Some outstanding physicists claimed this at the turn of the current century, at the very time when the discovery of radioactivity was opening a new era of atomic physics, making possible the atomic age! Spectacular advances of molecular biology in recent decades induced more than one scientist to make similar claims. Allegedly, the greatest ideas have already been advanced, and the fundamental discoveries have all been made. There are supposed to remain only some details to be filled in. Science is not endless, it is said: the limit can already be seen.

It is hard to confute this opinion, but not necessarily because it is true. Who knows what great ideas are to be conceived of, and what fundamentally new discoveries are waiting to be made? A new idea is unforeseeable until it has germinated in somebody's mind, and a new discovery is not guaranteed until at least a glimmer of it is seen. In short, ideas and discoveries that will open new paths to knowledge are unpredictable. Whether or not the epoch of great discoveries in science is past is a matter of personal faith or intuition. I, for one, believe that the limits of human knowledge are nowhere in sight.

# History and Tradition

## J. H. Plumb

J. H. Plumb, who is among the most distinguished of contemporary historians, is known to the general public chiefly through such books as *The Horizon Book of the Renaissance* (1961), *Men and Centuries* (1963), and *The Death of the Past* (1970). But his professional reputation is based on his studies of the eighteenth century. Among these are *England in the Eighteenth Century* (1950), *The Growth of Political Stability in England, 1675–1725* (1967), and a monumental life of Sir Robert Walpole, still to be completed, of which the first two volumes have been published.

Although he received his B.A. with first class honors in history from the University of London in 1933, Professor Plumb has made the greatest part of his academic career at Cambridge, where he is now professor of modern English history. He was visiting professor at Columbia University, New York City, in 1960 and distinguished visiting professor at the City University of New York in 1971–72. Awarded a D.Litt. from Cambridge in 1957 for his work in eighteenth-century English history, he is a fellow of the British Academy and an honorary foreign member of the American Academy of Arts and Sciences.

History is Janus-faced, but the faces are far from being identical. One is wrinkled with deep lines, as old as the distant ages of mankind; the other is youthful, vigorous, and in the full flood time of early maturity. These faces represent two very different types of history. The former is obviously riddled with traditional attitudes enshrined in works whose fame has lasted for milleniums. The latter, too, is old enough to have established traditions of working and methods of expression, some of which, though not all, continue to be powerful. Two types, therefore, of history need to be considered. One is the way man has always looked at his past. He has turned to it to explain the roots of his society, to tell him its story; he searches it, as his forebears did, for examples of human behavior, and often he scrutinizes the past in the hope that it will enlighten him about the future. This is basically what Voltaire called philosophic history, whose truth may lie deeper than facts. And this for centuries on end was the totality of historical practice—sometimes simple, sometimes sophisticated and complex—not only in the West and throughout Islam but also in China and in Japan. As we shall see, this type of history persists, and rightly so, though the part tradition plays in it has grown at once more complex and weaker with time.

But the more youthful variety of history is easier to deal with and should be taken up first. When Chinese historians of the T'ang period looked back on the Han, or when Livy contemplated Roman history or Herodotus delved into the history of Egypt or of Persia, they were largely concerned to discover moral truths; although they had some concern for factual accuracy, it was not their prime concern. Herodotus, like Thucydides after him, thought nothing of inventing speeches and putting them in dead men's mouths. Similarly, the Chinese historians would deliberately switch the semi-miraculous happenings necessary for the birth of an emperor from father to son without any compunction, because they were necessary for moral emphasis, to demonstrate clearly that Heaven itself supported the new emperor, this being presumed in light of the fact that the emperor had successfully established a dynasty. And so, in the Middle Ages, the monastic chroniclers accepted, not incredulously but because of their belief in God's will and purpose, the miracles of founding abbots or

of the saints who had embellished their orders. At the same time, all of these historians put into their works a great deal that was accurate—factual truths about the lives of men and women and events of their societies and communities. But the pursuit of factual truth was not their primary aim. They were illustrating the purpose of God, the truths of morality in which fables, miracles, or myths are as valuable as facts.

The development of critical history—the youthful face of Janus—was highly complex, with slow beginnings, and had, like all mighty rivers, many tributaries. And it is a purely Western phenomenon. As I have written elsewhere, "The Chinese pursued erudition, but they never developed the critical historiography which is the signal achievement of Western historians over the last two hundred years. They never attempted, let alone succeeded, in treating history as objective understanding."*

Probably one of the basic reasons why Europe developed critical history was because its past had been badly fractured. There was a pagan past of Greece and Rome and the Christian past of the Bible that interlocked but did not properly fit, leaving for the critical mind a wealth of problems, chronological and technical as well as interpretative. Also, the half-obliterated pagan past was a wonderful hunting ground for antiquarians, those who were searching for categories of facts and so were discovering facts themselves. There was so much to collect and put in order: chronicles, literature, plays, poems, epigrams and epigraphs, medals, coins, wonderful fields of antiquarian specialization that, from the fifteenth century onward, began to be ever more precise and accurate. The earliest traditions of exact historical scholarship began with the antiquarians and with the critical examination of texts—for example, Lorenzo Valla's famous proof that the Donation of Constantine was a forgery—in the fifteenth century. Valla belonged to a school of lawyers, a school that grew and strengthened over the next hundred years, and that was concerned to discover precisely what legal phrases, even words, meant at the time they became inscribed in law. These lawyers realized that time itself eroded and changed meanings, and that to understand legal concepts of Rome one needed to use historical criticism, to learn how to strip off the coruscations of time. Both processes encouraged the growth of erudition; the recovery and ordering of more facts about the past and the spread of critical methods of handling words and documents within their own special frameworks of time grew steadily throughout the sixteenth century, primarily in Italy and France but also, during the seventeenth century, in England. In France particularly this gave rise to the establishment of techniques—paleographic and diplomatic—that have become a traditional part of scholarship. Similarly, some of the great works of scholarship—the *De Re Diplomatica* of Mabillon or the *Acta Sanctorum* of the Bollandists (still in course of publication after three hundred years)—remain important books for the medieval historian. Here

---

* J. H. Plumb, *The Death of the Past* (Boston: Houghton Mifflin, 1970), p. 13.

the tradition is firm; the growth of knowledge, through established techniques, steady.

Even so, there were rapid improvements in the eighteenth century, and the spearhead of critical history passed to Germany, particularly to the University of Göttingen. Elsewhere there was great improvement. Always historians had embedded charters, letters, and documents in their histories and annals to help give veracity to their argument. But instead of being occasional embellishments, often now the volumes of the documents supporting a history were longer than the history itself. This was particularly true of a great but neglected English historian, Archdeacon Coxe, whose exceptional documentation, accurately presented (at least for his age), not only has given his books enduring value but has also influenced generations of English historians. From Coxe's day, the editing and publishing of documents became an intense preoccupation of the growing number of professional historians of the nineteenth century. The *Monumenta Germaniae Historica,* whose first volume, edited by the great scholar G. H. Pertz, appeared in 1826, induced scholars in other countries to follow Pertz's lead (notably in the case of the Rolls series in Britain), and so was created a tradition of editing, and publication of fundamental sources, that is still assiduously followed. Indeed, one may say that a tradition of editing historical sources was established, if constantly refined, from 1826 until the present day. However, two factors have placed this tradition in jeopardy. One is the soaring costs of printing a text with elaborate critical appendixes; the other is the ease with which nowadays any scholar can get a reproduction of almost any document that he may want. Even so, such editing, like its counterparts in historical erudition, the creation of historical dictionaries and collation of varied historical materials, remains a fundamental part of the historical profession; in essence, the rules laid down by Mabillon, and developed by the great German textual editors, are still followed. Here the traditional methods of scholarship endure.

\*     \*     \*     \*     \*

The ambitions of the early professional historians were vast, however, and not confined to the editing of thousands of texts. The range of Leopold von Ranke was enormous; he planned a Universal History at the age of ninety. His work still retains considerable value, through the care with which he used sources, the lucidity of his writing, and the sharp intelligence that he exercised, particularly in diplomatic history. Before Ranke, historians such as Gibbon—in a sense the first great critical and professional historian—had taken immense themes for their subjects, and historians continued to do so throughout the nineteenth century. In America (one has only to think of Bancroft, Prescott, and Motley) they all happily embraced great periods of time, rich with complex and multitudinous sources. Multivolume narrative histories or biographies were a commonplace of historical literature by the mid-nineteenth century. Yet what seemed to be an established tradition by the 1870s had almost vanished by 1914.

The vast outpouring of archival material in the nineteenth century, combined with stronger professional standards of scholarly care and mastery of sources, naturally increased specialization. This in turn was encouraged by the great national historical reviews that were established. Germany, not surprisingly, was the first in the field with the *Historische Zeitschrift* in 1859; France followed in 1876 with the *Revue historique*. Both England and America were much tardier. The *English Historical Review* was first published in 1886, and the *American Historical Review* in 1895. They were all symptoms of a development in the discipline of history that is now so deep-rooted as to be the most traditional aspect of academic or professional history. From 1900, journals for academic history of every kind proliferated rapidly and still continue to increase. In these journals a professional historian can treat of a small historical problem or throw new light on an aspect of a large one. It permits him to establish a reputation without the need to produce a book. And these journals have profoundly influenced the whole nature of historical investigation, for they are largely concerned with the "whys" of history, concepts about how history happened, rather than a relation of events. This, too, is reflected in the books that great professional historians, bred in this new style of history, began to write at the turn of the century. They ceased to write great narrative histories on large historic themes and turned to more specialized concepts: the nature of feudalism, the origins of parliamentary government, the nature of the Renaissance, the causes of the Reformation, the influence of the frontier on American history. Indeed, Frederick Jackson Turner's famous essay on the frontier, published in 1894, was a turning point in American historiography. Then came the first light of the dawn of that "new history" publicized and promoted by James Harvey Robinson and Charles A. Beard, who taught the methods, the techniques, and the attitudes toward the past that had been established in European historiography. From these and other points stems the great river of professional history, as wide and as long as the Mississippi, that flows through the universities and colleges of America. The influence of these men, and their pupils' influence, is still paramount.

The establishment of high professional standards bred specialization, both vertical and horizontal; that is, aspects of human activity were easier to isolate and study than their complex relationships, so scholars devoted their lives to economic history, or ecclesiastical history, or the history of ideas, or the history of politics or law. And, of course, it was easier to deal with a short period such as that covered by the agrarian revolution in sixteenth-century England, or the role of the lawyers in seventeenth-century Toulouse, or the origins of the meat-packing industry in Chicago. This vertical and horizontal slicing of history has now hardened into a tradition, and is dominant in professional academic circles. Naturally, the strength of its hold varies from country to country. It dominates English academic life, where the work of Sir Lewis B. Namier, which was, in essentials, confined to a segment of political history of the 1760s, is regarded as one of the great achievements of professional history. His work on the history of parliament has spawned a host of imitators. In America this tradition is also very powerful, as it is in France and the rest of Europe. However, among some of the most gifted historians writing today there is a growing disenchantment with specialization that is too rigid in the orientation of the subject or too confined in time.

Many of the greatest academic historians of this century have always been deeply concerned by the limitations of high professional specialization. Lord Acton, who believed this could be overcome by great cooperative enterprises, planned the *Cambridge Modern History*, by which he hoped to create a synthesis from the best specialists. The result was useful but dull, a fourteen-volume work of reference, of exceptionally varying quality; yet some chapters were brilliant, some volumes even admirable. And so the cooperative history of specialists established itself, whether dealing with all human history, such as the wholly admirable Columbia University's *History of the World*—perhaps the finest achievement of this tradition —or significant and large sections of the human story that the great Cambridge histories have covered. It is a method, however, that is less widely practiced in Europe, and though now firmly established as a practice of the professional historians, and still dominated by the tradition established by Lord Acton, it has never proved wholly satisfactory, nor satisfied those historians who wish for closer contacts with the culture of their day.

Historians, since Gibbon's day, have been well aware of its Janus-faced nature. History has possessed since the earliest times of mankind a social purpose and yet, by its very nature, professional and highly specialized history can play only a very limited role. It is excellent for training the critical faculties; on occasion it can stimulate sympathy and understanding of societies and people different from ourselves; but most of it, perhaps 90 percent of it, is uninteresting, even unreadable, except for those involved in its academic disciplines.

Fortunately, men and women since Homer's day and beyond have craved to know about the past. Who made the world? Why is there evil? How is good achieved? Questions as to how and why have always haunted generations of men and women whose curiosity about the past is insatiable, giving us works whose role has long endured—among them, and above all, the Bible, which in essence is a history. There is, indeed, a great constellation of epics—Homer, the Sagas, the Vedas, the early annals of China—that no amount of historical criticism can ever destroy, that remain to delight and to instruct the intelligent and curious reader. These

"The half-obliterated pagan past was a wonderful hunting ground for antiquarians.
. . . There was so much to collect and put in order."

epics merge in times closer to our own into the great traditional histories —Gibbon, Hume, Macaulay, Ranke, Michelet, Prescott, Motley—that so delighted our grandfathers and that are still read more by nonhistorians, perhaps, than by trained professionals. And so we have a curious anomaly, a traditional historical literature that is rarely read by the professional historian for its own sake. When the professional historian studies Herodotus or Gibbon, he does so historiographically, that is, to understand either what the author's vision of history was and why or the way he reflected the intellectual forces of his day. Whereas the bulk of the readership of these works, which is nonprofessional, goes to them for entirely different reasons. These traditional works—particularly historians such as Prescott or Gibbon or Macaulay—are read because they are excellent narratives, telling, with excitement in pungent prose, what happened. The stories of the conquest of Mexico, or the decline and fall of Rome, or the English revolution are magnificent in themselves. And as well as stories, there are the historical characters—larger than life, who in their day dominated the human scene—from Alexander the Great to Napoleon. About all these books there is what the French call the "odor of man," the smell of life. We can, through these books, project ourselves into the lives of men who once walked this earth as we do and have now vanished, whereby we participate in what may be called the poetry of time, which is the poetry of history. It is because it affords us this opportunity that history is so enduring a part of literature, a part of the great tradition.

And that tradition still exists, but it has tragically weakened. Where today are the Michelets, the Prescotts, the Macaulays? Few remain, if any, even though history as literature, history to entertain, pours from the presses as never before. Much of it is effective, a delight to read. Sometimes a professionally trained historian wanders into the field of traditional historical writing, almost uniformly with excellent results. For example, Sir John Neale wrote a biography of Queen Elizabeth that is certainly open to technical criticism, as it idolizes the queen; but, nevertheless, it is a remarkable literary tour de force that millions of people have read with delight. The same is true of a young American scholar, Lacey Baldwin Smith, whose *Mask of Royalty*, a book about Henry VIII, like Garrett Mattingly's *Defeat of the Spanish Armada*, will become a part of the classical tradition and endure as a work of art. Yet there are few professional historians at work in traditional history—studies of great events, biographies, and the like—and the reasons are not hard to find.

Traditional history, to be effective, requires great literary gifts—mastery of narrative structure, analytical insight into the vagaries of human behavior, a capacity to evoke through the magic of words, landscape, the way life was lived—all of which are not in the least necessary for a professional historian engaged on precise and narrow issues. And traditional history cannot often be written within a small compass about a narrow issue, so the writer of traditional history has to take great risks. He can never master all of the sources; there will be too many documents, too many letters, too many monographs. No one now can read all that has been published about the conquest of Mexico or the rise of the Dutch Republic. Therefore, the professional historian is naturally shy of attempting to do what his whole training has conditioned him not to do: to use his imagination, his sense of human reality, to bet on his hunches without having full documentary proof.

The reluctance or inability of professional historians to write traditional history means that the writing of it is largely in the hands of amateur historians, working outside the universities and the professional bodies. The last great academic figure who insisted passionately on the premise that history was literature or nothing and indeed wrote great traditional histories throughout his long life was G. M. Trevelyan. But his influence within the professional faculties of history was almost negligible. Lacking professional training, somewhat daunted by the bibliographical and archival expertise that a professional would have entirely at his command, the traditional historian, almost always an amateur, moves insecurely and often disastrously. Never before have so many books of a traditional historical kind been written. Most of them are sitting targets for professional criticisms. Within a year or two they pass into oblivion.

So we have a sad situation: a public demand for traditional history, an extraordinarily large response in terms of books (indeed, not only books; historical television series also meet with vast acclaim in both America and England), and yet an almost complete decline in quality, scarcely a book worthy to sit on the same shelf as the great old masters. To be fair, the decline is not in literary skill. Many recent books—Gene Smith's *Maximilian and Carlota,* Stanley Loomis's *Paris in the Terror,* or Robert Lacey on *Sir Walter Ralegh*—are beautifully constructed and written with the verve and panache worthy of a Prescott or Trevelyan. They fail to establish themselves permanently in the great tradition of historical writing.

One obvious reason for this is their lack of scholarship in depth. The great old masters—under less economic necessity, perhaps, as well as under less social pressure—tended to limit themselves to a few works on great themes. Gibbon spent his lifetime on the *Decline and Fall,** Macaulay, a man of monumental vigor, decades on his history, and even the output of a Motley or a Prescott was not large. In consequence, they had time to delve as deeply as any professional of their day into the sources of their work. Now, sources are more multitudinous than they were, yet the pressure on literary historians is to write quickly, to produce salable one-volume works as frequently as they can. Hence, even to the untrained reader of history, there is often a sense of a lack of depth, of profound knowledge, no matter how skillful the literary craftsmanship.

There is, however, I think, a more subtle reason. There has been a

---

* *The Decline and Fall of the Roman Empire; GBWW,* Vols. 40 and 41.

sharp decline in the role that traditional history plays in modern society. History has been the great interpreter of the human destiny, the pantheon in which mankind has enshrined its heroes, the majestic story of the conflict of good and evil, or the more mundane tale of progress, both material and moral. And furthermore, in the nineteenth century, history became even more closely associated with national destiny—a national destiny, however, that was also providential. The great American historians saw America, freed from the corruptions of Europe, as the great torchbearer of freedom. And whether they were writing about the Dutch Republic or the Conquistadores, there is, in their works, a deep sense that the tidal forces of history led inevitably to the freedom, the maturity, and the intellectual life that nineteenth-century New England, at least, enjoyed. The same is true of the great English historians, who saw English history as a slow but successful struggle for political freedom and representative institutions. If we turn to France or Italy or Germany, we find the same deep chord of national destiny struck. Hence, when these historians were read by tens of thousands of their fellow countrymen, the response went far deeper than entertainment; they fortified belief in their nation's destiny, strengthened social confidence. And that, of course, is why historical studies spread so rapidly in schools and universities in the late nineteenth and early twentieth centuries, and why all governments felt that the history of their nation must be an essential part of education at every level. History had an immediate, an urgent social purpose.

That situation has ended. The time given to history in schools shrinks every year. The enrollment of students in universities for historical studies has ceased to grow, and in many countries has begun to decline sharply. If we turn to other social studies—from economics to sociology—there is far less concern with historical roots of problems than there was. Indeed, it is rare now for scholars, let alone the public at large, to look to history for an explanation of the problems of our time. And nothing is more in ruins than the tradition that the past explains the present, sanctifies its institutions, and indicates the future. That ordinary men and women still hunger for such explanations and such prognostications is apparent from the popularity of Arnold Toynbee's great work on *A Study of History,* and nothing indicates the decay of such an attitude better than the lack of any imitators or even rivals to that work.

And yet this is true only of the West. In the nineteenth century, Marx and Engels forged an interpretation of history—materialist, dialectic and inevitable—that, as developed by Lenin, has become a rigid tradition not only in the Communist countries of Eastern Europe and of China but also among Marxist scholars or politicians in the rest of the world. This interpretation is now as absolute, as revered, as the old Chinese historical interpretation of the Mandate of Heaven. Indeed, it is a curious paradox that as traditional history has begun to crumble, not only in democratic societies of Europe and America but also in Islam and in the less developed

Each year North Carolina residents recreate a part of their history by making a wagon train journey from North Wilkesboro to Boone in much the same manner as early settlers of the region. *"Men and women since Homer's time and beyond have*

craved to know about the past. . . . Questions as to how and why have always haunted generations of men and women whose curiosity about the past is insatiable."

countries of Africa and the East, interpretations of history in Marxist countries have hardened into a steel-like dogma. At times this has odd consequences, for human events and indeed human beings have a Houdini-like capacity to escape the clutches of an inevitable historical interpretation; one needs only to recall the problems created by a rigid Christian interpretation of history not merely in the nineteenth century but even in the far distant days of Eusebius to see the point. And so, events—the denunciation of Stalin by Khrushchev—create a constant need for revision of the accepted Marxist tradition, all creating cracks in the edifice, making for cynicism, perhaps the most powerful corroder of tradition of all.

History, therefore, and the practitioners of history are entangled in complexities and paradoxes. As the professional methods and attitudes to history harden into even stronger traditions, the old social purposes of history that stretch back to the very beginnings of written records lose their force. The traditional power of history weakens, even as curiosity about the people and the events of the past grows. This situation is, of course, dangerous—more dangerous than many professional historians realize—for no discipline can survive for very long or be the recipient of vast funds, unless it fulfills an obvious social purpose. What is needed is what happened to history in the eighteenth century, when antiquarianism and philosophic history fused. The result of that fusion was the great historical literature of the nineteenth century. If only professional history could break with some of its traditional attitudes and take upon itself the burden of the history that society needs, the prospect for academic historians and for history in the service of mankind would be brighter than it is.

# The Idea of Tradition in Great Books of the Western World

Tradition is not one of the Great Ideas in the *Syntopicon*. It is, however, included in the Inventory of Terms, where we find it noted as a subject of discussion in topics belonging to half a dozen of those ideas, and at least implied in topics related to eight or nine more. This does not mean that the word itself always appears in the passage referred to. The discussion is sometimes carried on in the name of "custom," "convention," "habit," or "example." Nor are such related terms without their differences of meaning. They have, nevertheless, a common connotation, which is the preservation of the past that the idea of tradition necessarily involves, and they may fairly be said to indicate a common concept, as to the definition of which there is no serious dispute in *Great Books of the Western World*, but only some disagreement over the question whether that preservation is a good or a bad thing, considered in all its aspects.

One such aspect appears in the idea that the Past claims some authority in the Present, where it may or may not be regarded with deference. This is taken up in the texts under History 2, which deal with the role of history in education and the guidance of human conduct; it is considered also, with respect to the intellectual tradition, in passages noted at Progress 6c; it figures again, more generally, in writings listed at Time 8b, which deal with historical epochs, the ages of man, and the relative character of modernity.

A second aspect of the past as something that extends into the present appears in the form of particular customs or creeds that are handed down in the expectation of obedience or belief. This is discussed in the texts at Custom and Convention 8, dealing with custom in relation to order and progress; it appears also in writings listed under Custom and Convention 2, which have to do with the transmission of customs, and in Law 8, where passages dealing with the historical development of law are noted.

Still a third aspect of the subject, the most interesting one for a reader of the great books, seems to reveal a community of discourse in the accumulation of human knowledge. We find this considered in the chapter on Truth at topic 6, which lists writings that have to do with the progress of human learning; it is of some concern also in the texts at Philosophy 7, which deal with the history of philosophy and the lives of philosophers in relation to their thought; it is a notion basic to the discussion in the texts noted under Memory and Imagination 4b, which have to do with what is remembered, through instinct, legend, and tradition, in the life of the group or race.

The idea of a surviving past appears also in writings mentioned in the chapter on Art at topic 12, which are devoted to the history and progress of the arts, and by texts at Poetry 2 and 3, which are concerned with the origins of poetry in myth and legend and the influence on the poet of the poetic tradition. And the passages listed variously at Education 9, Family 7b, and Language 3c all point to the further fact that some, perhaps all, human arts and institutions are to some extent conservative of the past.

We can divide these many texts, which range beyond the concern of this year's symposium, into two groups. In one group, "tradition" or one of its related terms is used or intended generally and reflects a preoccupation with human development or human character. Such is the case in certain discussions of custom that occur, for example, in the *Essays* of Montaigne. The same preoccupation appears in William James's account of habit in the *Principles of Psychology*. We see it also in Freud when he speaks of the role of the superego in the unconscious. What is said about "tradition" on these occasions extends to all human orders—everything that men do, or make, or think—and is applicable perennially, without respect to time or place. Thus Robert M. Hutchins in volume 1 of *Great Books of the Western World* speaks of the tradition of the West as a Great Conversation, recognized by "the common voice of mankind,"[1] which has endured from epoch to epoch. The *Syntopicon* itself is, of course, a monument to this conception, without which it could never have been made.

In the second group of texts, "tradition" or one of its related terms is used with respect to a particular human order or preoccupation, such as art, philosophy, or government, and is often limited to a particular time and place. Hence the application is frequently one in which a custom or tradition is noted as having come or gone, grown stronger or weaker, perhaps even disappeared. In the *Iliad*, Nestor laments the vanished days of his youth when, he says, men were equally accomplished in counsel and the arts of war. Dante speaks of a change that has come about in art, where "Cimabue thought to hold the field in painting, and now Giotto has the cry";[2] he mentions also a "sweet new style" that has emerged in the poetry of his age.[3] Of course there is more than mention in *Don Quixote* about the passing of knight errantry. There is more than mention, too, in Plato's *Dialogues* of Athenian education, with its literary bent and rote learning, of which the *Dialogues* may be read as a critique, and for which Plato in his Academy substituted the mathematics and speculative inquiry that laid the basis of Western thought. As great a change was later brought about by Saint Augustine in Roman education, of which it may be said that he found it pagan and left it Christian, through the example and influence of his writings. And comparable changes were accomplished still later by

Copernicus—first, perhaps, among those whose work has altered the traditional understanding of things—by William Harvey, who revolutionized Galenic medicine, and by Lavoisier, who laid the foundations of modern chemistry.

The role of tradition in a particular human order is judged to be bad by some of these authors, by others is thought to be good. Among the first, those whose concern is with science tend to be most cogent and most critical. In this order, the weight of tradition is usually protested on the ground that it inhibits or prevents the progress of learning. Bacon, for instance—noting "the overmuch credit" that is given to the authority of the ancients, "making them dictators, that their words should stand, and not consuls to give advice"—says, "the damage is infinite that the sciences have received thereby, as the principal cause that hath kept them low at a stay without growth or advancement."[4] In another passage, speaking of "idols [that] beset the human mind," he mentions the "many elements and axioms of sciences which have become inveterate by tradition," and which he includes among what he calls the "idols of the theatre," because they, like "all the systems of philosophy hitherto received or imagined, [are] so many plays brought out and performed, creating fictitious and theatrical worlds."[5] And still later he complains that not experience but "mere reports of experience, traditions as it were of dreams," are the basis of the still-medieval science that he sees, which must be "built anew" if the mind of man is to be purged of "credulity and accident, and the puerile notions it originally contracted."[6]

Hobbes is even more severe, condemning deference to the past not only in science but in nearly everything else. "There is nothing so absurd that the old philosophers (as Cicero saith, who was one of them) have not some of them maintained," he writes. "And I believe that scarce anything can be more absurdly said in natural philosophy than what now is called Aristotle's *Metaphysics;* nor more repugnant to government than much of what he saith in his *Politics;* nor more ignorantly than a great part of his *Ethics.*"[7] Pascal, in his "Preface" to the *Treatise on the Vacuum*—an important text, about which there will be occasion to say more later on—is unwilling to condemn ancient authority in the same broad way, but he too notes the bad effect it has had in what we would now call physics, where, accepting the ancient dictum that nature abhors a vacuum, men had not until his time troubled to find out whether it was, in nature, actually so.[8] Galileo's account of his experiment with falling bodies in effect makes the same point, but it is not accompanied by any general remarks about the pernicious effects of traditional ways of thought.[9] We find such remarks, however, in Lavoisier, who in establishing that water is a compound and not a simple substance observes:

> *It is very extraordinary that this fact should have hitherto been overlooked by natural philosophers and chemists: indeed, it strongly proves that, in chemistry*

> *as in moral philosophy, it is extremely difficult to overcome prejudices imbibed in early education and to search for truth in any other road than the one we have been accustomed to follow.*[10]

And to this may be added the passage, of more extended application, that occurs in the second chapter of *The Decline and Fall of the Roman Empire*, where Gibbon notes the intellectual stagnation that had overtaken the Empire in the age of the Antonines, when, he says,

> *the authority of Plato and Aristotle, of Zeno and Epicurus, still reigned in the schools; and their systems, transmitted with blind deference from one generation of disciples to another, precluded every generous attempt to exercise the powers, or enlarge the limits, of the human mind.*[11]

As the focus of texts that are critical of tradition is chiefly on science, though it is not confined to that (Gibbon goes on to observe that in the same period of the Empire "the beauties of the [ancient] poets and orators, instead of kindling a fire like their own, inspired only cold and servile imitations: or if any ventured to deviate from those models, they deviated at the same time from good sense and propriety"[12]), so the focus of texts that approve the role of tradition tends to be on politics, morals, and religion, though authors can be found who judge that the weight of the past is a bad thing even in those orders. ("Prudence," said Jefferson, ". . . will dictate that governments long established should not be changed for light and transient causes,"[13] but the authors of *The Federalist* ask, "Is it not the glory of the people of America, that, whilst they have paid a decent regard to the opinions of former times and other nations, they have not suffered a blind veneration for antiquity, for custom, or for names, to overrule the suggestions of their own good sense, the knowledge of their own situation, and the lessons of their own experience?"[14]) As the ground for objecting to the role of tradition in science is chiefly that it prevents or inhibits progress, so the ground for supporting it in politics, morals, and religion is that it prevents or limits change. Montesquieu, for example, says that a democracy ought to have "a permanent body . . . to serve as a rule and pattern of manners; a senate, to which years, virtue, gravity, and eminent services procure admittance," which will "steadily adhere to the ancient institutions, and mind that the people and the magistrates never swerve from them."[15] And as the texts that oppose the role of tradition in science and certain other orders do so from the conviction, expressed or implied, that the past is inferior to the present, so the defenders of tradition do so from a conviction that at least in some orders the reverse is true. Again, it is Montesquieu who says,

> *The preservation of the ancient customs is a very considerable point in respect to manners. Since a corrupt people seldom perform any memorable actions, seldom establish societies, build cities, or enact laws; on the contrary,*

*since most institutions are derived from people whose manners are plain and simple, to keep up the ancient customs is the way to preserve the original purity of morals.*[16]

A regard for "ancient institutions" is as much needed when "by some revolution the state has happened to assume a new form" as in other circumstances, Montesquieu adds. For "even those who have been the instruments of the revolution were desirous it should be relished, which is difficult to compass without good laws."[17]

Authors who disapprove of tradition because of its effect on the progress of some human order such as science usually do so in the name of reason, which they oppose to it. This still allows tradition some room. Gibbon, observing how the Romans continued to worship the Greek gods as long as the Empire prospered, without any real belief that there was a connection between their fortunes and their faith, justifies such practice on the excuse—ironically intended, as to be sure it is—that "where reason cannot instruct, custom may be permitted to guide." Montaigne, however, finds reason *in* custom, insisting that there is "no so absurd or ridiculous fancy can enter into human imagination, that does not meet with some example of public practice, and that, consequently, our reason does not ground and back up."[18] What we regard as reasonable in this world is merely what we are accustomed to, he argues,

> *and the common fancies that we find in repute everywhere about us, and infused into our minds with the seed of our fathers, appear to be the most universal and genuine: from whence it comes to pass, that whatever is off the hinges of custom, is believed to be also off the hinges of reason; how unreasonably for the most part, God knows.*

Even "the laws of conscience, which we pretend to be derived from nature, proceed from custom," Montaigne says, so that "everyone, having an inward veneration for the opinions and manners approved and received amongst his own people, cannot, without very great reluctance, depart from them, nor apply himself to them without applause."[19] Such a doctrine, which denies that one custom is more reasonable than another, denies equally, of course, that reason can refute them. It is not therefore a surprise to find Montaigne saying, with respect to the political order, that men ought never to attempt to change their form of government so as to conform to some idea of what the best government is. Whatever plan is then conceived will be inferior in Montaigne's view to the wisdom embodied by time and trial in the government that exists, however bad that government is from an ideal point of view. "Not according to opinion," he insists, "but in truth and reality, the best and most excellent government for every nation is that under which it is maintained: its form and essential convenience depend upon custom." If we are displeased with our condition, yet we shall seek to alter it at our peril, for "nothing presses so hard upon a state as innovation: change only gives form to injustice and tyranny."[20]

Pascal disagrees with part of this. "Montaigne is wrong," he says, in offering such a rationale for custom. "Custom should be followed only because it is custom, and not because it is reasonable or just."[21] As we have seen, that for Pascal does not mean in science, where reason must rule and where men cannot accept any authority that is prejudicial to it. Customary beliefs, the authority of books, ancient teachings—these things belong in Pascal's view rather to history, to languages, and above all to religion, or more precisely to theology. For he says,

> *it is in theology that authority has its chief weight because there it is inseparable from truth, which we know only through it; so that to give absolute certainty to things which reason can grasp, it is sufficient to point them out in Holy Scripture (as, to show the uncertainty of the most probable things, we need only point out that they are not included there); because the principles of theology are above nature and reason, and the mind of man, too feeble to reach them by its own efforts, can arrive at this highest knowledge only if carried there by an all-powerful and supernatural force.*[22]

Because the tenor of these remarks is so very different from that with which Gibbon justifies the religion of Rome in the age of the Antonines, we may overlook the fact that they say the same thing. Of course Gibbon means that in matters that lie beyond the scope of reason, since no belief can be either true or false, any belief will do, or none; whereas for Pascal there is an order of things that includes a transcendent truth that reason cannot reach, that only faith can find. For both men, however, it is not in the order of reason and nature, but only in what lies beyond or above it, that what they call variously custom, tradition, opinion, or authority, in these and other texts, has its proper place.

The texts we have considered in which "tradition" or one of its related terms is said to be either a good or a bad thing in a particular human order are for the most part qualified, at least by implication, as expressions of the goodness or badness of "tradition" in general. Authors who approve or disapprove of custom or traditional authority in one order may accept or reject it in another, or in all others. Pascal, as we have seen, regards such authority as wrong in science but not in religion. Montaigne, who will not allow that any established government—that is, one sanctioned by custom—should be overthrown, even where the strongest reasons appear to exist for doing so, is eloquent on the folly of those who in dress or manners, "blinded and imposed upon by the authority of present usage," condemn any fashion but the current one, forgetting how often such things change.[23] And Bacon, who protests the authority of ancient learning in the experimental sciences, by no means rejects the means by which such learning survives. Indeed, he writes, "knowledge, whether it descend from divine inspiration, or spring from human sense, would soon perish and vanish to oblivion, if it were not preserved in books, traditions, conferences, and places appointed, as universities, colleges, and schools."[24]

There are, to be sure, a number of texts in which such qualifications do not appear, which take what may be called a comprehensive view of the subject. In some of them the role of "tradition" is regarded as beneficial in human character and circumstances generally, or in respect of some human order that is fundamental to such character and circumstances. These texts indicate that tradition, or custom, or whatever seems to convey the past into the present with authority, is an indispensable ingredient of human life considered as a whole, and therefore cannot or should not be denied.

One of these texts is in the *Laws* of Plato, who speaks in terms of custom and habit as well as of tradition itself. Elsewhere in that long dialogue, Plato asserts the importance of "unwritten customs, and what are termed the laws of our ancestors," which he calls "the bonds of the whole state";[25] he insists also upon the importance of religious traditions, "the least part of [which] ought not to be disturbed by the legislator";[26] he argues, as in *The Republic*, that no changes should ever be allowed in music and the forms of dance when they are expressive, as they ought always to be, of virtue;[27] and so forth. But in one particular passage he goes farther and maintains that

> *any change whatever except from evil is the most dangerous of all things; this is true in the case of the seasons and of the winds, in the management of our bodies and the habits of our minds—true of all things except, as I said before, of the bad. He who looks at the constitution of individuals accustomed to eat any sort of meat, or drink any drink, or to do any work which they can get, may see that they are first disordered by them, but afterwards, as time goes on, their bodies grow adapted to them, and they learn to know and like variety, and have good health and enjoyment of life; and if ever afterwards they are confined again to a superior diet, at first they are troubled with disorders, and with difficulty become habituated to their new food. A similar principle we may imagine to hold good about the minds of men and the natures of their souls. For when they have been brought up in certain laws, which by some Divine Providence have remained unchanged during long ages, so that no one has any memory or tradition of their being otherwise than they are, then everyone is afraid and ashamed to change that which is established.*

Therefore, Plato says, "the legislator must somehow find a way of implanting this reverence for antiquity," lest there be "frequent changes in the praise and censure of manners," which constitute "the greatest of evils."[28]

A second text in which "tradition" or one of its related terms is held to be good in a general sense is the famous passage in *The Principles of Psychology* where William James discourses on the subject of habit, which he calls "the enormous fly-wheel of society, its most precious conservative agent." The force of habit is such that no man can escape its effects, James asserts. And "on the whole," he adds, "it is best" that we should not escape. "It is well for the world that in most of us, by the age of thirty, the character has set like plaster, and will never soften again."[29]

Still a third text of the sort we are discussing is that in the *New Introductory Lectures on Psycho-Analysis* where Freud speaks of the superego as formed by the child's parents and thus as constituting "the vehicle of tradition and all the age-long values which have been handed down . . . from generation to generation." In conveying this tradition, Freud adds, the superego is "the representative of all moral restrictions, the advocate of the impulse towards perfection, in short . . . as much as we have been able to apprehend psychologically of what people call the 'higher' things in human life."[30] Similar statements appear later in the *Outline of Psychoanalysis*, where Freud again makes the point that the superego reflects the influence of the parents on the child's mind, and "includes not merely the personalities of the parents themselves, but also the racial, national, and family traditions handed on through them."[31] The same work contains a further interesting passage in which Freud adds:

> *In spite of their fundamental difference, the id and the superego have one thing in common: they both represent the influences of the past (the id the influence of heredity, the superego essentially the influence of what is taken over from other people), whereas the ego is principally determined by the individual's own experience, that is to say by accidental and current events.*[32]

There are also texts, however, quite as comprehensive as any of these, that take the opposite view, disputing the necessity and the worth of tradition in human affairs with the same lack of qualification. They regard tradition as inhibiting or as being otherwise detrimental to the progress of knowledge, the formation of human character, or the arrangement of human circumstances, and they argue or appeal for a reduction of its influence if they do not absolutely defy it.

One such text consists of the chapter called "Of Darkness from Vain Philosophy and Fabulous Traditions" in Part IV of Hobbes's *Leviathan*, from which a portion has already been quoted. In this chapter, Hobbes reviews with massive scorn a variety of errors or illusions that have survived by tradition through books and other means from ancient or medieval times. The defect of these errors or illusions—among which Hobbes lists the teachings of Aristotle, the commentaries of the Jews, and the dogmas of the Roman Church—is that they are based, or at least our acceptance of them is based, not on what Hobbes calls "reasoning," by which he means proceeding from "the manner of the generation of any-thing, to the properties; or from the properties, to some possible way of generation of the same," so as to be able to produce, "as far as matter and human force permit, such effects as human life requireth,"[33] but on suppo-sitions and distinctions that were faulty to begin with and have been handed down in books that neither understood the errors nor corrected them. All of which Hobbes rejects as tending to keep men in intellectual and spiritual darkness, ignorant alike of reason and the gospel, unfitted for the duties of a human Commonwealth and unready for the Kingdom of God to come.

To this may be added the statements in the *Discourse on Method* that tell how Descartes came to rely on his own intellectual resources rather than those of other men—statements purely personal in their intention, and significantly so, yet symptomatic of a cast of thought that has become wide-spread. For, Descartes says, after his experience of schools had convinced him that nothing was certainly known by the philosophers, and that the sciences grounded on their writings could therefore not be trusted, he resolved to seek no other knowledge than that which could be found in himself, on the assumption that

> *as regards all the opinions which up to this time I had embraced, I . . . could not do better than endeavour once for all to sweep them completely away, so that they might later on be replaced, either by others which were better, or by the same, when I had made them conform to the uniformity of a rational scheme. And I firmly believed that by this means I should succeed in directing my life much better than if I had only built on old foundations, and relied on prin-ciples of which I allowed myself in youth to be persuaded without having inquired into their truth.*[34]

On top of this must be added the remarks of John Stuart Mill—as strong an antitraditionalist in his way as Hobbes, though his tone is very different—who addresses himself to the subject in the essay *On Liberty*. There, in the chapter called "Of Individuality, as one of the Elements of Well-being," Mill asserts that

> *Where, not the person's own character, but the traditions or customs of other people are the rule of conduct, there is wanting one of the principal ingredients of human happiness, and quite the chief ingredient of individual and social progress.*[35]

The defect that Mill sees in the human society of his time is just its ten-dency to insist upon such sources of conduct and, as a result, to discourage individual and social development. "The despotism of custom," he writes, "is everywhere the standing hindrance to human advancement, being in unceasing antagonism to that disposition to aim at something better than customary, which is called, according to circumstances, the spirit of liberty, or that of progress or improvement."³⁶ Mill accepts certain limits to this spirit. "Nobody denies," he says,

> *that people should be so taught and trained in youth as to know and benefit by the ascertained results of human experience. But it is the privilege and proper condition of a human being, arrived at the maturity of his faculties, to use and interpret experience in his own way.*³⁷

If this does not happen, Mill argues, there cannot be any human development, for "the individuality is the same thing with development, and . . . it is only the cultivation of individuality which produces, or can produce, well-developed human beings."³⁸

It will be noted that in the passages we have considered from Plato, William James, and Freud, the value of tradition (or custom, or habit, as the case may be) is thought to lie mostly in its stabilizing influence, the restraint it provides in the cultural life of the race. For each of these authors, this is only the means to an end. James indicates how that is so in the relatively restricted terms that the idea of "habit" implies, as assuring social stability and making possible individual achievement. The function of the superego, Freud argues, is something greater, binding together not merely the social but what we may think of more comprehensively as the human order, and not only in respect of an individual lifetime, to which, of course, any habit is confined, but of the whole of human experience, which the superego makes available to, and brings to bear upon, the individual psyche. And Plato's frame of reference is larger still, being political and philosophical rather than historical or moral: the well-ordered State requires a "reverence for antiquity" as a body requires health—must, if it loses this reverence, become enfeebled and disordered, as a body without health becomes weakened or diseased—to the end that the laws and public institutions may survive and prosper and the citizens may live wise and virtuous lives.

The texts from Hobbes, Descartes, and J. S. Mill, which are as strongly against tradition as these passages are for it, likewise regard it not as an end in itself but as something intermediate in human affairs. But where Plato, Freud, and William James think tradition is enabling—is, indeed, the indispensable condition of a wise, good, and truly human life—for Hobbes, Descartes, and Mill it serves precisely the opposite function, is rather inhibiting if not absolutely preventive of that kind of life. Or, if some qualification is in order before we reach such a conclusion in the case of Hobbes and Descartes, the focus of whose concern may be said to be intellectual rather than moral—with what we know rather than with what we do (whatever difference that makes)—yet at least in the case of Mill there can be no doubt that we have a disagreement, with respect to Plato,

James, and Freud, that is both direct and profound. And this disagreement is at least implied in many of the other texts we have reviewed, so that it seems necessary to accept that, while the issue is not always exactly joined, when it is, the judgments of the authors of *Great Books of the Western World* on the subject are seriously conflicting.

There are, however, a number of texts in the set that endeavor to reconcile or transcend this disagreement, or that seem to provide grounds on which we may reconcile or transcend it ourselves—texts that indicate the fullest perception of the conflict that has been noted. This means, among other things, that they recognize the deadening effects that tradition can have in human affairs or on human understanding (for their focus is as much on knowledge as it is on action), and that they undertake to defend it only insofar as they can regard it as a vital force.

Such a text is Pascal's Preface to the *Treatise on the Vacuum*, of which some account has already been given. In this remarkable discussion that, brief as it is, seems to say nearly everything that can be said about tradition, Pascal distinguishes between the kind of knowledge that animals have and the kind that is peculiar to man. He observes that the knowledge animals have through instinct is complete but limited: nature teaches them whatever they need to know in order to accomplish their natural purpose, but no more; and as their knowledge does not need to be increased, so it cannot be preserved, being created afresh in each new member of the species. "It is different with man," Pascal says, "made only for infinity."

> *He is ignorant in his life's first age, but he never ceases to learn as he goes forward, for he has the advantage not only of his own experience but also of his predecessors', because he always keeps in his memory the knowledge he has once acquired, and that of the ancients is always at hand in the books they have left.*

In terms we have been using, this is to say that as man learns by reason rather than instinct, so the source of his knowledge is not nature but experience, both his own and that of his ancestors. The latter cannot limit us, Pascal insists, unless we make the mistake of treating it with reverence, as if, once the opinions of the ancients had been expressed, there were "no more truths to know." When we do this, in effect we treat such opinions as if they *were* instincts, and thus can learn nothing from them. The right way for man to regard the matter, Pascal argues, is to realize that "since he keeps his knowledge, he can also easily increase it," and that the men of any given time are, as one may say, in the same condition as the ancients would be if they had been able to continue their studies. For "the same thing happens in the succession of men as in the different ages of an individual," Pascal goes on, "so that the whole series of men during the course of so many centuries should be considered as one self-same man, always in existence and continually learning."[39]

A second text that seems to reconcile or transcend the conflict we have noted is from *The Critique of Judgment*, where Kant considers how an aesthetic judgment—that is, a judgment of taste, having to do with the excellence or beauty of a thing—can be arrived at. Such a judgment has no objective basis, yet lays claim to the agreement of everyone; can be verified only in the sense, and to the extent, that it agrees with the judgment of others, yet lays claim to autonomy, denying that other judgments are its source. "The fact that we recommend the works of the ancients as models," Kant says, "and rightly, too, and call their authors *classical*, as constituting a sort of nobility among writers that leads the way and thereby gives laws to the people, seems to indicate *a posteriori* sources of taste and to contradict the autonomy of taste in each individual."

> But we might just as well say that the ancient mathematicians, who, to this day, are looked upon as the almost indispensable models of perfect thoroughness and elegance in synthetic methods, prove that reason also is on our part only imitative, and that it is incompetent with the deepest intuition to produce of itself rigorous proofs by means of the construction of concepts.[40]

Kant allows that when we come to judge of anything, without considering what others have said before us, we are likely to blunder. It is not, however, "that predecessors make those who follow in their steps mere imitators, but by their methods they set others upon the track of seeking in themselves for the principles, and so of adopting their own, often better, course." They serve as examples rather than as rules, and the difference is that in judgments based on reason, such examples only reinforce the authority of concepts, whereas in aesthetic judgments, which are not based on concepts but are only expressions of taste, examples are our only guide, indicating "what has in the course of culture maintained itself longest in esteem." We follow such examples as precedents, Kant says, and this, so far as the influence of a particular author extends, "means no more than going to the same sources for a creative work as those to which he went for his creations, and learning from one's predecessor no more than the mode of availing oneself of such sources."[41]

To these observations of Kant's we may add the text—the last we have room to consider—provided by T. S. Eliot's essay "Tradition and the Individual Talent," which appears not in *Great Books of the Western World* but in *Gateway to the Great Books*, volume 5. For this essay, too, seems to reconcile or transcend the conflict we have observed. That is, it seems to rescue the idea of tradition from its deadening implications—not, as Pascal does, by asserting the continuity of humankind, and not as Kant does by invoking the notion of example or precedent, but with its perception that there is a particular order of human experience to which tradition belongs, and which may be said to comprise just that portion of the historical order that is always present and alive.

The context in which this perception of Eliot's occurs is that of art, in particular of poetry, as Pascal's context is scientific and Kant's is philosophical. But it is an idea with wider applications than Eliot gives it. It recognizes that there is a difference between the purely historical order and the order—the ideal order, as Eliot suggests it is—that is formed by "the existing monuments." This order is both temporal and timeless; it occurs within the historical order, but the parts of it, the achievements that comprise it, have a simultaneous existence. As such they constitute a tradition, Eliot says, that cannot be inherited, but can be obtained, if we chose, by great labor. If we are willing to put forth this labor, he adds, we acquire a historical sense that makes us conscious that as whatever work we undertake is affected by the tradition of which we have become aware, and in which our work takes its place, so the tradition is affected by that work, if ever so slightly—affected in the relationship that is thus established between the part and the whole, in the new intelligibility that each thereby acquires, and in the new value they take on in being measured by each other. For none of the works of man has its meaning alone, but each is significant in relation to the rest.

What we discern in these observations of Eliot's, as in Kant's remarks and those of Pascal, is an endeavor to distinguish between what may be called traditionalism, which forces the present, for good or ill, to adapt itself to the past, and a different sort of influence that places the present in a context that allows for—that requires—development. It is this latter meaning of tradition, implicit in many other texts besides those we have discussed, that a careful reading of *Great Books of the Western World* seems to bring out, as being the wisdom of the subject when it is squarely contemplated. That this should be so is consistent with the kind of tradition that the books themselves are thought to embody, of which Eliot in particular, though he has in mind a somewhat different order, gives such a good account. It is as if we had discovered in them the principle of their own vitality, which they had not often or lengthily troubled to explain, but which, when necessary, they could articulate and make manifest. "For books," as Milton says, "are not absolutely dead things, but do contain a potency of life in them to be as active as that soul whose progeny they are; nay, they do preserve as in a vial the purest efficacy and extraction of the living intellect that bred them."[42] In respect to the idea of tradition, as with so many other subjects, the *Great Books* seem able to show with special force how this is so.

[1] *GBWW*, Vol. 1, p. xi.
[2] *GBWW*, Vol. 21, p. 69d.
[3] Ibid., p. 90.
[4] *GBWW*, Vol. 30, p. 14c–d.
[5] Ibid., pp. 109, 110.
[6] Ibid., p. 126.
[7] *GBWW*, Vol. 23, pp. 268–69.
[8] *GBWW*, Vol. 33, p. 358.
[9] *GBWW*, Vol. 28, pp. 157 ff.
[10] *GBWW*, Vol. 45, p. 33.
[11] *GBWW*, Vol. 40, pp. 23–24.
[12] Ibid., p. 24.
[13] *GBWW*, Vol. 43, p. 1.
[14] Ibid., p. 62.
[15] *GBWW*, Vol. 38, p. 22a.
[16] Ibid., p. 22.
[17] Ibid.
[18] *GBWW*, Vol. 25, p. 44.
[19] Ibid., p. 46.
[20] Ibid., p. 463.
[21] *GBWW*, Vol. 33, p. 230.
[22] Ibid., p. 355.
[23] *GBWW*, Vol. 25, p. 143.
[24] *GBWW*, Vol. 30, p. 29.
[25] *GBWW*, Vol. 7, p. 716.
[26] Ibid., p. 692.
[27] Ibid., p. 654.
[28] Ibid., p. 718.
[29] *GBWW*, Vol. 53, p. 79.
[30] *GBWW*, Vol. 54, p. 834b–c.
[31] *An Outline of Psychoanalysis*, trans. James Strachey (New York: W. W. Norton & Co., 1949), p. 17.
[32] Ibid.
[33] *GBWW*, Vol. 23, p. 267.
[34] *GBWW*, Vol. 31, p. 45b–c.
[35] *GBWW*, Vol. 43, pp. 293–94.
[36] Ibid., p. 300.
[37] Ibid., p. 294.
[38] Ibid., p. 297.
[39] *GBWW*, Vol. 33, p. 357.
[40] *GBWW*, Vol. 42, pp. 513d–14a.
[41] Ibid., p. 514.
[42] *GBWW*, Vol. 32, p. 384.

# PART TWO

# Review
# of the
# Arts and Sciences

# Impasse for the Elementary-Particle Concept

## Geoffrey Chew

Geoffrey Chew, who began his scientific career at twenty with the Los Alamos Atomic Bomb project, on which he served as a research assistant (1944–46), has taught principally at the University of Illinois (1951–56) and the University of California at Berkeley, where he has been professor of physics since 1957 and since 1970 a theoretical group leader at the Lawrence Radiation Laboratory. He has been interested throughout in theoretical particle physics, scattering matrix theory, and the theory of strong interactions, all of which bear close relation to his discussion here of the elementary-particle concept and the dead end at which it has possibly arrived.

Professor Chew, who is the author of *S-Matrix Theory of Strong Interactions* (1961) and *The Analytic S Matrix: A Basis for Nuclear Democracy* (1966), is a consultant to both the Los Alamos and Brookhaven National Laboratories, a fellow of the American Physics Society, and a member of the American Academy of Arts and Sciences. In 1969 he received one of the Ernest O. Lawrence Memorial Awards for "especially meritorious contributions to the development, use or control of atomic energy" from the Atomic Energy Commission.

## Introduction

S cience ofttimes is likened to the peeling of layers from an onion, to see what lies "underneath." This figure of speech expresses the expectation that if a system be decomposed into "components," the laws governing the behavior of individual pieces will be revealed as simpler than those controlling the "larger" system. Western scientific thought from the time of the early Greek philosophers has been dominated by onion peeling — alternatively characterizable as the search for "elementary particles" — and the total record of success to this point is fabulous. Both in biological and in physical science the search for smaller and smaller units has yielded spectacular dividends, leading many thoughtful men to take for granted that a crucial frontier of scientific investigation will always lie in the quest for elementary entities.

Already in the first half of this century, on the other hand, Einstein's principle of relativity, in combination with the principles of quantum theory, showed signs of incompatibility with the notion of fundamental constituents of matter. Years of subsequent intensive study by the community of theoretical physicists have amplified doubts about the viability of the elementary-particle idea, doubts reinforced during the recent deluge of nuclear-particle discoveries by the failure to identify plausible candidates for elementary status. This essay proposes to review twentieth-century theoretical and experimental developments that suggest that the search for an elementary particle — obedient to a concept that has held sway over thousands of years of human intellectual activity — has reached the end of its road. The outline of an alternative idea, also thousands of years old but until recently not considered suitable for science, will be described.

Stephen Toulmin's "Physical Sciences" article in the 1967 issue of *The Great Ideas Today* (pp. 158–95) provides a survey of the dividends that, until the 1930s, flowed from the search for elementary particles. Toulmin goes on to identify certain of the difficulties subsequently encountered, but avoids dealing explicitly with the role of relativity, a principle lying at the heart of the elementary-particle impasse. In the present article we shall discuss relativity at the very beginning. As in doing so we shall avoid the use of mathematics, our discussion will suffer from lack of precision, and the reader must be prepared in the account that follows to encounter paradoxes. Such paradoxes are inevitable when ordinary language—designed to describe phenomena where all velocities are small compared to the velocity of light (186,000 miles per second)—is applied to situations where some velocities approach the value that Einstein identified as an absolute upper limit. An analogous difficulty is well known to arise from the use of everyday words to describe quantum phenomena. Since it is the union of quantum and relativity principles that we are to discuss, the language impediment promises to be formidable.

It must be acknowledged, however, that even with the help of a mathematical vocabulary the professional physicist has difficulty in unambiguously characterizing the puzzle treated in this article. It is likely that the question at issue will become clearly posable only at the moment when the answer to the question becomes apparent. The finding of appropriate language is the essence of the game.

## Equivalence of energy and mass

For the purposes of our review it will help to consider right at the start one special aspect of Einstein's relativity principle, the equivalence of mass and energy. This equivalence immediately raises problems for the concept of an elementary particle.

Einstein's 1905 theory, now thoroughly established by experiment, includes the statement that the mass of any object corresponds to the total energy of that object. This principle applies to both large and small objects —to baseballs and to atomic nuclei. If several objects are aggregated to form a larger system, the mass of the composite system corresponds to a total energy that combines the energies (masses) of the constituent objects with their energy of mutual interaction—often called the *potential energy*. If the component objects are in motion, the energy associated with this motion (kinetic energy) also is part of the total system's mass.*

For a concrete example we may consider the familiar Bohr picture of the hydrogen atom as a combination of a heavy nucleus, called the proton, and a light satellite called the electron, constrained to circulate around each other by the influence of an attractive electrical force. Such a picture we shall find later to be only a first approximation, but it serves to fix certain notions. The total mass of the atom in this picture is built up from five components: the mass of the proton, the mass of the electron, the kinetic energy (energy of motion) of the proton, the kinetic energy of the electron, and finally the energy associated with the attractive force between proton and electron. The latter component (potential energy) is negative and sufficiently large in magnitude that the total hydrogen-atom mass is smaller than the sum of electron and proton masses.

Experiments where the hydrogen atom acts as a unit do not differentiate the five ingredients; only the total mass is relevant. On the other hand, it is possible in certain experiments to supply sufficient energy so as to make up the difference between the atom's mass and the sum of electron and proton masses. The atom may then "dissociate" into its constituents. Such dissociation, of course, has been interpreted as evidence that atoms are not elementary particles.

Now let us ask the question: Is the proton elementary, or should it be considered as a composite in the same sense as an atom? Merely using the test of dissociability, the answer has clearly been given by experiment: With a sufficient supply of energy, a supply that has existed from particle accelerators since about 1950, the proton readily decomposes into combinations of other particles. It is true that the sum of the "constituent" masses is greater than the mass of the proton itself, but we have seen that such a circumstance already prevails for atoms.

It is, in fact, observed that as the available energy increases, the variety of proton constituent combinations also increases—apparently without limit. At the National Accelerator Laboratory (NAL) in Illinois, for example, proton dissociation into as many as five particles has been observed when extremely high kinetic energies are employed. Even higher energies are available at the European Center for Nuclear Research (CERN) in Geneva, and one there observes proton dissociation into correspondingly larger numbers of constituents.

Although the idea of a definite (finite) number of constituents for the proton is not tenable, neither is this idea tenable for the hydrogen atom. The latter decomposes uniquely into an electron and a proton if inadequate energy is available to allow other combinations, but with addition of further energy, new constituent possibilities inevitably become realized.

With the relativity principle's power to transform energy of motion into mass, any particle unavoidably possesses the capacity to "dissociate." It follows that if a meaning is to be found for the concept of "elementary particle," the meaning cannot rest on the impossibility of decomposing the particle. Even before the availability in the laboratory of the high kinetic energies needed to "dissociate" particles like the proton, physicists appreciated the above-described theoretical implications of Einstein's mass-energy equivalence. The experimental results at NAL and CERN, that is to say, come as no surprise. Why, then, was the idea of elementary particles not immediately abandoned when the principle of relativity became established? To answer this question we need to recall certain aspects of electromagnetic theory, where use of the elementary-particle concept has proved valuable even when kinetic energies are sufficient to allow particle dissociation.

---

* The term *rest mass* is used to denote the mass of an object whose center of gravity is motionless.

## Weakly interacting photons: quantum electrodynamics

It became understood during the nineteenth century that light constitutes one manifestation of electromagnetism: electric and magnetic waves propagating through space. With the early twentieth-century development of quantum theory, there arose the complementary notion of photons, which may be regarded as "particles of light." This dualism between waves and particles is one of the characteristic features of quantum theory; without consideration of both aspects, no description of electromagnetism is complete. The present stage of our discussion will nevertheless be expedited if we concentrate on the notion of photons as particles.

The photon differs from most particles in that it cannot be brought to rest; in fact, its velocity is always the same (the *velocity of light*), independent of how much energy the photon carries. Relativity theory permits a photon to possess any amount of energy, starting from zero, in contrast to a particle like the proton, whose energy may never be less than that corresponding to its mass when at rest (the *rest mass*). Creation of photons may consequently be accomplished by the expenditure of extremely small quantities of energy—less than needed to create ordinary particles.

Although in the pre-quantum-theory nineteenth century one did not speak of the "creation of photons" but rather of the "emission of electromagnetic radiation," it was a familiar idea before the discovery of relativity as a general principle that the kinetic energy of an ordinary particle such as an electron could be transformed into electromagnetic energy. In the language of the preceding section we would describe such a process as "dissociation" of an electron into an electron plus one or more photons.

We might correspondingly say that such dissociation implies a composite nature for the electron, one of its components being a photon-electron combination; doubt would then be cast on the status of an electron as an elementary particle. Use of such language may be avoided, however, if one recognizes a vital if elusive aspect of the photon, which is its weakness of coupling to other particles. Later in this essay we shall encounter profound significance for the very structure of science in the weakness of photon interactions. At the present stage of our discussion we point to this weakness as a fact of nature that allows a degree of usefulness for the elementary-particle concept.

What are we to understand by "weakness" of the photon interaction? Here our language must begin to reflect some aspects of quantum theory that require a probabilistic rather than deterministic characterization of experiments. If an electron, for example, passes close to some other electrically charged particle, there is a certain probability that the electron will dissociate into a particular combination of constituents—a chance, but not a certainty. If the energy is modest and we demand that the photons among the constituents carry off an appreciable fraction of the initial electron energy, it turns out that the probability of dissociation is very small.

In other words, any electron of energy available from present-day accelerators survives as a single particle most of the time, even though there is inevitably some small chance of its changing form. Because the probability of change is small, it is profitable for many purposes to speak of the electron as "elementary." Were the probability large, nothing would be gained by such a notion.

The smallness of the probability for creation of photons has allowed construction of an approximate but extremely accurate set of rules for predicting the moderate-energy behavior of electrons and photons in terms of the rest mass of the electron and its electric charge. These rules, known as "quantum electrodynamics," were the basis for the 1965 Nobel Prize awarded to Richard Feynman, Julian Schwinger, and Shinichiro Tomonaga. To the extent that the rules are self-contained and refer to no other particles than electrons and photons, they justify designation of these particles as "elementary." Many attempts have been made to find analogous rules for nuclear particles, but where the interactions are not weak the rules turn out to be useless. Even for photons and electrons the accuracy of the rules is limited and deteriorates as the energy increases, because the strength of photon coupling increases. Quantum electrodynamics cannot be the whole story even for these special particles.*

The success of quantum electrodynamics has nevertheless had a profound impact on the thinking of most twentieth-century theoretical physicists, many of whom have continued to hope for an extension of the sense in which photons and electrons may be regarded as elementary. This sense, however, is firmly tied to the mysterious weakness of the photon coupling. Nuclear particles, unlike electrons, are subject to interactions that are manyfold stronger than those of the photon.

## Nuclear particles and nuclear forces

What is meant by the term *nuclear particle*? Why are electrons and photons excluded from this category? To answer these questions one needs recall a major scientific discovery of the twentieth century: the existence of short-range forces between certain particles, of a strength much greater than possessed by electric or magnetic forces. Electromagnetic forces control the properties of atoms and molecules,† but are weak on the scale we are now considering. The first observation of strong short-range forces was between the nuclei of atoms, so these interactions were called *nuclear forces*.

---

* The plausibility of elementary status for the electron has further been undermined by the discovery of another particle, called the muon, that seems to differ from the electron only in its rest mass, which is 216 times as large. It is manifestly unreasonable to regard one of these particles as elementary and not the other, but regarding both as elementary would mean forgoing the possibility of understanding their puzzling mass ratio.

† We have mentioned above the electric force between electrons and atomic nuclei.

In this discussion we shall refer to *any* particle that is subject to such short-range forces as a *nuclear particle*. In fact there are known to exist many particles within this category that are unable to surround themselves with electrons and form the nucleus of an atom. The neutron, for instance, has properties similar to the proton with respect to short-range forces but, lacking electric charge, cannot attract and hold an electron, as a proton does in the hydrogen atom. We shall nevertheless refer to the neutron as a nuclear particle.

Electrons are not classified as nuclear particles because they are immune to strong short-range forces. Photons are similarly immune. At the same time, the great majority of the flood of particles discovered since the Second World War falls into the nuclear category; we shall have occasion later to identify the exceptions.

The entire class of nuclear particles shares many striking properties in common, encouraging a terminology that emphasizes at once their mutual similarity and their difference from nonnuclear particles. We shall not here find it necessary to go into detail regarding these properties;* it will suffice to emphasize the distinguishing characteristic of either being subject to, or immune to, nuclear forces. Needless to say, the origin of nuclear forces will be a main concern of this essay.

## "Weakly" interacting pions: classical nuclear physics

Nuclear particles such as protons dissociate into components so readily at the high energies already available at NAL and CERN as to render useless the notion that any nuclear particle is "elementary." But the only nuclear particle whose rest mass is so small that it can be easily created at *low* energy—a particle that has been named the *pion†*—has sufficiently weak interactions at low energy that it has proved possible to employ the elementary-particle concept in describing the low-energy behavior of atomic nuclei. The pion here plays a role analogous to that outlined earlier for the photon. Because pion interactions are much stronger than those of the photon, the associated elementarity concept for nuclear particles is much less accurate than for electrons, but such a concept nevertheless constitutes the basis for a branch of science called classical nuclear physics.

Classical nuclear physics regards neutrons and protons as the basic building blocks of nuclear matter, just as electrons (together with nuclei) are regarded as the basic constituents of atoms. According to this picture, one may join neutrons and protons into a variety of combinations to form the different atomic nuclei. The alpha particle or helium nucleus, for example, is pictured as a combination of two neutrons and two protons; the most common form of uranium nucleus is described as a combination of 92 protons and 146 neutrons, and so on. The arguments already given show that such a picture necessarily fails at high energies where the composite nature of neutrons and protons becomes revealed, but at low energies the model based on elementary neutrons and protons works well. Because of its small rest mass the pion is the most easily created nuclear particle, but the pion is sufficiently weakly coupled at low energy that its presence as a "component" of a neutron or proton may be treated as a small correction.

At the same time, in a sense first recognized in 1935 by Yukawa, the pion's presence as a component "within" neutrons and protons produces a force that binds together atomic nuclei. Speaking very loosely, a pion "attached" to one neutron or proton wanders about in the surrounding region, and if it encounters another neutron or proton the pion may transfer its allegiance. The net effect of such a transfer is to generate a force between donor and recipient. One may say, analogously, that the presence of the photon as a component of the electron is responsible for the attractive electrical force binding electrons within atoms, and such a connection between forces and component particles has been understood since the late fifties to be a completely general feature of quantum-relativity theory. This important point will receive repeated attention in what follows. The reader should note at once the implication that a truly elementary particle —completely devoid of internal structure—could not be subject to any forces that would allow us to detect its existence. The mere knowledge of a particle's existence, that is to say, indicates that the particle possesses internal structure, and implies that it cannot be "elementary" in a pristine sense.

One way to appreciate the need for particles as force mediators is to recognize that relativity precludes "action at a distance," signals never being allowed to travel faster than the velocity of light. Now, as we shall emphasize later, the meaning of *distance* becomes obscure when applied on the scale of nuclear particles, because there is no method of measuring distance at this level. Nevertheless, when careful analysis is made of the meaning of relativity in nuclear phenomena, one discovers that a force between two particles can arise only via other particles that bridge an intervening "gap." The electron in the hydrogen atom feels the attractive force of the proton through the photon component in the electron structure that "reaches out" to probe the surroundings. Similarly, a proton within a helium nucleus feels attracted by the two neutrons and the other proton through the pion component in the proton's structure.

In his 1935 analysis of the quantum-relativistic force problem—eventually rewarded by a Nobel Prize—Yukawa pointed out that the distance over which a force can be effective is inversely proportional to the rest

---

* A conscientious review of particle properties, replete with diagrams, may be found in Geoffrey F. Chew, Murray Gell-Mann, and Arthur H. Rosenfeld, "Strongly Interacting Particles," *Scientific American* 210 (February 1964): 74–93.

† The rest mass of the pion is roughly one-seventh as large as that of the proton or the neutron, whose rest masses are approximately equal to each other.

mass of the mediating particle; and because the pion is the least-massive nuclear particle, it produces the longest-range and most visible nuclear force.* Subsequent study showed that all types of particles make some contribution to the total interaction, but it turns out meaningless to maintain a picture of elementary neutrons and protons subject to mutual forces when the rest mass of the force-mediating particles becomes comparable to or larger than the rest masses of the original neutrons and protons. It is essential to classical nuclear physics that the pion rest mass is much smaller than that of neutrons and protons.

The classical nuclear-physics portrayal of atomic nuclei as composed of elementary neutrons and protons subject to Yukawa forces rests on the combination of a small pion rest mass (compared to that of neutrons and protons) and a (moderately) small low-energy pion coupling. It is the smallness of these parameters that determines the accuracy of the picture. Classical nuclear physics is correspondingly only approximate, even at low energy, and fails completely when the energy is large.

We now have encountered two different examples of approximate validity for the elementary-particle concept, and it is time to consider more broadly the status within physics of models that have utility even though these models violate some general principle of nature. A view of the general basis for physical models will allow an estimate of the chance for finding an elementary-particle model suitable when no interaction is weak.

## Physical models and small parameters: a closer look at onion peeling

Looking back over the history of physics from the time of Newton, who produced the first model of nature that was at once broad in scope, quantitative in content, and useful, we recognize that all dynamical schemes, including the most influential and valuable, have sooner or later proven to be flawed. Newton's description of the solar system is now recognized to violate relativity; Maxwell's nineteenth-century equations for electricity and magnetism ignore quantum requirements; the Bohr-Heisenberg-Schrödinger picture of the atom is nonrelativistic. Although it currently remains an unresolved question whether quantum electrodynamics—the previously noted set of rules for electrons and photons—is in violation of some established general principle, there are indications of trouble here with the probability interpretation of quantum mechanics, an interpretation that will be discussed when we consider quantum principles.

In the interest of clarity, a distinction should be drawn at this point between general principles of physics and dynamical models that include explicit statements about the detailed nature and strength of forces. General principles typically make no reference to numerical parameters, while each dynamical model is characterized by certain specific numbers, such as the mass and charge of the electron in the Bohr model of the atom. During the history of physical science there has been an evolution both of general principles and of dynamical models, the one type of development strongly influencing the other. In fact, flaws in some of the most important dynamical models of the past have turned out to be flaws in the general principles accepted at the time the model was invented. Newton's model of the solar system was based on space-time principles that were drastically revised by Einstein. Maxwell's model of electricity and magnetism took for granted classical principles of measurement that had to be modified with the advent of quantum theory.

At the time of their creation, the Newton and Maxwell models obeyed all known general principles. Certain other important dynamical models, on the other hand, such as that of Bohr, Heisenberg, and Schrödinger, were developed in the knowledge that they violated an accepted principle. In either event one is led to inquire how it is possible for models of nature that suffer from fundamental defects nevertheless to shed light.

The key to the usefulness of models that violate general principles resides inevitably in one or more small parameters—parameters whose magnitude the model is incapable of explaining but that allow the error of the model's predictions to be small when describing a limited range of phenomena. Newton's model of the solar system is useful because of the small magnitude of a parameter called the gravitational constant, which determines the attractive gravitational force between two bodies. Newton's model does not explain this magnitude, and were the gravitational constant much larger, his model would not give a recognizable representation of the solar system. It is believed that there exist within the universe regions of extremely high matter density where Newton's description is useless, but for the solar system, given the actual magnitude of the gravitational constant, the error in Newton's picture turns out to be less than one part in a hundred million.

Maxwell's (pre-quantum) equations for the propagation of electromagnetic radiation (light, radio waves, etc.) are useful when the proportion of the total electromagnetic energy carried by a single photon is small—or, equivalently, when many photons are present. It turns out in a host of important practical situations that such a large number of photons is involved as to make undetectable the error in Maxwell's picture, but there was no way for Maxwell to predict the small magnitude of the individual photon energy.

The nonrelativistic Bohr-Heisenberg-Schrödinger picture of the atom as consisting of electrons plus a nucleus depends, quite as much as does the improved picture given by quantum electrodynamics, on the smallness

---

* Because of its zero rest mass, the photon contributes a force of infinite range, but this electromagnetic force, which acts between nuclear particles as well as between electrons and nuclei, is much weaker at short distances than the nuclear force, transmitted via nuclear particles.

of the electric charge carried by the electron. This charge measures the strength of photon coupling to the electron, so we here are once again referring to the situation described above in our discussion of weakly coupled photons. That earlier discussion dwelt on the importance to the Bohr picture of the small electron charge. Here we emphasize additionally that the Bohr picture is incapable of explaining the magnitude of that charge.

The classical nuclear physics model, depicting atomic nuclei as composites of neutrons and protons, has been seen to depend on the (moderately) weak coupling of the pion as well as on the small pion mass. Analogously to our other examples of useful though imperfect models, classical nuclear physics gives no explanation of these pion properties, without which the model would not work.

We have drawn a distinction between general principles and dynamical models whose validity depends on the smallness of certain parameters; it is also possible to identify a hierarchical pattern within a sequence of models. That is, an early model may represent a less accurate version of a later model, the early version containing a larger number of arbitrary aspects and having a smaller domain of validity. The later edition may explain some of the parameters on which the early edition was based. Quantum electrodynamics, for example, explains why the magnetic interaction between electron and nucleus—ignored in the Bohr model—is much weaker than the electric interaction. The more recent model, furthermore, can describe situations involving high electron velocities where the Bohr version is inaccurate.

The Bohr model further assumes atomic nuclei to be indivisible without explaining why nuclei should require a higher energy for their dissociation than do atoms. Classical nuclear physics represents an improvement: it relates the stability of nuclei to properties (mass and coupling strength) of the pion and at the same time maintains all the predictive power of the Bohr model. For Bohr, each different atomic nucleus was a different elementary particle. Classical nuclear physics is less arbitrary in its assumption that there exist only three different elementary particles: electrons, protons, and neutrons.

The idea of a sequence of models, each more accurate and less arbitrary than the preceding, is equivalent to the notion of "onion peeling." The question being addressed in this essay is whether it is reasonable for particle physics to anticipate an indefinitely continuing sequence of models, each encompassing the ones preceding and giving improved accuracy with less arbitrariness. Our eventual answer will be in the negative, but let us for the moment consider what might seem a plausible next step in a chain of elementary-particle models—the next layer of the onion.

An immediate goal is a model that will explain the charge of the electron (i.e., the strength of electron-photon coupling) and the mass and coupling strength of the pion, at the same time encompassing all previous understanding. The new model would be expected itself to depend on some new unexplained parameters, dimensional reasoning suggesting as one of the new parameters a small (or large) ratio of rest masses. (The reciprocal of a small number is a large number.) There might, for example, be a new elementary particle with a rest mass that is either much smaller than the least massive ordinary nuclear particle or much larger than the most massive one. More will be said about these two possibilities after introduction of the quantum principles; we shall see how the combination of quantum theory and relativity makes either alternative appear unlikely.

## Quantum-relativistic principles for reaction probabilities

An important conceptual ingredient of quantum theory is the unification of "objects" and "events." The quantum concept of "particle" is defined not as an a priori entity but through experimental measurement of a "happening." In this respect the language used in this article may be misleading, since we have spoken of the electron, the proton, the photon, and so forth, as if they were objects in the ordinary sense. Even more dubious has been our reference to the "components" of a particle, phraseology that may conjure up an inappropriate geometrical picture.

Our knowledge of atomic and nuclear particles derives from experiments that measure velocity and energy (mass) while giving a rough meaning to the location and time of events. The combination of quantum theory and relativity precludes any precise meaning for space and time at the particle level; the Heisenberg uncertainty principle plays a key role in this regard, but so do the relativity constraints introduced by Einstein.

Heisenberg's celebrated principle places a lower limit on the product of the uncertainty in position and the uncertainty in momentum:* Accurate knowledge of the position of a particle must be accompanied by inaccurate knowledge of its momentum, and vice versa. It might seem that uncertainty in position might be made indefinitely small by sacrificing all knowledge of momentum, but momentum is related to energy (mass) and, according to Einstein, when the uncertainty in energy becomes larger than a particle's rest mass, one no longer can be certain that one is dealing with a single particle. Thus the combination of quantum and relativistic principles puts an absolute lower limit on the accuracy with which the position of an individual particle can be known. A pion, for example, may under no circumstances be localized more sharply than within an interval of about $10^{-13}$ inches. There is, however, no inhibition on the

---

* Momentum is the product of mass and velocity.

accurate measurement of energy and velocity; electric charge also may be determined.

The typical particle experiment consists of two successive measurements ("initial" and "final") of energies and velocities, interest focussing on a finding of results in the final measurement that differ from those in the initial measurement. When the initial and final results are different, one says that an intervening "collision" or "reaction" has taken place. Suppose, for example, that the initial measurement finds two particles, one with charge, energy, and velocity characteristic of a neutron and the other with attributes appropriate to a proton. The final measurement might detect three particles, two behaving like protons and one like a pion, none of the final velocities matching the initial one. If the experimenter has been careful to arrange his apparatus to avoid intrusion of extraneous particles, he describes his result as a "reaction" between a neutron and a proton, leading to two protons and a pion.

No experiment, no matter how careful, can give more than a rough statement as to "where" the reaction takes place* and at what time. The results, furthermore, are reproducible only in a statistical sense. That is, if the full (two-stage) experiment is repeated, with the initial measurement happening to yield the same result both times, there is no assurance that the two sets of final measurements will be the same. What must be done, in fact, is to repeat each (two-stage) experiment so many times that one is able to speak of the *probability* that a particular set of final measurements will follow a particular set of initial measurements.

Our entire knowledge of particles consists in determinations of such reaction probabilities. The discovery of new particles, for example, is most often accomplished by noticing a peculiarly high probability for certain special final configurations. These may be interpreted by saying that two successive and distinct reactions intervened between the initial and final measurements, a heretofore unknown particle being "created" in the first reaction and "absorbed" in the second. The new particle is not directly observed, but is inferred from the shape of a probability distribution.[†] Since any particle may play the role of intermediary in a two-step reaction, the concept of "particle" is seen to be interlocked with the concept of "reaction."

Although one may speak only of the *probability* that a particular result will be found in the final measurement, it is evident that the sum of the probabilities for every possible final result must equal 1. It is certain, in other words, that *something* is going to happen. This seemingly trivial common-sense statement turns out to be a major constraint on dynamical models.

There are other general principles to be satisfied. Physicists have long been aware in large-scale phenomena that energy, momentum, and angular momentum[‡] do not change, and corresponding conservation laws are obeyed in particle reactions. In the illustration cited above, for example, the sum of the energies of the initial neutron and proton would have to equal the sum of the energies of the final two protons and pion. A similar statement could be made both for momentum and for angular momentum.

It also must be true that if the experiment is performed by a moving experimenter—such an experimenter observing an altered set of particle velocities because of the effect of his own motion—the probabilities for corresponding reactions must remain the same as for the stationary observer. This requirement that physics not depend on the motion of the observer is called *Lorentz invariance*; the combination with the previously mentioned conservation laws is characterized as *Poincaré invariance*.

The term *invariance* in connection with conservation laws may seem strange. It turns out, nevertheless, that if the measured probabilities are to be independent of the time at which the two-stage experiment is begun (e.g., today or tomorrow), then energy must be conserved. If the entire apparatus can be uniformly shifted (e.g., from one side of the room to the other) without changing the probabilities, then momentum must be conserved. Finally, if probabilities are unchanged (invariant) when there is a rotation of the entire apparatus, angular momentum must be conserved.

Another general principle is related to the cause-effect property of events. Even though each reaction can be only approximately localized, we can still speak of a *succession* of reactions, having in mind the possibility that a particle produced in an "early" reaction may be absorbed in a "later" reaction. (We have in fact already discussed such a succession of reactions as a method for discovering new particles.) If we wish to guarantee that no particle produced in a later reaction will be absorbed in an earlier reaction, we speak of the requirement of *causality*. It proves surprisingly easy to invent noncausal quantum models even though the causality requirement seems no more than one of common sense.

We thus have identified three general principles for describing particle reactions: (1) a quantum-mechanical probability interpretation, (2) Poincaré invariance, and (3) causality. These principles combine Einstein's discoveries with those of Bohr and Heisenberg, and so far no violations have been observed. In searching for a dynamical model to explain the electron charge and the properties of the pion, one would hope to satisfy all three of these principles.

---

* The most precise spatial localization so far achieved is about one ten-thousandth of an inch. This is to be compared with the previously discussed "range" of the Yukawa force, which is a billion times smaller.

† Because particle energies and velocities are continuously variable, physicists usually display experimental results by plotting the probability of a reaction versus some parameter such as energy. We refer to such a diagram as a probability distribution.

‡ Angular momentum in the large is defined as the product of ordinary momentum and the perpendicular distance to some axis to which the angular motion is being referred.

## Refinement of concepts

Having introduced the quantum-relativistic framework for atomic and nuclear-particle phenomena, we shall attempt now to restate more precisely certain of the ideas expressed earlier in ordinary language. Some of these ideas are model-dependent, but the most important reflect no more than our general principles.

The term *particle dissociation*, used already in reference to high-energy proton experiments, is a euphemism for a special type of reaction in which there occurs, among the various final particles, a well-defined particle subgroup that can be unambiguously associated with *one* of the initial particles. The key to the association is the requirement that the final subgroup of particles should collectively carry almost the same amount of any conserved quantity, like electric charge, energy,* and momentum, as is carried into the reaction by the associated initial particle. It is *as if* the initial particle "falls to pieces" as a result of being "tickled," and the probability for different combinations of fragments may be regarded as revealing the "structure" of the initial particle. The term *structure* does not have a uniformly accepted meaning among particle physicists, but its use as a synonym for dissociation probabilities is better founded than most. Note that "dissociation" is only one special type of particle reaction, many reactions not being characterized by this term even though *any* reaction might be said to manifest *some* aspect of the "structure" of the particles involved.

For a specific illustration of dissociation we may refer to our earlier example of a reaction in which a neutron and a proton "collide" to produce a pion and two protons. At high energy one frequently finds the velocities of the three final particles in this type of reaction to be such that one of the final protons has almost the same momentum and energy as the initial proton, while the pion and the other final proton collectively have almost the same momentum and energy as the initial neutron. In such cases it is natural to describe the final proton-pion combination as "dissociation products" of the initial neutron. The initial proton in this illustration does not itself dissociate but provides a "tickle" that causes the neutron to reveal one aspect of its "structure."

The term *weak coupling* may readily be translated as meaning a small probability that certain reactions will occur. For example, the statement that the pion is weakly coupled to neutrons and protons at low energy means that reactions where the neutron dissociates into a proton and a pion are relatively improbable if the pion energy is low.

What is to be understood when we speak of the "range" of the interparticle force? How can a notion relating to the distance between particles have meaning when the spatial location of a reaction is intrinsically imprecise? Here we lean on angular momentum, which turns out not only to be definable in principle for particle reactions but measurable in practice. The technique of measurement is indirect and will not be described here, except to say that it requires probability distributions as a function of the angle at which final particles emerge. This angular dependence may be translated into a dependence of reaction probability on angular momentum, which may, if one chooses, be euphemistically regarded as a dependence on the "distance of closest approach."

The latter terminology is suggested by Newtonian mechanics where the mutual angular momentum of two particles is proportional to the smallest distance between the particles as their orbits pass one another. Quantum principles do not tolerate a precise meaning for particle *orbit,* but there is no harm in employing the term *distance of closest approach* as a synonym for *angular momentum.†* The dependence of reaction probability on angular momentum thus may be described as a dependence on distance of closest approach.

Now it turns out to be characteristic of each nuclear-particle reaction that its probability remains substantial for a certain limited range of angular momentum, but falls rapidly to zero when the angular momentum exceeds a characteristic maximum value. Such a property may be expressed by translating the maximum angular momentum into the "range" of the interaction (or force) between the initial particles. One then may employ ordinary language to say that if the distance of closest approach exceeds the range of the force, no reaction occurs. Of course such a statement is merely another euphemism, describing a feature of the reaction probability distribution.

Theoretical studies in the late fifties demonstrated that the magnitude of the maximum angular momentum (i.e., the range of the force) for each reaction is deducible from a combination of our three general principles, once the masses of the least-massive particles are known. The result is in accord with Yukawa's previously described rule for the range of the nuclear force, even though he employed a dynamical model, rather than general principles, as the basis for his 1935 reasoning. We shall return later to this important deduction, which has profound implications for the future of the elementary-particle concept. For the moment we content ourselves with the simple statement that the force range is determined through general principles by the least-massive particles, independently of the question as to which particles, if any, deserve to be called "elementary."

We see that the quantum framework of reaction probabilities, subject to our general principles, provides a meaning for such concepts as particle "structure" and the "range" and "strength" of interparticle forces. Thus far there has been no need to rely on a specific dynamical model. Let us

---

\* At very high energy, the Einstein formulas relating energy and mass allow the total energy of a final subgroup of particles to be only slightly different from the energy of the associated initial particle, even though the sum of the final rest masses may be much greater than the initial rest mass.

† The complete relation involves the magnitude of ordinary momentum as a factor.

inquire then as to what is added to the general picture by the model known as classical nuclear physics.

## The dynamical content of classical nuclear physics

Classical nuclear physics has been characterized as a dynamical model in which neutrons and protons are regarded as elementary building blocks, subject to forces arising from low-mass weakly coupled pions. As normally implemented, the model employs certain "equations of motion" for the neutrons and protons, equations patterned after the Bohr-Heisenberg-Schrödinger equations that describe atoms as composites of electrons and nuclei. These equations allow prediction of the properties of nuclei once the force between neutrons and protons has been specified. The model content going beyond principles thus seems threefold: (1) the designation of neutrons and protons as "elementary" pointlike entities—without structure, (2) the detailed specification of forces acting between neutrons and protons, and (3) the equations of motion.

Closer examination, however, reveals that the apparent added content is illusory. Our three general principles for reaction probabilities plus an experimental knowledge of the masses of neutron, proton, and pion and mutual coupling of these particles* probably allow all the same physical predictions as classical nuclear physics. The qualifier *probably* is used because the demonstration of equivalent physical content has so far been given only for two-particle systems. With currently available mathematical techniques, a general demonstration of equivalence becomes extremely complicated, but it seems overwhelmingly likely from studies of the two-particle problem carried out during the fifties that the entire dynamical content of classical nuclear physics already resides in our three general principles for quantum-relativistic reaction probabilities. There is no need to assume equations of motion! There is no need to assume a detailed law of force! There is no need to assume that neutrons, protons, and pions are elementary!

Even though the domain of relevance of classical nuclear physics involves neutrons and protons of such low velocities that relativity seems unimportant, relativistic aspects of our general principles are in fact crucial to their dynamical content. The simultaneous requirement of causality and Poincaré invariance turns out to enforce a unique relation between the law of force and the properties of low-mass particles; a knowledge of the particles that exist, in other words, implies a knowledge of interparticle forces. Whence arises the physical content equivalent to an equation of motion? Once again, causality and Poincaré invariance are vital, but now, in addition, there comes into play the quantum requirement of a probability interpretation. It is the combination of all three principles that does the trick.

The lack of any need for a quantum-relativistic equation of motion has enormous implications for the elementary-particle idea. Presupposing the need for a fundamental equation of motion, one must ask what the thing is whose motion is being described. Whatever the answer, the entity appearing in the fundamental equation plays the role characteristic of an elementary particle. But if no fundamental equation is needed, there may be no need to identify *any* entities as fundamental.

It is important to appreciate that the rules of classical nuclear physics, even though deducible from measured pion properties on the basis of general principles, do not completely satisfy these principles. The deduction depends on the small pion mass and relatively weak low-energy coupling to justify elimination from consideration of a vast variety of other nuclear particles. One can show that when neutron and proton velocities are small, the observed pion properties guarantee a small effect from other particles. Eliminating the remainder, however, leads to some violation of general principles even at low energy and to major violation when the energy is high.

The success of classical nuclear physics suggests that it would be worthwhile to extend the range of relevance and diminish the errors by keeping some of the neglected complications. Modest improvements have in fact been achieved, but as the energy increases, the complications grow so rapidly as to doom any approximation based on a small number of particles. A radically different approach is indicated.

## Indefinite particle sequences

An important aspect of current experimental knowledge about atomic and nuclear particles is that nearly all particles seem to fall into sequences of indefinite extent. The different members of a sequence differ in rest mass and angular momentum, but otherwise they possess similar attributes.

The sequence in which the ordinary hydrogen atom appears as the lowest-mass member was predicted by the Bohr-Heisenberg-Schrödinger model of an electron-proton composite; solving the equation of this model yields an infinite number of different though related atomic particles.[†] Solving the corresponding equations of classical nuclear physics similarly predicts indefinite sequences of nuclei, and huge numbers of particles on both atomic and nuclear sequences have for a long time been established.[‡] It was not, however, until the fifties that additional particles were discov-

---

* One also needs to know that no nuclear particles other than the pion exist with rest masses comparably small to that of the pion.

† The higher-mass particles in the hydrogen sequence are often described as "excited states" of hydrogen. The term *state* is to be understood as synonymous with *particle*.

‡ The study of the pattern of particle sequences is often called *spectroscopy* because the earliest work on atoms employed spectral analysis of the light emitted from these particles.

ered in the sequence that includes the neutron and proton as lowest-mass members. The intervals between rest masses on this particular sequence are so large that higher mass members could not be produced until accelerators of quite high energy became available. It was necessary to wait even longer to discover higher members of the sequence beginning with the pion, but at present, all nuclear particles can be associated with sequences that seem to extend indefinitely.

The only particles that continue to stand apart from such a pattern are the photon and the so-called leptons—a mysterious low-mass particle family of only finite extent (so far) that includes the electron.* From the standpoint of our discussion, the important characteristic of the leptons is their immunity to the strong forces that govern nuclear particles.

Before discovery of higher members along the nuclear sequence that includes the neutron and proton, there was a tendency to think of these latter particles as "elementary." When, however, it became apparent that neutrons and protons belong to indefinite sequences of the type predicted by classical nuclear physics, there evolved an inclination to think of neutrons and protons as "composite."† This tendency was reinforced by the phenomenon of dissociation that has been described above at length. A similar evolution of attitudes has surrounded the pion; at the present time, all known nuclear particles are generally regarded as "composite."

The question immediately arises: If the neutron is composite, of what is it composed? On the basis of dissociation experiments, we may define one component of the neutron structure to be a pion-proton combination. Another component would be two pions plus a neutron, and so on, as discussed several times already. But these are only words. The notion of structure is not useful unless it allows the correlation of experimental facts that would be otherwise unrelated. An obvious goal is prediction of the rest masses and other properties of particles lying on the neutron sequence, in the same spirit as the Bohr model predicts the hydrogen sequence.

What happens if we try to describe the neutron as a pion-proton composite, subject to forces dictated by the same general principles as dictate the forces of classical nuclear physics? This approach succeeds in predicting the properties of the next higher-mass particle in the neutron sequence, but there is failure thereafter. Analysis easily shows the reason: Components other than the pion-proton combination become important as the energy increases, the number of different components increasing so rapidly as quickly to exceed human calculational power.

In the present absence of human capacity to predict indefinite particle sequences on the basis of general principles, a variety of rules have evolved to represent empirical regularities.‡ A popular framework for certain of the most successful of these rules is the so-called quark model. Consideration of the quark model is essential to any current status assessment of the elementary-particle concept.

## The quark model

It is perhaps misleading to speak of *the* quark model. There are actually many versions, but all model variations share the common idea that particles like neutrons, protons, and pions, as well as the higher-mass members of the sequences to which these nuclear particles belong, can somehow be described as built from a small number of elementary entities—entities that so far have eluded direct observation. These hypothesized building blocks have been dubbed *quarks* by Murray Gell-Mann, using a humorously poetic term of James Joyce from *Finnegans Wake,* and although many alternative names have been proposed, it is *quark* that has caught on.

It turns out possible to assign appropriate properties, such as charge and angular momentum, to a small number of different quarks (three is the number most commonly used) so that putting together various quark combinations "explains" by simple addition the corresponding properties of many nuclear particles. The proton, for example, is commonly depicted as a three-quark combination.

To obtain the proton electric charge and angular momentum, one adds the charges and angular momenta of the three constituents; other properties are similarly handled. This approach cannot be dismissed as an empty game, because the number of different nuclear particles successfully described by quark constructs far exceeds the required number of different ingredient quarks. Especially impressive has been the prediction of the existence of certain particles before their experimental discovery.§

Not all quark combinations are manifested by the properties of observed nuclear particles; especially striking by their absence are particles corresponding to single quarks. The properties assigned to individual quarks would cause physical particles with such attributes to stand out in spectacular relief; the electric charge carried by one type of quark, for instance, is one-third the charge of an electron or proton. At the same time, consideration of our general principles and some firmly established experimental facts show that physical particles could not in any event be identified with the ingredient entities of quark models. The difficulty is associated with the forces needed to hold together a collection of constituent quarks.

In order to explain this point, we begin by noting that a key feature of quark models is their simple additivity. Thus to understand, say, the pro-

---

* The other leptons are the already mentioned electrically charged muon and two different electrically neutral and massless particles called neutrinos. For a discussion of neutrinos, see the 1967 *Great Ideas Today* article by Toulmin.

† The reasoning stems from the Bohr model of the atom and the classical model of the nucleus, where the indefinite sequence is associated with an internal structure that is capable of accepting unlimited amounts of kinetic energy.

‡ A detailed discussion of some of these rules may be found in Jeremy Bernstein, "Physical Sciences and Technology," *The Great Ideas Today,* 1965, pp 320–70.

§ Bernstein (ibid.) presents a detailed description of some quark-model predictions.

ton, in the spirit of the previously considered atomic and nuclear composite models, the proton structure must be dominated by a three-quark combination in the same sense that the hydrogen atom may be described as almost entirely a proton-electron combination. Such a statement in turn requires the sum of the three-quark rest masses to be approximately equal to the proton rest mass, because, as emphasized at the beginning of the article, should the total mass of a composite be much smaller than the sum of constituent masses, there must be a strong attractive force (potential energy) between constituents to supply a large negative increment to the total energy. But we have seen that general principles demand force to arise from *other* particles, and only if the forces were weak could one ignore the presence of these additional particles in the "structure" of the proton. Were the force strong, the associated particles would contribute substantially to the proton properties and upset the three-quark additivity.

Now, the notion of the proton as a composite of three "loosely bound" quarks, each less massive than the proton, conflicts violently with experimental facts about proton dissociation. When appropriately "tickled," the proton reveals a rich structure of components but no quarks, and since the 1950s ample energy has been available to dissociate protons into quarks if quarks were less massive than the proton. A search is under way at NAL and CERN, as well as in the cosmic radiation, for extremely massive particles with single-quark attributes, but even if such particles are discovered, our general principles will preclude their identification with the constituent entities appearing in quark models.

Another way to express the dilemma is to say that if quarks are nuclear particles, they are (by definition) subject to nuclear forces, and thus by our general principles they possess as much structure as any other nuclear particle. The properties assigned to the constituents of quark models, on the other hand, imply a structureless pointlike status for these constituents.

All proposed quark models conflict with one or more of our three general principles, so it is not surprising that even when a quark model gives a reasonably accurate description of some nuclear particle (such as the proton), the description is not perfect. There exist, moreover, vast families of nuclear particles for which quark models are meaningless. The pattern of success for the quark model in these respects is similar to that for other wrong though useful models.

What about the relationship to a hierarchical structure? Does the quark model systematically improve on previous nuclear models, encompassing all earlier achievement with less arbitrariness? The answer is no. The quark model explains neither the small mass of the pion nor the weak pion coupling, and so does not provide an underpinning for classical nuclear physics. Those nuclear-particle sequences, furthermore, that are successfully described by classical nuclear physics cannot be described by the quark model. The relation of these two models is not hierarchical but parallel. Each possesses its own limited domain of applicability.

We have seen that the content of classical nuclear physics can be deduced from general principles, once a few experimental facts are known. Can a similar statement be made about quark models? At present this question must be answered in the negative, the basis for the physical content of quark models not yet having been elucidated. Theoretical physicists have nevertheless uncovered hints of how a future explanation may be achieved.

The underlying small parameter appears to be a generalization of the weak pion coupling, extending the notion of such (moderate) weakness to other particles. The relationship between classical nuclear physics and the quark model might be characterized roughly as follows: Both models depend on weakness of coupling, but classical nuclear physics depends additionally on the small pion mass in order to justify ignoring, at low energy, particles other than neutrons, protons, and pions. The pion-induced force, although weak, has a relatively long range (because of the small pion mass) and so is capable at low energy of generating nuclear reactions with a high probability. The probability is so high that careful attention must be paid to the limitation, contained in our general principles, on the sum of all reaction probabilities. It has so far proved impossible to construct models that satisfy all three of the general principles, but if one or more principles is relaxed, the remainder may become tractable. Because classical nuclear physics forgoes description of high-velocity phenomena, it is possible to relax certain aspects of Poincaré invariance and causality without introducing excessive error. The model then succeeds in completely satisfying the requirement of a probability interpretation. On the other hand, if one is not especially interested in low velocities and large individual reaction probabilities, one may exploit the fact that average particle couplings are sufficiently weak to justify, for many purposes, ignoring the upper limit on reaction probabilities. Complete satisfaction of the remaining two general principles—Poincaré invariance and causality—is then much easier.

Theoretical physicists are finding indications that the physical content of the quark model may correspond to Poincaré invariance and causality when the probability constraint is disregarded. Approached in such a manner from general principles, theorists hope to show that the successful physical predictions of quark models are achievable without any implication of physical meaning for constituent quarks.

## Field theory: fundamental equations of motion

From a variety of points of view we have encountered a mismatch between the notion of elementarity and physically observable particles. The degree of mismatch is related to the strength of the forces acting on the particle and becomes intolerable for strongly interacting nuclear particles. In an effort to circumvent this dilemma, many theoretical physicists have sought to attach the concept of elementarity not to a particle but to a "field." What is meant by the term *field* when used by a particle physicist? An answer to this question is not easily given, even to an audience of specialists, but the effort will serve to illuminate further the elementary-particle impasse.

The original notion of "field" arose in the pre-quantum nineteenth-century description of electricity and magnetism. Before the notion of photons, the mechanism for electromagnetic transmission of forces (or signals, if the reader prefers) was described in terms of electric and magnetic fields—fields that can be precisely defined in terms of experimental measurements* and that may be regarded as "real" as any material object. With the advent of quantum theory came a recognition that for certain purposes it is convenient to speak of photons rather than electric and magnetic fields, but a notion called *quantum field* became involved early in the effort to deal with the quantum aspects of electromagnetism. Although the definition of a relativistic quantum field has never achieved precision, pursuit of such a concept has obsessed two successive generations of theoretical physicists.

The motivation lies in the perceived necessity for a fundamental equation of motion that is consistent with both quantum and relativistic requirements. Since the time of Newton, most physicists have taken for granted that forces and interactions must be described by equations of motion: Newton's equation for the motion of large bodies, Maxwell's equations for the motion of electric and magnetic fields, the Schrödinger and Dirac equations for the motion of atomic systems. The teaching of physics emphasizes this traditional attitude so strongly that professional physicists rarely consider any alternative. Now for reasons explained below, the quantum-relativistic general principles do not allow any equation of motion to be formulated for individual particles or even for finite groups of particles. On the other hand, Maxwell's equations for electric and magnetic fields accord completely with relativity, while at the same time the quantum content of electricity and magnetism is equivalent to photons—a special variety of particles; so perhaps the way to formulate quantum-relativistic equations of motion is to associate a field with the type of particle in question and then to construct equations for the field.

It was soon recognized that fields associated with particles other than photons cannot have a "real" interpretation in terms of direct physical measurement; electric and magnetic fields are unique in this respect. Nevertheless, in analogy with the Maxwell equations, it proved superficially possible to write down quantum-relativistic equations of motion for fields associated with *any* particles; the physics literature of the past forty years abounds in examples.

An essential attribute of a field, distinguishing it from a physical particle, is that a field is supposed to be definable at a *point* in space-time. Because, as we have repeatedly stressed, no precise meaning can be given to the position of a particle, there is no way to formulate a quantum-relativistic particle equation of motion. Quantum fields, on the other hand, not having any immediate physical significance, may be supposed arbitrarily to be sharply localized, and the formulation of field equations of motion then turns out to be straightforward. Of course it is another matter whether any of these equations has relevance to the physical world.

Quite apart from the difficulty of deciding which particles, among the enormous number of different nuclear species, deserve to be associated with a fundamental field equation of motion, it was eventually found that such equations probably do not, after all, lead to satisfaction of the general quantum-relativistic requirements. This fact is obscured by the lack of direct physical interpretation for quantum fields, allowing many sophisticated variations to be proposed for the connection between fields and particles. But no connection has yet proved satisfactory. The quantum significance of even the electromagnetic fields remains dubious. The previously discussed rules of quantum electrodynamics are framed in terms of particles, not of fields, and Maxwell's field equations have a clear meaning only in the classical sense in which they were originally proposed. Field equations associated with particles other than photons do not enjoy even this degree of physical significance.[†]

Because no definitive proof has been given that quantum-field equations are incapable of sensible physical implications, efforts to find such equations still occupy the energies of some theoretical physicists. The prevailing belief by now is that a field-particle association of the type originally envisaged is untenable, but not yet completely abandoned is the hope that the fundamental-field concept might somehow survive even if there were no associated fundamental particles. After all, if one accepts the necessity for an equation of motion, there must be some fundamental entity that "moves"; if this moving entity cannot be a particle it must be something else, perhaps a field. We have already argued, of course, that there may be no need for an equation of motion. If not, there may be no need for *any* fundamental entity, field or otherwise.


## Photon-nuclear collisions and nuclear fields

After a period of decline in the face of the above-described difficulties, interest in the concept of a "nuclear field," related somehow to the strong

---

[*] The electric field may be defined in terms of the force exerted on a motionless electrically charged object of small dimensions. The magnetic field may be defined through the additional force that is observed when the object is in motion.

[†] It has been conjectured that massless particles called gravitons may be associated with the gravitational field. If gravitons exist, they are coupled to other particles even more weakly than are photons and play no observable role in nuclear phenomena.

nuclear interactions, has recently been reawakened by the need to correlate high-energy experimental observations of collisions between nuclear
particles and electrons.* The resulting reactions stem from electromagnetic forces or, one might say, from the weak photon components "within"
the electron. It is possible, in fact, to simplify the discussion by ignoring the
electron and describing the reactions as if initiated through a nuclear
collision with one of these photons. Now there exists a set of rules—quantum electrodynamics—capable of describing with good accuracy, even at
the energies in question, the interaction between photons and particles
(like the electron) that may be regarded as approximately structureless.
But what are we to do for a high-energy collision between a photon and a
*nuclear* particle such as a proton? We would like a generalization of quantum electrodynamics that continues to treat photons as "elementary" to
the extent that photon couplings are weak, but one that at the same time
recognizes the composite nature of the proton.

What does it mean to say that the photon is "elementary" if we are to go
beyond its interaction with particles like the electron that are approximately pointlike? So far, a definitive answer to this question remains elusive. However, the rules of quantum electrodynamics were discovered by
attempting to reconcile the classical Maxwell field equations with quantum
principles,† and in the classical equations, relativity requirements demand
that the electric charge, which generates the electromagnetic field, be localized at points of space-time. Thus the only established procedures for
the formulation of elementary-photon reaction rules depend in a seemingly essential manner on the notion of point sources for the associated
electromagnetic field.

This situation is paradoxical in that the classical equations leading to the
point-source idea are physically relevant only for sources of large dimension. There is, in other words, no directly verifiable physical significance in
the concept of a point charge. Without the classical equations as a guide,
however, one does not know how to discover quantum rules for elementary-photon interactions. It is natural, then, that the urge to construct
dynamical models of high-energy photon-proton collisions has led to widespread use of the idea of a localizable charge "within" the proton.

A naive approach has associated this point charge with structureless
constituent quarks from which the proton is supposed to be built; we have
seen the difficulty with such a model. A more sophisticated approach associates a nuclear field with the required localizable charge, while avoiding
direct association of any individual nuclear particle with this field. The
nuclear field is supposed to act as a point source for the electromagnetic
field, allowing the photon to be treated as an elementary structureless
entity.

Is any distinctive physical content achieved by such an approach, which
some theorists argue does not necessarily imply a fundamental status for

the nuclear field?‡ A number of general experimental predictions about photon-nuclear reactions have been made on the basis of a localizable nuclear field, and so far these predictions seem in accord with experimental observations. Nevertheless, one can imagine that even if they are verified with precision, predictions such as these will in the future be shown to follow from more general principles that avoid the concept of a nuclear field and require no more than the notion of a weakly coupled photon. In the absence of evidence for elementary nuclear particles, it is difficult to conceive of any compelling experimental demonstration of necessity for the nuclear-field concept.

The reason for use of such a notion is the present dearth of theoretical ideas about high-energy photon interactions. Because in the past electromagnetism has come to be regarded as completely understood, there is a conviction that high-energy photon collisions with nuclear particles should be approached in the classically oriented framework that applies at lower energies. Such a framework depends on point sources for the electromagnetic field, and until a more general framework can be found, theoretical physicists will no doubt continue to study the possibility that such sources lie in a nuclear field, in spite of the difficulties known to be possessed by the latter concept, especially when the nuclear field is interpreted as a fundamental entity with an equation of motion.

## Neutrinos and the W

A more compelling stimulant to continued study of the quantum-field concept arises from experiments involving neutrinos, the electrically neutral and massless§ members of the lepton family. These remarkable particles are subject neither to the relatively strong short-range nuclear forces nor to the relatively weak long-range electromagnetic forces. Neutrinos must of course be susceptible to *some* force, or we would not know of their existence. This mysterious force is so extraordinarily weak at low energy that until recently neutrinos were almost invisible, but the force grows rapidly with increasing energy, so that with the huge NAL accelerator it is becoming possible to study neutrino properties in detail.

Physicists already know enough about the force acting on neutrinos to have recognized certain similarities to electromagnetism, and these

---

* Such measurements became possible after completion a decade ago of the three-mile-long linear accelerator at Stanford University.

† Although, as stated above, the effort has not been completely successful, the rules of quantum electrodynamics achieve compatibility to the extent that electromagnetic interactions are weak.

‡ That is, a simple equation of motion for the nuclear field is not necessarily implied.

§ Photons also are massless and electrically neutral but have an angular momentum different from that of neutrinos.

similarities have led theorists to conjecture the existence of a field that is analogous to the electromagnetic field, but whose associated particle, unlike the zero-mass photon, has a large rest mass.* This hypothetical particle is usually referred to as the W. Vigorous search for the W has to date been unsuccessful but is sure to continue as a major preoccupation of particle experimenters.

It has so far not been possible to predict the W mass, a circumstance indicative of the shaky nature of theoretical arguments for the existence of such a particle, but the associated quantum field is receiving furious attention, using the same techniques that were successful in constructing quantum electrodynamics. Although these techniques depend heavily on the weakness of the interaction, we have stressed that the neutrino force is in fact extremely weak. The concept of W field thus has a more plausible expectation of usefulness than does the nuclear-field concept.

Because of the weakness of the interaction in question, our general quantum-relativistic principles do not preclude identification of a physical particle with the W field. Even should the W particle exist, however, it could not serve as an elementary ingredient for nuclear particles, since it would not be subject to strong nuclear forces. The impasse posed by strong interactions for the elementary-particle concept would remain as severe as ever.

It should be remarked also that the use of electromagnetism as a motivating analogy for the W concept leaves a feeling of uneasiness. We have emphasized that the field concept has a secure meaning only in the large-scale (macroscopic) domain, and it can be shown that the zero photon mass is essential to the long-range aspects of electromagnetism. This extremely important fact will receive further emphasis in what follows, when we point to the extraordinary importance of large-scale electromagnetic effects to the very structure of science. Since the nonvanishing mass of the W particle precludes any large-scale (classical) manifestation of the W field, the analogy with electromagnetism is thin.

## The nuclear bootstrap:
## dissolution of the elementary-particle impasse

Readers who have not yet collapsed by the wayside should by this stage of our discussion have become impressed by the power of the quantum-relativistic general principles. Two extraordinary points have been made: (1) Given these principles, there may be no need for a fundamental equation of motion. (2) No model based on either primitive ingredients or an equation of motion or on both has succeeded in satisfying all three principles. Contemplation of these striking circumstances has motivated the scientifically revolutionary conjecture that the unique mechanism for collective satisfaction of the general principles may be the mechanism exhibited by nature. In other words, the observed collection of nuclear particles, with their assorted reaction probabilities, may represent the *only conceivable* fully consistent quantum-relativistic system.

The foregoing conjecture is often described as the "bootstrap" hypothesis, since each nuclear particle is supposed to support the existence of others, which in turn support it. Each nuclear particle may be seen in three different roles: (1) a *constituent* of some composite, (2) a contributor to the *force* that binds together a composite, or (3) an *entire composite*. We have seen how such language, although at first sight paradoxical, legitimately evokes different aspects of the physical content within the general principles.

According to the bootstrap hypothesis, no nuclear particle is intrinsically more significant than any other; "nuclear democracy" prevails. Dissolved is the impasse reached by the elementary-particle approach; instead of seeking an equation of motion for some will-o'-the-wisp primitive entity, we depend entirely on the requirement that natural phenomena be mutually self-consistent. All parameters (such as the pion mass and coupling) are supposed to be determined by self-consistency, no parameter being allowed to deviate from its observed value without violating some general principle.

It is important to distinguish the bootstrap hypothesis as a philosophical idea from its use as a scientific tool; one must correspondingly distinguish a "complete" bootstrap from a "partial" bootstrap, which applies to only a portion of nature. The notion of a complete bootstrap—all aspects of nature being interrelated and determined by mutual self-consistency—has enormous esthetic appeal and in fact constitutes an integral part of such ancient eastern philosophies as Mahayana Buddhism. Such a notion, however, is intrinsically unscientific.

To be pursued, science demands a language based on commonly shared perceptions of nature, so that questions may be formulated and experiments performed to answer the questions. Among currently unquestioned notions prerequisite to the conduct of science are:

(1) Three-dimensional space and a time flowing in only one direction, with an associated cause-effect relationship between events. (The existence of suitable measuring rods and clocks for measuring distance and time on a large scale is essential.)

(2) The arrangement of large-scale matter† into conglomerates of sufficiently well-defined shape and permanency such that the concept of isolated system or "object" has meaning. (The Poincaré invariance properties of space-time are essential here so that, for example, an object observed

---

\* The angular momentum of the W is supposed to be the same as that of a photon.

† As stressed in what follows, all actual measurements are performed "in the large." Even though we have spoken of measuring the velocity of a proton, what actually is done is to observe some effect produced in a relatively large clump of matter. There is no conceivable way to observe a nuclear particle directly.

today in a special location and orientation may be recognized as the same object tomorrow in a different setting.)

(3) The existence of extremely weak and long-range "probes," such as are provided by electromagnetism (photons), that allow a measurement to be made upon an "object" without the object being so changed by the probe as to lose its identity.

Although the foregoing detailed prerequisites may be summarized deceptively by a single word—*measurement*—the concept of measurement, on which hard science is based, is admissible only because of these special attributes of nature. A complete bootstrap could not assume such attributes on an a priori basis, but would be obliged to explain them as necessary components of self-consistency. In this sense the idea of a complete bootstrap is intrinsically unscientific. It is not ridiculous to suppose that any self-consistent nature must necessarily be built on the type of space-time structure that actually prevails, but consideration of such a proposition is unfeasible within the framework of hard science.

If we accept without question the measurement process and surrounding space-time attributes of nature, so as to operate within the conventional scientific framework, we are limited to the partial-bootstrap hypothesis that all *additional* aspects of nature should be fixed by self-consistency. Now there arises the delicate question of drawing a precise line between a priori attributes of nature, which are to be accepted as given, and the *additional* attributes that the partial bootstrap is to explain. In particular, it seems that the possibility of a suitable "probe" for objective measurement depends on the strength of the photon coupling and the photon rest mass. The logical basis for expecting such parameters to be determined by our partial bootstrap is then not compelling, because these parameters are already part of the framework that must preexist before the bootstrap constraints can be formulated.

A related but more delicate consideration further discourages the expectation that electromagnetism might emerge from a partial bootstrap based on our three general principles. These three principles represent not only the commonly accepted classical understanding of measurement in the large but also the probabilistic aspect of quantum phenomena. Now, the combination of classical and quantum ideas is fraught with contradiction. Einstein's celebrated remark that "God does not cast dice" dramatizes the conflict between quantum probability principles and the rational Western view of nature based on objectivity of measurement. How has it turned out possible to incorporate quantum principles into Western science? It becomes possible by hypothesizing a gap between the "real" world of measurement and the quantum world of particles. Repeatedly during this essay we have stressed that one never directly observes a particle; all actual observations deal with matter on a scale enormous with respect to individual particles. It is crucial, as Bohr never failed to emphasize, that on this large scale we accept the notion of objective measurement. The probabilistic aspect of quantum theory relates to our inability to predict with certainty the result of some (large-scale) measurement yet to be made on the basis of an already-performed (large-scale) measurement. In situations where this uncertainty is significant, physicists may say that they are "observing the quantum world," but each individual measurement is necessarily made in the real world without regard to quantum considerations.

It is at the same time evident that real and quantum worlds are not completely independent; electricity and magnetism in particular are very much a part of both domains. The large-scale aspects of electromagnetism were thoroughly appreciated before any hint appeared of the quantum world, and we have had ample occasion in this essay to stress its quantum aspects (i.e., the photon). In fact, electromagnetism is crucial to the contact between the two worlds that must exist before any knowledge about particles becomes possible.

Ultimately, all experiments characterizable as "measurements of particles" employ electromagnetism as the probe. An enormous variety of different particle-detection techniques have been invented, but each technique depends inevitably on the fact that some particles carry electric charge and interact thereby with low-energy photons, according to the rules of quantum electrodynamics. These rules permit a very large number of extremely low-energy photons to be involved without excessively "disturbing" the particle under observation. When the photon number is large, real-world language applies, and the interaction becomes interpretable as a "measurement"; the gap between the two worlds has been bridged.

Crucial to the bridging mechanism is the zero photon rest mass, which allows individual photons to carry arbitrarily small amounts of energy, and thus allows also an arbitrarily large number of photons to be involved, while maintaining the gentleness of the probe. It would therefore appear that among the a priori attributes of nature underlying the viability of the quantum principle, we should include the zero rest mass of the photon. Implicit in such an attitude is the assignment to the photon of an "aristocratic" status among particles; the photon is not simply one citizen in a democracy, and the partial-bootstrap hypothesis cannot be expected to explain electromagnetism as a necessary aspect of self-consistency. Electromagnetism, together with space-time, is an essential fiber within the fabric that underlies the scientific description of nature.

We remind the reader that nuclear particles, because none have zero rest mass, are incapable of bridging the gap between real and quantum spheres;* nuclear forces are not related immediately to those aspects of nature that underlie the possibility of scientific measurement.

---

* All four mysterious leptons also belong entirely to the quantum world, even though the neutrinos have zero rest mass. It turns out that the leptons' angular momentum precludes their playing a role like that of the photon.

We touch now on another subtle point: in providing a bridge between real and quantum worlds, electromagnetism disturbs the fabric of the latter. Quantum principles are predicated on the absence of forces whose range is so long as to encompass large-scale clumps of matter; the notion of particle (or of *quantum state*, an equivalent term) requires isolation from the surrounding environment. But the photon possesses the capability to serve as probe in particle measurements precisely because it transmits a coupling between particles and their large-scale environment. Another paradox!

Our first mention of quantum electrodynamics already identified the key to this problem: the weak coupling of the photon. The long-range forces are sufficiently gentle so that to a good degree of approximation they may be said not to alter the "structure" of nuclear particles. The quantum principle is nevertheless logically untenable except in the hypothetical limit of zero electromagnetic interaction, and we here recognize a difficulty with an effort to understand the electron through a partial bootstrap based on the quantum principle. Unlike nuclear particles such as the proton and the pion, the chief force felt by the electron (at short range as well as at long) is electromagnetic, so a hypothetical "turning off" of electromagnetism would presumably change the electron beyond recognition. A bootstrap explanation of the electron may thus have to wait until we have learned to formulate self-consistency without a priori assumption of the quantum principle.* Perhaps an Einstein of the distant future will elucidate a simultaneous bootstrap of space-time, quantum mechanics, electromagnetism, and the electron.

There remains the nuclear bootstrap hypothesis: the more immediate hope that by demanding consistency with our three general principles we might arrive at a complete understanding of the nuclear particles. Even such a limited program faces formidable difficulties in practice—difficulties that will be described in the remainder of this essay—but a conceptual impasse has nevertheless been breached.

## Modeling the nuclear bootstrap

Implied by the nuclear bootstrap hypothesis is the theoretical possibility of explaining all nuclear-particle properties (including their reaction probabilities) without requiring that any parameters, such as rest masses or strengths of coupling, be given in advance by experiment. Implied at the same time by nuclear democracy, however, is a requirement that the properties of a selected particle or group of particles be no more amenable to explanation than are the properties of any other particle or group. Since all nuclear particles are mutually interdependent in a bootstrap, an attempt to understand completely any individual particle requires an understanding of all particles. This "all or nothing" character of the hypothe-

sis makes elusive its definitive experimental test. Given, that is, the unbounded richness and complexity of observed nuclear phenomena, it is
manifestly beyond human capability to explain all details merely from
general principles, even if everything in fact flows uniquely from consistency with these principles.

Encouragement for the nuclear bootstrap idea is nevertheless being
derived from a variety of experimental observations, taken in combination
with a variety of approximate predictive schemes based on the quantum-
relativistic general principles. Each of these predictive schemes is a
"model" of some portion of the nuclear world, and the success of an ever
increasing number of such nuclear models—collectively spanning an ever
increasing proportion of the nuclear world—may eventually come to be
regarded as verification of the bootstrap hypothesis. Let us examine how
human limitations are being accommodated by a modeling of the nuclear
bootstrap.

Three essential characteristics of a bootstrap model are shared with any
physical model: (1) Each model becomes tractable to human powers by its
disregard of certain general principles. (2) The model consequently can at
best give only an approximate description of an experiment, but the error
may be small for a certain domain of phenomena. (3) The smallness of the
error may be traced to experimental facts (small parameters) that the
model cannot explain but must accept as given.

Bootstrap models ideally have an additional characteristic: Given the
underlying experimental facts, all predictions from a model are supposed
to follow from those quantum-relativistic general principles that are not
being disregarded. No ad hoc postulates, such as an equation of motion,
are required or permitted.

The adjective *bootstrap*, of course, is never completely appropriate for
any individual model, because each model necessarily accepts certain facts
as arbitrary input. It is only by combining different models that the appellation *bootstrap* acquires justification. Consider the example of classical nuclear physics: Here the existence and properties of the neutron, proton,
and pion are accepted as given; there is no possibility of classical nuclear
physics explaining these facts. Since, on the other hand, it appears that all
predictions of the model follow from general principles, plus the aforementioned facts, classical nuclear physics may be regarded as a member of
a family of bootstrap models.† Some other models in the family have the
capability of explaining the existence and properties of neutron, proton,
and pion. Each of these other models itself depends on certain given experimental facts, but these facts will hopefully in turn be explained by yet
different models.

---

* Because the other leptons seem closely related to the electron, it is implausible that we
shall understand their origin before that of the electron.

† If classical nuclear physics depended on an equation of motion that did not follow entirely
from general principles, we could not consider it part of the bootstrap family.

It is essential to such a pattern that, while each model possesses a distinctive domain of approximate validity, there be some overlapping of domains; examples of overlapping models already exist in abundance. The bootstrap hypothesis implies that there will gradually develop a more and more dense coverage of the nuclear world by interlocking models, no single model having preeminent status. Such a pattern might be characterized as a "democracy of models."*

How do quark models fit into such a picture? To the extent that certain aspects of quark models have not yet been deduced from a combination of experimental facts and general principles, these models cannot yet be regarded as part of the bootstrap family. We have noted, however, that future theoretical research may succeed in closing the gap. When and if such a development occurs, quark models will join the democracy. The precedent of classical nuclear physics should be noted: This model enjoyed an aristocratic status for almost thirty years, but eventually it was democratized.

We hasten to emphasize that the existence of a mosaic of models, each satisfying the bootstrap criterion, does not establish the validity of the bootstrap hypothesis. It still might be true that more than one set of experimental facts is consistent with an entire mosaic, and that some requirement beyond the quantum relativistic general principles is demanded.† In order to verify the bootstrap hypothesis one would need to show that consistency between interlocking models is possible only for the set of nuclear facts actually observed.

## The human element

A peculiar impediment to exploration of the bootstrap hypothesis is the finiteness of the individual human life span. Scientists are typically aggressive, ambitious personalities who require a sense of major accomplishment during their active professional life; discovery of a startling new phenomenon or of a powerful new theory is their dream. Unhappily, one cannot imagine any single development, experimental or theoretical, that would justify a press announcement of verification of the bootstrap hypothesis.‡ Verification, if it is ever achieved, will be the cumulative result of many steps stretching out over decades, at the least. The most talented physicists tend to be the most ambitious, so it is not surprising to find the bootstrap idea regarded with distaste by the flower of the profession. Few of the stars of the world of physics are content with the thought that their labors will constitute only a fraction of a vast mosaic that must be constructed before the complete picture becomes recognizable and understandable. The most gifted physicists tend to pursue one or another elusive "fundamental entity," preferring a gallant if futile struggle to what they regard as surrender to the mysteries of nature.

Fortunately for the development of the bootstrap approach, these quests for an "inner core," even though so far in vain, often yield insight into problems of self-consistency. Progress might nevertheless accelerate if humans were less impatient for a dramatic and decisive resolution of the quest for understanding. Patience is the name of the bootstrap game.

A political consideration is also inescapable. Particle physics is expensive; big accelerators cost big money, and it is necessary to persuade taxpayers of the value they will receive from research with these accelerators. It is fortunately no longer necessary to suggest that national defense is involved; the enlargement of human knowledge and understanding is becoming accepted as an appropriate end in itself. But from a public relations standpoint it is easier to justify an expensive research program by dangling the possibility of imminent discovery of a glamorous-sounding fundamental entity than by patiently explaining how the new facility will contribute a modest but useful increment to a pattern of collective understanding. The necessity for public support, as well as inner psychological need, drives physicists to visualize onion peeling as the essence of their goal.

Onion or bootstrap? When will we know? Despite the present vastness of human accumulated knowledge, a mighty effort is still demanded before the essential nature of the nuclear-particle world becomes revealed.

---

* Certain models are, of course, more powerful than others. The power of a model may be measured by the ratio of the domain of its coverage to the underlying input experimental information. The accuracy of the coverage should also be considered in assessing model power.

† If the additional requirement were itself in the nature of a general principle, not involving specification of a numerical parameter, the term *bootstrap* might still be appropriate.

‡ It is possible to imagine disproof of the hypothesis by construction of models that satisfy all the quantum-relativistic general principles without being in accord with nature.

# The Planning of the Future

Bertrand de Jouvenel

Bertrand de Jouvenel des Ursins, known simply as Bertrand de Jouvenel, is among the foremost living authorities on the study of the future. He was born in Paris in 1903, the son of Henry de Jouvenel des Ursins, a noted French diplomat of both practical and scholarly experience in international affairs. Trained in law, biology, and economics, the younger Jouvenel became known in the thirties as a journalist and writer concerned with European political and economic developments, but since the end of the Second World War his name has been increasingly associated with speculations and writings on what may be called alternative futures in their various aspects: political, economic, social, and ecological. He has served on many public commissions, and in 1961 was a founder of the organization called Futuribles. He and his wife are coeditors of *Analyse et prévision*, a journal of policy studies.

Distinguished as a scholar and writer, M. de Jouvenel is professor of economics at the University of Paris and has taught at many other universities around the world, among them Yale and the University of California at Berkeley. Of his various books, the following are available in English: *On Power* (1948), *Sovereignty: An Inquiry into the Political Good* (1957), and *The Art of Conjecture* (1967). This last volume is currently one of the standard readings in futures studies at American colleges and universities.

# Introduction

This paper deals with a major intellectual and social phenomenon: the explosion of interest in the future that has occurred in the West. The phenomenon can be roughly divided into three components: an increasing tendency among thoughtful men to speculate upon probable, possible, and feasible futures; an increasing disposition among leaders in various fields to invite these speculations so far as they bear upon specific problems; and finally, an eager reception by the general public of the projections that emerge, derived as they usually are from the mass media, where emphasis is laid upon their more sensational aspects.

It was in the sixties that this interest in the future reached such proportions as to make clear that it was something quite different from the bestirring of minds that is the immediate aftermath of every great historical convulsion, and that then peters out. This time, on the contrary, there was an ever more extensive involvement of scholars in what they had at first deemed intellectual adventurism; governments and intergovernmental organizations sought expert opinions on an ever wider scope of problems; a continuous discussion of the future established itself nationally and internationally. And this last, at the end of the sixties, broke through to large audiences and came to affect public opinion.

This is indeed a momentous novelty. Here is a profound change in the attitude and the role of the intellectual community, which is traditionally dedicated to the advancement and communication of knowledge, and which now constructs and conveys surmises (surmises based, to be sure, *on* knowledge). It indicates a profound change also in public attitudes, extending the public's interest to the dimension of time and coloring its judgments and demands as to the present with concern for the future.

This was a necessary development of both intellectual activity and social consciousness. What is puzzling is not its occurrence but its belatedness. As long ago as the beginning of the century (1905), Henry Adams observed that our society seems to obey a Law of Acceleration, as he called it, the result of an ever increasing command over the forces of nature. Since then there have been many who, observing this headlong rush, have asked where we were going, whether we wanted to go there, and if not, how we could go elsewhere. Sir Francis Bacon once said (1605), "The invention of the mariner's needle, which giveth the direction, is of no less benefit for navigation than the invention of the sails which give the motion."* In the present century we have had to consider where we might find the needle to guide our social development. How greatly we may need such a thing was indicated by Wesley Mitchell in 1923: "The doubtful fate of human kind hangs largely upon the question whether men can develop social sciences that will enable them to control social processes," he wrote. And in 1902, H. G. Wells called upon the social sciences, especially history and economics, to address their studies toward the future—an appeal that unfortunately went unheeded.

If it had developed earlier, the orientation toward the future that now at last has come about might have saved governments from some of the grievous errors that have afflicted our century. At least an early start would have advanced the difficult and hazardous art of conjecture beyond the rough practices that now mark its tardy infancy and precipitate manifestations. Also, what might be called future-mindedness would have percolated to the public at a more gradual pace before the rise of the mass media, and thus opinion would be in no danger of mistaking vague forecasts for hard and fast predictions, of confusing attempts at foresight, which are necessary ingredients of prudent decision, with the pretense of foreknowledge, which is a delusion.

Such an explosion of interest in the future raises many questions of great importance. They cannot all be dealt with properly within the compass of this paper. But it has seemed of interest to list them, as follows:

1. Wherein lies the novelty of this interest? It does not lie in the fact that there is concern for the future, since that has always been implicit in the actions and behavior of men. What has happened is rather that the concern has become explicit, is now the object of a distinct mental activity, one that bears upon real affairs. Of course the roots of this activity are to be found in quite primitive human dispositions, which should be considered as the source of present developments.

2. How did this futuristic cast of thought come about? What part was played in it by such major phenomena of the twentieth century as the growth of government and the accelerating pace of change; to what extent was the futuristic mood in the making before World War II; how did that disastrous event, and the Great Depression that preceded and prepared it, contribute to the subsequent development of future-mindedness; of what influence upon its growth was the appeal of governments for help during the war to physical and social scientists, and on the other hand, of what effect was the anxiety generated by new means of destruction and the increasing costliness of human errors?

3. What has happened over the last quarter century? What kinds of future-oriented writings have been embarked upon, with what specific purposes; by whom have they been written; to what audiences have they been addressed? What shifts have occurred in their subject matter?

4. Why did the phenomenon of future-mindedness occur so belatedly?

A major impediment was the sharp separation of the world of thought from the world of action. How did this arise; what were its justifications; why had it endured? What influence did the idea of progress have, and what is its influence now?

5. How does the new forecasting function of intellectuals affect the social sciences? How does it affect the social character of the intellectual community?

6. What services are rendered by these new intellectual activities to public opinion? What social and political consequences may follow, desirable or dangerous? What political and moral problems are posed by the involvement of these intellectuals?

It is impossible to do justice to all these questions. The following exposition will confine itself to the rise of futurism in relation to: (1) its ancient roots, (2) the idea of progress, (3) expanding governmental function, (4) the threat of world disaster in various forms, and (5) the new attitudes and functions of intellectuals.

## 1. The ancient sources of future-mindedness

Concern for the future is inherent in our species; indeed it was present in our prehuman forebears, otherwise we would not be here today. It is wonderful that the lineage from which we are descended could survive and develop when we consider the extraordinary burden placed upon adults by the slow maturation of their offspring. If we rank animal species according to the degree and duration of the dependence maintained by their young, we find at the lower extreme those forms of life whose survival is achieved by superabundant spawning and by the immediate autonomy of such of the issue as meet with favorable circumstances. At the other extreme has always stood our own kind, even in its earliest state. Its infants are for a number of years wholly dependent for nourishment and protection upon the adults, whose responsibility is complicated by the birth of new infants long before the older ones have matured, creating a continuous burden upon their parents.

Therein of course lies the origin of human societies, or to be more accurate, of the prehuman groupings in which man, properly so-called, arose. The groupings had to be permanent; hence language. The children had to be cared for over an extended interval; hence education. It is possible that the magic value attached to the figure of the circle from earliest times stemmed from the formation adopted by adults to beat back predators from offspring who as yet were unable to flee. But in any case the major handicap of our species provided its first principles of development.

It is important to stress that concern for the future has its earliest and

---

* *Advancement of Learning; GBWW*, Vol. 30, p. 47.

deepest roots in a collective concern for the preservation of the group's existence. It is the more important in that this earliest form of concern, inspired as it was by solicitude, and implying solidarity, was later overshadowed by concern of a very different kind.

Different indeed from the group primarily concerned with *existence* is the group devoted to *action*. The action group, formed initially for hunting and later for war, comprises only adult males. While the existence group is held together by an inward-looking and conservative attitude, the action group is governed by an outward-looking purpose, the acquisition of game, and later of spoils. The fundamental concern of the existence group is the avoidance of risk; the purpose of the action group necessarily involves risk-taking. As the action group is formed for specific achievement, success or failure is soon apparent; beyond even that, the degree of success is quantitatively measured. The action group is a force; the existence group is a community.

As the study of primitive societies has progressed, their inner complexity has been brought to light, dispelling the naive belief of the civilized world that they are very simple structures. This belief arose because ethnologists found it easier to formulate an objective justification for the institutions they studied than to understand the subjective explanations offered by members of these societies, who do not express themselves in the rational language familiar to the investigators. Nor is that surprising: these institutions were not laid down by mental planning, dear to men of thought, but have developed very slowly in the course of coping with the many diverse problems that affect a living community. The permanence of such a community depends upon its ability to survive various crises that have not been foreseen.

Quite different is the case of the action group. It is formed for a specific, short-term goal. Its activities are wholly addressed to the achievement of that goal. This focuses such mental faculties as are available upon a single problem: how to attain the goal. In the early part of this century, W. Köhler sought to exercise the mental faculties of chimpanzees by exposing an object of desire in successively less accessible places, thus urging the subjects to increase their mental efforts if they wished to attain what they sought. This is the very same process to which Hobbes has attributed the development of human intelligence.

> For the thoughts are to the desires, as scouts, and spies, to range abroad and find the way to the things desired: all steadiness of the mind's motion, and all quickness of the same proceeding from thence.*

There is a very modern name for this use of the mind. It is Operations Research. That name dates from World War II, but the practice itself goes back to the tactics of hunting and of battle, and has grown with the increasing magnitude of such activities.

The lure of a specific goal focuses attention, mobilizes the available mental faculties, and orders thoughts relative to the end sought. We can easily observe this process in animals and small children with respect to a visible objective. The process is of course superior in man, who has the capacity to form images of goals that are not perceptible to the eye. But that we are dealing with the same process is attested by language: we speak of a distant objective not only in terms of spatial distance but also of distance in time, and of both dimensions not only in relation to real things but as they apply to a creature of imagination.

We speak of obstacles to be met and overcome, eventually of adversary moves to be guessed and outmaneuvered. Our purpose operates as a powerful selector of information; only that which is relevant to the purpose is sought or welcomed; the more specific the purpose, the more precise the selection. Because the desired success requires systematic action, we develop first a plan of thought.

These features are most obviously apparent in military expeditions, wherein force is deployed according to calculations based upon available information. Assuredly, less thought went into William the Conqueror's landing in England in 1066 than into Eisenhower's landing in France of 1944, but it was the same type of thinking in both cases.

Instinctive concern for the community does not so naturally lead to mental programming. Community life gives rise to a great variety of problems that are not individually foreseen but are coped with as they appear. Insofar as they threaten the group, there is an instinctive disposition to nip them in the bud, a demand for the stabilization of behavior. The maxim of "playing it safe" rules, however unconsciously. And this is a natural attitude, since the fundamental purpose of the community is to protect the children and bring them to the condition achieved by their parents; a general concern for the future takes the form of ensuring repetition of the present.

This conservative mood has endured far beyond the tiny primitive communities in which it must have been something fundamental. Testimonies to it are the widespread myths obtaining in more advanced societies, referring to a wise founder whose institutions were to be preserved, whose precepts were sacrosanct. The contrast is stark with the adventurous spirit that looks outward and forward to the creation of a previously nonexisting situation. It is the generally accepted view that the larger political bodies with which history begins did not arise out of a friendly merging of initial communities, but by conquest. Every early political structure of which we know anything was created by the tribute exacted from subject communities.

There is a marked relation between the development of agriculture and the rise of empires. The former affords the latter an economic basis owing

---

* *Leviathan; GBWW*, Vol. 23, p. 68.

to the more or less regular production of sedentary, and thus controllable, rural communities. Great was the difference of scale between the size of the community and the power it exerted. Subjects of a conquered state did not thereby become part of the social community that overcame them. Their vital concerns remained local, while the conquerors, liberated from menial cares, could address themselves to the enjoyment of power, to disputes among themselves, and to seeking the enlargement of their dominion.

Why go back so far, which allows only a very rude sketch? In order to bring out clearly that the earliest concerns of the human species, which were community oriented and relatively inarticulate, were overrun by other, power-centered concerns, always more eloquent, which have now reigned for some thousands of years. Coincident with this change, the primitive deities bound up with features of life and nature were driven underground, superseded by gods bound up with power. At the beginning of this century, it was a trite criticism of history that it dealt almost exclusively with military and political events. But this did not occur without reason: it was because the only visible actors that history contained were those who had power, and their disputes referred to power. Presumably this explains the power connotation of such adjectives as *scheming* and *designing*. Surely there is ample occasion for schemes and designs tending to the common good. The unfavorable connotation of these adjectives must reflect the historical experience of such mental processes being most frequently used in power seeking.

Power seeking has indeed been the great motive for human action throughout history. It applies to the beginnings of economic development no less than to political and military affairs. Commerce did not develop out of neighborly exchange naturally limited in volume and kind but out of seafaring ventures in pursuit of the tempting outlets offered by distant power holders who were wealthy by virtue of their political dominion. The purpose of the merchant adventurers was not to make a living but to make a fortune, and to gain prestige, influence, and power at home. And as they created power, so were they secured by it. Their commerce required navies to lessen the risk of pirates and to maintain trade privileges.

Reviving in terms of large societies the community concerns that must have reigned in primitive times is a very recent undertaking. But precisely because it is so recent, we bring to the task ways of thinking that have developed in the service of power concerns. It is not insignificant that when we discuss policies tending to some social good, we are wont to name them "strategies," indicating thereby that the art of thinking in terms of the end-means relationship has its earliest manifestations in military affairs.

It seems timely to stress this, because the "good" of a society is multidimensional, and no easy agreement is possible as to the relative value of its various components, either as they exist in themselves or as they affect one another in the course of social development, concerning which we can say only that the ways of thought that were appropriate to the understanding of a single purpose are too simple to guide us in comprehending ends that are more complex. "Victory" and "gain" are simple criteria; "gradual improvement" is harder to analyze.

Human thinking with respect to futures has developed in the direction of single-purpose achievements, and has remained untrained and unequipped to deal with the fundamental problem of overall social evolution.

## 2. The idea of progress

When Auguste Comte uttered his slogan "Order and Progress," he thereby joined an age-old human concern with the new and ardent faith that characterizes modern society.

It has been pointed out that human society has its primeval root in the instinctive concern to secure the children; it has developed into something that provides a secure environment for adults. The nocturnal ring of fire against dangerous prowlers, the walls erected against nomads or invaders, are symbols of the guarantee that was sought against the unknown coming from outside, means of protection within which men could move in a known environment.

The Gestaltist Kurt Koffka has remarked, in a striking image, that "we lean with our eyes against the surroundings," and he gives many instances of dizziness and loss of equilibrium induced by the instability of the framework in various situations. This happens in the case of the social framework, certainly; we need its stability. When the established framework crumbles, many panic (the civilian panic in France of June 1940), and when the framework is threatened, there is a rush for order (the French elections of June 1968).

That whatever is familiar (and therefore reassuring) is subject to a process of decay was the thought magnificently expressed by Heraclitus, and in Europe the concern with decadence was one of the themes of classical education, as indeed it should have been, not only because of the sayings of classical authors but also because the history that was taught was that of the Hellenic and Roman civilizations that had decayed and died.

Momentous therefore was the development in Western Europe of a new faith in Progress, a faith that spread eventually to the whole world, the first creed to achieve universality.

The word *faith* is not excessive, for what occurred was nothing less than a new belief in man, in his earthly ascent, promised by some immanent Providence: an autolatry, as it may fairly be called, that has increased ever since it became established.

We are concerned here solely with the impact of this faith on conceptions of the future, so we need not dwell upon the formation of what amounts to a secular religion. Let us only note some traits that successively asserted themselves.

First we note a surge of boldness breaking out of established confines. Of this the most striking manifestation was the daring of navigators, who were sent forth by Prince Henry of Portugal as early as 1426 with the object of finding the way around Africa. Within a century, this venturing had resulted not only in finding a seaway to India but in the discovery of the New World—immense success in reward of such boldness. The same pattern was reproduced in other human concerns. There was boldness also, which was also successful, in the defiance, by reformers of the Church, of its power and its established doctrines.

These audacities were devastating in their results. As a consequence of the great navigations, Europeans displayed in the New World and in Africa every vice of which human nature is capable, while religious differences at home brought about a degree of savagery in warfare hitherto unknown.

Less spectacular but very much pleasanter to contemplate was the pattern of intellectual development. Here we find also a bold breaking away from established systems of thought. Intellectual work had been all too "confined and as it were imprisoned in the writings of certain authors" (so Bacon was to say in his *Novum Organum**), who were commented upon, interpreted, and resorted to for the purpose of developing every variety of abstract doctrine. Religious conflicts were no help in escaping from this kind of exercise, but its tone was much lowered when it undertook to address itself, by way of the decisive invention of printing, to a much larger public. It is noteworthy that social criticism (Erasmus, Sir Thomas More) preceded, save for a few isolated cases (Leonardo da Vinci), the growth of interest in knowledge of the material world. The time had not yet come when Bacon would reproach the "false estimation, that it should be as a diminution to the mind of man to be much conversant in experiences and particulars subject to sense and bound in matter, and which are laborious to search, ignoble to meditate, harsh to deliver, illiberal to practice."†

It is indicative that More's *Utopia* (1516) follows Plato in depicting a static society, once for all excellently ordained, where there is no advancement in science and technology, and no change in material conditions. This is in contrast to the idea of Progress as it was to be understood in the nineteenth century and in our own day. But it is interesting also that More's ideal society differs from Plato's in its social radicalism: though a static conception, it was static in populist terms.

Bacon was the first to formulate the idea of Progress as it was to triumph, taking knowledge as its engine—knowledge sought "not for truth but for operation . . . to increase the revenues and multiply the possessions of man."‡ And with this purpose in mind, Bacon set forth in 1603 a program that might as well be dated 1974. His idea is

> *to make distribution of sciences, arts, inventions, works, and their portions, according to the use and tribute which they yield and render to the conditions of man's life, and under these several uses, being as several offices of provisions, to charge and tax what may be reasonably exacted and demanded; . . . and then upon those charges and taxations to distinguish and present, as it were in several columns, what is extant and already found, and what is defective and further to be provided.*§

That Bacon's view of the use of knowledge for operational ends was widely received in England in the early years of the eighteenth century is attested by Swift's derision of it in his *Laputa*. But eighteenth-century authors, especially in France, were not as a rule Baconian in this respect. They conceived Progress mainly as Enlightenment, not as operation, and they thought that the condition of Enlightenment was the clearing from minds of superstitions, which condition they deemed themselves to have achieved. Hence it seemed to them that the natural light of Reason would henceforth show clearly the most important truths to their minds, unless these were further obfuscated by passion—an important proviso that Hume (after Hobbes) deemed unattainable. Such a triumph of Reason was called by Thomas Paine the right rule of Common Sense.

The marriage, in an all-embracing view of Progress, of sane moral judgments based upon self-evident truths with what we now term scientific and technological advances, was undertaken by the Encyclopaedists, principally Condorcet, who thus laid the foundations of the very first long-term view of the human future.

This comprehensive view formed the crowning part of Condorcet's *Sketch for a Historical Picture of the Progress of the Human Mind*, written in 1793, when he was outlawed by the National Convention after having been one of the leaders of the Revolution. It was a heroic effort, not only in metaphorical terms, for its scope was grandiose, but also psychologically, since the faith it manifested was proclaimed in circumstances that might have dashed the spirits of a lesser man—and when the "Sketch" was completed, Condorcet wandered out, unwilling to endanger any further the woman who had afforded him refuge, to find ultimately an obscure death in prison, under an assumed name.

Condorcet's vision blends moral with material progress. Equality among all the peoples of the world as well as in each nation, and an actual not merely a legal equality, is the goal toward which mankind is seen to be

---

\* *GBWW*, Vol. 30, p. 125.
† *Filum Labyrinthi.*
‡ *Valerius Terminus.*
§ *Valerius Terminus.*

moving. This movement is asserted to be coming about through the diffusion of practical arts as well as by their advancement through science. The progress of science shall be accelerated by universal education and consequently by a much larger recruitment of persons to be educated. Their understanding shall be served by a universal language of symbols. Social machinery will become sophisticated, based upon probability calculus and combinatorial analysis. Condorcet foretells in some detail institutions of mutual insurance. He predicts a considerable momentum of world population increase, but anticipates that reason will develop in time to brake it.

It is a lesson to us that this great mind quite failed to foresee the two great economic developments that were to characterize the nineteenth century: the spread of fuel-driven engines and the rise of business corporations.

A new era opens when Watt patents (1769) improvements that make practical the use of "the motive power of fire," as Denis Papin had already called it in 1690. From then onward, man would avail himself of ever increasing forces, machines of unprecedented weight moving at undreamed-of speeds. What an escape this was from previous limitations! And what a new conception of history as a progress of human power emerges! From all parts of the white man's world (as it then was), over six million visitors came in 1851 to admire man's works displayed at the Great Exhibition in London. The Paris Exposition of 1867 was of special interest in that it was so contrived as to lay stress upon man's progress: while the outer ring of exhibits displayed recent achievements, the inner ring was meant to take the visitor through human works going back to the Stone Age. Thus could men glory in their rise, as in that Darwinian time they liked to do, their new sense of what they were being expressed in the terms used by both Claparède and Broca: "I prefer to think of myself rather as a risen monkey than as a fallen Adam."

The year 1867 happens to be also the date of publication of *Das Kapital*, in which Marx displays with unexampled vigor the role of capital accumulation in the progress of human affairs. Of the capitalist he says:

> *Fanatically bent upon the expansion of exchange value, he relentlessly drives human beings to production for production's sake, thus bringing about a development of social productivity and the creation of those material conditions of production which can alone form the basis of a higher type of society, whose fundamental principle is the full and free development of every individual. Only as the personification of capital is the capitalist respectable.**

While it was pleasing to regard material progress as the result of inventiveness alone, such inventiveness was useless without the material means to apply it. Melancholy proof of this was evident in the failure of the Marquis de Jouffroy to establish the steamship, even though such a ship, designed by him, had operated successfully on the Saône River as early as 1775, shortly followed by another and better one: but then his personal funds gave out, and he could not raise more capital.

The fate of George Stephenson would have been no better, and there would have been no development of railways had it depended upon the efforts of an individual promoter limited to his private fortune. Even before Marx depicted the capitalist as the personification of capital, capital had found another personification in the business corporation, a gatherer of funds to build up equipment, which found, in selling the services thereby rendered, yet more funds to build yet more equipment.

It is very striking that while the whole tendency of the three hundred years before the eighteenth century had been to destroy the great concentration of assets in the hands of a vast self-perpetuating organization, the Church, the whole tendency of the nineteenth century was to favor in every way the concentration of assets in the hands of new organizations that likewise were undying. That an undying body must wax ever stronger had been Chancellor d'Aguesseau's argument of 1749, directed ostensibly against Foundations but meant against the Church, whose immense properties were later dispersed by the French Revolution among individual owners. The same argument could have been used to even greater effect when the undying body was of the sort that used its means to achieve profits and thereby gave itself new assets. In the nineteenth century a momentous change in the law favored the rise of corporations, and at the end of this century mergers further increased their size. The "battle of the trusts" was in fact lost by Theodore Roosevelt, as was predictable, these new corporate forms having already become the essential agents of ongoing capital development.

Thus, what Henry Adams saw in 1904 was the surge of energy and the proliferation of wealth accomplished by two great human agencies, the dynamo and the corporation. As Adams put it eloquently on returning to New York from Europe:

> *The outline of the city became frantic in its effort to explain something that defied meaning. Power seemed to have outgrown its servitude and to have asserted its freedom. The cylinder had exploded, and thrown great masses of stone and steam against the sky. The city had the air and movement of hysteria, and the citizens were crying, in every accent of anger and alarm, that the new forces must at any cost be brought under control. Prosperity never before imagined, power never yet wielded by man, speed never reached by anything but a meteor, had made the world irritable, nervous, querulous, unreasonable and afraid. All New York was demanding new men, and all the new forces, condensed into corporations, were demanding a new type of man—a man with*

---

* Bk. 1, pt. 7, chap. 24, sec. 3; *GBWW*, Vol. 50, p. 292.

> *ten times the endurance, energy, will and mind of the old type—for whom they*
> *were willing to pay millions at sight.\**

There was no doubt in Adams's mind that this combined development of huge forces and huge organizations would not only go on but would accelerate. Rather than Condorcet's vision, it was a Darwinian process that was being realized, transposed from living forms to social forms, and fantastically quickened: ever more complex organizations developing and creating conditions fatal to the older and simpler forms, the family-based industry, workshop, shop, and farm.

These new organizations, as Adams put it, "obnoxious because of their vigorous and unscrupulous energy ... tore society to pieces."† But also they were rebuilding it in their own image. The middle classes would not be destroyed as Marx had predicted, leaving a great uniform mass of oppressed workers to suffer from and ultimately to overthrow a small number of capitalists. The middle classes would reconstitute themselves by way of middle positions in the corporations, which needed, as great and efficient armies do, an ever increasing proportion of officers and technicians. The great moral revolt against the condition of the workers would be aided by the need of corporations to find consumers, who increasingly became, and were gradually seen to be, none other than the workers themselves.

Corporations are undying bodies that build up capital by the use of capital. They do this not only in financial terms but in tangible works, devoting financial resources obtained by the use of equipment to installing more or better equipment. It was but an extension of the same process that, in seeking markets, corporations found them by making consumers out of the same families whose members served them as workers. In time the social map came to have corporations as its backbone, with families that were workers by day becoming consumers, as it were, by night: indeed, this is how contemporary social organization is depicted in National Accounts (it is proper to mention that this great tool of vision was built up mainly by the National Bureau of Economic Research of New York).

The age of precipitate material growth in the industrialized countries brought in its wake a great number of problems, the character and extent of which may best be understood in the metaphor used by Henri de Saint-Simon in 1819. Saint-Simon saw progress as the march of the human caravan. This march did not have the same significance for all. Immensely advantageous and exciting to the leaders, it was less beneficial to those who, behind them, bore the burden—the workers. Saint-Simon was indignant that the leaders picked the fruits in this fashion while their servants had to be content with a pittance. So, even earlier (1812), was Robert Owen. And what of the material condition of the workers? This was the earliest problem of the Industrial Age, and the most pertinacious. Engels, observing Manchester in his youth, expected the explosion of workers to bring about a social revolution, which Marx predicted; it did not happen in the more advanced countries as Marx thought it would, but the resulting agitation did give rise to the unions, to labor laws, to the slow achievement of recognition and power by the wage earners. As for those whom age or sickness or unemployment precluded chronically or temporarily from earning any living at all, it took a long time to establish social insurance of the sort advocated by Condorcet.

Beyond even these disadvantaged were the people who could not adjust to the march at all, the apparently unemployable. It is only quite lately that this has been recognized as an important problem in itself. It had been optimistically believed that rising standards of living for workers, along with social insurance, would cover all needs. But matters turned out differently. While the most advanced country, the United States, was not the seat, as Marxian doctrine would have it, of a final class war between workers and capitalists, it proved to be the place where a large population unintegrated with the march was formed, living miserably on its margin and prone to disturbing behavior. Poverty was thus by no means eliminated, while crime rose to become a major problem.

As the livelihood of all families came to depend upon the march of the caravan, its halting at the time of the Great Depression proved a social disaster. From this the lesson was learned that public policies should be devised to keep the caravan moving. These policies were systematized at the end of World War II, and not only did they keep the caravan moving but they served to quicken its pace.

This was a great age of economists. The Depression had shaken them out of the apologetics of General Equilibrium, which taught that according to the "law" of supply and demand things would adjust themselves automatically in the best of possible worlds. Under the banner of Keynes, the economists sought the secret of uninterrupted growth, of perpetual enrichment, of a golden age of regular and unending progress of GNP, to be guaranteed by observing the golden rule of accumulation.

Thereupon it became usual to extrapolate the growth of national products, and this over longer and longer periods. Herman Kahn, beating all others at that game, forecast in the sixties what the national products of all various regions and countries would be in the year 2000. Here was the supreme manifestation of confidence in Progress, an assurance of its correctness as a term of social analysis.

But as early as the fifties, some faint voices had begun to ask: Progress toward what? Are we helping human beings to develop their potentialities, improving their relations with one another? Have we turned the earth into a garden, or are we so obsessed with *doing* that we have no time to ask

---

\* "Nunc Age (1905)" in *The Education of Henry Adams* (Boston: Houghton Mifflin, 1961), chap. 35, p. 499.

† Ibid., p. 500.

ourselves what deserves to be done, no leisure to seek the best means of its achievement? Are we so entranced by man's works that we cannot see the ruination of our land and the degradation of our characters, turned as we are into hustlers and hucksters? As our social powers increase, should not discrimination enter into their use?

The delay was short between the raising of these faint voices and the clamor, in France and elsewhere, of 1968. Shorter still was the delay between that and the outright declaration of war upon growth in the early seventies!

At the outset of this section, Progress was represented as a new faith, a secular religion. Looking at the matter in this light, the attitudes that have recently developed are analogous to the revolt against the Established Church that occurred in the sixteenth century.

Now, as then, the revolt takes a variety of forms, from appeals for the modification of established ideas to demands for their extirpation. It is a phenomenon of immense importance. History is made up mainly of conflicts of interests. Occasionally there are conflicts of beliefs. It has been observed throughout this section that since Bacon's time, faith in Progress has gradually evolved into a belief in ever rising production by way of technology and capital accumulation. This orthodoxy must now face heretics and negators, as well as those who wish only to reform it.

In this instance the former are making the greater noise. But as yet they offer no alternative, and the caravan cannot be halted without social disaster. The champions of reform, on the other hand, who desire not to overthrow progress but purify it, are concerned to find ways by which this may be done.

The march cannot be brought to a stop, but it can be reoriented. Starting from what one would like to see altered, one must seek what is feasible. Such an inquiry demands new habits of thought. How these have lately come to be acquired is the subject of the next two sections.

## 3. The expansion of governmental functions

An obvious phenomenon of the twentieth century is the great increase of governmental responsibility in fields such as education, health, income maintenance in old age or illness, the stabilization and promotion of economic growth, research and development, and most recently, the environment. The assumption of these and other human cares has an uneven history and order of development, having been carried more or less far, and administered in different ways, in different countries. In the United States, government support of health, for instance, is limited to Medicare for the aged and Medicaid for the poor, while in Britain there has been since 1946 a national health service free to all comers. Almost as comprehensive is the French system, in which, however, there is mainly a reimbursement of expenses (that is, monetary transfers). This support involves public spending corresponding to 2.6 percent of the gross national product in the United States, 4 percent in Britain, and 6.9 percent in France.

The growth of governmental responsibility is reflected, to some degree, in the vast increase of the funds that go through the hands of public institutions, measured as a percentage of the GNP, whether to support public activities or to achieve transfers. According to the OECD (that is the international Organization for Economic Cooperation and Development), these were lately (average of 1967–69) 30 percent for the United States, over 34 percent for France, with Sweden almost reaching 40 percent. Incidentally, no adverse effect has been observed on the pace of economic growth as a consequence of these expenditures; if anything, the reverse has occurred.

However impressive this financial commitment may appear, it still is an inadequate expression of government's increased social role, which is played also by means of mandatory instructions to individuals and private organizations telling them what they must or what they may not do, and how to proceed in whatever is to be done.

As one observes the enormous growth of governmental agencies and their powers, it is a natural and prudent reaction to consider its dangers. The greatest of these is that such a formidable assemblage of commanding levers may fall into evil hands: this concern inspired my book *On Power*, published in 1945. But the subtitle of that work stressed the fact that we have to deal here with a natural phenomenon. That this is what it is we see far more clearly twenty-eight years later. Observing the speed at which society is being transformed by the accelerating pace of technological progress, spurred by the equally accelerating pace of capital investment, governments are induced to greater and more diverse functions as contributors to the great social movement; they seek to improve the distribution of its benefits, to cope with the resulting injuries or anxieties, to sustain some sort of stability in a process of bewildering change.

It is relevant to stress that governments contribute considerably to the force exerted by these great agents of change, the business corporations. Governments have done this since the Great Depression, in response to its miseries (and its fatal political consequences in Germany), by very properly making full employment a political imperative. This ensures to business a continuing seller's market by making the pace of economic growth a measure of its success, which implies favoring productive investments (the only form of taxation that has in recent years declined in terms of its ratio to GNP is that of corporations, thanks to the increasing latitude of untaxed profits in the name of depreciation), and by heavily subsidizing research and development.

In these and other ways, governments have increased the impact of the commercial economy upon the people, both in its positive and in its negative aspects. And the people have had both aspects to cope with: more automobiles, more roads; more flying, more airports; changes in the character of labor, more education; more leisure, greater boredom with work; mobility of residence, more housing and new schools; the concentration of culture in cities, a piling up of population; increasing complexity, increasing regulations; increasing overall wealth, more care for the disfavored; more consumption, more waste to be dealt with; more intensive exploitation of nature, a more urgent problem of environment. We could go on. Contrary to the old assumption that there must be an opposition between the development of the private economy and of state action, what we have witnessed is a progress coupled with coincident problems.

It has been mentioned that the direst danger attending the growth of public power is the risk of its falling into mischievous hands. Strangely enough, the dreadful warning we have had in this respect—I mean the Fascist example—has not given rise to the creation of new political safeguards. An immensely enlarged arsenal of public powers is left as unguarded as it was in the period between the two world wars.

We seem to follow the course of Roman history, as foretold by Cournot in 1861. He described a dual process of increasing complexity in the organization of the administrative system, together with a reduction of the political system to the simplicity of its embodiment in one man, the principate. The first of these developments would have amazed the Romans of the Republican era, while the second would have appalled them.[1]

But let us not be prisoners of analogies, nor dwell upon the dangers of the principate, which are dealt with elsewhere. We are concerned with the extension of governmental activity, in our times, and what we want to stress is its association with forecasts and projections.

This impels us to consider, in the receding wake of the absolute monarchies of Europe, under which was begun the building of the modern State with its regular taxes and regular servants, two distinct eras that have succeeded them: one we may call the Age of Opinion, the other the Age of Information.

The Age of Opinion has been characterized by the rise and ultimate triumph of the following demands: that public decisions should be made according to rules carefully laid down and known to all (constitutionalism); that the decision-making process should be open to the view of all (public parliamentary debates); that this process should be responsible to and swayed by the active citizenry, primarily by means of free elections, whereby the citizens choose the decision makers, but also through current criticisms and demands addressed to these decision makers while they are at work (freedom of the press and other civil liberties).

Such are the features won by liberals (under whatever name they went) in the eighteenth and nineteenth centuries, which remain characteristic of what we call "free governments" (a misleading ellipsis: it is not the governments that are meant to be free).

A by-product of the emphasis upon opinion was the importance acquired by powers of expression. It is true, neither David Ricardo nor John Stuart Mill made much of a mark in the British Parliament, being deficient in oratory—an art that the example of Hitler has now taught us to distrust. But the chief means of disseminating opinion was the printing press, and let us remember that "freedom of the press" should be taken literally: it meant the right for anyone to resort for the expression of his views to a medium that was then extremely cheap. Three thousand copies of Marat's journal at the time of the French Revolution were produced at a cost equivalent to that of a lunch for four people at a fashionable restaurant. So small a circulation proved enough in times of crisis to raise a crowd for decisive demonstrations; in calmer times it also proved enough to feed the discussions of political circles.

The Encyclopaedists, who had done so much to promote the Age of Opinion, felt no doubt that it would promote general enlightenment. It is no refutation of their fundamental beliefs, and it implies no belittling of positive achievements, that "men of letters" all too often failed to live up to the trust placed in their apostolate. A collector and student of ancient journals of opinion must acknowledge, with great regret, that what the great majority of them expressed were "mere" opinions, which at worst were expressions of passion and at best were deductions from preconception. One finds all too few examples of argument based upon a solid sense of history such as there is in the Federalist papers.* And of course these opinions could not be based upon careful interpretation of collected current information, because there was no such collection of information.

Noisily celebrated today is the "Information Revolution," said to have been brought about by the computer, and in the fanfare celebrating this new wonder, voluntary testimonials are even more fervent than those of the commercial advertisers. Who indeed could deny that the computer is a wonder instrument, or belittle the services it may render? But it should not be represented as opening the Age of Information. On the contrary, the relationship is exactly the other way. It was the long-developing Age of Information that made such a machine necessary for the exploitation of the accumulated material.

The author is incompetent to form any picture of the computer's future achievements, or even to discuss its present functions in fields unfamiliar to him. But in the various areas of social affairs, what is the present func-

---

[1] Cournot puts it as follows: "The development of civilization, involving extreme division of labour, population growth, and the formation of large States, above all, the leveling of social conditions, brings about new institutions—military, financial, and administrative—often more complex and in all cases more stable and better informed. But as to politics itself, they rather fall back to simplicity. The administrative system of Diocletian was more scientific if not better conceived than that of Augustus . . . but the public law of ritualistic and patrician Rome was ever so much more complex than that of Rome, mistress of the world under Augustus and Diocletian." (A. Cournot's *Traité de l'enchaînement des idées fondamentales dans les sciences et dans l'histoire*, 2 vols. [Paris, 1861, 1912], p. 461.)

* *The Federalist*; GBWW, Vol. 43, pp. 29–259.

tion of the computer? It is to manipulate at lightning speed data that are fed to it, and to manipulate these in various ways prescribed to it. And this implies the antecedent collection of data, and a concern to make sense of it. It was that accumulation and that concern that brought on the Age of Information, and brought it slowly, without any fanfare.

How far we have come can be measured by quoting the alarm expressed by Montesquieu two and a half centuries ago (1721): "After having reckoned it as exactly as is possible in the order of things, I have found that the population of the Earth is scarcely a tenth of what it was in ancient times. And, what is most striking, depopulation proceeds, tending to make a desert ten centuries hence." As everyone is now aware, Montesquieu was wrong in both assertions: population had increased considerably and was increasing. But how could he have known? The information was not available.

A most important history, which is yet to be written, is that of the slow growth of information about human society. A preliminary stage of this was evident in the unique (and monumental) collection of descriptive reports about the various provinces of France drawn up at the order of Louis XIV in 1697. How did Western civilization move from that to the present availability of statistical series bearing upon an ever increasing number of social phenomena, series that, being kept up to date, indicate current trends, and that, being both extensive and numerous, permit the study of correlations? The heroes of this progression are unsung. One must delve into administrative archives to observe the rise of the Age of Information. For France, the starting point was the epoch that opened with the French Revolution and culminated in the authority of Napoleon. *There* was a master so avid for information that he would demand it of a minister called in the dead of night, and if dissatisfied, would turn him away and summon another who was better informed, so that his civil servants were not only afraid to disappoint him but were encouraged to suggest ways of increasing the information at their disposal, as I found incidentally in studying the Continental Blockade.

Here appears a link between Power and the demand for more and better Information. There is also an obvious link between the extension of state functions and a greater amount of information. But as to such an extension, the usual cause and effect relationship is reversed. While information is called for as the necessary servant of governmental action, informing the state of available means, information generated outside the governmental apparatus can be so significant as to show the need for government action. Such were the private investigations of working conditions conducted both in England and in France in the second quarter of the nineteenth century, culminating in a momentous survey, *Life and Labour of the People in London* (1889-1903), which, as Beatrice Webb states, was "carried on by Charles Booth (entirely at his own expense) over a period of seventeen years and published in as many volumes."

Although in the nineteenth century the searchers for social facts were few and their audiences tiny, their impact upon the twentieth century has been tremendous. Here we can easily distinguish, and might contrast, two different posterities springing from two different sources. On the one hand there is Marxism, the present importance of which needs no emphasis, and which may be said to have had its source in the critical examination made by Friedrich Engels in 1842–43 of the desperate condition of the working classes in England, whose plight he made known to Karl Marx, leading this powerful mind to develop his world-famous doctrine. On the other hand, we have the Welfare State, which has its source in the social expertise that originated in England with the Webbs. Not that anyone calls himself a Welfarist, much less a Webbist. Indeed, few would understand the reference to the powerful team formed in 1892 when Beatrice Potter, the daughter of a rich industrialist, cousin to Charles Booth and an associate in his social work, chose to marry, not the famous statesman Joseph Chamberlain, who had earlier thought of her, but an obscure civil service worker turned reformer, Sidney Webb. And yet much of the subsequent growth of governmental institutions in the West can be traced back to that couple's unrelenting effort to expose "the ill-instructed famous" to the factual knowledge of "the obscurely efficient" (as H. G. Wells put it when depicting the Webbs in his novel *The New Machiavelli*). While they shared Engels's social concern, the Webbs did not share the conviction of Marx that England, as the most industrially advanced country, must be the first to see a revolutionary overthrow of the capitalist class by the proletariat. They deemed the Establishment (as it is now called in Britain) solid but also permeable, and while they became active in the Labour Party, they also set about making themselves "a center of reference for all sorts of legislative proposals" (Wells again). They pinned their hopes for change not solely or indeed mainly upon a change in the party colors of elected representatives but upon their belief that elected bodies would have to appeal increasingly to the services of expert officials. And Wells quotes them (in the novel) as suggesting that "these expert officials must necessarily develop into a new class and a very powerful class in the community."

Whatever exaggeration there may be in the latter suggestion, it is true enough that elected representatives have during the twentieth century needed more expert advice. The expert is a feature of the Age of Information: witness the Congress of the United States, which is assisted by experts and which actively seeks information of all sorts. This is a logical necessity, and European parliaments have suffered greatly from not understanding it.

When governmental powers are exerted in a great variety of fields, each of which is changing, it is impossible for any public representative to have enough knowledge of each field to make intelligent decisions in it, or to estimate the consequences of the decisions he does make and their repercussions in related fields. Such a representative—such a decision maker—must resort to the services of experts.

The proper relationship between the decision maker and the experts, and the moral obligations that the latter have, their proper deontology, are important subjects, to be dealt with in another section relative to the intellectual. What must be stressed here is the significance of calling upon expert services. The significance is that responsible decision making requires much preliminary work, both in keeping information up to date and in making it available and intelligible when decisions are required. These are what nowadays we call inputs in the formation of the decision maker's opinion. They are costs in the Smithian sense of "toil and trouble," and nowadays they are also monetary costs.

Now let us consider the contrast between *this* sense of "opinion" and the sense that prevailed in the Age of Opinion. It was then proclaimed (and we still hold) that opinion should be "free"; but "free" has several meanings. It was then meant (and we now mean) that opinion should be "free" as to its expression (i.e., untrammeled). But "free" can also be taken to mean "costless," and in the Age of Opinion it was assumed to be just that. All men capable of expressing an opinion were assumed to be able to formulate it spontaneously, on the spur of the moment, and indeed eighteenth-century writers were wont to affirm that men could form a right opinion, according to right reason, if only their minds were purged of "superstitions." There was hardly any awareness then that an opinion should be formed on careful consideration of facts, requiring toil and trouble. This notion, which is still far from being as widespread as it should be, is a moral imperative that has occurred only with the Age of Information. It is a notion—or, again, a moral imperative—that has become a fundamental tenet of the generation that lived through and learned from the disastrous course of events from 1914 to 1944—thirty years that were for Europe the equivalent of the thirty years' war that debased Hellas.

We now come to the impact of these terrible events, which at the same time demonstrated dramatically the need for informed forethought and led to the extension of governmental functions, thus multiplying the need for information and its expert handling.

## 4. The threat of world disaster

Heedlessness in foreign affairs has dramatic results. A great master, Thucydides, taught this lesson for all time in his history of the Peloponnesian War.* While he did not live to see the end of that war, which lasted thirty years, Thucydides prophetically cast his tale as a tragedy leading to the wreck and ruin of the glory and importance of Hellas.

No thoughtful European who had seen the disastrous thirty years from 1914 to 1944 could fail to sense the analogy with the thirty years' war of

Greece, and therefore to understand the points made by Thucydides. For that historian, representing to us the debates in one or the other antagonistic city at the time of major decisions made in the course of the war, shows how decision makers were swayed by one-sided and heady visions of the results to be expected from daring recommendations. Thus, Alcibiades persuaded the Athenian Assembly to embark upon the expedition to Syracuse that was to prove the cemetery of Athenian prestige and power.

To make it quite clear that the course of his tragic tale turns upon lack of forethought, our great teacher, at an early stage of the conflict, puts key words in the mouth of Archidamus, addressing the Assembly of Lacedaemonians, who says: "We that must be thought the causers of events to come, good or bad, had better take heed to foresee them as far as possible."[†]

No such prudence was displayed by Europe's leaders in 1914, or indeed through the thirty disastrous years to 1944. How can this fail to impress upon us the need for a careful exploration of consequences?

World War I shook Europe to an utterly unexpected degree. While there had been a difference of opinion about the possibility of an armed conflict in Europe, all had agreed that if such a conflict occurred, it could not last more than a few weeks for economic reasons. It lasted over four years, practically every European family had its dead or maimed, whole regions were devastated, the political regimes of Russia, Germany, Austria-Hungary, and the Ottoman Empire were overturned, and in the end a great conference in Paris set about recasting the map of Europe on principles of nationalism.

To youthful minds entranced by the course of events, the Conference of Paris was proof positive that the world could be remade deliberately, and this well or badly. Keynes became our hero for denouncing the inherent absurdity both of interallied debts and reparations and of the extension of national debts. A further absurdity, of which I happened to be an indignant witness, was the humiliating manner in which the Treaty of Versailles was presented to the liberal representatives of a new German Republic, who were bidden to sign on the dotted line. This was unprecedented; nothing so degrading had ever occurred in the history of civilized Europe. The treaty also included the famous article 231 that charged Germany with exclusive responsibility for the war—an injustice of which Hitler was to make much. Any schoolboy could see that such inequities would have to be redressed, and that the Polish corridor was a dangerous device. But subsequent events only demonstrated the resistance of politicians and public opinion to a rectification of these obvious errors.

On the other side of the ledger was the League of Nations, more prom-

---

* *GBWW*, Vol. 6, pp. 349–593.
† Cf. *GBWW*, Vol. 6, p. 370.

isingly named in French the Society of Nations. It was a bliss at twenty to witness its September assembly, and an even greater joy to watch small clusters of delegates from different countries locked in friendly discussion. The scene at Geneva stretched on both sides of the Leman from the distant Secretariat to the hall of the Reformation, embracing the hotels housing the various delegations; to and fro went Jean Monnet, a creative go-between, inciting coalitions to advance the good work, inventing formulas. Here indeed was the building of the new world by men of good will! But had they power? It seemed that they did the next year (1924), when the prime ministers of Britain and France, Édouard Herriot and Ramsay Mac-Donald, both attended. Then it was that MacDonald had his great moment of oratory about the empty chair that Germany, he said, should come and fill—as it did.

Both of these statesmen gave their blessing to the great political achievement of the League, the Protocol for the Pacific Settlement of International Disputes, which bound signatories to abstain from war, to submit their disputes to arbitration, to proceed gradually to disarmament, and, in case of aggression, to apply sanctions to the aggressor and to cooperate in resistance to such aggression. This marked the culmination of efforts begun by Lord Robert Cecil and Henry de Jouvenel in 1922 to associate the principles of disarmament, arbitration, and security. It was a great triumph, but one devoid of any practical sequel. Power diplomacy went its own way, ignoring the display at Geneva, as could be seen the following year by the signing of the Pact of Locarno, so very different from the Protocol. Nor were even the commitments of this treaty, which bound the signatories to respect each other's boundaries, honored in 1936 when, Italy having invaded Ethiopia, Germany took advantage of the crisis to reoccupy the Rhineland.

In terms of international politics, then, Geneva was a complete failure. But in other terms it was immensely fruitful. Its support of economic studies brought together economists and statisticians of various countries, which had a seminal impact. The related International Labour Organisation was even more effective. Trade unionists of the member countries were brought together with representatives of employers and of governments, and this example had fruitful results in other, nonmember countries.

Geneva was also a meeting place for young people, some of them attached to the delegations in minor roles, many more attracted simply by curiosity and hope. From their common experience came views going beyond national frontiers, and a disposition to think and act in terms of the human race as a whole.

However, a lesson brought home by Geneva was that the available means of action were all strictly national. That is, they were in the hands of national governments, which were extraordinarily improvident. Though bound by bilateral treaties of 1921 and 1924 to come to the help of Poland

and Czechoslovakia in case of attack, the government of France presented to the Chamber of Deputies in May 1927 a law of military organization that, as the minister expressly stated, "is of a strictly defensive character." No wonder that France did not execute its obligation to Czechoslovakia in 1938 and gave no effective help to Poland in 1939! Similarly, in March 1936, Britain refused to intervene on the occasion of Hitler's remilitarization of the Rhineland, though bound to do so by the Locarno agreements. Many such failures of foresight prepared the catastrophe of 1940.

On the home front; things were no better. Great Britain, which had entered World War I against the fervent advice of the governor of the Bank of England to Prime Minister Asquith, emerged from it burdened with an enormous debt and overvalued currency (both against the advice of Keynes). England was afflicted throughout the twenties with massive unemployment, the rate of which (then known only among the members of trade unions) fell below 10 percent in only one year, 1924, after which it immediately started up again following Churchill's absurd revaluation of a pound already overvalued.

Thus, what had been the leading country of the West became a sorry laboratory of errors from which the younger generations learned in both ways: by seeing the facts and by the lucid explanations of some neglected critics.

Mismanagement in Germany was to have fatal consequences. The Dawes Plan had provided a new chance for postwar recovery, and American funds had flowed in, stimulating the economy; their outflow following the Wall Street crash constricted means of payment, and the number of unemployed was rising when Heinrich Brüning assumed the chancellorship in March 1930. Instead of reflating the mark, as was urgently needed, he concentrated during his more than two years of power upon balancing the budget, which helped to raise the number of unemployed from three million to six million and increased Nazi votes from fewer than one million in 1928 to almost fourteen million in the summer of 1932. To that extent Hitler was justified in saying when he rose to power: "We are the result of the distress for which the others are responsible."

Whoever lived through the intervening years and followed the mistaken steps that led to a second war as inevitable as the first had been avoidable —one still more inhuman and catastrophic—cannot fail to see the resemblance to the thirty years' war that brought down Hellas. Such a person must therefore regard prudence as the first necessity in statesmen. I use the old and modest term *prudence* in preference to the more fashionable *prescience*, or *prediction*, or even *future-mindedness*, for *prudence* combines all the activities of the mind that have as their end the beneficial conduct of human affairs.

It was clearly indicated at the close of hostilities in World War II (a fitting expression, since there was no formal peace) that certain mistakes were now understood. Among these were the wickedness of demanding reparations (to which Poincaré had clung) and of insisting upon interallied debts (to which the American Congress had clung). Instead, after World War II, the United States and Canada extended generous help to their allies and, after a loan to Britain had proved inadequate, a momentous further step in the form of the Marshall Plan was taken by the United States under President Truman.

This plan merits mention here, since it involved an exercise in forecasting that was to prove an important beginning. The idea sketched by Dean Acheson and announced by Secretary of State George Marshall was to provide, for a period of four years, the funds necessary to close the gap between the cost of the imports from the American continent that were needed by Europe for its recovery and Europe's capacity to pay. By way of implementation, the economic experts of the various countries accepting such aid were invited to get together for the purpose of spelling out and justifying their several requirements. This was an important exercise in itself, since it necessitated a four-year forecast by everyone, but it was also the germ of a continuing cooperation between governmental experts that has passed through several organizational formulations and now has come to exist, enlarged and institutionalized, as the international OECD.

As we come to the period that followed World War II, it should be observed that the future planning of the sixties came about in different forms because of the different circumstances that prevailed in the United States and in Europe, especially in continental Western Europe. Conditions in these two areas were utterly at variance. What had been the three first-rank powers of continental Europe—Germany, France, Italy—were now powerless, and in miserable material condition. Their first preoccupation had to be with the rebuilding of their economies.

On the other hand, the United States emerged from the war as by far the greatest power in the world. Its armed forces ringed Eurasia from Western Europe to Japan. They were fed by an unending flow of supplies proceeding from an industry that had long been the foremost in the world and that had developed mightily during the recent conflict, as against the destruction suffered by other industrial nations. Moreover, the United States had displayed a fearful weapon, the atom bomb, of which more anon. In so commanding a position, the United States had worldwide responsibilities, and these were keenly felt by President Truman, who went about attending to them, as they were then perceived. They were perceived both in humane and in political terms. Moscow had made a very unfavorable impression by imposing a government upon Poland, having earlier allowed the Germans to crush a non-Communist insurrection in Warsaw that might have provided postwar Polish leadership. The idea had been established that Moscow was out to impose its form of government as far as it could reach: hence the strategy of "containment," which Moscow saw as encirclement. It was believed at first that this containing function could be performed by Britain, the great war ally. But it was soon apparent that Britain had exhausted her forces in her heroic effort, and the United States stepped in, first in the case of Greece and Turkey.

World strategy was thus an important American concern, and the chief occasion for future planning. The vision of the Truman days can be summed up in two expressions. The first is "the free world," which was compounded of two ideas, (1) to shield countries from Soviet imperialism and (2) to promote their institutions of political freedom, which involved pressure upon former allies to liberate countries from colonial rule. As is well known, containment was successful, and colonial liberation occurred, but the expression "free world" is now derisive, given the character of many regimes supported by the United States. The second, later expression of Truman's time was "the underdeveloped countries," which referred to countries that were to be helped in their economic progress after the rehabilitation of Europe. Both of these expressions implied future concern—to foil Soviet expansion, to maintain or foster democratic systems of government, to promote economic development.

The United States was also, however, the seat of different preoccupations arising from the success of the Manhattan Project. The gigantic mushroom of the Hiroshima explosion was, so to speak, a monstrous advertisement for technology, proving its efficiency and warning of its dangers. In subsequent years two psychological reactions to the event fed two distinct strains of thought. The first was an unbounded confidence in the achievements that were anticipated from the marriage of science with technology, integrated in a continuous process of research and development. For all the verbal emphasis laid upon science from the end of the eighteenth century onward, the many practical inventions made then and through the nineteenth century were almost without exception owing to nonscientists, whose inventions were then developed by business firms. On the other hand, the Manhattan Project had at its source a purely scientific achievement (in Berlin) by Hahn and Strassmann,* and the project itself entrusted a scientific team with the task of inventing the means of application of the principles involved and of carrying out the application itself to its end result. Here was the promise of formidably accelerated innovations. And in this promise the American government invested sums that grew enormous.

By 1965, no less that 350,000 scientists and engineers were employed in research and development activities in American industry, 55 percent of which were financed by the federal government, while at the same time basic research had achieved political eminence in the manner described by Don K. Price's study, *The Scientific Estate*. Naturally enough, with such activities went technological forecasting: the anticipation of what can be achieved by what date. A memorable survey of long-range anticipations

---

* O. Hahn and F. Strassmann in 1938 had obtained isotopes of barium by bombarding uranium with neutrons, an important precedent for the scientists on the atom-bomb project.

was made by Theodore Gordon and Olaf Helmer in 1962. They asked what major achievements could be expected and when, and applied the Delphic method to such surveying; that is, they used several rounds of questions to narrow down initial differences of judgment. About the same time, a European investigator, Erich Jantsch, went around inquiring into the methods of technological forecasting when used in practice.

As against this, another strain of thought, represented in the *Bulletin of the Atomic Scientists*, was developed from considering the harm that could be done in war by the use of ever more advanced weapons—the harm to man and to his environment—of which bombing in Vietnam as well as defoliation offer a localized, but awesome, instance. But apart even from war, the atomic scientists thought of the disruptive effect upon mankind of a greatly accelerated social transformation and of the ruthless exploitation of nature that would attend it. And this strain of thought was later to link up with certain European ideas, arising from different sources.

While American preoccupations were bound up with American power, European preoccupations were determined by the neediness of Europe, of which the countries of the Continent were more aware than was Britain, which in the glory of its wartime achievement did not at first perceive the extent of its plight. True, it was in Britain that a great scheme of social insurance was first formulated (by Sir William Beveridge) and first adopted, to be copied soon afterward with some differences in France and then in the other countries of continental Western Europe. And similarly it was in Britain that guidelines for a future economic policy were first formulated (in the May 1944 White Paper entitled *Employment Policy*, a short but most important statement). But as the postwar period wore on, Britain fell far short of continental European achievements in this area.

As early as January 1947, the Plan Commissariat was created in France at the suggestion of Jean Monnet, who led it. This was to prove a major step. At the earliest stage of its organization, the situation being one of extreme scarcity and one therefore that required an authoritarian allocation of materials, there was a continuation of war economy, now addressed to reconstruction. It was reconstruction with a difference, for the aim was to create a pattern distinct from the prewar one, with emphasis on heavy industry, the lack of which had been recognized as a cause of French weakness in both war and peace. But novel as it was, this "command" stage of recovery was not by any means the main interest of Monnet. What he wished to do, and succeeded in doing, was to involve French opinion in economic growth.

The plan of the Plan Commissariat had to be carried out by private as well as by nationalized industries. They were called to the Commissariat's discussions and listened to. But so were the leaders of the unions, and this participation was subsequently to make a great difference in the conduct of French unions as compared with British unions in understanding the changes required within factories. To some degree, Monnet reproduced the ancient British pattern of "king in Parliament" decisions, mixing leaders of industry and the unions (no separation between an Upper and a Lower House). This had a considerable impact upon opinion, at least part of it.

Notably, it altered the mood of the French intellectual elite, which had traditionally looked down upon businessmen and spurned economic enterprise. Quite incapable of being excited by the commercial success of a firm, the educated Frenchman could be excited by the success of a National Plan. Economic activities could then be seen, not in the unfavorable light of profit seeking but in the favorable light of national achievement. Such in earlier times had been the attitude of Saint-Simon and his followers, too many of whom had become enmeshed, however, in the Second Empire. Such again, in the interwar period, had been the attitude of a few, led by Jean Coutrot. But now the attitude was generalized, and Jean Monnet saw to it that it remained so by keeping the Plan Commissariat itself small and calling upon all government departments and all manner of people to participate in its work.

Still, this new attitude toward economic activities (which was not shared by all: e.g., Sartre) did not amount to a complete espousal of business values. Profit seeking was accepted as a means, and essentially as a means to investment, which was likewise regarded as a means.

Means to what ends? Growth in itself was for a time a sufficient objective, the more so in that, after completion of the First Plan, protests against it, associated with demands for slackening the pace, had to be overcome. In view of the strong argument afforded to such opposition by the very high rate of inflation that had recurred, it is remarkable that the battle could so easily be won: it drew together all manner of people who looked to the future and who came to form an audience for discussion of the sort of future that could be achieved.

But even as the gospel of growth won acceptance, discussion of it led to further reflections. It was not difficult, in a formal discussion of how much housing could be achieved, to tag on questions as to the *kind* of housing, the question of environmental amenities, and the influence upon modes of life as against any mere standard of life. In the consideration of such things, businessmen, civil servants, and trade unionists, with a sprinkling of economic experts, grew familiar with each other, meeting in many agencies besides the Plan Commissariat, and learning the common language of National Accounting. They came gradually to consider what might lie beyond the forward surge of economic growth, what at that point were its social side effects, and what they felt should become its normative goals. Here were the makings of a forum to discuss social futures.

But however important this seemed to some, the problem of forms of government loomed even more urgently. The Third Republic had evolved toward a day-to-day dependence of the executive upon the confidence of Parliament. This feature was emphasized in the Fourth Republic, where a government could not be formed without a two-stage approval by the Chamber of Deputies. First, the man designated as the president of the republic had to win the approval of his person by the National Assembly; second, he had to come back before it with his team of ministers and gain a vote of confidence in the team, which, however, could be unseated at any moment. While this sensitivity to the Assembly had its virtues, it had also important disadvantages, which were clearly displayed when the creation of the European Defense Community (EDC), a French initiative, was laid aside by the Assembly without discussion, under a government whose leader let it go without a struggle, the leader being out of sympathy with his predecessors who had submitted it. It was seen that this form of government could not long endure, and some foresaw that it would lead to its very opposite, an executive that was too strong.

France was therefore the scene of much discussion as to forms of government, with much attention being paid in other countries to its difficulties. This was a time when liberal opinion in the United States was concerned over the prospects for liberal government everywhere, and when it seemed of particular interest that European institutions, after the defeat of EDC, were advancing by another, purely economic path, with striking implications for the emerging postcolonial countries whose governments were in the process of establishing themselves. Hence the choice in 1960, by the Ford Foundation, of France as the locus of speculations about the evolution of political institutions. (It is in order to explain this choice that emphasis, which otherwise would be excessive, has been laid on the French scene.)

The executive director of the international committee formed to govern this project saw the opportunity to develop a learning process among both political and social scientists. For he happened to sit as an expert on a variety of French agencies, and he was sensitive to the fact that he did so as an economist, that his partners were economists, and that no other social sciences were represented.

Now the call made upon economists was amply justified, not only because of the importance of economic activities but also because economists shared powerful intellectual tools that had been created for them by the great Wesley Clair Mitchell, his many eminent followers, and the National Bureau of Economic Research of New York, which he founded.

Other social scientists lacked this community of tools. It is revealing that a survey of studies of behavior under stress revealed the use by social scientists of no less than 349 and perhaps as many as 1,226 different concepts, according to some observers.[2] Here was anything but a community of language such as economists have invented, which is used by everyone who discusses economic situations. Nor did other social scientists have at their disposal the powerful intellectual machinery of econometrics, or a body of carefully accumulated and ordered information and an increasing flow of current data in their fields to draw upon. They lacked the spur of being called upon and the consequent occasion to gather, or at least to assert the need of, more information relevant to their concerns.

Was it not, however, desirable that these other social scientists should participate in the preparation of the future? Should that be left to economists alone, and be seen essentially in terms of quantitative increases in production, investment, and consumption? Was there not indeed a danger (perceived by the great Leontief) that the intellectual technology of econometrics, which had made economics so efficient, would direct all vision of the future away from sensitivity to human needs?

Such was the spirit of the Futuribles project that grew out of the Ford Foundation grant. The procedure adopted was to invite scholars of undisputed qualifications to submit essays expressing their personal views of the probable course of events within their fields. To a gathering of eminent scientists at Geneva in June 1961 it was explained that this procedure was in the nature of an experiment, that the essays were not to be thought of as "predictions" and were not to be publicized as such, that we would come together to discuss them and to analyze the methods implicit in their forecasts, that they would be circulated only among the participants and to colleagues designated by them, and that they would be eventually offered only to a limited public familiar with economic forecasting and aware of the difficulties of attempting it in untried fields.

Forecasting was not, indeed, the object of the exercise. The idea was to think back from the projections that had been expressed as "probable" to the reasons why they seemed so to those who had drawn them up, and from there to seek the sensitive points in their formulation—the points, that is to say, at which either exogenous happenings or voluntary intervention could alter them into other possible projections.

The name *Futuribles* (meaning possible futures) was coined by the present writer to express a fundamental belief that the purpose of predictive studies is not to give us "knowledge of the future," which in the ordinary meaning of that phrase is impossible, but an understanding of the ways in which it is possible to control the course of human affairs.

Many authors in many countries responded with contributions (some 130 essays were produced in the period of Ford support between 1961 and 1966), spreading the futuribles concept to their fellow social scientists, and an international network was established, which was afterward maintained and extended by means of an international association and a journal, *Analyse & prévision*.[3]

The justification for thus dwelling upon the Futuribles project is that it serves to prepare the discussion of possible approaches to futures re-

---

[2] See Samuel Z. Klausner (Bureau of Social Science Research, Washington, D.C.), "Rationalism and Empiricism in Studies of Behavior in Stressful Situations," *Behavioral Science* 11, no. 5 (September 1966): 329–41.

[3] Both the association and this journal are housed at the Maison des Futuribles, 52 rue des Saints-Pères, Paris 7, with a library and a data center on futures research.

search. Among such approaches it stands at the opposite extreme from attempts to produce a grandiose view of the future, almost an "Authorized Version"! Nor was it intended to generate a special breed of social scientists who would be specialists of the future, of the kind implied in the now popular term *futurologists*. Rather, the object was to create in all manner of social scientists a disposition to submit their knowledge of the present to a forum that would undertake to evaluate their indications of feasible goods and avoidable harms.

It is indeed striking that a variety of projects that contributed to the building up of futures research during the postwar period had each a distinct character, arising from different circumstances and often bearing fruits beyond the original intention. While it is quite impossible to review all of these projects, some at least should be discussed.

Pride of place should be given to the Paley report* conducted in the United States from 1950 to 1952 by Philip Coombs. This report was called for by President Truman because of the raw materials panic caused by the outbreak of the Korean War, then interpreted by many as the opening of the Third World War. Raw materials were bought up in the United States to build up stocks, and this proceeded at such a rate as to make the materials scarce, with the result that their cost rose to dizzy heights.

To abate the fears of 1950, President Truman demanded an investigation of the fuel and other raw material inputs that both the United States and Western Europe would need in the future (that is, to 1975). The results were quite reassuring. But this investigation, though in itself an exercise in futures research, was still more important in its indirect consequences. After the report had been handed in (June 1952), it seemed to the Ford Foundation that the resources problem should be regarded as a continuing one: hence the creation of Resources for the Future, an organization that, thanks to the efforts of certain individuals, was moved to consider economic processes not as monetary transactions but in terms of actual materials passing through various stages from extraction and transformation to consumption and then to—what? To rejection, which was found to have occurred not only after consumption but at every stage of the economic process. Rejection is a phenomenon of the human body, of any human agglomeration, but to quite a gigantic degree of heavily urbanized and heavily industrialized society. As early as 1952, this phenomenon was noted by a reader of the Paley report when he saw the enormous mass of concrete inputs per capita in the United States. This seemed to be somewhat over two hundred times the weight of every human body in the country. A fantastic picture presented itself, which was worked out in its implications by Kneese and Ayers.[4] This in turn set in a general framework the special problem of pollutions (that is, rejects that are noticed because of their inconvenient place or specially obnoxious nature).

What suddenly became clear were the destructive aspects of our productivity and consumption. It was recognized that with these we are sending forth an ever growing Ganges of filth, not to mention the devastation of landscapes, which had long worried the British but which caused an American outcry in the sixties. It is notable that only the Americans were capable of turning into a national issue problems about which others in other countries had been deeply worried, but inefficiently.

Next we must notice the Buchanan report (*Traffic in Towns*[†]) called for by a British transport minister, Ernest Marples. This clearly set out the problem raised by extensive motorization in countries with far greater density of population than the United States has, and where urban agglomeration greatly antedated the age of the automobile. The echo of this report rang through Europe.

That was in 1962. In that same year, the then commissioner of the French plan, Pierre Massé, persuaded his government to set up a so-called 1985 work group. This group was to assume that the very swift ongoing rate of economic growth (4.7% per capita) would be sustained up to 1985. The question to be faced was, what problems would arise if that happened? Among the things to be considered was the pressure upon workers to change jobs and location. What should be done to provide them with the new skills or qualifications that were called for? What should be done, beyond mere housing facilities, to provide environmental amenities? What of crowding and transport? What of the appalling uglification of town and country? What of the partition of France into congested centers of activity and pollution, on the one hand, and on the other, into depressed and deserted regions where it would be impossible for anyone to earn a living? What of the new causes of inequality arising from growth? These and many other questions were raised, with little immediate result but with a good deal of later influence.

Then Daniel Bell, who had been an active participant in the Futuribles venture, proceeded, after the related Yale symposium, to constitute his Commission on the Year 2000, too well known in the United States to call for any recounting.[‡] But it should be noted that this was the occasion of an important discussion between Herman Kahn and Wassily Leontief. Where Kahn was the champion of forecasting by way of extrapolation, Leontief objected that unless we seek to understand the whole system of social relationships, we cannot control or influence forward movement. The famous Kahn-Wiener book was an output linked to the commission: it illustrates the method of extrapolation.[§]

---

[*] U.S. President's Materials Policy Commission, *Resources for Freedom: A Report to the President* (Washington, D.C: U.S. Government Printing Office, 1952).

[4] In Robert U. Ayers and Allen V. Kneese, "Production, Consumption, and Externalities," *American Economic Review* 59 (1969): 282.

[†] British Ministry of Transport, *Traffic in Towns: A Study of the Long Term Problems of Traffic in Urban Areas* (London: H.M. Stationery Office, 1963).

[‡] See *Toward the Year 2000: Work in Progress, Daedalus* 96, no. 3 (Summer 1967).

[§] Herman Kahn and Anthony J. Wiener, *The Year 2000: A Framework for Speculation on the Next Thirty-three Years* (New York: The Macmillan Co., 1967).

In the latter part of the sixties, interest in the future spread like an explosion. It was thus all the more remarkable that the great organizations that underlie social and economic development were not much affected, as if that development were something independent from the power centers. This omission tended to endow the course of human affairs with a character of inevitability, as beyond social control. And that in turn evoked the sense of revolt pointed to in Section 2.

## 5. The new attitudes and functions of intellectuals

The term *intellectual* is here taken to embrace all those who, in one way or another, formulate our understanding of the human scene. It would be illogical to start with an enumeration of the categories this includes, since the purpose here is to stress how the function has over the course of time devolved upon different sorts of persons, and has been performed in different ways.

Over much the longest part of European history, the intellectuals were churchmen, as is noted in the inscription on the college gates at Harvard:

> *After God had carried us safe to New England and wee had builded our houses, provided necessaries for our livelihood, rear'd convenient places for God's worship, and settled the Civill Government; One of the new things we longed for, and looked after was to advance* Learning, *and perpetuate it to posterity; dreading to leave an illiterate Ministry to the Church, when our present Ministers lie in the dust.*

Here are literacy, learning, and preaching bound together, a perfect expression of the medieval conception of the intellectual. It is important to dwell awhile upon this conception, both because of its perseverance up to our own day, where it appears in different forms, and because of certain interesting contrasts that are evident in these various manifestations.

Let us go back to Saint Augustine's all-important declaration of severance between the Terrestrial City that is given up to the Demon and the passion he excites, and the City of God that is formed of His servants. As is well known, Augustine was moved to write his *City of God** by the disastrous fall of Rome to the Barbarians (410), but the idea of such severance was prior, and implicit in the teaching of Jesus. From it comes the famous prescription of canon law that the cleric should stand aloof from the turmoil of temporal affairs. Not all clerics actually did so, but it was an essential part of their *idealtypus*. And let us add that right up to World War II it was also part of the different *idealtypus* of the scientist, who shut himself up in his laboratory, unconcerned with the march of history (however much he or his predecessors contributed to it indirectly).

But there are two kinds of aloofness. There is the aloofness of the monk absorbed in contemplation and possibly in theological controversy with his peers, or of the pure scientist absorbed in his research and possibly in controversy with his peers, and there is the aloofness of the preacher who stands above worldly interests but admonishes.

An interesting example of the first is offered to us by Eckermann in his *Conversations with Goethe*. On learning of the July 1830 revolution in France, Eckermann excitedly rushed to see Goethe and found that to Goethe the "great news" was that of Geoffroy Saint-Hilaire's victory over Baron Cuvier in a dispute at the French Academy of Sciences over the transformation of species. As it happened, Goethe's judgment was the better one!

The second form of aloofness implies a concern with temporal affairs, but as these are looked upon from above the turmoil, by the preacher, who seeks to awaken individual consciences and call men to a more godly life—in short to invite them to the City of God—and also to castigate evil, denounce wickedness, and thunder against corruption. Leaning now the one way and now the other, such a preacher calls or condemns according to his temperament.

It is quite obviously condemnation that has been favored by most intellectuals of recent times—those who in the process are commonly designated the *intelligentsia*. With a few great exceptions, their preaching has been concerned less with the improvement of their readers than with the denunciation of evil ways and bad institutions.

In the energetic age of the Renaissance, some preachers—Savonarola in Florence and Calvin in Geneva, for example—undertook to establish the City of God in temporal affairs; and it is rather sad that it was the milder of the two who failed in his political attempt. For an analogue to them, after the rise of the intelligentsia, we may look to Lenin. There have been others since Lenin, of course, in other countries. But it is a quite remarkable phenomenon that the triumph of the intelligentsia, wherever it has occurred, has led to its subsequent authoritarian silencing.

Denouncing present evils is, of course, a necessary social function, and it can be quite effectively performed by way of the novel: stories are more impressive than statements, as *Uncle Tom's Cabin* proved. The nineteenth century was marked by the development of the social novel, in which authors moved from telling tales of individual character or action to works that explored the social context and described society, as in the case of Balzac and Trollope. Such descriptions could be the result of strong moral feeling, as it was in the case of Dickens and Zola. The emphasis in such works is upon situations that illustrate social evils.

In the twentieth century, the novel has been used to warn of social evils to come: one thinks, for instance, of Aldous Huxley and George Orwell. This can be done by laying heavy emphasis on present social features that are clearly in process of developing and projecting them to an extreme.

---

* *GBWW*, Vol. 18, pp. 129–618.

And just as Dickens and Zola performed great social services in stressing the evils of their times, so have Huxley and Orwell in giving us notice of dangers; but their works are forebodings rather than forecasts.

At the turn of the century, H. G. Wells opened the age of social forecasting, using alternately the two modes of the novel and the essay. His work as a novelist has unfortunately come to overshadow his work as an essayist, and the more so as it has generated a far more direct and earlier posterity in the form of the massive development of so-called science fiction, now recognized as an important social phenomenon. Of course, the great majority of writers in this field merely use assumed technological advances (feasible or fanciful) to support tales of adventure; and so far as it has not amounted to more than that, the proliferation of science fiction is interesting only as it expresses the strength of a belief in the unlimited achievements of man through technology. But the genre has also been used by some in the spirit of Wells, that is for "social fiction." This has created a literature of quality that has been all too long ignored, though its importance is now acknowledged. This literature, going back to the twenties, antedates scholarly research by a whole generation and may have worked to delay such research beyond the point at which it would otherwise have begun.

Why so? Because students of society were greatly concerned after the seventies or eighties of the last century to move away from the once glorious stance of humanists to the increasingly desirable status of scientists, an achievement that, they felt, would be compromised if, as one writer put it as late as 1960, they "came to dabble in speculations which pertain to the pulp literature of science fiction." That this could be said at so recent a point in time makes it understandable that Wells's appeal to social scientists, particularly historians, should have been neglected when he made it as long ago as 1902, while he was known essentially for his futuristic novels.

In view of Wells's important role, it is worth recounting in his own words the start of his attempt to deal with the future by way of both the novel and the essay. "The future depicted in *The Time Machine\** (1894)," he said,

> *was a mere fantasy based on the idea of the human species developing about divergent lines, but the future in* When the Sleeper Awakes *(1898) was essentially an exaggeration of contemporary tendencies: higher buildings, bigger towns, wickeder capitalists and labour more downtrodden than ever and more desperate. Everything was bigger, quicker and more crowded; there was more and more flying and the wildest financial speculation. It was our contemporary world in a state of highly inflamed distension. Very much the same picture is given in* A Story of the Days to Come *(1899) and* A Dream of Armageddon *(1903). I suppose that is the natural line for an imaginative writer to take, in an age of material progress and political sterility.*[5]

Wells went on to describe his first nonfiction attempt (1900), called *Anticipations* (and in book form, *Anticipations of the Reaction of Mechanical and Scientific Progress upon Human Life and Thought*):

> *It was the first attempt to forecast the human future as a whole and to estimate the relative power of this and that great system of influence. Partial forecasts and forebodings existed in abundance already; we had estimates for instance, of the length of time it would take to exhaust the world's coal supply, of the prospects of population congestion if the birth-rate remained stable, of the outlook for this planet as the solar system cooled, as it was then supposed to be doing, very rapidly; but most of the conclusions were based upon such narrowly conditioned calculations that they could be dismissed quite easily by challenging the validity of the assumptions. A comprehensive attempt to state and weigh and work out a general resultant for the chief forces of social change throughout the world, sober forecasting, that is to say, without propaganda, satire or extravaganza, was so much a novelty that my book, crude though it was and smudgily vague, excited quite a number of people.*[6]

Such a vision of "The Future" as Wells thus offered went far beyond what social scientists even in our day would acknowledge as "sober forecasting." A social scientist would reserve that term for his calculated anticipation of the way in which the phenomena that constituted his specific field of study might develop. This would be an expert opinion as to some specific future, not knowledge but drawn from knowledge; and the credibility thereby attached to this surmise would make it suggestive of action to be taken, or of action tending to preclude the realization of the surmise if the development were thought undesirable. Such a social scientist would think of more ambitious efforts as best left to philosophers.

Two eminent French contemporaries of Wells in 1899 tried their hand at deducing some features of the twentieth century from the social forces of which they were aware. Each of their views contains insights, but it is of interest to note the contrast between their political predictions. Thus, Émile Faguet saw the history of the twentieth century as likely to be "less arbitrary, less picturesque, and less dramatic [!]" The great conqueror, the great reformer, the great legislator "were on their way out [!]"[7] On the other hand, Gabriel Tarde stated:

> *We can predict with assurance that the future will see personifications of Authority and Power overshadowing the greatest despots of the past. . . . There are greater means of prestige than ever, which can support a statesman in*

---

* See *The Great Ideas Today*, 1971, pp. 446–505.

[5] *Experiment in Autobiography* (London: Victor Gollancz Ltd., 1934), vol. 2, chap. 9, p. 645.

[6] Ibid., pp. 645–46.

[7] The Faguet essay is reproduced in *Futuribles*, no. 32 (June 20, 1962).

> *carrying out political and social programs the boldness of which would have frightened Bismarck himself.*[8]

The event verified Tarde's vision. But consider the nature of its impact at the time of utterance: it was thought provoking, not suggestive of some action to be taken. And we may thus draw the line between anticipations and forecasts. Furthermore, we immediately see that those in the seat of power have use for forecasts to guide their decisions, while anticipations must find an audience in the public at large. It is therefore not surprising that established powers, political or economic, should have become the clientele of more and more extensive forecasting operations, conducted by ever larger teams with increasingly heavy equipment, while anticipations remained the work of individual authors who found many readers or not, as they could. Whatever influence anticipations may exert upon the course of things is by way of public opinion. It is only insofar as they make an impression upon public opinion that they may come indirectly to be noticed by decision makers, while forecasts, on the contrary, are direct instruments of decision making.

As forecasts are increasingly in demand by established centers of decision, they are attempted by many different groups, but their variety is limited by the fact that they must be tailored to the concerns of those who commission them. Whether there be a national plan or merely something in the way of an interprofessional communication, specific forecasts tend to coalesce into an overall picture, an advanced view of the general situation. This is natural and desirable, but it is not without serious drawbacks. The overall picture may be seriously skewed. Important aspects of change may be left out of the picture. I am not aware of any government that invites and favors political science forecasts on the deterioration of the governmental system, pointing, for instance, to the likelihood of a palatine form of government, concentrated and secluded. But going beyond omissions as natural as they are deplorable, governments distribute their commissions most unequally among various kinds of expertise, with economists getting far and away the largest share of them. There is ample reason for this in the talent of that profession and the accuracy of reasoning it develops, and in the fundamental character of our society. But it may be that economic concepts go too far in shaping the vision of our society's march and leave inadequate room for other aspects of the picture. It is important that people should fare well as consumers; it is not unimportant that they should live pleasantly as inhabitants, which, incidentally, is the capacity in which they are citizens. We can glory in our machines, but do we not need fauna and flora? It was through anticipations of where we might be going, not by any forecast, that the environmentalist theme broke forth. And here the role of mass media is striking. Slight had been the impact of books; enormous was the impact of television that showed the spoiling of the land upon which our descendants must live.

Upon this climate came the Meadows report, which is in the nature of an anticipation, and which was not so much a scientific as a political achievement.[9] It gave proof that the public can be moved to consider and question the very march of our civilization. (Regarding ourselves as impelled by forces over which we have no control is the great modern superstition.) Skeptics, however, could point out that this result was obtained only by crying "Fire!"

Some fundamental questions about the political character of our modern societies follow. All adults are citizens by law, but few are active citizens. Of those who are active, moreover, many are active only in the service of some specific cause, and while the cause may be a good one, that is not enough to make them attentive to diverse aspects of the march of the caravan and ready to consider the effects on one part of it of action in another. Hence we have the phenomenon quite improperly designated as *technocracy*, a term that confuses two different features, one of which is the concentration of power that has proceeded to extremes (in the business field, which is not here considered, as well as in the political order, to which the following remarks are addressed), and the other of which is the existence of an all too narrow elite, neither of power nor of riches but of information. The members of this elite are of different origins, and whatever may have been their subsequent experience or education, their competence is largely acquired by self-teaching and communication with one another. Among them, some are honored with the term *expert*, while a very few are promoted to the status of *wise man*!

It is quite wrong to regard such people as wielding power (which is implied in the suffix "-cracy"). It is true, however, that with few exceptions they stand near to the seats of power, upon which they exert influence by virtue of their information and advice. But what are their positions? In Europe the overwhelming majority of them are permanent civil servants, which has the advantage of making them professionally independent of those who at any given time hold power. To these civil servants, add the members of consultative bodies, which governments try to make representative of the range of public opinions. So far so good. But formally the duty of civil servants is to respond to the demands of politicians in power while the function of consultative bodies is to deal only with questions that are submitted to them (though in France the Economic and Social Council, with a membership of two hundred persons made up of representatives of the various economic and social interests may, besides responding, take initiatives). Informally, of course, civil servants do make suggestions, discreetly, while members of consultative bodies do so openly. But this is in vain if they do not strike a responsive chord in those who hold positions of power. That is why there will always be bodies such as the Council of

---

[8] Cf. Gabriel Tarde, *Les Transformations du pouvoir* (Paris: Félix Alcan, 1899).

[9] D. H. Meadows et al., *The Limits to Growth* (New York: Universe Books, 1972).

Economic Advisers in the United States, whose members in fact are picked by the president, and likewise in Europe, ministers will draw to their immediate company those members of their department who have the greater affinity with their views.

While it seems, therefore, a gross exaggeration to speak of technocracy, we would do well to consider what truth may lie behind that expression. It is true that the minister conducts affairs within his department, and among other departments and agencies with which he must deal, in a language different from that which he uses in his public addresses; and this tends to a new version of Disraeli's "two nations," consisting of the informed and the uninformed. It is also true that the more technical "in" language may be misused to "prove" that objective analysis points to a certain course, while that "objective analysis" is in fact loaded with the subjective preferences or interests of those who have demanded or chosen it.

Our societies are immensely complicated; it is most difficult to grasp how things hang upon one another. They are also moving very fast. It is convenient for those at the helm to prove that the way things are moving is the best of possible courses, and glib intellectual salesmen can always be found to offer an impressive demonstration that this is so. But is it the best course? In terms of what interests, of what values, of what time horizon? What other courses are possible; by what means could they be realized; with what promises; and at what costs? We should come to political discussion on those terms—which implies, among many other things, that public servants should be free to communicate their knowledge to the public, whose indirect servants they are, not merely to the power holders they serve directly. It is the current tendency of citizens in our democratic societies to press for recognition and redress only of their present particular cares and needs, while leaving their future in the hands of their rulers. This is neither democratic nor prudent.

# PART THREE

# Contemporary Status
# of a Great Idea

# The Idea of Justice

## Otto Bird

Otto Bird was born and raised in Ann Arbor, Michigan. He attended the university there, from which he graduated in 1935 with honors in English and from which he received a master's degree in comparative literature the following year. In 1937 he went to the University of Chicago to study philosophy, and took a doctorate two years later in philosophy and literature at the Medieval Institute of the University of Toronto.

From 1947 to 1950 he worked with Mortimer Adler as associate editor of the *Syntopicon* for *Great Books of the Western World*. In the latter year he joined the faculty at the University of Notre Dame, where he was director of the General Program of Liberal Studies, a great books program, until 1963. He served as executive editor of *The Great Ideas Today* from 1964 to 1970 (he is now consulting editor), when he was appointed university professor of arts and letters at Notre Dame.

He has written three books, *The Canzone d'Amore of Guido Cavalcante with the Commentary of Dino del Garbo* (1942), *Syllogistic and Its Extensions* (1964), and *The Idea of Justice* (1967), and has published a number of articles on the history and theory of the liberal arts and the humanities. In addition, he was a major contributor to the *Propaedia*, or Outline of Knowledge, of the new fifteenth edition of the *Encyclopaedia Britannica*.

In 1973–74 he lived and worked at the Institute for Ecumenical and Cultural Research, St. John's University, Collegeville, Minnesota, where he combined the fruits of many years of study and teaching in a book on the development of Western culture, which he has just completed.

Time is one measure of the greatness of an idea, just as it is of the greatness of a book. A great idea, like a great book, possesses to a high degree the ability to survive. It is able to prove itself under diverse conditions, to show that it is useful, indeed indispensable, to men as they contemplate their human nature, the conditions of their life and livelihood, their relations to one another and to God.

Yet even great ideas are not entirely free from the vicissitudes of time and place. Some arise early in man's intellectual history, at once come into prominence, and then drop away, perhaps to be forgotten for centuries. The idea of democracy is of this sort. Appearing early in Greek thought, it quickly won great importance, but then with the advent of the Roman empire it retired, in effect, and did not emerge again to exercise controlling force till modern times. Other ideas, like that of equality, are, as it were, late starting, and do not attract much attention until well along the intellectual tradition, when they have a great impact on human history.[1] Still others early achieve greatness and continue without interruption to maintain their hold upon the minds of men. A prominent example of this last type is the idea of justice.

Ample and eloquent evidence of how the idea of justice has endured is provided by the *Syntopicon*. Its 42d chapter is devoted to this idea, and in the references the chapter provides to discussions of justice that occur in *Great Books of the Western World*, the reader will find that the whole of our intellectual tradition is represented, from the very beginning among the ancient Greeks down to the present day. There is no age in which men have not thought and written about justice. They are continuing to do so in the last third of the twentieth century, when a new concern for civil rights and a fresh perception of inequality have intensified interest in the subject.

The evidence provided by the *Syntopicon* of the perennial and enduring character of the idea of justice is sound, however, and proves the point only on one condition. This is that the discussions of various topics of justice cited there can be shown to deal with one common subject, that they are not merely passages in which the same word is used with such wide differences of meaning as to indicate that it really intends different things. We may think it intends the same thing simply because the same word is used, though the word is often not the original term that the writer employed but only a translation. If this should be so, if the common element in the passages is merely verbal, any claim of continuity and perdurability of the idea itself is bogus. We are dealing not with one idea but with many.

That such in fact is the case is the claim advanced by what is sometimes called philosophical relativism. It is a claim that deserves consideration not only for its bearing on our analysis of the idea of justice but because it implies an objection to the use, not to say the validity, of such a work as the *Syntopicon*. Thus the British philosopher R. G. Collingwood attacks as a vulgar and baseless error the notion that there are any "permanent" or "eternal" problems in philosophy. In support of this contention, he offers, as examples from political philosophy, Plato's *Republic* and Hobbes's *Leviathan*—two works that figure prominently in the theory of justice. Noting that "the political theories they set forth are not the same," Collingwood asks, "Do they represent two different theories of the same thing? Can you say that the *Republic* gives one account of 'the nature of the State' and the *Leviathan* another?" Collingwood answers "no" to both these questions on the ground that Plato's "State" is the Greek *polis* while Hobbes's is the absolutist state of the seventeenth century—political entities so different, Collingwood thinks, that they cannot be understood in the same terms, notwithstanding our (and his) use of such terms in referring to them.[2]

Collingwood's position amounts to saying that the ideas of any given age are so enculturated in the ways of that age as to make it impossible to compare them with ideas that appear earlier or later in history. In this view, where Plato in *The Republic* writes about what is translated as "justice," it would be mistaken to think that he is writing about what we understand by that term, or even what Hobbes understood. For the context in which Plato thought and wrote was vastly different from the one in which Hobbes worked, as the context of our thinking in the technological world of the twentieth century is different from both. These differences are so great, Collingwood thinks, as to leave nothing that can be taken as a common subject of discussion and controversy among writers widely separated in time. It is only an illusion, he believes, to think that such writers are talking about the same thing, or that what they say can be of help in arriving at an understanding of whatever it is we mean nowadays by the term *justice*.

Whether or not this is so (and quite apart from the fact that it contradicts the experience of men who have derived their idea of justice from these very sources) can be determined, at least up to a point, if we put the question to the test—if, that is, we examine the writers on "justice" to see if they do not offer some basis, however minimal it may be, for carrying on a discussion, and more, whether there are not fundamental issues on which they take positions that can be construed as agreements and disagreements.

The simplest way to do this is to look at the earliest great book that purportedly deals with the subject of justice—with, that is to say, Plato's *Republic*—and see if the questions it asks and the questions we ourselves ask are the same. If they are, then the thing the questions are about, though called by different names in different languages, is also recognizably the same.

## The common subject

As in most of the Platonic dialogues, the discussion in *The Republic* is presented as a search for a definition. Socrates is led to elaborate his own theory only after a number of preliminary attempts have been made to say what justice (*dikaiosyne*) is. Thus justice, we are told by Cephalus, consists in speaking the truth and paying one's debts (331e). Thrasymachus counters this description by claiming that it is simple compliance with the interest of the stronger, i.e., of the ruling class, as expressed in law (339a). Glaucon then intervenes with the proposition that justice is a mean or compromise between the best of all, which is to do wrong and not be punished, and the worst of all, which is to suffer wrong without the power of retaliation (359a). Against all of these, Socrates is called upon not only to provide a more adequate definition but also to prove that justice is a good in itself for the individual, apart from any social benefits that may result from it (367). The effort is to show that the just man, even if he possessed Gyges' magic ring of invisibility, which would enable him to commit all the unjust acts that he wished without any fear of discovery and harm to his reputation, nevertheless would, and should, choose justice because justice in itself is preferable and better (359–360).

From even so brief a statement as this of the setting for Socrates' discourse, we can see that what is understood by justice, or *dikaiosyne*, has several distinguishing notes or characteristics. First, it applies to men in their relations to one another, since it is with respect to another that one tells the truth, pays debts, obeys the law, or abides by a compromise. Second, it is a social norm in that it establishes a course of conduct that one ought to follow in his relations with other men. The three preliminary definitions agree upon this fact, although they conceivably imply different reasons for it. That is, the first definition implies that justice is a good that ought to be done for no other reason, the second says that it comes about through—is only another name for—the sanctions of superior force, and the third sees it as a social good brought about by a certain compromise. But all the definitions agree that justice is something praiseworthy, though again for different reasons according to the different definitions that are given of it—good and praiseworthy for itself, or for society, or for the individual himself and not only in his social relations.

From the preliminary groundwork preparing for the discussion of *The Republic* we see that justice, or *dikaiosyne,* is taken to be a social norm that is both obligatory and approbative. Further, it is important to note that this much is granted even by the three different accounts that have been offered of justice. But this is to say that we have here at the very beginning of the first comprehensive treatise on the subject a record of a controversy over a common subject. Let us admit that it is a controversy over *dikaiosyne* and that *dikaiosyne* is not in every respect what we mean today in twentieth-century English by *justice.* (No translation can ever hope to be exactly and fully in every respect the same as the original.) Nevertheless, it already appears that we do have here a common subject that we can discuss with Plato. For in even the little that we have so far considered, it is clear that he is talking about justice in a way that we still do; i.e., as a social norm that is both obligatory and approbative. And this much suffices, as the remainder of this essay will attempt to show, to provide a common subject for a controversy, a basis, despite objections such as Collingwood's, for analyzing, comparing, and contrasting the theories of justice across the ages and across cultures.

## Basic issues and positions

It has been claimed that the whole of Western philosophy consists of little more than a series of footnotes to Plato, and that Aristotle wrote most of the footnotes.[3] The controversy concerning justice abundantly bears out this claim. For Plato, in *The Republic,* not only established the subject of the continuing and ongoing controversy; he also sketched the basic issues as well as the basic positions that have come to be taken in the course of it.

We can find representative and even paradigmatic expressions of each of these basic positions in theories of justice that are set forth in *Great Books of the Western World.* For example, the definition offered in *The Republic* by Thrasymachus raises an issue regarding the relation between justice and legality. Thrasymachus maintains that justice is the "interest of the stronger," because power is "in every state in the hands of the ruling class, which makes laws in its own interest . . . (and) in making these laws defines as just for their subjects what is to the interest of themselves, and if anyone breaks their laws, he is punished for violation of justice" (338c–e). Justice, in other words, is identified with obedience to the positive law, and we may accordingly call this the Positive Law theory of justice. In the great books tradition, Hobbes is a vigorous proponent of this position.

On the other hand, in the social contract theory put forward by Glaucon we have the adumbration of what may be called the Social Good theory of justice.[4] Justice is said to be the result of a compact or compromise that men make in order to live together. Glaucon agrees with Thrasymachus that men would like to be strong enough to do anything they wish without fear of retaliation. But he denies that this determines their sense of what is just, which is based, he thinks, on the recognition that they cannot as individuals achieve such power. Glaucon's contention is that, having learned from experience both what it is to do wrong and to suffer it, men have found that suffering wrong outweighs the good of inflicting it (358c). Hence they have joined together in society and agreed with one another neither to do nor to suffer wrong. Such, Glaucon says, is "the origin and nature of justice, . . . midway between what is most desirable, i.e. to do wrong and avoid punishment, and what is most undesirable, to suffer wrong without redress" (359b). Justice is thus in effect a social arrangement or utility. And it is among the utilitarian philosophers that this Social Good position on justice has received its most comprehensive development.

The third basic position regarding justice—which we will call the Natural Right theory—is also formulated in *The Republic*. It is implicit in the description of justice that Cephalus gives, but becomes explicit in the reformulation of that in the words of the ancient poet Simonides: "It is just to render to each what is due to him" (331e).[5] This is substantially the same as the definition, undoubtedly the most famous and influential in the entire discussion of justice, that the Roman lawyers enshrined in the Justinian Code: "Justice is the constant and perpetual will of rendering to each his right (*jus*)," where the Latin word for *right* makes manifest that it is the root of *justice*. The definition that Socrates himself finally develops is in effect a version of this: minding one's proper business, both in external relations with others and in the internal ordering of the soul (434a, 443d). A clearer and more representative version of the Natural Right position is provided by Aristotle's theory of justice. The essential note—hence the name—is that justice consists in rendering a man what is his by virtue of his nature as a man.

We thus have three basic positions regarding justice, according as its basis is taken to be positive law, the social good, or natural right. Each of these positions can be found, although admittedly in a rudimentary form, in the record of the controversy concerning justice that is found in *The Republic*. It is our claim that these three positions have remained basic or fundamental throughout the entire history of the controversy, from Plato down to Professor John Rawls, whose book, *A Theory of Justice*, published in 1971, is the most comprehensive theory of its subject written in the twentieth century. These positions are basic in the sense that it is with reference to them that the controversy concerning justice can be most readily and clearly understood. They provide the coordinates for mapping the controversy as a whole and indicating the points of agreement and disagreement.

## The Positive Law theory of justice

A full and complete statement of the Positive Law theory of justice calls for two distinct considerations. One is an account of justice in terms of positive law, the other a theory of meaning that explains, or rather explains away, uses of the terms that appear to involve more than law. It is seldom, however, and not until quite recently, that we find equal attention paid to both these aspects of the subject. Usually, a proponent of the theory deals only with the first aspect. Such is the case with the strong and vigorous assertion of the theory that is found in the work of Thomas Hobbes.

At the heart of this position lies the claim that positive law can explain all the important uses of the term *justice*. The attempt to justify this claim can be viewed as containing three moments: first, the assertion that justice depends upon law and is posterior to it; second, that law itself, being prior to justice, cannot be judged in terms of it; and third, that law constitutes the whole measure of justice so that justice consists in nothing but conformity to law.

To support the position that justice depends on law, Hobbes proposes to describe what conditions would be like if no law existed. In such a situation, he maintains, there would be "no common power," no organized society capable of issuing and enforcing commands; men would be living in a "state of nature." In the absence of any overriding social rules, men would confront one another merely as individuals, and, according to Hobbes, it is characteristic of men as individuals to be avid for gain, safety, and reputation, and to seek nothing but their own advantage. Yet as individuals they are so equal in power that no one enjoys a clear advantage; nor is anyone truly safe or secure; the life of all is "solitary, poor, nasty, brutish, and short."[6] Thus the state of nature amounts to a state of war, and "such a war as is of every man against every man."[7]

In this state of nature, not only is there no common power able to make and enforce laws; there is no justice or injustice. "Before the names of *just* and *unjust* can have place," Hobbes writes, "there must be some coercive power to compel men equally to the performance of their covenants." As long as "there is a fear of not performance on either part," there can be no question of justice. "Injustice actually there can be none till the cause of such fear be taken away."[8] In a state of war a man may do anything he can to preserve his own life, hence "nothing can be unjust."[9]

Hobbes supports his assertion that justice depends upon the existence of a superior power by this counterfactual argument: "If we could suppose a great multitude of men to consent in the observation of justice ... without a common power to keep them all in awe, we might as well suppose all mankind to do the same; and then there neither would be nor need to be any civil government or Commonwealth at all."[10] That this could occur is absurd to expect, and it is therefore too obvious to require saying that men need government to order their relations with one another.

Such a requirement comes about, Hobbes argues, as the result of "an ill condition which man by mere nature is actually placed in." What is wanting is a common power, and this is obtained through the establishment of a "commonwealth," or what we would usually now call a civil society or state but which Hobbes also calls "Leviathan," to emphasize its power. Such a leviathan comes into being when men reach a common agreement to abandon the state of nature in which they are living. This agreement, according to Hobbes, is "a covenant of every man with every man, in such manner as if every man should say to every man: 'I authorise and give up my right of governing myself to this man, or to this assembly of men, on this condition; that thou give up thy right to him, and authorise all his actions in like manner.' " In this way Leviathan is born and "hath the use of so much power and strength conferred on him that, by terror thereof, he is enabled to form the wills of them all, to peace at home and mutual aid against their enemies abroad."[11] Since there now exists "coercive power to compel men equally to the performance of their covenants," there is also occasion for justice.[12]

Hobbes is willing to accept "the ordinary definition of justice" as giving to every man his own, but only on the condition that what is one's own is understood to depend upon the coercive power of law. In the state of "mere nature," Hobbes claims, "every man has right to everything," and this is tantamount to having no right at all. But "where there is no *own*, that is, no propriety, there is no injustice; and where there is no coercive power erected, that is, where there is no Commonwealth, there is no propriety, all men having right to all things: therefore where there is no Commonwealth, there nothing is unjust."[13]

If we think of men as existing in a condition where they are utterly without law, then, according to the Positive Law theory we will see that there can be no question of justice or injustice. In other words, justice and injustice presuppose the existence of civil society and its positive law. This brings us to the second fundamental assertion of the theory, which is that justice is not and cannot be a criterion of law. "No law can be unjust," Hobbes declares.[14] Laws can be good or bad, but they cannot be just or unjust. Their goodness or badness depends upon how well or ill they fulfill the purpose for which they are made, and this purpose, according to Hobbes, is identical with that of the fundamental compact underlying the founding of the state, namely the establishment and maintenance of peace and order.

Hobbes's theory is that the relation between law and justice is the very reverse of what it is sometimes thought to be. Far from being a measure of law, justice is itself the creature of law. The laws, Hobbes declares, "are the rules of just and unjust," and "nothing [is] reputed unjust that is not contrary to some law."[15] When we say of a man that he is just, what we mean is that he is one "that in his actions observeth the laws of his country."[16]

There is also no question that the law referred to here is man-made positive law, or what Hobbes calls the "civil law." Such law, he says, "is to every subject those rules which the Commonwealth hath commanded him, by word, writing, or other sufficient sign of the will, to make use of for the distinction of right and wrong; that is to say, of what is contrary, and what is not contrary to the rule."[17]

Hobbes does talk about natural law as well as natural right, and the interpretation of his doctrine dealing with those concepts has long posed a famous crux for Hobbesian scholarship. It is clearly far removed, however, from the position on justice taken by the proponents of what we have called the Natural Right theory. In terms of this theory, natural right provides the basis of justice, whereas positive law fulfills that function for Hobbes.

Justice consists in conformity to the law, Hobbes maintains, and injustice in the lack of such conformity as "the committing by deed or word of that which the law forbiddeth, or the omission of what it hath commanded."[18] For Hobbes, the critical term for the analysis of justice is not right but covenant or law, law being "brought into the world for nothing else but to limit the natural liberty of particular men," and to deprive them of that "right of nature, that is, the natural liberty of man."[19] When Hobbes declares that a law of nature is "the fountain and original of *justice*," it is only by way of describing the antecedent condition of men that led to the establishment of civil society and positive law.[20]

Hobbes's doctrine of the essential dependence of justice upon law provides a typical and representative example of the way a Positive Law theory accounts for justice as a social norm: Law is that norm. Positive Law theory also has its own distinctive manner of accounting for the obligatoriness of justice. To ask why one ought to be just is to ask why one ought to obey the law. The answer Hobbes gives to this question is likewise typical of the Positive Law position in the way it combines the sanctions of coercion and agreement. Without the existence of coercive power to compel men to act, covenants are "but words and breath," he declares, and of themselves "have no force to oblige, contain, constrain, or protect any man."[21] Yet Hobbes also holds that there is "no obligation on any man which ariseth not from some act of his own."[22] But the law, even reaching to the original compact on which it rests, is something to which its subjects have agreed. "The law is made by the sovereign power, and all that is done by such power is warranted and owned by every one of the people; and that which every man will have so, no man can say is unjust."[23] And they have done so and continue so to do in order to secure peace. Indeed, it is their agreement that establishes the coercive power behind the law. Thus, for Hobbes—and in this he is typical of the whole position—ultimately the obligatory or binding power of justice is legal force and social approval. There is no appeal to any kind of distinctive moral *ought*: One ought to be just in order to avoid punishment and to achieve a socially approved aim.

The entire thrust of the Positive Law theory is toward the identification of justice with obedience; the just man is the law-abiding citizen. Hobbes prefers, however, to describe justice as the "keeping of covenant," or fulfillment of promises.[24] This follows upon his Social Contract theory of society, not from his Positive Law theory of justice, and, as we shall see, the contractual theory is not an essential element of the Positive Law theory. In effect, too, the "keeping of covenant" for Hobbes reduces to obeying the sovereign law.

To complete the exposition of the Positive Law theory we need to see how it handles meanings of *justice* that clearly cannot be reduced to legality. In doing so, we will also be considering how the theory accounts for the approbative character of justice. Hobbes does not tell us very much about this. It is something, however, about which contemporary adherents to the theory have much to say, thereby making their own distinctive contribution to the Positive Law position. For an understanding of that contribution we will draw mainly upon the work of Professor Alf Ross, a leading representative of the Scandinavian school of legal positivists, whose book *On Law and Justice* appeared in 1958.

By equating justice with legality, the Positive Law theory is compelled, as other theories are not, to account for the senses in which the "just" clearly means something different from "legal." We may admit that a certain action is legal without thereby approving of it, as we also may disapprove of those who take advantage of the law to their own profit, if not to the actual hurt of another. Yet we claim that such actions and persons are unjust, and so too we also say of some laws that they are unjust. How does the Positive Law theory account for such facts in the realm of discourse?

Alf Ross holds as strongly as Hobbes does that law, strictly and properly speaking, cannot be just or unjust, precisely because it is the measure and source of justice. When then men do so speak, Ross claims, they are saying something not about the law but about their relation to it. "A person who maintains that a certain rule or order—for example, a system of taxation —is unjust, does not indicate any discernible quality in the order; he does not provide any reasons for his attitude, but merely gives to it an emotional expression. *A* says: 'I am against this rule because it is unjust.' What he should say is: 'This rule is unjust because I oppose it.' To invoke injustice is the same thing as banging on the table: an emotional expression which turns one's demand into an absolute postulate."[25] Such a statement has "emotive meaning," but it does not have any "descriptive meaning."

The language of this distinction reveals that Ross is an advocate of what has come to be called the emotive theory of value, which is concerned with the meaning of normative, approbative forms. Endorsement of this theory is not a necessary and characteristic feature of the Positive Law theory of justice; it is questionable, for example, how far Hobbes would subscribe to it. Ross's position, however, is illuminating in that it shows how the Positive Law theory can identify justice with legality and still maintain that the one word cannot entirely replace the other. To predicate justice of something is to indicate one's approval of it in a way that merely calling it legal does not.

With this we complete our exposition of the Positive Law theory of justice. In summary and minimal form, the propositions that are characteristic of it and make it one of the basic positions on justice are the following:

1. Justice and injustice are dependent on positive law.
2. Law itself is independent of justice.
3. Justice consists in conformity to positive law.
4. Justice, apart from legality, implies no more than approbation.
5. Justice is obligatory ultimately only because of legal and political sanctions.
6. Justice as a virtue is identical with obedience.

A writer on justice counts as an advocate of the Positive Law theory if he would tend to assert each of these six propositions. He need not do so explicitly, and indeed it is seldom that any one writer expressly addresses all six of the underlying issues. In fact, none of the three proponents that we have cited in expounding the theory did so. Yet it is usually clear from what they say where they would stand with respect to the issues on which they do not speak expressly. For Positive Law theory, the crucial issue is that regarding the relation between justice and law.[26]

## The Social Good theory of justice

The classical exponents of this theory in the great books tradition are Hume and Mill, and for our exposition of it we will rely mainly on their work. But we will also call frequently upon the Cambridge philosopher, Henry Sidgwick, whose analysis of justice, which first appeared in 1874, is an extension and completion of theirs. We will postpone consideration of contemporary representatives of the position until we come to study combinations of Social Good theory and the theory of Natural Right.

It is on the relation of justice and law that Social Good theory differs most sharply from that of Positive Law. According to those who hold the Social Good theory, justice cannot be identified with conformity to the law. Mill argues that in both our public and private life there are many occasions on which we appeal to justice without any reference to law. "Mankind considers the idea of justice and its obligations as applicable to many things which neither are, nor is it desired that they should be, regulated by law," he writes. "Nobody desires that laws should interfere with the whole detail of private life; yet everyone allows that in all daily conduct a person may and does show himself to be either just or unjust."[27] So too, Mill claims, there are many occasions in public life on which justice appears without law. As examples, he cites the fact that "it is universally considered just that each person should obtain that (whether good or evil) which he *deserves;* . . . [that it is] unjust to *break faith* with anyone . . . [and] inconsistent with justice to be *partial.*" Further, not only is law not constitutive of justice but justice itself provides a criterion for determining the goodness or badness of a law. Opinions may differ "as to the justice or injustice of infringing" a law, Mill notes, but, he declares, "it seems to be universally admitted that there may be unjust laws, and that law, consequently, is not the ultimate criterion of justice."[28]

Justice, according to the Social Good theory, is a wider notion than that of law, and it is so because society and its good is wider than that of law. Proponents of the Social Good theory may differ among themselves about the social good and its determination, but all agree that what is just is ultimately decided only by determining what is good for society, and that, whenever a course of action runs counter to that good, it is to that extent unjust. No law, no right, falls outside the scope of this criterion. Laws and rights are just or unjust according as they do or do not establish and promote the social good.

If by what is conventional we understand something that is the result of the agreement of men associated together in a society, then justice, according to this theory, is conventional and not natural. While admitting that justice is prior to government and its law and hence could exist without them, the Social Good theory denies that there is any justice or any basis for it apart from society. An individual man, considered apart from society, is in no way just or unjust. He becomes just or unjust by and in society, and all the rights and rules of justice come about as a result of the work of society. In this sense, the Social Good theory denies that any such thing as natural right is the basis of justice.

Proponents of the Social Good theory assert the dependence of justice upon society in different ways. Hume does so by claiming that justice is an "artificial virtue," not a "natural virtue." Mill accomplishes the same purpose by claiming that justice has its origin in a social feeling. Sidgwick denies that natural right provides a basis for justice. All three writers agree that there is no basis for justice other than society and its good.

Hume maintains that justice is an "artificial virtue," hence unlike benevolence or sympathy, which are "instincts originally implanted in our natures."[29] To substantiate this claim, he offers several reasons, only one of which we will consider here. It is argued that if justice were natural to man and not dependent upon a special social situation, we could expect to find it wherever we find man. Yet, Hume contends, it is easy to imagine situations in which justice would not exist, as in the golden age of the poets, where men enjoy an abundance of all that they want, or in a society of saints, where every man has perfect benevolence, or, again, in a condition of such extreme indigence that there is not enough to prevent most of its members from starving—a society of ruffians, Hobbes's "state of nature"—

or where there is a solitary man who has everything. In any of these situations, Hume maintains, there would be no question of justice at all, since there would be no function for it to perform.[30]

The need for justice, according to Hume, depends "entirely on the particular condition in which men are placed," that is, a condition of a scarcity of material goods and security in which man's wants and desires are always more than he can satisfy individually by himself. His acquisitive passions are so strong as greatly to threaten a peaceable and secure life with others of his kind. Hence these passions must be brought under control by regulating the possession of the material goods that are their object. But this can be done, Hume claims, "after no other manner than by a convention entered into by all the members of society to bestow stability on the possession of those external goods and leave everyone in the peaceable enjoyment of what he may acquire by his fortune and industry."[31] Justice, which results, thus has its origin in "a kind of convention or agreement, i.e. by a sense of interest supposed to be common to all, and where every single act is performed in expectation that others are to perform the like."[32] Justice, then, is conventional, not natural.

Mill does not declare explicitly that justice is a social convention, but he clearly implies as much in the account he offers of the origin of the sentiment of justice. This sentiment, as he sees it, has two essential ingredients: "the desire to punish a person who has done harm, and the knowledge or belief that there is some definite individual or individuals to whom harm has been done." But this desire to punish is itself "a spontaneous outgrowth from two sentiments . . . the impulse of self-defense and the feeling of sympathy . . . [since] it is natural to resent, and to repel or retaliate, any harm done or attempted against ourselves or against those with whom we sympathise." Yet at this stage the feeling of sympathy "has nothing moral in it." It does not become moral until there is "the exclusive subordination of it to the social sympathies, so as to wait on and obey their call." Our natural feeling becomes moral by becoming socialized so that it "only acts in the directions conformable to the general good." Since the sentiment of justice is a moral feeling, it must accordingly be rooted in a concern for the general or social good. A person feeling resentment at a harm done, "if he is regarding the act solely as it affects him individually, . . . is not consciously just; he is not concerning himself about the justice of his actions."[33] For Mill, as for Hume, justice always implies the "interest of society."

Those who base the idea of justice on the social good thereby deny that its basis is in nature. Sidgwick argues strongly to this effect. "No definition that has ever been offered of the Natural exhibits this notion as really capable of furnishing an independent ethical first principle," he declares.[34] He allows that "justice is generally, though somewhat vaguely, held to prescribe the fulfilment of all such expectations (of services, etc.) as arise naturally and normally out of the relations, voluntary or involuntary, in which we stand towards other human beings."[35] But he contends that this notion of natural expectation, besides being indefinite, also conceals a "fundamental conflict of ideas,"

> *. . . for the word* natural, *as used in this connexion, covers and conceals the whole chasm between the actual and the ideal—what is and what ought to be. . . . The term seems, as ordinarily used, to contain the distinct ideas of (1) the common as opposed to the exceptional, and (2) the original or primitive as contrasted with the result of later conventions and institutions. But it is also used to signify . . . "what would exist in an ideal state of society."*[36]

With such confusion, it is plain, Sidgwick thinks, that the natural provides no criterion for determining the just.

Because it denies any connection between justice and nature, the Social Good theory tends to dismiss the Roman definition of justice as unsatisfactory. This definition is wrong, Hume writes, because it assumes that right and property exist independent of justice, whereas their true relation is the very reverse: it is the social convention, the basis of justice, that establishes right and property.[37]

Any adequate definition of justice, according to the Social Good theory, would have to indicate its dependence on society. Sidgwick, who thinks that Hume and Mill do not appreciate the full complexity of the subject, holds that this dependence involves at least four distinct elements: (1) law-observance, (2) equality, whether in the distribution or allotment of rewards and burdens, or impartiality and the avoidance of arbitrary inequality in making and carrying out the law, (3) fulfillment of contract and of natural and normal expectations, and (4) reward and punishment according to desert.[38] In claiming that these are the elements of justice, Sidgwick does not mean that they are signified or implied in every use of the word, only that they are different ways in which the word may be used; nor does he say that any one of them is adequate by itself to convey what justice is. What makes it possible in his view to recognize them as parts of one complex whole is utilitarianism, which "furnishes us with a common standard to which the different elements included in the notion of Justice may be reduced."[39]

By "utilitarianism," Sidgwick ordinarily means the principle he accepts from Bentham and Mill of promoting the greatest happiness of the greatest number. Since he uses this principle as that to which the various elements of justice can be reduced, however, it is clear that he means by it no more than the social good, i.e., the good of society.

The social good provides an objective norm of justice and one that, according to the utilitarian proponents of the theory, is susceptible to calculation. Thus the social approbativeness of justice, even apart from legality and as a criterion of it, has an objective basis. On this issue, the Social Good theory sides with that of Natural Right against the Positive Law theory.

Proponents of the Social Good theory, however, take different ways in defending the objectivity of justice apart from legality. Among these ways, two main ones can be distinguished. The first, which is the way taken by Hume, bases justice on the common feeling of the society regarding what is good. The second, preferred by Sidgwick, bases it on a rational judgment concerning what is for the social good.

Hume's argument that the moral component of justice is based on feeling is similar to that advanced by some proponents of the Positive Law theory; in fact, Hume's work is an important source for the emotivist theory of moral judgments. The approbation or blame implicit in judgments of justice is not a work of reason, Hume claims, "but of the heart; and is not a speculative proposition or affirmation, but an active feeling or sentiment."[40] To say that an act is just is to have both a motive and an obligation to act. But only feeling, and never reason, is capable of providing motive and obligation. The feeling that underlies justice, however, is not a subjective one that is restricted and relative only to the individual. It is a social and public feeling that arises in any man's breast when he is confronted with circumstances that involve a question of the social good. Sympathy with the public interest, Hume writes, is "inviolably established in the nature of man, and of the world, in which he lives."[41] And again, "The convenience, or rather necessity, which leads to justice is so universal, and everywhere points so much to the same rules, that the habit takes place in all societies."[42] Hence, Hume claims, "the rules of justice are not arbitrary."[43] For the same reason, the approbation implicit in a judgment of justice is not subjective, since it is based on the common feeling of the society regarding what should or should not be approved.

In common with Hume, and with Mill too, Sidgwick holds that a judgment that X is just contains at least two perceptions: (1) that X is for the social good, and (2) that what is for the social good ought to be done. For the first of these, concerning the determination of a matter of fact, all three writers would agree that reason and deliberation are needed. But whereas Hume and Mill regard the second perception as a feeling, Sidgwick maintains that it too is a work of reason and knowledge. The moral faculty by which we are aware of what ought to be done cannot be a sense, he argues, because if it were, two people could differ completely about it without either ever being in error. Moral judgments are based on more than feelings because they are intrinsically universal, and it would be unreasonable not to do their bidding. But they rest, Sidgwick claims, on an intuition; not on a reasoning from fact or principle, but a seeing that such-and-such is so: "the power of seeing clearly that certain kinds of actions are right and reasonable in themselves, apart from their consequences."[44] But there is nothing special and inherently private about such an intuition; it is objective and open to all.

The norm of justice is a moral rule declaring what ought to be done. If now we ask why one ought to be just, the question for the Social Good position amounts to asking why one ought to do what conforms to the social good, or why one should do what is socially useful. Of course, if one does not, one becomes subject to the sanctions of society. But, according to the Social Good theory, the obligatoriness of justice rests on more than the threat of sanctions.

Sidgwick distinguishes four senses or ways in which we use the expression "X ought to be done." (1) It may mean that X is "the fittest or only fit means to the realization of some end"; this is a teleological *ought* inasmuch as the judgment involved has the form: If you want Y, then X ought to be done. (2) The expression may affirm "no more than the existence of a specific emotion in the mind of the person who utters it . . . a feeling of approbation or satisfaction"; this is the approbative *ought*, since the reason that one has for asserting that X ought to be done is his approval of X. (3) Again, when we say that X ought to be done, we may "mean that [we are] bound under penalties to do it," in which case we have a penal or punitive *ought*. (4) Finally, we have a distinctively moral *ought* when, in judging that X ought to be done, we give expression to a notion that is "too elementary to admit of any formal definition," although it implies that X is thought to be capable of being brought about voluntarily or, at least, of serving as an ideal or pattern to follow, and that the judgment that it ought to be done "gives an impulse or motive to action" that it would be unreasonable not to follow.[45]

The judgment that X is just and ought to be done is not truly a moral judgment unless it includes this distinctively moral *ought*, Sidgwick holds, and he claims that it is a shortcoming in the accounts of Hume and Mill that they have tried to do without such an ought. Hume attempts to explain the obligatoriness of justice by means of an approbative *ought*—one that is social rather than merely individual in character, yet still approbative only. Mill offers an explanation that in effect combines a teleological with a punitive *ought*. Neither, according to Sidgwick, has succeeded in accounting for what is distinctively moral in the obligatoriness of justice, since they have failed to include the fundamental intuition of the moral *ought*. Knowing that X is for the social good does not of itself impose the duty of doing X, unless we also know that what is for the social good ought to be done. But in any case, according to Sidgwick, we must finally reach a distinctively moral *ought*.

Sidgwick's position with regard to this moral intuition is summed up in the statement that "there are certain absolute practical principles, the truth of which, when they are explicitly stated, is manifest; but they are of too abstract a nature, and too universal in their scope to enable us to ascertain by immediate application of them what we ought to do in any particular case; particular duties have still to be determined by some other method."[46] The method Sidgwick defends is that of determining what in the concrete instance is for the greater good, which, on his understanding of it, is the method of utilitarianism.

In his account of moral obligation Sidgwick comes close to the position held by the Natural Right theory, whereas Hume leans in the opposite direction toward the theory of Positive Law. (Indeed, Sidgwick criticizes Hume for tending to make justice the same as law-observance,[47] though Hume is otherwise to be classified, as we have seen, with Social Good theorists.)

The Social Good theory holds that justice is a distinct virtue, but it shows a tendency to assimilate justice to benevolence, just as the Positive Law theory tends to assimilate it to obedience. For the Social Good theory, justice is like benevolence in both source and end. Both justice and benevolence are rooted in the instinct or feeling of sympathy that we have for our fellowman, what Hume calls our "natural philanthropy," and both aim at the good of others as a common good. How then do they differ from one another? The Social Good authors answer the question in different ways.

Hume locates the difference, as we have already seen, in the fact that benevolence is a "natural virtue," where justice is "artificial" in that it requires reason, forethought, design, and social union.[48] Benevolence "applies directly by instinct to simple particular objects," whereas justice supposes "a whole scheme or system concurred in by the whole, or the greater part of society."[49] Unlike benevolence, which may be exercised whenever and wherever we wish to help another, justice may demand of us actions that we do not want to perform and that we may even find displeasing, as when "judges take from a poor man to give to a rich . . . bestow on the dissolute the labor of the industrious, and put into the hands of the vicious the means of harming both themselves and others."[50] The justice of such actions may lie in their being advantageous to society in the long run, once all things are taken into account.

Mill places the difference between the two virtues in a feature implicit in Hume's account, namely, the fact that the services dictated by justice can be claimed as a right by their recipient, whereas beneficence, as he calls it, is essentially unconstrained. This difference corresponds, in Mill's view, to the difference between what some ethical writers denote by "duties of perfect and of imperfect obligation; the latter being those in which, though the act is obligatory, the particular occasions of performing it are left to our choice; as in the case of charity or beneficence, which we are indeed bound to practise, but not towards any definite person, nor at any prescribed time." But "duties of perfect obligation are those duties in virtue of which a correlative *right* resides in some person or persons." It is the existence of such a right that constitutes "the specific difference between justice, and generosity or beneficence."[51]

According to Sidgwick, justice differs from benevolence rather in that it "involves allotment of something considered as advantageous or disadvantageous: whether it be money or other material means of happiness; or praise, or affection, or other immaterial good, or some merited pain or loss."[52]

Nevertheless, however differently these three authors account for the virtue of justice, all would agree that ultimately it consists in serving and promoting the social good.

This completes the exposition of the Social Good theory of justice. In summary form it can be characterized as holding the following propositions:

1. Justice and injustice are not exclusively dependent on positive law but also have application in areas such as private life where law does not and should not apply.
2. Justice provides a criterion of law so that it makes sense to describe a law as just or unjust.
3. Justice derives exclusively from society, not from natural right, and consists ultimately in promoting the social good.
4. Justice, even apart from legality, is an objective norm for human actions.
5. Justice imposes a moral duty based on the social good, not merely on legal and social sanctions.
6. Justice is a distinct virtue, but it is similar to benevolence, and disposes one to act for the social good.[53]

## The Natural Right theory of justice

Of the three basic theories of justice, the Natural Right theory is by far the most complex. There is accordingly much variation to be found among the expressions given to it by its proponents. To see clearly the main lines of the theory, we must disregard the many ways in which individual writers differ and center our attention upon the significant points on which they agree.

Three notes, two of them negative and one positive, suffice to identify the Natural Right theory and distinguish it from the other two basic theories. The theory denies, first, that justice is identical with legality and, second, that the interest or good of society provides its fundamental basis. It asserts, third, that justice is based on the nature of man and answers to needs that he has because of the kind of being that he is.

Many proponents of the theory also hold that there is such a thing as natural law. This assertion, however, is not a necessary and identifying note of the theory as such. A writer may in fact deny the existence of natural law and yet adhere to the Natural Right position. Julius Stone, for example, maintains that there are certain "quasi-absolutes of justice," and yet denies that they belong to or derive from any natural law. In his account of these absolutes, he declares that the basic one is the precept that "social arrangements should as a minimum (even if only as a minimum) respect every man's claim to form, entertain, and articulate his own interests."[54] In thus holding that every man has a right to such a claim, and one to which he can appeal against society and its laws, Stone thereby shows that he subscribes to the Natural Right theory of justice.

For our construction of the Natural Right theory we will draw upon the work of Aristotle, Aquinas, and Locke in the great books tradition and from among contemporaries the writings of Jacques Maritain and Mortimer J. Adler.

The classic Roman definition of justice as rendering to each his right is fully endorsed by the Natural Right theory. This is in contrast to the Positive Law and Social Good theories, which would accept such a definition only with reservations, since they exclude the notion of right as primitive for the analysis of justice. Aquinas is representative of the entire Natural Right position when he writes that "rendering each his right states the proper object and matter of justice."[55]

Although Aristotle has much to say about justice, he does not actually cite this definition, a form of which was available to him in the quotation from Simonides quoted by Plato. Yet he would accept it, since as we shall see, he holds that there are things naturally just that a man may claim as his right or his own. Locke does not elaborate a theory of justice as such, and what he thinks about the nature of justice has to be gathered mainly from what he has to say about society and government. But from this it is clear that he would accept the classical definition. He maintains that "where there is no property there is no injustice," but by "property" he understands "a right to anything," so that injustice consists in "the invasion or violation of that right."[56] Justice then is the observance of one's right.

Maritain, of the authors we are now considering, has the most to say about right. "The notion of justice is enveloped in that of right," he declares, but then he notes that "it is there in an implicit state, and it is by means of the very notion of right that it is disengaged and brought to light. Justice is defined by means of right as rendering to each *his due.*"[57] Maritain here brings together *right* and *due*. Frequently, to these two terms a third is added, that namely of *one's own*. The essential part of the classical definition of justice may accordingly be formulated in three ways, as rendering to each his right, his due, or his own. We may ask what reason there is for thinking that these three formulations are equivalent, and what difference it makes to use one rather than another. On this matter Maritain says much that is relevant and brings us close to the heart of the Natural Right position.

*Right* is undoubtedly the most ambiguous of the three terms. Indeed, it has the same ambiguity as *just*. It has a general use in which it can apply to any action that is judged to be morally good; it can apply to any virtuous action. Thus it can be said of a man that he did right in ceasing to drink before he became drunk, or that it is right to be temperate. Corresponding to this adjectival use, there is the substantival use in the expression "I have the right to do so," where it means, according to Maritain, "only that in acting so I would do nothing wrong or prohibited by law."[58] In this sense, *right* has as its opposite the word *wrong*, and there is nothing in it that is peculiar to justice. Justice enters when *right* has a more particular sense, as when we speak of a right to such things as life, liberty, and the pursuit of happiness. It is used thus, Maritain says, when we speak of "rights that one possesses and can lay a claim to," rights such as are personal or pertain to property. The opposite of *right* in this sense is not *wrong* but *no-right*. A person has a right to the house he owns, but no right at all to a house that is owned by another.

This twofold sense of *right* corresponds to the distinction Aristotle draws between general and particular justice.[59] In the general sense, right includes all that is morally good. Of right in the particular sense, in which it is allied with particular justice, Maritain provides the following definition: "A right is a demand or claim emanating from a self in regard to something as *his* due and which other moral agents are obliged in conscience not to frustrate."[60]

This definition makes clear that there are at least three elements involved in the notion of right. First, there is an object, something that is due to one in virtue of his having such and such a right. The owner of a house has the right to privacy, to be secure against trespass, and to sell, bequeath, or give it away. The objects in these cases consist in forbearances on the part of others or in actions that the possessor of the right can by right perform. This element in right is called by Maritain, following Aquinas, the *debitum,* or that which is due. Second, there is the subject of the right, the person who has or possesses the right. Third, there is the obligation laid upon others to respect that right and to observe it either by way of forbearance or of positive action. Thus, corresponding to the possession of a right, there is a correlative duty imposed upon others.

By so distinguishing and identifying these three elements contained in the notion of right, it becomes clear that the three different ways of formulating the Roman definition of justice are equivalent and differ only in emphasizing one of the elements over the others. Thus, for example, we may speak of the suffrage as a *right* of the citizen and thereby emphasize its character as a power that the voter enjoys; to refer to it as *his own* stresses the subject, his possession of it, his property; while to speak of it as something that is due him stresses the obligation or duty laid upon others to allow him to exercise that right.

Any theory of justice admits that justice has something to do with rights. What is unique about the Natural Right theory is that it makes *right* the absolutely first and basic term for the analysis of justice, and prior to law as well as to the conventions of society. This priority of right is asserted by claiming a basis in nature rather than in law or society.

The basis of justice in natural right can be asserted in many different ways. Thus it may be claimed that natural right is something that a man possesses as an individual apart from and even before he enters into civil society. Or the natural basis of justice may be asserted by distinguishing natural from conventional justice and claiming that the latter depends upon the former. More frequent, especially among modern proponents of the theory, is the practice of distinguishing different kinds of rights and identifying the basic kind as natural, human, moral, inalienable, personal, or a priori.

Locke takes the first way and describes the condition of men in a state of nature, apart from civil society and government. That is, he writes,

> *a state of perfect freedom to order their actions, and dispose of their possessions and persons as they think fit, within the bounds of the law of Nature, without asking leave or depending upon the will of any other man. . . . But though this be a state of liberty, yet it is not a state of licence; though man in that state have an uncontrollable liberty to dispose of his person or possessions, yet he has not liberty to destroy himself or so much as any creature in his possession. . . . The state of Nature has a law of Nature to govern it which obliges every one, and reason, which is that law, teaches all mankind who will but consult it, that being all equal and independent, no one ought to harm another in his life, health, liberty or possessions.*

Furthermore, Locke claims, every man in the state of nature has the right to do what is necessary to restrain others from invading his rights.[61] The state of society differs from that of nature only with regard to this last right, that of securing the observance of the former rights and punishing their violation.

Aristotle does not use the expression "natural right." He speaks, as Aquinas points out, of natural and legal justice, where the jurists talk of natural and positive right.[62] According to Aristotle, the naturally just is "that which has the same power everywhere and does not depend on our accepting it or not, whereas the legally just is that which in the beginning might have been settled indifferently either way, but, once settled, is no longer indifferent."[63] Of the instances of what is naturally just, he gives most attention to that of equality. "That the equal should not go to the equal and the like to the like is contrary to nature," he writes.[64]

Aristotle links together equality and law as the basic elements of justice, saying "the just is the lawful and the equal, (or fair) and the unjust is the unlawful and the unequal."[65] Equality is obviously a different kind of principle from law. It is, by itself, a purely formal principle in that, without further specification, it provides no criterion of relevance or of applicability; it does not say which respects are to count as relevant for consideration with regard to equality. Men are never equal in every respect, and which respect is to be taken as the relevant one, Aristotle claims, "is a political question."[66] Democrats hold that men should be treated as equal in every respect because they are equal in one, namely, in citizenship, whereas oligarchs argue that because men are unequal in the one respect of wealth, they should be treated as though they were unequal in all. Both are in error, Aristotle maintains, because they overlook the fact that in justice and politics only certain kinds of equality and inequality are relevant.

Although the criterion of relevance may change, it is with respect to the exchange and distribution of material goods that equality is most often proclaimed as a principle of justice. Aristotle takes this to be the standard case of justice or injustice, and defines the unjust man as one who "takes more than his share, not of any and all goods, but of those on which good and bad fortune depend," and takes more of the good things or less of the bad.[67] Underlying this emphasis upon equality as a basic principle of justice there seems to be the presumption that equal treatment among men insofar as they are equal is to be expected and that any departure from it calls for justification. In this sense, the right of equals to equal treatment is sometimes called a prima-facie right—that is, a right that cannot be denied or violated without some justification.

The basic justification for unequal treatment, according to Aristotle, is the existence of some inequality in desert or merit. Such a difference Aristotle accommodates to the principle of equality by basing it on proportionate rather than arithmetic equality. Thus if two persons A and B are unequal, their shares of good, honors, or whatever, x and y, should also in justice be unequal. Hence when A is greater than B, his share, x, should accordingly be greater than B's share, y, and less when it is respectively less. Not all proponents of the Natural Right theory would agree that the principle of desert can be accommodated under the notion of equality, even granted that an equality of ratios is in question. Some look upon desert or merit as a distinct principle and contrast meritorian with equalitarian justice. Aristotle does not, but this may derive, at least in part, from the fact that his Greek makes the word for "equal" (*isos*) also do the work of "fair." In any case, the equal and the fair are for Aristotle principles of justice that are prior to social convention and positive law. In this sense they are rights that are natural.

Maritain makes natural right the basis of justice by attributing it to the nature of man as a person. "The human person possesses rights because of the very fact that it is a person, a whole, master of itself and of its acts," he writes,

> *and which consequently is not merely a means to an end, but an end, an end which must be treated as such. The dignity of the human person? The expression means nothing if it does not signify that by virtue of natural law, the human person has the right to be respected, is the subject of rights, possesses rights. There are things which are owed to man because of the very fact that he is man.*[68]

More stringently, in claiming that "real goods make natural rights," Mortimer Adler correlates the notion of natural right with that of natural need —that is, a need founded on the specific nature of man. A real as distinct from an apparent good is one that answers to a natural need rather than to a passing desire; it is a good that is indispensable to a good human life and one that man ought to pursue, since, according to Adler, man is morally bound to pursue a good human life for himself. Thus, for Adler, there is "a set of basic notions that are inseparably connected with one another:"

> *(a) natural needs, (b) real goods, (c) the duties or moral obligations I have in the conduct of my own life, (d) moral or natural rights, and (e) the duties or moral obligations I have in my conduct toward others. Natural needs make certain things really good for me; the things that are really good for me impose moral obligations on me in the conduct of my private life; these, in turn, give me certain moral or natural rights, and my having such rights imposes moral obligations on others with respect to me.*[69]

Natural Right authors differ among themselves regarding the extent to which the natural rights of man can be specified and detailed apart from actual embodiment in social institutions and laws. Some of the seventeenth- and eighteenth-century theorists, including Jefferson and the founding fathers of the United States, descend to considerable detail in specifying these rights. Others are more restrained and cite as natural rights only a few general principles, sometimes only one of them, the right to be free. Adler distinguishes the primary natural right—"our right to the pursuit of happiness"—from "subsidiary natural rights—rights to life, security of life and limb, a decent livelihood, freedom from coercion, political liberty, educational opportunities, medical care, sufficient free time for the pursuits of leisure," all of which, he claims, "stem from my right to the pursuit of happiness and from my obligation to make a good life for myself."[70]

Differences and disagreements over the number and specification of natural rights indicate differences in the relation between natural right on the one side and society and positive law on the other. All proponents of Natural Right theory would agree, however, that justice provides a criterion of goodness for both society and law. According to Aristotle, constitutions, as well as laws, "must be good or bad, just or unjust." He undertakes to show how constitutions can be classified according to their justice, the best state being the one that has men who are just absolutely and not according to some particular standard.[71] As the possessor of natural rights, man is not subject to his society in all that he is and has. This is as much as to say that he has rights on his own that do not derive from society and its laws, but to which he can appeal as a criterion by which to judge both.

In this position the Natural Right theory joins that of the Social Good in common opposition to the Positive Law theory. Both contend that justice is something more than law and applies to areas where there is no question of law. As evidence, Maritain cites two imaginary examples: the case of an employer who agrees to pay his workers a certain fee and then lives up to his agreement, and that of a chief of a primitive tribe who is hard and severe, but who treats each member impartially according to his deeds. In neither case is there any reference to law; yet, according to Maritain, "the common man faced with these examples would know that the employer or tribal chief is *just* and that to be just is *good*."[72]

These are examples, respectively, of what Aristotle and Aquinas call commutative and distributive justice, by which they mean justice between private individuals as distinct from justice between the head of a community and its members, respectively. Aristotle makes still another division of justice that shows it extending to matters outside the reach of law. Thus he contrasts domestic with political justice, the first being that which applies within the household; he also distinguishes despotic justice between master and slave, paternal justice between father and child, and conjugal justice between husband and wife.[73] In each case, he holds that there is an area of human relations in which a person can be just or unjust, even though there is no positive law (or none existed in his time) to limit the person's acts.

Natural Right theory asserts the objectivity of justice by holding that justice provides a norm of what is due to man that is both natural and moral: natural as based on his nature and moral as obliging him to observe it. According to Locke, "[there] is a fixed and permanent rule of morals, which reason itself pronounces, and which persists, being a fact so firmly rooted in the soil of human nature." And Locke continues, "since man has been made such as he is, equipped with reason and his other faculties and destined for this mode of life, there necessarily result from his inborn constitution some definite duties for him, which cannot be other than they are."[74]

The pertinent fact for the theory is the kind of being that man is. He has such dignity that what is ultimately due him is logically prior to any social agreement or public enactment or institution. To make this point, Locke appeals to man in a state of nature apart from civil society and its government. But such an appeal is not essential to the theory, and none of the other authors we are discussing resorts to it in claiming that there are things that are due to man as man, not to man as citizen or as subject of the law. All would hold with Adler that one need only "appeal to the facts of a specific nature common to all men."[75]

From our preliminary analysis of right, we have seen that the element of obligation is essential to it. A right by the very fact of being a right obliges others to respect it. When one goes on to ask why one ought to do what is just, the characteristic answer of the Natural Right theory is that the obligation arises because what requires to be done is itself good and just. No further justification is needed: Seeing what is just entails the obligation to do it. Thus, according to this theory, not only are there things that are naturally just; there are also natural obligations.

Locke, after noting that the jurists define obligation as "the bond of law whereby one is bound to render what is due," declares that the law in question must be "the bond of natural law whereby one is bound to discharge a natural obligation, that is, to fulfil the duty which it lies upon one to perform by reason of one's nature." Although he traces this law back to the will of God, he also declares that it is "not fear of punishment, but a rational apprehension of what is right, [that] puts us under an obligation."[76]

Aristotle has nothing to say directly about obligation, but he declares that "the good man does what he ought, since intelligence always chooses for itself that which is best, and the good man obeys his intelligence"; and among goods he holds that the best is the virtuous good (*bonum honestum*), which is superior to pleasure (*bonum delectabile*) because nobler, and better than the useful (*bonum utile*) because an intrinsic good, which is good in itself and not merely good as a means to a further end.[77]

This *bonum honestum*, Maritain writes, is "the quality of an act that is morally good in virtue of what it is and of the relation that it has to man, independent of every consideration of advantage or utility or pleasure, and independent also of all pressures that can weigh upon us and of all the emotions and aspirations that stir us." It constrains and obliges just because it is good.[78]

The obligation of justice, according to the Natural Right theory, is a distinctly moral *ought*, not to be confused with any other such as the teleological, the punitive, or the approbative ought. But proponents of the theory differ as to how the obligation comes about. Some follow Kant and make moral duty a categorical imperative; one must act justly because it is one's duty. For others, like Locke, one must do one's duty because it is the will of God. Others make the obligation of justice depend upon the fulfillment or realization of the needs of human nature. Thus Adler claims that "the fundamental normative truth [is] that I ought to make a really good life for myself or, in other words, that a whole life that is really good is the ultimate normative end, the *totum bonum*, that I am categorically obliged to pursue. All other normative truths—all other true ought-statements—are propositions about the goods that ought to be sought as constitutive parts of a whole good life or as means to the *totum bonum* which is the ultimate end." And justice is such a good because it is a requisite for the good society, which the individual needs for the achievement of a truly good human life.[79]

According to the Natural Right theory, justice is a distinct virtue, and there is no tendency to confuse it with either obedience or benevolence. Thus Adler writes: "It is love, not justice, that impels us to act benevolently toward those whom we regard as our friends. The duties of justice relate only to the rights of others that we are obliged to respect, and this is but another way of saying that justice requires us not to injure them by depriving them of the things they need," whereas love, or benevolence, "unlike justice, does not consist in rendering to others what is their due . . . [but] consists in giving them generously more than is their due."[80]

For Aristotle, justice is one of the virtues that later come to be called cardinal. Like other moral virtues, it is a habit of conduct; but, unlike courage and temperance, it is a habit of action and not of the passions. It is that settled inclination by which "the just man is said to be a doer, by choice, of that which is just, and one who will distribute either between himself and another or between two others not so as to give more of what is desirable to himself and less to his neighbour (and conversely with what is harmful), but so as to give what is equal in accordance with proportion."[81] Unlike other moral virtues, the justice of an act can be determined without taking into account the condition of the agent. How much wine a person can drink without becoming intemperate depends on the person, but what one owes the bartender depends on how much has been drunk. Hence, Aquinas declares that justice is the only virtue that implies the notion of the *debitum*, of what is due to another.[82]

Not all the proponents of the Natural Right theory would agree with Aristotle and Aquinas in their analysis of virtue. But all would agree that the virtue of justice cannot simply be identified with obedience to the law. The two are the same only when the just coincides with the legal, but, on this theory, such is not always the case. Aquinas accordingly places obedience among the virtues "annexed to justice," i.e., as agreeing with it in some respects, but falling short of it in others.[83]

We have now seen the position that the Natural Right theory takes on the fundamental issues regarding justice. This position is summarized in the following leading propositions:

1. Justice and injustice do not ultimately derive from positive law.
2. Justice provides a criterion for the goodness of law.
3. Justice is based on natural right and consists in rendering to each his due.
4. Justice is an objective norm for human actions.
5. Justice is obligatory in itself apart from social and legal sanctions.
6. Justice is a special virtue distinct from all other virtues.[84]

## Combinations of basic theories

The positions of the three basic theories of justice have now been sketched in their main lines. These theories are basic in that they establish a position from which the entire controversy regarding justice may be viewed and analyzed, and provide types or paradigms according to which any theory may be measured and identified. Most theories of justice are more in accord with one of the three basic ones than they are with either of the others. Yet it must be admitted that some authors develop theories that do not fit well and easily under any of the three paradigms, notwithstanding that the distinctions between these, developed in the preceding pages, would seem to be sharp enough to disallow the possibility that any theory could be consistent if it tried to cross lines. What seems to lead to this result is the fact that each of the three basic theories is complex in requiring several principles for its delineation, so that, in applying them, certain authors can resist or refuse to be caught within the network that the distinctions provide, and can appear to merge and combine at the very points where we have found that other authors cut and separate. The great books tradition contains two eminent examples of this tendency: Hegel, who seems to combine Natural Right and Positive Law theory, and Kant, who brings together the theories of Natural Right and Social Good.

Hegel is notoriously difficult to understand, and *The Philosophy of Right*, in which he develops his theory of justice, is characteristically dense. To ask whether right or law is the more primitive term for the analysis of justice is to pose a question Hegel's theory seems designed to deny. He appears to want to claim that both right and law are primitive and need to be reconciled in the higher synthesis that his system provides. He asserts emphatically that "law and right are identical,"[85] so that his theory of justice is sometimes equated with that of Hobbes, thus making him an adherent of the Positive Law theory.[86] Yet he also admits that man has rights not only antecedent to civil society but also against it, thus seeming to allow that there is a basis for right apart from law.[87] Further, he distinguishes the natural law from positive law, but denies that there is any opposition between them, claiming that "the relation between them is much more like that between Institutes and Pandects."[88] By this comparison with the basic works of Roman law, it would appear that Hegel is saying that the natural law is related to the positive law as the general is to the particular—the Institutes being understood to supply the general principles on which the detailed case law of the Pandects is based. The positive law of the State, which for Hegel is the culmination of reason, makes particular and concrete what is general and indefinite. Thus, Hegel can claim that no opposition is possible between natural right and positive law.

The theory of justice that Kant develops in his *Science of Right* may be viewed as a combination of Natural Right and Social Good theory. Kant admits that the Roman definition expresses "the law of justice," but he maintains that if this were translated simply as " 'Give everyone *his own*,' it would express an absurdity, for we cannot *give* anyone what he already has." Hence Kant proposes the following reformulation: "Enter into a state in which everyone can have what is his own secured against the action of every other."[89] The state referred to here is that of civil society under government, which is characterized by the presence of distributive justice with a judge who rules over this sphere and has the task of "assigning every one what is his own."[90] Kant does not hesitate to claim that the state of man apart from this is *status justitiae vacuus* (a state void of justice).[91] From such statements it would appear that Kant is making justice the creation of society and hence should be counted as a proponent of the Social Good theory.

To conclude so, however, would be overhasty. He also maintains that the work of a civil constitution establishing a civil society is "only the juridical condition under which every one has what is his own merely secured to him, as distinguished from its being specially assigned and determined to him," which is to say that right is not created but is only guaranteed by society.[92] More than this, Kant expresses a doctrine of natural right, by distinguishing innate from acquired rights and by declaring that the former is "that right which belongs to every one by nature, independent of all juridical acts," whereas acquired right is created by a judicial act. Yet he also claims that there is "only one Innate Right, the Birthright of Freedom," which is also described as "an innate equality belonging to every man which consists in his right to be independent of being bound by others to anything more than that to which he may also reciprocally bind them."[93] Man thus possesses at least one right that is his by virtue of his nature and is not the product of society and its conventions, and this is a claim that is characteristic of the Natural Right theory.

Kant's position here is obviously not typical of the Natural Right theory as represented, for instance, by Aquinas, Locke, and Maritain. For none of these writers does the natural right that provides the basis of justice reduce to a right of equal freedom, and all would hold that nature establishes still other rights. Since for Kant such rights would all be the work of society, it appears that his theory should be considered a combination of the Natural Right and Social Good theories.[94]

## Natural Right and Social Good

Many of the recent theories of justice, especially those put forward by the predominant school of Anglo-American philosophers, are best understood as efforts to combine Social Good and Natural Right theory. This school has been strongly influenced by the utilitarian philosophers, who, as we have seen, are typical representatives of the Social Good theory of justice. The attempt to meet criticisms of the utilitarian position has resulted in the addition of some form of Natural Right theory as a qualification and correction. For a review of recent utilitarian theories, as well as a criticism of them and a proposed alternative, we may turn to Nicholas Rescher's *Distributive Justice*, which provides a good introduction.

The attraction of the utilitarian approach, Professor Rescher notes, has been that "it lays the groundwork for introducing into the discussion [of distributive justice] mathematical and quantitative modes of thought, greatly to the benefit of the exactness and clarity of the reasoning we can bring to bear on the issues."[95] This has been especially true of the development of utilitarian thought in economics, and above all in that branch known as welfare economics. The original formulation of the principle— "which asserts that utility (or . . . simply the good things of this life) should be distributed according to the rule of 'the greatest good of the greatest number' "—has come under increasing criticism, however, as both "imprecise and indeed inadequate."[96]

The principle is "imprecise," Rescher says, because it does not determine in a case of doubt whether a greater total good is to be chosen or a pattern of distribution that benefits the greater number, e.g., between "a less populous world with a higher per capita average utility, and a more populous world with a lower per capita average utility."[97] The principle is most clearly "inadequate" in that "it leaves wholly out of account that essential reference to claims, merit, and desert without which no theory of distributive justice fulfills the requisite for serious consideration."[98] Thus, on the one hand, to seek only the greatest good of the greatest number does not recognize the claim in justice "to minimize the number of persons in a state of genuine *deprivation*," which is to hold that "diminishing the number of those who simply do not have enough is a more fundamental element of the concept of justice than diminishing the gap between the 'haves' and the 'have-nots'."[99] On the other hand, such an aim leaves out of account the "proportionality qualification" that one person may deserve more than another because of a claim based on effort, need, ability, or any other legitimate basis.[100] Without the principles of proportionality and deservingness, utilitarianism, according to Rescher, can lead to results that are unjust because manifestly unfair.

In advancing his "canon of claims," Rescher is, in effect, calling for recognition of natural right, even though he does not use the term. The closest he comes to it is in his assertion that "certain unearned claims can be taken to be inherent in the human condition, being treated, like life and liberty, as 'inalienable rights.' "[101]

Rescher maintains that there is one situation, however, in which the principle of utility—and hence that of the social good—remains supreme. That is the situation now prevailing in the Western world for those governments that enjoy an economy of abundance and "an essentially fixed amount of 'utility' to distribute (so that there is no way of benefiting all by adopting a less equitable alternative division of a larger amount) among a group of potential recipients whose claims are essentially identical, and all of whom are 'deserving.' " In such a situation, all are "in the same boat," and hence the principle of deservingness is irrelevant, especially where the public assets and facilities are such as to "benefit everyone alike: fire protection, air-pollution control, traffic safety, mail service, public health, etc."[102]

Rescher sums up his theory of justice in the proposition that "there are two distinct senses of *justice,* corresponding to two diverse articulations of the concept itself. There is *justice in the narrower sense of fairness,* on the one hand, and on the other, *justice in a wider sense, taking account of the general good.*"[103] The first, based on the principle of proportionality and deservingness, amounts to a recognition of natural right. The second, where the principle of utility rules, adopts the Social Good position. Hence, Rescher's theory may be looked upon as a combination of Natural Right and Social Good principles.

The position taken by Professor John Rawls in his ambitious *A Theory of Justice*—in scope and size the most comprehensive treatise on the subject since the works of the great scholastics—is also best understood as a combination of Social Good and Natural Right ideas. Although Rawls expressly proposes his theory as an alternative to utilitarianism, and acknowledges his obligation to Kant, in developing his conception he has clearly been influenced by the utilitarian thinkers and especially by the welfare economists. With them he shares the desire for a conception of justice that is sufficiently precise, even calculable, so as to be readily applicable, particularly in the distributive order. He criticizes Natural Right theories, which are included for the most part under what he calls "intuitionistic theories," as well as various versions of qualified utilitarianism, including that of Rescher, for not meeting the standards of precision and exactness that he claims may be expected. Thus he would seem to agree with those "intuitionists" for whom the classical definition of giving every man his due is said to "reduce to triviality."[104]

Rawls erects his whole theory upon two basic principles. They are given various formulations, as he presents them, from the simplest to the fullest. In their simplest expression they are summed up in the proposition that "all social values—liberty and opportunity, income and wealth, and the bases of self-respect—are to be distributed equally unless an unequal distribution of any, or all, of these values is to everyone's advantage."[105] Breaking this down into its parts, Rawls formulates his principles in their fullest expression as follows:

> First Principle [*of Equal Liberty*]: *Each person is to have an equal right to the most extensive total system of equal basic liberties compatible with a similar system of liberty for all.*
> Second Principle [*the Difference Principle*]: *Social and economic inequalities are to be arranged so that they are both: (a) to the greatest benefit of the least advantaged, consistent with the just savings principle, and (b) attached to offices and positions open to all under conditions of fair equality of opportunity.*[106]

In case of conflict between the two, the first is always to have priority over the second, while the second takes priority over efficiency and welfare.

The principles are by no means self-evident. They also appear to be much more conditioned by a certain conception of political and economic society, and intended to apply to a more particularized situation, than any of the previous conceptions we have been considering. Aristotle's theory, as we have seen, allows a large place for equality, but Rawls goes much further and not only drops the notion of proportionate equality but specifies a criterion for judging equality and inequality, which according to Aristotle, is always a political question. Furthermore, as is shown by the reference to a "savings principle," which is meant to assure that justice is done to future generations, it seems clear that we are also supposed to be operating in a modern economy of abundance. These observations by themselves are not a criticism of Rawls; he admits that he is providing a conception of justice for a definite kind of society, that of modern, Western, libertarian, democratic countries with economies of abundance. Conceivably, he might maintain that this society is also the most just that has yet existed (but I do not find that he ever says so expressly), since the literal application of his principles would result in condemning all the great cultures of the past as unjust for allowing slavery or for not working to the advantage of the least advantaged. At any rate, the assumptions underlying Rawls's principles seem to make his theory much more restricted—less philosophical and more political—than the previous theories of justice that we have been considering.

Why then should these two principles be accepted as basic for justice? Rawls gives many reasons, developed at great length, but they finally reduce to this: it is the rational thing to accept such principles, being what rational persons would do if they were put in a situation in which the minimum conditions of justice were clearly visible. In this methodological respect, Rawls's procedure bears some similarity to that of Plato in *The Republic,* where Socrates puts forward a hypothetical ideal state in which the principles of justice would be "writ large" and plain enough for any rational man to see. Rawls's conception of a rational man, however, as well as the position in which he is locating him for the sake of discovering justice, is vastly different from Plato's.

The special notion of rationality adopted by Rawls as "the standard one familiar in social theory" (we are referred to the welfare economists) is controlling for his position. The rational person is one who has "a coherent set of preferences between the options open to him. He ranks these options according to how well they further his purposes; he follows the plan which will satisfy more of his desires rather than less, and which has the greater chance of being successfuly executed."[107] Placed in a situation of risk and great uncertainty, the rational person is the sort who would adopt the "maximin rule" and rank alternatives by their worst possible outcomes, and who would then choose the alternative whose worst imaginable outcome would be better than the worst outcome of the others.[108]

The hypothetical situation we are to imagine is the one familiar in social contract doctrine where men are engaged in agreeing upon the principles by which they will be bound in the association they are establishing. Rawls introduces a special feature in what he calls "the veil of ignorance," whereby each person is supposed to be ignorant of "his place in society, his class position or social status; . . . his fortune in the distribution of natural assets and abilities, his intelligence and strength, and the like . . . his conception of the good, the particulars of his rational plan of life, or even the special features of his psychology . . . [and] the particular circumstances of their own society . . . its economic or political situation, or the level of civilization and culture it has been able to achieve." Such persons are further assumed to "have no information as to which generation they belong." However, they do know "the general facts about human society. They understand political affairs and the principles of economic theory; they know the basis of social organization and the laws of human psychology."[109] This knowledge (which is incidentally of a very contemporary kind, such as only men of our own time can be supposed to possess or even recognize) does much, of course, to counteract if not cancel the aforementioned ignorance. But there is a further special feature in that the persons are supposed also to know that "their society is subject to the circumstances of justice and whatever this implies." These circumstances are conditions of moderate scarcity, in which the parties strive for their own good without being bound by "prior moral ties to each other." Justice, for Rawls as for Hume, exists only where there is conflict, and where competing interests exist; hence there is no such thing as justice in heaven.[110]

Why in such a situation would it be "rational" for rational persons, so understood, to accept these two principles over all others as the basis of justice, i.e., as the basic rules for governing their relations with one another? They would accept them, Rawls argues, because such principles satisfy the "maximin rule" of assuring the best possible outcome if the worst should eventuate, since they are the principles that "a person would choose for the design of a society in which his enemy is to assign him his place."[111] As autonomous individuals, these rational persons will want to assure themselves of liberty to direct their lives as they wish. Knowing that men differ in their ideals of the good life, and not knowing, behind their "veil of ignorance," the ideals of the other participants, "equal liberty of conscience is the only principle that the persons in the original position can acknowledge," Rawls claims, and this is assured by adoption of the first principle, that of equal liberty.[112] Ignorant, too, of their own individual social, economic, and psychological position, they do not know that they are not the "least advantaged," and hence they want to assure that any inequalities in the social structure based on these respects redound to the benefit of the least advantaged, and this outcome is secured by adoption of the second principle.[113]

Acceptance of these two principles amounts to recognition of liberty and equality as two natural rights, and though Rawls does not seem to care much for the term, he does say, in a footnote, that his theory has "the characteristic marks of a natural rights theory" in that it is ultimately based "solely on certain natural attributes the presence of which can be ascertained by natural reason using common sense methods of inquiry ... established independently from social conventions and legal norms."[114] There is no question that his conception of justice is independent of law as well as a criterion of it, and hence is opposed to the Positive Law theory. One may well question, however, the extent of its independence from social convention and the features that characterize the Social Good position.

The principles that underlie justice for Rawls are presented as the result of a contract drawn up for the establishment of a society, a contract under which the parties are supposed to have "no prior moral ties to each other" and to want to be as free as they can be to do as they like. This differs strikingly from a typical Natural Right theory such as Locke's, where men have moral obligations to one another prior to the social contract, and whose liberty, as distinct from license, is constrained by natural law. Justice, for Locke, is prior to society, and that is typical of the Natural Right position.

In contrast, for Rawls, liberty and equality are principles that control justice, and both are prior to it. This is the very reverse of what is maintained by typical Natural Right theory. For example, Adler maintains that "the controlling principle is justice, not liberty and equality; for without justice, liberty cannot be restrained from becoming license, and the personal inequalities among men cannot be prevented from producing an inequitable inequality of conditions."[115] That is the opposite idea.

Rawls also, in contrast to the Natural Right theorists, strongly emphasizes the subordination of justice to society. For him, it is not human nature but the social scheme that determines one's due, "that is, it [a just scheme] allots to each what he is entitled to as defined by the scheme itself."[116] Rawls recognizes the existence of "natural duties," such as the duty to uphold justice, to provide mutual aid, not to injure another — principles that "have no necessary connection with [our] institutions or social practices,"[117] — but he regards such duties as subordinate for individuals to what may be established by institutions.[118] He maintains that principles of justice are the result of choice and agreement, and that they demand unanimity because they are procedural, not contentual, insofar as they involve an ideal of the good,[119] all of which are tenets more characteristic of the Social Good than of the Natural Right position on justice.

In still other respects than that of the relation between justice and liberty, Rawls reverses the typical Natural Right position. The principles of justice are not based on the notion of respect for persons or a recognition of their inherent worth and dignity but rather the other way round—that is, the conception of what is due the person is derived solely from what the principles of justice dictate.[120] Nor are inequalities in effort or ability recognized as having any inherent right to differential treatment, except as granted by society. This revises Aristotle's natural principle of equality that equals should be treated equally and unequals unequally. The unequal, too, are to be equally treated, the undeserving alike with the deserving. Indeed, Rawls is highly suspicious of desert or deservingness as a principle of justice. Inequalities of natural endowment, as well as those of social condition, are viewed by him as arbitrary accidents if not actual injustices; even the greater effort that a man might exert is attributed to a fortunate family background and dismissed as any basis for desert.[121] In fact, Rawls conceives the task of justice as largely one of nullifying and mitigating, even of redressing, the inequalities of nature and society.[122]

If, then, Rawls's theory includes some element of natural right—in its principles of liberty and equality—this is mixed with the idea of social good, and is nearly if not actually dominated by it. Rawls is thus in the same class as Rescher, who likewise holds a theory of justice that combines natural right and social good. But the two men differ strongly in their basic principles. Both emphasize justice as fairness, but they mean very different things by *fairness*. For Rescher, fairness consists in recognizing the equality of men in their essential worth, with a consequent right to a "utility floor" consisting of the minimum goods needed for leading a good life. But he gives equal weight to the principle of proportionality, or desert based on inequality, as establishing a title to right that is independent of social convention. He also holds that just distribution will have to vary with the condition of the society—that of an economy of scarcity differing, for example, from that in an economy of abundance, where the total good could take precedence over that of the "least advantaged."[123] Fairness for Rawls, however, involves an overriding emphasis upon equality, and requires the subordination of the principle of desert or proportionate equality to a distribution consistent with a certain conception of society, a conception implicit in his Difference Principle.

In connection with the theories of Rescher and Rawls, it is illuminating to consider the work of Professor Chaim Perelman on justice. For Perelman has developed a theory primarily in response to the Positive Law position, whereas Rescher and Rawls, as we have seen, were responding mainly to the utilitarian idea of the social good. Perelman is also much more concerned than either of the American writers is with the question of the degree of certitude that may be looked for in matters of justice.

Taking a judge deciding a case before him as the paradigm of the determination of justice, Perelman acknowledges that the identification of justice with the rule of law would satisfy the need for uniformity, security, and predictability; but he maintains that "it is not enough to satisfy our need for justice," since we may legitimately demand whether the juridical order and the law itself is just.[124] But if it is wrong to demand of justice the certitude that is found in positive law, so too it is a mistake to look for an absolutely just system of rules that would be recognized as such by all reasonable men, and this is the charge that Perelman directs against the theory of Rawls.

Perelman deals with Rawls's earlier papers that preceded his book, and some of his particular criticisms have now been met, but the main one about certitude still applies. In effect, Perelman claims that Rawls wants more certitude than the matter of justice allows. Justice is a moral matter, and in morals as in philosophy, in contrast with the situation in science, Perelman argues that unanimity as to what constitutes the reasonable thing is not to be expected. "If there were an objective criterion, expressible in quantitative terms . . . of what in each case was the best reason, then a single judgment would be reasonable, namely, to conform one's behavior to the quantitatively determined result."[125] But this is not the case regarding justice, Perelman claims, and criticizes Rawls for using a model from game theory in a situation where it does not apply. On the contrary, Perelman argues, such a model entirely leaves out of account the fact that many rights "are for the most part products of a historic past" that men will not readily be persuaded to forgo "in the name of abstract principles." It would be gratuitous to apply Rawls's principles to the world community and "try from the start to establish equal justice among the inhabitants of the earth, by suppressing as far as possible the inequalities in wealth and ability that now exist among the various regions of the world," Perelman argues. What evidence is there, he asks, to persuade men "that it is just to give up the advantages thus far obtained for them by their historical situation"?[126]

Perelman's own position on justice is also best regarded as a combination of Social Good and Natural Right theory. The just act, Perelman holds, is one that is " 'compatible with the greatest number—and the greatest intensity—of values and beliefs' . . . of the community in whose name political power is being exercised." But such an act must also be rational and, hence, not "partial to sectional interests, with no regard for values accepted by the universal audience."[127] By this appeal to "the universal audience," Perelman would avoid "the relativization of the notion of political justice" and would thus establish a standard based on man as such.[128]

## The three-sided controversy about justice

It has become clear, especially in the formulations of the most recent theories, that the degree of certitude to be sought in matters of justice constitutes an issue on which there is major disagreement. The Positive

Law theory demands the most certitude. In fact, it might be claimed that this theory is led to identify justice with legality because of its great desire to have a standard and norm of action that is certain, objective, applicable, and capable of providing a definite decision, all of which are qualities possessed by the positive law. By the same token, the main argument of the Positive Law theory against the other theories is that they are so imprecise and inexact that no question of justice can ever be decided definitely and unequivocally, the "social good" as well as "natural right" being susceptible of different and opposed interpretations.

Social Good theory tolerates less certitude than Positive Law theory does. This is so for Rawls, notwithstanding that he includes quantifiable factors in his formulation. Thus his Difference Principle is indeterminate and inapplicable even when some definition, say by law, is given of the "least advantaged." For if this minimum social position is identified, as Rawls suggests, with that of the unskilled worker or those with less than half of the median income,[129] the question still remains open regarding what is to count as "the benefit of the least advantaged," as well as the question of who is to decide it, the least advantaged themselves or somebody else.

With respect to certitude, Natural Right theory is still more indeterminate, and this for several reasons. In the first place, there is no agreement among Natural Right authors regarding the number of natural rights, whether there is one only, or many. Then, too, there is disagreement about the specificity of such rights, and how they are to be determined. Even when they are spelled out, as in a bill of rights, the question of priority remains undecided, without any method of determining in case of conflict which is to have priority over the others. A still further complication is to be found in the unique status of the very notion of natural right. No one in the controversy over justice ever denies all content to such terms as *law* or the *social good*, though different interpretations and different weight may be given to it. But according to some writers on justice, there is no such thing as a "natural" right; the notion is empty of meaning. Thus, as we have seen, two of the three theories that represent basic and paradigmatic positions in the controversy as a whole manage to account for justice without any reference to natural right. Yet, despite this fact, many authors, as we have also seen, do adopt what we have identified as the Natural Right position.

The special status of natural right within the controversy also indicates that the underlying issue is the relation between justice and society, whether it is based on nature or convention—a very old question that was argued among the ancient Greeks as the issue between *Physis* and *Nomos*. In all theories of the subject, justice is a social virtue and a norm governing man's conduct toward others. But one group of theories holds that it is based exclusively on the conventions of society and its laws and the good they seek, whereas another group of theories maintains that justice is ultimately based on the nature of man, on what he is, and not on what he has agreed to in society.

This basic division shows up in the position taken toward the classical definition of justice as rendering to each his due. One group of theories holds that there is something due to man as man, while the other group denies this and declares that what is due is only and entirely what has been determined within society by its laws or its aims.

The same fundamental division appears again in the accounts given by the various theories of the approbative and obligatory character of justice. For one position, the just thing elicits approval and imposes an obligation ultimately because it is seen to be just, i.e., a good, and a good to be done. For the other position, both the approbation and the obligatoriness belonging to justice stem ultimately from social conventions, and except that it is for the good of others or that of their association, there is no reason to approve of justice and no obligation to conform one's actions to its norm.

Although the division with regard to natural right is fundamental, this does not mean that the entire controversy over justice is at best a two-sided one. For it must be remembered that the issue regarding law also serves to divide all theories of justice into two groups, those that make positive law the fundamental criterion of justice and those that do not. This is an important division, not only because it yields a strong, clearly delineated group of theories but also because one extreme within it unequivocally bases justice on force. Nevertheless, the theories clearly holding the Positive Law position on justice are few in number. The issue regarding natural right is thus more pervasive in its influence, and for that reason merits further attention.

If natural right is held to provide the basis of justice, it does so in the sense that human nature itself shows what is due to man—not human nature as empirically given with a variety of abilities, talents, dispositions, and qualities of many degrees but human nature as seen in the ideal of the good man, which can serve, as Aristotle argues, to constitute an ethical norm.[130] That human nature so conceived shows how man should be treated, shows what is due him and hence what is his right, is the basic and identifying proposition of the Natural Right theory. Proponents of the theory differ widely in their understanding of how these rights come to be known. Some Natural Right authors hold that man would know them even if he lived entirely outside society, whereas others maintain that men ordinarily learn about their rights through living in society under its laws. What is essential to the position is not agreement on how men come to know their natural rights but that such rights exist and that they are the ultimate basis of justice.

Opposition to the doctrine of natural right sometimes seems to be based on little more than a prejudice against the use of the word *nature*. In this regard, Dewey once wrote: " 'Give a dog a bad name and hang him.' Human nature has been the dog of professional moralists, and consequences accord with the proverb."[131] Some writers prefer to speak of "moral" or of "human" or "inalienable" rights, but such terms function in their theories just as "natural" right would, and allow them to be counted in the Natural Right group.

Insofar as the opposition is substantial and not merely verbal, the arguments against the Natural Right position can be reduced to three: the argument from variability, from indefiniteness, and from the mode of justification.

The argument from variability rests on the claim that there is no general, unchanging agreement to be found among men regarding the content of natural right. What is declared to be natural right in one society is denied in another, or the same society will both affirm and deny it at different times, or within the same society at any one time some men will assert what others deny as a natural right. Thus only a few generations ago Americans were deeply and bitterly divided over whether it was naturally unjust to hold a person in chattel slavery. In the ancient world, it was widely held, as Aristotle argued, that some men are naturally slaves and hence could justly be treated as such, whereas today there is practically worldwide agreement that slavery is unjust because man by virtue of what he is possesses the right of personal freedom.

Against this argument from variability, the Natural Right theory advances a two-part answer. On the one hand, it denies that the variation and disagreement are as great as is charged. On the other hand, it offers an explanation of why disagreement should be expected with regard to natural right. Thus, on the first point, it is claimed that agreement and invariability are to be found among all men in all cultures and at all times regarding certain principles of social conduct, based on such convictions as the following: that taking a human life differs in seriousness from taking any other kind of life; that sexual relations need some kind of regulation; that men need rules and prohibitions to lead a common life. The different formulations and specifications of such principles in a wide diversity of customs and laws are no argument, it is maintained, against the general agreement on the principles themselves. It is argued further that even if disagreement over natural right were as great as claimed, this fact by itself would not prove that the rights themselves are variable, any more than disagreement over the shape of the earth would prove that the earth did not have one shape.

Disagreement about natural right is regarded as understandable. Natural right is not as evident as the sensible qualities of a physical object. Knowledge of it may sometimes be difficult to acquire. But the difficulty of knowing it is no argument against its existence, any more than the difficulty of deciding a law case is an argument against the existence of the law.

The charge of indefiniteness, as we have seen, is also frequently urged as an argument against the Natural Right position. Proponents of this position, however, while admitting the fact, deny that it constitutes an argument against the existence or standing of natural right as a norm. Men, sharing in the same specific nature, have the same natural needs, such as the need for bodily health and vigor, for a means of livelihood, and for the goods of pleasure and of individual and social improvement. These needs are the same for all men even though men in different times and places and according to their differing temperaments satisfy them in different ways. The natural right rooted in these natural needs provides, as it were, only the general principle, and it is through working out solutions to the problems of their daily lives that men discover how the principle is to be specified and applied. Laws and social practices may thus be considered as special applications and determinations of natural right. This feature shows, it is claimed, how progress may occur in the knowledge of natural right, and that men can come to know better, to see more clearly, what their natural rights are.

The third argument, concerning the justification of natural right, underlies both the arguments from variability and from indefiniteness. It is also the point at which the Positive Law and the Social Good theories begin to diverge in their disagreement with the Natural Right theory. Up to here, the arguments against the Natural Right position can be and are advanced by the proponents of both the opposing theories indistinguishably. Both also agree in charging that the Natural Right position is weak in its account of the way in which natural right is known and justified, but they do so finally for different reasons.

Beyond this point, it is argued that natural right is without rational justification, since it has no objective basis that is knowable in a way that can be verified or confirmed by any disinterested observer. Natural right, it is claimed, seems to be more a matter of faith than of evidence, and the appeal to intuition and self-evidence is dismissed as a repudiation of reason, a confession of ignorance. The notion that natural right is an inescapable if indemonstrable first principle is dismissed as irrational. But Positive Law and Social Good theories differ as to why this is so. The Positive Law position denies the objectivity of all moral or value judgments and, hence, the rationality of natural right as a moral principle. The Social Good position does not deny the objectivity of all moral judgments; it simply rejects the idea that nature, rather than society and its conventions, can establish justice as an objective norm.

When we have got that far, however, the controversy comes to a standstill as we face what seems to be a matter of fact rather than of argument. The Natural Right theory maintains, in effect, that one need only see what man is to recognize that he has a right to life, that his life must be respected in a way that is fundamentally different from that of other living things, and may not be taken without compelling justification. Against this claim, the other two theories maintain that they see no such thing; there is no natural right, there is only the right men have created as a result of their social and legal activity.

Between these two claims, how can we decide? Men obviously now learn of their rights through living and being educated in society. To escape this limitation, Natural Right authors frequently invent ways in which primitive man might have acquired knowledge of right, or imagine as a kind of ideal experiment what man would be like living outside the bounds of society. But Positive Law and Social Good theorists dismiss such examples as "desert island" cases, of questionable value in themselves and without any force as evidence. The controversy concerning justice thus comes up against the fundamental question of what is to count as acceptable moral reasoning and good evidence in deciding questions of value.

Positive Law theory takes the simplest position by basing justice on law and reducing moral judgments to personal choice, even subjective choice based on subjective feeling. The Social Good position is more complex; while admitting that justice may sometimes be a question of law, it subjects the law itself to the standard of the social good. The Natural Right position is the most complex of the three inasmuch as it includes both the legal and the social good within its account of justice, but bases both of them on what it holds to be a basic right, one that is rooted in the nature of man.

---

[1] See "The Idea of Equality," in *The Great Ideas Today,* 1968, pp. 303–4.

[2] R. G. Collingwood, *An Autobiography* (Oxford: Oxford University Press, 1939; reprint ed. 1970), p. 61.

[3] The claim as to Aristotle is that of Mortimer Adler, referring to a well-known remark of A. N. Whitehead's about Plato.

[4] Since Glaucon claims to be restating the position of Thrasymachus, one might interpret his theory as a variant of the Positive Law position, as I did in my book, *The Idea of Justice* (1967), p. 69.

[5] *To ta opheilómena hekásto apodidónai dikaion esti*—the similarity with the classical definition is lost in Jowett's translation of it as "the re-payment of a debt is just" (*GBWW*, Vol. 7, p. 297).

[6] *Leviathan; GBWW*, Vol. 23, pp. 84, 85.

[7] Ibid., p. 85.

[8] Ibid., p. 91.

[9] Ibid., p. 86.

[10] Ibid., p. 99.

[11] Ibid., p. 100.

[12] Ibid., p. 91.

[13] Ibid., p. 91.

[14] Ibid., p. 157.

[15] Ibid., p. 130.

[16] Ibid., p. 55.

[17] Ibid., p. 130.

[18] Ibid., p. 139.

[19] Ibid., p. 131.

[20] Ibid., p. 91.

[21] Ibid., p. 102.

[22] Ibid., p. 115.

[23] Ibid., p. 157; cf. p. 115.

[24] Ibid., p. 92.

25 Alf Ross, *On Law and Justice* (Berkeley: University of California Press, 1959), p. 274.

26 Many representatives of the Positive Law position could be cited, especially from England and America, in addition to those we have discussed. Any list of them would extend from the ancient Greek sophist Thrasymachus down to the contemporary legal philosopher Hans Kelsen and the Scandinavian jurist Alf Ross. It would include men who hold different philosophies: Spinoza is a rationalist, Hobbes an empiricist, John Austin (1790–1859) a utilitarian and founder of the analytical school of jurisprudence; also, Kelsen is a Kantian, while Wesley Hohfield (1879–1918) and Oliver Wendell Holmes (1841–1935) were indebted to pragmatism, yet all subscribe to the Positive Law theory of justice.

27 *Utilitarianism; GBWW*, Vol. 43, p. 467.

28 Ibid., p. 466.

29 *A Treatise of Human Nature*, bk. 2, pt. 3, sec. 3 (Oxford: Clarendon Press, 1888; reprint ed. 1955), p. 417.

30 *An Enquiry concerning the Principles of Morals*, sec. 3, pt. 1 (Oxford: Clarendon Press, 1894), pp. 183–92.

31 *Treatise*, bk. 3, pt. 2, sec. 2, p. 489.

32 Ibid., p. 498.

33 *Utilitarianism; GBWW*, Vol. 43, p. 470.

34 Henry Sidgwick, *The Methods of Ethics*, 7th ed. (London: Macmillan & Co., 1907; reprint ed. 1962), p. 83.

35 Ibid., p. 269.

36 Ibid., pp. 272–73.

37 *Treatise*, bk. 3, pt. 2, sec. 6, p. 526; cf. pp. 490–91.

38 *Methods*, pp. 265–94.

39 Ibid., p. 447.

40 *Enquiry*, app. 1, no. 240, p. 290.

41 Ibid., sec. 4, no. 171, p. 210.

42 Ibid., sec. 3, pt. 2, no. 162, p. 203.

43 *Treatise*, bk. 3, pt. 2, sec. 1, p. 484.

44 *Methods*, p. 200.

45 Ibid., pp. 32–37.

46 Ibid., p. 379.

47 Ibid., p. 440.

48 *Enquiry*, app. 3, no. 258, p. 307.

49 Ibid., app. 3, no. 256, p. 304.

50 *Treatise*, bk. 3, pt. 3, sec. 1, p. 579.

51 *Utilitarianism; GBWW*, Vol. 43, p. 469.

52 *Methods*, p. 268.

53 The Social Good theory of justice has had many adherents, particularly in Great Britain and the United States. Besides Hume and the classical utilitarians, Bentham, Mill, and Sidgwick, it has among its advocates the English radical and utopian anarchist William Godwin (1756–1836) and the leader of the "New Liberals" in British politics, L. T. Hobhouse (1864–1929). In the U.S., it has counted among its representatives the "legal realist" and former dean of Harvard Law School Roscoe Pound (1870–1964) as well as the Yale idealist philosopher Brand Blanshard (1892–    ).

54 Julius Stone, *Human Law and Human Justice* (London: Stevens & Sons, 1965), p. 333; cf. pp. 340–41.

55 *Summa Theologica* II–II, Qu. 51, art. 1.

56 *An Essay concerning Human Understanding*, bk. 4, chap. 3, p. 18; *GBWW*, Vol. 35, p. 318.

57 *Neuf Leçons sur les notions premières de la philosophie morale* (Paris: P. Téqui, 1949), p. 167.

58 Ibid., p. 163.

59 *Nicomachaean Ethics* 1130a2–20; *GBWW*, Vol. 9, p. 377.

60 *Neuf Leçons*, pp. 166–67.

61 *Concerning Civil Government*, chap. 2, pp. 4–7; *GBWW*, Vol. 35, pp. 25–26.

62 *Commentary on the Nicomachaean Ethics*, no. 1016.

63 *Ethics* 1134b19; cf. *GBWW*, Vol. 9, p. 382.

64 *Politics* 1325b7; cf. *GBWW*, Vol. 9, p. 529.

65 *Ethics* 1129b1; cf. *GBWW*, Vol. 9, p. 376.

66 *Politics* 1282b22; cf. *GBWW*, Vol. 9, p. 480.

67 *Ethics* 1129b1; cf. *GBWW*, Vol. 9, p. 376.

[68] *The Rights of Man and Natural Law* (New York: Charles Scribner's Sons, 1943), p. 65.

[69] M. J. Adler, *The Time of Our Lives* (New York: Holt, Rinehart & Winston, 1970), pp. 141–42.

[70] Ibid., p. 143.

[71] *Politics* 1279a17 (*GBWW*, Vol. 9, p. 476); 1282b10 (*GBWW*, Vol. 9, pp. 479–80).

[72] *Neuf Leçons*, p. 54.

[73] *Ethics* 1134b9; *GBWW*, Vol. 9, p. 382.

[74] *Essays on the Law of Nature* (Oxford: Clarendon Press, 1954; reprint ed. 1958), p. 199.

[75] M. J. Adler, *The Time of Our Lives*, p. 295.

[76] *Essays on the Law of Nature*, pp. 181, 185.

[77] *Ethics* 1169a15 (*GBWW*, Vol. 9, p. 422); 1155b19 (*GBWW*, Vol. 9, p. 406).

[78] *La Philosophie morale* (Paris: Librairie Gallimard, 1960), pp. 535–36; cf. p. 538.

[79] M. J. Adler, *The Time of Our Lives*, pp. 158, 175–76.

[80] Ibid., p. 183.

[81] *Ethics* 1134a1–6; *GBWW*, Vol. 9, p. 381.

[82] *Summa Theologica* I–II, Qu. 99, art. 5, reply obj. 1; *GBWW*, Vol. 20, p. 250.

[83] Ibid., II–II, Qu. 80, art. 1.

[84] Of the three basic positions, the Natural Right theory comprehends the greatest diversity among its proponents. Extending in time from antiquity down to the present, it includes philosophers, theologians, jurists, and political leaders. Among philosophers, it counts not only Plato, Aristotle, Cicero, and Aquinas, but also Locke, the empiricist, Leibniz, the rationalist, the French neo-Thomist writers Jacques Maritain (1882–1973) and Yves Simon (1903–61), the German phenomenologist Max Scheler (1874–1928), and the contemporary American moral philosopher William Frankena (1908–    ). Among theologians, it includes Catholics such as Aquinas, Protestants such as the Swiss Reformed theologian Emil Brunner (1889–1966), and the post-Reformation jurists Hugo Grotius (1583–1645) and Samuel von Pufendorf (1632–94). Lawyers and legal philosophers who have taken this position, besides Cicero and Montesquieu, are the commentator on the English common law Sir William Blackstone (1723–80), the Italian jurist and scholar Giorgio del Vecchio (1878–    ), and the Australian lawyer and professor Julius Stone (1907–    ). Among politicians, it includes not only the conservative Edmund Burke (1729–97) but also the American Revolutionary leaders Thomas Jefferson (1743–1826) and Thomas Paine (1737–1809).

[85] *The Philosophy of Right*, "Additions," no. 137, par. 217; *GBWW*, Vol. 46, p. 138.

[86] G. del Vecchio, *Justice: An Historical and Philosophical Essay* (Edinburgh: Edinburgh University Press, 1952), chap. 11, n. 12, p. 131.

[87] *Right*, no. 44 (*GBWW*, Vol. 46, p. 23); no. 238 (*GBWW*, Vol. 46, p. 76); "Additions," no. 146 (*GBWW*, Vol. 46, p. 140).

[88] Ibid., no. 3; *GBWW*, Vol. 46, p. 10.

[89] *The Science of Right*; *GBWW*, Vol. 42, p. 401.

[90] Ibid., pp. 432, 433, 436.

[91] Ibid., p. 435.

[92] Ibid., p. 409.

[93] Ibid., p. 401.

[94] In my book I classified both Kant and Hegel among proponents of the Natural Right theory, but noted that they were notoriously resistant to classification; p. 121.

[95] Nicholas Rescher, *Distributive Justice* (Indianapolis: The Bobbs-Merrill Company, 1966), p. 11.

[96] Ibid., p. 8.

[97] Ibid., pp. 26–27.

[98] Ibid., p. 48.

[99] Ibid., p. 29.

[100] Ibid., pp. 56, 62.

[101] Ibid., pp. 66–67.

[102] Ibid., pp. 118–20.

[103] Ibid., p. 90.

[104] John Rawls, *A Theory of Justice* (Cambridge, Mass.: Harvard University Press, Belknap Press, 1971), p. 39.

[105] Ibid., p. 62.

[106] Ibid., pp. 302–3.

[107] Rawls, p. 143.

[108] Ibid., pp. 152–53.
[109] Ibid., p. 137.
[110] Ibid., pp. 128–29.
[111] Ibid., p. 152.
[112] Ibid., p. 207.
[113] Ibid., p. 151.
[114] Ibid., pp. 505–6 n.
[115] M. J. Adler, *The Common Sense of Politics* (New York: Holt, Rinehart & Winston, 1971), p. 130.
[116] Rawls, p. 313.
[117] Ibid., p. 114; cf. p. 108.
[118] Ibid., pp. 334–35; cf. p. 10.
[119] Ibid., pp. 446–47.
[120] Ibid., pp. 585–86.
[121] Ibid., p. 104.
[122] Ibid., pp. 15, 72, 100, 511, 585.
[123] Rescher, pp. 117–20.
[124] Chaim Perelman, *Justice* (New York: Random House, 1967), pp. 25–26.
[125] Ibid., p. 108.
[126] Ibid., p. 48.
[127] Ibid., pp. 67, 86.
[128] Ibid., p. 68.
[129] Rawls, p. 98.
[130] *Ethics*, 1176a15; *GBWW*, Vol. 9, p. 430.
[131] John Dewey, *Human Nature and Conduct* (New York: Henry Holt & Co., 1922), p. 1.

## BIBLIOGRAPHY

This bibliography is restricted to books published since 1950. For books published before that date, the reader should consult the bibliography provided in the *Syntopicon*, following Chapter 42 on JUSTICE, and the author's book, *The Idea of Justice* (1967), of which the present essay is at once a development, a condensation, and an updating.

BAIER, KURT. *The Moral Point of View.* New York: Random House, 1965.

BAYLIS, C. A. *Ethics.* New York: Holt, Rinehart & Winston, 1958.

BENN, S. I., and PETERS, R. S. *Social Principles and the Democratic State.* London: George Allen & Unwin, 1959.

BLANSHARD, BRAND. *Reason and Goodness.* London: George Allen & Unwin, 1961.

BODENHEIMER, EDGAR. *Treatise on Justice.* New York: Philosophical Library, 1967.

BOWIE, N. E. *Towards a New Theory of Distributive Justice.* Amherst: University of Massachusetts Press, 1971.

BRANDT, R. B. *Ethical Theory.* Englewood Cliffs, N.J.: Prentice-Hall, 1959.

———. *Social Justice.* Englewood Cliffs, N.J.: Prentice-Hall, 1962.

COHEN, F. S. *Ethical Systems and Legal Ideals.* Ithaca, N.Y.: Cornell University Press, 1959.

DEL VECCHIO, GIORGIO. *Justice: An Historical and Philosophical Essay.* Edited by A. H. CAMPBELL. Edinburgh: Edinburgh University Press, 1952.

DRUMMOND, WILLIAM F. *Social Justice.* Milwaukee: Bruce Publishing Co., 1955.

EWING, A. C. *Ethics.* London: English Universities Press, 1957.

FRANKENA, W. K. *Some Beliefs about Justice.* Lawrence: University of Kansas Press, 1966.

FREUND, P. A. *On Law and Justice.* Cambridge, Mass.: Harvard University Press, Belknap Press, 1973.

FRIEDRICH, C. J. *The Philosophy of Law in Historical Perspective.* 2d ed. Chicago: University of Chicago Press, 1963.

FULLER, LON LUVOIS. *The Morality of Law.* New Haven: Yale University Press, 1964.

GINSBERG, MORRIS. *On Justice in Society.* Ithaca, N.Y.: Cornell University Press, 1965.

JAFFE, RAYMOND. *The Pragmatic Conception of Justice.* Berkeley: University of California Press, 1960.

KELSEN, HANS. *General Theory of Law and State.* Translated by ANDERS WEDBERG. New York: Russell & Russell, 1961.

———. *What Is Justice?* Berkeley: University of California Press, 1957.

KIEFER, H. E., and MUNITZ, MILTON K. *Ethics and Social Justice.* Albany: State University of N.Y. Press, 1970.

MABBOTT, J. D. *An Introduction to Ethics.* London: Hutchinson University Library, 1966.

MARITAIN, JACQUES. *Man and the State.* Chicago: University of Chicago Press, 1951.

———. *La Philosophie morale.* Paris: Librairie Gallimard, 1960.

MELDEN, A. I. *Rights and Right Conduct.* Oxford: Basil Blackwell, 1959.

NATHAN, N. M. L. *The Concept of Justice.* London: The Macmillan Press, 1971.

NELSON, LEONARD. *System of Ethics.* Translated by NORBERT GUTERMAN. New Haven: Yale University Press, 1956.

NOMOS VI. *Justice.* Edited by C. J. FRIEDRICH, J. W. CHAPMAN. New York: Atherton Press, 1963.

OLAFSON, FREDERICK, ed. *Justice and Social Policy.* Englewood Cliffs, N.J.: Prentice-Hall, 1961.

———. *Principles and Persons: An Ethical Interpretation of Existentialism.* Baltimore: Johns Hopkins Press, 1967.

PERELMAN, CHAIM. *Justice.* New York: Random House, 1967.

PIEPER, JOSEF. *Justice.* Translated by L. E. LYNCH. London: Faber & Faber, 1957.

POUND, ROSCOE. *Jurisprudence.* St. Paul, Minn.: West Publishing Co., 1959.

RAPHAEL, D. DAICHES. *Moral Judgement.* London: George Allen & Unwin, 1955.

RAWLS, JOHN. *A Theory of Justice.* Cambridge, Mass.: Harvard University Press, Belknap Press, 1971.

RESCHER, NICHOLAS. *Distributive Justice.* Indianapolis: Bobbs-Merrill, 1966.

ROSS, ALF. *On Law and Justice.* Berkeley: University of California Press, 1959.

SCHUTZ, ALFRED. *The Phenomenology of the Social World.* Evanston, Ill.: Northwestern University Press, 1967.

SIMON, YVES. *The Tradition of Natural Law.* Edited by VUKAN KUIC. New York: Fordham University Press, 1965.

STONE, JULIUS. *Human Law and Human Justice.* London: Stevens & Sons, 1965.

STRAUSS, LEO. *Natural Right and History.* Chicago: University of Chicago Press, 1953.

STROLL, AVRUM. *The Emotive Theory of Ethics.* Berkeley: University of California Press, 1954.

TILLICH, PAUL. *Love, Power, and Justice.* New York: Oxford University Press, 1954.

VON WRIGHT, G. H. *An Essay in Deontic Logic and the General Theory of Action.* Acta Philosophica Fennica, fasc. 21. Amsterdam: North-Holland Publishing Co., 1968.

———. *The Varieties of Goodness.* London: Routledge & Kegan Paul, 1963.

## NOTE TO THE READER

JUSTICE is the subject of Chapter 42 of the *Syntopicon*. Of particular relevance to Mr. Bird's essay are the readings listed under Topic 6, "Justice and liberty: the theory of human rights." See also Topics 9a and 9b, devoted to aspects of political justice, and Topics 10a and 10b, which deal with justice and law. Among the cross-references that follow the listings of references, those under "Problems of justice in government and law" would be the most useful to look up.

Several of the works in *GGB* deal with justice of one kind or another. See Dickens, "A Full and Faithful Report of the Memorable Trial of Bardell against Pickwick" (Vol. 2, pp. 391– 448); the "Meditation on the Divine Will," "The Gettysburg Address," and the "Second Inaugural Address" of Abraham Lincoln (Vol. 6, pp. 758–61); Melville's "Billy Budd" (Vol. 3, pp. 31–98); and both the essay on "Civil Disobedience" and "A Plea for Captain John Brown" by Henry David Thoreau (Vol. 6, pp. 695–732).

# PART FOUR

# Three Classics of Science

*Two New Sciences*
Galileo Galilei

*The Loadstone
and
Magnetic Bodies*
William Gilbert

*The Motion
of the
Heart and Blood*
William Harvey

# Three Classics of Science

William A. Wallace

Father Wallace, a member of the Dominican Order, is professor of history and philosophy of science at the Catholic University of America in Washington, D.C. Educated at Manhattan College, New York City, the Catholic University of America (Ph.D. in philosophy, 1952), and the University of Fribourg, Switzerland (Th.D., 1961), he has been an indefatigable researcher and a prolific writer in the history and philosophy of science for over twenty years. He is particularly interested in medieval and early modern science and in the development of scientific methodology, on which he has written numerous articles for learned journals and several books. Among the latter, a two-volume work entitled *Causality and Scientific Explanation* (1972–73), which surveys the development of science since medieval times, has been called "a revolutionary work of major proportions" and an "exceptionally important book" by authorities in the field.

Active in religious as well as in scientific and scholarly pursuits, Father Wallace has also published *The Role of Demonstration in Moral Theology* (1962) and *Cosmogony* (vol. 10 of the English edition of the *Summa Theologiae*, 1967), among other works. He is past president of the American Catholic Philosophical Association (1969), and has been associate editor of *The Thomist* since 1962.

t is a commonplace to salute such thinkers as Galileo, Harvey, and Gilbert as "the founders of modern science," but few who use this expression attempt to acquaint themselves with the works these men have authored, the classical contributions that first made science a reality in the West. Within the covers of Volume 28 of the *Great Books* three such writings invite our attention, and the purpose of this review is to make them accessible to the reader who would like to meet these "founding fathers" in the forum where they present themselves best, viz., in their own masterworks. All three of the great books featured here were written within the first thirty-eight years of the seventeenth century, and none can be properly appreciated without some knowledge of the thought currents of those times. Even readers with good scientific backgrounds must make conceptual adjustments to understand arguments such as those presented by Galileo. The following essay aims to facilitate such adjustments; it aims also to provide the *praenotamina* required for a fuller understanding of the works, to bridge over the more difficult passages so that their essential messages may be grasped as a whole. Perhaps the reader who uses the essay as a companion in reading Volume 28 will come to see too that many of the issues vexing scientists and philosophers of science in the present day were already implicit in the writings of science's founders, and that in some cases the solutions they insinuated were not notably different from those we now pride ourselves on having attained.

In scope the three great books range over the physical and biological sciences, treating in detail the basic concepts of mechanics, magnetism and electricity, and biology and medicine. In point of time Galileo's *Two New Sciences* was the last work written, and yet we shall begin with it and devote more space to it since it is the most seminal for modern thought and offers the greatest difficulty to the reader, if for no other reason than because of the mathematics it employs. Then we shall take up Gilbert's work on the magnet, which presents some interesting contrasts to Galileo's treatise and yet complements it by supplying a needed ingredient for the later work of Kepler and Newton that would finally lay bare the "System of the World."

We shall conclude with Harvey's classic on the circulation of the blood, as having elements in common with the two previous works while inaugurating new directions in experimental research that would serve as paradigms throughout the continuing development of the biological and medical sciences.

## Galileo: Two New Sciences

The last work of Galileo Galilei,[1] the *Two New Sciences*, came off the press of the Elzevir publishing company at Leiden, Holland, in July of 1638. At the time Galileo was seventy-four years of age, had already gone blind, and was to live out his house arrest in Arcetri, near Florence, but a few more years. The great book, his masterpiece, was produced under the most difficult of circumstances. As the title claims, it marked a new beginning: it heralded the birth of experimental science as we now know it; it dethroned Aristotle as the supreme authority in the schools; and it continued the momentous struggle its author had initiated against any external restriction being placed, by God or by man, on rational inquiry. Perhaps more than any other work it laid the foundations for modern thought; and within its pages it bears the unmistakable signs of the birth pangs that attended the delivery of the new era. Ironically, John Milton witnessed some of this travail during his journeys in Italy, where he had "found and visited the famous Galileo, grown old a prisoner to the Inquisition,"* unabashed in his pity for the great scientist, unaware that he too would be sightless before the composition of his own greatest work, *Paradise Lost*. As between the Puritan Milton and the Catholic Galileo it would be hard to decide who coupled the greater genius with the more indomitable will. Fortunately the decision need not be made, since we can allow a debt to both for the ideals, in literature and science, respectively, that they persevered in passing to us as their distinctive heritages.

The ideas that lie behind the *Two New Sciences* are partly methodological and partly substantive. To the first category pertain Galileo's use of mathematical reasoning and his insistence on experimentation for laying bare the secrets of nature, while to the second pertain two principles of mechanics, presumably found through the application of this twofold method, namely, the principle of inertia and the law of falling bodies. It is these ideas that will continually occupy us as we page through the *Two New Sciences*. Historians of science are unanimous that they constitute Galileo's essential achievement and that they are best set forth in this book with which he brought his life's work to completion. Paradoxically, not one of the four ideas is stated clearly and unambiguously at any place in the text that presents itself to our eyes.[2] Yet they are indeed present in the *Two New Sciences*, and their discovery will become a fascinating game once we read the work and begin to penetrate the thought it contains.

Unlike William Shakespeare, who was born in the same year as Galileo but who left no diaries or personal letters from which one might glimpse the intimate details of his life, Galileo bequeathed a mass of personal correspondence, notes, and calculations that shed light on almost every page of his masterwork. These materials were gathered and preserved by Galileo's faithful disciple, Vincenzio Viviani, and the larger portion of them can still be consulted today in the manuscript room of the Biblioteca Nazionale Centrale in Florence. Between 1890 and 1909 the dedicated Italian scholar, Antonio Favaro, produced a splendid edition in twenty volumes of *Le Opere di Galileo Galilei* (hereafter referred to simply as *Opere*), wherein much of this material may be found in print.[3] More recent scholarship, mainly within the past few years, has concentrated on fragments not included in the *Opere* and on certain clues, such as the watermarks of the sheets on which Galileo wrote both notes and letters, the latter usually dated, in order to trace more accurately the chronological development of his thought.

Such a resurgence of interest in the *Two New Sciences* in the 1970s attests to the fundamental importance of the work and its enduring appeal. The results of the investigations confirm an earlier suspicion that the discoveries therein reported by Galileo were made over a long period of time, extending back to his professorship at Padua and even to his earliest writings while at Pisa. When putting these results in final form, Galileo decided for several reasons to write partly in Italian and partly in Latin. His earlier academic writings, as was customary at the time, had been done mainly in Latin, whereas the controversial *Dialogues concerning the Two Chief World Systems* and most of his other polemical writings had been written in the vernacular. It is perhaps a sign of Galileo's hardiness that he elected to return to the form of the Italian dialogue for the first two days of the discussions reported in the *Two New Sciences*, and then on the third and fourth days to have the dialogists discuss, in Italian, a manuscript written in Latin by an unidentified author, whom they refer to as "the Academician" but who is clearly Galileo himself. The more technical and systematic exposition thus appeared in Latin, and so could be read by all interested scholars throughout Europe, whereas the surrounding discussions, more probing and tentative, were made available only to readers of Italian. This device also enabled Galileo to utilize materials already at hand and worked up in the two languages, which he wished to incorporate in his final treatise.

The translation we shall be using was prepared by Henry Crew and Alfonso de Salvio in 1914. It is highly readable and, though not entirely literal, for the most part conveys accurately the sense of Galileo's thought to modern readers. An Italian proverb, *traduttore-traditore*, reminds us however that all translators are traitors, or at least that the interpretations they

---

place on expressions can inadvertently falsify or distort the author's original meaning. We shall have occasion to return to this point when discussing one or two disputed passages in the translation and some alternative readings that have subsequently been suggested.

*Dedication*

Galileo's words are not always to be taken at face value, and perhaps nowhere is this more readily seen than in the dedicatory letter with which he begins the *Two New Sciences* (p. 129). On reading it one quickly gains the impression of an abject old man, complying with the sentence of the Holy Office that no more of his work is ever to be published again, wishing only to leave a manuscript somewhere for posterity, and expressing surprise that the Elzevirs now have the manuscript in hand and are preparing to publish it, only awaiting from him a letter of dedication. With the exception of his dejected state, none of these impressions is actually correct. Galileo was thoroughly crushed in spirit by the debacle in which had ended his prolonged efforts from 1609 to 1632 to gain acceptance of Copernicanism by the Church, and he was personally even more desolate from the sudden and cruel loss of his favorite daughter, Virginia. Born like his other two children out of wedlock, Virginia had been placed as a child in a convent at Arcetri for safekeeping; there she had flourished and eventually become a nun, taking the name of Sister Maria Celeste. Her letters to her father through the years are a delight to read, and their frequent visits during his stays in Florence were his major source of joy. One of the few consolations of his imprisonment at Arcetri, in fact, was that he was now again close to this beloved daughter. But early in 1634 Sister Maria Celeste fell mortally ill, and on April 2 she passed from this life, not yet having reached her thirty-fourth year. Galileo's grief over her death was inconsolable, and he fell into a mood of complete dejection. On April 27, 1634, he wrote to Geri Bocchineri that the state of his health had become most wretched:

> *My hernia has returned and is larger than before, my pulse is irregular with palpitations of the heart, a sadness and a great melancholy have overcome me, no appetite whatever, loathesome even to myself, and worst of all I keep hearing myself continually called by the voice of my beloved daughter.*[4]

Yet, despite these crushing burdens, by a heroic effort Galileo lifted himself out of the depression and soon, with remarkable equanimity, had started work on what was to become the *Two New Sciences*. In December 1634 the French ambassador, Francis Count of Noailles, asked the pope to release him from his sentence, and around the same time other foreigners, notably Father Marin Mersenne, secured the publication of some of his earlier writings in Paris, Strasbourg, and Leiden. By June 1635 Galileo had finished the first two days of the *Two New Sciences* and had begun to think of possibilities of having it too published, when completed, perhaps at Venice, or better, in Austria, Germany, or France, or better still in Holland, far out of reach of the Inquisition. During the summer of 1636 he entertained a representative of the Elzevirs at Arcetri, daringly discussed with him the possibility of having his press take the new work, and even entrusted to him the portions of the manuscript already completed. That same year in October he met the Count of Noailles personally, and sometime afterward decided to dedicate the *opus magnum* to him. Thus encouraged, Elzevir began to set the book in type early in 1637, though the fourth day of the dialogue was not yet finished at that time. By the end of the year it was finally done; by then Galileo had also suffered his last great personal misfortune, the loss of sight in both eyes.[5] But he was beyond the possibility of being further crushed, for his most important work was now concluded and the world had only to await its eventual publication.

The title under which it ultimately appeared, *Discorsi e dimostrazioni matematiche intorno a due nuove scienze attenenti alla mecanica & i movimenti locali,* rendered by Crew and Salvio simply as *Dialogues concerning the Two New Sciences*, is unfortunate both in its original form and in English translation. The clumsy original, which is translated more accurately as "Discourses and mathematical demonstrations concerning two new sciences pertaining to mechanics and local motion," was not Galileo's but one that the Elzevirs had put in its place. Galileo's proposed caption has been lost, but it is known that Galileo complained about this "low and common title" that had been substituted "for the noble and dignified one carried upon the title page."[6] Crew and Salvio, moreover, confused matters somewhat by mistranslating "Discourses" as "Dialogues." Galileo scholars usually distinguish between the *Dialogi* and the *Discorsi*, using the former to designate the *Dialogues concerning the Two Chief World Systems* of 1632 and the latter to designate the *Discourses concerning the Two New Sciences* of 1638. Both works, it is true, are written as dialogues, although the latter not only is that but contains a systematic exposition, whereas the former makes exclusive use of this Platonic mode of discourse.

### First day

The discussion of the first day opens with such a dialogue, and once again we meet the famous interlocutors, Salviati, Sagredo, and Simplicio, who figured so prominently in the *Two Chief World Systems* (p. 131). For those unacquainted with their earlier appearance it may be noted that Salviati and Sagredo are named after real personages who had been friends of Galileo, whereas Simplicio is a fictitious character. The first was a nobleman of Florence, Filippo Salviati, who died in 1614 and to whom Galileo had already dedicated his work on sunspots; in the *Two Chief World Systems* he had spoken the part of a militant Copernican, and here we can expect him to be a skilled proponent of Galileo's new views. The second was the

# DISCORSI
### E
# DIMOSTRAZIONI
## MATEMATICHE,

*intorno à due nuoue scienze*

Attenenti alla

## MECANICA & i MOVIMENTI LOCALI;

*del Signor*

## GALILEO GALILEI LINCEO,

Filosofo e Matematico primario del Serenissimo
Grand Duca di Toscana.

*Con vna Appendice del centro di grauità d'alcuni Solidi.*

### IN LEIDA,
Appresso gli Elseviri. M. D. C. XXXVIII.

Title page of the original edition of Galileo's *Discorsi*

patrician of Venice, Giovanfrancesco Sagredo, who had died in 1620 and in whose palace at Venice the earlier dialogue had been staged; he plays the role of a gracious but intelligent amateur, open to the new ideas and already half-converted to their acceptance. The last is Simplicio, ostensibly the name of the famous sixth-century commentator on Aristotle but also taking on, in Italian, the connotation of "simpleton," who is the somewhat dogmatic Aristotelian, objecting to the new doctrines as one might expect the peripatetic professors in the universities to do, and relentlessly being convinced, if not discredited, in the course of the discussions. The scene of the dialogue has changed from the palace to Venice's "famous arsenal," where the three are looking at ships and weapons under construction—a prophetic scene, heralding even then the alliance between science and the military that would continue to our own day. The setting also reveals Galileo's interest in practical mechanics and the engineering arts, which had occupied much of his time while a professor at Padua.

From the way the conversation begins we see that the first "new science" is to be concerned with the strength or resistance of materials; a series of topics relating to this subject occupies the entire first day, but the results are inconclusive and the matter is resumed on the second. A subsidiary theme, and this leading up to the second "new science" to be discussed on the third and fourth days, is the role of mathematics in physics. The fact that "mechanics has its foundation in geometry" (p. 131c) seems to be at variance with the experience of artisans in the arsenal who note that, although the geometry of large and small structures is similar, the materials of which they are constructed seem to make the small structure stronger than the large, and thus the principle requires investigation and deeper theoretical justification.

Galileo's use of the dialogue form permits him to make full use of his rhetorical skill—and here his style is of course at the opposite pole from modern scientific writing—but it also allows him to take up a variety of topics that are not rigorously connected. So we encounter fragmentary discussions, digressions, personal asides, lengthy expositions and proofs, regressions to material already discussed, etc., all presented in relatively undisciplined fashion. The range of topics, however, reveals the fertility of Galileo's mind and the way in which he was able to see a few underlying principles as having application through a wide range of phenomena.

The burden of the first discussion, as Sagredo points out, is to learn "what is the binding material which holds together the parts of solids so that they can scarcely be separated" (p. 134a). Earlier the same speaker had indicated an interest in what caused materials to resist breakage or fracture, and Salviati had hastened to assure him that "our Academician," meaning Galileo himself,

> had thought much upon this subject and according to his custom had demon-
> strated everything by geometrical methods so that one might fairly call this a

> *new science. For, although some of his conclusions had been reached by others, first of all by Aristotle, these are not the most beautiful and, what is more important, they had not been proven in a rigid manner from fundamental principles [p. 133b].*

The reference here is to the pseudo-Aristotelian *Questions in Mechanics*, which formed the basis for Galileo's early *Le Meccaniche*, written about 1594. In his reworking of this material Galileo now attempts an answer by reasoning that matter must be made up of finite divisible parts whose separation would cause a vacuum. Since it is axiomatic that nature abhors a vacuum, nature on the strength of this axiom must generate a force preventing such separation whose quantity and quality can be investigated by experiment (p. 135c–d). In a similar way Galileo further wishes to explain the failure of siphons and suction pumps to raise water to a height beyond eighteen cubits,[7] for if nature employs such a mechanism to resist the breaking of solids, it will do so in the case of liquids also, and so water will be found to have a tensile strength analogous to that of fibrous materials. Curiously, Galileo does not invoke the weight of air to explain suction phenomena, although he knew that air has weight and even devised methods for measuring it (pp. 164d–65c); moreover, the possibility of this alternative explanation had even been suggested to him by a contemporary.[8] But in this matter Galileo was still tied to medieval modes of thought, and so the discovery of the true explanation of siphoning and other barometric phenomena had to await the experimental work of his brilliant pupil, Evangelista Torricelli.

The foregoing consideration of minute vacua in matter prompts Salviati to make the assertion that "within a finite extent it is possible to discover an infinite number of vacua" (p. 139b–c), and this diverts the group to an extended discussion of the structure of mathematical continua, how lines may be made up of infinite numbers of points, etc., and various paradoxes that arise when comparing infinities of different types. The exposition that ensues is Aristotelian in inspiration, and Salviati again refers to the *Questions in Mechanics* for a good selection of related problems and their solutions. A more systematic account is to be found in the sixth book of Aristotle's *Physics*, which the interested reader may consult with profit at this point.* It is in a context such as this that we encounter Galileo's first mathematical demonstrations of the *Two New Sciences*, demonstrations that are somewhat complex for the sparse results to which they come (pp. 139c–41b, 151d–53a). The conclusions, as it turns out, are not essential for advancing the main argument, and so the proofs may be skipped if they offer any difficulty.[9]

Such a showing of mathematical skill, however, serves a useful purpose, for it elicits from Simplicio, who has been trying to follow the proofs and to see how they can be applied to an explanation of rarefaction and condensation, the pertinent criticism:

*The arguments and demonstrations which you have advanced are mathematical, abstract, and far removed from concrete matter; and I do not believe that when applied to the physical and natural world these laws will hold [p. 153b].*

Rising to the challenge, Salviati thereupon details a number of demonstrations relating the surfaces of bodies to the volumes they contain, and shows how these can find ready application when solving physical problems, among them calculations of the surface resistance bodies encounter when they fall through various media.[10] In the face of this display Simplicio must reluctantly admit:

*I am quite convinced; and, believe me, if I were again beginning my studies, I should follow the advice of Plato and start with mathematics, a science which proceeds very cautiously and admits nothing as established until it has been rightly demonstrated [p. 169d].*

It is remarks such as this that foster the interpretation that Galileo was a Platonist at heart, subscribing to the rationalist ideal of a deductive science that relies on mathematical insight rather than having to make inductive appeals to experience.

Yet, the opposite impression is created by the detailed examination given this same day to Aristotle's treatment of falling motion, and this with particular reference to free fall in a vacuum. Here the focus quickly turns to experimental evidence and its role in arriving at truths about nature. Since the ensuing discussion, beginning at p. 157b, has great bearing on the second "new science" to be introduced on the third day, it deserves careful reading. Simplicio, in the context of the exposition relating to vacua, has been asked to explain why Aristotle was opposed to them and why he thought their existence would render motion impossible. Thereupon Simplicio explains the doctrine of chapter 8 of the fourth book of the *Physics*, where Aristotle presents two quasi-mathematical arguments; Simplicio reverses the order of the arguments, but otherwise summarizes them accurately.[†] Basic to Aristotle's reasoning is the assumption, probably held by his Greek adversaries, that the velocity of fall of a heavy object is directly proportional to its weight and inversely proportional to the resistance it encounters in passing through a medium. The inverse proportionality part of this assumption provides Aristotle's basis for rejecting vacua, for if, in accordance with the accepted premise, the medium offers no resistance whatever, as would be true of a vacuum, falling motion would be instantaneous, and this is contrary to fact. The debate does not turn on the inverse proportionality part of the premise, however, but concentrates on Aristotle's seeming admission that, in any one medium, two bodies of

---

* *GBWW*, Vol. 8, pp. 312–25.
† *GBWW*, Vol. 8, p. 295.

different weights will move "with different speeds which stand to one another in the same ratio as the weights; so that, for example, a body which is ten times as heavy as another will move ten times as rapidly as the other" (p. 157b–c). These figures, it should be noted, are not in Aristotle's text, but, taking on face value Simplicio's implication that they are actually there, Salviati immediately objects:

> *I greatly doubt that Aristotle ever tested by experiment whether it be true that two stones, one weighing ten times as much as the other, if allowed to fall, at the same instant, from a height of, say, 100 cubits, would so differ in speed that when the heavier had reached the ground, the other would not have fallen more than 10 cubits [p. 157d].*

In reply Simplicio is more simplistic than he need be, indicating his acceptance of the figures as experimentally established, and even conceding that Aristotle's "language would seem to indicate that he had tried the experiment."[11] Sagredo interrupts at this juncture and states unequivocally that he has performed the experiment and that the results are quite different from Aristotle's:

> *But I, Simplicio, who had made the test can assure you that a cannon ball weighing one or two hundred pounds, or even more, will not reach the ground by as much as a span ahead of a musket ball weighing only half a pound, provided both are dropped from a height of 200 cubits [p. 157d].*

Were Galileo the empiricist that some have claimed, one should expect Salviati, speaking for Galileo, to provide more precise experimental details at this point. Curiously, however, he does not, and proceeds instead to give an a priori, deductive refutation of Aristotle's so-called dynamic law, asserting that

> *even without further experiment, it is possible to prove clearly, by means of a short and conclusive argument, that a heavier body does not move more rapidly than a lighter one provided both bodies are of the same material and in short such as those mentioned by Aristotle [p. 157d].*

The "short and conclusive argument" then given is very similar to one offered by Giovanni Battista Benedetti in 1554, which makes no appeal to experiment whatever. Yet, using this as a basis, Salviati hopes to prove "that large and small bodies move with the same speed provided they are of the same specific gravity" (p. 158c). This he regards as true whenever the resistive effects of the medium through which the bodies fall can be neglected, for he feels that he has proved "that in a medium totally devoid of resistance all bodies would fall with the same speed" (p. 161d). Salviati admits, however, that resistive effects will retard the smaller body more than the larger, and thus there will be a slight observable difference in their moments of impact. Otherwise, employing his principle of equal speeds of fall, he is confident that one will "find a much closer agreement of experiment with our computation than with that of Aristotle" (p. 163c).[12]

These passages illustrate some of the difficulties involved in laying bare the methodological content of the *Two New Sciences*. Such difficulties unfortunately are not cleared up as we read further and see the evidence adduced on the basis of experiments seemingly performed with pendulums and vibrating strings. Working with crude equipment and long before the advent of the stopwatch, to say nothing of stroboscopic lighting and other experimental techniques now available in a high-school science laboratory, Galileo had to use great ingenuity to detect the differences he suspected between the rates of fall of heavy and light bodies. Apparently he first experimented with balls rolling down inclined planes so as "to employ the slowest speeds possible and thus reduce the change which the resisting medium produces upon the simple effect of gravity" (p. 167a). With inclined planes, however, there is always the problem of friction, and so we must further admire his inventiveness when he proposes to approximate the roll of balls down their inclines by the swings of similar balls along the arcs of pendulums. This procedure has the decided advantage, as Salviati explains for Galileo, that it enables him "to repeat many times the fall through a small height in such a way [as to] accumulate all those small intervals of time that elapse between the arrival of the heavy and the light bodies respectively at their common terminus, so that this sum makes an interval of time which is not only observable, but easily observable" (p. 167a). Following out this experimental plan, Salviati goes on,

> I took two balls, one of lead and one of cork, the former more than a hundred times heavier than the latter, and suspended them by means of two equal fine threads, each four or five cubits long. Pulling each ball aside from the perpendicular, I let them go at the same instant, and they, falling along the circumferences of circles having these equal strings for semi-diameters, passed beyond the perpendicular and returned along the same path. This free vibration repeated a hundred times showed clearly that the heavy body maintains so nearly the period of the light body that neither in a hundred swings nor even in a thousand will the former anticipate the latter by as much as a single moment, so perfectly do they keep step [p. 167a–b].

Continuing along in this passage we note Galileo's additional indications that he experimented with a wide variety of arcs of swings for both the lead and the cork ball, ranging from four to ninety degrees from the perpendicular.

These citations would seem to offer proof positive that Galileo had performed experiments accurately and thus had an empirical basis for his assertions. But Alexandre Koyré, studying the passages carefully and noting Father Mersenne's difficulty in verifying Galileo's results, questions whether Galileo actually did observe, as he seems to say he did, one thousand oscillations of his pendulums.[13] Koyré's conclusion is that he probably did not, for although it is true that the period of a pendulum swinging through small arcs is a function of its length alone and not of the weight of its bob, this isochronous feature is not true when large amplitudes of swing are involved—a fact later shown experimentally by Mersenne and proved theoretically by Christiaan Huygens.[14] Had Galileo therefore observed a thousand, or even a hundred, swings of his pendulums, he must surely have observed the difference between the durations of the long and the short oscillations. Koyré surmises either that he did not make such prolonged observations or that, if he did, he idealized his results and suppressed the observed deviation. And he is not to be blamed for doing so, concludes this eminent historian of science, "for it is not by following experiment, but by outstripping experiment, that the scientific mind makes progress."[15]

These few selections from the first day of the dialogue give food for thought as to Galileo's methodology and the foundations on which his "new science" was actually laid. Other passages that amply repay study are those relating to light and its velocity, with the account of the attempt to measure that velocity and its null result (pp. 148c–49b); Galileo's awareness that bodies falling through a medium reach a terminal velocity (pp. 170c–71a); and the various experiments that he reports with vibrating strings (pp. 172d–77c). Scholars are agreed that the experiences on which Galileo drew when writing these passages took place, for the most part, many years before the composition of the *Two New Sciences*. The work with vibrating strings, for example, goes back to experiments performed by Galileo's father, Vincenzio Galilei, who was an accomplished musician and was involved in several disputes over the matters discussed in this portion of his son's work.[16] Galileo himself was an amateur musician, and as a young mathematician interested in ratios, either watched his father's experimentation closely or helped with the experiments while at home between 1585 and 1589.[17] But these and the other observations are not of recent vintage, nor are the latter reported with the precision and objectivity a modern scientist might expect, so one can only wonder, at this stage of the dialogue, how importantly they figured in Galileo's own estimate of the "new sciences" he was then in the process of founding.

*Second day*

The second day resumes the discussion on the strength of materials, and this now proceeds more systematically than on the preceding day. True to his promise Salviati brings with him "some papers in which I have set down in an orderly way the theorems and propositions dealing with the various phases of this subject, matters which, from memory alone, I could not present in the proper order" (p. 170b). The exposition based on these papers is brief; few of the intriguing philosophical questions raised earlier are pursued; and the style is very classical, much after the fashion of a

Euclidean or Archimedean treatise—possibly signs of an earlier composition that Galileo is here weaving into his master thesis. Indeed, an examination of the manuscript fragments relating to the second day suggests that the materials here reported were already worked out by 1608, a full thirty years before they were finally published. This makes them no less interesting, for they provide an insight into Galileo's enduring interest in Archimedes and his long-term attempts to reduce physics to geometry.

The scope of the discussion is signaled by Salviati at the outset when he limits attention to the resistance solids offer to bending stresses alone and not to longitudinal pulls. A beam that is mortised or cantilevered into a wall functions somewhat like a lever when forces are applied at the free end. This is precisely the case Galileo wishes to investigate, since it enables him to take a variety of resistive phenomena and reduce them to problems that can be solved by the consistent application of lever principles (p. 178b).[18]

The entire program of the second day is to reduce the "new science" of strength of materials to a branch of statics, a subject already well understood by classical geometers. Thus it is actually designed to reinforce Galileo's thesis that geometry is the most powerful tool available for the solution of physical problems. The propositions and demonstrations that make up this new discipline are not difficult to understand, once this aim is appreciated. Eight propositions are presented in systematic fashion, all of them concerned with the strength of cantilevered beams of various shapes and encompassing three different cases. In the first case an external force acts at the end of the beam, but the weight of the beam is neglected; in the second the beam's weight is also taken into account; and in the third the external force is neglected and only the beam's weight considered. Following this a number of theorems are developed less systematically relating to beams supported at both ends and the ways in which these should be designed for maximum strength across a span. The reader should note the illustrations for the various cases, all of which are reproduced from the original Elzevir edition. Most interesting is Galileo's application of the principles he discovers to the field of biophysics, for he makes many fascinating observations on the relative strength and sizes of land and aquatic animals, on nature's use of hollow bone structures in birds, and on the different type of material that would be required in the bones of a giant, as compared to an ordinary man, if he were to retain the same proportions of limb and not fall and be crushed under his own weight (pp. 187b–88c). Through all this Galileo shows his tacit acceptance of nature as a principle of operation, and indeed acknowledges its wisdom in making correct use of mechanical principles.

Several times during the discussions of this day Galileo mentions the parabola and its properties, and in one such case provides a further clue as to his experimental methods. The occasion is a question from Sagredo as to how "a mechanician might draw a parabola upon a plane surface"

(p. 195a). Salviati replies that there are two methods, the first of which he describes as follows:

> *I take a perfectly round brass ball about the size of a walnut and project it along the surface of a metallic mirror held in a nearly upright position, so that the ball in its motion will press slightly upon the mirror and trace out a fine sharp parabolic line; this parabola will grow longer and narrower as the angle of elevation increases. The above experiment furnishes clear and tangible evidence that the path of a projectile is a parabola; a fact first observed by our friend [Galileo] and demonstrated by him in his book on motion which we shall take up at our next meeting. In the execution of this method, it is advisable to slightly heat and moisten the ball by rolling in the hand in order that its trace upon the mirror may be more distinct [p. 195b].*

The mirror to which he has reference, unlike modern glass mirrors, was polished on its top surface and thus would register the passage of the ball —a truly ingenious way of anticipating the photographic techniques now employed to study similar trajectories. Salviati's second method, unfortunately, gives erroneous results, for it is based on the idea that a chain suspended from two nails at the same height on a wall will "assume the form of a parabola" (p. 195c), whereas the curve such a chain takes is actually a catenary. A similar error occurs earlier, when Galileo asserts that a beam of uniform bearing strength and having no excess material to increase its weight would be parabolic in shape; the curve that fills these requirements is an ellipse, as was subsequently noted by his critics (p. 192b).

Background material for understanding the discussions of the second and subsequent days will be found in Volume 11 of the *Great Books*, which contains the basic treatises of Euclid and Archimedes on which Galileo relied for his mathematics. Also noteworthy in the same volume is Apollonius of Perga's *Conics*, which is the classical exposition of the properties of the parabola and other conic sections, and to which Sagredo will make reference at the beginning of the fourth day (p. 238b). Again, Nicomachus of Gerasa's *Introduction to Arithmetic* is helpful for understanding Galileo's use of the classical and medieval language of ratios; for example, his mention of a "sesquialteral ratio" (pp. 183b, 184c), that of 3 to 2, as explained by Nicomachus in his first book.[19]

*Third day*

The discussions of the third and fourth days report what, in Galileo's estimation, was his most revolutionary achievement, the sketching out of "a very new science dealing with a very ancient subject" (p. 197a). The subject of motion is indeed quite ancient, and this is revealed by the title Galileo uses to introduce the second "new science." Here the three interlocutors leave aside their native Italian and start to read Galileo's Latin treatise, which begins with the caption *De motu locali,* correctly rendered as "Change of Position." The Latin title, however, better indicates Galileo's ancient source, which is Aristotle, who developed in his *Physics* an extensive treatment of motion or change (*kinēsis*) and enumerated its three species or kinds: change of quality, change of quantity, and change of position.* The scholastics referred to the first two types as *alteratio* and *augmentatio,* and to the last as *motus localis.* Much had been written about this "local motion," or displacement of a body from one position to another, so it is difficult to see at the outset why Galileo should refer to his treatise as "a very new science." In his mind, however, the striking results to which he had come and the mathematical methods he had used in reaching them, as he will explain at the end of the third day's discussion (p. 236d), provided ample justification for his claim. For the moment he simply states that he has discovered some properties of local motion "which are worth knowing and which have not hitherto been either observed or demonstrated" (p. 197a). The English translation has him claiming that he discovered these properties "by experiment," but these words are an interpolation of the translators whereby they apparently hoped to clarify the novelty of Galileo's contribution by stressing its experimental character.

The Latin treatise is divided into three books, the first concerned with uniform motion (*De motu aequabili*), the second with naturally accelerated motion (*De motu naturaliter accelerato*), and the third—whose discussion is postponed until the fourth day—with the motion of projectiles (*De motu proiectorum*). Of these the second book is the most difficult, being concerned with the problem of a body's free fall under the influence of gravity, but it is this that also led to Galileo's most significant findings for the science of dynamics. The first and third books are important for their contributions to kinematics and for the illumination they provide for understanding the second book. Material pertaining to the Latin treatise is introduced without the name of a dialogist; where such a name appears in the text, the original was composed in Italian. The English translation, of course, does not reveal from which language it was made, although this does have a bearing on the interpretation accorded some of the passages.

The first book, dealing with uniform or "steady" (i.e., equable) motion, is brief, axiomatic in structure, and sufficiently self-evident, in Galileo's opinion, not to require discussion by the participants. It begins with a definition of uniform motion, from this deduces four axioms, and then uses these to prove six different propositions, all of which are stated as theorems. The definition is implicit in propositions already used by Archimedes when treating uniform motion in his work *On Spirals;*† the formulation Galileo refers to here as "the old definition" (p. 197c), however, is probably of medieval origin. Uniform motion is that in which equal

---

* *GBWW,* Vol. 8, pp. 306b–7a.
† *GBWW,* Vol. 11, p. 484.

distances are traversed during equal time intervals, and from this it follows that the distances traversed vary, for a given velocity, directly with the time (Axioms I and II), and, for a given time interval, directly with the velocities (Axioms III and IV). The Latin *velocitas* is rendered as "speed," an acceptable translation, particularly when one considers that the present-day distinction between velocity and speed was unknown to Galileo and his contemporaries. Using these axioms, the first three theorems establish simple ratios between the three quantities: speed or *velocitas* (V), distance or *spatium* (S), and time or *tempus* (T).[20] Stated mathematically in the form of ratios, they read as follows:

Theorem I: if $V_1 = V_2$, then $T_1/T_2 = S_1/S_2$

Theorem II: if $T_1 = T_2$, then $V_1/V_2 = S_1/S_2$

Theorem III: if $S_1 = S_2$, then $V_1/V_2 = T_2/T_1$

The first two theorems express a direct proportion between ratios, and the third, an inverse proportion. In proving the first theorem Galileo makes use of Euclid's teaching on ratios in Book V of the *Elements*, and particularly his fifth definition (p. 198b);* Archimedes uses the same definition to prove his first proposition on uniform motion.† The Euclidean doctrine on ratios thus becomes fundamental for the subsequent development, a circumstance that, while conferring rigor on the treatment, enormously complicates the proofs for the modern reader. For example, according to Euclid's third definition only magnitudes "of the same kind" can stand in a proper ratio; thus it is impossible for Galileo to abbreviate his first three theorems as $V = S/T$, an expression readily understood by the modern reader but violating the third definition in that it relates magnitudes of different kinds, S and T. The last three theorems involve compound rather than simple, ratios, and they are stated mathematically as follows:

Theorem IV: $S_1/S_2 = (V_1/V_2)(T_1/T_2)$

Theorem V: $T_1/T_2 = (S_1/S_2)(V_2/V_1)$

Theorem VI: $V_1/V_2 = (S_1/S_2)(T_2/T_1)$

It may be noted that only the first four theorems are used in the proofs that follow on accelerated and projectile motion, so that the last two are superfluous, apparently being worked out by Galileo to complete the symmetry of his proofs.

With this Book I comes to an end, and Sagredo introduces the second book, on naturally accelerated motion, as "a new and more discriminating consideration" of the type of motion "generally experienced by heavy falling bodies" (p. 200a). The second book is far more complicated than the first, and, while patterned after a Euclidean-Archimedean mathematical treatise, is not as coherent as it appears on the surface. Since the exposition is frequently interrupted for discussion and clarification by the dialogists, a brief overview at this point may put its development in perspective. To the definition and axioms of Book I Galileo first adds one definition, that of uniformly accelerated motion, and explicitly assumes one principle, called on this account the "assumption" or "postulate." Other important principles, however, are introduced informally in the subsequent discussion, whereas still others are never formulated explicitly. From these premises thirty-eight propositions are deduced, and interspersed among these are also a number of corollaries and scholia. The propositions themselves are of two types, theorems and problems. The difference between a theorem and a problem is usually this: a theorem is a basic proposition of relatively simple formulation, whereas a problem is a more complex proposition that requires some type of construction for its proof, and therefore is posited as a query whose solution elicits the required construction.[22] Despite some lapses, the treatment is remarkably rigorous considering the circumstances under which Galileo assembled, and made his final redaction of, materials on which he had been working for more than fifty years.

The definition with which Galileo opens Book II is proposed as "best fitting natural phenomena," specifically "the phenomena of bodies falling with acceleration such as actually occurs in nature" (p. 200a–b).[23] Stated simply, a uniformly accelerated motion is one wherein equal increments of speed are acquired in equal time intervals (p. 200d). Galileo's justification for the definition is twofold: experimental results are seen to agree with it; and nature acts by means that are simple, easy, and obvious. In his view nothing could be more simple than a relation between motion and time that "repeats itself always in the same manner" (p. 200c).[24] Sagredo and Salviati thereupon discuss experimental evidence that seems to conflict with the proposed definition; this interchange leads Salviati to stress the importance of interpreting experiments properly since "the same experiment which at first glance seemed to show one thing, when more carefully examined, assures us of the contrary" (p. 201c). He then proceeds to claim that "without depending upon the above experiment . . . it ought not to be difficult to establish such a fact by reasoning alone" (p. 201d). Galileo's justification of this key definition is thus typical of his methodological indecision: results are seemingly established by experiment, but even without experiment, human reason can penetrate to a knowledge of their truth.

Immediately following this comes another interesting dispute regarding the role of causality in scientific explanation. Having apparently agreed on

---

\* *GBWW*, Vol. 11, p. 81.
† *GBWW*, Vol. 11, p. 484.

the mathematical description of naturally accelerated motion, Sagredo suggests that this may now lead to "a proper solution of the problem discussed by philosophers, namely, what causes the acceleration in the natural motion of heavy bodies?" (p. 202a). Simplicio and Sagredo exchange views on this subject, only to have the discussion terminated rather abruptly by Salviati, speaking for Galileo himself, who asserts that the present is not "the proper time to investigate the cause of the acceleration of natural motion," since such investigation "is not really worthwhile" (p. 202d). Some have seen in this statement an attitude that characterizes the mature Galileo, as opposed to the author of the earlier writings, wherein he has totally abandoned the search for causes and opted instead for a positivist approach to scientific investigation. This interpretation does not square, however, with other of Galileo's statements, and a more acceptable view is that he wished here to bracket, or suspend, the search for physical causes until the mathematical properties of phenomena were well established, and the ground thereby prepared for a more successful search.[25]

Up to this point, attention has centered on the definition of uniformly accelerated motion. Now it passes to the postulate, or assumption, on which the entire subsequent development will depend. Galileo states this as follows:

> *The speeds acquired by one and the same body moving down planes of different inclinations are equal when the heights of these planes are equal* [*p. 203d*].

Of the truth of this statement he seems to have been convinced between 1600 and 1604, but he could never work out a satisfactory proof and thus presents it here hypothetically. This does not prevent him, however, from hinting at its obvious and self-evident character, for he has Sagredo observe that it is "so reasonable that it ought to be conceded without question" (p. 204a). Salviati agrees that it is "very plausible," and then briefly details an experimental confirmation that is calculated to increase its probability so as to "be little short of a rigid demonstration" (p. 204b). The experiment is one with which Galileo had long been fascinated, wherein a simple pendulum is allowed to swing from a nail driven into a vertical wall so that its plane of oscillation is parallel to the wall and only "two fingerbreadths" in front of it. When a horizontal line is drawn on the wall from the point at which the bob is released, it is found that the bob practically reaches the same line on its upswing, with the "slight shortage being caused by the resistance of the air and the string" (p. 204b; see fig. 46). If, now, the length of the pendulum is effectively shortened at the moment when it passes the vertical by having another nail driven in the wall at a point below the horizontal line, the bob will be seen to attempt to reach the level of the horizontal line. Galileo speaks of the bob's acquired "momentum" as the cause of this phenomenon—and here he obviously adumbrates the concept of kinetic energy—but the proof for which he was looking had to await the more detailed analysis later provided by Huygens.

On the basis of this assumption Galileo is now ready to proceed with his theorems. The first of these, sometimes referred to as the "mean-speed" theorem, states that the time in which any space is traversed by a uniformly accelerating body is equal to the time in which the same body would traverse the same space when moving uniformly at a speed, as we read in the Crew and Salvio translation, "whose value is the mean of the highest speed and the speed just before acceleration began" (p. 205b). So stated, the mean-speed theorem is far from new, being known to fourteenth-century English writers at Merton College, Oxford, and being amply demonstrated by Nicole Oresme at Paris in manuscripts that were widely diffused throughout Europe.[26] The diagram Galileo employs (fig. 47) is remarkably similar to Oresme's, and when one couples this with the fact that Domingo de Soto, a Spanish scholastic who had studied at Paris, explicitly applied the rule to free fall in a book written in 1545, with which Galileo was also acquainted, it seems plausible to see here an influence of medieval science on the founder of modern mechanics.[27] This influence is generally acknowledged by historians of science, but recently Professor Drake has questioned it, holding that the medieval concept of "mean speed" was not actually used by Galileo in his statement and proof of the first theorem—a fact that has passed unnoticed by historians, in his view, because they have been using an incorrect translation of the theorem. In place of the expression "a uniform speed whose value is the mean of the highest speed and the speed just before acceleration began," which occurs in the Crew and Salvio translation, Drake would therefore substitute the clause "by a uniform motion whose degree of speed is as one-half to the highest and last degree of speed."[28] The difference in translation calls attention to the fact that Galileo spoke only of ratios between degrees of speed that can actually be measured, and so made no mention of a "mean" speed, which cannot be directly observed. This suggests the further inference that medieval writers were referring to a type of theoretical entity when they used the expression "mean speed," whereas Galileo, consistent with his Euclidean mathematics, wrote only of ratios between observable velocities. Whether such an inference regarding the medievals is correct or not may be debatable, but Drake's concern with the concepts behind the words is nonetheless legitimate, and his criticisms are of particular significance for showing how English translations of scientific classics may inadvertently color the interpretations later put on the texts.

The second theorem is then the famous "times-squared" theorem, which Galileo hit upon in 1604 but whose proof eluded him at that time. The demonstration he now offers (p. 206b–c) should be studied carefully, with pencil and paper if necessary, to trace the steps whereby he arrives at this classic law.[29] His diagram (fig. 48, p. 206a) is clear, but unlike modern graphs it shows both the time axis and the distance axis drawn vertically, side by side, with the time line AB to the left of the distance line HI. All that Galileo requires for the proof is the first theorem just given and the fourth theorem of the first book (p. 198d). Especially noteworthy is the fact that the conclusion of the demonstration is expressed formally in the language of ratios: "Hence the ratio of the spaces traversed is the same as the squared ratio of the time-intervals. Q.E.D." (p. 206c). From this important result a number of other interesting consequences follow, and Galileo now presents one as his first corollary, generally referred to as the "odd-number" rule. This states that, in uniformly accelerated motion, whereas the velocities increase as the natural numbers during equal intervals of time, "the increments in the distances traversed during these equal time-intervals are to one another as the odd numbers beginning with unity" (p. 206d). The proof of this and the diagram associated with it (fig. 49, p. 207a) again show similarities to those of Oresme, although there are also significant differences; both, however, adumbrate modern techniques whereby mathematical integration is applied to physical quantities to obtain significant results. Galileo may not have been the first to employ this type of reasoning, but his "new science" showed how it could be put to work to develop a mathematical physics, and in this achievement lay his true genius.

Up to this point the exposition has centered on the reading of the Latin treatise, but here Simplicio makes a most important intervention. The treatise has proceeded thus far in a very a priori fashion, like a rigid mathematical deduction, with little attention to experimental confirmation. Notice that it is the Aristotelian who now exhibits the empiricist bent by asking for experimental verification of the times-squared law. Similarly noteworthy is the fact that whenever experiments or agreement with experience is discussed in the *Two New Sciences*, this is done in the Italian dialogue and not in the classical treatise composed by Galileo. Some have seen in this a further confirmation of Galileo's Platonic inclinations, or at least his satisfaction with deductivist explanations based on self-evident principles rather than on appeals to experience. From Simplicio's remark, however, it is obvious that Galileo had performed some experiments to verify this law, and in reply we are now given an account of one. This is the celebrated inclined-plane experiment, which Salviati now describes together with the techniques Galileo used for measuring distances and times of travel (p. 208). It should be observed, of course, that a ball rolling down an inclined plane is not the same as a freely falling body, since complications are introduced in the former case by resistance and rotational inertia. Noting such complications, Koyré has questioned whether these experiments were actually "repeated a full hundred times," as Galileo states (p. 208b), and whether they were indeed capable of confirming his famous law.[30] Following his criticism, most historians of science have held that such experiments merely suggested the times-squared law to Galileo, who obtained his generalization by disregarding the discrepancies and simply stating what would happen in the ideal case. Some dozen years ago, however, an attempt was made to duplicate Galileo's findings with apparatus similar to that which he describes, leaving aside all present-day analytical refinements and attempting only to show that, for a given inclination of the plane, the distances a ball travels down it are in direct proportion to the squares of the times of its roll, i.e., $S_1/S_2 = T_1^2/T_2^2$. Stated in this form of Euclidean ratios, the units of measurement, the value of g in s $= \frac{1}{2}gt^2$, and the factor introduced by rotational inertia all cancel out, and it is possible to obtain consistent numerical results. Thomas Settle, who performed the experiments, sees no reason to doubt Galileo's account of them, and argues that they indeed supplied an experimental basis for the famous law.[31]

Among the remaining propositions two are especially worthy of comment. The first is presented as Theorem VI, commonly referred to as the "law of chords," which we have seen already stated during the discussions of the first day (p. 171d). Galileo had hit upon this result by 1602 but apparently did not find a rigorous proof until later; it is possible that the discovery of this proof, together with the final formulation of the first two theorems, was what enabled him to synthesize his more fragmentary findings into the form in which we now have the *Two New Sciences*. The second is Theorem XXII, the last theorem of Book II (p. 234b), which also was known to Galileo in 1602, when he was working on the classical problem of the brachistochrone, or "the path of quickest descent from one point to another." At that time he thought he succeeded in showing that this "is not the shortest path, namely, a straight line, but the arc of a circle," a result that is erroneous (the correct curve is a cycloid) but that he appends as a scholium to this last theorem (p. 235b). Thus one should beware of thinking that the propositions are arranged in the chronological order of their discovery, since it seems that this was far from the actual case.

With this we have sketched the essential elements of Book II, with the exception of one principle that is here introduced informally but is extremely important for an understanding of projectile motion, to be discussed in Book III. This is the principle of inertia, which we find stated in a scholium following Problem IX as follows:

> *any velocity once imparted to a moving body will be rigidly maintained as long as the external causes of acceleration or retardation are removed, a condition which is found only on horizontal planes* [*p. 224d*].

This sounds very much like Newton's first law of motion,* but there are difficulties in equating the two, as will be noticed in connection with the discussions of the fourth day. For the moment, suffice it to mention that in the early *De motu* of 1590 Galileo was working in the thought context of medieval impetus theory, according to which a projectile is moved by a force impressed on it by the projector; he thought then that this force would gradually diminish with distance of travel and ultimately bring the

---

* *GBWW*, Vol. 34, p. 14a.

projectile to rest. By the time he wrote the letters on sunspots in 1613, however, Galileo had come to the conclusion that heavy bodies are "indifferent" to horizontal motion, meaning by this a motion that carries them neither toward nor away from the center of the earth, and once set in such motion should continue forever. So he asserts:

> *All external impediments removed, a heavy body on a spherical surface concentric with the earth will be indifferent to rest and to movements towards any part of the horizon. And it will maintain itself in that state in which it has once been placed; that is, if placed in a state of rest, it will conserve that; and if placed in movement toward the west (for example), it will maintain itself in that movement. Thus a ship, for instance, having once received some impetus through the tranquil sea, would move continually around our globe without ever stopping; and placed at rest it would perpetually remain at rest, if in the first case all extrinsic impediments could be removed, and in the second case no external cause of motion were added.*[32]

A concept of inertia is clearly implied in this passage, but historians usually refer to it as "circular inertia," since it seemingly endows terrestrial bodies with the same capacity for eternal movement in a circle that Aristotle and medieval cosmologists attributed to the heavenly spheres. Whether Galileo has abandoned such "circular inertia" in the passage quoted from the third day (p. 224d) is much debated by historians. Arguments bearing on this precise point are resumed on the fourth day, however, and so to this we now turn.

*Fourth day*

Book III of *De motu locali* is the focus of attention on this day, and as noted it is devoted to the study of the motion of projectiles. In it Galileo proposes to show that such motion "is compounded of two other motions, namely, one uniform and one naturally accelerated" (p. 238a). With regard to the uniform component, this is illustrated by a "particle projected along a horizontal plane without friction," which then, "from what has been more fully explained in the preceding pages, ... will move along this same plane with a motion which is uniform and perpetual, provided the plane has no limits" (p. 238a). The reference here is to the passage in the third day's discussion to which attention has just been directed. In that same passage it should now be noted that Galileo also enunciated another principle, the principle of superposition of motions, when he asserted that

> *we have here the superposition of two different states, namely, the velocity ... which if acting alone would carry the body at a uniform rate to infinity, and the velocity which results from a natural acceleration downwards common to all bodies* [*p. 224d*].

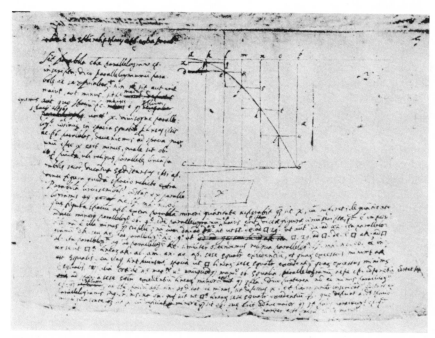

Galileo's manuscript drawing of the parabolic path followed by a falling
projectile, showing the two components of its motion (folio 102v, volume 72,
MSS Galileiani)

At the beginning of this fourth day's discussion he now employs these principles of inertia and of superposition to define projectile motion as "compounded of one [motion] which is uniform and horizontal and of another which is vertical and naturally accelerated" (p. 238b). Such motion turns out to have interesting properties, and these are thus the subject of further demonstrations.

In structure the third book is simple and orderly, consisting of only fourteen propositions, of which the first five are the most fundamental. Propositions VI through XI describe the main mathematical properties of parabolic paths, whereas the remaining three propositions supply directions for the computation of trajectories based on such properties. All propositions except the last are identified as theorems or problems, but not all the theorems and problems are numbered consecutively as in Book II.

Of the five initial propositions, the first three are entitled theorems despite the fact that a formal statement of the third is lacking. The first theorem establishes that the path of a projectile, consequent on the definition of its motion, must be a semiparabola—undoubtedly one of Galileo's most important discoveries. The next two theorems spell out the further implications of the superposition principle, with the second supplying the rule of "vector addition" for the composition of velocities. The precise content of the third theorem is not clear, but recent work shows that it is probably connected with refined experimental investigations conducted by Galileo in 1609, which will be explained momentarily.

The details of Galileo's proof of his first, or "parabolic path," theorem need not concern us, but the discussion that follows the proof is noteworthy, for it is here that important remarks are made on the subject of inertia. Following Salviati's explanation of the demonstration, which assumes that the horizontal component of the motion remains uniform and that the vertical increases with "the square of the time," both Sagredo and Simplicio object that these rectangular components do not correspond to the physical geometry of the universe, and thus that the curve along which projectiles will move near the surface of the earth is not a perfect semiparabola. Sagredo's objection is based on the projectile's tendency to seek the center of gravity of the earth during its fall. Assuming that it begins its parabolic path at some point directly above the earth's center, the further it travels along the parabola the more it departs from the earth's center, and this is contrary to its natural tendency (pp. 240d–41a). Implicit in Sagredo's argument is the contention that the body's natural tendency will effectively exert a retarding influence on the horizontal component that will prevent its being uniform and perpetual.

Simplicio's objection is made along similar lines, but is more pointedly addressed to the problem of locating a perfectly horizontal plane anywhere on the earth's surface. As he formulates it, the difficulty *is that we suppose the horizontal plane, which slopes neither up nor down, to be represented by a straight line as if each point on the line were equally distant from the [earth's] centre, which is not the case; for as one starts from the middle and goes towards either end, he departs farther and farther from the centre [of the earth] and is therefore constantly going uphill. Whence it follows that the motion cannot remain uniform through any distance whatever, but must continually diminish [p. 241a].*

A related difficulty also mentioned by Simplicio is that the motion would have to be performed in a resistanceless medium, and such media are never found in practice.

Salviati's reply to these objections is straightforward. He is quite willing to admit the difficulties, and even to go further and acquiesce to them on the part of "our Author," Galileo:

*All these difficulties and objections which you urge are so well founded that it is impossible to remove them; and, as for me, I am ready to admit them all, which indeed I think our Author would also do. I grant that these conclusions proved in the abstract will be different when applied in the concrete and will be fallacious to this extent, that neither will the horizontal motion be uniform nor the natural acceleration be in the ratio assumed, nor the path of the projectile a parabola, etc. [p. 241b].*

Salviati goes on, however, to urge his companions not to begrudge these principles to "our Author, . . . even if not strictly true." A consideration that may make their assumption permissible is the fact that

*in practice, our instruments and the distances involved are so small in comparison with the enormous distance from the centre of the earth that we may consider a minute of arc on a great circle as a straight line, and may regard the perpendiculars let fall from its extremities as parallel. [p. 241b–c].*

It is on the basis of texts such as these that historians dispute whether Galileo had completely broken the bonds of Aristotelian cosmology to enunciate a principle of "rectilinear inertia," as this is found in Newton, or whether he merely arrived at the concept of "circular inertia," and thus marked only a first step, admittedly an essential one, in the direction of the Newtonian synthesis. Much can be said for both sides, but for our purposes the very existence of the dispute illustrates the complexity of such an apparently simple concept as inertia, and the difficulties that were early encountered in giving that concept accurate formulation.[33]

Earlier we noted one experimental technique used by Galileo to verify the parabolic path of projectiles. (p. 195b). Since no experiments are explicitly discussed during the fourth day, it has been generally assumed that

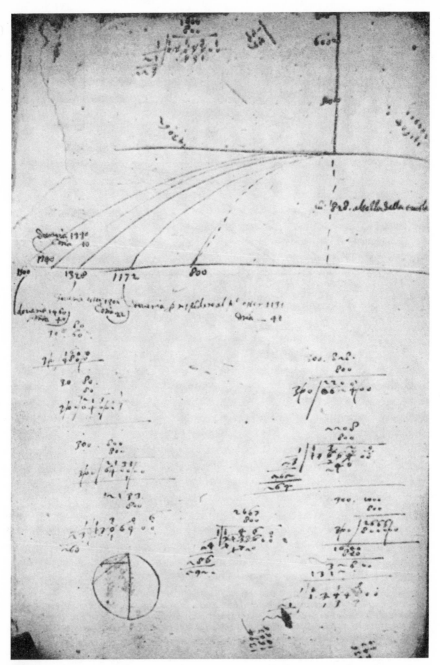

Galileo's calculations and test results showing that he verified parabolic paths and distances of travel by experiments with falling bodies (folio 116v, volume 72, MSS Galileiani)

no further measurements were performed by Galileo when investigating parabolic trajectories. A study just recently published, however, shows that this is not the case, and that in fact some of Galileo's best experimental work was done in this context, possibly in connection with the third theorem on projectile motion. This discovery was made by Professor Drake from an analysis of unpublished manuscript diagrams and calculations, on the basis of which he was able to reconstruct Galileo's apparatus and check his numerical results.[34] The experiment consisted of dropping a ball from different heights to a deflector located on a table, at which point the ball was given different horizontal velocities depending on the length of its fall. Apparently Galileo had computed the horizontal distances the ball should travel depending on the velocity imparted to it, and then had actually measured points of impact to verify his calculations. Like Settle before him, Drake reconstructed the apparatus and repeated the measurements, and found good agreement not only between Galileo's actual and calculated distances but also between these results and those provided by modern theory and computer calculations. Watermarks and other clues indicate that all of this work was done in 1609, and, of course, this new evidence gives strong support to the claim that Galileo was empirically minded and was not a pure Platonist, as has hitherto been claimed.

Such an important discovery as Drake's should nonetheless not blind us to other evidences that attest to multiple facets in Galileo's character and especially to his rationalist bent. One passage that gives pause comes just after a corollary following Proposition VII, wherein Galileo shows that a projectile shot from the earth's surface will attain maximum range when fired at an elevation of 45°. Here Sagredo is very appreciative of the proof, and acknowledges that "the force of rigid demonstrations such as occur only in mathematics fills me with wonder and delight" (p. 252a). Already gunners had provided him with knowledge of this fact, he admits, "but to understand why this happens far outweighs the mere information obtained by the testimony of others, or even by repeated experiment." This preference for knowledge through causes answering to the question "why" over merely descriptive knowledge answering only to the "that" or the "how" elicits from Salviati a very surprising response:

> *What you say is very true. The knowledge of a single fact acquired through a discovery of its causes prepares the mind to understand and ascertain other facts without need of recourse to experiment [p. 252b].*

Presumably Salviati is speaking for Galileo, as is his wont, and thus is here affirming the author's ultimate ideal of scientific knowledge.

A similar mentality is evident in the brief digression on cosmogenesis that concludes the discussion after the third theorem on projectile motion. Here Sagredo points out an agreement between Galileo's thought and Plato's regarding the origins of the universe. Specifically, he speculates that

God may have put the heavenly bodies in their proper orbits by first having them fall from a height and then deflecting them into circular orbits, where they will rotate uniformly forever—a conception that shows remarkable affinity with the experiments Galileo himself had been conducting (p. 245b–c). A related idea was mentioned in the *Two Chief World Systems*, and it is noteworthy that these cosmological speculations of Galileo were even known to Isaac Newton and discussed by him at length in his letters to Richard Bentley regarding proposed new proofs for God's existence.[35] Also, earlier in the *Two New Sciences*, after stating and proving the "law of chords," Simplicio suggests that this too may have cosmological applications, "that there may be some great mystery hidden in these true and wonderful results, a mystery related to the creation of the universe . . . and related also to the seat of the first cause" (p. 214d). Salviati again is not adverse to this:

> *I have no hesitation in agreeing with you. But profound considerations of this kind belong to a higher science than ours. We must be satisfied to belong to that class of less worthy workmen who procure from the quarry the marble out of which, later, the gifted sculptor produces those masterpieces which lay hidden in this rough and shapeless exterior* [*p. 214d*].

Perhaps here Galileo is signaling what he considers to be the division of labor between scientist and metaphysician. But if so, it is noteworthy that his is not the statement of one who rejects causes entirely or who regards their search as meaningless; rather, it reflects the mentality of one who places such deeper knowledge at the summit of human understanding.

The remainder of the propositions of Book III draw out the implications and applications of the first three theorems. Unfortunately, but again prophetically, they return to the problems of military engineering with which the first day's dialogue opened, only now concerned more explicitly with ordnance and ballistics. Galileo here computes tables of altitude and distance for given muzzle velocities and for various angles of elevation. It should be noted that because of the great air resistance encountered at high velocities his tables had to assume low initial speeds and thus were of no practical use to gunners. But, like so much of his work, the published tables gave incentive to others, and soon ballistics became an accepted field of application for the new mathematical physics.

At the very end of the *Two New Sciences* Salviati appends Galileo's theorems on the center of gravity of solids, his first technical essay whose favorable review by Christopher Clavius and by Guidobaldo del Monte had launched him on his scientific career.[36] The inclusion of this work, written over fifty years earlier, as an appendix to the author's masterpiece, illustrates how Galileo valued everything he wrote; it also supplies some insight into this man who was a "paper saver," and who left us such an abundance of manuscript remains on which to base our researches. Galileo assembled the materials for the fourth day's discussion in a great rush, as we have seen, while Elzevir was already setting the book in type. Other materials he designated for possible fifth and sixth days of the *Discorsi*, and these still exist in manuscript form. The "fifth day" was to be concerned with a thorough treatment of the Euclidean theory of ratios, and this was completed in a work by Galileo's faithful disciple, Vincenzio Viviani, published in 1674. The "sixth day" was to take up the difficult problem of impact force, or force of percussion, and attempt to evaluate the effect of a hammer's weight and its velocity on its percussive effects.

Neither of these last two days' discussions was finished by Galileo himself, although he was working on them only a few months before his death. In November of 1641 a slight fever and palpitations of the heart overtook him, and he was confined to bed. "After two months of illness that little by little consumed his spirit," writes Viviani,

> *on Wednesday the eighth of January in the year of the Incarnation 1642, at four o'clock in the morning, at an age of seventy-seven years, ten months, and twenty days, he returned his soul to his Creator with philosophical and Christian perseverance. He sent it, as he liked to believe, to enjoy and to gaze more closely on those eternal and changeless marvels he had so eagerly, if impatiently, by means of a fragile instrument, brought closer to our mortal eyes.*[37]

So passed from his earthly prison, with tranquil dignity and a great sense of accomplishment, this most celebrated founder of modern science.

## Gilbert: The Loadstone and Magnetic Bodies

William Gilbert,[38] the author of *De magnete* and Galileo's chief competitor for the title of "father of experimental science," was twenty years the latter's senior and had completed most of his experimental work before the Florentine physicist began his. Like Harvey, Gilbert was a physician of note, both men having persevered in medicine, the profession Galileo abandoned after four years of study at the University of Pisa. Apparently Gilbert had conserved all of his books, notes, and experimental equipment, since he bequeathed these to the Royal College of Physicians for their library in London, but the library and all its contents were destroyed in the Great Fire of 1666. Thus there is a paucity of source material relating to Gilbert's classic, and most of our information will have to be drawn from an analysis of its text. Like Newton, Gilbert never married, but materials on which he had been working at the time of his death were assembled by his half-brother, also named William, and published in Amsterdam in 1651 under the title *De mundo*. The two Williams are differentiated by their place of birth: our author is known as William Gilbert of Colchester; his half-brother, as William Gilbert of Melford.

The work on the loadstone, whose fuller title translates literally as "On the magnet and magnetic bodies, and on the great magnet, the earth, a new natural philosophy (*physiologia*), demonstrated by many reasonings and experiments," was published by Peter Short of London in 1600, fittingly perhaps, for it thus auspiciously inaugurated the seventeenth century and heralded the dawn of an experimental era. The book was an immediate success and, interestingly enough, was republished by the Elzevirs in 1628, the same year that Harvey's classic on the motion of the heart and blood also appeared on the Continent. Written in Latin, it was not translated into English until 1893, at which time P. Fleury Mottelay rendered it in the form in which we have it in our *Great Books* edition. This is an accurate though not literal translation; it reads very easily and, like the original, is well illustrated, so that it can be understood without detailed commentary. The observations that follow will hopefully assist the reader by picking out salient points in the text and relating these to other developments in the history of science.

*Preface*

From his prefatory comments, we know that Gilbert wishes to do more than recount his many experiments with magnets; indeed, he wishes to use this work as a base on which to erect an entirely new philosophy of nature. Aware that it is not easy to gain acceptance in such an undertaking, particularly for "doctrines that are novel, unheard-of, and opposed to everybody's opinions" (p. 2a), he nonetheless addresses himself hopefully "to the candid reader, studious of the magnetic philosophy." Aware too that "philosophy is for the few" (p. 2a), he must signal out those who would be "true philosophers, ingenuous minds, who not only in books but in things themselves look for knowledge," and dedicate to them "these foundations of magnetic science" (p. 1d). Gilbert's tone here may have encouraged Galileo in the latter's extravagant claims for his "new sciences," for Gilbert announces that his also is "a new style of philosophizing" (p. 1d), that only a few writers before him have published "meagre accounts of certain magnetic forces," and thus that his "natural philosophy . . . is almost a new thing, unheard of before" (p. 2b). As such it is a great advance over the learning of the ancients and the Greeks, and it will probably turn out to be an "inadmissible philosophy to the judgment of men who have taken oath to follow the opinions of others" (p. 1d)—a barb, like Galileo's many, aimed at the peripatetic professors in the universities.

This new philosophy, then, will have difficulty gaining a hearing, and Gilbert seems particularly aware that there will be no easy acceptance of his extension of that philosophy to the whole of cosmology, to be outlined in his concluding book (p. 2d). So as to ease the path toward its acceptance, therefore, he urges the reader to note the "great multitude of experiments and discoveries" on which the work is based. "We have dug them up and demonstrated them," he writes, "with much pains and sleepless nights and great money expense" (pp. 1d–2a). This is no idle boast for Gilbert, nor can there be any doubt, as there may be in the case of Galileo, of his

# GVILIELMI GIL-
## BERTI COLCESTREN-
### SIS, MEDICI LONDI-
### NENSIS,

## DE MAGNETE, MAGNETI-
### CISQVE CORPORIBVS, ET DE MAG-
no magnete tellure ; Phyſiologia noua,
*plurimis & argumentis, & expe-*
rimentis demonſtrata.

## LONDINI
**EXCVDEBAT** Petrvs Short **ANNO**
## MDC.

Title page of the original edition of Gilbert's *De magnete*

commitment to empirical method and to the actual performance of experiments. The treatise we are reading, in fact, can lay claim to being the first laboratory manual, or book of experiments, wherein directions are given for the student to verify the stated results. To call attention to this feature, Gilbert announces that "we have set over against our discoveries and experiments larger and smaller asterisks according to their importance and their subtility" (p. 2a). Unfortunately, these asterisks are not shown in our translation, but they are there in the original edition, standing out boldly in the margins, continually inviting the reader to confirm these novel findings by his own personal appeal to experience.

Gilbert makes note of geometry in his preface (p. 1b), but his is not the enthusiastic endorsement of mathematical method that was Galileo's. There is evidence that Galileo read the *De magnete*, even making a marginal note in his copy, and the magnetic philosophy is actually featured in the third day's dialogue of the *Two Chief World Systems*. There Salviati expresses his admiration for Gilbert, noting that he is joined in this by "every man who has attentively read his book and carried out his experiments."[39] Some of these experiments are then discussed and indications given that Galileo actually performed them and, characteristically, obtained results superior to Gilbert's. Obviously Galileo has "the highest praise, admiration, and envy for this author," and yet he must voice a slight criticism through the mouth of Salviati:

> *What I might have wished for in Gilbert would be a little more of the mathematician, and especially a thorough grounding in geometry, a discipline which would have rendered him less rash about accepting as rigorous proofs those reasons which he puts forward as verae causae for the correct conclusions he himself had observed. His reasons, candidly speaking, are not rigorous, and lack that force which must unquestionably be present in those adduced as necessary and eternal scientific conclusions.*[40]

This criticism may tell as much about Galileo as it does about Gilbert, for it hints that in Galileo's mind a combination of experimental and mathematical methodology should ultimately lead to a knowledge of these same "true causes."

Francis Bacon was also an admirer of Gilbert, and illustrated his *Novum Organum* with experiments drawn from Gilbert's treatise,* but he too was critical of Gilbert's attempt to extend his magnetic theory to the whole of the cosmos. Undoubtedly Gilbert was precipitate in this respect, probably influenced by Neoplatonist and animistic notions that had found their way into the literature on magnetism, along with other strains deriving from magic and the Hermetic tradition. This supplied what may be referred to as the rationalist element in Gilbert's thought, which led him to generalize too extensively on the basis of his experiments and to set forth some questionable results, in his words, "*in probabilibus hypothesibus,*" well translated by Mottelay as "in hypotheses that are provable" (p. 2d), thereby reminding us that *probabile* had a different meaning for Gilbert than for ourselves, who are now prone to settle for conjectural and probable explanations in matters as difficult as these.

## Book first

The first book is introductory in character, recounting the sources on which the work is based and outlining the characteristics of the loadstone in a general way. The style of writing is typical of the schools, and quite different in this respect from all except the earliest of Galileo's compositions.[41] It gives credence to the opinion, otherwise with little support, that Gilbert had studied not only at Cambridge but also on the Continent, probably in an Italian university. Despite the advertised newness of *De magnete*, considerable had been written about the magnet in ancient and medieval times, and Gilbert here provides a good survey of all this material. A surprising amount of it is contained in the *Great Books*, so the interested reader can consult at first hand Plato's comments on the magnet in the *Ion* and the *Timaeus*,† Aristotle's remarks in the *Physics* and in *On the Soul*,‡ Galen's fuller analysis in his *On the Natural Faculties*,§ and Lucretius's most complete explanation in his didactic poem, *On the Nature of Things*.‖ The work that most influenced Gilbert's own, however, was the less-well-known *Letter on the Magnet* of Petrus Peregrinus, alias Peter of Maricourt, which was composed in 1269 and is acknowledged by Gilbert as "a pretty erudite book considering the time" (p. 5b). This was one of the best experimental treatises to come out of the Middle Ages, and many of the experiments described in it are taken over and refined by Gilbert.[42] It is interesting to note that Gilbert, who shows traces of English chauvinism throughout the work, sees Roger Bacon as behind Peter's work, whereas in truth this *magister experimentorum* was actually the inspiration behind Roger's own writing.[43] Others whom Gilbert had read carefully include Girolamo Cardano, whose name Gilbert anglicizes as Cardan, and Giovanni Battista Della Porta, whom he refers to variously as Baptista Porta or Porta throughout the exposition. Both of these men were Renaissance Neoplatonists, imbued with animistic and vitalistic notions, and thus much interested in the lifelike properties of the magnet. Cardano's most important contributions were to mathematics, but in his encyclopedic *De subtilitate rerum*, published in 1550, he described some properties of magnets, adumbrated the distinction between magnetic and electric phenomena that Gilbert was to establish in definitive fashion, and proposed the theory that magnetic declination was caused by the pull of a magnetic star in the tail of the constellation Ursa Major. Della Porta is of similar interest for his

---

* *GBWW*, Vol. 30, pp. 163c–d, 166c–67a, 181b–c, 182b–c, 184a.
† *GBWW*, Vol. 7, pp. 144b, 471b–c.
‡ *GBWW*, Vol. 8, pp. 354b–c, 634c.
§ *GBWW*, Vol. 10, pp. 177a–78c.
‖ *GBWW*, Vol. 12, pp. 92b–94c.

*Magia naturalis*, first published in 1558 and thereafter going through many editions, whose very title reveals its concern with the occult. This was a collection of novelties, tricks, and illusions, but it dealt with optical and magnetic phenomena also, and indeed reported some interesting measurements with magnets. Among the Englishmen Gilbert acknowledges mention should be made of Robert Norman (p. 5d), whose book on magnetism, *The New Attractive*, published in 1581, was the first to discuss the phenomenon of magnetic dip; in it Norman gives instructions for making a compass needle that will not be affected by dip but will remain horizontal in its operation.[44] Another is Edward Wright (p. 7a), who wrote an introduction following Gilbert's preface for the 1600 edition of *De magnete*, wherein he asserted that the earth's rotation, as taught by Gilbert in his sixth book, was not in conflict with Holy Scripture.

Following some descriptive material in Chapter 2, various properties of the loadstone are investigated, beginning in Chapter 3 with the first experiment, marked with a large asterisk in the margin, which contains instructions for making a spherical magnet. This Gilbert maintains "is a true homogeneous offspring of the earth and is of the same shape" (p. 9d), and it will henceforth serve as his primary instrument for bringing to the knowledge of mankind "many abstruse and unheeded truths of philosophy, hid in deplorable darkness" (p. 10a). Gilbert invents a special name for this magnet, calling it a *terrella*, or in Greek *microgē*, which significantly, as Mottelay tells us, means "earthkin" or "little earth." Instructions are then given for finding the poles of the *terrella*, using essentially the methods of Peter of Maricourt, and then a little experiment (i.e., one marked with a small asterisk) is detailed explaining how a "fine iron wire as long as a barley corn" can be made to stand erect when it is directly over one of the poles (p. 10c). In succeeding chapters, series of tests are performed with loadstones of this type, and other magnetic phenomena are investigated with iron ore, wrought iron, smelted iron, etc. All of this leads up to the concluding chapter of the first book, wherein Gilbert lays out the basic idea on which his magnetic philosophy will be built, namely, that the earth (*tellus*) itself is essentially magnetic and so is a giant loadstone, with properties similar to the *terrella*, properties that serve to explain why it "lies ever in the same direction in the universe" (p. 23b). This is "the real foundation of terrestrial philosophy," which Gilbert wishes to submit "to the judgment of scholars" and which, when examined thoroughly, "will stand as firm as aught that ever was proposed in philosophy, backed by ingenious argumentation, or buttressed by mathematical demonstrations" (p. 23b–c). The arguments that follow are based negatively on the failure to find anywhere the Aristotelian element earth (pp. 24a, 25b) and positively on the fact that both *tellus* and *terrella* have poles and an equator, and draw objects to themselves along similar geometrical paths. In this last observation, of course, Gilbert conflates gravitational properties with magnetic properties, an identification we now see as an error, but which proved to be remarkably suggestive for those who came after him. James Joyce once remarked that a man of genius makes no mistakes, that his errors are portals of discovery. This saying is remarkably apposite here, for Gilbert's error really started the search for a missing cosmological ingredient, namely, the physical cause or force that holds together the system of the world, in which Galileo feigned disinterest, but which Kepler pursued in terms of the model Gilbert provided, and which Newton finally attained in his law of universal gravitation.

### Book second

If the first book reveals Gilbert as a creative scientist of insight and genius, the second shows him as the patient experimenter who clearly differentiated magnetic from electric phenomena and separated out the class of substances that behave as amber does when rubbed; he names these *electrica* or "electrics," thereby introducing the root term electric into the English language and marking its study as a special field of investigation. Gilbert's starting point here was the classification of various movements, which he multiplied from Aristotle's two (toward and away from the center) to the following five: coition, direction, variation, declination, and revolution. The first of these he treats in the present book, and each of the others becomes the subject of concern in succeeding books.

Coition is the word Gilbert prefers to the more common attraction, and it is the examination of the different ways in which bodies seem to attract one another that he is able to distinguish the amber effect from the magnetic. Detailed experiments are necessary to make the differentiation; to perform them, a large asterisk in the margin directs attention to instructions for building a test instrument, called the *versorium*, itself a primitive electroscope (pp. 27d–28a). Also intensely interested in determining the causes of both types of attraction, Gilbert shows his scholastic heritage by attributing electrical effects to a material cause and magnetic ones to a formal cause. The former is some type of effluvium emitted by amber and similar substances that engulfs small particles and draws them toward the parent body, whereas the latter is a primal form (*forma praecipua*) that generates an orb of virtue around the magnetic substance. Gilbert apparently avoided the term attraction so as to bypass the problem of action at a distance, and probably for the same reason he concentrated on formal and material causes rather than on efficient causes when explaining coition. Magnets approach each other, not because one pulls the other but because there exists in nature a harmonious action or mutual tendency whereby they come together. Such an explanation is not that of classical mechanics, but it shows some kinship with Einstein's general theory of relativity, wherein space-time geodesics replace Newtonian attractive forces.[45] Gilbert's account also has elements in common with that of Thomas Aquinas, whose opinion he cites favorably in this context (p. 36b–c) and whom earlier he has complimented by speculating that "with his godlike and perspicacious mind he would have developed many a point had he been acquainted with magnetic experiments" (p. 4b). On the matter of experiments, Gilbert is not at all deficient in this second book, for the margins are adorned with five large asterisks and no less than 97 small asterisks. (It would be an interesting exercise to attempt to identify these from a simple reading of the English text, without having recourse to the original edition.) Most of the demonstrations are concerned with investigating the geometry of magnetic forces, increasing the strength of magnets through the use of caps or armatures, and establishing generalizations such as the following: "The velocity of the movement of a magnetic body to a loadstone is in proportion to the strength of the loadstone, or its mass, or its shape, or the nature of the medium, or the distance within the magnetic sphere of action" (p. 55a). The experimental study of magnetism and electricity, and eventually of gravitation, was thus well under way by the time Gilbert had completed work on this book.

*Book third*

Now begins the detailed treatment of other movements apart from coition, and first of these is that by which a magnetized needle assumes its orientation in the plane parallel to the earth's surface. In effect, this is a treatment of the behavior of the magnetic compass, which Gilbert well knows to be irregular, pointing sometimes to the celestial poles and sometimes not, depending on the latitude and longitude of its location. Continuing his resolution in terms of causes, however, he breaks down this orientation into two factors, one a true direction, which will be ascertained in the present book (*De directione*), and the other the deviation from that direction, known as variation, which will be treated in the following book (*De variatione*). In adopting this solution, Gilbert rejects the explanations of Peter of Maricourt and Cardano, who located the source of the magnet's orientation in the celestial poles or particular stars, and also that of "others" who more correctly "have come down to rocks and I know not what 'magnetic mountains'" for their explanation (p. 60d). In Gilbert's view, true direction is caused by the magnetic needle simply aligning itself with the earth's north and south poles, for the earth is a large loadstone, and needles on its surface and within its orb of virtue must behave just as they do on the surface of the *terrella* (p. 61c).

Most of the third book is thereupon concerned with investigating the directive or versorial force that acts on a needle and brings it into alignment with the north-south axis. Gilbert invents a special term for this force, calling it *verticitas*, a word that Mottelay anglicizes as verticity (p. 62b). To study this experimentally, Gilbert adapts his electroscope by substituting a magnetized needle for the electric indicator, making of it a "magnetized versorium." The titles of the subsequent chapters from 3 through 16 show the extent of Gilbert's study of this basic orienting force. Particularly noteworthy are his experiments with heat and friction as inducing magnetic effects; the cut on page 71, for example, shows a black-smith magnetizing a length of iron by hammering it while oriented toward the north (*septentrio* or *septentriones*) and south (*auster*). This drawing, as the Latin inscriptions hint, is reproduced from the original edition of 1600. Since magnetized versoriums are indispensable for verifying such effects, and must be sensitive in order to do so, Gilbert devotes his concluding chapter to the care of these instruments and of magnetic compasses, providing full details regarding "the best process for rubbing and magnetically exciting them and the proper method of applying the process" (p. 75a).

### Book fourth

The importance of the magnetic compass for navigation was recognized by sailors long before the end of the sixteenth century, and considerable empirical information had been gathered by them with respect to the needle's variation from true north. No satisfactory explanation had yet been given of this deviation from the meridian, however, and it is to this problem that Gilbert addresses himself in his fourth book. He rejects the possibility that such variation is caused by concentrations of loadstone in "magnetic mountains or a certain magnetic rock" (p. 77d), and even rules out the existence of magnetic islands or mines filled with loadstone deep in the earth's interior (p. 81b–c). His preferred explanation is similar to that for verticity, being suggested by experiments he can perform on the *terrella*. If a *terrella* is not a perfect sphere, a magnetic needle will be found to vary its orientation depending upon the mass of matter that protrudes beyond the basic spherical core. Similarly, the purity of the magnetic material located in protruding masses must influence the needle's orientation in much the same way that a strong loadstone exerts greater influence than a weak one. Such reasoning led Gilbert to locate the true cause of magnetic variation in inequalities of mass and magnetic purity among the earth's elevations (p. 79a) and, as a corollary, to maintain that the variation is constant at a given place on the earth's surface (p. 80d). Noteworthy in this book is the chapter devoted to the construction of compasses (p. 83b), and another, to the design of an instrument that can be used to measure variation accurately at sea in the most adverse weather conditions (p. 86d). Gilbert's explanation of variation is of course faulty, and his error in this matter is exacerbated by his proneness to dismiss lack of agreement between theory and observation on the carelessness, falsity, and general unreliability of reports made by seamen—whence his concern for the construction and use of more accurate instruments (p. 89a).

### Book fifth

Although Gilbert was not the first to discover magnetic declination or dip, he was the first to attempt to explain it, seeking its causes in his fifth book (*De declinatione*). Consistent with his previous explanations, he accounted for this also in terms of "natural verticity," or the magnetic properties of the earth as manifested by experiments with the *terrella*. He invented the first instrument to measure dip (*instrumentum declinationis*), pictured on page 93. From experiments with a large *terrella* he was able to show that the dip at the equator is zero and that it increases uniformly as the needle reaches the pole, at which point it becomes perpendicular (p. 94d). The diagram on page 95d is noteworthy for its indication of the "orb of virtue" (*orbis virtutis*) that surrounds the *terrella* and that determines the needle's orientation; Gilbert is explicit "that dip is not caused by . . . attraction" (p. 97c). Also noteworthy is his instrument for showing the degree of dip that should be experienced at any latitude on a sphere (p. 96) and Gilbert's application of this to a new method of determining latitude at sea "in any part of the world, without the help of the heavenly bodies, sun, planets, or fixed stars, and in foggy weather as well as in darkness" (p. 100c). The chart he proposed to use for this purpose was similar in precision to that shown on page 100, but was inserted as a fold-out in the Latin edition of 1600. Gilbert was quite enthusiastic about this proposal, claiming that from it "we can see how far from idle is the magnetic philosophy; on the contrary, how delightful, how beneficial, how divine!" (p. 101a). Here too, however, his explanation was incorrect; yet there was no way of his knowing this, as the dip effect had only recently been noted and there were no observations on which he could have based a correct theory, such as were available for magnetic variation. Believing, then, that he has solved all of the problems of the earth's magnetism, in the last two chapters of this book Gilbert waxes enthusiastic over "the formal magnetic act spherically effused" (p. 102d), and is led to make the extravagant claim that "the magnetic force is animate, or imitates a soul; in many respects it surpasses the human soul while that is united to an organic body" (p. 104b). From this and similar statements one can see that, for all his empiricist inclinations, Gilbert was effectively won over by the vitalist and animistic philosophy of Cardano and Della Porta, who explained all cosmic phenomena in terms of an *anima mundi* or world soul.

*Book sixth*

The foregoing thus prepared for Gilbert's daring last book, entitled *De telluris globo, magno magnete*, "Of the earth as a large magnet," wherein he draws out the cosmological implications of his doctrine. In the early chapters we see that Gilbert knew of Copernicus's teaching and that he studied the astronomical observations of others, including the Prutenic Tables of Erasmus Rheinhold (cf. note on p. 118b). It is in the second chapter, where Gilbert mentions Copernicus's teacher, Dominicus Maria of Ferrara (p. 106d), that Galileo made his marginal note calling attention to the falsity of Dominicus's observations and explaining how they can be disproved.[46]

Basing himself on the earlier teaching of Peter of Maricourt, Gilbert was convinced that revolution or rotation was one of the magnetic movements,

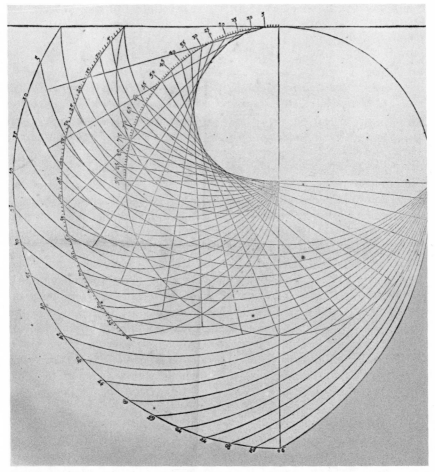

The chart Gilbert prepared for using magnetic dip to determine latitude at sea, which was to be inserted "betwixt the 200 and 201 folioes" of the original Latin edition

although he denied that a *terrella* could be converted into a perpetual motion machine, as Peter had believed (p. 112b). The uniform revolution every twenty-four hours that Peter attributed to a *terrella* perfectly balanced along a north-south axis, however, Gilbert applied to the earth, and so used magnetism to explain its diurnal rotation. It should be noted here that while Gilbert taught the earth's rotation, he did not explicitly argue that either the earth or the sun was at the center of the universe. He seems, however, to have been partial to the Copernican system, as the following passage suggests:

> *Thus, inasmuch as the sun itself is the mover and inciter of the universe, the other planets that are situate within the sphere of its forces, being impelled and set in motion, do also with their own forces determine their own courses and revolve in their own periods, according to the amplitude of their greater rotation and the differences of the forces effused and the perception of a greater good* [*p. 116b–c*].

Other phenomena, such as the inclination of the earth's axis and the precession of the equinoxes, Gilbert tried to explain in terms of his magnetic theory, but he ran into serious difficulties in so doing and was forced to admit that "we cannot assign with certainty any natural causes" for these effects (p. 121c).

The boldness of Gilbert's speculations in this last book left him open to criticism, but there can be no denying that his proposals provided a much needed step in the development of gravitational theory. His influence on Galileo has already been mentioned, but much more impressive was the stimulus he provided to Kepler for working out the physical causes of planetary motion. Kepler's *Epitome of Copernican Astronomy* is written in the form of questions and answers, and one of the queries asks whether or not it is "unbelievable" that the heavenly bodies act as huge magnets. In reply, Kepler urges the questioner to

> *read the philosophy of magnetism of the Englishman William Gilbert; for in that book, although the author did not believe that the Earth moved among the stars, nevertheless he attributes a magnetic nature to it, by very many arguments, and he teaches that its magnetic threads or filaments extend in straight lines from south to north.\**

Kepler then goes on to apply this doctrine of magnetic filaments to explain the motion of the planets in their orbits under the sun's influence.† Admittedly, this was still a long way from Newton's *Principia*, but one must concede that the seminal idea was Gilbert's and thus that he too had a role to play in founding the science of celestial mechanics.[47]

However historians of science evaluate this contribution, there can be no doubt that Gilbert provides an excellent example of pre-Baconian experimental philosophy. It has been said that Gilbert's home in London was the scene of meetings of a group of scientists who discussed their work each month and so were the precursors of the Royal Society. There is no historical basis for this claim, and yet it cannot be denied that when the Royal Society eventually was founded, and experimental science came into its own, Englishmen could look back on their own countryman, William Gilbert, and see in him one who exemplified, par excellence, the ideals the society had come to represent. In their eyes, at least, his would have to be the strongest claim for recognition as the father of experimental science.

## Harvey: The Motion of the Heart and Blood

The founder of modern biological and medical science, William Harvey,[48] was the youngest of the three men whose masterworks we are here reviewing. To locate him temporally with respect to Gilbert and Galileo, he was born just after William Gilbert's admission to the Royal College of Physicians—a college in which he himself was to become a fellow after Gilbert's death and in which he would take a lifelong interest. Harvey was also Galileo's junior by fourteen years, being a medical student at Padua while Galileo was a professor of mathematics there. Having already studied both arts and medicine at Cambridge, Harvey journeyed to the Continent in 1600, the year the *De magnete* appeared, to finish his training at what was then the most renowned medical school in Europe, the University of Padua. There his principal professor was the great anatomist, Girolamo Fabrici of Acquapendente, the Latin of whose name is Hieronymus Fabricius. It is unlikely that Galileo taught Harvey, since the mathematics and astronomy Galileo was then teaching were elementary in character, and Harvey would be presumed to have covered these before beginning his advanced studies.

Unlike Gilbert and Galileo, Harvey had great respect for Aristotle and used him as a methodological guide throughout his life's work. It is not known from whom Harvey acquired his knowledge of, and appreciation for, Aristotle, although Aristotelians had been strong in the arts faculty at Padua, particularly since the time of Jacopo Zabarella, and Harvey may have attended the lectures of Zabarella's successor, Cesare Cremonini. Professors in faculties of medicine at that time were generally more partial to Galen than to Aristotle, but at Padua even in medicine there were strong Aristotelians such as Andrea Cesalpino, who had taught that subject at Pisa when Galileo studied there, and Caspar Hofmann, with whom Harvey later had lengthy correspondence (cf. note on p. 284d). Fabricius, however, was the professor Harvey most referred to as his teacher, ac-

---

* *GBWW*, Vol. 16, p. 935b.
† *GBWW*, Vol. 16, pp. 941b–42a.

knowledging his twofold debt to Aristotle and to Fabricius, "the former as my leader, the latter as my informant of the way" (p. 337c).

After his return to England in 1602, Harvey practiced medicine in London, served as physician at St. Bartholomew's Hospital, and lectured on surgery at the Royal College during a career that lasted over forty years. He also was royal physician to both James I and Charles I, and had many influential friends and acquaintances, among them Robert Boyle, Thomas Hobbes, and Francis Bacon, the last of whom he attended as personal physician. Harvey married in 1604 but had no children; he survived his wife, spending his last decade as a widower and living with his brothers, who were successful London merchants.

Harvey's greatest work is his treatise on *The Motion of the Heart and Blood in Animals*, published in Latin at Frankfurt am Main in 1628, with the title *Exercitatio anatomica de motu cordis et sanguinis in animalibus.* An English version appeared in London in 1653; the standard translation, which is that included in the *Great Books*, was prepared by Robert Willis for the Sydenham Society of London in 1847. This work on the heart was Harvey's first published writing. It is known from his notes that he did extensive research on respiration, the brain, the locomotion and generation of animals, and a variety of other topics. He probably planned to publish treatises on all these subjects, but that on *Animal Generation* was the only one to find its way into print, at London in 1651. Many of his manuscripts and notes were confiscated and destroyed at the outbreak of the Civil War in 1642, and the rest are presumed burned, along with Gilbert's legacy, in the conflagration of 1666. Harvey's anatomical lecture notes were preserved, however, as were drafts of projected treatises on muscles and on animal locomotion; from these materials and from surviving correspondence, historians of science attempt to reconstruct the chronology of his discovery of the blood's circulation.

Although *The Motion of the Heart and Blood* is much briefer than *Animal Generation*, it is compactly written, and its technical terminology requires explanation to be understood by the reader not trained in biology or medicine. The lengthy *Animal Generation*, on the other hand, abounds in descriptive material that can be readily comprehended by the general reader. For this reason the commentary that follows will be concerned mainly with *The Motion of the Heart and Blood*; only brief guidelines will be given for reading the letters to Riolan, which contain further comments on the circulation of the blood and thus clarify the teaching in Harvey's original treatise.

*Dedications*

Harvey was a royalist sympathizer, having served as physician extraordinary to King James I and in higher positions under King Charles I, to whom his first published work is dedicated (p. 267). Harvey was on par-

# EXERCITATIO,
# ANATOMICA DE
## MOTV CORDIS ET SAN-
## GVINIS IN ANIMALI-
### BVS,

*GVILIELMI HARVEI ANGLI,*
*Medici Regii, & Professoris Anatomiæ in Col-*
*legio Medicorum Londinensi.*

*FRANCOFVRTI,*
Sumptibus GVILIELMI FITZERI.

*ANNO M. DC. XXVIII.*

Title page of Harvey's *De motu cordis*

ticularly friendly terms with Charles, who took him along on his travels, was interested in his scientific investigations, and provided animals from the royal park for his experiments; characteristically outspoken, Harvey did not conceal his admiration for Charles even after the latter's execution. The dedication to this patron and friend is thus genuine and straightforward. Worthy of special note is Harvey's likening the place of the heart in animals to that of the king in his realm and the sun in the universe, an analogy popular at the time and not without Copernican overtones. Harvey's emphasis on the primacy of the heart here, however, gave way in his more mature thought to an emphasis on the primacy of the blood, which he came to regard as the principal vital agent in animals.

The second dedication is to Dr. John Argent and to his colleagues, "other learned physicians," at the Royal College. This is a stylized letter, written with the expected humility, revealing an awareness of departure from the accepted anatomical tradition, denying any arrogance in so doing, and giving assent to publication only because of the importunate "requests, I might say entreaties, of many" (p. 267). The conventional form, however, does not falsify what Harvey has to say in these dedicatory remarks. Argent had been one of Harvey's examiners when he sought admission to the college in 1603, and remained a constant friend thereafter; his presidency of the Royal College at the time only gave Harvey an additional reason, out of courtesy, for dedicating the book to him.

Whether or not this dedication incorporates actual statements of fact has important consequences because of Harvey's opening assertion that he has already presented his "new views of the motion and function of the heart in [his] anatomical lectures" at the college, and that he has "now for nine years and more confirmed these views by multiplied demonstrations" in the presence of his colleagues (p. 267b). Harvey was the Lumleian lecturer on surgery at the Royal College from 1615 onwards, and still extant are his lecture notes of 1616, to which he apparently made additions over the next ten years. There is no unambiguous record of the discovery of the circulation in these lecture notes, nor is there any correspondence or any record of a physician at the Royal College who attended Harvey's dissections that acknowledges or comments on this revolutionary find. If Harvey's "nine years and more" are taken on face value, however, he came upon the circulation no later than 1619. Yet he need not have worked out all of its details at that time, and some historians prefer on the basis of other evidence to date the conclusive proof between 1625 and 1627.[49] The observational data reported in the early chapters, it is generally admitted, are in close agreement with the anatomical lecture notes, and thus date from the period Harvey here identifies.

Also noteworthy in this dedication is Harvey's characteristic respect for tradition, for authorities of the past such as Aristotle and Galen—a virtue. in which he far surpasses Gilbert, to say nothing of Galileo. Harvey was not prone on this account, as were many of the anatomists of the time, to direct his researches only toward a vindication of such authorities, but stressed instead the continued need to observe and experiment so as to make additions to the body of truth possessed from antiquity. It is in this spirit that he professes "both to learn and to teach anatomy, not from books but from dissections; not from the positions of philosophers but from the fabric of nature" (p. 268c). In all this, he does not "think it right or proper to strive to take from the ancients any honour that is their due, nor yet to dispute with the moderns, and enter into controversy with those who have excelled in anatomy and been my teachers" (p. 268c). So he simply avows himself "the partisan of truth alone," to whose acquisition he has devoted all his labors (p. 268d). As will become clear from what follows, and consonant with these statements, Harvey was a great experimentalist and comparative anatomist, but this did not exclude a distinct speculative bent that enabled him to see connections between the new science and ancient philosophy, and so to produce the remarkably synthetic work we are about to read.

*Introductory material*

The *De motu cordis* comprises an introduction and seventeen chapters, the first of which merely outlines the author's motives for writing and so may be included here as part of the introductory material. The introduction itself was probably written at the end of Harvey's researches, and, unlike the rest of the work, is devastating in its critique of prevailing medical theories. The reason for this is Harvey's desire to call attention to the seriousness of the errors being propagated in medical schools, and the need for a complete rethinking of the relation between the heart's beating and the process of respiration. The chief target is Galen, the second-century Greek physician, whose basic work is among the *Great Books* and can be consulted with profit at this point.* Galen had criticized the earlier anatomist, Erasistratos, who flourished in the third century B.C., but he persisted in maintaining that the heart's pulsation and respiration were ordained to the same end, namely, the ventilation of the blood (p. 268d). Even Fabricius, whose *De respiratione* had appeared in 1615, assigns the lungs a role in cooling the heart, and so continues to associate the systole and diastole of the heart with the movement of the lungs (p. 269a). The terms systole and diastole used here are extremely important, for they recur frequently throughout the work and their understanding is requisite to its comprehension. Systole is the contraction of the heart wherein blood is forced out of its chambers, whereas diastole is the expansion or dilatation of the heart wherein the cavities again fill with blood. The two movements occur rhythmically, and it is their alternation that is referred

---

* *GBWW*, Vol. 10, pp. 213a–15d; see also pp. 179d–85a and 188a–d.

to as the beating of the heart. An analogous contraction and dilatation takes place in the arteries, also referred to as systole and diastole, and this similarly accounts for the beating of the pulse.

The burden of Harvey's attack against the Galenists consists in showing that the arteries contain, not air or spirits, but simply blood. Here he pits Galen himself against the Galenic thesis (p. 270a), and draws on other experimental evidence that will be detailed more fully in the body of the work itself. Note his mention of Riolanus, or John Riolan (p. 271a), the French anatomist who is the addressee of the two letters on *The Circulation of the Blood*, and who will occupy us later. From this Harvey passes to problems associated with a comparatively recent discovery, that of Realdus Columbus (p. 271d), in whose *De re anatomica*, published at Venice in 1559, is contained a fairly accurate description of the heart's movement. Columbus is credited with discovering the minor or pulmonary circuit of the blood, which Harvey will also examine later, in Chapters 6 and 7 of this work. Another author whom Harvey now cites is Andreas Laurentius, who published a *Historia anatomica* at Frankfurt in 1600, and who there revived the Galenic theory that pus from the chest, rather than being voided directly through the urine, is "absorbed from the cavities of the chest into the pulmonary vein" and thence passes through the heart to the kidneys (p. 273b). If such "heterogeneous matter" can be discharged through the heart, Harvey wonders why Laurentius had not seen the same route as a proper passage for the blood itself. It is the existence of such difficulties and numerous inconsistencies in current anatomical teaching that prompts Harvey to research this entire problem anew and come to his present solution.

The first chapter adds little to what has already been said. It attests to the many difficulties involved, particularly in observing the times at which systole and diastole take place in rapidly beating hearts (p. 273c), notes Laurentius's confirmation of the complexity of the problem (p. 273d), and reminds the reader of the entreaties of his friends and the indifference of others, both impelling him to make his results available (p. 274a). Finally, conscious of the apparent slight to his teacher Fabricius in the introduction (p. 269a), he here makes amends and notes that, although Fabricius had treated "almost every one of the several parts of animals in a special work, [he] has left the heart alone untouched" (p. 274a), thereby happily leaving this topic free for the investigation of his student.

*Factual observations*

The first substantive portion of *De motu cordis*, chapters 2 through 7, shows Harvey the experimentalist at his best. Chapters 2 through 4 describe his detailed investigations of the ventricles, the arteries, and the auricles, respectively; chapter 5 presents a summary of the conclusions to which these investigations lead; and chapters 6 and 7 propose a corollary that follows from them relating to the pulmonary circuit of the blood. In all of this the observations are carefully made and the inferences drawn with logical precision, thus setting up a firm factual base on which the demonstration of the blood's circulation is to be erected.

Harvey's initial point of attack is the study of the heart's movements in systole and diastole to establish "the very opposite of opinions commonly received" (p. 275a). To overcome the observational difficulty posed by rapidly beating hearts, Harvey, a pioneer in comparative anatomy, notes that he made his experiments on the "colder animals, such as toads, frogs, serpents, small fishes, crabs, shrimps, snails, and shell-fish," and also on "warm-blooded animals, such as the dog and hog," when they were near death and their heartbeats had slowed appreciably (p. 274b). In such circumstances "it is made much more easy to perceive and unravel what the motions really are, and how they are performed" (p. 274c). The conclusion to which these observations come is that the heart acts like a muscle, and that its primary motion is one of constriction during which it squeezes out the blood it contains. Thus, when the heart beats it tenses up, causing its apex to strike against the chest, where it can be felt externally; when this occurs, moreover, it is in systole, forcing blood out of its chambers, and not in its expanded state. Harvey's surprising conclusion is that "the motion which is generally regarded as the diastole of the heart, is in truth its systole" (p. 275a). Once he establishes this, he is able to explain the shortcomings in the explanation of the heart's movement offered by the great Paduan anatomist, Vesalius (p. 275b), and can also dispose of a notion on which Vesalius's explanation was based, namely, that the heart "has the power of drawing the blood into the ventricles" (p. 275c).

Harvey's next step is to analyze the movement of the arteries and to see how this is related to the motion of the heart. This too leads to a surprising conclusion, namely, that "at the moment the heart contracts, and when the breast is struck, when, in short, the organ is in its state of systole, the arteries are dilated, yield a pulse, and are in the state of diastole" (p. 275d). Observation of the ventricles confirms this, for when they contract the arteries are distended, whereas when they cease to act the pulse in the arteries is scarcely perceptible. Again the conclusion, although "in opposition to commonly received opinions," is inescapable, namely, "that the diastole of the arteries corresponds with the time of the heart's systole" (p. 276a). So Harvey can confidently state:

> *It is in virtue of one and the same cause, therefore, that all the arteries of the body pulsate, viz., the contraction of the left ventricle; in the same way as the pulmonary artery pulsates by the contraction of the right ventricle* [*p. 276a*].

These results lead Harvey to a further study of the motion of the heart's auricles, providing one of the finest series of observations in the entire work. John Riolan and Caspar Bauhin, on whose textbook, *Theatrum anatomicum*, published at Frankfurt in 1605, Harvey had based his anatomical lectures, both taught that the heart has four movements, two proper to the auricles and two to the ventricles. Harvey's detailed observations of hearts that were slowed up, even up to and including the point of death, enabled him to show that what appear to be four movements are actually only two; for the two auricles move simultaneously, and immediately after they move so do the two ventricles. Thus the beat of the heart actually begins with the constriction of the auricles, and then extends to the ventricles. Strictly speaking, therefore, one should not say that the heart, as a whole, is "the first part to live, the last to die, but rather its auricles, or the part which corresponds to the auricles in serpents, fishes, &c., which both lives before the heart and dies after it" (pp. 277d–78a). Having come to this result, Harvey further suggests that perhaps the blood is the real life-giving principle, a noteworthy observation, signaling here an insight he was to pursue in his later writings (p. 278a).

On the basis of these factual observations, Harvey is now prepared to summarize what he has ascertained concerning the action and function of the heart. An ample supply of blood is contained at "the head of the veins," and when the heart beats this is thrown by the auricle into the ventricle, at whose contraction it is discharged to the arteries; the right ventricle expels its blood through the vena arteriosa (now known as the pulmonary artery) into the lungs, whereas the left ventricle propels its blood into the aorta, and thence "by the arteries to the body at large" (p. 278d). The motions of the ventricles and auricles take place consecutively and rhythmically, and the overall effect is a kind of deglutition, or swallowing, which brings about "a transfusion of the blood from the veins to the arteries" (p. 279b). This then is the proper motion of the heart, and its one action "is the transmission of the blood and its distribution, by means of the arteries, to the very extremities of the body" (p. 279c). Most of the confusion about this movement, Harvey continues, arises from the fact that anatomists have identified the action of the heart with that of the lungs, essentially one of respiration. Following Galen, they thought that blood passed from the liver through the vena cava to the right ventricle, and from there through the vena arteriosa to the lungs for their nutrition. This posed the problem, however, as to how blood reaches the left ventricle, and to explain this Galenic anatomists had to posit the existence of small pores in the septum, the membrane that separates the two ventricles, and to maintain that "the blood made its way from the right to the left ventricle by sweating through the septum of the heart" (p. 280b). Vesalius, however, had searched for such pores in the septum and failed to find them. Harvey himself feels that he has already excluded this explanation in his introduction, where he asserts

> *In faith, no such pores can be demonstrated, neither, in fact, do any such exist. For the septum of the heart is of a denser and more compact structure than any portion of the body, except the bones and sinews [p. 272d].*

Apart from this statement, however, he offers no detailed observational or experimental proof—a failure that was not passed over by his critics, who made it a point of continuing controversy.

The two chapters that follow next (6 and 7) are concerned with the passage of the blood through the lungs, and there is some reason to believe that they were composed in an order the reverse of that in which they now appear.[50] The point of both chapters is to show that, if the blood cannot travel from the right to the left ventricle through pores in the septum, it must do so by percolating through the parenchyma or pulpy tissue of the lungs (p. 282d). Arguing in a variety of ways, Harvey supports his conclusion by observations first on animals without lungs, then on fetal hearts, and finally on the hearts of more perfect animals of mature age; he also confirms it by analogies drawn from the percolation of fluids through the liver and kidney, and by detailed examination of the structure of the valves situated at the orifice of the pulmonary artery. Although not as well organized as the material in other chapters, the exposition nonetheless contains all the factual information requisite for understanding Harvey's great discovery, which he is now ready to explain.

*Discovery of the circulation*

Chapter 8 occupies the central position in Harvey's classic, and it is indeed the key chapter, for in it he relates how he went beyond his earlier observational analyses to the first suspicion of the blood's circulation. The chapter is a classic of scientific writing, for not only does it trace accurately the steps involved but it manages to convey some idea of the workings of the mind, some of the spirit and excitement, that attend the making of a new discovery. After all his observations, as he tells us, what began to impress itself on his consciousness was the huge quantity of blood that passes through the heart in a relatively short period of time (p. 285c). Harvey's attention may have been drawn to this realization by his reading of Aemilius Parisanus's *Nobilium exercitationum de subtilitate libri*, published at Venice in 1623, a work that calls attention to a similar fact, and that Harvey knew and later cited, although in a different context[51] (p. 364b). However this may be, he now sees that the supply of blood to the heart would be quickly exhausted if blood did not return in some way from the arteries back to the veins. So he writes:

> *And sooth to say, when I surveyed my mass of evidence, . . . I frequently and seriously bethought me, and long revolved in my mind, what might be the quantity of blood which was transmitted, in how short a time its passage must be effected, and the like; and not finding it possible that this could be [done] . . . unless the blood should somehow find its way from the arteries into the veins, and so return to the right side of the heart; I began to think whether there might not be a motion, as it were, in a circle. Now this I afterwards found to be true [p. 285c–d].*

The two steps involved in Harvey's momentous discovery are here clearly indicated: first, the suspicion, based on quantitative analysis, that there must be a return flow to the veins, and secondly, the realization that a quasi-circular motion is necessary to account for this. The latter insight Harvey acknowledges as deriving from Aristotle, who referred to the rain-and-water-evaporation cycle as circular in much the same sense:

> *Which motion we may be allowed to call circular, in the same way as Aristotle says that the air and the rain emulate the circular motion of the superior bodies [p. 285d].*

Two remarks may be made with respect to this account of the discovery, one relating to how the concept of circularity may have influenced it, the other to how the notion of a mechanical pump may have done likewise. With regard to the first, it is unlikely that Harvey was the type of Aristotelian who would have been preoccupied a priori with the idea of circular motion and that this preoccupation here stimulated his discovery. On the other hand, it seems plausible that what enabled him to see through the complexity of his observational data and solve the quantitative problem was the concept of motion in a circle. Thus it is probable that circularity functioned as the key concept in the discovery, for although first suggested a posteriori by observations, it was the unifying idea that permitted everything else to fall into place. With regard to the pump concept, on the other hand, there is no evidence here that Harvey was influenced by the mechanical philosophy in any way, although he is frequently cited in its support. In his anatomical lecture notes, however, there is an interesting passage, written partly in Latin and partly in English, that seems to hint at such influence. It reads as follows:

> *WH constat per fabricam cordis sanguinem per pulmones in aortam perpetuo transferri, as by two clacks of a water bellows to rayse water, constat per ligaturum transitum sanguinis ab arteriis ad venas unde △ perpetuum sanguinis motum in circulo fieri pulsu cordis.*

This may be translated:

> *WH is certain from the structure of the heart that the blood is perpetually carried across through the lungs into the aorta as by two clacks of a water bellows to raise water. It is certain from the experiment of the ligature that there is a passage of blood from the arteries to the veins. It is thus demonstrated that a perpetual motion of the blood in a circle is caused by the heart beat.[52]*

On the basis of this manuscript, historians at one time thought that Harvey's discovery of the circulation dated from as early as 1616, when the lecture notes were thought to be composed in their entirety; now the more common opinion is that this is a subsequent addition, inserted some ten years later. It has been further surmised that the pumping action Harvey refers to in the notes was suggested by a pump he had seen in a fire engine of a type that was not in use in London until about 1625.[53] Yet, even with these emendations, it cannot be said that Harvey entertained a mechanical view of nature, and particularly not of living things. The heart, for him, "is the beginning of life; the sun of the microcosm," and its motion has a "final cause" that far exceeds that of any mechanical contrivance (p. 286a).

*Confirmation and proof*

Having presented his discovery in this fashion, Harvey proceeds to point out three presuppositions that it entails, and notes that if he is able to confirm these, as he puts it, "I conceive that the truth I contend for will follow necessarily, and appear as a thing obvious to all" (p. 286c). He thereupon devotes two chapters apiece to the first two suppositions and one to the third, providing ample proofs and in so doing clearing up problems that have puzzled anatomists for centuries.

The first supposition is that "the blood is incessantly transmitted by the action of the heart from the vena cava to the arteries in such quantities that it cannot be supplied from the ingesta, and in such wise that the whole mass must very quickly pass through the organ" (p. 286c). Chapters 9 and 10 report confirmations of this through measurements of the actual quantity of blood transported, establishing that the heart expels at least "one drachm of blood . . . at each pulse"[54] and that "in the course of half an hour, the heart will have made more than one thousand beats" (p. 286d). These calculations are deliberately conservative, and yet they yield the irrefutable result that in a brief period the heart will have transmitted far more blood than any ingested food could possibly supply. Other experiments are detailed showing how quickly blood is emptied from an animal through a large artery, and how the pinching of the vena cava and the aorta of a live snake yields exactly the results to be expected from the supposed transmission.

The second supposition is that "the blood under the influence of the arterial pulse enters and is impelled in a continuous, equable, and incessant stream through every part and member of the body, in much larger quantity than were sufficient for nutrition, or than the whole mass of fluids could supply" (p. 286c). Harvey demonstrates the truth of this in chapters 11 and 12 through the use of ligatures, whereby he is able to show that there must be some passage from the arteries to the veins at the body's extremities. The experimentation here is ingenious, and altogether necessary since Harvey had no microscope and thus could not observe, as Malpighi was able to do in 1661, that the return flow is made through capillaries too small to be seen with the unaided eye. By successfully applying ligatures to the arm, however, and seeing under what circumstances the arteries and veins are swollen with blood, Harvey was able to verify not only the direction of flow but also the rough quantity of blood transmitted from the heart to the arteries and then returned to the veins.

The third supposition is directly concerned with the latter process, for it states that "the veins in like manner return this blood incessantly to the heart from all parts and members of the body" (p. 286c). Here his experimental work, detailed in chapter 13, is based on an examination of "the valves which are found in the cavities of the veins themselves" (p. 293a). These valves were discovered either by Fabricius, "a most skilful anatomist, and venerable old man," or by Jacobus Silvius, but neither of these rightly understood their function (p. 293b). Harvey then reports the effect of the valves on the venous flow, testing this with ligatures and with pressure exerted by the finger at various points along the vein. The drawings used to illustrate these experiments, it may be noted, are facsimiles of the originals appearing in the 1628 edition (p. 295).

With all of these arguments now assembled, in chapter 14 Harvey draws the obvious conclusion of the demonstration, which he states apodictically in the famous words:

> *it is absolutely necessary to conclude that the blood in the animal body is impelled in a circle, and is in a state of ceaseless motion; that this is the act or function which the heart performs by means of its pulse; and that it is the sole and only end of the motion and contraction of the heart* [*p. 296a*].

Not satisfied with this, however, in the remaining three chapters he offers further proofs: those in chapter 15 confirming the conclusion by probable reasons; those in chapter 16, by arguments a posteriori, which also serve to clear up a number of previously unexplained phenomena; and those in chapter 17, by a detailed examination of the structure of the heart. Having thus accounted for all these cardiac *phaenomena* or "appearances," Harvey is confident that he has illustrated and confirmed "the truth contended for throughout these pages," for otherwise "it would be very difficult to explain in any other way to what purpose all is constructed and arranged as we have seen it to be" (p. 304c). The expression "to what purpose" is Willis's translation of Harvey's "quam ob causam," which inadvertently conceals the latter's enduring concern for causal explanation. In fact, it may be argued that the entire structure of the *De motu cordis* is dictated by the methodology of Aristotle's *Posterior Analytics*, that the demonstration of the circulation is itself made through a material cause, i.e., the quantity of blood in the body, and that the work finally terminates in a complete definition of the heart that is given in terms of all four of Aristotle's causes.[55] This methodological commitment to Aristotle is not explicit in the text, however, although it becomes quite apparent in the introduction to *Animal Generation* (pp. 331–37).

*Letters to Riolan*

There was considerable discussion of Harvey's phenomenal discovery in the years following its publication, much of it favorable, although some Galenists remained unconvinced and so pressed to the attack. Among these was a French physician who had published a number of important works on anatomy, and for whom Harvey had great respect; this was John Riolan the Younger, called such to distinguish him from his father of the same name, who also had written a textbook on anatomy. In 1648 Riolan put out a small work at Leiden entitled *Encheiridium anatomicum et pathologicum*, which criticized the circulatory movement as now newly proposed. On receiving a copy, Harvey took occasion to reply to all his critics, and a few months later, in 1649, published a small book containing two anatomical disquisitions on *The Circulation of the Blood*, presented in the form of two letters to Riolan. The first is a point-by-point reply to the criticisms voiced in the *Encheiridium*, whereas the second is a more systematic treatise, probably composed prior to the appearance of Riolan's book, and now published as though it was addressed explicitly to Riolan but actually replying to Harvey's remaining critics.

The first letter is brief and mainly of interest for showing how deeply imbedded were Galenic notions in the medical profession of the time, and how patient Harvey could be in dealing with those who failed to comprehend his teaching. The second letter is more informative, for at its outset Harvey mentions that he omitted much material from his original treatise "as redundant and unnecessary," and that he is now making this available "for the sake of the studious" (p. 313c). There are no chapter headings or clearcut divisions of the text, but a number of topics are taken up that shed further light on the circulation. The first, beginning at page

An illustration from the collected lectures of William Harvey demonstrating the circulation of the blood and the action of valves in the veins of the arm

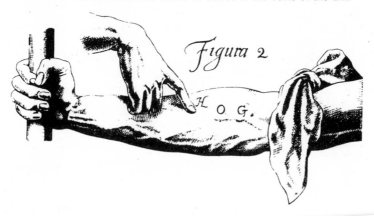

313d, provides additional proofs that the arterial pulse is actually caused by the motion of the heart. Then follows, beginning at page 315b, a detailed examination of the alleged differences between the kind of blood found in the arteries and that found in the veins, a topic that much interested the Galenists. This in turn leads into a fascinating disquisition, beginning at page 316b, on the subject of vital spirits, innate heat, and other factors adduced to explain the action of the heart and blood. From this Harvey passes to a related question, that of the purpose or final cause of the circulation, beginning at page 319c. It should be noted here that Harvey's early views on this subject had been criticized by Caspar Hofmann, and that in his correspondence with Hofmann he admitted that he was not completely satisfied with them either; but he maintained to Hofmann, as he does here, that his inability to supply a complete answer regarding the final cause of the circulation should be no reason for denying its existence. Harvey then resumes his arguments and experiments confirming the flow of blood in the arteries and veins. Noteworthy here is his mention of dissecting a deer in the presence of King Charles I (p. 321a), and his observations on the physiology of "a man within two hours after his execution by hanging" (p. 321c; cf. p. 327a)—a gruesome reminder that most of his public dissections at the Royal College were performed on the bodies of executed criminals. Finally, after a very good summary of the circulation (p. 326d), Harvey launches into a detailed critique of Descartes and his view on the heart and blood, beginning at page 327b. In his *Discourse on Method*, Descartes had discussed the movement of the blood as proposed by the "English physician," and then returned to this same topic in his *Objections and Replies*.* Harvey, having read the former, rightly criticizes Descartes for his failure properly to observe the heart's systole and diastole, and for his inability to assign the proper efficient cause of each.

*    *    *

With this we conclude our reading of three classics of the founders of modern science. The works are important in themselves, but even more in the influence they have exerted on thinking men down through the ages. Galileo's initial impact was in Italy, first with his disciples, Castelli, Viviani, Torricelli, and Cavalieri, and then with the students they formed and influenced. His ideas were also propagated in France almost immediately, through the efforts of such intermediaries as Marin Mersenne and Pierre Gassendi, and only slightly later in Germany through Johannes Kepler. John Wilkins and John Wallis were his first enthusiasts in England; there also Isaac Newton read his *Dialogue concerning the Two Chief World Systems* and knew enough of his other works through secondary sources to credit them, though somewhat inaccurately, in his *Principia*.† For the Enlightenment, of course, Galileo was best known as a symbol of rational inquiry courageously persevering in the face of religious persecution. But his enduring contribution was to show how mathematics and experimentation could be successfully joined in a new scientific enterprise, and thus to lay secure foundations on which a systematic mathematical physics could be erected that would serve as the model for all future scientific reasoning.

William Gilbert's claim to fame need be only a bit more modest than Galileo's, and this because his was not the mathematical genius of the Florentine. But where Galileo was at times indecisive, precisely because the mathematical ideal tugged strongly at him and made him uncertain of the ultimate value of experimentation in science, Gilbert came out loud and clear on the side of empirical modes of inquiry. His was therefore the earliest and most unambiguous example of pre-Baconian experimental philosophy. Like all good experimentalists, he was a man of vision and imagination. His mind was not confined within the limits of his laboratory, but reached far out into the universe to see there the magnetism it understood so well as a type of cosmic glue, thereby providing the model for comprehending gravitational phenomena that was to stimulate Kepler and Newton in their final framing of the system of the universe.

Harvey's genius lay in another, more difficult area of scientific investigation, that of complex living organisms. But his too was a commitment to close observation and critical experimentation, coupled, oddly enough, with a thorough understanding and appreciation of the wisdom of past ages. His work on the circulation of the blood, after some initial opposition in France and on the Continent, quickly came to be regarded as a classic. Thus the effect of his researches was to revolutionize physiology, to give inspiration to succeeding generations of anatomists and physicians who would apply his methods to all the tracts of the human body. And his reliance on experimentation and ocular demonstration exemplified the ideals of the Royal Society, thereby giving impetus to the growth of the "new science" in Britain. Francis Bacon is credited with providing a philosophy for the new movement, but his minimal knowledge of the heart's movement[‡] possibly explains the low opinion Harvey entertained of him as a scientist. Moreover, Harvey had great powers of synthesis and, as the editors of the *Syntopicon* remark, his insistence "on the necessity of finding a functional purpose for an organic structure stands as the classic rejoinder to Francis Bacon's recommendation that formal and final causes be separated from material and efficient causes in the study of nature."[§] Withal, Harvey was a man with remarkable scientific and philosophical insight, and he stands as a model for anyone who would effect a harmonious understanding of these two great disciplines.

---

[*] *GBWW*, Vol. 31, pp. 56b–59a, 156c–d.
[†] *Mathematical Principles of Natural Philosophy; GBWW*, Vol. 34, p. 19b.
[‡] *GBWW*, Vol. 30, p. 186d.
[§] *GBWW*, Vol. 2, p. 22a.

The appreciative judgment of critical readers over almost three centuries has thus put its stamp of approval on the three classics we have just reviewed. Each is a momentous contribution. Each reveals to a remarkable degree the character and personality of its composer. And each exhibits in its own way the enduring character of the great ideas, ideas that formed the intellectual inheritance of these men who stood at the dawn of a new era, who wrestled with and transformed what they themselves had been taught, and who had the genius to extract therefrom the new ideas on which our world of science and technology would be built.[56]

---

[1] For details of Galileo's life, *see* the Biographical Note, *GBWW*, Vol. 28, pp. 125–26. A fuller account is Stillman Drake's article in the *Dictionary of Scientific Biography* (New York: Charles Scribner's Sons, 1970–   ), 5 : 237–50, which includes a good guide to bibliography. Other important studies are Ludovico Geymonat, *Galileo Galilei: A Biography and Inquiry into his Philosophy of Science*, trans. Stillman Drake (New York: McGraw-Hill Book Co., 1965); Alexandre Koyré, *Metaphysics and Measurement: Essays in the Scientific Revolution* (Cambridge, Mass.: Harvard University Press, 1968); Stillman Drake, *Galileo Studies: Personality, Tradition, and Revolution* (Ann Arbor: University of Michigan Press, 1970); William R. Shea, *Galileo's Intellectual Revolution: Middle Period, 1610–1632* (New York: Science History Publications, 1972); and Jerome J. Langford, *Galileo, Science and the Church*, rev. ed. (Ann Arbor: University of Michigan Press, 1971).

[2] Recent interpreters still argue strenuously over the relative priority of the two components that seem to characterize Galileo's methodology, the mathematical and the experimental. Some, with Alexandre Koyré, urge that Galileo was primarily a Platonist who saw the book of nature written in the language of mathematics; others, of whom Stillman Drake is representative, see him mainly as the empiricist or positivist who came to his principles only by a process of careful experimentation. Again, with regard to the principle of inertia, although Sir Isaac Newton credited Galileo with its discovery, recent historians question Newton's accuracy and prefer rather to acknowledge Descartes for adumbrating the principle Newton was later to formulate as his first law of motion (*GBWW*, Vol. 34, p. 14). With regard to the law of falling bodies, finally, this is nowhere stated in the familiar form known to every college freshman, $s = \frac{1}{2}gt^2$, but has to be disengaged from a series of statements and geometrical demonstrations that are far from transparent to the modern reader.

[3] Originally published by G. Barbèra in Florence, 1890–1909, and then reprinted by the same publisher, 1929–39, again in 1964–66, and yet again in 1968 when the reprinted edition was destroyed in the flood of 1966.

[4] *Opere*, 16 : 84–85.

[5] The words in which he writes of his blindness to Elia Diodati on January 2, 1638, are most poignant: "Think of the affliction in which I find myself, particularly when you consider that the very sky, the world, and the universe which, by my surprising observations and lucid demonstrations I have opened out a hundred or a thousand times beyond anything seen by the savants of all centuries past, is now compressed and confined for me to within a space no larger than that occupied by my own person." (*Opere*, 17 : 247.)

[6] *Opere*, 17 : 370, 373.

[7] The English term cubit is used in our edition to translate the Italian *braccio*, or arm, a distance of about 20 inches; the Florentine cubit is thus slightly longer than the English measure, usually given as equivalent to 18 inches.

[8] *See* the correspondence between Galileo and G. B. Baliani, *Opere*, 14 : 128, 158–59, and 18 : 68–71.

[9] Readers with training in mathematics, however, will discover matters of interest in them; they may be surprised, for instance, to find Galileo making implicit use of the notion of "one-to-one correspondence" in comparing infinite sets, or to note his explicit statement that "we cannot speak of infinite quantities as being the one greater or less than or equal to another" (p. 144b). Such findings seem to adumbrate the discoveries of modern mathemati-

cians such as Georg Cantor, but they are not original with Galileo, being already part of the medieval scholastic tradition deriving from Thomas Bradwardine, and thus being generally known to Renaissance mathematicians.

[10] Note that in explaining such calculations Galileo acknowledges having studied "the sphere of Sacrobosco with the aid of a learned commentator" (p. 155c), undoubtedly referring to the Jesuit mathematician of the Collegio Romano, Christopher Clavius, whom he had met and admired in his Pisan days. Also noteworthy is Sagredo's comment that computations of this type satisfy the ideal of a "demonstrative science that . . . springs from and grows out of principles well-known, understood, and conceded by all" (p. 168b), a veiled reference to Aristotle's *Posterior Analytics* (see *GBWW*, Vol. 8, p. 98a), with which Galileo was well acquainted and on which he had composed a detailed series of questions also while at Pisa.

[11] In so doing he is referring to the passage in the *Physics*, "We see that bodies which have a greater impulse either of weight or of lightness, if they are alike in other respects, move faster over an equal space, and in the ratio which their magnitudes bear to each other" (*GBWW*, Vol. 8, p. 295d). Simplicio points here to the word *see* as providing an experimental basis for Aristotle's statement.

[12] Several comments may be in order regarding this preliminary discussion of falling bodies. The first bears on the strongly quantitative interpretation there given to Aristotle's statements in the fourth book of the *Physics*. Thomas Aquinas, who commented on these passages around 1267, rejected such a literal interpretation of the text, seeing it as a dialectical attempt to refute Democritean atomism and thus as not implying precise dynamic laws of motion. Earlier, however, Arab commentators such as Avempace and Averroes had given the same passages quantitative readings, and indeed argued as to the precise type of mathematical proportionality Aristotle meant to use when formulating these dynamic laws. By the middle of the fourteenth century, owing to the work of Thomas Bradwardine and his disciples, it had become quite common to give the type of interpretation advanced by Simplicio, and indeed even more sophisticated mathematical formulations of Aristotle's so-called dynamic laws occur in commentaries and questionaries on his *Physics* and in separate treatises on motion used in European universities in the early sixteenth century. Thus the Aristotelian doctrine presented by Simplicio is not necessarily that of the Greek Aristotle, whereas it has a definite kinship with that of the late medieval and Renaissance Aristotelian tradition.

Also noteworthy throughout the discussion is the fact that all participants seem interested in the facts of experience, and even in a general way in quantitative measurements, but that very few precise details are given by any discussant. There are occasional references to differences of fall of "a span" (p. 157d) or of "less than four finger-breadths" (p. 159d) and to time intervals of "one or two pulse-beats" (pp. 160a, 168c), but one is left wondering whether these are arbitrary figures made up by the speakers or the results of actual measurement.

Again, since Salviati is Galileo's spokesman, it should be noted that he seems disposed to argue on the basis more of abstract principles than of experimental tests. He does enunciate, in passing, one version of the law of free fall (p. 162d), which will occupy us later. But this he states as a principle only, not maintaining that bodies actually move in this way, but merely that they have "an inherent tendency" to do so. Moreover, as we have seen, he feels that he can argue his case "even without further experiment" and this apparently on the basis of some insight into what makes bodies move as they do.

[13] *Metaphysics and Measurement*, p. 77, n. 3.

[14] Ibid., pp. 76–80. For a more detailed study, *see* Piero Ariotti, "Galileo on the Isochrony of the Pendulum," *Isis*, 59 (1968): 414–26.

[15] Ibid., p. 80.

[16] For more details on Vincenzio Galilei, *see* the article by Stillman Drake in the *Dictionary of Scientific Biography*, 5 : 249–50.

[17] *See* Stillman Drake, *Galileo Studies*, p. 57.

[18] The law of the lever, namely, "that the force bears to the resistance the inverse ratio of the distances which separate the fulcrum from the force and the resistance respectively" (p. 178b), was formulated and proved, as Simplicio here points out, in the Aristotelian treatise *Questions in Mechanics*. This proof has been studied by recent historians of science, who see it as being based on an application of dynamic principles and so employing concepts much like those of virtual displacement and virtual velocity that did not receive their modern formulation until the eighteenth century. Galileo is well aware of the Aristotelian demonstration, but here he unequivocally indicates his preference for the more static type of proof worked out

by Archimedes in his tract *On the Equilibrium of Planes* (*GBWW*, Vol. 11, pp. 502–19). This is not, of course, Galileo's first contact with Archimedes, for in 1586 he had studied and annotated Archimedes's *De sphaera et cylindro*, and his own early writings on the center of gravity of solids and on motion, as well as his *Discourse on Floating Bodies* of 1612, show a heavy indebtedness to this author. In the *De motu*, for example, he speaks of the "divine Archimedes," and asserts that against his adversaries he will take refuge under "the protecting wings of the super-human Archimedes, whose name I never mention without a feeling of awe." Galileo had similar feelings toward Euclid, whose *Elements* he had long taught at Pisa and Padua.

[19] See *GBWW*, Vol, 11, p. 823a. Other details may provide some insight into Galileo's personality, namely, the identities of the author of the lines quoted on p. 187c and of the two contemporary mathematicians mentioned by name in the text. The verse is from the *Orlando Furioso* of Ariosto, and its quotation by Salviati reveals Galileo's enduring interest in poetry. In his youth he had annotated a copy of this work, as he did a copy of Tasso's *Gerusalemma Liberata*, and had engaged in debates over the relative merits of the two authors, preferring Ariosto for his greater imagination and originality. Luca Valerio (c. 1552–1618), referred to by Sagredo as "the Archimedes of our age" (p. 194d), was an eminent mathematician who taught in Rome, a member of the Accademia dei Lincei, and Galileo's friend and frequent correspondent. He composed a treatise *De centro gravitatis* that so impressed Galileo that it caused him to discard his own juvenile essay on this subject. Giovanni di Guevara (1561–1641) published at Rome in 1627 an excellent commentary on the pseudo-Aristotle's *Mechanics*, which was known to Galileo (pp. 185b, 139c). Guevara was a Neapolitan of Spanish parents who entered the religious order of Clerks Regular Minor, later became its general, and was made bishop of Teano by Urban VIII—a circumstance that apparently did not diminish Galileo's admiration for his work as a mathematician.

[20] Note that the initial letters still used in modern textbooks to designate these variables are taken from the Latin terms and not from their English equivalents.

[21] As a consequence, each proposition is assigned two numbers, one locating it among either theorems or problems and the other among propositions. Thus Theorem XXII, the last of the theorems, is Proposition XXXVI (p. 234b), whereas Problem XVI, the last of the problems, is Proposition XXXVIII (p. 236b).

[22] However, Winifred Lovell Wisan, in her recent doctoral dissertation on "Galileo's *De motu locali*," has noted that there are exceptions to this general rule, that Galileo's proofs rarely respect the requirements of elegance and simplicity, that complex propositions not infrequently precede simple ones, and that his tendency is to regard the results of his earlier investigations as theorems and his more recent findings as problems. A revised version of Dr. Wisan's work will appear shortly in the *Archive for History of Exact Sciences*.

[23] In his earliest *De motu*, Galileo regarded falling motion as essentially uniform, a type of terminal velocity determined by the difference between the specific gravity of the falling body and of the medium through which it falls, thus combining Aristotelian dynamics with Archimedean buoyancy principles. Later he seems to have thought that the velocity would continue to increase, but would do this directly as the distance of fall. (*See* note 25, infra.)

[24] The reference to nature as a principle of operation is very scholastic, and suggests that the source of Galileo's definition may have been Domingo de Soto's *Questions on the Physics of Aristotle*, which was known to Galileo, and wherein a similar definition of uniformly accelerated motion is illustrated as applying to falling bodies. In any event, the definition is discussed by the three interlocutors, and some attention is given to the scholastic problem, treated in Soto's and other questionaries, as to how motion can start from rest, i.e., from infinite slowness, and pass through an infinite number of very small increments to reach a finite value.

[25] Yet another interesting digression occurs at this point of the text. Sagredo suggests the possibility that a better definition of naturally accelerated motion would have velocity increase in direct proportion to the space traversed and not to the time of fall. Salviati quickly welcomes this "companion in error," having apparently entertained this possibility himself, and admitting that "our Author ... had for some time shared the same fallacy" (p. 203a). The reference here is to Galileo's earlier teaching, contained in a letter to Paolo Sarpi in 1604, where he tried to prove the times-squared law for falling bodies on the erroneous supposition that the velocity increase is directly proportional to the distance traversed rather than to the time of fall. The modern reader with a knowledge of calculus will recognize immediately

that one can obtain $s = \frac{1}{2}gt^2$ by integrating, with respect to t, the equation $v=ds/dt=gt$, whereas it is mathematically impossible to obtain the same result by integrating the equation $v=gs$. Galileo, of course, did not have these powerful analytical tools, and so had to resort to a more involved proof employing Euclidean ratios.

[26] On this *see* Marshall Clagett, *The Science of Mechanics in the Middle Ages* (Madison: University of Wisconsin Press, 1959), especially pp. 421–582.

[27] Fuller details are given by William A. Wallace in "The Enigma of Domingo de Soto: *Uniformiter difformis* and Falling Bodies in Late Medieval Physics," *Isis*, 59 (1968): 384–401; "Mechanics from Bradwardine to Galileo," *Journal of the History of Ideas*, 32 (1971): 15–28; and "Experimental Science and Mechanics in the Middle Ages," *Dictionary of the History of Ideas*, ed. P. P. Wiener, 4 vols. (New York: Charles Scribner's Sons, 1973), 2 : 196–205.

[28] *Galileo Studies*, p. 222. This, of course, is a correct translation of the passage, and is equivalent to that also given by Marshall Clagett in his emendation of the Crew and Salvio reading—see *The Science of Mechanics in the Middle Ages*, p. 409.

[29] Some helpful notes are given by Charles C. Gillispie, *The Edge of Objectivity: An Essay in the History of Scientific Ideas* (Princeton: Princeton University Press, 1960), pp. 3–7.

[30] *Metaphysics and Measurement*, pp. 89–117, especially pp. 92–95.

[31] Thomas B. Settle, "An Experiment in the History of Science," *Science*, 6 January 1961, pp. 19–23.

[32] Quoted from Stillman Drake, trans., *Discoveries and Opinions of Galileo* (Garden City, N.Y.: Doubleday & Co., Doubleday Anchor Books, 1957), pp. 113–14.

[33] *See* Stillman Drake, *Galileo Studies*, pp. 257–78, for the latest contribution to this controversy.

[34] "Galileo's Experimental Confirmation of Horizontal Inertia: Unpublished Manuscripts," (Galileo Gleanings XXII), *Isis*, 64 (1973): 290–305.

[35] *See* Alexandre Koyré, *Newtonian Studies* (Cambridge, Mass.: Harvard University Press, 1965), p. 201 ff.

[36] This is entitled *Theoremata circa centrum gravitatis solidorum* and is found in Galileo's *Opere*, 1 : 179–208.

[37] *Opere*, 19 : 623.

[38] For an account of Gilbert's life and works, *see* the "Biographical Note," *GBWW*, Vol. 28, pp. ix–x. More details are given by Suzanne Kelly in her article on Gilbert in the *Dictionary of Scientific Biography*, 5 : 396–401. Other significant studies are Duane H. D. Roller, *The De magnete of William Gilbert* (Amsterdam: Menno Hertzberger, 1959), and Suzanne Kelly, *The De mundo of William Gilbert* (Amsterdam: Menno Hertzberger, 1965).

[39] *Dialogue concerning the Two Chief World Systems,* trans. Stillman Drake (Berkeley: University of California Press, 1962), p. 400.

[40] Ibid., p. 406.

[41] These are usually referred to as Galileo's "Juvenilia" and are published in his *Opere*, 1 : 7–177.

[42] For a summary description of the work and its contents, *see* William A. Wallace, *Causality and Scientific Explanation*, vol. 1, *Medieval and Early Classical Science* (Ann Arbor: University of Michigan Press, 1972), pp. 88–94.

[43] Ibid., pp. 88–91.

[44] In this connection it may be noted that Galileo had not read Gilbert carefully, for he attributes the discovery of magnetic dip to Gilbert (*Dialogue concerning the Two Chief World Systems,* trans. Stillman Drake, p. 411), whereas Gilbert himself acknowledges that this discovery had been made earlier by Norman (p. 7a).

[45] For a discussion of Einstein's gravitational theory and its relation to earlier cosmological speculations, *see* William A. Wallace, *Causality and Scientific Explanation*, vol. 2, *Classical and Contemporary Science* (Ann Arbor: University of Michigan Press, 1974), pp. 287–97.

[46] The note is transcribed by Favaro in *Opere*, 8 : 625.

[47] Kepler himself acknowledges Gilbert as a major source of his inspiration; see *GBWW*, Vol. 16, p. 908.

[48] Some facts of Harvey's life are given in the "Biographical Note," *GBWW*, Vol. 28, pp. 263–64. For more details and an up-to-date bibliography, *see* the article by Jerome J. Bylebyl in the *Dictionary of Scientific Biography*, 6 : 150–62. A recent study that supplies even fuller background is Gweneth Whitteridge, *William Harvey and the Circulation of the Blood*, (New York: American Elsevier, 1971).

[49] *See* Whitteridge, p. 105, and Bylebyl, p. 156c.

[50] Whitteridge, p. 120.

[51] Bylebyl, p. 155c.

[52] Cf. Whitteridge, p. 169.

[53] Ibid., p. 171.

[54] A "drachm," or dram, is an apothecary's measure equivalent to about one-eighth of an ounce.

[55] See *Causality and Scientific Explanation*, 1:184–93.

[56] The research on which much of this study was based has been supported by the National Science Foundation, whose assistance the author wishes here to acknowledge. He also expresses his indebtedness to Prof. Stillman Drake, for previews and preprints of his many contributions to Galileo scholarship, and to Dr. Winifred Wisan, for the loan of her doctoral dissertation on the *De motu locali*, which proved of great value in preparing the foregoing commentary on the *Two New Sciences*. He thanks also Prof. Duane H. D. Roller, as well as Professors Drake and Wisan, for going over a draft of this review and saving him from a number of errors.

## NOTE TO THE READER

Chapter 83 of the *Syntopicon*, SCIENCE, is relevant to all three of the books that Professor Wallace discusses. See in particular Topic 1c, devoted to "the issue concerning science and philosophy: the distinction and relation between experimental and philosophical science, or between empirical and rational science"; also Topics 4d and 4e, which deal with aspects of the nature of scientific knowledge; and Topic 5, which is concerned with scientific method. In addition, in Chapter 36, HYPOTHESIS, Topic 4b deals with the purpose of hypotheses in science, and in Chapter 39, INDUCTION, Topic 5 is concerned with the role of induction in the development of science.

With respect to Gilbert and Galileo, Chapter 67, PHYSICS, would be useful to read. See especially the readings under Topic 4b on the experimental method in the study of nature. Even more to the point is Chapter 54, MECHANICS, in which see the readings at Topics 1a and 1b concerned with the foundations of mechanics, at Topic 2, which deals with its logic and method, at Topics 5b and 5f, which cover mechanical problems taken up by Galileo, and at Topic 7d, which has to do with magnetism and the great magnet of the earth—of special relevance to Gilbert.

Concerning Harvey, Chapter 2, ANIMAL, is helpful. See the readings under Topic 5b, devoted to "the circulatory system: the motions of the heart, blood, and lymph."

In *GGB*, see Galileo's "The Starry Messenger" (Vol. 8, pp. 330–55) and "The Rise and Decline of Classical Physics," by Albert Einstein and Leopold Infeld (ibid., pp. 490–560).

# PART FIVE

# Additions
# to the
# Great Books Library

# St. Thomas Aquinas

G. K. Chesterton

## Editor's Introduction

Few more brilliant or more engaging figures have appeared on the literary scene in the twentieth century than G. K. Chesterton, whose centennial
we celebrate this year. Few have claimed attention on so many counts. For
more than three decades, from his first volume of essays, called *The Defendant*, in 1901 (there had been a volume of poems published the year before)
to the *Autobiography* he completed just before his death in 1936, as well as
in the countless lectures he gave and the many public debates in which he
engaged (and not forgetting the two periodicals that at different times he
edited and largely wrote), Chesterton was an acute and witty commentator
on men and events, a respected literary critic, and, particularly toward the
end of his life, a considerable champion in the field of theology and religious argument. He found time also to write a great number of stories,
among which five volumes devoted to the exploits of Father Brown, the
little priest-detective through whom he delivered many of his characteristic judgments, may turn out, notwithstanding his other real achievements,
to be his lasting one.

It is no easier now than it would have been in Chesterton's heyday, half
a century and more ago, to define such an exuberant and prolific person
as he managed to be. He was of the last, or very nearly the last, generation
of Englishmen—the generation that included Shaw, Wells, and Hilaire
Belloc, as well as Max Beerbohm—that could believe that whatever it had
to say on any subject it found worth talking about was of interest not only
to the society in which it lived and moved but to the whole civilized world.
The titles Chesterton gave to some of the volumes in which he collected
the succession of essays he contributed to newspapers and periodicals—
titles such as *All Things Considered, A Miscellany of Men, Alarms and Discursions,
Tremendous Trifles*—suggest (not without humor) the extent of his concerns.
So many were these that it sometimes seems as if in the course of his
career he touched on every subject there is.

Yet he was no dilettante, any more than Shaw was one, or Wells. Like
any good journalist, Chesterton took his occasions where he found them,
but he always meant what he said. What he said so many times and in so
many ways was that the world is a hugely interesting place, far richer and
more various than some men—critics, moralists, would-be saviors of
humankind—seemed to know. Chesterton ridiculed the utopianism of
Wells and the scientific socialism for which he stood. Such a philosophy

sprang, Chesterton argued, from a conviction that humanity was sick and needed treatment, as if the way to cure the many ills that society exhibits were to create a different kind of human being instead of different social circumstances. Chesterton could be critical of human conditions, but he had no quarrel with human nature. And many human follies—cheap fiction, pompous public statues, meaningless information supplied by the press—he defended as having their own use and rightness, as being proper to the infinite variety of human wants. Chesterton found much to complain of in human affairs—indeed, one of his books was called *What's Wrong with the World*—but what he disapproved of most were efforts to alter or improve human life that in his view reflected an inadequate or mistaken conception of what it is.

What human life is can be understood, Chesterton maintained, only in a context that is ultimately religious, apart from which, he argued, it makes no sense at all. That one who thought so much of man should at the same time have insisted on the greater glory of God may seem strange, but the paradox, if it is one, would have pleased Chesterton to acknowledge, since he delighted in surprising juxtapositions and frequently employed them. He himself saw no contradiction in the fact that so genial and in some ways so worldly a person as he was should have been serious about religion, or that he should have regarded the conversion to Catholicism that he underwent in 1922 as the most important thing that ever happened to him. He was aware that many persons in his skeptical, free-thinking age found this embarassing, or rather, that they found embarrassing the fact that Chesterton publicly and joyously professed his faith. "Religious liberty might be supposed to mean that everybody is free to discuss religion," he once typically remarked. "In practice it means that hardly anybody is allowed to mention it." He for his part mentioned it all the time, or at least whenever it pleased him to do so, and if the Church has had more profound defenders, it has seldom had one who was more intelligent or more agreeable.

Chesterton's biography of St. Thomas Aquinas, which was first published in 1933, is perhaps the best short account of its subject in English, and though written without claim of special competence in either philosophy or theology has been highly praised by such a Thomistic scholar as Étienne Gilson, among others. It is reprinted here not only in recognition of Chesterton but in homage also to Aquinas, of whose death the year 1974 marks the seven-hundredth anniversary.

# St. Thomas Aquinas

## Author's Introductory Note

This book makes no pretence to be anything but a popular sketch of a great historical character who ought to be more popular. Its aim will be achieved, if it leads those who have hardly even heard of St. Thomas Aquinas to read about him in better books. But from this necessary limitation certain consequences follow, which should perhaps be allowed for from the start.

First, it follows that the tale is told very largely to those who are not of the communion of St. Thomas; and who may be interested in him as I might be in Confucius or Mahomet. Yet, on the other hand, the very need of presenting a clean-cut outline involved its cutting into other outlines of thought, among those who may think differently. If I write a sketch of Nelson mainly for foreigners, I may have to explain elaborately many things that all Englishmen know, and possibly cut out, for brevity, many details that many Englishmen would like to know. But, on the other side, it would be difficult to write a very vivid and moving narrative of Nelson, while entirely concealing the fact that he fought with the French. It would be futile to make a sketch of St. Thomas and conceal the fact that he fought with heretics; and yet the fact itself may embarrass the very purpose for which it is employed. I can only express the hope, and indeed the confidence, that those who regard me as the heretic will hardly blame me for expressing my own convictions, and certainly not for expressing my hero's convictions. There is only one point upon which such a question concerns this very simple narrative. It is the conviction, which I have expressed once or twice in the course of it, that the sixteenth-century schism was really a belated revolt of the thirteenth-century pessimists. It was a backwash of the old Augustinian Puritanism against the Aristotelian liberality. Without that, I could not place my historical figure in history. But the whole is meant only for a rough sketch of a figure in a landscape; and not of a landscape with figures.

Second, it follows that in any such simplification I can hardly say much of the philosopher, beyond showing that he had a philosophy. I have only, so to speak, given samples of that philosophy. Lastly, it follows that it is practically impossible to deal adequately with the theology. A lady I know picked up a book of selections from St. Thomas, with a commentary; and began hopefully to read a section with the innocent heading, "The Simplicity of God." She then laid down the book with a sigh and said, "Well, if that's His simplicity, I wonder what His complexity is like." With all respect to that excellent Thomistic commentary, I have no desire to have this book laid down, at the very first glance, with a similar sigh. I have taken the view that the biography is an introduction to the philosophy, and that the philosophy is an introduction to the theology; and that I can only carry the reader just beyond the first stage of the story.

Third, I have not thought it necessary to notice those critics who, from time to time, desperately play to the gallery by reprinting paragraphs of medieval demonology in the hope of horrifying the modern public merely by an unfamiliar language. I have taken it for granted that educated men know that Aquinas and all his contemporaries, and all his opponents for centuries after, did believe in demons, and similar facts, but I have not thought them worth mentioning here, for the simple reason that they do not help to detach or distinguish the portrait. In all that, there was no disagreement between Protestant or Catholic theologians, for all the hundreds of years during which there was any theology; and St. Thomas is not notable as holding such views, except in holding them rather mildly. I have not discussed such matters, not because I have any reason to conceal them, but because they do not in any way personally concern the one person whom it is here my business to reveal. There is hardly room, even as it is, for such a figure in such a frame.

## CONTENTS

# I  On two friars

Let me at once anticipate comment by answering to the name of that notorious character, who rushes in where even the Angels of the Angelic Doctor might fear to tread. Some time ago I wrote a little book of this type and shape on St. Francis of Assisi; and some time after (I know not when or how, as the song says, and certainly not why) I promised to write a book of the same size, or the same smallness on St. Thomas Aquinas. The promise was Franciscan only in its rashness; and the parallel was very far from being Thomistic in its logic. You can make a sketch of St. Francis: you could only make a plan of St. Thomas, like the plan of a labyrinthine city. And yet in a sense he would fit into a much larger or a much smaller book. What we really know of his life might be pretty fairly dealt with in a few pages; for he did not, like St. Francis, disappear in a shower of personal anecdotes and popular legends. What we know, or could know, or may eventually have the luck to learn, of his work, will probably fill even more libraries in the future than it has filled in the past. It was allowable to sketch St. Francis in an outline; but with St. Thomas everything depends on the filling up of the outline. It was even medieval in a manner to illuminate a miniature of the Poverello, whose very title is a diminutive. But to make a digest, in the tabloid manner, of the Dumb Ox of Sicily passes all digestive experiments in the matter of an ox in a tea-cup. But we must hope it is possible to make an outline of biography, now that anybody seems 'capable of writing an outline of history or an outline of anything. Only in the present case the outline is rather an outsize. The gown that could contain the colossal friar is not kept in stock.

I have said that these can only be portraits in outline. But the concrete contrast is here so striking, that even if we actually saw the two human figures in outline, coming over the hill in their friar's gowns, we should find that contrast even comic. It would be like seeing, even afar off, the silhouettes of Don Quixote and Sancho Panza, or of Falstaff and Master Slender. St. Francis was a lean and lively little man; thin as a thread and vibrant as a bowstring; and in his motions like an arrow from the bow. All his life was a series of plunges and scampers; darting after the beggar, dashing naked into the woods, tossing himself into the strange ship, hurling himself into the Sultan's tent and offering to hurl himself into the fire. In appearance he must have been like a thin brown skeleton autumn leaf dancing eternally before the wind; but in truth it was he that was the wind.

St. Thomas was a huge heavy bull of a man, fat and slow and quiet; very mild and magnanimous but not very sociable; shy, even apart from the humility of holiness; and abstracted, even apart from his occasional and carefully concealed experiences of trance or ecstasy. St. Francis was so fiery and even fidgety that the ecclesiastics, before whom he appeared quite suddenly, thought he was a madman. St. Thomas was so stolid that the scholars, in the schools which he attended regularly, thought he was a dunce. Indeed, he was the sort of schoolboy, not unknown, who would much rather be thought a dunce than have his own dreams invaded, by more active or animated dunces. This external contrast extends to almost every point in the two personalities. It was the paradox of St. Francis that while he was passionately fond of poems, he was rather distrustful of books. It was the outstanding fact about St. Thomas that he loved books and lived on books; that he lived the very life of the clerk or scholar in *The Canterbury Tales,* who would rather have a hundred books of Aristotle and his philosophy than any wealth the world could give him. When asked for what he thanked God most, he answered simply, "I have understood every page I ever read." St. Francis was very vivid in his poems and rather vague in his documents; St. Thomas devoted his whole life to documenting whole systems of Pagan and Christian literature; and occasionally wrote a hymn like a man taking a holiday. They saw the same problem from different angles, of simplicity and subtlety; St. Francis thought it would be enough to pour out his heart to the Mohammedans, to persuade them not to worship Mahound. St. Thomas bothered his head with every hair-splitting distinction and deduction, about the Absolute or the Accident, merely to prevent them from misunderstanding Aristotle. St. Francis was the son of a shopkeeper, or middle class trader; and while his whole life was a revolt against the mercantile life of his father, he retained none the less, something of the quickness and social adaptability which makes the market hum like a hive. In the common phrase, fond as he was of green fields, he did not let the grass grow under his feet. He was what American millionaires and gangsters call a live wire. It is typical of the mechanistic moderns that, even when they try to imagine a live thing, they can only think of a mechanical metaphor from a dead thing. There is such a thing as a live worm; but there is no such thing as a live wire. St. Francis would have heartily agreed that he was a worm; but he was a very live worm. Greatest of all foes to the go-getting ideal, he had certainly abandoned getting, but he was still going. St. Thomas, on the other hand, came out of a world where he might have enjoyed leisure, and he remained one of those men whose labour has something of the placidity of leisure. He was a hard worker, but nobody could possibly mistake him for a hustler. He had something indefinable about him, which marks those who work when they need not work. For he was by birth a gentleman of a great house, and such repose can remain as a habit, when it is no longer a motive. But in him it was expressed only in its most amiable elements; for instance, there was possibly something of it in his effortless courtesy and patience. Every saint is a man before he is a saint; and a saint may be made of every sort or kind of man; and most of us will choose between these different types according to our different tastes. But I will confess that, while the romantic glory of St. Francis has lost nothing of its glamour for me, I have in later years grown to feel almost as much affection, or in some aspects even more, for this man who unconsciously inhabited a large heart and a large head, like one inheriting a large house, and exercised there an equally generous if rather more absentminded hospitality. There are moments when St. Francis, the most unworldly man who ever walked the world, is almost too efficient for me.

St. Thomas Aquinas has recently reappeared, in the current culture of the colleges and the salons, in a way that would have been quite startling even ten years ago. And the mood that has concentrated on him is doubtless very different from that which popularised St. Francis quite twenty years ago.

The Saint is a medicine because he is an antidote. Indeed that is why the saint is often a martyr; he is mistaken for a poison because he is an antidote. He will generally be found restoring the world to sanity by exaggerating whatever the world neglects, which is by no means always the same element in every age. Yet each generation seeks its saint by instinct; and he is not what the people want, but rather what the people need. This is surely the very much mistaken meaning of those words to the first saints, "Ye are the salt of the earth," which caused the Ex-Kaiser to remark with all solemnity that his beefy Germans were the salt of the earth; meaning thereby merely that they were the earth's beefiest and therefore best. But salt seasons and preserves beef, not because it is like beef; but because it is very unlike it. Christ did not tell his apostles that they were only the excellent people, or the only excellent people, but that they were the exceptional people; the permanently incongruous and incompatible people; and the text about the salt of the earth is really as sharp and shrewd and tart as the taste of salt. It is because they were the exceptional people, that they must not lose their exceptional quality. "If salt lose its savour, wherewith shall it be salted?" is a much more pointed question than any mere lament over the price of the best beef. If the world grows too worldly, it can be rebuked by the Church; but if the Church grows too worldly, it cannot be adequately rebuked for worldliness by the world.

Therefore it is the paradox of history that each generation is converted by the saint who contradicts it most. St. Francis had a curious and almost uncanny attraction for the Victorians; for the nineteenth century English who seemed superficially to be most complacent about their commerce and their common sense. Not only a rather complacent Englishman like Matthew Arnold, but even the English Liberals whom he criticised for their complacency, began slowly to discover the mystery of the Middle Ages through the strange story told in feathers and flames in the hagiographical pictures of Giotto. There was something in the story of St. Francis that pierced through all those English qualities which are most famous and fatuous, to all those English qualities which are most hidden and human: the secret softness of heart; the poetical vagueness of mind; the love of landscape and of animals. St. Francis of Assisi was the only medieval Catholic who really became popular in England on his own merits. It was largely because of a subconscious feeling that the modern world had neglected those particu-

lar merits. The English middle classes found their only missionary in the figure, which of all types in the world they most despised; an Italian beggar.

So, as the nineteenth century clutched at the Franciscan romance, precisely because it had neglected romance, so the twentieth century is already clutching at the Thomist rational theology; because it has neglected reason. In a world that was too stolid, Christianity returned in the form of a vagabond; in a world that has grown a great deal too wild, Christianity has returned in the form of a teacher of logic. In the world of Herbert Spencer men wanted a cure for indigestion; in the world of Einstein they want a cure for vertigo. In the first case, they dimly perceived the fact that it was after a long fast that St. Francis sang the Song of the Sun and the praise of the fruitful earth. In the second case, they already dimly perceived that, even if they only want to understand Einstein, it is necessary first to understand the use of the understanding. They begin to see that, as the eighteenth century thought itself the age of reason, and the nineteenth century thought itself the age of common sense, the twentieth century cannot as yet even manage to think itself anything but the age of uncommon nonsense. In those conditions the world needs a saint; but above all, it needs a philosopher. And these two cases do show that the world, to do it justice, has an instinct for what it needs. The earth was really very flat, for those Victorians who most vigorously repeated that it was round, and Alverno of the Stigmata stood up as a single mountain in the plain. But the earth is an earthquake, a ceaseless and, apparently endless earthquake, for the moderns for whom Newton has been scrapped along with Ptolemy. And for them there is something more steep and even incredible than a mountain; a piece of really solid ground; the level of the level-headed man. Thus in our time the two saints have appealed to two generations, an age of romantics and an age of sceptics; yet in their own age they were doing the same work; a work that has changed the world.

Again, it may be said truly that the comparison is idle, and does not fit in well even as a fancy; since the men were not properly even of the same generation or the same historic moment. If two friars are to be presented as a pair of Heavenly Twins, the obvious comparison is between St. Francis and St. Dominic. The relations of St. Francis and St. Thomas were, at nearest, those of uncle and nephew; and my fanciful excursus may appear only a highly profane version of "Tommy make room for your uncle". For if St. Francis and St. Dominic were the great twin brethren, Thomas was obviously the first great son of St. Dominic, as was his friend Bonaventure of St. Francis. Nevertheless, I have a reason (indeed two reasons) for taking as a text the accident of two title-pages; and putting St. Thomas beside St. Francis, instead of pairing him off with Bonaventure the Franciscan. It is because the comparison, remote and perverse as it may seem, is really a sort of short cut to the heart of history; and brings us by the most rapid route to the real question of the life and work of St. Thomas Aquinas. For most people now have a rough but picturesque picture in their minds of the life and work of St. Francis of Assisi. And the shortest way of telling the other story is to say that, while the two men were thus a contrast in almost every feature, they were really doing the same thing. One of them was doing it in the world of the mind and the other in the world of the worldly. But it was the same great medieval movement; still but little understood. In a constructive sense, it was more important than the Reformation. Nay, in a constructive sense, it was the Reformation.

About this medieval movement there are two facts that must first be emphasised. They are not, of course, contrary facts, but they are perhaps answers to contrary fallacies. First, in spite of all that was once said about superstition, the Dark Ages and the sterility of Scholasticism, it was in every sense a movement of enlargement, always moving towards greater light and even greater liberty. Second, in spite of all that was said later on about progress and the Renaissance and forerunners of modern thought, it was almost entirely a movement of orthodox theological enthusiasm, unfolded from within. It was *not* a compromise with the world, or a surrender to heathens or heretics, or even a mere borrowing of external aids, even when it did borrow them. In so far as it did reach out to the light of common day, it was like the action of a plant which by its own force thrusts out its leaves into the sun; not like the action of one who merely lets daylight into a prison.

In short, it was what is technically called a Development in doctrine. But there seems to be a queer ignorance, not only about the technical, but the natural meaning of the word Development. The critics of Catholic theology seem to suppose that it is not so much an evolution as an evasion; that it is at best an adaptation. They fancy that its very success is the success of surrender. But that is not the natural meaning of the word Development. When we talk of a child being well-developed, we mean that he has grown bigger and stronger with his own strength; not that he is padded with borrowed pillows or walks on stilts to make him look taller. When we say that a puppy develops into a dog, we do not mean that his growth is a gradual compromise with a cat; we mean that he becomes more doggy and not less. Development is the expansion of all the possibilities and implications of a doctrine, as there is time to distinguish them and draw them out; and the point here is that the enlargement of medieval theology was simply the full comprehension of that theology. And it is of primary importance to realise this fact first, about the time of the great Dominican and the first Franciscan, because their tendency, humanistic and naturalistic in a hundred ways, was truly the development of the supreme doctrine, which was also the dogma of all dogmas. It is in this that the popular poetry of St. Francis and the almost rationalistic prose of St. Thomas appear most vividly as part of the same movement. They are both great growths of Catholic development, depending upon external things only as every living and growing thing depends on them; that is, it digests and transforms them, but continues in its own image and not in theirs. A Buddhist or a Communist might dream of two things which simultaneously eat each other, as the perfect form of unification. But it is not so with living things. St. Francis was content to call himself the Troubadour of God; but not content with the God of the Troubadours. St. Thomas did not reconcile Christ to Aristotle; he reconciled Aristotle to Christ.

Yes; in spite of the contrasts that are as conspicuous and even comic as the comparison between the fat man and the thin man, the tall man and the short; in spite of the contrast between the vagabond and the student, between the apprentice and the aristocrat, between the book-hater and the book-lover, between the wildest of all missionaries and the mildest of all professors, the great fact of medieval history is that these two great men were doing the same great work; one in the study and the other in the street. They were not bringing something new into Christianity, in the sense of something heathen or heretical into Christianity; on the contrary, they were bringing Christianity into Christendom. But they were bringing it back against the pressure of certain historic tendencies, which had hardened into habits in many great schools and authorities in the Christian Church; and they were using tools and weapons which seemed to many people to be associated with heresy or heathenry. St. Francis used Nature much as St. Thomas used Aristotle; and to some they seemed to be using a Pagan goddess and a Pagan sage. What they were really doing, and especially what St. Thomas was really doing, will form the main matter of these pages; but it is convenient to be able to compare him from the first with a more popular saint; because we may thus sum up the substance of it in the most popular way. Perhaps it would sound too paradoxical to say that these two saints

saved us from Spirituality; a dreadful doom. Perhaps it may be misunderstood if I say that St. Francis, for all his love of animals, saved us from being Buddhists; and that St. Thomas, for all his love of Greek philosophy, saved us from being Platonists. But it is best to say the truth in its simplest form; that they both reaffirmed the Incarnation, by bringing God back to earth.

This analogy, which may seem rather remote, is really perhaps the best practical preface to the philosophy of St. Thomas. As we shall have to consider more closely later on, the purely spiritual or mystical side of Catholicism had very much got the upper hand in the first Catholic centuries; through the genius of Augustine, who had been a Platonist, and perhaps never ceased to be a Platonist; through the transcendentalism of the supposed work of the Areopagite; through the Oriental trend of the later Empire and something Asiatic about the almost pontifical kinghood of Byzantium; all these things weighed down what we should now roughly call the Western element; though it has as good a right to be called the Christian element; since its common sense is but the holy familiarity of the word made flesh. Anyhow, it must suffice for the moment to say that theologians had somewhat stiffened into a sort of Platonic pride in the possession of intangible and untranslatable truths within; as if no part of their wisdom had any root anywhere in the real world. Now the first thing that Aquinas did, though by no means the last, was to say to these pure transcendentalists something substantially like this.

"Far be it from a poor friar to deny that you have these dazzling diamonds in your head, all designed in the most perfect mathematical shapes and shining with a purely celestial light; all there, almost before you begin to think, let alone to see or hear or feel. But I am not ashamed to say that I find my reason fed by my senses; that I owe a great deal of what I think to what I see and smell and taste and handle; and that so far as my reason is concerned, I feel obliged to treat all this reality as real. To be brief, in all humility, I do not believe that God meant Man to exercise only that peculiar, uplifted and abstracted sort of intellect which you are so fortunate as to possess: but I believe that there is a middle field of facts which are given by the senses to be the subject matter of the reason; and that in that field the reason has a right to rule, as the representative of God in Man. It is true that all this is lower than the angels; but it is higher than the animals, and all the actual material objects Man finds around him. True, man also can be an object; and even a deplorable object. But what man has done man may do; and if an antiquated old heathen called Aristotle can help me to do it I will thank him in all humility."

Thus began what is commonly called the appeal to Aquinas and Aristotle. It might be called the appeal to Reason and the Authority of the Senses. And it will be obvious that there is a sort of popular parallel to it in the fact that St. Francis did not only listen for the angels, but also listened to the birds. And before we come to those aspects of St. Thomas that were very severely intellectual, we may note that in him as in St. Francis there is a preliminary practical element which is rather moral; a sort of good and straightforward humility; and a readiness in the man to regard even himself in some ways as an animal; as St. Francis compared his body to a donkey. It may be said that the contrast holds everywhere, even in zoological metaphor, and that if St. Francis was like that common or garden donkey who carried Christ into Jerusalem, St. Thomas, who was actually compared to an ox, rather resembled that Apocalyptic monster of almost Assyrian mystery; the winged bull. But again, we must not let all that can be contrasted eclipse what was common; or forget that neither of them would have been too proud to wait as patiently as the ox and ass in the stable of Bethlehem.

There were of course, as we shall soon see, many other much more curious and complicated ideas in the philosophy of St. Thomas; besides this primary idea of a central common sense that is nourished by the five senses. But at this stage, the point of the story is not only that this was a Thomist doctrine, but that it is a truly and eminently Christian doctrine. For upon this point modern writers write a great deal of nonsense; and show more than their normal ingenuity in missing the point. Having assumed without argument, at the start, that all emancipation must lead men away from religion and towards irreligion, they have just blankly and blindly forgotten what is the outstanding feature of the religion itself.

It will not be possible to conceal much longer from anybody the fact that St. Thomas Aquinas was one of the great liberators of the human intellect. The sectarians of the seventeenth and eighteenth centuries were essentially obscurantists, and they guarded an obscurantist legend that the Schoolman was an obscurantist. This was wearing thin even in the nineteenth century; it will be impossible in the twentieth. It has nothing to do with the truth of their theology or his; but only with the truth of historical proportion, which begins to reappear as quarrels begin to die down. Simply as one of the facts that bulk big in history, it is true to say that Thomas was a very great man who reconciled religion with reason, who expanded it towards experimental science, who insisted that the senses were the windows of the soul and that the reason had a divine right to feed upon facts, and that it was the business of the Faith to digest the strong meat of the toughest and most practical of pagan philosophies. It is a fact, like the military strategy of Napoleon, that Aquinas was thus fighting for all that is liberal and enlightened, as compared with his rivals, or for that matter his successors and supplanters. Those who, for other reasons, honestly accept the final effect of the Reformation will none the less face the fact, that it was the Schoolman who was the Reformer; and that the later Reformers were by comparison reactionaries. I use the word not as a reproach from my own standpoint, but as a fact from the ordinary modern progressive standpoint. For instance, they riveted the mind back to the literal sufficiency of the Hebrew Scriptures; when St. Thomas had already spoken of the Spirit giving grace to the Greek philosophies. He insisted on the social duty of works; they only on the spiritual duty of faith. It was the very life of the Thomist teaching that Reason can be trusted: it was the very life of the Lutheran teaching that Reason is utterly untrustworthy.

Now when this fact is found to be a fact, the danger is that all the unstable opposition will suddenly slide to the opposite extreme. Those who up to that moment have been abusing the Schoolman as a dogmatist will begin to admire the Schoolman as a Modernist who diluted dogma. They will hastily begin to adorn his statue with all the faded garlands of progress, to present him as a man in advance of his age, which is always supposed to mean in agreement with our age; and to load him with the unprovoked imputation of having produced the modern mind. They will discover his attraction, and somewhat hastily assume that he was like themselves, because he was attractive. Up to a point this is pardonable enough; up to a point it has already happened in the case of St. Francis. But it would not go beyond a certain point in the case of St. Francis. Nobody, not even a Freethinker like Renan or Matthew Arnold, would pretend that St. Francis was anything but a devout Christian, or had any other original motive except the imitation of Christ. Yet St. Francis also had that liberating and humanising effect upon religion; though perhaps rather on the imagination than the intellect. But nobody says that St. Francis was loosening the Christian code, when he was obviously tightening it; like the rope round his friar's frock. Nobody says he merely opened the gates to sceptical science, or sold the pass to heathen humanism, or looked forward only to the Renaissance or met the Rationalists half way. No biographer pretends that St. Francis, when he is reported to have opened the Gospels at random and read the great texts about Poverty, really only opened the *Aeneid*

and practised the *Sors Virgiliana* out of respect for heathen letters and learning. No historian will pretend that St. Francis wrote *The Canticle of the Sun* in close imitation of a Homeric Hymn to Apollo or loved birds because he had carefully learned all the tricks of the Roman Augurs.

In short, most people, Christian or heathen, would now agree that the Franciscan sentiment was primarily a Christian sentiment, unfolded from within, out of an innocent (or, if you will, ignorant) faith in the Christian religion itself. Nobody, as I have said, says that St. Francis drew his primary inspiration from Ovid. It would be every bit as false to say that Aquinas drew his primary inspiration from Aristotle. The whole lesson of his life, especially of his early life, the whole story of his childhood and choice of a career, shows that he was supremely and directly devotional; and that he passionately loved the Catholic worship long before he found he had to fight for it. But there is also a special and clinching instance of this, which once more connects St. Thomas with St. Francis. It seems to be strangely forgotten that both these saints were in actual fact imitating a Master, who was not Aristotle let alone Ovid, when they sanctified the senses or the simple things of nature; when St. Francis walked humbly among the beasts or St. Thomas debated courteously among the Gentiles.

Those who miss this, miss the point of the religion, even if it be a superstition; nay, they miss the very point they would call most superstitious. I mean the whole staggering story of the God-Man in the Gospels. A few even miss it touching St. Francis and his unmixed and unlearned appeal to the Gospels. They will talk of the readiness of St. Francis to learn from the flowers or the birds as something that can only point onward to the Pagan Renaissance. Whereas the fact stares them in the face; first, that it points backwards to the New Testament, and second that it points forward, if it points to anything, to the Aristotelian realism of the *Summa* of St. Thomas Aquinas. They vaguely imagine that anybody who is humanising divinity must be paganising divinity; without seeing that the humanising of divinity is actually the strongest and starkest and most incredible dogma in the Creed. St. Francis was becoming more like Christ, and not merely more like Buddha, when he considered the lilies of the field or the fowls of the air; and St. Thomas was becoming more of a Christian, and not merely more of an Aristotelian, when he insisted that God and the image of God had come in contact through matter with a material world. These saints were, in the most exact sense of the term, Humanists; because they were insisting on the immense importance of the human being in the theological scheme of things. But they were not Humanists marching along a path of progress that leads to Modernism and general scepticism; for in their very Humanism they were affirming a dogma now often regarded as the most superstitious Superhumanism. They were strengthening that staggering doctrine of Incarnation, which the sceptics find it hardest to believe. There cannot be a stiffer piece of Christian divinity than the divinity of Christ.

This is a point that is here very much to the point; that these men became more orthodox, when they became more rational or natural. Only by being thus orthodox could they be thus rational and natural. In other words, what may really be called a liberal theology was unfolded from within, from out of the original mysteries of Catholicism. But that liberality had nothing to do with liberalism; in fact it cannot even now coexist with liberalism.* The matter is so cogent, that I will take one or two special ideas of St. Thomas to illustrate what I mean. Without anticipating the elementary sketch of Thomism that must be made later, the following points may be noted here.

For instance, it was a very special idea of St. Thomas that Man is to be studied in his whole manhood; that a man is not a man without his body, just as he is not a man without his soul. A corpse is not a man; but also a ghost is not a man. The earlier school of Augustine and even of Anselm had rather neglected this, treating the soul as the only necessary treasure, wrapped for a time in a negligible napkin. Even here they were less orthodox in being more spiritual. They sometimes hovered on the edge of those Eastern deserts that stretch away to the land of transmigration; where the essential soul may pass through a hundred unessential bodies; reincarnated even in the bodies of beasts or birds. St. Thomas stood up stoutly for the fact that a man's body is his body as his mind is his mind; and that *he* can only be a balance and union of the two. Now this is in some ways a naturalistic notion, very near to the modern respect for material things; a praise of the body that might be sung by Walt Whitman or justified by D. H. Lawrence: a thing that might be called Humanism or even claimed by Modernism. In fact, it may be Materialism; but it is the flat contrary of Modernism. It is bound up, in the modern view, with the most monstrous, the most material, and therefore the most miraculous of miracles. It is specially connected with the most startling sort of dogma, which the Modernist can least accept; the Resurrection of the Body.

Or again, his argument for Revelation is quite rationalistic; and on the other side, decidedly democratic and popular. His argument for Revelation is not in the least an argument against Reason. On the contrary, he seems inclined to admit that truth could be reached by a rational process, if only it were rational enough; and also long enough. Indeed, something in his character, which I have called elsewhere optimism, and for which I know no other approximate term, led him rather to exaggerate the extent to which all men would ultimately listen to reason. In his controversies, he always assumes that they will listen to reason. That is, he

---

* I use the word liberalism here in the strictly limited theological sense, in which Newman and other theologians use it. In its popular political sense, as I point out later, St. Thomas rather tended to be a Liberal, especially for his time.

does emphatically believe that men can be convinced by argument; when they reach the end of the argument. Only his common sense also told him that the argument never ends. I might convince a man that matter as the origin of Mind is quite meaningless, if he and I were very fond of each other and fought each other every night for forty years. But long before he was convinced on his deathbed, a thousand other materialists would have been born, and nobody can explain everything to everybody. St. Thomas takes the view that the souls of all the ordinary hard-working and simple-minded people are quite as important as the souls of thinkers and truth-seekers; and he asks how all these people are possibly to find time for the amount of reasoning that is needed to find truth. The whole tone of the passage shows both a respect for scientific enquiry and a strong sympathy with the average man. His argument for Revelation is not an argument against Reason; but it is an argument for Revelation. The *conclusion* he draws from it is that men must receive the highest moral truths in a miraculous manner; or most men would not receive them at all. His arguments are rational and natural; but his own deduction is all for the supernatural; and, as is common in the case of his argument, it is not easy to find any deduction except his own deduction. And when we come to that, we find it is something as simple as St. Francis himself could desire; the message from heaven; the story that is told out of the sky; the fairytale that is really true.

It is plainer still in more popular problems like Free Will. If St. Thomas stands for one thing more than another, it is what may be called subordinate sovereignties or autonomies. He was, if the flippancy may be used, a strong Home Ruler. We might even say he was always defending the independence of dependent things. He insisted that such a thing could have its own rights in its own region. It was his attitude to the Home Rule of the reason and even the senses; "Daughter am I in my father's house; but mistress in my own." And in exactly this sense he emphasised a certain dignity in Man, which was sometimes rather swallowed up in the purely theistic generalisations about God. Nobody would say he wanted to divide Man from God; but he did want to distinguish Man from God. In this strong sense of human dignity and liberty there is much that can be and is appreciated now as a noble humanistic liberality. But let us not forget that its upshot was that very Free Will, or moral responsibility of Man, which so many modern liberals would deny. Upon this sublime and perilous liberty hang heaven and hell, and all the mysterious drama of the soul. It is distinction and not division; but a man *can* divide himself from God, which, in a certain aspect, is the greatest distinction of all.

Again, though it is a more metaphysical matter, which must be mentioned later, and then only too slightly, it is the same with the old philosophical dispute about the Many and the One. Are things so different that they can never be classified; or so unified that they can never be distinguished? Without pretending to answer such questions here, we may say broadly that St. Thomas comes down definitely on the side of Variety, as a thing that is real as well as Unity. In this, and questions akin to this, he often departs from the great Greek philosophers who were sometimes his models; and entirely departs from the great Oriental philosophers who are in some sense his rivals. He seems fairly certain that the difference between chalk and cheese, or pigs and pelicans, is not a mere illusion, or dazzle of our bewildered mind blinded by a single light; but is pretty much what we all feel it to be. It may be said that this is mere common sense; the common sense that pigs are pigs; to that extent related to the earthbound Aristotelian common sense; to a human and even a heathen common sense. But note that here again the extremes of earth and heaven meet. It is also connected with the dogmatic Christian idea of the Creation; of a Creator who created pigs, as distinct from a Cosmos that merely evolved them.

In all these cases we see repeated the point stated at the start. The Thomist movement in metaphysics, like the Franciscan movement in morals and manners, was an enlargement and a liberation, it was emphatically a growth of Christian theology from within; it was emphatically *not* a shrinking of Christian theology under heathen or even human influences. The Franciscan was free to be a friar, instead of being bound to be a monk. But he was more of a Christian, more of a Catholic, even more of an ascetic. So the Thomist was free to be an Aristotelian, instead of being bound to be an Augustinian. But he was even more of a theologian; more of an orthodox theologian; more of a dogmatist, in having recovered through Aristotle the most defiant of all dogmas, the wedding of God with Man and therefore with Matter. Nobody can understand the greatness of the thirteenth century, who does not realise that it was a great growth of new things produced by a living thing. In that sense it was really bolder and freer than what we call the Renaissance, which was a resurrection of old things discovered in a dead thing. In that sense medievalism was not a Renascence, but rather a Nascence. It did not model its temples upon the tombs, or call up dead gods from Hades. It made an architecture as new as modern engineering: indeed it still remains the most modern architecture. Only it was followed at the Renaissance by a more antiquated architecture. In that sense the Renaissance might be called the Relapse. Whatever may be said of the Gothic and the Gospel according to St. Thomas, they were not a Relapse. It was a new thrust like the titanic thrust of Gothic engineering; and its strength was in a God who makes all things new.

In a word, St. Thomas was making Christendom more Christian in making it more Aristotelian. This is not a paradox but a plain truism, which can only be missed by those who may know what is meant by an Aristotelian, but have simply forgotten what is meant by a Christian. As compared with a Jew, a Moslem, a Buddhist, a Deist, or most obvious alternatives, a Christian *means* a man who believes that deity or sanctity has attached to matter or entered the world of the senses. Some modern writers, missing this simple point, have even talked as if the acceptance of Aristotle was a sort of concession to the Arabs; like a Modernist vicar making a concession to the Agnostics. They might as well say that the Crusades were a concession to the Arabs as say that Aquinas rescuing Aristotle from Averrhoes was a concession to the Arabs. The Crusaders wanted to recover the place where the body of Christ had been, because they believed, rightly or wrongly, that it was a Christian place. St. Thomas wanted to recover what was in essence the body of Christ itself; the sanctified body of the Son of Man which had become a miraculous medium between heaven and earth. And he wanted the body, and all its senses, because he believed, rightly or wrongly, that it was a Christian thing. It might be a humbler or homelier thing than the Platonic mind; that is why it was Christian. St. Thomas was, if you will, taking the lower road when he walked in the steps of Aristotle. So was God, when He worked in the workshop of Joseph.

Lastly, these two great men were not only united to each other but separated from most of their comrades and contemporaries by the very revolutionary character of their own revolution. In 1215, Dominic Guzman, the Castilian, founded an Order very similar to that of Francis; and, by a most curious coincidence of history, at almost exactly the same moment as Francis. It was directed primarily to preaching the Catholic philosophy to the Albigensian heretics; whose own philosophy was one of the many forms of that Manicheanism with which this story is much concerned. It had its roots in the remote mysticism and moral detachment of the East; and it was therefore inevitable that the Dominicans should be rather more a brotherhood of philosophers, where the Franciscans were by comparison a brotherhood of poets. For this and other reasons, St. Dominic and his followers are little known or understood in modern England; they were involved eventually in a religious war, which followed on a theological argument; and there was something in the atmosphere of our country, during the last century or so, which made the theological argument even more incomprehensible than the religious war. The ultimate effect is in some ways curious; because St. Dominic, even more than St. Francis, was marked by that intellectual independence, and strict standard of virtue and veracity, which Protestant cultures are wont to regard as specially Protestant. It was of him that the tale was told, and would certainly have been told more widely among us if it had been told of a Puritan, that the Pope pointed to his gorgeous Papal Palace and said, "Peter can no longer say 'Silver and gold have I none' "; and the Spanish friar answered, "No, and neither can he now say, 'Rise and walk.' "

Thus there is another way in which the popular story of St. Francis can be a sort of bridge between the modern and medieval world. And it is based on that very fact already mentioned: that St. Francis and St. Dominic stand together in history as having done the same work, and yet are divided in English popular tradition in the most strange and startling way. In their own lands they are like Heavenly Twins, irradiating the same light from heaven, seeming sometimes to be two saints in one halo, as another order depicted Holy Poverty as two knights on one horse. In the legends of our own land, they are about as much united as St. George and the Dragon. Dominic is still conceived as an Inquisitor devising thumbscrews; while Francis is already accepted as a humanitarian deploring mousetraps. It seems, for instance, quite natural to us, and full of the same associations of flowers and starry fancies, that the name of Francis should belong to Francis Thompson. But I fancy it would seem less natural to call him Dominic Thompson; or find that a man, with a long record of popular sympathies and practical tenderness to the poor, could bear such a name as Dominic Plater. It

would sound as if he had been called Torquemada Thompson.

Now there must be something wrong behind this contradiction; turning those who were allies at home into antagonists abroad. On any other question, the fact would be apparent to common sense. Suppose English Liberals or Free-Traders found that, in remote parts of China, it was generally held that Cobden was a cruel monster but Bright a stainless saint. They would think there was a mistake somewhere. Suppose that American Evangelicals learned that in France or Italy, or other civilizations impenetrable by Moody and Sankey, there was a popular belief that Moody was an angel but Sankey a devil; they would guess that there must be a muddle somewhere. Some other later accidental distinction must have cut across the main course of a historical tendency. These parallels are not so fantastic as they may sound. Cobden and Bright have actually been called 'child-torturers', in anger at their alleged callousness about the evils amended by the Factory Acts; and some would call the Moody and Sankey sermon on hell a hellish exhibition. All that is a matter of opinion; but both men held the same sort of opinion, and there must be a blunder in an opinion that separates them so completely. And of course there is a complete blunder in the legend about St. Dominic. Those who know anything about St. Dominic know that he was a missionary and not a militant persecutor; that his contribution to religion was the Rosary and not the Rack; that his whole career is meaningless, unless we understand that his famous victories were victories of persuasion and not persecution. He did believe in the justification of persecution; in the sense that the secular arm could repress religious disorders. So did everybody else believe in persecution; and none more than the elegant blasphemer, Frederick II who believed in nothing else. Some say he was the first to burn heretics; but anyhow, he thought it was one of his imperial privileges and duties to persecute heretics. But to talk as if Dominic did nothing but persecute heretics, is like blaming Father Mathew, who persuaded millions of drunkards to take a temperance pledge, because the accepted law sometimes allowed a drunkard to be arrested by a policeman. It is to miss the whole point; which is that this particular man had a genius for conversion, quite apart from compulsion. The real difference between Francis and Dominic, which is no discredit to either of them, is that Dominic did happen to be confronted with a huge campaign for the conversion of heretics, while Francis had only the more subtle task of the conversion of human beings. It is an old story that, while we may need somebody like Dominic to convert the heathen to Christianity, we are in even greater need of somebody like Francis, to convert the Christians to Christianity. Still, we must not lose sight of St. Dominic's special problem, which was that of dealing with a whole population, kingdoms and cities and countrysides, that had drifted from the Faith and solidified into strange and abnormal new religions. That he did win back masses of men so deceived, merely by talking and preaching, remains an enormous triumph worthy of a colossal trophy. St. Francis is called humane because he tried to convert Saracens and failed; St. Dominic is called bigoted and besotted because he tried to convert Albigensians and succeeded. But we happen to be in a curious nook or corner of the hills of history, from which we can see Assisi and the Umbrian hills, but are out of sight of the vast battle-field of the Southern Crusade; the miracle of Muret and the greater miracle of Dominic, when the roots of the Pyrenees and the shores of the Mediterranean saw defeated the Asiatic despair.

But there is an earlier and more essential link between Dominic and Francis, which is more to the immediate purpose of this book. They were in later times bracketed in glory, because they were in their own time bracketed in infamy; or at least in unpopularity. For they did the most unpopular thing that men can do; they started a popular movement. A man who dares to make a direct appeal to the populace always makes a long series of enemies—beginning with the populace. In proportion as the poor begin to understand that he means to help and not hurt them, the solid classes above begin to close in, resolved to hinder and not help. The rich, and even the learned, sometimes feel not unreasonably that the thing will change the world, not only in its worldliness or its worldly wisdom, but to some extent perhaps in its real wisdom. Such a feeling was not unnatural in this case; when we consider, for instance, St. Francis's really reckless attitude about rejecting books and scholarship; or the tendency that the Friars afterwards showed to appeal to the Pope in contempt of local bishops and ecclesiastical officers. In short, St. Dominic and St. Francis created a Revolution, quite as popular and unpopular as the French Revolution. But it is very hard today to feel that even the French Revolution was as fresh as it really was. The Marseillaise once sounded like the human voice of the volcano or the dance-tune of the earthquake, and the kings of the earth trembled, some fearing that the heavens might fall; some fearing far more that justice might be done. The Marseillaise is played today at diplomatic dinner-parties, where smiling monarchs meet beaming millionaires, and is rather less revolutionary than "Home, Sweet Home". Also, it is highly pertinent to recall, the modern revolutionists would now call the revolt of the French Jacobins insufficient, just as they would call the revolt of the Friars insufficient. They would say that neither went far enough; but many, in their own day, thought they went very much too far. In the case of the Friars, the higher orders of the State, and to some extent even of the Church, were profoundly shocked at such a loosening of wild popular preachers among the people. It is not at all easy for us to feel that distant events were thus disconcerting and even disreputable. Revolutions turn into institutions; revolts that renew the youth of old societies in their turn grow old; and the past, which was full of new things, of splits and innovations and insurrections, seems to us a single texture of tradition.

But if we wish for one fact that will make vivid this shock of change and challenge, and show how raw and ragged, how almost rowdy in its reckless novelty, how much of the gutter and how remote from refined life, this experiment of the Friars did really seem to many in its own day, there is here a very relevant fact to reveal it. It shows how much a settled and already ancient Christendom did feel it as something like the end of an age; and how the very roads of the earth seem to shake under the feet of the new and nameless army; the march of the Beggars. A mystic nursery rhyme suggests the atmosphere of such a crisis; "Hark, hark, the dogs do bark; the Beggars are coming to town". There were many towns that almost fortified themselves against them and many watchdogs of property and rank did really bark, and bark loudly, when those Beggars went by; but louder was the singing of the Beggars who sang their Canticle to the Sun, and louder the baying of the Hounds of Heaven; the *Domini canes* of the medieval pun; the Dogs of God. And if we would measure how real and rending seemed that revolution, what a break with the past, we can see it in the first and most extraordinary event in the life of St. Thomas Aquinas.

## II  The runaway abbot

Thomas Aquinas, in a strange and rather symbolic manner, sprang out of the very centre of the civilised world of his time; the central knot or coil of the powers then controlling Christendom. He was closely connected with all of them; even with some of them that might well be described as destroying Christendom. The whole religious quarrel, the whole international quarrel, was for him, a family quarrel. He was born in the purple; almost literally on the hem of the imperial purple; for his own cousin was the Holy Roman Emperor. He could have quartered half the kingdoms of Europe on

his shield—if he had not thrown away the shield. He was Italian and French and German and in every way European. On one side, he inherited from the energy that made the episode of the Normans, whose strange organising raids rang and rattled like flights of arrows in the corners of Europe and the ends of the earth; one flight of them following Duke William far northward through the blinding snows to Chester; another treading in Greek and Punic footsteps through the island of Sicily to the gates of Syracuse. Another bond of blood bound him to the great Emperors of the Rhine and Danube who claimed to wear the crown of Charlemagne; Red Barbarossa, who sleeps under the rushing river, was his great uncle, and Frederick II, the Wonder of the World, his second cousin, and yet he held by a hundred more intimate ties to the lively inner life, the local vivacity, the little walled nations and the thousand shrines of Italy. While inheriting this physical kinship with the Emperor, he maintained far more firmly his spiritual kinship with the Pope. He understood the meaning of Rome, and in what sense it was still ruling the world; and was not likely to think that the German Emperors of his time, any more than the Greek Emperors of a previous time, would be able to be really Roman in defiance of Rome. To this cosmopolitan comprehensiveness in his inherited position, he afterwards added many things of his own, that made for mutual understanding among the peoples, and gave him something of the character of an ambassador and interpreter. He travelled a great deal; he was not only well known in Paris and the German universities, but he almost certainly visited England; probably he went to Oxford and London; and it has been said that we may be treading in the footsteps of him and his Dominican companions, whenever we go down by the river to the railway-station that still bears the name of Blackfriars. But the truth applies to the travels of his mind as well as his body. He studied the literature even of the opponents of Christianity much more carefully and impartially than was then the fashion; he really tried to understand the Arabian Aristotelianism of the Moslems; and wrote a highly humane and reasonable treatise on the problem of the treatment of the Jews. He always attempted to look at everything from the inside; but he was certainly lucky in having been born in the inside of the state system and the high politics of his day. What he thought of them may perhaps be inferred from the next passage in his history.

St. Thomas might thus stand very well for the International Man, to borrow the title of a modern book. But it is only fair to remember that he lived in the International Age; in a world that was international in a sense not to be suggested in any modern book, or by any modern man. If I remember right, the modern candidate for the post of International Man was Cobden, who was an almost abnormally national man; a narrowly national man; a very fine type, but one which can hardly be imagined except as moving between Midhurst and Manchester. He had an international policy, and he indulged in international travel; but if he always remained a national person, it was because he remained a normal person; that is, normal to the nineteenth century. But it was not so in the thirteenth century. There a man of international influence, like Cobden, could be also almost a man of international nationality. The names of nations and cities and places of origin did not connote that deep division that is the mark of the modern world. Aquinas as a student was nicknamed the ox of Sicily, though his birthplace was near Naples; but this did not prevent the city of Paris regarding him so simply and solidly as a Parisian, because he had been a glory of the Sorbonne, that it proposed to bury his bones when he was dead. Or take a more obvious contrast with modern times. Consider what is meant in most modern talk by a German Professor. And then realise that the greatest of all German Professors, Albertus Magnus, was himself one of the glories of the University of Paris; and it was in Paris that Aquinas supported him. Think of the modern German Professor being famous throughout Europe for his popularity when lecturing in Paris.

Thus, if there was war in Christendom, it was international war in the special sense in which we speak of international peace. It was not the war of two nations; but the war of two internationalisms: of two World States: the Catholic Church and the Holy Roman Empire. The political crisis in Christendom affected the life of Aquinas at the start in one sharp disaster, and afterwards in many indirect ways. It had many elements; the Crusades; the embers of the Albigensian pessimism, over which St. Dominic had triumphed in argument and Simon de Montfort in arms; the dubious experiment of an Inquisition which started from it; and many other things. But, broadly speaking, it is the period of the great duel between the Popes and the Emperors, that is the German Emperors who called themselves Holy Roman Emperors, the House of Hohenstaufen. The particular period of the life of Aquinas, however, is entirely overshadowed by the particular Emperor who was himself more an Italian than a German; the brilliant Frederick II who was called the Wonder of the World. It may be remarked, in passing, that Latin was the most living of languages at this time, and we often feel a certain weakness in the necessary translation. For I seem to have read somewhere that the word used was stronger than the Wonder of the World; that his medieval title was *Stupor Mundi*, which is more exactly the Stupefaction of the World. Something of the sort may be noted later of philosophical language, and the weakness of translating a word like *Ens* by a word like Being. But for the moment the parenthesis has another application; for it might well be said that Frederick did indeed stupefy the world; that there was something stunning and blinding about the blows he struck at religion, as in that blow which almost begins the biography of Thomas Aquinas. He may also be called stupefying in another sense; in that his very brilliancy has made some of his modern admirers very stupid.

For Frederick II is the first figure, and that a rather fierce and ominous figure, who rides across the scene of his cousin's birth and boyhood: a scene of wild fighting and of fire. And it may be allowable to pause for a parenthesis upon his name, for two particular reasons: first that his romantic reputation, even among modern historians, covers and partly conceals the true background of the time; and second that the tradition in question directly involves the whole status of St. Thomas Aquinas. The nineteenth century view, still so strangely called the modern view by many moderns, touching such a man as Frederick II, was well summed up by some solid Victorian, I think by Macaulay; Frederick was "a statesman in an age of Crusaders; a philosopher in an age of monks." It may be noted that the antithesis involves the assumption that a Crusader cannot easily be a statesman; and that a monk cannot easily be a philosopher. Yet, to take only that special instance, it would be easy to point out that the cases of two famous men in the age of Frederick II would alone be strong enough to upset both the assumption and the antithesis. St. Louis, though a Crusader and even an unsuccessful Crusader, was really a far more successful statesman than Frederick II. By the test of practical politics, he popularised, solidified and sanctified the most powerful government in Europe, the order and concentration of the French Monarchy; the single dynasty that steadily increased in strength for five hundred years up to the glories of the Grand Siècle, whereas Frederick went down in ruin before the Papacy and the Republics and a vast combination of priests and peoples. The Holy Roman Empire he wished to found was an ideal rather in the sense of a dream; it was certainly never a fact like the square and solid State which the French statesman did found. Or, to take another example from the next generation, one of the most strictly practical statesmen in history, our own Edward I, was also a Crusader.

The other half of the antithesis is even more false and here even more relevant. Frederick II was not a philosopher in the age of monks. He was a gentleman dabbling in philosophy in the age of the monk Thomas Aquinas. He was doubtless an intelligent and even brilliant gentleman; but if he did leave any notes on the nature of Being and Becoming, or the precise sense in which realities can be relative to Reality, I do not imagine those notes are now exciting undergraduates at Oxford or literary men in Paris, let alone the little groups of Thomists who have already sprung up even in New York and Chicago. It is no disrespect to the Emperor to say that he certainly was not a philosopher in the sense in which Thomas Aquinas was a philosopher, let alone so great or so universal or so permanent a philosopher. And Thomas Aquinas lived in that very age of monks, and in that very world of monks, which Macaulay talks of as if it were incapable of producing philosophy.

We need not dwell on the causes of this Victorian prejudice, which some still think so very advanced. It arose mainly from one narrow or insular notion; that no man could possibly be building up the best of the modern world, if he went with the main movement of the medieval world. These Victorians thought that only the heretic had ever helped humanity; only the man who nearly wrecked medieval civilisation could be of any use in constructing modern civilisation. Hence came a score of comic fables; as that the cathedrals must have been built by a secret society of Freemasons; or that the epic of Dante must be a cryptogram referring to the political hopes of Garibaldi. But the generalisation is not in its nature probable and it is not in fact true. This medieval period was rather specially the period of communal or corporate thinking, and in some matters it was really rather larger than the individualistic modern thinking. This could be proved in a flash from the mere fact of the use of the word 'statesman'. To a man of Macaulay's period, a statesman *always* meant a man who maintained the more narrow national interests of his own state against other states, as Richelieu maintained those of France, or Chatham of England, or Bismarck of Prussia. But if a man actually wanted to defend all these states, to combine all these states, to make a living brotherhood of all these states, to resist some outer peril as from the Mongolian millions—then that poor devil, of course, could not really be called a statesman. He was only a Crusader.

In this way it is but fair to Frederick II to say that he was a Crusader; if he was also rather like an Anti-Crusader. Certainly he was an international statesman. Indeed he was a particular type, which may be called an international soldier. The international soldier is always very much disliked by internationalists. They dislike Charlemagne and Charles V and Napoleon; and everybody who tried to create the World State for which they cry aloud day and night. But Frederick is more dubious and less doubted; he was supposed to be the head of the Holy Roman Empire; and accused of wanting to be the head of a very Unholy Roman Empire. But even if he were Antichrist, he would still be a witness to the unity of Christendom.

Nevertheless, there is a queer quality in that time; which, while it was international was also internal and intimate. War, in the wide modern sense, is possible, not because more men disagree, but because more men agree. Under the peculiarly modern coercions, such as Compulsory Education and Conscription, there are such very large *peaceful* areas, that they can all agree upon War. In that age men disagreed even about war; and peace might break out anywhere. Peace was interrupted by feuds and feuds by pardons. Individuality wound in and out of a maze; spiritual extremes were walled up with one another in one little walled town; and we see the great soul of Dante divided, a cloven flame; loving and hating his own city. This individual complexity is intensely vivid in the particular story we have here to tell, in a very rough outline. If anyone wishes to know what is meant by saying that

action was more individual, and indeed incalculable, he may well note some of the stages in the story of the great feudal house of Aquino, which had its castle not far from Naples. In the mere hasty anecdote we have now to tell, we shall note in succession five or six stages of this sort. Landulf of Aquino, a heavy feudal fighter typical of the time, rode in armour behind the imperial banners, and attacked a monastery, because the Emperor regarded the monastery as a fortress held for his enemy the Pope. Later, we shall see, the same feudal lord sent his own son to the same monastery; probably on the friendly advice of the same Pope. Later still, another of his sons, entirely on his own, rebelled against the Emperor, and went over to the armies of the Pope. For this he was executed by the Emperor, with promptitude and despatch. I wish we knew more about that brother of Thomas Aquinas who risked and lost his life to support the cause of the Pope; which was in all human essentials the cause of the People. He may not have been a saint; but he must have had some qualities of a martyr. Meanwhile, two other brothers, still ardent and active apparently, in the service of the Emperor who killed the third brother, themselves proceeded to kidnap another brother, because they did not approve of his sympathy with the new social movements in religion. That is the sort of tangle in which this one distinguished medieval family found itself. It was not a war of nations; but it was a rather widespread family quarrel.

The reason for dwelling here, however, upon the position of the Emperor Frederick, as a type of his time, in his culture and his violence, in his concern for philosophy and his quarrel with religion, is not merely concerned with these things. He may here be the first figure that crosses the stage, because one of his very typical actions precipitated the first action, or obstinate inaction, which began the personal adventures of Thomas Aquinas in this world. The story also illustrates the extraordinary tangle in which a family like that of the Count of

Aquino found itself; being at once so close to the Church and so much at odds with it. For Frederick II, in the course of those remarkable manoeuvres, military and political, which ranged from burning heretics to allying himself with Saracens, made a swoop as of a predatory eagle (and the Imperial eagle was rather predatory) upon a very large and wealthy monastery; the Benedictine Abbey of Monte Cassino; and stormed and sacked the place.

Some miles from the monastery of Monte Cassino stood a great crag or cliff, standing up like a pillar of the Apennines. It was crowned with a castle that bore the name of The Dry Rock, and was the eyrie in which the eaglets of the Aquino branch of the Imperial family were nursed to fly. Here lived Count Landulf of Aquino, who was the father of Thomas Aquinas and some seven other sons. In military affairs he doubtless rode with his family, in the feudal manner; and apparently had something to do with the destruction of the monastery. But it was typical of the tangle of the time, that Count Landulf seems afterwards to have thought that it would be a tactful and delicate act to put in his son Thomas as Abbot of the monastery. This would be of the nature of a graceful apology to the Church, and also, it would appear, the solution of a family difficulty.

For it had been long apparent to Count Landulf that nothing could be done with his seventh son Thomas, except to make him an Abbot or something of that kind. Born in 1226, he had from childhood a mysterious objection to becoming a predatory eagle, or even to taking an ordinary interest in falconry or tilting or any other gentlemanly pursuits. He was a large and heavy and quiet boy, and phenomenally silent, scarcely opening his mouth except to say suddenly to his schoolmaster in an explosive manner, "What is God?" The answer is not recorded but it is probable that the asker went on worrying out answers for himself. The only place for a person of this kind was the Church and presumably the cloister; and so

far as that went, there was no particular difficulty. It was easy enough for a man in Count Landulf's position to arrange with some monastery for his son to be received there; and in this particular case he thought it would be a good idea if he were received in some official capacity, that would be worthy of his worldly rank. So everything was smoothly arranged for Thomas Aquinas becoming a monk, which would seem to be what he himself wanted; and sooner or later becoming Abbot of Monte Cassino. And then the curious thing happened.

In so far as we may follow rather dim and disputed events, it would seem that the young Thomas Aquinas walked into his father's castle one day and calmly announced that he had become one of the Begging Friars, of the new order founded by Dominic the Spaniard; much as the eldest son of the squire might go home and airily inform the family that he had married a gypsy; or the heir of a Tory Duke state that he was walking tomorrow with the Hunger Marchers organised by alleged Communists. By this, as has been noted already, we may pretty well measure the abyss between the old monasticism and the new, and the earthquake of the Dominican and Franciscan revolution. Thomas had appeared to wish to be a Monk; and the gates were silently opened to him and the long avenues of the abbey, the very carpet, so to speak, laid for him up to the throne of the mitred abbot. He said he wished to be a Friar, and his family flew at him like wild beasts; his brothers pursued him along the public roads, half-rent his friar's frock from his back and finally locked him up in a tower like a lunatic.

It is not very easy to trace the course of this furious family quarrel, and how it eventually spent itself against the tenacity of the young Friar; according to some stories, his mother's disapproval was short-lived and she went over to his side; but it was not only his relatives that were embroiled. We might say that the central governing class of Europe, which partly consisted of his family, were in a turmoil over the deplorable youth; even the Pope was asked for tactful intervention, and it was at one time proposed that Thomas should be allowed to wear the Dominican habit while acting as Abbot in the Benedictine Abbey. To many this would seem a tactful compromise; but it did not commend itself to the narrow medieval mind of Thomas Aquinas. He indicated sharply that he wished to be a Dominican in the Dominican Order, and not at a fancy-dress ball; and the diplomatic proposal appears to have been dropped.

Thomas of Aquino wanted to be a Friar. It was a staggering fact to his contemporaries; and it is rather an intriguing fact even to us; for this desire, limited literally and strictly to this statement, was the one practical thing to which his will was clamped with adamantine obstinacy till his death. He would not be an Abbot; he would not be a Monk; he would not even be a Prior or ruler in his own fraternity; he would not be a prominent or important Friar; he would be a Friar. It is as if Napoleon had insisted on remaining a private soldier all his life. Something in this heavy, quiet, cultivated, rather academic gentleman would not be satisfied till he was, by fixed authoritative proclamation and official pronouncement, established and appointed to be a Beggar. It is all the more interesting because, while he did more than his duty a thousand times over, he was not at all like a Beggar; not at all likely to be a good Beggar. He had nothing of the native vagabond about him, as had his great precursors; he was not born with something of the wandering minstrel, like St. Francis; or something of the tramping missionary, like St. Dominic. But he insisted upon putting himself under military orders, to do these things at the will of another, if required. He may be compared with some of the more magnanimous aristocrats who have enrolled themselves in revolutionary armies; or some of the best of the poets and scholars who volunteered as private soldiers in the Great War. Something in the courage and consistency of Dominic and Francis had challenged his deep sense of justice; and while remaining a very reasonable person, and even a diplomatic one, he never let anything shake the iron immobility of this one decision of his youth; nor was he to be turned from his tall and towering ambition to take the lowest place.

The first effect of his decision, as we have seen, was much more stimulating and even startling. The General of the Dominicans, under whom Thomas had enrolled himself, was probably well aware of the diplomatic attempts to dislodge him and the worldly difficulties of resisting them. His expedient was to take his young follower out of Italy altogether; bidding him proceed with a few other friars to Paris. There was something prophetic even about this first progress of the travelling teacher of the nations; for Paris was indeed destined to be in some sense the goal of his spiritual journey; since it was there that he was to deliver both his great defence of the Friars and his great defiance to the antagonists of Aristotle. But this his first journey to Paris was destined to be broken off very short indeed. The friars had reached a turn of the road by a wayside fountain, a little way north of Rome, when they were overtaken by a wild cavalcade of captors, who seized on Thomas like brigands, but who were in fact only rather needlessly agitated brothers. He had a large number of brothers: perhaps only two were here involved. Indeed he was the seventh; and friends of Birth Control may lament that this philosopher was needlessly added to the noble line of ruffians who kidnapped him. It was an odd affair altogether. There is something quaint and picturesque in the idea of kidnapping a begging friar, who might in a sense be called a runaway abbot. There is a comic and tragic tangle in the motives and purposes of such a trio of strange kinsmen. There is a sort of Christian cross-purposes in the contrast between the feverish illusion of the importance of things, always marking men who are called practical; and the much more practical pertinacity of the man who is called theoretical.

Thus at least did those three strange brethren stagger or trail along their tragic road, tied together, as it were, like criminal and constable; only that the criminals were making the arrest. So their figures are seen for an instant against the horizon of history; brothers as sinister as any since Cain and Abel. For this queer outrage in the great family of Aquino does really stand out symbolically, as representing something that will forever make the Middle Ages a mystery and a bewilderment; capable of sharply contrasted interpretations like darkness and light. For in two of those men there raged, we might say screamed, a savage pride of blood and blazonry of arms, though they were princes of the most refined world of their time, which would seem more suitable to a tribe dancing round a totem. For the moment they had forgotten everything except the name of a family, that is narrower than a tribe, and far narrower than a nation. And the third figure of that trio, born of the same mother and perhaps visibly one with the others in face or form, had a conception of brotherhood broader than most modern democracy, for it was not national but international; a faith in mercy and modesty far deeper than any mere mildness of manners in the modern world; and a drastic oath of poverty, which would now be counted quite a mad exaggeration of the revolt against plutocracy and pride. Out of the same Italian castle came two savages and one sage; or one saint more pacific than most modern sages. That is the double aspect confusing a hundred controversies. That is what makes the riddle of the medieval age; that it was not one age but two ages. We look into the moods of some men, and it might be the Stone Age; we look into the minds of other men, and they might be living in the Golden Age; in the most modern sort of Utopia. There were always good men and bad men; but in this time good men who were subtle lived with bad men who were simple. They lived in the same family; they were brought up in the same nursery; and they came out to struggle, as the brothers of Aquino strug-

gled by the wayside, when they dragged the new friar along the road and shut him up in the castle on the hill.

When his relations tried to despoil him of his friar's frock he seems to have laid about them in the fighting manner of his fathers, and it would seem successfully, since this attempt was abandoned. He accepted the imprisonment itself with his customary composure, and probably did not mind very much whether he was left to philosophise in a dungeon or in a cell. Indeed there is something in the way the whole tale is told, which suggests that through a great part of that strange abduction, he had been carried about like a lumbering stone statue. Only one tale told of his captivity shows him merely in anger; and that shows him angrier than he ever was before or after. It struck the imagination of his own time for more important reasons; but it has an interest that is psychological as well as moral. For once in his life, for the first time and the last, Thomas of Aquino was really *hors de lui;* riding a storm outside that tower of intellect and contemplation in which he commonly lived. And that was when his brothers introduced into his room some specially gorgeous and painted courtesan, with the idea of surprising him by a sudden temptation, or at least involving him in a scandal. His anger was justified, even by less strict moral standards than his own; for the meanness was even worse than the foulness of the expedient. Even on the lowest grounds, he knew his brothers knew, and they knew that he knew, that it was an insult to him as a gentleman to suppose that he would break his pledge upon so base a provocation; and he had behind him a far more terrible sensibility; all that huge ambition of humility which was to him the voice of God out of heaven. In this one flash alone we see that huge unwieldy figure in an attitude of activity, or even animation; and he was very animated indeed. He sprang from his seat and snatched a brand out of the fire, and stood brandishing it like a flaming sword. The woman not unnaturally shrieked and fled, which was all that he wanted; but it is quaint to think of what she must have thought of that madman of monstrous stature juggling with flames and apparently threatening to burn down the house. All he did, however, was to stride after her to the door and bang and bar it behind her; and then, with a sort of impulse of violent ritual, he rammed the burning brand into the door, blackening and blistering it with one big black sign of the cross. Then he returned, and dropped it again into the fire; and sat down on that seat of sedentary scholarship, that chair of philosophy, that secret throne of contemplation, from which he never rose again.

## III The Aristotelian revolution

Albert, the Swabian, rightly called the Great, was the founder of modern science. He did more than any other man to prepare that process, which has turned the alchemist into the chemist, and the astrologer into the astronomer. It is odd that, having been in his time, in this sense almost the first astronomer, he now lingers in legend almost as the last astrologer. Serious historians are abandoning the absurd notion that the medieval Church persecuted all scientists as wizards. It is very nearly the opposite of the truth. The world sometimes persecuted them as wizards, and sometimes ran after them as wizards; the sort of pursuing that is the reverse of persecuting. The Church alone regarded them really and solely as scientists. Many an enquiring cleric was charged with mere magic in making his lenses and mirrors; he was charged by his rude and rustic neighbours; and would probably have been charged in exactly the same way if they had been Pagan neighbours or Puritan neighbours or Seventh-Day Adventist neighbours. But even then he stood a better chance when judged by the Papacy, than if he had been merely lynched by the laity. The Catholic Pontiff did not denounce Albertus Magnus as a magician. It was the half-heathen tribes of the north who admired him as a

magician. It is the half-heathen tribes of the industrial towns today, the readers of cheap dream-books, and quack pamphlets, and newspaper prophets, who still admire him as an astrologer. It is admitted that the range of his recorded knowledge, of strictly material and mechanical facts, was amazing in a man of his time. It is true that, in most other cases, there was a certain limitation to the data of medieval science; but this certainly had nothing to do with medieval religion. For the data of Aristotle, and the great Greek civilisation, were in many ways more limited still. But it is not really so much a question of access to the facts, as of attitude to the facts. Most of the Schoolmen, if informed by the only informants they had that a unicorn has one horn or a salamander lives in the fire, still used it more as an illustration of logic than an incident of life. What they really said was, "If a unicorn has one horn, two unicorns have as many horns as one cow." And that is not one inch the less a fact because the unicorn is a fable. But with Albertus in medieval times, as with Aristotle in ancient times, there did begin something like the idea of emphasising the question: "But *does* the unicorn only have one horn or the salamander a fire instead of a fireside?" Doubtless when the social and geographical limits of medieval life began to allow them to search the fire for salamanders or the desert for unicorns, they had to modify many of their scientific ideas. A fact which will expose them to the very proper scorn of a generation of scientists which has just discovered that Newton is nonsense, that space is limited, and that there is no such thing as an atom.

This great German, known in his most famous period as a professor in Paris, was previously for some time professor at Cologne. In that beautiful Roman city, there gathered round him in thousands the lovers of that extraordinary life; the student life of the Middle Ages. They came together in great groups called Nations; and the fact illustrates very well the difference between medieval nationalism and modern nationalism. For although there might any morning be a brawl between the Spanish students and the Scottish students, or between the Flemish and the French, and swords flash or stones fly on the most purely patriotic principles, the fact remains that they had all come to the same school to learn the same philosophy. And though that might not prevent the starting of a quarrel, it might have a great deal to do with the ending of it. Before these motley groups of men from the ends of the earth, the father of science unrolled his scroll of strange wisdom; of sun and comet, of fish and bird. He was an Aristotelian developing, as it were, the one experimental hint of Aristotle; and in this he was entirely original. He cared less to be original about the deeper matters of men and morals; about which he was content to hand on a decent and Christianised Aristotelianism; he was even in a sense ready to compromise upon the merely metaphysical issue of the Nominalists and the Realists. He would never have maintained alone the great war that was coming, for a balanced and humanised Christianity; but when it came, he was entirely on its side. He was called the Universal Doctor, because of the range of his scientific studies; yet he was in truth a specialist. The popular legend is never quite wrong; if a man of science is a magician, he was a magician. And the man of science has always been much *more* of a magician than the priest; since he would "control the elements" rather than submit to the Spirit who is more elementary than the elements.

Among the students thronging into the lecture-rooms there was one student, conspicuous by his tall and bulky figure, and completely failing or refusing to be conspicuous for anything else. He was so dumb in the debates that his fellows began to assume an American significance in the word dumbness; for in that land it is a synonym for dullness. It is clear that, before long, even his imposing stature began to have only the ignominious immensity of the big boy left behind in the lowest form. He was called the Dumb Ox. He was the object, not merely of mockery, but of pity. One good-natured student pitied him so much as to try to help him with his lessons, going over the elements of logic like an alphabet in a horn-book. The dunce thanked him with pathetic politeness; and the philanthropist went on swimmingly, till he came to a passage about which he was himself a little doubtful; about which, in point of fact, he was wrong. Whereupon the dunce, with every appearance of embarrassment and disturbance, pointed out a possible solution which happened to be right. The benevolent student was left staring, as at a monster, at this mysterious lump of ignorance and intelligence; and strange whispers began to run round the schools.

A regular religious biographer of Thomas Aquinas (who, needless to say, was the dunce in question) has said that by the end of this interview "his love of truth overcame his humility"; which, properly understood, is precisely true. But it does not, in the secondary psychological and social sense, describe all the welter of elements that went on within that massive head. All the relatively few anecdotes about Aquinas have a very peculiar vividness if we visualise the type of man; and this is an excellent example. Amid those elements was something of the difficulty which the generalising intellect has in adapting itself suddenly to a tiny detail of daily life; there was something of the shyness of really well-bred people about showing off; there was something even, perhaps, of that queer paralysis, and temptation to prefer even misunderstandings to long explanations, which led Sir James Barrie, in his amusing sketch, to allow himself to be saddled with a Brother Henry he never possessed, rather than exert himself to put in a word of warning. These other elements doubtless worked with the very extraordinary humility of this very extraordinary man; but another element worked with his equally unquestionable 'love of truth' in bringing the misunderstanding to an end. It is an element that must never be left out of the make-up of St. Thomas. However dreamy or distracted or immersed in theories he might be, he had any amount of Common Sense; and by the time it came, not only to being taught, but to being taught wrong, there was something in him that said sharply, 'Oh, this has got to stop!'

It seems probable that it was Albertus Magnus himself, the lecturer and learned teacher of all these youths, who first suspected something of the kind. He gave Thomas small jobs to do, of annotation or exposition; he persuaded him to banish his bashfulness so as to take part in at least one debate. He was a very shrewd old man and had studied the habits of other animals besides the salamander and the unicorn. He had studied many specimens of the most monstrous of all monstrosities; that is called Man. He knew the signs and marks of the sort of man, who is in an innocent way something of a monster among men. He was too good a schoolmaster not to know that the dunce is not always a dunce. He learned with amusement that this dunce had been nicknamed the Dumb Ox by his schoolfellows. All that is natural enough; but it does not take away the savour of something rather strange and symbolic, about the extraordinary emphasis with which he spoke at last. For Aquinas was still generally known only as one obscure and obstinately unresponsive pupil, among many more brilliant and promising pupils, when the great Albert broke silence with his famous cry and prophecy; "You call him a Dumb Ox; I tell you this Dumb Ox shall bellow so loud that his bellowings will fill the world".

To Albertus Magnus, as to Aristotle or Augustine or any number of other and older teachers, St. Thomas was always ready, with the hearty sort of humility, to give thanks for all his thinking. None the less, his own thinking was an advance on Albertus and the other Aristotelians, just as it was an advance on Augustine and the Augustinians. Albert had drawn attention to the direct study of natural facts, if only through fables like the unicorn and the salamander but the

monster called Man awaited a much more subtle and flexible vivi-section. The two men, however, became close friends and their friendship counts for a great deal in this central fight of the Middle Ages. For, as we shall see, the rehabilitation of Aristotle was a revolution almost as revolutionary as the exaltation of Dominic and Francis; and St. Thomas was destined to play a striking part in both.

It will be realised that the Aquino family had ultimately abandoned its avenging pursuit of its ugly duckling; who, as a black friar, should perhaps be called its black sheep. Of that escape some picturesque stories are told. The black sheep generally profits at last by quarrels among the white sheep of a family. They begin by quarrelling with him, but they end by quarrelling with each other. There is a rather confusing account concerning which members of his family came over to his side, while he was still imprisoned in the tower. But it is a fact that he was very fond of his sisters, and therefore probably not a fable that it was they who engineered his escape. According to the story, they rigged up a rope to the top of the tower, attached to a big basket, and it must have been rather a big basket if he was indeed lowered in this fashion from his prison, and escaped into the world. Anyhow, he did escape by energy, external or internal. But it was only an individual energy. The world was still pursuing and persecuting the Friars, quite as much as when they fled along the road to Rome. Thomas Aquinas had the good fortune to gather under the shadow of the one great outstanding Friar, whose respectability it was difficult to dispute, the learned and orthodox Albertus; but even he and his were soon troubled by the growing storm that threatened the new popular movements in the Church. Albertus was summoned to Paris, to receive the degree of a Doctor; but everyone knew that every move in that game had the character of a challenge. He made only the request, which probably looked like an eccentric request, that he should take his Dumb Ox along with him. They set out, like ordinary Friars or religious vagabonds; they slept in such monasteries as they could find; and finally in the monastery of St. James in Paris, where Thomas met another Friar who was also another friend.

Perhaps under the shadow of the storm that menaced all Friars, Bonaventure, the Franciscan, grew into so great a friendship with Thomas the Dominican, that their contemporaries compared them to David and Jonathan. The point is of some interest; because it would be quite easy to represent the Franciscan and the Dominican as flatly contradicting each other. The Franciscan may be represented as the Father of all the Mystics; and the Mystics can be represented as men who maintain that the final fruition or joy of the soul is rather a sensation than a thought. The motto of the Mystics has always been, "Taste and see". Now St. Thomas also began by saying, "Taste and see"; but he said it of the first rudimentary impressions of the human animal. It might well be maintained that the Franciscan puts Taste last and the Dominican puts it first. It might be said that the Thomist begins with something solid like the taste of an apple, and afterwards deduces a divine life for the intellect; while the Mystic exhausts the intellect first, and says finally that the sense of God is something like the taste of an apple. A common enemy might claim that St. Thomas begins with the taste of fruit and St. Bonaventure ends with the taste of fruit. But they are both right; if I may say so, it is a privilege of people who contradict each other in their cosmos to be both right. The Mystic is right in saying that the relation of God and Man is essentially a love-story; the pattern and type of all love-stories. The Dominican rationalist is equally right in saying that the intellect is at home in the topmost heavens; and that the appetite for truth may outlast and even devour all the duller appetites of man.

At the moment Aquinas and Bonaventure were encouraged in the possibility that they were both right; by the almost universal agreement that they were both wrong. It

was in any case a time of wild disturbance, and, as is common in such times, those who were trying to put things right were most vigorously accused of putting things wrong. Nobody knew who would win in that welter; Islam, or the Manichees of the Midi; or the two-faced and mocking Emperor; or the Crusades; or the old Orders of Christendom. But some men had a very vivid feeling that everything was breaking up; and that all the recent experiments or excesses were part of the same social dissolution; and there were two things that such men regarded as signs of ruin; one was the awful apparition of Aristotle out of the East, a sort of Greek god supported by Arabian worshippers; and the other was the new freedom of the Friars. It was the opening of the monastery and the scattering of the monks to wander over the world. The general feeling that they wandered like sparks from a furnace hitherto contained; the furnace of the abnormal love of God: the sense that they would utterly unbalance the common people with the counsels of perfection; that they would drift into being demagogues; all this finally burst out in a famous book called *The Perils of the Latter Times*, by a furious reactionary, William de St. Amour. It challenged the French King and the Pope, so that they established an enquiry. And Aquinas and Bonaventure, the two incongruous friends, with their respectively topsy-turvy universes, went up to Rome together, to defend the freedom of the Friars.

Thomas Aquinas defended the great vow of his youth, for freedom and for the poor; and it was probably the topmost moment of his generally triumphant career; for he turned back the whole backward movement of his time. Responsible authorities have said that, but for him, the whole great popular movement of the Friars might have been destroyed. With this popular victory the shy and awkward student finally becomes a historical character and a public man. After that, he was identified with the Mendicant Orders. But while St. Thomas may be said to have made his name in the defence of the

Mendicant Orders against the reactionaries, who took the same view of them as his own family had taken, there is generally a difference between a man making his name and a man really doing his work. The work of Thomas Aquinas was yet to come; but less shrewd observers than he could already see that it was coming. Broadly speaking, the danger was the danger of the orthodox, or those who too easily identify the old order with the orthodox, forcing a final and conclusive condemnation of Aristotle. There had already been rash and random condemnations to that effect, issued here and there, and the pressure of the narrower Augustinians upon the Pope and the principal judges became daily more pressing. The peril had appeared, not unnaturally, because of the historical and geographical accident of the Moslem proximity to the culture of Byzantium. The Arabs had got hold of the Greek manuscripts before the Latins who were the true heirs of the Greeks. And Moslems, though not very orthodox Moslems, were turning Aristotle into a pantheist philosophy still less acceptable to orthodox Christians. This second controversy, however, requires more explanation than the first. As is remarked on an introductory page, most modern people do know that St. Francis at least was a liberator of larger sympathies; that, whatever their positive view of medievalism, the Friars were in a relative sense a popular movement, pointing to greater fraternity and freedom; and a very little further information would inform them that this was every bit as true of the Dominican as of the Franciscan Friars. Nobody now is particularly likely to start up in defence of feudal abbots or fixed and stationary monks, against such impudent innovators as St. Francis and St. Thomas. We may therefore be allowed to summarise briefly the great debate about the Friars, though it shook all Christendom in its day. But the greater debate about Aristotle presents a greater difficulty; because there are modern misconceptions about it which can only be approached with a little more elaboration.

Perhaps there is really no such thing as a Revolution recorded in history. What happened was always a Counter-Revolution. Men were always rebelling against the last rebels; or even repenting of the last rebellion. This could be seen in the most casual contemporary fashions, if the fashionable mind had not fallen into the habit of seeing the very latest rebel as rebelling against all ages at once. The Modern Girl with the lipstick and the cocktail is as much a rebel against the Woman's Rights Woman of the '80's, with her stiff stick-up collars and strict teetotalism, as the latter was a rebel against the Early Victorian lady of the languid waltz tunes and the album full of quotations from Byron; or as the last, again, was a rebel against a Puritan mother to whom the waltz was a wild orgy and Byron the Bolshevist of his age. Trace even the Puritan mother back through history and she represents a rebellion against the Cavalier laxity of the English Church, which was at first a rebel against the Catholic civilisation, which had been a rebel against the Pagan civilisation. Nobody but a lunatic could pretend that these things were a progress; for they obviously go first one way and then the other. But whichever is right, one thing is certainly wrong; and that is the modern habit of looking at them only from the modern end. For that is only to see the end of the tale; they rebel against they know not what, because it arose they know not when; intent only on its ending, they are ignorant of its beginning; and therefore of its very being. The difference between the smaller cases and the larger, is that in the latter there is really so huge a human upheaval that men start from it like men in a new world; and that very novelty enables them to go on very long; and generally to go on too long. It is *because* these things start with a vigorous revolt that the intellectual impetus lasts long enough to make them seem like a survival. An excellent example of this is the real story of the revival and the neglect of Aristotle. By the end of the medieval time, Aristotelianism did eventually grow stale. Only a very fresh and successful novelty ever gets quite so stale as that.

When the moderns, drawing the blackest curtain of obscurantism that ever obscured history, decided that nothing mattered much before the Renaissance and the Reformation, they instantly began their modern career by falling into a big blunder. It was the blunder about Platonism. They found, hanging about the courts of the swaggering princes of the sixteenth century (which was as far back in history as they were allowed to go) certain anti-clerical artists and scholars who said they were bored with Aristotle and were supposed to be secretly indulging in Plato. The moderns, utterly ignorant of the whole story of the medievals, instantly fell into the trap. They assumed that Aristotle was some crabbed antiquity and tyranny from the black back of the Dark Ages, and that Plato was an entirely new Pagan pleasure never yet tasted by Christian men. Father Knox has shown in what a startling state of innocence is the mind of Mr. H. L. Mencken, for instance, upon this point. In fact, of course, the story is exactly the other way round. If anything, it was Platonism that was the old orthodoxy. It was Aristotelianism that was the very modern revolution. And the leader of that modern revolution was the man who is the subject of this book.

The truth is that the historical Catholic Church began by being Platonist; by being rather too Platonist. Platonism was in that very golden Greek air that was breathed by the first great Greek theologians. The Christian Fathers were much more like the Neo-Platonists than were the scholars of the Renaissance; who were only Neo-Neo-Platonists. For Chrysostom or Basil it was as ordinary and normal to think in terms of the Logos, or the Wisdom which is the aim of philosophers, as it is to any men of any religion today to talk about social problems or progress or the economic crisis throughout the world. St. Augustine followed a natural mental evolution when he was a Platonist before he was a Manichean, and a Mani-

chean before he was a Christian. And it was exactly in that last association that the first faint hint, of the danger of being *too* Platonist, may be seen.

From the Renaissance to the nineteenth century, the Moderns have had an almost monstrous love of the Ancients. In considering medieval life, they could never regard the Christians as anything but the pupils of the Pagans; of Plato in ideas, or Aristotle in reason and science. It was not so. On some points, even from the most monotonously modern standpoint, Catholicism was centuries ahead of Platonism or Aristotelianism. We can see it still, for instance, in the tiresome tenacity of Astrology. On that matter the philosophers were all in favour of superstition; and the saints and all such superstitious people were against superstition. But even the great saints found it difficult to get disentangled from this superstition. Two points were always put by those suspicious of the Aristotelianism of Aquinas; and they sound to us now very quaint and comic, taken together. One was the view that the stars are personal beings, governing our lives; the other the great general theory that men have one mind between them; a view obviously opposed to immortality; that is, to individuality. Both linger among the Moderns; so strong is still the tyranny of the Ancients. Astrology sprawls over the Sunday papers, and the other doctrine has its hundredth form in what is called Communism; or the Soul of the Hive.

For on one preliminary point, this position must not be misunderstood. When we praise the practical value of the Aristotelian Revolution, and the originality of Aquinas in leading it, we do not mean that the Scholastic philosophers before him had not been philosophers, or had not been highly philosophical, or had not been in touch with ancient philosophy. In so far as there was ever a bad break in philosophical history, it was not before St. Thomas, or at the beginning of medieval history; it was after St. Thomas and at the beginning of modern history. The great intellectual tradition that comes down to us from Pythagoras and Plato was never interrupted or lost through such trifles as the sack of Rome, the triumph of Attila or all the barbarian invasions of the Dark Ages. It was only lost after the introduction of printing, the discovery of America, the founding of the Royal Society and all the enlightenment of the Renaissance and the modern world. It was there, if anywhere, that there was lost or impatiently snapped the long thin delicate thread that had descended from distant antiquity; the thread of that unusual human hobby; the habit of thinking. This is proved by the fact that the printed books of this later period largely had to wait for the eighteenth century, or the end of the seventeenth century, to find even the names of the new philosophers; who were at the best a new kind of philosophers. But the decline of the Empire, the Dark Ages and the early Middle Ages, though too much tempted to neglect what was opposed to Platonic philosophy, had never neglected philosophy. In that sense St. Thomas, like most other very original men, has a long and clear pedigree. He himself is constantly referring back to the authorities from St. Augustine to St. Anselm, and from St. Anselm to St. Albert, and even when he differs, he also defers.

A very learned Anglican once said to me, not perhaps without a touch of tartness, "I can't understand why everybody talks as if Thomas Aquinas were the beginning of the Scholastic philosophy. I could understand their saying he was the end of it." Whether or no the comment was meant to be tart, we may be sure that the reply of St. Thomas would have been perfectly urbane. And indeed it would be easy to answer, with a certain placidity, that in his Thomist language, the end of a thing does not mean its destruction, but its fulfilment. No Thomist will complain, if Thomism is the end of our philosophy, in the sense in which God is the end of our existence. For that does not mean that we cease to exist, but that we become as perennial as the *philosophia perennis*. Putting this claim on one side, however, it is impor-

tant to remember that my distinguished interlocutor was perfectly right, in that there had been whole dynasties of doctrinal philosophers before Aquinas, leading up to the day of the great revolt of the Aristotelians. Nor was even that revolt a thing entirely abrupt and unforeseen. An able writer in the *Dublin Review* not long ago pointed out that in some respects the whole nature of metaphysics had advanced a long way since Aristotle, by the time it came to Aquinas. And that it is no disrespect to the primitive and gigantic genius of the Stagirite to say that in some respects he was really but a rude and rough founder of philosophy, compared with some of the subsequent subtleties of medievalism; that the Greek gave a few grand hints which the Scholastics developed into the most delicate fine shades. This may be an overstatement, but there is a truth in it. Anyhow, it is certain that even in Aristotelian philosophy, let alone Platonic philosophy, there was already a tradition of highly intelligent interpretation. If that delicacy afterwards degenerated into hairsplitting, it was none the less delicate hairsplitting; and work requiring very scientific tools.

What made the Aristotelian Revolution really revolutionary was the fact that it was really religious. It is the fact, so fundamental that I thought it well to lay it down in the first few pages of this book; that the revolt was largely a revolt of the most Christian elements in Christendom. St. Thomas, every bit as much as St. Francis, felt subconsciously that the hold of his people was slipping on the solid Catholic doctrine and discipline, worn smooth by more than a thousand years of routine; and that the Faith needed to be shown under a new light and dealt with from another angle. But he had no motive except the desire to make it popular for the salvation of the people. It was true, broadly speaking, that for some time past it had been too Platonist to be popular. It needed something like the shrewd and homely touch of Aristotle to turn it again into a religion of common sense. Both the motive and the method are illustrated in the war of Aquinas against the Augustinians.

First, it must be remembered that the Greek influence continued to flow from the Greek Empire; or at least from the centre of the Roman Empire which was in the Greek city of Byzantium, and no longer in Rome. That influence was Byzantine in every good and bad sense; like Byzantine art, it was severe and mathematical and a little terrible; like Byzantine etiquette, it was Oriental and faintly decadent. We owe to the learning of Mr. Christopher Dawson much enlightenment upon the way in which Byzantium slowly stiffened into a sort of Asiatic theocracy, more like that which served the Sacred Emperor in China. But even the unlearned can see the difference, in the way in which Eastern Christianity flattened everything, as it flattened the faces of the images into icons. It became a thing of patterns rather than pictures; and it made definite and destructive war upon statues. Thus we see, strangely enough, that the East was the land of the Cross and the West was the land of the Crucifix. The Greeks were being dehumanised by a radiant symbol, while the Goths were being humanised by an instrument of torture. Only the West made realistic pictures of the greatest of all the tales out of the East. Hence the Greek element in Christian theology tended more and more to be a sort of dried up Platonism; a thing of diagrams and abstractions; to the last indeed noble abstractions, but not sufficiently touched by that great thing that is by definition almost the opposite of abstraction: Incarnation. Their Logos was the Word; but not the Word made Flesh. In a thousand very subtle ways, often escaping doctrinal definition, this spirit spread over the world of Christendom from the place where the Sacred Emperor sat under his golden mosaics; and the flat pavement of the Roman Empire was at last a sort of smooth pathway for Mahomet. For Islam was the ultimate fulfilment of the Iconoclasts. Long before that, however, there was this tendency to make the Cross merely decorative like the Crescent; to make it a pattern like the Greek Key or the Wheel of Buddha. But there is something passive about such a world of patterns, and the Greek Key does not open any door, while the Wheel of Buddha always moves round and never moves on.

Partly through these negative influences, partly through a necessary and noble asceticism which sought to emulate the awful standard of the martyrs, the earlier Christian ages had been excessively anti-corporeal and too near the danger-line of Manichean mysticism. But there was far less danger in the fact that the saints macerated the body than in the fact that the sages neglected it. Granted all the grandeur of Augustine's contribution to Christianity, there was in a sense a more subtle danger in Augustine the Platonist than even in Augustine the Manichee. There came from it a mood which unconsciously committed the heresy of dividing the substance of the Trinity. It thought of God too exclusively as a Spirit who purifies or a Saviour who redeems; and too little as a Creator who creates. That is why men like Aquinas thought it right to correct Plato by an appeal to Aristotle; Aristotle who took things as he found them, just as Aquinas accepted things as God created them. In all the work of St. Thomas the world of positive creation is perpetually present. Humanly speaking, it was he who saved the human element in Christian theology, if he used for convenience certain elements in heathen philosophy. Only, as has already been urged, the human element is also the Christian one.

The panic upon the Aristotelian peril, that had passed across the high places of the Church, was probably a dry wind from the desert. It was really filled rather with fear of Mahomet than fear of Aristotle. And this was ironic, because there was really much more difficulty in reconciling Aristotle with Mahomet than in reconciling him with Christ. Islam is essentially a simple creed for simple men; and nobody can ever really turn pantheism into a simple creed. It is at once too abstract and too complicated. There are simple believers in a personal

God; and there are atheists more simple-minded than any believers in a personal God. But few can, in mere simplicity, accept a godless universe as a god. And while the Moslem, as compared with the Christian, had perhaps a less human God, he had if possible a more personal God. The will of Allah was very much of a will, and could not be turned into a stream of tendency. On all that cosmic and abstract side the Catholic was more accommodating than the Moslem —up to a point. The Catholic could admit at least that Aristotle was right about the impersonal elements of a personal God. Hence, we may say broadly of the Moslem philosophers, that those who became good philosophers became bad Moslems. It is not altogether unnatural that many bishops and doctors feared that the Thomists might become good philosophers and bad Christians. But there were also many, of the strict school of Plato and Augustine, who stoutly denied that they were even good philosophers. Between those rather incongruous passions, the love of Plato and the fear of Mahomet, there was a moment when the prospects of any Aristotelian culture in Christendom looked very dark indeed. Anathema after anathema was thundered from high places; and under the shadow of the persecution, as so often happens, it seemed for a moment that barely one or two figures stood alone in the storm-swept area. They were both in the black and white of the Dominicans; for Albertus and Aquinas stood firm.

In that sort of combat there is always confusion; and majorities change into minorities and back again, as if by magic. It is always difficult to date the turn of the tide, which seems to be a welter of eddies; the very dates seeming to overlap and confuse the crisis. But the change, from the moment when the two Dominicans stood alone to the moment when the whole Church at last wheeled into line with them, may perhaps be found at about the moment when they were practically brought before a hostile but a not unjust judge. Stephen Tempier, the Bishop of Paris, was apparently a rather fine specimen of the old fanatical Churchman, who thought that admiring Aristotle was a weakness likely to be followed by adoring Apollo. He was also, by a piece of bad luck, one of the old social conservatives, who had intensely resented the popular revolution of the Preaching Friars. But he was an honest man; and Thomas Aquinas never asked for anything but permission to address honest men. All around him there were other Aristotelian revolutionaries of a much more dubious sort. There was Siger, the sophist from Brabant, who learned all his Aristotelianism from the Arabs; and had an ingenious theory about how an Arabian agnostic could also be a Christian. There were a thousand young men of the sort that had shouted for Abelard; full of the youth of the thirteenth century and drunken with the Greek wine of Stagira. Over against them, lowering and implacable, was the old Puritan party of the Augustinians; only too delighted to class the rationalistic Albert and Thomas with the equivocal Moslem metaphysicians.

It would seem that the triumph of Thomas was really a personal triumph. He withdrew not a single one of his propositions; though it is said that the reactionary Bishop did condemn some of them after his death. On the whole, however, Aquinas convinced most of his critics that he was quite as good a Catholic as they were. There was a sequel of squabbles between the Religious Orders, following upon this controversial crisis. But it is probably true to say that the fact, that a man like Aquinas had managed even partially to satisfy a man like Tempier, was the end of the essential quarrel. What was already familiar to the few became familiar to the many; that an Aristotelian could really be a Christian. Another fact assisted in the common conversion. It rather curiously resembles the story of the translation of the Bible; and the alleged Catholic suppression of the Bible. Behind the scenes, where the Pope was much more tolerant than the Paris Bishop, the friends of Aquinas had been hard at work producing a new translation of Aristotle. It demonstrated that in many ways the heretical translation had been a very heretical translation. With the final consummation of this work, we may say that the great Greek philosophy entered finally into the system of Christendom. The process has been half humourously described as the Baptism of Aristotle.

We have all heard of the humility of the man of science; of many who were very genuinely humble; and of some who were very proud of their humility. It will be the somewhat too recurrent burden of this brief study that Thomas Aquinas really did have the humility of the man of science; as a special variant of the humility of the saint. It is true that he did not himself contribute anything concrete in the experiment or detail of physical science; in this, it may be said, he even lagged behind the last generation, and was far less of an experimental scientist than his tutor Albertus Magnus. But for all that, he was historically a great friend to the freedom of science. The principles he laid down, properly understood, are perhaps the best that can be produced for protecting science from mere obscurantist persecution. For instance, in the matter of the inspiration of Scripture, he fixed first on the obvious fact, which was forgotten by four furious centuries of sectarian battle, that the meaning of Scripture is very far from self-evident; and that we must often interpret it in the light of other truths. If a literal interpretation is really and flatly contradicted by an obvious fact, why then we can only say that the literal interpretation must be a false interpretation. But the fact must really be an obvious fact. And unfortunately, nineteenth-century scientists were just as ready to jump to the conclusion that any guess about nature was an obvious fact, as were seventeenth-century sectarians to jump to the conclusion that any guess about Scripture was the obvious explanation. Thus, private theories about what the Bible ought to mean, and premature theories about what the world ought to mean, have met in loud and widely advertised controversy, especially in the Victorian

time; and this clumsy collision of two very impatient forms of ignorance was known as the quarrel of Science and Religion.

But St. Thomas had the scientific humility in this very vivid and special sense; that he was ready to take the lowest place; for the examination of the lowest things. He did not, like a modern specialist, study the worm as if it were the world; but he was willing to begin to study the reality of the world in the reality of the worm. His Aristotelianism simply meant that the study of the humblest fact will lead to the study of the highest truth. That for him the process was logical and not biological, was concerned with philosophy rather than science, does not alter the essential idea that he believed in beginning at the bottom of the ladder. But he also gave, by his view of Scripture and Science, and other questions, a sort of charter for pioneers more purely practical than himself. He practically said that if they could really prove their practical discoveries, the traditional interpretation of Scripture must give way before those discoveries. He could hardly, as the common phrase goes, say fairer than that. If the matter had been left to him, and men like him, there never would have been any quarrel between Science and Religion. He did his very best to map out two provinces for them, and to trace a just frontier between them.

It is often cheerfully remarked that Christianity has failed, by which is meant that it has never had that sweeping, imperial and imposed supremacy, which has belonged to each of the great revolutions, every one of which has subsequently failed. There was never a moment when men could say that every man was a Christian; as they might say for several months that every man was a Royalist or a Republican or a Communist. But if sane historians want to understand the sense in which the Christian character has succeeded, they could not find a better case than the massive moral pressure of a man like St. Thomas, in support of the buried rationalism of the heathens, which had as yet only been dug up for the amusement of the heretics. It was, quite strictly and exactly, because a new kind of man was conducting rational enquiry in a new kind of way, that men forgot the curse that had fallen on the temples of the dead demons and the palaces of the dead despots; forgot even the new fury out of Arabia against which they were fighting for their lives; because the man who was asking them to return to sense, or to return to their senses, was not a sophist but a saint. Aristotle had described the magnanimous man, who is great and knows that he is great. But Aristotle would never have recovered his own greatness, but for the miracle that created the more magnanimous man; who is great and knows that he is small.

There is a certain historical importance in what some would call the heaviness of the style employed. It carries a curious impression of candour, which really did have, I think, a considerable effect upon contemporaries. The saint has sometimes been called a sceptic. The truth is that he was very largely tolerated as a sceptic because he was obviously a saint. When he seemed to stand up as a stubborn Aristotelian, hardly distinguishable from the Arabian heretics, I do seriously believe that what protected him was very largely the prodigious power of his simplicity and his obvious goodness and love of truth. Those who went out against the haughty confidence of the heretics were stopped and brought up all standing, against a sort of huge humility which was like a mountain; or perhaps like that immense valley that is the mould of a mountain. Allowing for all medieval conventions, we can feel that with the other innovators, this was not always so. The others, from Abelard down to Siger of Brabant, have never quite lost, in the long process of history, a faint air of showing off. Nobody could feel for a moment that Thomas Aquinas was showing off. The very dullness of diction, of which some complain, was enormously convincing. He could have given wit as well as wisdom; but he was so prodigiously in earnest that he gave his wisdom without his wit.

After the hour of triumph came the moment of peril. It is always so with alliances, and especially because Aquinas was fighting on two fronts. His main business was to defend the Faith against the abuse of Aristotle; and he boldly did it by supporting the use of Aristotle. He knew perfectly well that armies of atheists and anarchists were roaring applause in the background at his Aristotelian victory over all he held most dear. Nevertheless, it was never the existence of atheists, any more than Arabs or Aristotelian pagans, that disturbed the extraordinary controversial composure of Thomas Aquinas. The real peril that followed on the victory he had won for Aristotle was vividly presented in the curious case of Siger of Brabant; and it is well worth study, for anyone who would begin to comprehend the strange history of Christendom. It is marked by one rather queer quality; which has always been the unique note of the Faith, though it is not noticed by its modern enemies, and rarely by its modern friends. It is the fact symbolised in the legend of Antichrist, who was the double of Christ; in the profound proverb that the Devil is the ape of God. It is the fact that falsehood is never so false as when it is very nearly true. It is when the stab comes near the nerve of truth, that the Christian conscience cries out in pain. And Siger of Brabant, following on some of the Arabian Aristotelians, advanced a theory which most modern newspaper readers would instantly have declared to be the same as the theory of St. Thomas. That was what finally roused St. Thomas to his last and most emphatic protest. He had won his battle for a wider scope of philosophy and science; he had cleared the ground for a general understanding about faith and enquiry; an understanding that has generally been observed among Catholics, and certainly never deserted without disaster. It was the idea that the scientist should go on exploring and experimenting freely, so long as he did not claim an infallibility and finality which it was against his own principles to claim. Meanwhile the Church should go on developing and defining, about supernatural things, so long as she did not claim a right to alter the deposit of faith, which it was against her own principles to claim. And when he had said this, Siger of Brabant got up and said something so horribly like it, and so horribly unlike, that (like Antichrist) he might have deceived the very elect.

Siger of Brabant said this: the Church must be right theologically, but she can be wrong scientifically. There are two truths; the truth of the supernatural world, and the truth of the natural world, which contradicts the supernatural world. While we are being naturalists, we can suppose that Christianity is all nonsense; but then, when we remember that we are Christians, we must admit that Christianity is true even if it is nonsense. In other words, Siger of Brabant split the human head in two, like the blow in an old legend of battle; and declared that a man has two minds, with one of which he must entirely believe and with the other may utterly disbelieve. To many this would at least seem like a parody of Thomism. As a fact, it was the assassination of Thomism. It was not two ways of finding the same truth; it was an untruthful way of pretending that there are two truths. And it is extraordinarily interesting to note that this is the one occasion when the Dumb Ox really came out like a wild bull. When he stood up to answer Siger of Brabant, he was altogether transfigured, and the very style of his sentences, which is a thing like the tone of a man's voice, is suddenly altered. He had never been angry with any of the enemies who disagreed with him. But these enemies had attempted the worst treachery: they had made him agree with them.

Those who complain that theologians draw fine distinctions could hardly find a better example of their own folly. In fact, a fine distinction can be a flat contradiction. It was notably so in this case. St. Thomas was willing to allow the one truth to be approached by two paths, precisely *because* he was sure there was only one truth. Because the Faith was the one truth, nothing discov-

ered in nature could ultimately contradict the Faith. Because the Faith was the one truth, nothing really deduced from the Faith could ultimately contradict the facts. It was in truth a curiously daring confidence in the reality of his religion; and though some may linger to dispute it, it has been justified. The scientific facts, which were supposed to contradict the Faith in the nineteenth century, are nearly all of them regarded as unscientific fictions in the twentieth century. Even the materialists have fled from materialism; and those who lectured us about determinism in psychology are already talking about indeterminism in matter. But whether his confidence was right or wrong, it was specially and supremely a confidence that there is one truth which cannot contradict itself. And this last group of enemies suddenly sprang up, to tell him they entirely agreed with him in saying that there are two contradictory truths. Truth, in the medieval phrase, carried two faces under one hood; and these double-faced sophists practically dared to suggest that it was the Dominican hood.

So, in his last battle and for the first time, he fought as with a battle-axe. There is a ring in the words altogether beyond the almost impersonal patience he maintained in debate with so many enemies. "Behold our refutation of the error. It is not based on documents of faith, but on the reasons and statements of the philosophers themselves. If then anyone there be who, boastfully taking pride in his supposed wisdom, wishes to challenge what we have written, let him not do it in some corner nor before children who are powerless to decide on such difficult matters. Let him reply openly if he dare. He shall find me there confronting him, and not only my negligible self, but many another whose study is truth. We shall do battle with his errors or bring a cure to his ignorance."

The Dumb Ox is bellowing now; like one at bay and yet terrible and towering over all the baying pack. We have already noted why, in this one quarrel with Siger of Brabant, Thomas Aquinas let loose such thunders of purely moral passion; it was because the whole work of his life was being betrayed behind his back, by those who had used his victories over the reactionaries. The point at the moment is that this is perhaps his one moment of personal passion, save for a single flash in the troubles of his youth; and he is once more fighting his enemies with a firebrand. And yet, even in this isolated apocalypse of anger, there is one phrase that may be commended for all time to men who are angry with much less cause. If there is one sentence that could be carved in marble, as representing the calmest and most enduring rationality of his unique intelligence, it is a sentence which came pouring out with all the rest of this molten lava. If there is one phrase that stands before history as typical of Thomas Aquinas, it is that phrase about his own argument: "It is not based on documents of faith, but on the reasons and statements of the philosophers themselves." Would that all Orthodox doctors in deliberation were as reasonable as Aquinas in anger! Would that all Christian apologists would remember that maxim; and write it up in large letters on the wall, before they nail any theses there. At the top of his fury, Thomas Aquinas understands, what so many defenders of orthodoxy will not understand. It is no good to tell an atheist that he is an atheist; or to charge a denier of immortality with the infamy of denying it; or to imagine that one can force an opponent to admit he is wrong, by proving that he is wrong on somebody else's principles, but not on his own. After the great example of St. Thomas, the principle stands, or ought always to have stood established; that we must either not argue with a man at all, or we must argue on his grounds and not ours. We may do other things *instead* of arguing, according to our views of what actions are morally permissible; but if we argue we must argue 'on the reasons and statements of the philosophers themselves.' This is the common sense in a saying attributed to a friend of St. Thomas, the great St. Louis, King of

France, which shallow people quote as a sample of fanaticism; the sense of which is, that I must either argue with an infidel as a real philosopher can argue, or else 'thrust a sword through his body as far as it will go.' A real philosopher (even of the opposite school) will be the first to agree that St. Louis was entirely philosophical.

So, in the last great controversial crisis of his theological campaign, Thomas Aquinas contrived to give his friends and enemies not only a lesson in theology, but a lesson in controversy. But it was in fact his last controversy. He had been a man with a huge controversial appetite, a thing that exists in some men and not others, in saints and in sinners. But after this great and victorious duel with Siger of Brabant, he was suddenly overwhelmed with a desire for silence and repose. He said one strange thing about this mood of his to a friend, which will fall into its more appropriate place elsewhere. He fell back on the extreme simplicities of his monastic round and seemed to desire nothing but a sort of permanent retreat. A request came to him from the Pope that he should set out upon some further mission of diplomacy or disputation; and he made ready to obey. But before he had gone many miles on the journey, he was dead.

## IV   A meditation on the Manichees

There is one casual anecdote about St. Thomas Aquinas which illuminates him like a lightning-flash, not only without but within. For it not only shows him as a character, and even as a comedy character, and shows the colours of his period and social background; but also, as if for an instant, makes a transparency of his mind. It is a trivial incident which occurred one day, when he was reluctantly dragged from his work, and we might almost say from his play. For both were for him found in the unusual hobby of thinking, which is for some men a thing much more intoxicating than mere drinking. He had declined any number of society invitations, to the courts of kings and princes, not because he was unfriendly, for he was not; but because he was always glowing within with the really gigantic plans of exposition and argument which filled his life. On one occasion, however, he was invited to the court of King Louis IX of France, more famous as the great St. Louis; and for some reason or other, the Dominican authorities of his Order told him to accept; so he immediately did so, being an obedient friar even in his sleep; or rather in his permanent trance of reflection.

It is a real case against conventional hagiography that it sometimes tends to make all saints seem to be the same. Whereas in fact no men are more different than saints; not even murderers. And there could hardly be a more complete contrast, given the essentials of holiness, than between St. Thomas and St. Louis. St. Louis was born a knight and a king; but he was one of those men in whom a certain simplicity, combined with courage and activity, makes it natural, and in a sense easy, to fulfil directly and promptly any duty or office, however official. He was a man in whom holiness and healthiness had no quarrel; and their issue was in action. He did not go in for thinking much, in the sense of theorising much. But, even in theory, he had that sort of presence of mind, which belongs to the rare and really practical man when he has to think. He never said the wrong thing; and he was orthodox by instinct. In the old pagan proverb about kings being philosophers or philosophers kings, there was a certain miscalculation, connected with a mystery that only Christianity could reveal. For while it is possible for a king to wish very much to be a saint, it is not possible for a saint to wish very much to be a king. A good man will hardly be always dreaming of being a great monarch; but, such is the liberality of the Church, that she cannot forbid even a great monarch to dream of being a good man. But Louis was a straightforward soldierly sort of person who did not particularly mind being a king, any more than he would have

minded being a captain or a sergeant or any other rank in his army. Now a man like St. Thomas would definitely dislike being a king, or being entangled with the pomp and politics of kings; not only his humility, but a sort of subconscious fastidiousness and fine dislike of futility, often found in leisurely and learned men with large minds, would really have prevented him making contact with the complexity of court life. Also, he was anxious all his life to keep out of politics; and there was no political symbol more striking, or in a sense more challenging, at that moment, than the power of the King in Paris.

Paris was truly at that time an *aurora borealis*; a Sunrise in the North. We must realise that lands much nearer to Rome had rotted with paganism and pessimism and Oriental influences of which the most respectable was that of Mahound. Provence and all the South had been full of a fever of nihilism or negative mysticism, and from Northern France had come the spears and swords that swept away the unchristian thing. In Northern France also sprang up that splendour of building that shines like swords and spears: the first spires of the Gothic. We talk now of grey Gothic buildings; but they must have been very different when they went up white and gleaming into the northern skies, partly picked out with gold and bright colours; a new flight of architecture, as startling as flying-ships. The new Paris ultimately left behind by St. Louis must have been a thing white like lilies and splendid as the oriflamme. It was the beginning of the great new thing: the nation of France, which was to pierce and overpower the old quarrel of Pope and Emperor in the lands from which Thomas came. But Thomas came very unwillingly, and, if we may say it of so kindly a man, rather sulkily. As he entered Paris, they showed him from the hill that splendour of new spires beginning, and somebody said something like, "How grand it must be to own all this." And Thomas Aquinas only muttered, "I would rather have that Chrysostom MS. I can't get hold of."

Somehow they steered that reluctant bulk of reflection to a seat in the royal banquet hall; and all that we know of Thomas tells us that he was perfectly courteous to those who spoke to him, but spoke little, and was soon forgotten in the most brilliant and noisy clatter in the world: the noise of French talking. What the Frenchmen were talking about we do not know; but they forgot all about the large fat Italian in their midst, and it seems only too possible that he forgot all about them. Sudden silences will occur even in French conversation; and in one of these the interruption came. There had long been no word or motion in that huge heap of black and white weeds, like motley in mourning, which marked him as a mendicant friar out of the streets, and contrasted with all the colours and patterns and quarterings of that first and freshest dawn of chivalry and heraldry. The triangular shields and pennons and pointed spears, the triangular swords of the Crusade, the pointed windows and the conical hoods, repeated everywhere that fresh French medieval spirit that did, in every sense, come to the point. But the colours of the coats were gay and varied, with little to rebuke their richness; for St. Louis, who had himself a special quality of coming to the point, had said to his courtiers, "Vanity should be avoided; but every man should dress well, in the manner of his rank, that his wife may the more easily love him."

And then suddenly the goblets leapt and rattled on the board and the great table shook, for the friar had brought down his huge fist like a club of stone, with a crash that startled everyone like an explosion; and had cried out in a strong voice, but like a man in the grip of a dream, "And *that* will settle the Manichees!"

The palace of a king, even when it is the palace of a saint, has its conventions. A shock thrilled through the court, and every one felt as if the fat friar from Italy had thrown a plate at King Louis, or knocked his crown sideways. They all looked timidly at the terrible seat, that was for a thousand years the throne of the Capets; and many there were

presumably prepared to pitch the big black-robed beggarman out of the window. But St. Louis, simple as he seemed, was no mere medieval fountain of honour or even fountain of mercy; but also the fountain of two eternal rivers; the irony and the courtesy of France. And he turned to his secretaries, asking them in a low voice to take their tablets round to the seat of the absent-minded controversialist, and take a note of the argument that had just occurred to him; because it must be a very good one and he might forget it. I have paused upon this anecdote, first, as has been said, because it is the one which gives us the most vivid snapshot of a great medieval character; indeed of two great medieval characters. But it is also specially fitted to be taken as a type or a turning-point, because of the glimpse it gives of the man's main preoccupation; and the sort of thing that might have been found in his thoughts, if they had been thus surprised at any moment by a philosophical eavesdropper or through a psychological keyhole. It was not for nothing that he was still brooding, even in the white court of St. Louis, upon the dark cloud of the Manichees.

This book is meant only to be the sketch of a man; but it must at least lightly touch, later on, upon a method and a meaning; or what our journalism has an annoying way of calling a message. A few very inadequate pages must be given to the man in relation to his theology and his philosophy; but the thing of which I mean to speak here is something at once more general and more personal even than his philosophy. I have therefore introduced it here, before we come to anything like technical talk about his philosophy. It was something that might alternatively be called his moral attitude, or his temperamental predisposition, or the purpose of his life so far as social and human effects were concerned: for he knew better than most of us that there is but one purpose in this life, and it is one that is beyond this life. But if we wanted to put in a picturesque and simplified form what he wanted for the world, and what was his work in history, apart from theoretical and theological definitions, we might well say that it really was to strike a blow and settle the Manichees.

The full meaning of this may not be apparent to those who do not study theological history; and perhaps even less apparent to those who do. Indeed it may seem equally irrelevant to the history and the theology. In history St. Dominic and Simon de Montfort between them had already pretty well settled the Manichees. And in theology, of course, an encyclopaedic doctor like Aquinas dealt with a thousand other heresies besides the Manichean heresy. Nevertheless, it does represent his main position and the turn he gave to the whole history of Christendom.

I think it well to interpose this chapter, though its scope may seem more vague than the rest; because there is a sort of big blunder about St. Thomas and his creed, which is an obstacle for most modern people in even beginning to understand them. It arises roughly thus. St. Thomas, like other monks, and especially other saints, lived a life of renunciation and austerity; his fasts, for instance, being in marked contrast to the luxury in which he might have lived if he chose. This element stands high in his religion, as a manner of asserting the will against the power of nature; of thanking the Redeemer by partially sharing his sufferings, of making a man ready for anything as a missionary or martyr, and similar ideals. These happen to be rare in the modern industrial society of the West, outside his communion; and it is therefore assumed that they are the whole meaning of that communion. Because it is uncommon for an alderman to fast forty days, or a politician to take a Trappist vow of silence, or a man about town to live a life of strict celibacy, the average outsider is convinced, not only that Catholicism is nothing except asceticism, but that asceticism is nothing except pessimism. He is so obliging as to explain to Catholics why they hold this heroic virtue in respect; and is ever ready to point out that the

philosophy behind it is an Oriental hatred of anything connected with Nature, and a purely Schopenhauerian disgust with the Will to Live. I read in a "high-class" review of Miss Rebecca West's book on St. Augustine, the astounding statement that the Catholic Church regards sex as having the nature of sin. How marriage can be a sacrament if sex is a sin, or why it is the Catholics who are in favour of birth and their foes who are in favour of birth-control, I will leave the critic to worry out for himself. My concern is not with that part of the argument; but with another.

The ordinary modern critic, seeing this ascetic ideal in an authoritative Church, and not seeing it in most other inhabitants of Brixton or Brighton, is apt to say, "This is the result of Authority; it would be better to have Religion without Authority." But in truth, a wider experience outside Brixton or Brighton would reveal the mistake. It is rare to find a fasting alderman or a Trappist politician, but it is still more rare to see nuns suspended in the air on hooks or spikes; it is unusual for a Catholic Evidence Guild orator in Hyde Park to begin his speech by gashing himself all over with knives; a stranger calling at an ordinary presbytery will seldom find the parish priest lying on the floor with a fire lighted on his chest and scorching him while he utters spiritual ejaculations. Yet all these things are done all over Asia, for instance, by voluntary enthusiasts acting solely on the great impulse of Religion; of Religion, in their case, not commonly imposed by any immediate Authority; and certainly not imposed by this particular Authority. In short, a real knowledge of mankind will tell anybody that Religion is a very terrible thing; that it is truly a raging fire, and that Authority is often quite as much needed to restrain it as to impose it. Asceticism, or the war with the appetites, is itself an appetite. It can never be eliminated from among the strange ambitions of Man. But it can be kept in some reasonable control; and it is indulged in much saner proportion under Catholic Authority than in

Pagan or Puritan anarchy. Meanwhile, the whole of this ideal, though an essential part of Catholic idealism when it is understood, is in some ways entirely a side issue. It is not the primary principle of Catholic philosophy; it is only a particular deduction from Catholic ethics. And when we begin to talk about primary philosophy, we realise the full and flat contradiction between the monk fasting and the fakir hanging himself on hooks.

Now nobody will begin to understand the Thomist philosophy, or indeed the Catholic philosophy, who does not realise that the primary and fundamental part of it is entirely the praise of Life, the praise of Being, the praise of God as the Creator of the World. Everything else follows a long way after that, being conditioned by various complications like the Fall or the vocation of heroes. The trouble occurs because the Catholic mind moves upon two planes; that of the Creation and that of the Fall. The nearest parallel is, for instance, that of England invaded; there might be strict martial law in Kent because the enemy had landed in Kent, and relative liberty in Hereford; but this would not affect the affection of an English patriot for Hereford or Kent, and strategic caution in Kent would not affect the love of Kent. For the love of England would remain, both of the parts to be redeemed by discipline and the parts to be enjoyed in liberty. Any extreme of Catholic asceticism is a wise, or unwise, precaution against the evil of the Fall; it is *never* a doubt about the good of the Creation. And *that* is where it really does differ, not only from the rather excessive eccentricity of the gentleman who hangs himself on hooks, but from the whole cosmic theory which is the hook on which he hangs. In the case of many Oriental religions, it really is true that the asceticism is pessimism; that the ascetic tortures himself to death out of an abstract hatred of life; that he does not merely mean to control Nature as he should, but to contradict Nature as much as he can. And though it takes a milder form than hooks in

millions of the religious populations of Asia, it is a fact far too little realised, that the dogma of the denial of life does really rule as a first principle on so vast a scale. One historic form it took was that great enemy of Christianity from its beginning: the Manichees.

What is called the Manichean philosophy has had many forms; indeed it has attacked what is immortal and immutable with a very curious kind of immortal mutability. It is like the legend of the magician who turns himself into a snake or a cloud; and the whole has that nameless note of irresponsibility, which belongs to much of the metaphysics and morals of Asia, from which the Manichean mystery came. But it is always in one way or another a notion that nature is evil; or that evil is at least rooted in nature. The essential point is that as evil has roots in nature, so it has rights in nature. Wrong has as much right to exist as right. As already stated this notion took many forms. Sometimes it was a dualism, which made evil an equal partner with good; so that neither could be called an usurper. More often it was a general idea that demons had made the material world, and if there were any good spirits, they were concerned only with the spiritual world. Later, again, it took the form of Calvinism, which held that God had indeed made the world, but in a special sense, made the evil as well as the good: had made an evil will as well as an evil world. On this view, if a man chooses to damn his soul alive, he is not thwarting God's will but rather fulfilling it. In these two forms, of the early Gnosticism and the later Calvinism, we see the superficial variety and fundamental unity of Manicheanism. The old Manicheans taught that Satan originated the whole work of creation commonly attributed to God. The new Calvinists taught that God originates the whole work of damnation commonly attributed to Satan. One looked back to the first day when a devil acted like a god, the other looked forward to a last day when a god acted like a devil. But both had the idea that the creator of the earth was primarily the creator of the evil, whether we call him a devil or a god.

Since there are a good many Manicheans among the Moderns, as we may remark in a moment, some may agree with this view, some may be puzzled about it, some may only be puzzled about why we should object to it. To understand the medieval controversy, a word must be said of the Catholic doctrine, which is as modern as it is medieval. That 'God looked on all things and saw that they were good' contains a subtlety which the popular pessimist cannot follow, or is too hasty to notice. It is the thesis that there are no bad things, but only bad uses of things. If you will, there are no bad things but only bad thoughts; and especially bad intentions. Only Calvinists can really believe that hell is paved with good intentions. That is exactly the one thing it cannot be paved with. But it is possible to have bad intentions about good things; and good things, like the world and the flesh have been twisted by a bad intention called the devil. But he cannot make *things* bad; they remain as on the first day of creation. The work of heaven alone was material; the making of a material world. The work of hell is entirely spiritual.

This error then had many forms; but especially, like nearly every error, it had two forms, a fiercer one which was outside the Church and attacking the Church, and a subtler one, which was inside the Church and corrupting the Church. There has never been a time when the Church was not torn between that invasion and that treason. It was so, for instance, in the Victorian time. Darwinian "competition," in commerce or race conflict, was every bit as brazen an atheist assault, in the nineteenth century, as the Bolshevist No-God movement in the twentieth century. To brag of brute prosperity, to admire the most muddy millionaires who had cornered wheat by a trick, to talk about the 'unfit' (in imitation of the scientific thinker who would finish them off because he cannot even finish his own sentence—unfit for what?)—all that is as simply and openly Anti-Christian as the Black Mass. Yet some weak and worldly Catholics did

use this cant in defence of Capitalism, in their first rather feeble resistance to Socialism. At least they did until the great Encyclical of the Pope on the Rights of Labour put a stop to all their nonsense. The evil is always both within and without the Church; but in a wilder form outside and a milder form inside. So it was, again, in the seventeenth century, when there was Calvinism outside and Jansenism inside. And so it was in the thirteenth century, when the obvious danger outside was in the revolution of the Albigensians; but the potential danger inside was in the very traditionalism of the Augustinians. For the Augustinians derived only from Augustine, and Augustine derived partly from Plato, and Plato was right, but not quite right. It is a mathematical fact that if a line be not perfectly directed towards a point, it will actually go further away from it as it comes nearer to it. After a thousand years of extension, the miscalculation of Platonism had come very near to Manicheanism.

Popular errors are nearly always right. They nearly always refer to some ultimate reality, about which those who correct them are themselves incorrect. It is a very queer thing that "Platonic Love" has come to mean for the unlettered something rather purer and cleaner than it means for the learned. Yet even those who realise the great Greek evil may well realise that perversity often comes out of the wrong sort of purity. Now it was the inmost lie of the Manichees that they identified purity with sterility. It is singularly contrasted with the language of St. Thomas, which always connects purity with fruitfulness; whether it be natural or supernatural. And, queerly enough, as I have said, there does remain a sort of reality in the vulgar colloquialism that the affair between Sam and Susan is "quite Platonic." It is true that, quite apart from the local perversion, there was in Plato a sort of idea that people would be better without their bodies; that their heads might fly off and meet in the sky in merely intellectual marriage, like cherubs in a picture. The ultimate phase of this "Platonic" philosophy was what inflamed poor D. H. Lawrence into talking nonsense, and he was probably unaware that the Catholic doctrine of marriage would say much of what he said, without talking nonsense. Anyhow, it is historically important to see that Platonic love did somewhat distort both human and divine love, in the theory of the early theologians. Many medieval men, who would indignantly deny the Albigensian doctrine of sterility, were yet in an emotional mood to abandon the body in despair; and some of them to abandon everything in despair.

In truth, this vividly illuminates the provincial stupidity of those who object to what they call "creeds and dogmas." It was precisely the creed and dogma that saved the sanity of the world. These people generally propose an alternative religion of intuition and feeling. If, in the really Dark Ages, there had been a religion of feeling, it would have been a religion of black and suicidal feeling. It was the rigid creed that resisted the rush of suicidal feeling. The critics of asceticism are probably right in supposing that many a Western hermit did *feel* rather like an Eastern fakir. But he could not really *think* like an Eastern fakir; because he was an orthodox Catholic. And what kept his thought in touch with healthier and more humanistic thought was simply and solely the Dogma. He could not deny that a good God had created the normal and natural world; he could not say that the devil had made the world; because he was not a Manichee. A thousand enthusiasts for celibacy, in the day of the great rush to the desert or the cloister, might have called marriage a sin, if they had only considered their individual ideals, in the modern manner, and their own immediate feelings about marriage. Fortunately, they had to accept the Authority of the Church, which had definitely said that marriage was not a sin. A modern emotional religion might at any moment have turned Catholicism into Manichaeism. But when Religion would have maddened men, Theology kept them sane.

In this sense St. Thomas stands up simply as the great orthodox theologian, who reminded men of the creed of Creation, when many of them were still in the mood of mere destruction. It is futile for the critics of medievalism to quote a hundred medieval phrases that may be supposed to sound like mere pessimism, if they will not understand the central fact; that medieval men did not care about being medieval and did not accept the authority of a mood, because it was melancholy, but did care very much about orthodoxy, which is not a mood. It was because St. Thomas could *prove* that his glorification of the Creator and His creative joy was more orthodox than any atmospheric pessimism, that he dominated the Church and the world, which accepted that truth as a test. But when this immense and impersonal importance is allowed for, we may agree that there was a personal element as well. Like most of the great religious teachers, he was fitted individually for the task that God had given him to do. We can if we like call that talent instinctive; we can even descend to calling it temperamental.

Anybody trying to popularise a medieval philosopher must use language that is very modern and very unphilosophical. Nor is this a sneer at modernity; it arises from the moderns having dealt so much in moods and emotions, especially in the arts, that they have developed a large but loose vocabulary, which deals more with atmosphere than with actual attitude or position. As noted elsewhere, even the modern philosophers are more like the modern poets; in giving an individual tinge even to truth, and often looking at all life through different coloured spectacles. To say that Schopenhauer had the blues, or that William James had a rather rosier outlook, would often convey more than calling the one a Pessimist or the other a Pragmatist. This modern moodiness has its value, though the moderns overrate it; just as medieval logic had its value, though it was overrated in the later Middle Ages. But the point is that to explain the medievals to the moderns, we must often use this modern language of mood. Otherwise the character will be missed, through certain prejudices and ignorances about all such medieval characters. Now there is something that lies all over the work of St. Thomas Aquinas like a great light; which is something quite primary and perhaps unconscious with him, which he would perhaps have passed over as an irrelevant personal quality; and which can now only be expressed by a rather cheap journalistic term, which he would probably have thought quite senseless.

Nevertheless, the only working word for that atmosphere is Optimism. I know that the word is now even more degraded in the twentieth century than it was in the nineteenth century. Men talked lately of being Optimists about the issue of War; they talk now of being Optimists about the revival of Trade; they may talk tomorrow of being Optimists about the International Ping-pong Tournament. But men in the Victorian time did mean a little more than that, when they used the word Optimist of Browning or Stevenson or Walt Whitman. And in a rather larger and more luminous sense than in the case of these men, the term was basically true of Thomas Aquinas. He did, with a most solid and colossal conviction, believe in Life; and in something like what Stevenson called the great theorem of the livableness of life. It breathes somehow in his very first phrases about the reality of Being. If the morbid Renaissance intellectual is supposed to say, "To be or not to be—that is the question," then the massive medieval doctor does most certainly reply in a voice of thunder, "To be—that is the answer." The point is important; many not unnaturally talk of the Renaissance as the time when certain men began to believe in Life. The truth is that it was the time when a few men, for the first time, began to disbelieve in Life. The medievals had put many restrictions, and some excessive restrictions, upon the universal human hunger and even fury for Life. Those restrictions had often been expressed in fanatical and rabid terms; the terms of

those resisting a great natural force; the force of men who desired to live. Never until modern thought began, did they really have to fight with men who desired to die. That horror had threatened them in Asiatic Albigensianism, but it never became normal to them—until now.

But this fact becomes very vivid indeed, when we compare the greatest of Christian philosophers with the only men who were anything like his equals, or capable of being his rivals. They were people with whom he did not directly dispute; most of them he had never seen; some of them he had never heard of. Plato and Augustine were the only two with whom he could confer as he did with Bonaventure or even Averrhoes. But we must look elsewhere for his real rivals, and the only real rivals of the Catholic theory. They are the heads of the great heathen systems; some of them very ancient, some very modern, like Buddha on the one hand or Nietzsche on the other. It is when we see his gigantic figure against this vast and cosmic background, that we realise, first, that he was the only optimist theologian, and second, that Catholicism is the only optimist theology. Something milder and more amiable may be made out of the deliquescence of theology, and the mixture of the creed with everything that contradicts it; but among consistent cosmic creeds, this is the only one that is entirely on the side of Life.

Comparative religion has indeed allowed us to compare religions—and to contrast them. Fifty years ago, it set out to prove that all religions were much the same; generally proving, alternately, that they were all equally worthy and that they were all equally worthless. Since then this scientific process has suddenly begun to be scientific, and discovered the depths of the chasms as well as the heights of the hills. It is indeed an excellent improvement that sincerely religious people should respect each other. But respect has discovered difference, where contempt knew only indifference. The more we really appreciate the noble revulsion and renunciation of Buddha, the more we see that intellectually it was the converse and almost the contrary of the salvation of the world by Christ. The Christian would escape from the world into the universe: the Buddhist wishes to escape from the universe even more than from the world. One would uncreate himself; the other would return to his Creation; to his Creator. Indeed it was so genuinely the converse of the idea of the Cross as the Tree of Life, that there is some excuse for setting up the two things side by side, as if they were of equal significance. They are in one sense parallel and equal; as a mound and a hollow, as a valley and a hill. There is a sense in which that sublime despair is the only alternative to that divine audacity. It is even true that the truly spiritual and intellectual man sees it as a sort of dilemma; a very hard and terrible choice. There is little else on earth that can compare with these for completeness. And he who will not climb the mountain of Christ does indeed fall into the abyss of Buddha.

The same is true, in a less lucid and dignified fashion, of most other alternatives of heathen humanity; nearly all are sucked back into that whirlpool of recurrence which all the ancients knew. Nearly all return to the one idea of returning. That is what Buddha described so darkly as the Sorrowful Wheel. It is true that the sort of recurrence which Buddha described as the Sorrowful Wheel, poor Nietzsche actually managed to describe as the Joyful Wisdom. I can only say that if bare repetition was his idea of Joyful Wisdom, I should be curious to know what was his idea of Sorrowful Wisdom. But as a fact, in the case of Nietzsche, this did not belong to the moment of his breaking out, but to the moment of his breaking down. It came at the end of his life, when he was near to mental collapse; and it is really quite contrary to his earlier and finer inspirations of wild freedom or fresh and creative innovation. Once at least he had tried to break out; but he also was only broken—on the wheel.

Alone upon the earth, and lifted and liberated from all the wheels and whirlpools of the earth, stands up the faith of St. Thomas; weighted and balanced indeed with more than Oriental metaphysics and more than Pagan pomp and pageantry; but vitally and vividly alone in declaring that life is a living story, with a great beginning and a great close; rooted in the primeval joy of God and finding its fruition in the final happiness of humanity; opening with the colossal chorus in which the sons of God shouted for joy, and ending in that mystical comradeship, shown in a shadowy fashion in those ancient words that move like an archaic dance; "For His delight is with the sons of men."

It is the fate of this sketch to be sketchy about philosophy, scanty or rather empty about theology, and to achieve little more than a decent silence on the subject of sanctity. And yet it must none the less be the recurrent burden of this little book, to which it must return with some monotony, that in this story the philosophy did depend on the theology, and the theology did depend on the sanctity. In other words, it must repeat the first fact, which was emphasised in the first chapter: that this great intellectual creation was a Christian and Catholic creation and cannot be understood as anything else. It was Aquinas who baptised Aristotle, when Aristotle could not have baptised Aquinas; it was a purely Christian miracle which raised the great Pagan from the dead. And this is proved in three ways (as St. Thomas himself might say), which it will be well to summarise as a sort of summary of this book.

First, in the life of St. Thomas, it is proved in the fact that only his huge and solid orthodoxy could have supported so many things which then seemed to be unorthodox. Charity covers a multitude of sins; and in that sense orthodoxy covers a multitude of heresies; or things which are hastily mistaken for heresies. It was precisely because his personal Catholicism was so convincing, that his impersonal Aristotelianism was given the benefit of the doubt. He did not smell of the faggot because he did smell of the firebrand; of the firebrand he had so instantly and instinctively snatched up, under a real assault on essential Catholic ethics. A typically cynical modern phrase refers to the man who is so good that he is good for nothing. St. Thomas was so good that he was good for everything; that his warrant held good for what others considered the most wild and daring speculations, ending in the worship of nothing. Whether or no he baptised Aristotle, he was truly the godfather of Aristotle; he was his sponsor; he swore that the old Greek would do no harm; and the whole world trusted his word.

Second, in the philosophy of St. Thomas, it is proved by the fact that everything depended on the new Christian *motive* for the study of facts, as distinct from truths. The Thomist philosophy began with the lowest roots of thought, the senses and the truisms of the reason; and a Pagan sage might have scorned such things, as he scorned the servile arts. But the materialism, which is merely cynicism in a Pagan, can be Christian humility in a Christian. St. Thomas was willing to begin by recording the facts and sensations of the material world, just as he would have been willing to begin by washing up the plates and dishes in the monastery. The point of his Aristotelianism was that even if common sense about concrete things really was a sort of servile labour, he must not be ashamed to be *servus servorum Dei*. Among heathens the mere sceptic might become the mere cynic; Diogenes in his tub had always a touch of the tub-thumper; but even the dirt of the cynics was dignified into dust and ashes among the saints. If we miss that, we miss the whole meaning of the greatest revolution in history. There was a new *motive* for beginning with the most material, and even with the meanest things.

Third, in the theology of St. Thomas, it is proved by the tremendous truth that supports all that theology; or any other Christian theology. There really was a new reason for regarding the senses, and the sensations of the body, and the experiences of the common man, with a reverence at which great Aristotle would have stared, and no man in the ancient world could have begun to understand. The Body was no longer what it was when Plato and Porphyry and the old mystics had left it for dead. It had hung upon a gibbet. It had risen from a tomb. It was no longer possible for the soul to despise the senses, which had been the organs of something that was more than man. Plato might despise the flesh; but God had not despised it. The senses had truly become sanctified; as they are blessed one by one at a Catholic baptism. "Seeing is believing" was no longer the platitude of a mere idiot, or common individual, as in Plato's world; it was mixed up with real conditions of real belief. Those revolving mirrors that send messages to the brain of man, that light that breaks upon the brain, these had truly revealed to God himself the path to Bethany or the light on the high rock of Jerusalem. These ears that resound with common noises had reported also to the secret knowledge of God the noise of the crowd that strewed palms and the crowd that cried for Crucifixion. After the Incarnation had become the idea that is central in our civilisation, it was inevitable that there should be a return to materialism, in the sense of the serious value of matter and the making of the body. When once Christ had risen, it was inevitable that Aristotle should rise again.

Those are three real reasons, and very sufficient reasons, for the general support given by the saint to a solid and objective philosophy. And yet there was something else, very vast and vague, to which I have tried to give a faint expression by the interposition of this chapter. It is difficult to express it fully, without the awful peril of being popular, or what the Modernists quite wrongly imagine to be popular; in short, passing from religion to religiosity. But there is a general tone and temper of Aquinas, which it is as difficult to avoid as daylight in a great house of windows. It is that *positive* position of his mind, which is filled and soaked as with sunshine with the warmth of the wonder of created things. There is a certain private audacity, in his communion, by which men add to their private names the tremendous titles of the Trinity and the Redemption; so that some nun may be called "of the Holy Ghost"; or a man bear such a burden as the title of St. John of the Cross. In this sense, the man we study may specially be called St. Thomas of the Creator. The Arabs have a phrase about the hundred names of God; but they also inherit the tradition of a tremendous name unspeakable because it expresses Being itself, dumb and yet dreadful as an instant inaudible shout; the proclamation of the Absolute. And perhaps no other man ever came so near to calling the Creator by His own name, which can only be written I Am.

## V The real life of St. Thomas

At this point, even so crude and external a sketch of a great saint involves the necessity of writing something that cannot fit in with the rest; the one thing which it is important to write and impossible to write. A saint may be any kind of man, with an additional quality that is at once unique and universal. We might even say that the one thing which separates a saint from ordinary men is his readiness to be one with ordinary men. In this sense the word ordinary must be understood in its native and noble meaning; which is connected with the word order. A saint is long past any desire for distinction; he is the only sort of superior man who has never been a superior person. But all this arises from a great central fact, which he does not condescend to call a privilege, but which is in its very nature a sort of privacy; and in that sense almost a form of private propery. As with all sound private property, it is enough for him that he has it, he does not desire to limit the number of people who have it. He is always trying to hide it, out of a sort of celestial good manners; and Thomas Aquinas tried to hide it more than most. To reach it, in so far as we can reach it, it will be best to begin with the upper strata; and reach what was in the inside from what was most conspicuous on the outside.

The appearance or bodily presence of St. Thomas Aquinas is really easier to resurrect than that of many who lived before the age of portrait painting. It has been said that in his bodily being or bearing there was little of the Italian; but this is at the best, I fancy, an unconscious comparison between St. Thomas and St. Francis; and at worst, only a comparison between him and the hasty legend of vivacious organ-grinders and incendiary ice-cream men. Not all Italians are vivacious organ-grinders, and very few Italians are like St. Francis. A nation is never a type, but it is nearly always a tangle of two or three roughly recognizable types. St. Thomas was of a certain type, which is not so much common in Italy, as common to uncommon Italians. His bulk made it easy to regard him humorously as the sort of walking wine-barrel, common in the comedies of many nations; he joked about it himself. It may be that he, and not some irritated partisan of the Augustinian or Arabian parties, was responsible for the sublime exaggeration that a crescent was cut out of the dinner-table to allow him to sit down. It is quite certain that it was an exaggeration; and that his stature was more remarked than his stoutness; but, above all, that his head was quite powerful enough to dominate his body. And his head was of a very real and recognisable type, to judge by the traditional portraits and the personal descriptions. It was that sort of head with the heavy chin and jaws, the Roman nose and the big rather bald brow, which, in spite of its fullness, gives also a curious concave impression of hollows here and there, like caverns of thought. Napoleon carried that head upon a short body. Mussolini carries it today, upon a rather taller but equally active one. It can be seen in the busts of several Roman Emperors, and occasionally above the shabby shirt-front of an Italian waiter; but he is generally a head waiter. So unmistakable is the type, that I cannot but think that the most vivid villain of light fiction, in the Victorian shocker called *The Woman in White*, was really sketched by Wilkie Collins from an actual Italian Count; he is so complete a contrast to the conventional skinny, swarthy and gesticulating villain whom the Victorians commonly presented as an Italian Count. Count Fosco, it may be remembered (I hope) by some, was a calm, corpulent, colossal gentleman, whose head was exactly like a bust of Napoleon of heroic size. He may have been a melodramatic villain; but he was a tolerably convincing Italian—of that kind. If we recall his tranquil manner, and the excellent common sense of his everyday external words and actions, we shall probably have a merely material image of the type of Thomas Aquinas; given only the slight effort of faith required to imagine Count Fosco turned suddenly into a saint.

The pictures of St. Thomas, though many of them painted long after his death, are all obviously pictures of the same man. He rears himself defiantly, with the Napoleonic head and the dark bulk of body, in Raphael's 'Dispute About the Sacrament.' A portrait by Ghirlandajo emphasises a point which specially reveals what may be called the neglected Italian quality in the man. It also emphasises points that are very important in the mystic and the philosopher. It is universally attested that Aquinas was what is commonly called an absent-minded man. That type has often been rendered in painting, humorous or serious; but almost always in one of two or three conventional ways. Sometimes the expression of the eyes is merely vacant, as if absent-mindedness did really mean a permanent absence of mind. Sometimes it is rendered more respectfully as a wistful expression, as of one yearning for something afar off, that he cannot see and can only faintly desire. Look at the eyes in Ghirlandajo's portrait of St. Thomas; and you will see a sharp difference. While the eyes are indeed completely torn away from the immediate surroundings, so that the pot of flowers above the philosopher's head might fall on it without attracting his attention, they are not in the least wistful, let alone vacant. There is kindled in them a fire

of instant inner excitement; they are vivid and very Italian eyes. The man is thinking about something; and something that has reached a crisis; not about nothing or about anything; or, what is almost worse, about everything. There must have been that smouldering vigilance in his eyes, the moment before he smote the table and startled the banquet hall of the King.

Of the personal habits that go with the personal physique, we have also a few convincing and confirming impressions. When he was not sitting still, reading a book, he walked round and round the cloisters and walked fast and even furiously, a very characteristic action of men who fight their battles in the mind. Whenever he was interrupted, he was very polite and more apologetic than the apologizer. But there was that about him, which suggested that he was rather happier when he was not interrupted. He was ready to stop his truly Peripatetic tramp: but we feel that when he resumed it, he walked all the faster.

All this suggests that his superficial abstraction, that which the world saw, was of a certain kind. It will be well to understand the quality, for there are several kinds of absence of mind, including that of some pretentious poets and intellectuals, in whom the mind has never been noticeably present. There is the abstraction of the contemplative, whether he is the true sort of Christian contemplative, who is contemplating Something, or the wrong sort of Oriental contemplative, who is contemplating Nothing. Obviously St. Thomas was not a Buddhist mystic; but I do not think his fits of abstraction were even those of a Christian mystic. If he had trances of true Christian mysticism, he took jolly good care that *they* should not occur at other people's dinner-tables. I think he had the sort of bemused fit, which really belongs to the practical man rather than the entirely mystical man. He uses the recognised distinction between the active life and the contemplative life, but in the cases concerned here, I think even his contemplative life was an active life. It had nothing to do with his higher life, in the sense of ultimate sanctity. It rather reminds us that Napoleon would fall into a fit of apparent boredom at the Opera, and afterwards confess that he was thinking how he could get three army corps at Frankfurt to combine with two army corps at Cologne. So, in the case of Aquinas, if his daydreams were dreams, they were dreams of day; and dreams of the day of battle. If he talked to himself, it was because he was arguing with somebody else. We can put it another way, by saying that his daydreams, like the dreams of a dog, were dreams of hunting; of pursuing the error as well as pursuing the truth; of following all the twists and turns of evasive falsehood, and tracking it at last to its lair in hell. He would have been the first to admit that the erroneous thinker would probably be more surprised to learn where his thought came from, than anybody else to discover where it went to. But this notion of *pursuing* he certainly had, and it was the beginning of a thousand mistakes and misunderstandings that pursuing is called in Latin Persecution. Nobody had less than he had of what is commonly called the temper of a persecutor; but he had the quality which in desperate times is often driven to persecute; and that is simply the sense that everything lives somewhere, and nothing dies unless it dies in its own home. That he did sometimes, in this sense, "urge in dreams the shadowy chase" even in broad daylight, is quite true. But he was an active dreamer, if not what is commonly called a man of action; and in that chase he was truly to be counted among the *domini canes;* and surely the mightiest and most magnanimous of the Hounds of Heaven.

There may be many who do not understand the nature even of this sort of abstraction. But then, unfortunately, there are many who do not understand the nature of any sort of argument. Indeed, I think there are fewer people now alive who understand argument than there were twenty or thirty years ago; and St. Thomas might have preferred the society of the atheists of the early nineteenth century, to that of the blank sceptics of the early twentieth. Anyhow, one of the real disadvantages of the great and glorious sport, that is called argument, is its inordinate length. If you argue honestly, as St. Thomas always did, you will find that the subject sometimes seems as if it would never end. He was strongly conscious of this fact, as appears in many places; for instance his argument that most men must have a revealed religion, because they have not time to argue. No time, that is, to argue fairly. There is always time to argue unfairly; not least in a time like ours. Being himself resolved to argue, to argue honestly, to answer everybody, to deal with everything, he produced books enough to sink a ship or stock a library; though he died in comparatively early middle age. Probably he could not have done it at all, if he had not been thinking even when he was not writing; but above all thinking *combatively*. This, in his case, certainly did not mean bitterly or spitefully or uncharitably; but it did mean combatively. As a matter of fact, it is generally the man who is not ready to argue, who is ready to sneer. That is why, in recent literature, there has been so little argument and so much sneering.

We have noted that there are barely one or two occasions on which St. Thomas indulged in a denunciation. There is not a single occasion on which he indulged in a sneer. His curiously simple character, his lucid but laborious intellect, could not be better summed up than by saying that he did not know how to sneer. He was in a double sense an intellectual aristocrat: but he was never an intellectual snob. He never troubled at all whether those to whom he talked were more or less of the sort whom the world thinks worth talking to; and it was apparent by the impression of his contemporaries that those who received the ordinary scraps of his wit or wisdom were quite as likely to be nobodies as somebodies, or even quite as likely to be noodles as clever people. He was interested in the souls of all his fellow creatures, but not in classifying the minds of any of them; in a sense it was too personal and in another sense too arrogant for his particular mind and temper. He was very much interested in the subject he was talking about; and may sometimes have talked for a long time, though he was probably silent for a much longer time. But he had all the unconscious contempt which the really intelligent have for an intelligentsia.

Like most men concerned with the common problems of men, he seems to have had a considerable correspondence; considering that correspondence was so much more difficult in his time. We have records of a great many cases in which complete strangers wrote to ask him questions, and sometimes rather ridiculous questions. To all of these he replied with a characteristic mixture of patience and that sort of rationality, which in most rational people tends to be impatience. Somebody, for instance, asked him whether the names of all the blessed were written on a scroll exhibited in heaven. He wrote back, with untiring calm; "So far as I can see, this is not the case; but there is no harm in saying so."

I have remarked on the portrait of St. Thomas by an Italian painter, which shows him alert even in abstraction; and only silent as if about to speak. Pictures in that great tradition are generally full of small touches that show a very large imagination. I mean the sort of imagination on which Ruskin remarked, when he saw that in Tintoretto's sunlit scene of the Crucifixion the face of Christ is dark and undecipherable; but the halo round his head unexpectedly faint and grey like the colour of ashes. It would be hard to put more powerfully the idea of Divinity itself in eclipse. There is a touch, which it may be fanciful to find equally significant, in the portrait of Thomas Aquinas. The artist, having given so much vividness and vigilance to the eyes, may have felt that he stressed too much the merely combative concentration of the saint; but anyhow for some reason he has blazoned upon his breast a rather curious emblem, as if it were some third symbolic and cyclopean eye. At least it is no normal Christian sign; but something more like the disk of the sun such as held the face of a heathen god; but the face itself is dark and occult, and only the rays breaking from it are a ring of fire. I do not know whether any traditional meaning has been attached to this; but its imaginative meaning is strangely apt. That secret sun, dark with excess of light, or not showing its light save in the enlightenment of others, might well be the exact emblem of that inner and ideal life of the saint, which was not only hidden by his external words and actions, but even hidden by his merely outward and automatic silences and fits of reflection. In short, this spiritual detachment is not to be confused with his common habit of brooding or falling into a brown study. He was a man entirely careless of all casual criticism of his casual demeanour; as are many men built on a big masculine model and unconsciously inheriting a certain social splendour and largesse. But about his real life of sanctity he was intensely secretive. Such secrecy has indeed generally gone with sanctity; for the saint has an unfathomable horror of playing the Pharisee. But in Thomas Aquinas it was even more sensitive, and what many in the world would call morbid. He did not mind being caught woolgathering over the wine-cups of the King's banquet; for that was merely upon a point of controversy. But when there was some question of his having seen St. Paul in a vision, he was in an agony of alarm lest it should be discussed; and the story remains somewhat uncertain in consequence. Needless to say, his followers and admirers were as eager to collect these strictly miraculous stories as he was eager to conceal them; and one or two seem to be preserved with a fairly solid setting of evidence. But there are certainly fewer of them, known to the world, than in the case of many saints equally sincere and even equally modest, but more preoccupied with zeal and less sensitive about publicity.

The truth is that about all such things, in life and death, there is a sort of enormous quiet hanging about St. Thomas. He was one of those large things who take up little room. There was naturally a certain stir about his miracles after his death; and about his burial at the time when the University of Paris wished to bury him. I do not know in detail the long history of the other plans of sepulture, which have ultimately ended with his sacred bones lying in the church of St. Sernin in Toulouse; at the very base of the battlefields where his Dominicans had warred down the pestilence of pessimism from the East. But somehow, it is not easy to think of his shrine as the scene of the more jolly, rowdy and vulgar devotion either in its medieval or modern form. He was very far from being a Puritan, in the true sense; he made a provision for a holiday and banquet for his young friends, which has quite a convivial sound. The trend of his writing, especially for his time, is reasonable in its recognition of physical life; and he goes out of his way to say that men must vary their lives with jokes and even with pranks. But for all that, we cannot somehow see his personality as a sort of magnet for mobs; or the road to the tomb of St. Thomas at Toulouse having always been a long street of taverns, like that to the tomb of St. Thomas at Canterbury. I think he rather disliked noise; there is a legend that he disliked thunderstorms; but it is contradicted by the fact that in an actual shipwreck he was supremely calm. However that may be, and it probably concerned his health, in some ways sensitive, he certainly was very calm. We have a feeling that we should gradually grow conscious of his presence; as of an immense background.

Here, if this slight sketch could be worthy of its subject, there should stand forth something of that stupendous certitude, in the presence of which all his libraries of philosophy, and even theology, were but a litter of pamphlets. It is certain that this thing was in him from the first, in the form of conviction, long before it could possibly have even begun to take the form of controversy. It was very vivid in his childhood; and his were exactly the circumstances in which the anecdotes of the nursery and the playground are likely enough to have been really preserved. He had from the first that full and final test of truly orthodox Catholicity; the impetuous, impatient, intolerant passion for the poor; and even that readiness to be rather a nuisance to the rich, out of a hunger to feed the hungry. This can have had nothing to do with the intellectualism of which he was afterwards accused; still less with any habit of dialectic. It would seem unlikely that at the age of six he had any ambition to answer Averrhoes, or that he knew what Effective Causality is; or even that he had worked out, as he did in later life, the whole theory by which a man's love of himself is Sincere and Constant and Indulgent; and that this should be transferred intact (if possible) to his love of his neighbour. At this early age he did not understand all this. He only did it. But all the atmosphere of his actions carries a sort of conviction with it. It is beautifully typical, for instance, of that sort of aristocratic *ménage*, that his parents seem to have objected mildly, if at all, to his handing out things to beggars and tramps; but it was intensely disliked by the upper servants.

Still, if we take the thing as seriously as all childish things should be taken, we may learn something from that mysterious state of innocence, which is the first and best spring of all our later indignations. We may begin to understand why it was that there grew steadily with his growing mind, a great and very solitary mind, an ambition that was the inversion of all the things about him. We shall guess what had continuously swelled within him, whether in protest or prophecy or prayer for deliverance, before he startled his family by flinging away not only the trappings of nobility, but all forms of ambition, even ecclesiastical ambition. His childhood may contain the hint of that first stride of his manhood, from the house onto the highway; and his proclamation that he also would be a Beggar.

There is another case of a sort of second glimpse or sequel, in which an incident well known in the external sense gives us also a glimpse of the internal. After the affair of the firebrand, and the woman who tempted him in the tower, it is said that he had a dream; in which two angels girded him with a cord of fire, a thing of terrible pain and yet giving a terrible strength; and he awoke with a great cry in the darkness. This also has something very vivid about it, under the circumstances; and probably contains truths that will be some day better understood, when priests and doctors have learned to talk to each other without the stale etiquette of nineteenth-century negations. It would be easy to analyse the dream, as the very nineteenth-century doctor did in *Armadale*, resolving it into the details of the past days; the cord from his struggle against being stripped of his Friar's frock; the thread of fire running through the tapestries of the night, from the firebrand he had snatched from the fireside. But even in *Armadale* the dream was fulfilled mystically as well, and the dream of St. Thomas was fulfilled very mystically indeed. For he did in fact remain remarkably untroubled on that side of his human nature after the incident; though it is likely enough that the incident had caused an upheaval of his normal humanity, which produced a dream stronger than a nightmare. This is no place to analyse the psychological fact, which puzzles Non-Catholics so much: of the way in which priests do manage to be celibate without ceasing to be virile. Anyhow, it seems probable that in this matter he was less troubled than most. This has nothing to do with true virtue, which is of the will; saints as holy as he have rolled themselves in brambles to distract the pressure of passion; but he never needed much in the way of a counter-irritant; for the simple reason that in this way, as in most ways, he was not very often irritated. Much must remain unexplained, as part of the mysteries of grace; but there is probably some truth in the psychological idea of "sublimation"; that is the lifting of a lower energy to higher ends; so that appetite almost faded in the furnace of his intellectual energy. Between supernatural and natural causes, it is probable that he never knew or suffered

greatly on this side of his mind.

There are moments when the most orthodox reader is tempted to hate the hagiographer as much as he loves the holy man. The holy man always conceals his holiness; that is the one invariable rule. And the hagiographer sometimes seems like a persecutor trying to frustrate the holy man; a spy or eavesdropper hardly more respectful than an American interviewer. I admit that these sentiments are fastidious and one-sided, and I will now proceed to prove my penitence by mentioning one or two of the incidents that could only have come to common knowledge in this deplorable way.

It seems certain that he did live a sort of secondary and mysterious life; the divine double of what is called a double life. Somebody seems to have caught a glimpse of the sort of solitary miracle which modern psychic people call Levitation; and he must surely have either been a liar or a literal witness, for there could have been no doubts or degrees about such a prodigy happening to such a person; it must have been like seeing one of the huge pillars of the church suspended like a cloud. Nobody knows, I imagine, what spiritual storm of exaltation or agony produces this convulsion in matter or space; but the thing does almost certainly occur. Even in the case of ordinary Spiritualist mediums, for whatever reason, the evidence is very difficult to refute. But probably the most representative revelation of this side of his life may be found in the celebrated story of the miracle of the crucifix; when in the stillness of the church of St. Dominic in Naples, a voice spoke from the carven Christ, and told the kneeling Friar that he had written rightly, and offered him the choice of a reward among all the things of the world.

Not all, I think, have appreciated the point of this particular story as applied to this particular saint. It is an old story, in so far as it is simply the offer made to a devotee of solitude or simplicity, of the pick of all the prizes of life. The hermit, true or false, the fakir, the fanatic or the cynic, Stylites on his column or Diogenes in his tub, can all be pictured as tempted by the powers of the earth, of the air or of the heavens, with the offer of the best of everything; and replying that they want nothing. In the Greek cynic or stoic it really meant the mere negative; that he wanted nothing. In the Oriental mystic or fanatic, it sometimes meant a sort of positive negative; that he wanted Nothing; that Nothing was really what he wanted. Sometimes it expressed a noble independence, and the twin virtues of antiquity, the love of liberty and the hatred of luxury. Sometimes it only expressed a self-sufficiency that is the very opposite of sanctity. But even the stories of real saints, of this sort, do not quite cover the case of St. Thomas. He was not a person who wanted nothing; and he was a person who was enormously interested in everything. His answer is not so inevitable or simple as some may suppose. As compared with many other saints, and many other philosophers, he was avid in his acceptance of Things; in his hunger and thirst for Things. It was his special spiritual thesis that there really are things; and not only the Thing; that the Many existed as well as the One. I do not mean things to eat or drink or wear, though he never denied to these their place in the noble hierarchy of Being; but rather things to think about, and especially things to prove, to experience and to know. Nobody supposes that Thomas Aquinas, when offered by God his choice among all the gifts of God, would ask for a thousand pounds, or the Crown of Sicily, or a present of rare Greek wine. But he might have asked for things that he really wanted; and he was a man who could want things; as he wanted the lost manuscript of St. Chrysostom. He might have asked for the solution of an old difficulty; or the secret of a new science; or a flash of the inconceivable intuitive mind of the angels; or any one of a thousand things that would really have satisfied his broad and virile appetite for the very vastness and variety of the universe. The point is that for him, when the voice spoke from between

the outstretched arms of the Crucified, those arms were truly opened wide, and opening most gloriously the gates of all the worlds; they were arms pointing to the east and to the west, to the ends of the earth and the very extremes of existence. They were truly spread out with a gesture of omnipotent generosity; the Creator himself offering Creation itself; with all its millionfold mystery of separate beings, and the triumphal chorus of the creatures. That is the blazing background of multitudinous Being that gives the particular strength, and even a sort of surprise, to the answer of St. Thomas, when he lifted at last his head and spoke with, and for, that almost blasphemous audacity which is one with the humility of his religion; "I will have Thyself."

Or, to add the crowning and crushing irony to this story, so uniquely Christian for those who can really understand it, there are some who feel that the audacity is softened by insisting that he said, "*Only* Thyself."

Of these miracles, in the strictly miraculous sense, there are not so many as in the lives of less immediately influential saints; but they are probably pretty well authenticated; for he was a well-known public man in a prominent position, and, what is even more convenient for him, he had any number of highly incensed enemies, who could be trusted to sift his claims. There is at least one miracle of healing; that of a woman who touched his gown; and several incidents that may be variants of the story of the crucifix at Naples. One of these stories, however, has a further importance as bringing us to another section of his more private, personal or even emotional religious life; the section that expressed itself in poetry. When he was stationed at Paris, the other Doctors of the Sorbonne put before him a problem about the nature of the mystical change in the elements of the Blessed Sacrament, and he proceeded to write, in his customary manner, a very careful and elaborately lucid statement of his own solution. Needless to say, he felt with hearty simplicity the heavy responsibility and gravity of such a judicial decision; and not unnaturally seems to have worried about it more than he commonly did over his work. He sought for guidance in more than usually prolonged prayer and intercession; and finally, with one of those few but striking bodily gestures that mark the turning points of his life, he threw down his thesis at the foot of the crucifix on the altar, and left it lying there; as if awaiting judgment. Then he turned and came down the altar steps and buried himself once more in prayer; but the other Friars, it is said, were watching; and well they might be. For they declared afterwards that the figure of Christ had come down from the cross before their mortal eyes; and stood upon the scroll, saying "Thomas, thou hast written well concerning the Sacrament of My Body." It was after this vision that the incident is said to have happened, of his being borne up miraculously in mid-air.

An acute observer said of Thomas Aquinas in his own time, "He could alone restore all philosophy, if it had been burnt by fire." That is what is meant by saying that he was an original man, a creative mind; that he could have made his own cosmos out of stones and straws, even without the manuscripts of Aristotle or Augustine. But there is here a not uncommon confusion, between the thing in which a man is most original and that in which he is most interested; or between the thing that he does best and the thing that he loves most. Because St. Thomas was a unique and striking philosopher, it is almost unavoidable that this book should be merely, or mainly, a sketch of his philosophy. It cannot be, and does not pretend to be, a sketch of his theology. But this is because the theology of a saint is simply the theism of a saint; or rather the theism of all saints. It is less individual, but it is much more intense. It is concerned with the common origin; but it is hardly an occasion for originality. Thus we are forced to think first of Thomas as the maker of the Thomist philosophy; as we think first of Christopher Columbus as the discoverer of America,

though he may have been quite sincere in his pious hope to convert the Khan of Tartary; or of James Watt as the discoverer of the steam-engine, though he may have been a devout fire-worshipper, or a sincere Scottish Calvinist, or all kinds of curious things. Anyhow, it is but natural that Augustine and Aquinas, Bonaventure and Duns Scotus, all the doctors and the saints, should draw nearer to each other as they approach the divine unity in things; and that there should in that sense be less difference between them in theology than in philosophy. It is true that, in some matters, the critics of Aquinas thought his philosophy had unduly affected his theology. This is especially so, touching the charge that he made the state of Beatitude too intellectual, conceiving it as the satisfaction of the love of truth; rather than specially as the truth of love. It is true that the mystics and the men of the Franciscan school, dwelt more lovingly on the admitted supremacy of love. But it was mostly a matter of emphasis; perhaps tinged faintly by temperament; possibly (to suggest something which is easier to feel than to explain), in the case of St. Thomas, a shadowy influence of a sort of shyness. Whether the supreme ecstasy is more affectional than intellectual is no very deadly matter of quarrel among men who believe it is both, but do not profess even to imagine the actual experience of either. But I have a sort of feeling that, even if St. Thomas had thought it was as emotional as St. Bonaventure did, he would never have been so emotional about it. It would always have embarrassed him to write about love at such length.

The one exception permitted to him was the rare but remarkable output of his poetry. All sanctity is secrecy; and his sacred poetry was really a secretion; like the pearl in a very tightly closed oyster. He may have written more of it than we know; but part of it came into public use through the particular circumstance of his being asked to compose the office for the Feast of Corpus Christi: a festival first established after the controversy to which he had contributed, in the scroll that he laid on the altar. It does certainly reveal an entirely different side of his genius; and it certainly was genius. As a rule, he was an eminently practical prose writer; some would say a very prosaic prose writer. He maintained controversy with an eye on only two qualities; clarity and courtesy. And he maintained these because they were entirely practical qualities; affecting the probabilities of conversion. But the composer of the Corpus Christi service was not merely what even the wild and woolly would call a poet; he was what the most fastidious would call an artist. His double function rather recalls the double activity of some great Renaissance craftsman, like Michelangelo or Leonardo da Vinci, who would work on the outer wall, planning and building the fortifications of the city; and then retire into the inner chamber to carve or model some cup or casket for a reliquary. The Corpus Christi Office is like some old musical instrument, quaintly and carefully inlaid with many coloured stones and metals; the author has gathered remote texts about pasture and fruition like rare herbs; there is a notable lack of the loud and obvious in the harmony; and the whole is strung with two strong Latin lyrics. Father John O'-Connor has translated them with an almost miraculous aptitude; but a good translator will be the first to agree that no translation is good; or, at any rate, good enough. How are we to find eight short English words which actually stand for "*Sumit unus, sumunt mille; quantum isti, tantum ille*"? How is anybody really to render the sound of the "*Pange Lingua*", when the very first syllable has a clang like the clash of cymbals?

There was one other channel, besides that of poetry, and it was that of private affections, by which this large and shy man could show that he had really as much *Caritas* as St. Francis; and certainly as much as any Franciscan theologian. Bonaventure was not likely to think that Thomas was lacking in the love of God, and certainly he was never lacking in the love of Bonaventure. He felt for his whole family a steady, we might say a

stubborn tenderness; and, considering how his family had treated him, this would seem to call not only for charity, but for his characteristic virtue of patience. Towards the end of his life, he seems to have leaned especially on his love of one of the brethren, a Friar named Reginald, who received from him some strange and rather startling confidences, of the kind that he very seldom gave even to his friends. It was to Reginald that he gave that last and rather extraordinary hint, which was the end of his controversial career, and practically of his earthly life; a hint that history has never been able to explain.

He had returned victorious from his last combat with Siger of Brabant; returned and retired. This particular quarrel was the one point, as we may say, in which his outer and his inner life had crossed and coincided; he realised how he had longed from childhood to call up all allies in the battle for Christ; how he had only long afterwards called up Aristotle as an ally; and now in that last nightmare of sophistry, he had for the first time truly realised that some might really wish Christ to go down before Aristotle. He never recovered from the shock. He won his battle, because he was the best brain of his time, but he could not forget such an inversion of the whole idea and purpose of his life. He was the sort of man who hates hating people. He had not been used to hating even their hateful ideas, beyond a certain point. But in the abyss of anarchy opened by Siger's sophistry of the Double Mind of Man, he had seen the possibility of the perishing of all idea of religion, and even of all idea of truth. Brief and fragmentary as are the phrases that record it, we can gather that he came back with a sort of horror of that outer world, in which there blew such wild winds of doctrine, and a longing for the inner world which any Catholic can share, and in which the saint is not cut off from simple men. He resumed the strict routine of religion, and for some time said nothing to anybody. And then something happened (it is said while he was celebrating Mass) the nature of which will never be known among mortal men.

His friend Reginald asked him to return also to his equally regular habits of reading and writing, and following the controversies of the hour. He said with a singular emphasis, "I can write no more." There seems to have been a silence; after which Reginald again ventured to approach the subject; and Thomas answered him with even greater vigour, "I can write no more. I have seen things which make all my writings like straw."

In 1274, when Aquinas was nearly fifty, the Pope, rejoicing in the recent victory over the Arabian sophists, sent word to him, asking him to come to a Council on these controversial matters, to be held at Lyons. He rose in automatic obedience, as a soldier rises; but we may fancy that there was something in his eyes that told those around him that obedience to the outer command would not in fact frustrate obedience to some more mysterious inner command; a signal that only he had seen. He set out with his friend on the journey, proposing to rest for the night with his sister, to whom he was deeply devoted; and when he came into her house he was stricken down with some unnamed malady. We need not discuss the doubtful medical problems. It is true that he had always been one of those men, healthy in the main, who are overthrown by small illnesses; it is equally true that there is no very clear account of this particular illness. He was eventually taken to a monastery at Fossanuova; and his strange end came upon him with great strides. It may be worth remarking, for those who think that he thought too little of the emotional or romantic side of religious truth, that he asked to have The Song of Solomon read through to him from beginning to end. The feelings of the men about him must have been mingled and rather indescribable; and certainly quite different from his own. He confessed his sins and he received his God; and we may be sure that the great philosopher had entirely forgotten philosophy. But it was not

entirely so with those who had loved him, or even those who merely lived in his time. The elements of the narrative are so few, yet so essential, that we have a strong sense in reading the story of the two emotional sides of the event. Those men must have known that a great mind was still labouring like a great mill in the midst of them. They must have felt that, for that moment, the inside of the monastery was larger than the outside. It must have resembled the case of some mighty modern engine, shaking the ramshackle building in which it is for the moment enclosed. For truly that machine was made of the wheels of all the worlds; and revolved like that cosmos of concentric spheres which, whatever its fate in the face of changing science, must always be something of a symbol for philosophy; the depth of double and triple transparencies more mysterious than darkness; the sevenfold, the terrible crystal. In the world of that mind there was a wheel of angels, and a wheel of planets, and a wheel of plants or of animals; but there was also a just and intelligible order of all earthly things, a sane authority and a self-respecting liberty, and a hundred answers to a hundred questions in the complexity of ethics or economics. But there must have been a moment, when men knew that the thunderous mill of thought had stopped suddenly; and that after the shock of stillness that wheel would shake the world no more; that there was nothing now within that hollow house but a great hill of clay; and the confessor, who had been with him in the inner chamber, ran forth as if in fear, and whispered that his confession had been that of a child of five.

## VI  The approach to Thomism

The fact that Thomism is the philosophy of common sense is itself a matter of common sense. Yet it wants a word of explanation, because we have so long taken such matters in a very uncommon sense. For good or evil, Europe since the Reformation, and most especially England since the Reformation, has been in a peculiar sense the home of paradox. I mean in the very peculiar sense that paradox was at home, and that men were at home with it. The most familiar example is the English boasting that they are practical *because* they are not logical. To an ancient Greek or a Chinaman this would seem exactly like saying that London clerks excel in adding up their ledgers, because they are not accurate in their arithmetic. But the point is not that it is a paradox; it is that paradoxy has become orthodoxy; that men repose in a paradox as placidly as in a platitude. It is not that the practical man stands on his head, which may sometimes be a stimulating if startling gymnastic; it is that he *rests* on his head; and even sleeps on his head. This is an important point, because the use of paradox is to awaken the mind. Take a good paradox, like that of Oliver Wendell Holmes: "Give us the luxuries of life and we will dispense with the necessities." It is amusing and therefore arresting; it has a fine air of defiance; it contains a real if romantic truth. It is all part of the fun that it is stated almost in the form of a contradiction in terms. But most people would agree that there would be considerable danger in basing the whole social system on the notion that necessaries are not necessary; as some have based the whole British Constitution on the notion that nonsense will always work out as common sense. Yet even here, it might be said that the invidious example has spread, and that the modern industrial system does really say, "Give us luxuries like coal-tar soap, and we will dispense with necessities like corn."

So much is familiar; but what is not even now realised is that not only the practical politics, but the abstract philosophies of the modern world have had this queer twist. Since the modern world began in the sixteenth century, nobody's system of philosophy has really corresponded to everybody's sense of reality; to what, if left to themselves, common men would call common sense. Each started with a paradox; a peculiar point of view demanding the sacrifice of what they would call a sane point of view. That is the one thing common to Hobbes and Hegel, to Kant and Bergson, to Berkeley and William James. A man had to believe something that no normal man would believe, if it were suddenly propounded to his simplicity; as that law is above right, or right is outside reason, or things are only as we think them, or everything is relative to a reality that is not there. The modern philosopher claims, like a sort of confidence man, that if once we will grant him this, the rest will be easy; he will straighten out the world, if once he is allowed to give this one twist to the mind.

It will be understood that in these matters I speak as a fool; or, as our democratic cousins would say, a moron; anyhow as a man in the street; and the only object of this chapter is to show that the Thomist philosophy is nearer than most philosophies to the mind of the man in the street. I am not, like Father D'Arcy, whose admirable book on St. Thomas has illuminated many problems for me, a trained philosopher, acquainted with the technique of the trade. But I hope Father D'Arcy will forgive me if I take one example from his book, which exactly illustrates what I mean. He, being a trained philosopher, is naturally trained to put up with philosophers. Also, being a trained priest, he is naturally accustomed, not only to suffer fools gladly, but (what is sometimes even harder) to suffer clever people gladly. Above all, his wide reading in metaphysics has made him patient with clever people when they indulge in folly. The consequence is that he can write calmly and even blandly sentences like these. "A certain likeness can be detected between the aim and method of St. Thomas and those of Hegel. There are, however, also remarkable differences. For St. Thomas it is impossible that contradictories should exist together, and again reality and intelligibility correspond, but a thing must first be, to be intelligible."

Let the man in the street be forgiven, if he adds that the "remarkable difference" seems to him to be that St. Thomas was sane and Hegel was mad. The moron refuses to admit that Hegel can both exist and not exist; or that it can be possible to understand Hegel, if there is no Hegel to understand. Yet Father D'Arcy mentions this Hegelian paradox as if it were all in the day's work; and of course it is, if the work is reading all the modern philosophers as searchingly and sympathetically as he has done. And this is what I mean by saying that a modern philosophy starts with a stumbling-block. It is surely not too much to say that there *seems* to be a twist, in saying that contraries are not incompatible; or that a thing can "be" intelligible and not as yet "be" at all.

Against all this the philosophy of St. Thomas stands founded on the universal common conviction that eggs are eggs. The Hegelian may say that an egg is really a hen, because it is a part of an endless process of Becoming; the Berkeleian may hold that poached eggs only exist as a dream exists; since it is quite as easy to call the dream the cause of the eggs as the eggs the cause of the dream; the Pragmatist may believe that we get the best out of scrambled eggs by forgetting that they ever were eggs, and only remembering the scramble. But no pupil of St. Thomas needs to addle his brains in order adequately to addle his eggs; to put his head at any peculiar angle in looking at eggs, or squinting at eggs, or winking the other eye in order to see a new simplification of eggs. The Thomist stands in the broad daylight of the brotherhood of men, in their common consciousness that eggs are not hens or dreams or mere practical assumptions; but things attested by the Authority of the Senses, which is from God.

Thus, even those who appreciate the metaphysical depth of Thomism in other matters have expressed surprise that he does not deal at all with what many now think the main metaphysical question; whether we can prove that the primary act of recognition of any reality is real. The answer is that St. Thomas recognised instantly, what so many modern sceptics have begun to suspect rather laboriously; that a man must either answer that question in the affirmative, or else never answer any question, never ask any question, never even exist intellectually, to answer or to ask. I suppose it is true in a sense that a man can be a fundamental sceptic, but he cannot be anything else; certainly not even a defender of fundamental scepticism. If a man feels that all the movements of his own mind are meaningless, then his mind is meaningless, and he is meaningless; and it does not mean anything to attempt to discover his meaning. Most fundamental sceptics appear to survive, because they are not consistently sceptical and not at all fundamental. They will first deny everything and then admit something, if for the sake of argument—or often rather of attack without argument. I saw an almost startling example of this essential frivolity in the professor of final scepticism, in a paper the other day. A man wrote to say that he accepted nothing but Solipsism, and added that he had often wondered it was not a more common philosophy. Now Solipsism simply means that a man believes in his own existence, but not in anybody or anything else. And it never struck this simple sophist, that if his philosophy was true, there obviously were no other philosophers to profess it.

To this question "Is there anything?" St. Thomas begins by answering "Yes"; if he began by answering "No", it would not be the beginning, but the end. That is what some of us call common sense. Either there is no philosophy, no philosophers, no thinkers, no thought, no anything; or else there is a real bridge between the mind and reality. But he is actually less exacting than many thinkers, much less so than most rationalist and materialist thinkers, as to what that first step involves; he is content, as we shall see, to say that it involves the recognition of Ens or Being as something definitely beyond ourselves. Ens is Ens: Eggs are eggs, and it is not tenable that all eggs were found in a mare's nest.

Needless to say, I am not so silly as to suggest that all the writings of St. Thomas are simple and straightforward; in the sense of being easy to understand. There are passages I do not in the least understand myself; there are passages that puzzle much more learned and logical philosophers than I am; there are passages about which the greatest Thomists still differ and dispute. But that is a question of a thing being hard to read or understand: not hard to accept when understood. That is a mere matter of "The Cat sat on the Mat" being written in Chinese characters; or "Mary had a Little Lamb" in Egyptian hieroglyphics. The only point I am stressing here is that Aquinas is almost always on the side of simplicity, and supports the ordinary man's acceptance of ordinary truisms. For instance, one of the most obscure passages, in my very inadequate judgment, is that in which he explains how the mind is certain of an external object and not merely of an impression of that object; and yet apparently reaches it through a concept, though not merely through an impression. But the only point here is that he does explain that the mind is certain of an external object. It is enough for this purpose that his conclusion is what is called the conclusion of common sense; that it is his purpose to justify common sense; even though he justifies it in a passage which happens to be one of rather uncommon subtlety. The problem of later philosophers is that their conclusion is as dark as their demonstration; or that they bring out a result of which the result is chaos.

Unfortunately, between the man in the street and the Angel of the Schools, there stands at this moment a very high brick wall, with spikes on the top, separating two men who in many ways stand for the same thing. The wall is almost a historical accident; at least it was built a very long time ago, for reasons that need not affect the needs of normal men today; least of all the greatest need of normal men; which is for a normal philosophy. The first difficulty is merely a difference of form; not in the medieval but in the modern sense. There is first a simple obstacle of language; there is then a rather more subtle obstacle of logical method. But the language itself counts for a great deal; even when it is translated, it is still a foreign language; and it is, like other foreign languages, very often translated wrong. As with every other literature from another age or country, it carried with it an atmosphere which is beyond the mere translation of words, as they are translated in a traveller's phrase-book. For instance, the whole system of St. Thomas hangs on one huge and yet simple idea; which does actually cover everything there is, and even everything that could possibly be. He represented this cosmic conception by the word *Ens*; and anybody who can read any Latin at all, however rudely, feels it to be the apt and fitting word; exactly as he feels it in a French word in a piece of good French prose. It ought only to be a matter of logic; but it is also a matter of language.

Unfortunately there is no satisfying translation of the word *Ens*. The difficulty is rather verbal than logical, but it is practical. I mean that when the translator says in English 'being', we are aware of a rather different atmosphere. Atmosphere ought not to affect these absolutes of the intellect; but it does. The new psychologists, who are almost eagerly at war with reason, never tire of telling us that the very terms we use are coloured by our subconsciousness, with something we meant to exclude from our consciousness. And one need not be so idealistically irrational as a modern psychologist, in order to admit that the very shape and sound of words do make a difference, even in the baldest prose, as they do in the most beautiful poetry. We can not quite prevent the imagination from remembering irrelevant associations even in the abstract sciences like mathematics. Jones Minimus, hustled from history to geometry, may for an instant connect the Angles of the isosceles triangle with the Angles of the Anglo-Saxon Chronicle; and even the mature mathematician, if he is as mad as the psychoanalyst hopes, may have in the roots of his subconscious mind something material in his idea of a root. Now it unfortunately happens that the word 'being', as it comes to a modern Englishman, through modern associations, has a sort of hazy atmosphere that is not in the short and sharp Latin word. Perhaps it reminds him of fantastic professors in fiction, who wave their hands and say, "Thus do we mount to the ineffable heights of pure and radiant Being:" or, worse still, of actual professors in real life, who say, "All Being is Becoming; and is but the evolution of Not-Being by the law of its Being." Perhaps it only reminds him of romantic rhapsodies in old love stories; "Beautiful and adorable being, light and breath of my very being". Anyhow it has a wild and woolly sort of sound; as if only very vague people used it; or as if it might mean all sorts of different things.

Now the Latin word *Ens* has a sound like the English word *End*. It is final and even abrupt; it is nothing except itself. There was once a silly gibe against Scholastics like Aquinas, that they discussed whether angels could stand on the point of a needle. It is at least certain that this first word of Aquinas is as sharp as the point of a pin. For that also is, in an almost ideal sense, an End. But when we say that St. Thomas Aquinas is concerned fundamentally with the idea of Being, we must not admit any of the cloudier generalisations that we may have grown used to, or even grown tired of, in the sort of idealistic writing that is rather rhetoric than philosophy. Rhetoric is a very fine thing in its place, as a medieval scholar would have willingly agreed, as he taught it along with logic in the schools; but St. Thomas Aquinas himself is not at all rhetorical. Perhaps he is hardly even sufficiently rhetorical. There are any number of purple patches in Augustine; but there are no purple patches in Aquinas. He did on certain definite occasions drop into poetry; but he very seldom dropped into oratory. And so little was he in touch with some modern tendencies, that whenever he did write poetry, he actually put it into poems. There is

another side to this, to be noted later. He very specially possessed the philosophy that inspires poetry; as he did so largely inspire Dante's poetry. And poetry without philosophy has only inspiration, or, in vulgar language, only wind. He had, so to speak, the imagination without the imagery. And even this is perhaps too sweeping. There is an image of his, that is true poetry as well as true philosophy; about the tree of life bowing down with a huge humility, because of the very load of its living fruitfulness; a thing Dante might have described so as to overwhelm us with the tremendous twilight and almost drug us with the divine fruit. But normally, we may say that his words are brief even when his books are long. I have taken the example of the word *Ens*, precisely because it is one of the cases in which Latin is plainer than plain English. And his style, unlike that of St. Augustine and many Catholic Doctors, is always a penny plain rather than twopence coloured. It is often difficult to understand, simply because the subjects are so difficult that hardly any mind, except one like his own, can fully understand them. But he never darkens it by using words without knowledge, or even more legitimately, by using words belonging only to imagination or intuition. So far as his method is concerned, he is perhaps the one real Rationalist among all the children of men.

This brings us to the other difficulty; that of logical method. I have never understood why there is supposed to be something crabbed or antique about a syllogism; still less can I understand what anybody means by talking as if induction had somehow taken the place of deduction. The whole point of deduction is that true premises produce a true conclusion. What is called induction seems simply to mean collecting a larger number of true premises, or perhaps, in some physical matters, taking rather more trouble to see that they are true. It may be a fact that a modern man can get more out of a great many premises, concerning microbes or asteroids than a medieval man could get out of a very few premises about salamanders and unicorns. But the process of deduction from the data is the same for the modern mind as for the medieval mind; and what is pompously called induction is simply collecting more of the data. And Aristotle or Aquinas, or anybody in his five wits, would of course agree that the conclusion could only be true if the premises were true; and that the more true premises there were the better. It was the misfortune of medieval culture that there were not enough true premises, owing to the rather ruder conditions of travel or experiment. But however perfect were the conditions of travel or experiment, they could only produce premises; it would still be necessary to deduce conclusions. But many modern people talk as if what they call induction were some magic way of reaching a conclusion, without using any of those horrid old syllogisms. But induction does not lead us to a conclusion. Induction only leads us to a deduction. Unless the last three syllogistic steps are all right, the conclusion is all wrong. Thus, the great nineteenth century men of science, whom I was brought up to revere ("accepting the conclusions of science", it was always called), went out and closely inspected the air and the earth, the chemicals and the gases, doubtless more closely than Aristotle or Aquinas, and then came back and embodied their final conclusion in a syllogism. "All matter is made of microscopic little knobs which are indivisible. My body is made of matter. Therefore my body is made of microscopic little knobs which are indivisible." They were not wrong in the form of their reasoning; because it is the only way to reason. In this world there is nothing except a syllogism—and a fallacy. But of course these modern men knew, as the medieval men knew, that their conclusions would not be true unless their premises were true. And that is where the trouble began. For the men of science, or their sons and nephews, went out and took another look at the knobby nature of matter; and were surprised to find that it was not knobby at all. So they came back and completed the process with their syllogism; "All matter is made of whirling protons and electrons. My body is made of matter. Therefore my body is made of whirling protons and electrons." And that again is a good syllogism; though they may have to look at matter once or twice more, before we know whether it is a true premise and a true conclusion. But in the final process of truth there is nothing else except a good syllogism. The only other thing is a bad syllogism; as in the familiar fashionable shape; "All matter is made of protons and electrons. I should very much like to think that mind is much the same as matter. So I will announce, through the microphone or the megaphone, that my mind is made of protons and electrons." But that is not induction; it is only a very bad blunder in deduction. That is not another or new way of thinking; it is only ceasing to think.

What is really meant, and what is much more reasonable, is that the old syllogists sometimes set out the syllogism at length; and certainly that is not always necessary. A man can run down the three steps much more quickly than that; but a man cannot run down the three steps if they are not there. If he does, he will break his neck, as if he walked out of a fourth-story window. The truth about this false antithesis of induction and deduction is simply this; that as premises or data accumulated, the emphasis and detail was shifted to them, from the final deduction to which they lead. But they did lead to a final deduction; or else they led to nothing. The logician had so much to say about electrons or microbes that he dwelt most on these data and shortened or assumed his ultimate syllogism. But if he reasoned rightly, however rapidly, he reasoned syllogistically.

As a matter of fact, Aquinas does not usually argue in syllogisms; though he always argues syllogistically. I mean he does not set out all the steps of the logic in each case; the legend that he does so is part of that loose and largely unverified legend of the Renaissance; that the Schoolmen were all crabbed and mechanical medieval bores. But he does argue with a certain austerity, and disdain of ornament, which may make him seem monotonous to anyone specially seeking the modern forms of wit or fancy. But all this has nothing to do with the question asked at the beginning of this chapter and needing to be answered at the end of it; the question of what he is arguing for. In that respect it can be repeated, most emphatically, that he is arguing for common sense. He is arguing for a common sense which would even now commend itself to most of the common people. He is arguing for the popular proverbs that seeing is believing; that the proof of the pudding is in the eating; that a man cannot jump down his own throat or deny the fact of his own existence. He often maintains the view by the use of abstractions; but the abstractions are no more abstract than Energy or Evolution or Space-Time; and they do not land us, as the others often do, in hopeless contradictions about common life. The Pragmatist sets out to be practical, but his practicality turns out to be entirely theoretical. The Thomist begins by being theoretical, but his theory turns out to be entirely practical. That is why a great part of the world is returning to it today.

Finally, there is some real difficulty in the fact of a foreign language; apart from the ordinary fact of the Latin language. Modern philosophical terminology is not always exactly identical with plain English; and medieval philosophical terminology is not at all identical even with modern philosophical terminology. It is not really very difficult to learn the meaning of the main terms; but their medieval meaning is sometimes the exact opposite of their modern meaning. The obvious example is in the pivotal word "form". We say nowadays, "I wrote a formal apology to the Dean", or "The proceedings when we wound up the Tip-Cat Club were purely formal." But we mean that they were purely fictitious; and St. Thomas, had he been a member of the Tip-Cat Club, would have meant just the opposite. He would have meant that the proceedings dealt with the very heart and soul and secret of the whole being of the Tip-Cat Club; and that

the apology to the Dean was so essentially apologetic that it tore the very heart out in tears of true contrition. For "formal" in Thomist language means actual, or possessing the real decisive quality that makes a thing itself. Roughly when he describes a thing as made out of Form and Matter, he very rightly recognises that Matter is the more mysterious and indefinite and featureless element; and that what stamps anything with its own identity is its Form. Matter, so to speak, is not so much the solid as the liquid or gaseous thing in the cosmos; and in this most modern scientists are beginning to agree with him. But the form is the fact; it is that which makes a brick a brick, and a bust a bust, and not the shapeless and trampled clay of which either may be made. The stone that broke a statuette, in some Gothic niche, might have been itself a statuette; and under chemical analysis, the statuette is only a stone. But such a chemical analysis is entirely false as a philosophical analysis. The reality, the thing that makes the two things real, is in the idea of the image and in the idea of the image-breaker. This is only a passing example of the mere idiom of the Thomist terminology; but it is not a bad prefatory specimen of the truth of Thomist thought. Every artist knows that the form is not superficial but fundamental; that the form is the foundation. Every sculptor knows that the form of the statue is not the outside of the statue, but rather the inside of the statue; even in the sense of the inside of the sculptor. Every poet knows that the sonnet-form is not only the form of the poem; but the poem. No modern critic who does not understand what the medieval Schoolman meant by form can meet the Schoolman as an intellectual equal.

## VII  The permanent philosophy

It is a pity that the word Anthropology has been degraded to the study of Anthropoids. It is now incurably associated with squabbles between prehistoric professors (in more senses than one) about whether a chip of stone is the tooth of a man or an ape; sometimes settled as in that famous case, when it was found to be the tooth of a pig. It is very right that there should be a purely physical science of such things; but the name commonly used might well, by analogy, have been dedicated to things not only wider and deeper, but rather more relevant. Just as, in America, the new Humanists have pointed out to the old Humanitarians that their humanitarianism has been largely concentrated on things that are *not* specially human, such as physical conditions, appetites, economic needs, environment and so on— so in practice those who are called Anthropologists have to narrow their minds to the materialistic things that are *not* notably anthropic. They have to hunt through history and pre-history something which emphatically is not *Homo Sapiens,* but is always in fact regarded as *Simius Insipiens. Homo Sapiens* can only be considered in relation to *Sapientia;* and only a book like that of St. Thomas is really devoted to the intrinsic idea of *Sapientia.* In short, there ought to be a real study called Anthropology corresponding to Theology. In this sense St. Thomas Aquinas, perhaps more than he is anything else, is a great anthropologist.

I apologise for the opening words of this chapter to all those excellent and eminent men of science, who are engaged in the real study of humanity in its relation to biology. But I rather fancy that they will be the last to deny that there has been a somewhat disproportionate disposition, in popular science, to turn the study of human beings into the study of savages. And savagery is not history: it is either the beginning of history or the end of it. I suspect that the greatest scientists would agree that only too many professors have thus been lost in the bush or the jungle; professors who wanted to study anthropology and never got any further than anthropophagy. But I have a particular reason for prefacing this suggestion of a higher anthropology by an apology to any genuine biologists who might seem to be included, but are certainly not included, in a protest against cheap popular science. For the first thing to be said about St. Thomas as an anthropologist, is that he is really remarkably like the best sort of modern biological anthropologist; of the sort who would call themselves Agnostics. This fact is so sharp and decisive a turning point in history, that the history really needs to be recalled and recorded.

St. Thomas Aquinas closely resembles the great Professor Huxley, the Agnostic who invented the word Agnosticism. He is like him in his way of starting the argument, and he is unlike everybody else, before and after, until the Huxleyan age. He adopts almost literally the Huxleyan definition of the Agnostic method; "To follow reason as far as it will go"; the only question is—where does it go? He lays down the almost startlingly modern or materialist statement; "Everything that is in the intellect has been in the senses". This is where he began, as much as any modern man of science, nay, as much as any modern materialist who can now hardly be called a man of science; at the very opposite end of enquiry from that of the mere mystic. The Platonists, or at least the Neo-Platonists, all tended to the view that the mind was lit entirely from within; St. Thomas insisted that it was lit by five windows, that we call the windows of the senses. But he wanted the light from without to shine on what was within. He wanted to study the nature of Man, and not merely of such moss and mushrooms as he might see through the window, and which he valued as the first enlightening experience of man. And starting from this point, he proceeds to climb the House of Man, step by step and story by story, until he has come out on the highest tower and beheld the largest vision.

In other words, he is an anthropologist, with a complete theory of Man, right or wrong. Now the modern Anthropologists, who called themselves Agnostics, completely failed to be Anthropologists at all. Under their limitations, they could not get a complete theory of Man, let alone a complete theory of nature. They began by ruling out something which they called the Unknowable. The incomprehensibility was almost comprehensible, if we could really understand the Unknowable in the sense of the Ultimate. But it rapidly became apparent that all sorts of things were Unknowable, which were exactly the things that a man has got to know. It is necessary to know whether he is responsible or irresponsible, perfect or imperfect, perfectible or unperfectible, mortal or immortal, doomed or free, not in order to understand God, but in order to understand Man. Nothing that leaves these things under a cloud of religious doubt can possibly pretend to be a Science of Man; it shrinks from anthropology as completely as from theology. Has a man free will; or is his sense of choice an illusion? Has he a conscience, or has his conscience any authority; or is it only the prejudice of the tribal past? Is there any real hope of settling these things by human reason; and has *that* any authority? Is he to regard death as final; and is he to regard miraculous help as possible? Now it is all nonsense to say that these are unknowable in any remote sense, like the distinction between the Cherubim and the Seraphim, or the Procession of the Holy Ghost. The Schoolmen may have shot too far beyond our limits in pursuing the Cherubim and Seraphim. But in asking whether a man can choose or whether a man will die, they were asking ordinary questions in natural history; like whether a cat can scratch or whether a dog can smell. Nothing calling itself a complete Science of Man can shirk them. And the great Agnostics did shirk them. They may have said they had no scientific evidence; in that case they failed to produce even a scientific hypothesis. What they generally did produce was a wildly unscientific contradiction. Most Monist moralists simply said that Man has no choice; but he must think and act heroically as if he had. Huxley made morality, and even Victorian morality, in the exact sense, supernatural. He said it had arbitrary rights above nature; a sort of theology without theism.

I do not know for certain why St. Thomas was called the Angelic Doctor: whether it was that he had an angelic temper, or the intellectuality of an Angel; or whether there was a later legend that he concentrated on Angels—especially on the points of needles. If so, I do not quite understand how this idea arose; history has many examples of an irritating habit of labelling somebody in connection with something, as if he never did anything else. Who was it who began the inane habit of referring to Dr. Johnson as 'our lexicographer'; as if he never did anything but write a dictionary? Why do most people insist on meeting the large and far-reaching mind of Pascal at its very narrowest point; the point at which it was sharpened into a spike by the spite of the Jansenists against the Jesuits? It is just possible, for all I know, that this labelling of Aquinas as a specialist was an obscure depreciation of him as a universalist. For that is a very common trick for the belittling of literary or scientific men. St. Thomas must have made a certain number of enemies, though he hardly ever treated them as enemies. Unfortunately, good temper is sometimes more irritating than bad temper. And he had, after all, done a great deal of damage, as many medieval men would have thought; and, what is more curious, a great deal of damage to both sides. He had been a revolutionist against Augustine and a traditionalist against Averrhoes. He might appear to some to have tried to wreck that ancient beauty of the city of God, which bore some resemblance to the Republic of Plato. He might appear to others to have inflicted a blow on the advancing and levelling forces of Islam, as dramatic as that of Godfrey storming Jerusalem. It is possible that these enemies, by way of damning with faint praise, talked about his very respectable little work on Angels: as a man might say that Darwin was really reliable when writing on coral-insects; or that some of Milton's Latin poems were very creditable indeed. But this is only a conjecture, and many other conjectures are possible. And I am disposed to think that St. Thomas really was rather specially interested in the nature of Angels, for the same reason that made him even more interested in the nature of Men. It was a part of that strong personal interest in things subordinate and semidependent, which runs through his whole system: a hierarchy of higher and lower liberties. He was interested in the problem of the Angel, as he was interested in the problem of the Man, because it was a problem; and especially because it was a problem of an intermediate creature. I do not pretend to deal here with this mysterious quality, as he conceives it to exist in that inscrutable intellectual being, who is less than God but more than Man. But it was this quality of a link in the chain, or a rung in the ladder, which mainly concerned the theologian, in developing his own particular theory of degrees. Above all, it is this which chiefly moves him, when he finds so fascinating the central mystery of Man. And for him the point is always that Man is not a balloon going up into the sky, nor a mole burrowing merely in the earth; but rather a thing like a tree, whose roots are fed from the earth, while its highest branches seem to rise almost to the stars.

I have pointed out that mere modern free-thought has left everything in a fog, including itself. The assertion that thought is free led first to the denial that will is free; but even about that there was no real determination among the Determinists. In practice, they told men that they must treat their will as free though it was not free. In other words, Man must live a double life; which is exactly the old heresy of Siger of Brabant about the Double Mind. In other words, the nineteenth century left everything in chaos; and the importance of Thomism to the twentieth century is that it may give us back a cosmos. We can give here only the rudest sketch of how Aquinas, like the Agnostics, beginning in the cosmic cellars, yet climbed to the cosmic towers.

Without pretending to span within such limits the essential Thomist idea, I may be allowed to throw out a sort of rough version of the fundamental question, which I think I have known myself, consciously or unconsciously since my childhood. When a child looks out of the nursery window and sees anything, say the green lawn of the garden, what does he actually know; or does he know anything? There are all sorts of nursery games of negative philosophy played round this question. A brilliant Victorian scientist delighted in declaring that the child does not see any grass at all; but only a sort of green mist reflected in a tiny mirror of the human eye. This piece of rationalism has always struck me as almost insanely irrational. If he is not sure of the existence of the grass, which he sees through the glass of a window, how on earth can he be sure of the existence of the retina, which he sees through the glass of a microscope? If sight deceives, why can it not go on deceiving? Men of another school answer that grass is a mere green impression on the mind; and that he can be sure of nothing except the mind. They declare that he can only be conscious of his own consciousness; which happens to be the one thing that we know the child is not conscious of at all. In that sense, it would be far truer to say that there is grass and no child, than to say that there is a conscious child but no grass. St. Thomas Aquinas, suddenly intervening in this nursery quarrel, says emphatically that the child is aware of *Ens*. Long before he knows that grass is grass, or self is self, he knows that something is something. Perhaps it would be best to say very emphatically (with a blow on the table), "There *is* an Is". That is as much monkish credulity as St. Thomas asks of us at the start. Very few unbelievers start by asking us to believe so little. And yet, upon this sharp pin-point of reality, he rears by long logical processes that have never really been successfully overthrown, the whole cosmic system of Christendom.

Thus, Aquinas insists very profoundly, but very practically, that there *instantly* enters, with this idea of affirmation, the idea of contradiction. It is instantly apparent, even to the child, that there cannot be both affirmation and contradiction. Whatever you call the thing he sees, a moon or a mirage or a sensation or a state of consciousness, when he sees it, he knows it is not true that he does not see it. Or whatever you call what he is supposed to be doing, seeing or dreaming or being conscious of an impression, he knows that if he is doing it, it is a lie to say he is not doing it. Therefore there has already entered *something* beyond even the first fact of being; there follows it like its shadow the first fundamental creed or commandment; that a thing cannot be and not be. Henceforth, in common or popular language, there is a false and true. I say in popular language, because Aquinas is nowhere more subtle than in pointing out that being is not strictly the same as truth; seeing truth must mean the appreciation of being by some mind capable of appreciating it. But in a general sense there has entered that primeval world of pure actuality, the division and dilemma that brings the ultimate sort of war into the world; the everlasting duel between Yes and No. This is the dilemma that many sceptics have darkened the universe and dissolved the mind, solely in order to escape. They are those who maintain that there is something that is both Yes and No. I do not know whether they pronounce it Yo.

The next step following on this acceptance of actuality or certainty, or whatever we call it in popular language, is much more difficult to explain in that language. But it represents exactly the point at which nearly all other systems go wrong, and in taking the third step abandon the first. Aquinas has affirmed that our first sense of fact is a fact; and he cannot go back on it without falsehood. But when we come to look at the fact or facts, as we know them, we observe that they have a rather queer character; which has made many moderns grow strangely and restlessly sceptical about them. For instance, they are largely in a state of change, from being one thing to being another; or their qualities are relative to other things; or they appear to move incessantly; or they ap-

pear to vanish entirely. At this point, as I say, many sages lose hold of the first principle of reality, which they would concede at first; and fall back on saying that there is nothing except change; or nothing except comparison; or nothing except flux; or in effect that there is nothing at all. Aquinas turns the whole argument the other way, keeping in line with his first realisation of reality. There is no doubt about the being of being, even if it does sometimes look like becoming; that is because what we see is not the fullness of being; or (to continue a sort of colloquial slang) we never see being being as much as it can. Ice is melted into cold water and cold water is heated into hot water; it cannot be all three at once. But this does not make water unreal or even relative; it only means that its being is limited to being one thing at a time. But the fullness of being is everything that it can be; and without it the lesser or approximate forms of being cannot be explained as anything; unless they are explained away as nothing.

This crude outline can only at the best be historical rather than philosophical. It is impossible to compress into it the metaphysical proofs of such an idea; especially in the medieval metaphysical language. But this distinction in philosophy is tremendous as a turning point in history. Most thinkers, on realising the apparent mutability of being, have really forgotten their own realisation of the being, and believed only in the mutability. They cannot even say that a thing changes into another thing; for them there is no instant in the process at which it is a thing at all. It is only a change. It would be more logical to call it nothing changing into nothing, than to say (on these principles) that there ever was or will be a moment when the thing is itself. St. Thomas maintains that the ordinary thing at any moment is something; but it is not everything that it could be. There is a fullness of being, in which it could be everything that it can be. Thus, while most sages come at last to nothing but naked change, he comes to the ultimate thing that is unchangeable, because it is all the other things at once. While they describe a change which is really a change in nothing, he describes a changelessness which includes the changes of everything. Things change because they are not complete; but their reality can only be explained as part of something that is complete. It is God.

Historically, at least, it was round this sharp and crooked corner that all the sophists have followed each other while the great Schoolman went up the high road of experience and expansion; to the beholding of cities, to the building of cities. They all failed at this early stage because, in the words of the old game, they took away the number they first thought of. The recognition of something, of a thing or things, is the first act of the intellect. But because the examination of a thing shows it is not a fixed or final thing, they inferred that there is nothing fixed or final. Thus, in various ways, they all began to see a thing as something thinner than a thing; a wave; a weakness; an abstract instability. St. Thomas, to use the same rude figure, saw a thing that was thicker than a thing; that was even more solid than the solid but secondary facts he had started by admitting as facts. Since we know them to be real, any elusive or bewildering element in their reality cannot really be unreality; and must be merely their relation to the real reality. A hundred human philosophies, ranging over the earth from Nominalism to Nirvana and Maya, from formless evolutionism to mindless quietism, all come from this first break in the Thomist chain; the notion that, because what we see does not satisfy us or explain itself, it is not even what we see. That cosmos is a contradiction in terms and strangles itself; but Thomism cuts itself free. The defect we see, in what is, is simply that it is not all that is. God is more actual even than Man; more actual even than Matter; for God with all His powers at every instant is immortally in action.

A cosmic comedy of a very curious sort occurred recently; involving the views of very brilliant men, such as Mr. Bernard Shaw and the Dean of St. Paul's. Briefly, freethinkers of many sorts had often said they had no need of a Creation, because the cosmos had always existed and always would exist. Mr. Bernard Shaw said he had become an atheist because the universe had gone on making itself from the beginning, or without a beginning; Dean Inge later displayed consternation at the very idea that the universe could have an end. Most modern Christians, living by tradition where medieval Christians could live by logic or reason, vaguely felt that it was a dreadful idea to deprive them of the Day of Judgment. Most modern agnostics (who are delighted to have their ideas called dreadful) cried out all the more, with one accord, that the self-producing, self-existent, truly scientific universe had never needed to have a beginning and could not come to an end. At this very instant, quite suddenly, like the look-out man on a ship who shouts a warning about a rock, the *real* man of science, the expert who was examining the facts, announced in a loud voice that the universe *was* coming to an end. He had not been listening, of course, to the talk of the amateurs; he had been actually examining the texture of matter; and he said it was disintegrating: the world was apparently blowing itself up by a gradual explosion called energy; the whole business would certainly have an end and had presumably had a beginning. This was very shocking indeed; not to the orthodox, but rather specially to the unorthodox; who are rather more easily shocked. Dean Inge, who had been lecturing the orthodox for years on their stern duty of accepting all scientific discoveries, positively wailed aloud over this truly tactless scientific discovery; and practically implored the scientific discoverers to go away and discover something different. It seems almost incredible; but it is a fact that he asked what God would have to amuse Him, if the universe ceased. That is a measure of how much the modern mind needs Thomas Aquinas. But even without Aquinas, I can hardly conceive any educated man, let alone such a learned man, believing in God at all without assuming that God contains in Himself every perfection including eternal joy; and does not require the solar system to entertain him like a circus.

To step out of these presumptions, prejudices and private disappointments, into the world of St. Thomas, is like escaping from a scuffle in a dark room into the broad daylight. St. Thomas says, quite straightforwardly, that he himself believes this world has a beginning and end; because such seems to be the teaching of the Church; the validity of which mystical message to mankind he defends elsewhere with dozens of quite different arguments. Anyhow, the Church said the world would end; and apparently the Church was right; always supposing (as we are always supposed to suppose) that the latest men of science are right. But Aquinas says he sees no particular reason, in reason, why this world should not be a world without end; or even without beginning. And he is quite certain that, if it were entirely without end or beginning, there would still be exactly the same logical need of a Creator. Anybody who does not see that, he gently implies, does not really understand what is meant by a Creator.

For what St. Thomas means is not a medieval picture of an old king; but this second step in the great argument about *Ens* or Being; the second point which is so desperately difficult to put correctly in popular language. That is why I have introduced it here in the particular form of the argument that there must be a Creator even if there is no Day of Creation. Looking at Being as it is now, as the baby looks at the grass, we see a second thing about it; in quite popular language, it *looks* secondary and dependent. Existence exists; but it is not sufficiently self-existent; and would never become so merely by going on existing. The same primary sense which tells us it is Being, tells us that it is not perfect Being; not merely imperfect in the popular controversial sense of containing sin or sorrow; but imperfect as Being; less actual than the actuality it implies. For instance, its Being is often only Becoming; beginning to Be or ceasing to Be; it implies a more constant or complete thing of which it gives in itself no example. That is the meaning of that basic medieval phrase, "Everything that is moving is moved by another"; which, in the clear subtlety of St. Thomas, means inexpressibly more than the mere Deistic "somebody wound up the clock" with which it is probably often confounded. Anyone who thinks deeply will see that motion has about it an essential incompleteness, which approximates to something more complete.

The actual argument is rather technical; and concerns the fact that potentiality does not explain itself; moreover, in any case, unfolding must be of something folded. Suffice it to say that the mere modern evolutionists, who would ignore the argument, do not do so because they have discovered any flaw in the argument; for they have never discovered the argument itself. They do so because they are too shallow to see the flaw in their own argument; for the weakness of their thesis is covered by fashionable phraseology, as the strength of the old thesis is covered by old-fashioned phraseology. But for those who really think, there is always something really unthinkable about the whole evolutionary cosmos, as they conceive it; because it is something coming out of nothing; an ever-increasing flood of water pouring out of an empty jug. Those who can simply accept that, without even seeing the difficulty, are not likely to go so deep as Aquinas and see the solution of his difficulty. In a word, the world does not explain itself, and cannot do so merely by continuing to expand itself. But anyhow, it is absurd for the Evolutionist to complain that it is unthinkable for an admittedly unthinkable God to make everything out of nothing, and then pretend that it is *more* thinkable that nothing should turn itself into everything.

We have seen that most philosophers simply fail to philosophise about things because they change; they also fail to philosophise about things because they differ. We have no space to follow St. Thomas through all these negative heresies; but a word must be said about Nominalism, or the doubt founded on the things that differ. Everyone knows that the Nominalist declared that things differ too much to be really classified; so that they are only labelled. Aquinas was a firm but moderate Realist, and therefore held that there really are general qualities; as that human beings are human, and other paradoxes. To be an extreme Realist would have taken him too near to being a Platonist. He recognized that individuality is real, but said that it coexists with a common character making some generalisation possible; in fact, as in most things, he said exactly what all common sense would say, if no intelligent heretics had ever disturbed it. Nevertheless, they still continue to disturb it. I remember when Mr. H. G. Wells had an alarming fit of Nominalist philosophy; and poured forth book after book to argue that everything is unique and untypical; as that a man is so much an individual that he is not even a man. It is a quaint and almost comic fact, that this chaotic negation especially attracts those who are always complaining of social chaos, and who propose to replace it by the most sweeping social regulations. It is the very men who say that nothing can be classified, who say that everything must be codified. Thus Mr. Bernard Shaw said that the only golden rule is that there is no golden rule. He prefers an iron rule; as in Russia.

But this is only a small inconsistency in some moderns as individuals. There is a much deeper inconsistency in them as theorists in relation to the general theory called Creative Evolution. They seem to imagine that they avoid the metaphysical doubt about mere change by assuming (it is not very clear why) that the change will always be for the better. But the mathematical difficulty of finding a corner in a curve is not altered by turning the chart upside down, and saying that a downward curve is now an upward curve. The point is that there is no point in the curve; no place at which we have a logical right to say that the curve has reached its climax, or revealed its origin, or

come to its end. It makes no difference that they choose to be cheerful about it, and say, "It is enough that there is always a beyond"; instead of lamenting, like the more realistic poets of the past, over the tragedy of mere Mutability. It is not enough that there is always a beyond; because it might be beyond bearing. Indeed the only defence of this view is that sheer boredom is such an agony, that any movement is a relief. But the truth is that they have never read St. Thomas, or they would find, with no little terror, that they really agree with him. What they really mean is that change is not mere change; but is the unfolding of something; and if it is thus unfolded, though the unfolding takes twelve million years, it must be there already. In other words, they agree with Aquinas that there is everywhere potentiality that has not reached its end in act. But if it is a definite potentiality, and if it can only end in a definite act, why then there is a Great Being, in whom all potentialities already exist as a plan of action. In other words, it is impossible even to say that the change is for the better, unless the best exists somewhere, both before and after the change. Otherwise it is indeed mere change, as the blankest sceptics or the blackest pessimists would see it. Suppose two entirely new paths open before the progress of Creative Evolution. How is the evolutionist to know which Beyond is the better; unless he accepts from the past and present some standard of the best? By their superficial theory everything can change; everything can improve, even the nature of improvement. But in their submerged common sense, they do not really think that an ideal of kindness could change to an ideal of cruelty. It is typical of them that they will sometimes rather timidly use the word Purpose; but blush at the very mention of the word Person.

St. Thomas is the very reverse of anthropomorphic, in spite of his shrewdness as an anthropologist. Some theologians have even claimed that he is too much of an agnostic; and has left the nature of God too much of an intellectual abstraction. But we do not need even St. Thomas, we do not need anything but our own common sense, to tell us that if there has been from the beginning anything that can possibly be called a Purpose, it must reside in something that has the essential elements of a Person. There cannot be an intention hovering in the air all by itself, any more than a memory that nobody remembers or a joke that nobody has made. The only chance for those supporting such suggestions is to take refuge in blank and bottomless irrationality; and even then it is impossible to prove that anybody has any right to be unreasonable, if St. Thomas has no right to be reasonable.

In a sketch that aims only at the baldest simplification, this does seem to me the simplest truth about St. Thomas the philosopher. He is one, so to speak, who is faithful to his first love; and it is love at first sight. I mean that he immediately recognised a real quality in things; and afterwards resisted all the disintegrating doubts arising from the nature of those things. That is why I emphasise, even in the first few pages, the fact that there is a sort of purely Christian humility and fidelity underlying his philosophic realism. St. Thomas could as truly say, of having seen merely a stick or a stone, what St. Paul said of having seen the rending of the secret heavens, "I was not disobedient to the heavenly vision". For though the stick or the stone is an earthly vision, it is through them that St. Thomas finds his way to heaven; and the point is that he is obedient to the vision; he does not go back on it. Nearly all the other sages who have led or misled mankind do, on one excuse or another, go back on it. They dissolve the stick or the stone in chemical solutions of scepticism; either in the medium of mere time and change; or in the difficulties of classification of unique units; or in the difficulty of recognising variety while admitting unity. The first of these three is called debate about flux or formless transition; the second is the debate about Nominalism and Realism, or the existence of general ideas; the third is called the ancient metaphysical riddle of the One and the

Many. But they can all be reduced under a rough image to this same statement about St. Thomas. He is still true to the first truth and refusing the first treason. He will not deny what he has seen, though it be a secondary and diverse reality. He will not take away the numbers he first thought of, though there may be quite a number of them.

He has seen grass; and will not say he has not seen grass, because it today is and tomorrow is cast into the oven. That is the substance of all scepticism about change, transition, transformism and the rest. He will not say that there is no grass but only growth. If grass grows and withers, it can only mean that it is part of a greater thing, which is even more real; not that the grass is less real than it looks. St. Thomas has a really logical right to say, in the words of the modern mystic, A.E.: "I begin by the grass to be bound again to the Lord".

He has seen grass and grain; and he will not say that they do not differ, because there is something common to grass and grain. Nor will he say that there is nothing common to grass and grain, because they do really differ. He will not say, with the extreme Nominalists, that because grain can be differentiated into all sorts of fruitage, or grass trodden into mire with any kind of weed, therefore there can be no *classification* to distinguish weeds from slime or to draw a fine distinction between cattle-food and cattle. He will not say with the extreme Platonists, on the other hand, that he saw the perfect fruit in his own head by shutting his eyes, *before* he saw any difference between grain and grass. He saw one thing and then another thing, and then a common quality; but he does not really pretend that he saw the quality before the thing.

He has seen grass and gravel; that is to say, he has seen things really different; things not classified together like grass and grain. The first flash of fact shows us a world of really strange things; not merely strange to us, but strange to each other. The separate things need have nothing in common except Being. Everything is Being; but it is not true that everything is Unity. It is here, as I have said, that St. Thomas does definitely, one might say defiantly, part company with the Pantheist and the Monist. All things are; but among the things that are is the thing called difference, quite as much as the thing called similarity. And here again we begin to be bound again to the Lord, not only by the universality of grass, but by the incompatibility of grass and gravel. For this world of different and varied beings is especially the world of the Christian Creator; the world of created things, like things made by an artist; as compared with the world that is only one thing, with a sort of shimmering and shifting veil of misleading change; which is the conception of so many of the ancient religions of Asia and the modern sophistries of Germany. In the face of these, St. Thomas still stands stubborn in the same obstinate objective fidelity. He has seen grass and gravel; and he is not disobedient to the heavenly vision.

To sum up; the reality of things, the mutability of things, the diversity of things, and all other such things that can be attributed to things, is followed carefully by the medieval philosopher, without losing touch with the original point of the reality. There is no space in this book to specify the thousand steps of thought by which he shows that he is right. But the point is that, even apart from being right he is real. He is a realist in a rather curious sense of his own, which is a third thing, distinct from the almost contrary medieval and modern meanings of the word. Even the doubts and difficulties about reality have driven him to believe in more reality rather than less. The *deceitfulness* of things which has had so sad an effect on so many sages, has almost a contrary effect on this sage. If things deceive us, it is by being more real than they seem. As ends in themselves they always deceive us; but as things tending to a greater end, they are even more real than we think them. If they seem to have a relative unreality (so to speak) it is because they are potential and not actual;

they are unfulfilled, like packets of seeds or boxes of fireworks. They have it in them to be more real than they are. And there is an upper world of what the Schoolman called Fruition, or Fulfillment, in which all this relative relativity becomes actuality; in which the trees burst into flower or the rockets into flame.

Here I leave the reader, on the very lowest rung of those ladders of logic, by which St. Thomas besieged and mounted the House of Man. It is enough to say that by arguments as honest and laborious, he climbed up to the turrets and talked with angels on the roofs of gold. This is, in a very rude outline, his philosophy; it is impossible in such an outline to describe his theology. Anyone writing so small a book about so big a man, must leave out something. Those who know him best will best understand why, after some considerable consideration, I have left out the only important thing.

## VIII   The sequel to St. Thomas

It is often said that St. Thomas, unlike St. Francis, did not permit in his work the indescribable element of poetry: As, for instance, that there is little reference to any pleasure in the actual flowers and fruit of natural things, though any amount of concern with the buried roots of nature. And yet I confess that, in reading his philosophy, I have a very peculiar and powerful impression analogous to poetry. Curiously enough, it is in some ways more analogous to painting, and reminds me very much of the effect produced by the *best* of the modern painters, when they throw a strange and almost crude light upon stark and rectangular objects, or seem to be groping for rather than grasping the very pillars of the subconscious mind. It is probably because there is in his work a quality which is Primitive, in the best sense of a badly misused word; but anyhow, the pleasure is definitely not only of the reason, but also of the imagination.

Perhaps the impression is connected with

the fact that painters deal with things without words. An artist draws quite gravely the grand curves of a pig; because he is not thinking of the *word* pig. There is no thinker who is so unmistakably thinking about things, and not being misled by the indirect influence of words, as St. Thomas Aquinas. It is true in that sense that he has not the advantage of words, any more than the disadvantage of words. Here he differs sharply, for instance, from St. Augustine who was, among other things, a wit. He was also a sort of prose poet, with a power over words in their atmospheric and emotional aspect; so that his books abound with beautiful passages that rise in the memory like strains of music; the *illi in vos saeviant;* or the unforgettable cry, "Late I have loved thee, O Ancient Beauty!" It is true that there is little or nothing of this kind in St. Thomas; but if he was without the higher uses of the mere magic of words, he was also free from that abuse of it, by mere sentimentalists or self-centred artists, which can become merely morbid and a very black magic indeed. And truly it is by some such comparison with the purely introspective intellectual, that we may find a hint about the real nature of the thing I describe, or rather fail to describe; I mean the elemental and primitive poetry that shines through all his thoughts; and especially through the thought with which all his thinking begins. It is the intense rightness of his sense of the relation between the mind and the real thing outside the mind.

That *strangeness* of things, which is the light in all poetry, and indeed in all art, is really connected with their otherness; or what is called their objectivity. What is subjective must be stale; it is exactly what is objective that is in this imaginative manner strange. In this the great contemplative is the complete contrary of that false contemplative, the mystic who looks only into his own soul, the selfish artist who shrinks from the world and lives only in his own mind. According to St. Thomas, the mind acts freely of itself, but its freedom exactly consists in finding a way out to liberty and the

light of day; to reality and the land of the living. In the subjectivist, the pressure of the world forces the imagination inwards. In the Thomist, the energy of the mind forces the imagination outwards, but because the images it seeks are real things. All their romance and glamour, so to speak, lies in the fact that they are real things; things *not* to be found by staring inwards at the mind. The flower is a vision because it is not only a vision. Or, if you will, it is a vision because it is not a dream. This is for the poet the strangeness of stones and trees and solid things; they are strange because they are solid. I am putting it first in the poetical manner, and indeed it needs much more technical subtlety to put it in the philosophical manner. According to Aquinas, the object becomes a part of the mind; nay, according to Aquinas, the mind actually becomes the object. But, as one commentator acutely puts it, it only becomes the object and does not create the object. In other words, the object *is* an object; it can and does exist outside the mind, or in the absence of the mind. And *therefore* it enlarges the mind of which it becomes a part. The mind conquers a new province like an emperor; but only because the mind has answered the bell like a servant. The mind has opened the doors and windows, because it is the natural activity of what is inside the house to find out what is outside the house. If the mind is sufficient to itself, it is insufficient for itself. For this feeding upon fact *is* itself; as an organ it has an object which is objective; this eating of the strange strong meat of reality.

Note how this view avoids both pitfalls; the alternative abysses of impotence. The mind is not merely receptive, in the sense that it absorbs sensations like so much blotting-paper; on that sort of softness has been based all that cowardly materialism, which conceives man as wholly servile to his environment. On the other hand, the mind is not purely creative, in the sense that it paints pictures on the windows and then mistakes them for a landscape outside. But the mind is active, and its activity consists in following, so far as the will chooses to follow, the light outside that does really shine upon real landscapes. That is what gives the indefinably virile and even adventurous quality to this view of life; as compared with that which holds that material inferences pour in upon an utterly helpless mind, or that which holds that psychological influences pour out and create an entirely baseless phantasmagoria. In other words, the essence of the Thomist common sense is that two agencies are at work; reality and the recognition of reality; and their meeting is a sort of marriage. Indeed it is very truly a marriage, because it is fruitful; the only philosophy now in the world that really is fruitful. It produces practical results, precisely because it is the combination of an adventurous mind and a strange fact.

M. Maritain has used an admirable metaphor, in his book *Theonas,* when he says that the external fact *fertilises* the internal intelligence, as the bee fertilises the flower. Anyhow, upon that marriage, or whatever it may be called, the whole system of St. Thomas is founded; God made Man so that he was capable of coming in contact with reality; and those whom God hath joined, let no man put asunder.

Now, it is worthy of remark that it is the only working philosophy. Of nearly all other philosophies it is strictly true that their followers work in spite of them, or do not work at all. No sceptics work sceptically; no fatalists work fatalistically; all without exception work on the principle that it is possible to assume what it is not possible to believe. No materialist who thinks his mind was made up for him, by mud and blood and heredity, has any hesitation in making up his mind. No sceptic who believes that truth is subjective has any hesitation about treating it as objective.

Thus St. Thomas's work has a constructive quality absent from almost all cosmic systems after him. For he is already building a house, while the newer speculators are still at the stage of testing the rungs of a ladder, demonstrating the hopeless softness of the unbaked bricks, chemically analysing the spirit in the spirit-level, and generally quarrelling about whether they can even make the tools that will make the house. Aquinas is whole intellectual aeons ahead of them, over and above the common chronological sense of saying a man is in advance of his age; he is ages in advance of our age. For he has thrown out a bridge across the abyss of the first doubt, and found reality beyond and begun to build on it. Most modern philosophies are not philosophy but philosophic doubt; that is, doubt about whether there can be any philosophy. If we accept St. Thomas's fundamental act or argument in the acceptance of reality, the further deductions from it will be equally real; they will be things and not words. Unlike Kant and most of the Hegelians, he has a faith that is not merely a doubt about doubt. It is not merely what is commonly called a faith about faith; it is a faith about fact. From this point he can go forward, and deduce and develop and decide, like a man planning a city and sitting in a judgment-seat. But never since that time has any thinking man of that eminence thought that there is any real evidence for anything, not even the evidence of his senses, that was strong enough to bear the weight of a definite deduction.

From all this we may easily infer that this philosopher does not merely touch on social things, or even take them in his stride to spiritual things; though that is always his direction. He takes hold of them, he has not only a grasp of them, but a grip. As all his controversies prove, he was perhaps a perfect example of the iron hand in the velvet glove. He was a man who always turned his full attention to anything; and he seems to fix even passing things as they pass. To him even what was momentary was momentous. The reader feels that any small point of economic habit or human accident is for the moment almost scorched under the converging rays of a magnifying lens. It is impossible to put in these pages a thousandth part of the decisions on details of life that may be found in his work; it would be like reprinting the law-reports of an incredible century of just judges and sensible magistrates. We can only touch on one or two obvious topics of this kind.

I have noted the need to use modern atmospheric words for certain ancient atmospheric things; as in saying that St. Thomas was what most modern men vaguely mean by an Optimist. In the same way, he was very much what they vaguely mean by a Liberal. I do not mean that any of his thousand political suggestions would suit any such definite political creed; if there are nowadays any definite political creeds. I mean, in the same sense, that he has a sort of atmosphere of believing in breadth and balance and debate. He may not be a Liberal by the extreme demands of the moderns for we seem always to mean by the moderns the men of the last century, rather than this. He was very much of a Liberal compared with the most modern of all moderns; for they are nearly all of them turning into Fascists and Hitlerites. But the point is that he obviously preferred the sort of decisions that are reached by deliberation rather than despotic action; and while, like all his contemporaries and co-religionists, he has no doubt that true authority may be authoritative, he is rather averse to the whole savour of its being arbitrary. He is much less of an Imperialist than Dante, and even his Papalism is not very Imperial. He is very fond of phrases like "a mob of free men" as the essential material of a city; and he is emphatic upon the fact that law, when it ceases to be justice, ceases even to be law.

If this work were controversial, whole chapters could be given to the economics as well as the ethics of the Thomist system. It would be easy to show that, in this matter, he was a prophet as well as a philosopher. He foresaw from the first the peril of that mere reliance on trade and exchange, which was beginning about his time; and which has culminated in a universal commercial collapse in our time. He did not merely assert that Usury is unnatural, though in saying that he only followed Aristotle and obvious common sense, which was never contradicted by anybody until the time of the commercialists, who have involved us in the collapse. The modern world began by Bentham writing the Defence of Usury, and it has ended after a hundred years in even the vulgar newspaper opinion finding Finance indefensible. But St. Thomas struck much deeper than that. He even mentioned the truth, ignored during the long idolatry of trade, that things which men produce only to sell are likely to be worse in quality than the things they produce in order to consume. Something of our difficulty about the fine shades of Latin will be felt when we come to his statement that there is always a certain *inhonestas* about trade. For *inhonestas* does not exactly mean dishonesty. It means approximately "something unworthy," or, more nearly perhaps, "something not quite handsome." And he was right; for trade, in the modern sense, does mean selling something for a little more than it is worth, nor would the nineteenth century economists have denied it. They would only have said that he was not practical; and this seemed sound while their view led to practical prosperity. Things are a little different now that it has led to universal bankruptcy.

Here, however, we collide with a colossal paradox of history. The Thomist philosophy and theology, quite fairly compared with other philosophies like the Buddhist or the Monist, with other theologies like the Calvinist or the Christian Scientist, is quite obviously a working and even a fighting system; full of common sense and constructive confidence; and therefore normally full of hope and promise. Nor is this hope vain or this promise unfulfilled. In this not very hopeful modern moment, there are no men so hopeful as those who are today looking to St. Thomas as a leader in a hundred crying questions of craftsmanship and ownership and economic ethics. There is undoubtedly a hopeful and creative Thomism in our time. But we are none the less puzzled by the fact that this did not immediately follow on St. Thomas's time. It is true that there was a great march of progress in the thirteenth century; and in some things, such as the status of the peasant, matters had greatly improved by the end of the Middle Ages. But nobody can honestly say that Scholasticism had greatly improved by the end of the Middle Ages. Nobody can tell how far the popular spirit of the Friars had helped the later popular medieval movements; or how far this great Friar, with his luminous rules of justice and his lifelong sympathy with the poor, may have indirectly contributed to the improvement that certainly occurred. But those who followed his method, as distinct from his moral spirit, degenerated with a strange rapidity; and it was certainly not in the Scholastics that the improvement occurred. Of some of the Scholastics we can only say that they took everything that was worst in Scholasticism and made it worse. They continued to count the steps of logic; but every step of logic took them further from common sense. They forgot how St. Thomas had started almost as an agnostic; and seemed resolved to leave nothing in heaven or hell about which anybody could be agnostic. They were a sort of rabid rationalists, who would have left no mysteries in the Faith at all. In the earliest Scholasticism there is something that strikes a modern as fanciful and pedantic; but, properly understood, it has a fine spirit in its fancy. It is the spirit of freedom; and especially the spirit of free will. Nothing seems more quaint, for instance, than the speculations about what would have happened to every vegetable or animal or angel, if Eve had chosen *not* to eat the fruit of the tree. But this was originally full of the thrill of choice; and the feeling that she might have chosen otherwise. It was this detailed detective method that was followed, without the thrill of the original detective story. The world was cumbered with countless tomes, proving by logic a thousand things that can be known only to God. They developed all that was really sterile in Scholasticism, and left for us all that is really fruitful in Thomism.

There are many historical explanations. There is the Black Death, which broke the back of the Middle Ages; the consequent decline in clerical culture, which did so much to provoke the Reformation. But I suspect that there was another cause also; which can only be stated by saying that the contemporary fanatics, who controverted with Aquinas, left their own school behind them; and in a sense that school triumphed after all. The really narrow Augustinians, the men who saw the Christian life only as the narrow way, the men who could not even comprehend the great Dominican's exultation in the blaze of Being, or the glory of God in all his creatures, the men who continued to insist feverishly on every text, or even on every truth, that appeared pessimistic or paralysing, these gloomy Christians could not be extirpated from Christendom; and they remained and waited for their chance. The narrow Augustinians, the men who would have no science or reason or rational use of secular things, might have been defeated in controversy, but they had an accumulated passion of conviction. There was an Augustinian monastery in the North where it was near to explosion.

Thomas Aquinas had struck his blow; but he had not entirely settled the Manichees. The Manichees are not so easily settled; in the sense of settled forever. He had insured that the main outline of the Christianity that has come down to us should be supernatural but not antinatural; and should never be darkened with a false spirituality to the oblivion of the Creator and the Christ who was made Man. But as his tradition trailed away into less liberal or less creative habits of thought, and as his medieval society fell away and decayed through other causes, the thing against which he had made war crept back into Christendom. A certain spirit or element in the Christian religion, necessary and sometimes noble but always needing to be balanced by more gentle and generous elements in the Faith, began once more to strengthen, as the framework of Scholasticism stiffened or split. The Fear of the Lord, that is the beginning of wisdom, and therefore belongs to the beginnings, and is felt in the first cold hours before the dawn of civilisation; the power that comes out of the wilderness and rides on the whirlwind and breaks the gods of stone; the power before which the eastern nations are prostrate like a pavement; the power before which the primitive prophets run naked and shouting, at once proclaiming and escaping from their god; the fear that is rightly rooted in the beginnings of every religion, true or false: the fear of the Lord, that is the beginning of wisdom; but not the end.

It is often remarked, as showing the ironical indifference of rulers to revolutions, and especially the frivolity of those who are called the Pagan Popes of the Renaissance, in their attitude to the Reformation, that when the Pope first heard of the first movements of Protestantism, which had started in Germany, he only said in an offhand manner that it was "some quarrel of monks". Every Pope of course was accustomed to quarrels among the monastic orders; but it has always been noted as a strange and almost uncanny negligence that he could see no more than this in the beginnings of the great sixteenth century schism. And yet, in a somewhat more recondite sense, there is something to be said for what he has been blamed for saying. In one sense, the schismatics had a sort of spiritual ancestry even in medieval times.

It will be found earlier in this book; and it *was* a quarrel of monks. We have seen how the great name of Augustine, a name never mentioned by Aquinas without respect but often mentioned without agreement, covered an Augustinian school of thought naturally lingering longest in the Augustinian Order. The difference, like every difference between Catholics, was only a difference of emphasis. The Augustinians stressed the idea of the impotence of man before God, the omniscience of God about the destiny of man, the need for holy fear and the humiliation of intellectual pride, more than the opposite and corresponding truths of free will or human dignity or good works. In this

they did in a sense continue the distinctive note of St. Augustine, who is even now regarded as relatively the determinist doctor of the Church. But there is emphasis and emphasis; and a time was coming when emphasising the one side was to mean flatly contradicting the other. Perhaps, after all, it did begin with a quarrel of monks; but the Pope was yet to learn how quarrelsome a monk could be. For there was one particular monk, in that Augustinian monastery in the German forests, who may be said to have had a single and special talent for emphasis; for emphasis and nothing except emphasis; for emphasis with the quality of earthquake. He was the son of a slatecutter; a man with a great voice and a certain volume of personality; brooding, sincere, decidedly morbid; and his name was Martin Luther. Neither Augustine nor the Augustinians would have desired to see the day of that vindication of the Augustinian tradition; but in one sense, perhaps, the Augustinian tradition was avenged after all.

It came out of its cell again, in the day of storm and ruin, and cried out with a new and mighty voice for an elemental and emotional religion, and for the destruction of all philosophies. It had a peculiar horror and loathing of the great Greek philosophies, and of the Scholasticism that had been founded on those philosophies. It had one theory that was the destruction of all theories; in fact it had its own theology which was itself the death of theology. Man could say nothing to God, nothing from God, nothing about God, except an almost inarticulate cry for mercy and for the supernatural help of Christ, in a world where all natural things were useless. Reason was useless. Will was useless. Man could not move himself an inch any more than a stone. Man could not trust what was in his head any more than a turnip. Nothing remained in earth or heaven, but the name of Christ lifted in that lonely imprecation; awful as the cry of a beast in pain.

We must be just to those huge human figures, who are in fact the hinges of history.

However strong, and rightly strong, be our own controversial conviction, it must never mislead us into thinking that something trivial has transformed the world. So it is with that great Augustinian monk, who avenged all the ascetic Augustinians of the Middle Ages; and whose broad and burly figure has been big enough to block out for four centuries the distant human mountain of Aquinas. It is not, as the moderns delight to say, a question of theology. The Protestant theology of Martin Luther was a thing that no modern Protestant would be seen dead in a field with; or if the phrase be too flippant, would be specially anxious to touch with a barge-pole. That Protestantism was pessimism; it was nothing but bare insistence on the hopelessness of all human virtue, as an attempt to escape hell. That Lutheranism is now quite unreal; more modern phases of Lutheranism are rather more unreal; but Luther was not unreal. He was one of those great elemental barbarians, to whom it is indeed given to change the world. To compare those two figures bulking so big in history, in any philosophical sense, would of course be futile and even unfair. On a great map like the mind of Aquinas, the mind of Luther would be almost invisible. But it is not altogether untrue to say, as so many journalists have said without caring whether it was true or untrue, that Luther opened an epoch; and began the modern world.

He was the first man who ever consciously used his consciousness; or what was later called his Personality. He had as a fact a rather strong personality. Aquinas had an even stronger personality; he had a massive and magnetic presence; he had an intellect that could act like a huge system of artillery spread over the whole world; he had that instantaneous presence of mind in debate, which alone really deserves the name of wit. But it never occurred to him to use anything except his wits, in defence of a truth distinct from himself. It never occurred to Aquinas to use Aquinas as a weapon. There is not a trace of his ever using his personal advantages, of birth or body or brain or breeding,

in debate with anybody. In short, he belonged to an age of intellectual unconsciousness, to an age of intellectual innocence, which was very intellectual. Now Luther did begin the modern mood of depending on things not merely intellectual. It is not a question of praise or blame; it matters little whether we say that he was a strong personality, or that he was a bit of a big bully. When he quoted a Scripture text, inserting a word that is not in Scripture, he was content to shout back at all hecklers: "Tell them that Dr. Martin Luther will have it so!" That is what we now call Personality. A little later it was called Psychology. After that it was called Advertisement or Salesmanship. But we are not arguing about advantages or disadvantages. It is due to this great Augustinian pessimist to say, not only that he did triumph at last over the Angel of the Schools, but that he did in a very real sense make the modern world. He destroyed Reason; and substituted Suggestion.

It is said that the great Reformer publicly burned the *Summa Theologica* and the works of Aquinas; and with the bonfire of such books this book may well come to an end. They say it is very difficult to burn a book; and it must have been exceedingly difficult to burn such a mountain of books as the Dominican had contributed to the controversies of Christendom. Anyhow, there is something lurid and apocalyptic about the idea of such destruction, when we consider the compact complexity of all that encyclopaedic survey of social and moral and theoretical things. All the close-packed definitions that excluded so many errors and extremes; all the broad and balanced judgments upon the clash of loyalties or the choice of evils; all the liberal speculations upon the limits of government or the proper conditions of justice; all the distinctions between the use and abuse of private property; all the rules and exceptions about the great evil of war; all the allowances for human weakness and all the provisions for human health; all this mass of medieval humanism shrivelled and curled up in smoke before the eyes of its enemy; and that great passionate peasant rejoiced darkly, because the day of the Intellect was over. Sentence by sentence it burned, and syllogism by syllogism; and the golden maxims turned to golden flames in that last and dying glory of all that had once been the great wisdom of the Greeks. The great central Synthesis of history, that was to have linked the ancient with the modern world, went up in smoke and, for half the world, was forgotten like a vapour.

For a time it seemed that the destruction was final. It is still expressed in the amazing fact that (in the North) modern men can still write histories of philosophy, in which philosophy stops with the last little sophists of Greece and Rome; and is never heard of again until the appearance of such a third-rate philosopher as Francis Bacon. And yet this small book, which will probably do nothing else, or have very little other value, will be at least a testimony to the fact that the tide has turned once more. It is four hundred years after; and this book, I hope (and I am happy to say I believe) will probably be lost and forgotten in the flood of better books about St. Thomas Aquinas, which are at this moment pouring from every printing-press in Europe, and even in England and America. Compared with such books it is obviously a very slight and amateurish production; but it is not likely to be burned, and if it were, it would not leave even a noticeable gap in the pouring mass of new and magnificent work, which is now daily dedicated to the *philosophia perennis;* to the Everlasting Philosophy.

# On Crimes and Punishments

Cesare Beccaria

## Editor's Introduction

In the summer of 1764, in Leghorn, Italy, an anonymous treatise was published on crimes and punishments (*Dei delitti e delle pene*). Highly critical of the prevailing practice of criminal law for its extreme brutality, the book met with immediate and immense success. Within a year it had gone through three editions in Italian. More importantly, it had been welcomed by the *philosophes* in Paris. Published in a French translation, its fame spread rapidly throughout Europe until it was read and admired from Sweden to Spain and from England to Russia. Voltaire wrote a commentary on it, in which he turned its principles against the punishment of heretics. Jeremy Bentham, the English legal reformer and father of Utilitarianism, hailed its author as his "master, first evangelist of Reason," and the book, in fact, contains in its introduction a statement that anticipates the best-known slogan of the Utilitarian program: "the greatest happiness of the greatest number." In Russia, Catherine the Great made the book a basis of her program of legal reform.

The book was first published anonymously out of fear that the author might be subjected to punitive measures from the authorities responsible for upholding the laws he criticized. His identity soon became known, however, perhaps as a result of the proddings of his friends and collaborators, the Counts Pietro and Alessandro Verri of Milan. He was Cesare Beccaria, the son of an ancient noble Lombard family, and, as events were to prove, his timid nature could hardly bear the burden that fate had suddenly placed upon it.

Beccaria was born in Milan on March 15, 1738. He received his first education from the Jesuits at Parma and then studied law at the University of Padua, from which he received a degree in 1758. An indifferent student while at school, he experienced his first intellectual awakening upon reading *The Persian Letters* of Montesquieu. After that he began reading seriously and extensively in the luminaries of the French enlightenment. His favorite authors, besides Montesquieu, were Rousseau, Hume, and the writers most closely associated with the great French *Encyclopédie*—Diderot, D'Alembert, Helvétius, Condillac.

Beccaria's intellectual development was immeasurably aided by his friendship with the Verri family. Their house was the center of a study group dedicated to the causes of enlightenment and reform, which they promoted through a periodical, *Il caffè,* modeled on the *Spectator* of London. Under their urging, Beccaria directed his studies of public policy to the problem of criminal law. Count Alessandro Verri, in his office as protector of prisoners, provided firsthand evidence of prison conditions, while the elder brother inspired him, Beccaria said, with "the same enthusiasm of friendship that Montaigne felt for Étienne de La Boëtie." The book that was to win him lasting fame was composed with the help of the two brothers. It represented the substance of conversations held in the Verri household between March 1763 and January 1764.

The fame of the book won its author an invitation from Paris to visit and be feted by the authors he admired most. His personal reluctance to venture forth was overcome by the insistence of Pietro Verri. In the fall of 1766, accompanied by Alessandro (since duties made it impossible for Pietro to leave Italy), Beccaria received a triumphal welcome in Paris. But to Beccaria himself the occasion was a constant trial, and to restore his tranquillity, after scarcely two months he fled back to Milan. There he found life more to his liking, first as professor of political economy in the Palatine college of Milan, and then in various public offices under the Austrian government of Lombardy—offices that amounted to sinecures and yet drew upon his knowledge of civil and criminal law and its reform.

In 1766, Beccaria against his father's wishes married Teresa de' Blasco by whom he had two daughters, one of whom became the mother of Italy's most famous novelist, Alessandro Manzoni. Beccaria died of an apoplectic stroke November 28, 1794.

*On Crimes and Punishments* is presented here in the translation of Edward D. Ingraham, from the second American edition, Philadelphia, 1819. This edition follows the editing and rearranging of the original that was made by Abbé Morellet for the first French translation of 1766—the version in which the work won its great fame and which had the approval of the author. The frontispiece showing Justice horrified at torture was chosen by Beccaria himself.

# CONTENTS

INTRODUCTION

In every human society, there is an effort continually tending to confer on one part the height of power and happiness, and to reduce the other to the extreme of weakness and misery. The intent of good laws is to oppose this effort, and to diffuse their influence universally and equally. But men generally abandoned the care of their most important concerns to the uncertain prudence and discretion of those whose interest it is to reject the best and wisest institutions; and it is not till they have been led into a thousand mistakes in matters the most essential to their lives and liberties, and are weary of suffering, that they can be induced to apply a remedy to the evils with which they are oppressed. It is then they begin to conceive and acknowledge the most palpable truths, which, from their very simplicity, commonly escape vulgar minds, incapable of analysing objects, accustomed to receive impressions without distinction, and to be determined rather by the opinions of others than by the result of their own examination.

If we look into history we shall find that laws, which are, or ought to be, conventions between men in a state of freedom, have been, for the most part, the work of the passions of a few, or the consequences of a fortuitous or temporary necessity; not dictated by a cool examiner of human nature, who knew how to collect in óne point the actions of a multitude, and had this only end in view, *the greatest happiness of the greatest number.* Happy are those few nations who have not waited till the slow succession of human vicissitudes should, from the extremity of evil, produce a transition to good; but by prudent laws have facilitated the progress from one to the other! And how great are the obligations due from mankind to that philosopher, who, from the obscurity of his closet, had the courage to scatter among the multitude the seeds of useful truths, so long unfruitful!

The art of printing has diffused the knowledge of those philosophical truths, by which the relations between sovereigns and their subjects, and between nations are discovered. By this knowledge commerce is animated, and there has sprung up a spirit of emulation and industry, worthy of rational beings. These are the produce of this enlightened age; but the cruelty of punishments, and the irregularity of proceedings in criminal cases, so principal a part of the legislation, and so much neglected throughout Europe, has hardly ever been called in question. Errors, accumulated through many centuries, have never yet been exposed by ascending to general principles; nor has the force of acknowledged truths been ever opposed to the unbounded licentiousness of ill-directed power, which has continually produced so many authorised examples of the most unfeeling barbarity. Surely, the groans of the weak, sacrificed to the cruel ignorance and indolence of the powerful, the barbarous torments lavished and multiplied with useless severity, for crimes either not proved, or in their nature impossible, the filth and horrors of a prison, increased by the most cruel tormentor of the miserable, uncertainty, ought to have roused the attention of those whose business is to direct the opinions of mankind.

The immortal Montesquieu has but slightly touched on this subject.* Truth, which is eternally the same, has obliged me to follow the steps of that great man; but the studious part of mankind, for whom I write, will easily distinguish the superstructure from the foundation. I shall be happy if, with him, I can obtain the secret thanks of the obscure and peaceful disciples of reason and philosophy, and excite that tender emotion in which sensible minds sympathise with him who pleads the cause of humanity.

---

* *The Spirit of the Laws,* esp. bks. 7 and 12; *GBWW,* Vol. 38, pp. 33a–43d and 84b–92b.

# On Crimes and Punishments

## I  Of the origin of punishments

Laws are the conditions under which men, naturally independent, united themselves in society. Weary of living in a continual state of war, and of enjoying a liberty, which became of little value, from the uncertainty of its duration, they sacrificed one part of it, to enjoy the rest in peace and security. The sum of all these portions of the liberty of each individual constituted the sovereignty of a nation and was deposited in the hands of the sovereign, as the lawful administrator. But it was not sufficient only to establish this deposit; it was also necessary to defend it from the usurpation of each individual, who will always endeavour to take away from the mass, not only his own portion, but to encroach on that of others. Some motives, therefore, that strike the senses were necessary to prevent the despotism of each individual from plunging society into its former chaos. Such motives are the punishments established against the infractors of the laws. I say that motives of this kind are necessary; because experience shows, that the multitude adopt no established principle of conduct; and because society is prevented from approaching to that dissolution (to which, as well as all other parts of the physical and moral world, it naturally tends) only by motives that are the immediate objects of sense, and which being continually presented to the mind, are sufficient to counterbalance the effects of the passions of the individual which oppose the general good.

Neither the power of eloquence nor the sublimest truths are sufficient to restrain, for any length of time, those passions which are excited by the lively impressions of present objects.

## II  Of the right to punish

Every punishment which does not arise from absolute necessity, says the great Montesquieu, is tyrannical.* A proposition which may be made more general thus: every act of authority of one man over another, for which there is not an absolute necessity, is tyrannical. It is upon this then that the sovereign's right to punish crimes is founded; that is, upon the necessity of defending the public liberty, entrusted to his care, from the usurpation of individuals; and punishments are just in proportion, as the liberty, preserved by the sovereign, is sacred and valuable.

Let us consult the human heart, and there we shall find the foundation of the sovereign's right to punish, for no advantage in moral policy can be lasting which is not founded on the indelible sentiments of the heart of man. Whatever law deviates from this principle will always meet with a resistance which will destroy it in the end; for the smallest force continually applied will overcome the most violent motion communicated to bodies.

---

* Cf. *GBWW*, Vol. 38, p. 85b.

No man ever gave up his liberty merely for the good of the public. Such a chimera exists only in romances. Every individual wishes, if possible, to be exempt from the compacts that bind the rest of mankind.

The multiplication of mankind, though slow, being too great for the means which the earth, in its natural state, offered to satisfy necessities which every day became more numerous, obliged men to separate again, and form new societies. These naturally opposed the first, and a state of war was transferred from individuals to nations.

Thus it was necessity that forced men to give up a part of their liberty. It is certain, then, that every individual would choose to put into the public stock the smallest portion possible, as much only as was sufficient to engage others to defend it. The aggregate of these, the smallest portions possible, forms the right of punishing; all that extends beyond this, is abuse, not justice.

Observe that by *justice* I understand nothing more than that bond which is necessary to keep the interest of individuals united, without which men would return to their original state of barbarity. All punishments which exceed the necessity of preserving this bond are in their nature unjust. We should be cautious how we associate with the word *justice* an idea of any thing real, such as a physical power, or a being that actually exists. I do not, by any means, speak of the justice of God, which is of another kind, and refers immediately to rewards and punishments in a life to come.

## III Consequences of the foregoing principles

The laws only can determine the punishment of crimes; and the authority of making penal laws can only reside with the legislator, who represents the whole society united by the social compact. No magistrate then (as he is one of the society), can, with justice, inflict on any other member of the same society punishment that is not ordained by the laws. But as a punishment, increased beyond the degree fixed by the law, is the just punishment with the addition of another, it follows that no magistrate, even under a pretence of zeal, or the public good, should increase the punishment already determined by the laws.

If every individual be bound to society, society is equally bound to him, by a contract which, from its nature, equally binds both parties. This obligation, which descends from the throne to the cottage, and equally binds the highest and lowest of mankind, signifies nothing more than that it is the interest of all that conventions, which are useful to the greatest number, should be punctually observed. The violation of this compact by any individual is an introduction to anarchy.

The sovereign, who represents the society itself, can only make general laws to bind the members; but it belongs not to him to judge whether any individual has violated the social compact, or incurred the punishment in consequence. For in this case there are two parties, one represented by the sovereign, who insists upon the violation of the contract, and the other is the person accused, who denies it. It is necessary then that there should be a third person to decide this contest; that is to say, a judge, or magistrate, from whose determination there should be no appeal; and this determination should consist of a simple affirmation or negation of fact.

If it can only be proved, that the severity of punishments, though not immediately contrary to the public good, or to the end for which they were intended, viz. to prevent crimes, be useless, then such severity would be contrary to those beneficent virtues, which are the consequence of enlightened reason, which instructs the sovereign to wish rather to govern men in a state of freedom and happiness than of slavery. It would also be contrary to justice and the social compact.

## IV Of the interpretation of laws

Judges, in criminal cases, have no right to interpret the penal laws, because they are not legislators. They have not received the laws from our ancestors as a domestic tradition, or as the will of a testator, which his heirs and executors are to obey; but they receive them from a society actually existing, or from the sovereign, its representative. Even the authority of the laws is not founded on any pretended obligation, or ancient convention; which must be null, as it cannot bind those who did not exist at the time of its institution; and unjust, as it would reduce men in the ages following, to a herd of brutes, without any power of judging or acting. The laws receive their force and authority from an oath of fidelity, either tacit or expressed, which living subjects have sworn to their sovereign, in order to restrain the intestine fermentation of the private interest of individuals. From hence springs their true and natural authority. Who then is their lawful interpreter? The sovereign, that is, the representative of society, and not the judge, whose office is only to examine if a man have or have not committed an action contrary to the laws.

In every criminal cause the judge should reason syllogistically. The *major* should be the general law; the *minor,* the conformity of the action, or its opposition to the laws; the *conclusion,* liberty, or punishment. If the judge be obliged by the imperfection of the laws, or chooses to make any other or more syllogisms than this, it will be an introduction to uncertainty.

There is nothing more dangerous than the common axiom, *the spirit of the laws is to be considered.* To adopt it is to give way to the torrent of opinions. This may seem a paradox to vulgar minds, which are more strongly affected by the smallest disorder before their eyes, than by the most pernicious though remote consequences produced by one false principle adopted by a nation.

Our knowledge is in proportion to the number of our ideas. The more complex these are, the greater is the variety of positions in which they may be considered. Every man hath his own particular point of view, and, at different times, sees the same objects in very different lights. The spirit of the laws will then be the result of the good or bad logic of the judge; and this will depend on his good or bad digestion, on the violence of his passions, on the rank or condition of the accused, or on his connections with the judge, and on all those little circumstances which change the appearance of objects in the fluctuating mind of man. Hence we see the fate of a delinquent changed many times in passing through the different courts of judicature, and his life and liberty victims to the false ideas or ill humour of the judge, who mistakes the vague result of his own confused reasoning for the just interpretation of the laws. We see the same crimes punished in a different manner at different times in the same tribunals, the consequence of not having consulted the constant and invariable voice of the laws, but the erring instability of arbitrary interpretation.

The disorders that may arise from a rigorous observance of the letter of penal laws are not to be compared with those produced by the interpretation of them. The first are temporary inconveniences which will oblige the legislature to correct the letter of the law, the want of preciseness and uncertainty of which has occasioned these disorders; and this will put a stop to the fatal liberty of explaining, the source of arbitrary and venal declamations. When the code of laws is once fixed, it should be observed in the literal sense, and nothing more is left to the judge than to determine whether an action be or be not conformable to the written law. When the rule of right, which ought to direct the actions of the philosopher, as well as the ignorant, is a matter of controversy, not of fact, the people are slaves to the magistrates. The despotism of this multitude of tyrants is more insupportable the less the distance is between the oppressor and the oppressed, more fatal than that of one, for the tyranny of many is not to be shaken off but by having recourse to that of one alone. It is more cruel, as it meets with more opposition, and the cruelty of a tyrant is not in proportion to his strength, but to the obstacles that oppose him.

These are the means by which security of person and property is best obtained, which is just, as it is the purpose of uniting in society; and it is useful as each person may calculate exactly the inconveniences attending every crime. By these means, subjects will acquire a spirit of independence and liberty, however it may appear to those who dare to call the weakness of submitting blindly to their capricious and interested opinions by the sacred name of virtue.

These principles will displease those who have made it a rule with themselves to transmit to their inferiors the tyranny they suffer from their superiors. I should have every thing to fear if tyrants were to read my book; but tyrants never read.

## V  Of the obscurity of laws

If the power of interpreting laws be an evil, obscurity in them must be another, as the former is the consequence of the latter. This evil will be still greater if the laws be written in a language unknown to the people; who, being ignorant of the consequences of their own actions, become necessarily dependent on a few, who are interpreters of the laws, which, instead of being public and general, are thus rendered private and particular. What must we think of mankind when we reflect, that such is the established custom of the greatest part of our polished and enlightened Europe? Crimes will be less frequent in proportion as the code of laws is more universally read and understood; for there is no doubt but that the eloquence of the passions is greatly assisted by the ignorance and uncertainty of punishments.

Hence it follows, that, without written laws, no society will ever acquire a fixed form of government, in which the power is vested in the whole, and not in any part of the society; and in which the laws are not to be altered but by the will of the whole, nor corrupted by the force of private interest. Experience and reason show us that the probability of human traditions diminishes in proportion as they are distant from their sources. How then can laws resist the inevitable force of time, if there be not a lasting monument of the social compact.

Hence we see the use of printing, which alone makes the public, and not a few individuals, the guardians and defenders of the laws. It is this art which, by diffusing literature, has gradually dissipated the gloomy spirit of cabal and intrigue. To this art it is owing that the atrocious crimes of our ancestors, who were alternately slaves and tyrants, are become less frequent. Those who are acquainted with the history of the two or three last centuries may observe, how from the lap of luxury and effeminacy have sprung the most tender virtues, humanity, benevolence, and toleration of human errors. They may contemplate the effects of what was so improperly called ancient simplicity and good faith; humanity groaning under implacable superstition, the avarice and ambition of a few staining with human blood the thrones and palaces of kings, secret treasons and public massacres, every noble a tyrant over the people, and the ministers of the gospel of Christ bathing their hands in blood in the name of the God of all mercy. We may talk as we please of the corruption and degeneracy of the present age, but happily we see no such horrid examples of cruelty and oppression.

## VI  Of the proportion between crimes and punishments

It is not only the common interest of mankind that crimes should not be committed, but that crimes of every kind should be less frequent, in proportion to the evil they produce to society. Therefore the means made use of by the legislature to prevent crimes should be more powerful, in proportion as they are destructive of the public safety and happiness, and as the inducements to commit them are stronger. Therefore there ought to be a fixed proportion between crimes and punishments.

It is impossible to prevent entirely all the disorders which the passions of mankind cause in society. These disorders increase in proportion to the number of people and the opposition of private interests. If we consult history, we shall find them increasing, in every state, with the extent of dominion. In political arithmetic, it is necessary to substitute a calculation of probabilities to mathematical exactness. That force which continually impels us to our own private interest, like gravity, acts incessantly, unless it meets with an obstacle to oppose it. The effects of this force are the confused series of human actions. Punishments, which I would call political obstacles, prevent the fatal effects of private interest, without destroying the impelling cause, which is that sensibility inseparable from man. The legislator acts, in this case, like a skilful architect, who endeavours to counteract the force of gravity by combining the circumstances which may contribute to the strength of his edifice.

The necessity of uniting in society being granted, together with the conventions which the opposite interests of individuals must necessarily require, a scale of crimes may be formed, of which the first degree should consist of those which immediately tend to the dissolution of society, and the last of the smallest possible injustice done to a private member of that society. Between these extremes will be comprehended all actions contrary to the public good which are called criminal, and which descend by insensible degrees, decreasing from the highest to the lowest. If mathematical calculation could be applied to the obscure and infinite combinations of human actions, there might be a corresponding scale of punishments, descending from the greatest to the least; but it will be sufficient that the wise legislator mark the principal divisions, without disturbing the order, lest to crimes of the *first* degree be assigned punishments of the *last*. If there were an exact and universal scale of crimes and punishments, we should there have a common measure of the degree of liberty and slavery, humanity and cruelty, of different nations.

Any action which is not comprehended in the above mentioned scale will not be called a crime, or punished as such, except by those who have an interest in the denomination. The uncertainty of the extreme points of this scale hath produced a system of morality which contradicts the laws, a multitude of laws that contradict each other, and many which expose the best men to the severest punishments, rendering the ideas of *vice* and *virtue* vague and fluctuating, and even their existence doubtful. Hence that fatal lethargy of political bodies, which terminates in their destruction.

Whoever reads, with a philosophic eye, the history of nations, and their laws, will generally find, that the ideas of virtue and vice, of a good or bad citizen, change with the revolution of ages, not in proportion to the alteration of circumstances, and consequently conformable to the common good, but in proportion to the passions and errors by which the different lawgivers were successively influenced. He will frequently observe that the passions and vices of one age are the foundation of the morality of the following; that violent passion, the offspring of fanaticism and enthusiasm, being weakened by time, which reduces all the phenomena of the natural and moral world to an equality, becomes, by degrees, the prudence of the age, and an useful instrument in the hands of the powerful or artful politician. Hence the uncertainty of our notions of honour and virtue; an uncertainty which will ever remain, because they change with the revolutions of time, and names survive the things they originally signified; they change with the boundaries of states, which are often the same both in physical and moral geography.

Pleasure and pain are the only springs of actions in beings endowed with sensibility. Even amongst the motives which incite men to acts of religion, the invisible legislator has ordained rewards and punishments. From a partial distribution of these will arise that contradiction, so little observed, because so common, I mean that of punishing by the laws the crimes which the laws have occasioned. If an equal punishment be ordained for two crimes that injure society in different degrees, there is nothing to deter men from committing the greater as often as it is attended with greater advantage.

## VII  Of estimating the degree of crimes

The foregoing reflections authorise me to assert that crimes are only to be measured by the injury done to society.

They err, therefore, who imagine that a crime is greater or less according to the intention of the person by whom it is committed; for this will depend on the actual impression of objects on the senses, and on the previous disposition of the mind; both which will vary in different persons, and even in the same person at different times, according to the succession of ideas, passions, and circumstances. Upon that system it would be necessary to form, not only a particular code for every individual, but a new penal law for every crime. Men, often with the best intention, do the greatest injury to society, and, with the worst, do it the most essential services.

Others have estimated crimes rather by the dignity of the person offended than by their consequences to society. If this were the true standard, the smallest irreverence to the Divine Being ought to be punished with infinitely more severity than the assassination of a monarch.

In short, others have imagined, that the greatness of the sin should aggravate the crime. But the fallacy of this opinion will appear on the slightest consideration of the relations between man and man, and between God and man. The relations between man and man are relations of equality. Necessity alone hath produced, from the opposition of private passions and interests, the idea of public utility, which is the foundation of human justice. The other are relations of dependence, between an imperfect creature and his Creator, the most perfect of beings, who has reserved to himself the sole right of being both lawgiver and judge; for he alone can, without injustice, be, at the same time, both one and the other. If he hath decreed eternal punishments for those who disobey his will, shall an insect dare to put himself in the place of divine justice, or pretend to punish for the Almighty, who is himself all sufficient, who cannot receive impressions of pleasure or pain, and who alone, of all other beings, acts without being acted upon? The degree of sin depends on the malignity of the heart, which is impenetrable to finite beings. How then can the degree of sin serve as a standard to determine the degree of crimes? If that were admitted, men may punish when God pardons, and pardon when God condemns; and thus act in opposition to the Supreme Being.

## VIII  Of the division of crimes

We have proved, then, that crimes are to be estimated by *the injury done to society*. This is one of those palpable truths which though evident to the meanest capacity, yet by a combination of circumstances, are only known to a few thinking men in every nation, and in every age. But opinions, worthy only of the despotism of Asia, and passions, armed with power and authority, have, generally by insensible, and sometimes by violent impressions on the timid credulity of men, effaced those simple ideas which perhaps constituted the first philosophy of an infant society. Happily the philosophy of the present enlightened age seems again to conduct us to the same principles, and with that degree of certainty which is obtained by a rational examination and repeated experience.

A scrupulous adherence to order would require, that we should now examine and distinguish the different species of crimes and the modes of punishment; but they are so variable in their nature, from the different circumstances of ages and countries, that the detail would be tiresome and endless. It will be sufficient for my purpose to point out the most general principles, and the most common and dangerous errors, in order to undeceive as well those who, from a mistaken zeal for liberty, would introduce anarchy and confusion, as those who pretend to reduce society in general to the regularity of a covenant.

Some crimes are immediately destructive of society, or its representative; others attack the private security of the life, property, or honour of individuals; and a third class consists of such actions as are contrary to the laws which relate to the general good of the community.

The first, which are of the highest degree, as they are most destructive to society, are called crimes of *lese-majesty*.[1] Tyranny and ignorance, which have confounded the clearest terms and ideas, have given this appellation to crimes of a different nature, and consequently have established the same punishment for each; and, on this occasion, as on a thousand others, men have been sacrificed victims to a word. Every crime, even of the most private nature, injures society; but every crime does not threaten its immediate destruction. Moral as well as physical actions have their sphere of activity differently circumscribed, like all the movements of nature, by time and space; it is therefore a sophistical interpretation, the common philosophy of slaves, that would confound the limits of things established by eternal truth.

To these succeed crimes which are destructive of the security of individuals. This security being the principal end of all society, and to which every citizen hath an undoubted right, it becomes indispensably necessary, that to these crimes the greatest of punishments should be assigned.

The opinion, that every member of society has a right to do any thing that is not contrary to the laws, without fearing any other inconveniences than those which are the natural consequences of the action itself, is a political dogma, which should be defended by the laws, inculcated by the magistrates, and believed by the people; a sacred dogma, without which there can be no lawful society, a just recompense for our sacrifice of that universal liberty of action common to all sensible beings, and only limited by our natural powers. By this principle our minds become free, active, and vigorous; by this alone we are inspired with that virtue which knows no fear, so different from that pliant prudence, worthy of those only who can bear a precarious existence.

Attempts, therefore, against the life and liberty of a citizen are crimes of the highest nature. Under this head we comprehend not only assassinations and robberies committed by the populace, but by grandees and magistrates, whose example acts with more force, and at a greater distance destroying the ideas of justice and duty among the subjects, and substituting that of the right of the strongest, equally dangerous to those who exercise it and to those who suffer.

## IX  Of honour

There is a remarkable difference between the civil laws, those jealous guardians of life and property, and the laws of what is called *honour,* which particularly respects the opinion of others. Honour is a term which has been the foundation of many long and brilliant reasonings, without annexing to it any precise or fixed idea. How miserable is the condition of the human mind, to which the most distant and least essential matters, the revolutions of the heavenly bodies, are more distinctly known than the most inter-

---

[1] High treason.

esting truths of morality, which are always confused and fluctuating, as they happen to be driven by the gales of passion, or received and transmitted by ignorance! But this will cease to appear strange, if it be considered, that as objects, when too near the eye appear confused, so the too great vicinity of the ideas of morality is the reason why the simple ideas of which they are composed are easily confounded, but which must be separated before we can investigate the phenomena of human sensibility; and the intelligent observer of human nature will cease to be surprised, that so many ties, and such an apparatus of morality, are necessary to the security and happiness of mankind.

Honour, then, is one of those complex ideas which are an aggregate not only of simple ones, but of others so complicated, that, in their various modes of affecting the human mind, they sometimes admit and sometimes exclude part of the elements of which they are composed, retaining only some few of the most common, as many algebraic quantities admit one common divisor. To find this common divisor of the different ideas attached to the word honour, it will be necessary to go back to the original formation of society.

The first laws and the first magistrates owed their existence to the necessity of preventing the disorders which the natural despotism of individuals would unavoidably produce. This was the object of the establishment of society, and was, either in reality or in appearance, the principal design of all codes of laws, even the most pernicious. But the more intimate connexions of men, and the progress of their knowledge, gave rise to an infinite number of necessities and mutual acts of friendship between the members of society. These necessities were not foreseen by the laws, and could not be satisfied by the actual power of each individual. At this epoch began to be established the despotism of opinion, as being the only means of obtaining those benefits which the law could not procure, and of removing those evils

against which the laws were no security. It is opinion, that tormentor of the wise and the ignorant, that has exalted the appearance of virtue above virtue itself. Hence the esteem of men becomes not only useful but necessary to every one, to prevent his sinking below the common level. The ambitious man grasps at it, as being necessary to his designs; the vain man sues for it, as a testimony of his merit; the honest man demands it, as his due; and most men consider it as necessary to their existence.

Honour, being produced after the formation of society, could not be a part of the common deposit, and therefore, whilst we act under its influence, we return, for that instant, to a state of nature, and withdraw ourselves from the laws, which, in this case, are insufficient for our protection.

Hence it follows, that, in extreme political liberty, and in absolute despotism, all ideas of honour disappear, or are confounded with others. In the first case, reputation becomes useless from the despotism of the laws; and in the second, the despotism of one man, annulling all civil existence, reduces the rest to a precarious and temporary personality. Honour, then, is one of the fundamental principles of those monarchies which are a limited despotism; and in these, like revolutions in despotic states, it is a momentary return to state of nature and original equality.

## X   Of duelling

From the necessity of the esteem of others have arisen single combats, and they have been established by the anarchy of the laws. They are thought to have been unknown to the ancients, perhaps because they did not assemble in their temples, in their theatres, or with their friends, suspiciously armed with swords; and, perhaps, because single combats were a common spectacle, exhibited to the people by gladiators, who were slaves, and whom freemen disdained to imitate.

In vain have the laws endeavoured to abolish this custom by punishing the offenders with death. A man of honour, deprived of the esteem of others, foresees that he must be reduced either to a solitary existence, insupportable to a social creature, or become the object of perpetual insult; considerations sufficient to overcome the fear of death.

What is the reason that duels are not so frequent among the common people as amongst the great? not only because they do not wear swords, but because to men of that class reputation is of less importance than it is to those of a higher rank, who commonly regard each other with distrust and jealousy.

It may not be without its use to repeat here what has been mentioned by other writers, viz. that the best method of preventing this crime is to punish the aggressor, that is, the person who gave occasion to the duel, and to acquit him who, without any fault on his side, is obliged to defend that which is not sufficiently secured to him by the laws.

## XI   Of crimes which disturb the public tranquillity

Another class of crimes are those which disturb the public tranquillity and the quiet of the citizens; such as tumults and riots in the public streets, which are intended for commerce and the passage of the inhabitants; the discourses of fanatics, which rouse the passions of the curious multitude, and gain strength from the number of their hearers, who, though deaf to calm and solid reasoning, are always affected by obscure and mysterious enthusiasm.

The illumination of the streets during the night at the public expense, guards stationed in different quarters of the city, the plain and moral discourses of religion reserved for the silence and tranquillity of churches, and protected by authority, and harangues in support of the interest of the public, delivered only at the general meetings of the nation, in parliament, or where the sovereign resides, are all means to prevent the dangerous effects of the misguided passions of the people. These should be the principal objects of the vigilance of a magistrate, and which the French call *police;* but if this magistrate should act in an arbitrary manner, and not in conformity to the code of laws, which ought to be in the hands of every member of the community, he opens a door to tyranny, which always surrounds the confines of political liberty.

I do not know of any exception to this general axiom, that *Every member of society should know when he is criminal and when innocent.* If censors, and, in general, arbitrary magistrates, be necessary in any government, it proceeds from some fault in the constitution. The uncertainty of crimes hath sacrificed more victims to secret tyranny than have ever suffered by public and solemn cruelty.

What are, in general, the proper punishments for crimes? Is the punishment of death really *useful,* or necessary for the safety or good order of society? Are tortures and torments consistent with *justice,* or do they answer the *end* proposed by the laws? Which is the best method of preventing crimes? Are the same punishments equally useful at all times? What influence have they on manners? These problems should be solved with that geometrical precision, which the mist of sophistry, the seduction of eloquence, and the timidity of doubt, are unable to resist.

If I have no other merit than that of having first presented to my country, with a greater degree of evidence, what other nations have written and are beginning to practise, I shall account myself fortunate; but if, by supporting the rights of mankind and of invincible truth, I shall contribute to save from the agonies of death one unfortunate victim of tyranny, or of ignorance, equally fatal, his blessing and tears of transport will be a sufficient consolation to me for the contempt of all mankind.

## XII    Of the intent of punishments

From the foregoing considerations it is evident that the intent of punishments is not to torment a sensible being, nor to undo a crime already committed. Is it possible that torments and useless cruelty, the instrument of furious fanaticism or the impotency of tyrants, can be authorised by a political body, which, so far from being influenced by passion, should be the cool moderator of the passions of individuals? Can the groans of a tortured wretch recall the time past, or reverse the crime he has committed?

The end of punishment, therefore, is no other than to prevent the criminal from doing further injury to society, and to prevent others from committing the like offence. Such punishments, therefore, and such a mode of inflicting them, ought to be chosen, as will make the strongest and most lasting impressions on the minds of others, with the least torment to the body of the criminal.

## XIII    Of the credibility of witnesses

To determine exactly the credibility of a witness, and the force of evidence, is an important point in every good legislation. Every man of common sense, that is, every one whose ideas have some connection with each other, and whose sensations are conformable to those of other men, may be a witness; but the credibility of his evidence will be in proportion as he is interested in declaring or concealing the truth. Hence it appears how frivolous is the reasoning of those who reject the testimony of women, on account of their weakness; how puerile it is not to admit the evidence of those who are under sentence of death, because they are dead in law; and how irrational to exclude

persons branded with infamy; for in all these cases they ought to be credited, when they have no interest in giving false testimony.

The credibility of a witness, then, should only diminish in proportion to the hatred, friendship, or connections, subsisting between him and the delinquent. One witness is not sufficient for, whilst the accused denies what the other affirms, truth remains suspended, and the right that every one has to be believed innocent turns the balance in his favour.

The credibility of a witness is the less as the atrociousness of the crime is greater, from the improbability of its having been committed; as in cases of witchcraft, and acts of wanton cruelty. The writers on penal laws have adopted a contrary principle, viz. that the credibility of a witness is greater as the crime is more atrocious. Behold their inhuman maxim, dictated by the most cruel imbecility. *In atrocissimis, leviores conjecturæ sufficiunt, et licit judici jura transgredi.* Let us translate this sentence, that mankind may see one of the many unreasonable principles to which they are ignorantly subject. *In the most atrocious crimes, the slightest conjectures are sufficient, and the judge is allowed to exceed the limits of the law.* The absurd practices of legislators are often the effect of timidity, which is a principal source of the contradictions of mankind. The legislators (or rather lawyers, whose opinions when alive were interested and venal, but which after their death become of decisive authority, and are the sovereign arbiters of the lives and fortunes of men), terrified by the condemnation of some innocent person, have burdened the law with pompous and useless formalities, the scrupulous observance of which will place anarchical impunity on the throne of justice; at other times, perplexed by atrocious crimes of difficult proof, they imagined themselves under a necessity of superseding the very formalities established by themselves; and thus, at one time with despotic impatience, and at another with feminine timidity, they transform their solemn judgments into a game of hazard.

But, to return: in the case of witchcraft, it is much more probable that a number of men should be deceived than that any person should exercise a power which God hath refused to every created being. In like manner, in cases of wanton cruelty, the presumption is always against the accuser; for no man is cruel without some interest, without some motive of fear or hate. There are no spontaneous or superfluous sentiments in the heart of man; they are all the result of impressions on the senses.

The credibility of a witness may also be diminished by his being a member of a private society, whose customs and principles of conduct are either not known or are different from those of the public. Such a man has not only his own passions, but those of the society of which he is a member.

Finally, the credibility of a witness is null when the question relates to the words of a criminal; for the tone of voice, the gesture, all that precedes, accompanies, and follows the different ideas which men annex to the same words, may so alter and modify a man's discourse, that it is almost impossible to repeat them precisely in the manner in which they were spoken. Besides, violent and uncommon actions, such as real crimes, leave a trace in the multitude of circumstances that attend them, and in their effects; but words remain only in the memory of the hearers, who are commonly negligent or prejudiced. It is infinitely easier, then, to found an accusation on the words than on the actions of a man; for in these the number of circumstances urged against the accused afford him variety of means of justification.

## XIV   Of evidence and the proofs of a crime, and of the form of judgment

The following general theorem is of great use in determining the certainty of a fact.

When the proofs of a crime are dependent on each other, that is, when the evidence of each witness, taken separately, proves nothing, or when all the proofs are dependent upon one, the number of proofs neither increase nor diminish the probability of the fact; for the force of the whole is no greater than the force of that on which they depend, and if this fails, they all fall to the ground. When the proofs are independent on each other, the probability of the fact increases in proportion to the number of proofs; for the falsehood of the one does not diminish the veracity of another.

It may seem extraordinary that I speak of probability with regard to crimes, which to deserve a punishment, must be certain. But this paradox will vanish when it is considered, that, strictly speaking, moral certainty is only probability, but which is called a certainty, because every man in his senses assents to it from an habit produced by the necessity of acting, and which is anterior to all speculation. That certainty which is necessary to decide that the accused is guilty is the very same which determines every man in the most important transactions of his life.

The proofs of a crime may be divided into two classes, perfect and imperfect. I call those perfect which exclude the possibility of innocence; imperfect, those which do not exclude this possibility. Of the first, one only is sufficient for condemnation; of the second, as many are required as form a perfect proof; that is to say, that though each of these, separately taken, does not exclude the possibility of innocence, it is nevertheless excluded by their union. It should be also observed, that the imperfect proofs, of which the accused, if innocent, might clear himself, and does not, become perfect.

But it is much easier to feel this moral certainty of proofs than to define it exactly. For this reason, I think it an excellent law which establishes assistants to the principal judge, and those chosen by lot; for that ignorance which judges by its feelings is less subject to error than the knowledge or the laws which judges by opinion. Where the laws are clear and precise, the office of the judge is merely to ascertain the fact. If, in examining the proofs of a crime, acuteness and dexterity be required, if clearness and precision be necessary in summoning up the result, to judge of the result itself nothing is wanting but plain and ordinary good sense, a less fallacious guide than the knowledge, of a judge, accustomed to find guilty, and to reduce all things to an artificial system borrowed from his studies. Happy the nation where the knowledge of the law is not a science!

It is an admirable law which ordains that every man shall be tried by his peers; for, when life, liberty and fortune, are in question, the sentiments which a difference of rank and fortune inspires should be silent; that superiority with which the fortunate look upon the unfortunate, and that envy with which the inferior regard their superiors, should have no influence. But when the crime is an offence against a fellow-subject, one half of the judges should be peers to the accused, and the other peers to the person offended: so that all private interest, which, in spite of ourselves, modifies the appearance of objects, even in the eyes of the most equitable, is counteracted, and nothing remains to turn aside the direction of truth and the laws. It is also just that the accused should have the liberty of excluding a certain number of his judges; where this liberty is enjoyed for a long time, without any instance to the contrary, the criminal seems to condemn himself.

All trials should be public, that opinion, which is the best, or perhaps the only cement of society, may curb the authority of the powerful, and the passions of the judge, and that the people may say, "We are protected by the laws; we are not slaves," a sentiment which inspires courage, and which is the best tribute to a sovereign who knows his real interest. I shall not enter into particulars. There may be some persons who expect that I should say all that can

be said upon this subject; to such what I have already written must be unintelligible.

## XV   Of secret accusations

Secret accusations are a manifest abuse, but consecrated by custom in many nations, where, from the weakness of the government, they are necessary. This custom makes men false and treacherous. Whoever suspects another to be an informer, beholds in him an enemy; and from thence mankind are accustomed to disguise their real sentiments; and, from the habit of concealing them from others, they at last even hide them from themselves. Unhappy are those who have arrived at this point! without any certain and fixed principles to guide them, they fluctuate in the vast sea of opinion, and are busied only in escaping the monsters which surround them: to those the present is always embittered by the uncertainty of the future; deprived of the pleasures of tranquillity and security, some fleeting moments of happiness, scattered thinly through their wretched lives, console them for the misery of existing. Shall we, amongst such men, find intrepid soldiers, to defend their king and country? Amongst such men shall we find incorruptible magistrates, who, with the spirit of freedom and patriotic eloquence, will support and explain the true interest of their sovereign; who, with the tributes, offer up at the throne the love and blessing of the people, and thus bestow on the palaces of the great and the humble cottage peace and security, and to the industrious a prospect of bettering their lot—that useful ferment and vital principle of states?

Who can defend himself from calumny, armed with that impenetrable shield of tyranny, secrecy? What a miserable government must that be where the sovereign suspects an enemy in every subject, and, to secure the tranquillity of the public, is obliged to sacrifice the repose of every individual.

By what argument is it pretended that *secret accusations* may be justified? The public safety, say they, and the security and maintenance of the established form of government. But what a strange constitution is that where the government, which hath in its favour not only power, but opinion, still more efficacious, yet fears its own subjects? *The indemnity of the informer;* do not the laws defend him sufficiently? and are there subjects more powerful than the laws? *The necessity of protecting the informer from infamy;* then secret calumny is authorised, and punished only when public. *The nature of the crime;* if actions, indifferent in themselves, or even useful to the public, were called crimes, both the accusation and the trial could never be too secret. But can there be any crime committed against the public which ought not to be publicly punished? I respect all governments; and I speak not of any one in particular. Such may sometimes be the nature of circumstances, that, when abuses are inherent in the constitution, it may be imagined, that to rectify them would be to destroy the constitution itself. But, were I to dictate new laws in a remote corner of the universe, the good of posterity, ever present to my mind, would hold back my trembling hand, and prevent me from authorising *secret accusations.*

Public accusations, says Montesquieu, are more conformable to the nature of a republic, where zeal for the public good is the principal passion of a citizen, than of a monarchy, in which, as this sentiment is very feeble, from the nature of the government, the best establishment is that of *commissioners,* who, in the name of the public, accuse the infractors of the laws. But in all governments, as well in a republic as in a monarchy, the punishment due to the crime of which one accuses another ought to be inflicted on the informer.*

## XVI  Of torture

The torture of a criminal during the course of his trial is a cruelty consecrated by custom in most nations. It is used with an intent either to make him confess his crime, or to explain some contradictions into which he had been led during his examination, or discover his accomplices, or for some kind of metaphysical and incomprehensible purgation of infamy, or, finally, in order to discover other crimes of which he is not accused, but of which he may be guilty.

No man can be judged a criminal until he be found guilty; nor can society take from him the public protection until it have been proved that he has violated the conditions on which it was granted. What right, then, but that of power, can authorise the punishment of a citizen so long as there remains any doubt of his guilt? This dilemma is frequent. Either he is guilty, or not guilty. If guilty, he should only suffer the punishment ordained by the laws, and torture becomes useless, as his confession is unnecessary. If he be not guilty, you torture the innocent; for, in the eye of the law, every man is innocent whose crime has not been proved. Besides, it is confounding all relations to expect that a man should be both the accuser and accused; and that pain should be the test of truth, as if truth resided in the muscles and fibres of a wretch in torture. By this method the robust will escape, and the feeble be condemned. These are the inconveniences of this pretended test of truth, worthy only of a cannibal, and which the Romans, in many respects barbarous, and whose savage virtue has been too much admired, reserved for the slaves alone.

What is the political intention of punishments? To terrify and be an example to others. Is this intention answered by thus privately torturing the guilty and the innocent? It is doubtless of importance that no crime should remain unpunished; but it is useless to make a public example of the author of a crime hid in darkness. A crime already committed, and for which there can be no remedy, can only be punished by a political society with an intention that no

---

* Cf. *GBWW,* Vol. 38, p. 37c.

hopes of impunity should induce others to commit the same. If it be true, that the number of those who from fear or virtue respect the laws is greater than of those by whom they are violated, the risk of torturing an innocent person is greater, as there is a greater probability that, *cæteris paribus* [other things being equal], an individual hath observed, than that he hath infringed the laws.

There is another ridiculous motive for torture, namely, *to purge a man from infamy*. Ought such an abuse to be tolerated in the eighteenth century? Can pain, which is a sensation, have any connection with a moral sentiment, a matter of opinion? Perhaps the rack may be considered as the refiner's furnace.

It is not difficult to trace this senseless law to its origin; for an absurdity, adopted by a whole nation, must have some affinity with other ideas established and respected by the same nation. This custom seems to be the offspring of religion, by which mankind, in all nations and in all ages, are so generally influenced. We are taught by our infallible church, that those stains of sin contracted through human frailty, and which have not deserved the eternal anger of the Almighty, are to be purged away in another life by an incomprehensible fire. Now infamy is a stain, and if the punishments and fire of purgatory can take away all spiritual stains, why should not the pain of torture take away those of a civil nature? I imagine, that the confession of a criminal, which in some tribunals is required as being essential to his condemnation, has a similar origin, and has been taken from the mysterious tribunal of penitence, where the confession of sins is a necessary part of the sacrament. Thus have men abused the unerring light of revelation; and, in the times of tractable ignorance, having no other, they naturally had recourse to it on every occasion, making the most remote and absurd applications. Moreover, infamy is a sentiment regulated neither by the laws nor by reason, but entirely by opinion; but torture renders the victim infamous, and therefore cannot take infamy away.

Another intention of torture is to oblige the supposed criminal to reconcile the contradictions into which he may have fallen during his examination; as if the dread of punishment, the uncertainty of his fate, the solemnity of the court, the majesty of the judge, and the ignorance of the accused, were not abundantly sufficient to account for contradictions, which are so common to men even in a state of tranquillity, and which must necessarily be multiplied by the perturbation of the mind of a man entirely engaged in the thoughts of saving himself from imminent danger.

This infamous test of truth is a remaining monument of that ancient and savage legislation, in which trials by fire, by boiling water, or the uncertainty of combats, were called *judgments of God;* as if the links of that eternal chain, whose beginning is in the breast of the first cause of all things, could ever be disunited by the institutions of men. The only difference between torture and trials by fire and boiling water is, that the event of the first depends on the will of the accused, and of the second on a fact entirely physical and external: but this difference is apparent only, not real. A man on the rack, in the convulsions of torture, has it as little in his power to declare the truth, as, in former times, to prevent without fraud the effects of fire or boiling water.

Every act of the will is invariably in proportion to the force of the impression on our senses. The impression of pain, then, may increase to such a degree, that, occupying the mind entirely, it will compel the sufferer to use the shortest method of freeing himself from torment. His answer, therefore, will be an effect as necessary as that of fire or boiling water, and he will accuse himself of crimes of which he is innocent: so that the very means employed to distinguish the innocent from the guilty will most effectually destroy all difference between them.

It would be superfluous to confirm these

reflections by examples of innocent persons who, from the agony of torture, have confessed themselves guilty: innumerable instances may be found in all nations, and in every age. How amazing that mankind have always neglected to draw the natural conclusion! Lives there a man who, if he has carried his thoughts ever so little beyond the necessities of life, when he reflects on such cruelty, is not tempted to fly from society, and return to his natural state of independence?

The result of torture, then, is a matter of calculation, and depends on the constitution, which differs in every individual, and it is in proportion to his strength and sensibility; so that to discover truth by this method, is a problem which may be better solved by a mathematician than by a judge, and may be thus stated: *The force of the muscles and the sensibility of the nerves of an innocent person being given, it is required to find the degree of pain necessary to make him confess himself guilty of a given crime.*

The examination of the accused is intended to find out the truth; but if this be discovered with so much difficulty in the air, gesture, and countenance of a man at ease, how can it appear in a countenance distorted by the convulsions of torture? Every violent action destroys those small alterations in the features which sometimes disclose the sentiments of the heart.

These truths were known to the Roman legislators, amongst whom, as I have already observed, slaves only, who were not considered as citizens, were tortured. They are known to the English, a nation in which the progress of science, superiority in commerce, riches, and power, its natural consequences, together with the numerous examples of virtue and courage, leave no doubt of the excellence of its laws. They have been acknowledged in Sweden, where torture has been abolished. They are known to one of the wisest monarchs in Europe, who, having seated philosophy on the throne by his beneficent legislation, has made his subjects free, though dependent on the laws; the only freedom that reasonable men can desire in the present state of things. In short, torture has not been thought necessary in the laws of armies, composed chiefly of the dregs of mankind, where its use should seem most necessary. Strange phenomenon! that a set of men, hardened by slaughter, and familiar with blood, should teach humanity to the sons of peace.

It appears also that these truths were known, though imperfectly, even to those by whom torture has been most frequently practised; for a confession made during torture, is null, if it be not afterwards confirmed by an oath, which if the criminal refuses, he is tortured again. Some civilians and some nations permit this infamous *petitio principii* to be only three times repeated, and others leave it to the discretion of the judge; therefore, of two men equally innocent, or equally guilty, the most robust and resolute will be acquitted, and the weakest and most pusillanimous will be condemned, in consequence of the following excellent mode of reasoning. *I, the judge, must find some one guilty. Thou, who art a strong fellow, hast been able to resist the force of torment; therefore I acquit thee. Thou, being weaker, hast yielded to it; I therefore condemn thee. I am sensible, that the confession which was extorted from thee has no weight; but if thou dost not confirm by oath what thou hast already confessed, I will have thee tormented again.*

A very strange but necessary consequence of the use of torture is, that the case of the innocent is worse than that of the guilty. With regard to the first, either he confesses the crime which he has not committed, and is condemned, or he is acquitted, and has suffered a punishment he did not deserve. On the contrary, the person who is really guilty has the most favourable side of the question; for, if he supports the torture with firmness and resolution, he is acquitted, and has gained, having exchanged a greater punishment for a less.

The law by which torture is authorised, says, *Men, be insensible to pain. Nature has indeed given you an irresistible self-love, and an unalienable right of self-preservation; but I create in you a contrary sentiment, an heroical hatred of yourselves. I command you to accuse yourselves, and to declare the truth, amidst the tearing of your flesh and the dislocation of your bones.*

Torture is used to discover whether the criminal be guilty of other crimes besides those of which he is accused, which is equivalent to the following reasoning. *Thou art guilty of one crime, therefore it is possible that thou mayest have committed a thousand others; but the affair being doubtful I must try it by my criterion of truth. The laws order thee to be tormented because thou art guilty, because thou mayest be guilty, and because I choose thou shouldst be guilty.*

Torture is used to make the criminal discover his accomplices; but if it has been demonstrated that it is not at a proper means of discovering truth, how can it serve to discover the accomplices, which is one of the truths required? Will not the man who accuses himself yet more readily accuse others? Besides, is it just to torment one man for the crime of another? May not the accomplices be found out by the examination of the witnesses, or of the criminal; from the evidence, or from the nature of the crime itself; in short, by all the means that have been used to prove the guilt of the prisoner? The accomplices commonly fly when their comrade is taken. The uncertainty of their fate condemns them to perpetual exile, and frees society from the danger of further injury; whilst the punishment of the criminal, by deterring others, answers the purpose for which it was ordained.

## XVII  Of pecuniary punishments

There was a time when all punishments were pecuniary. The crimes of the subjects were the inheritance of the prince. An in-

jury done to society was a favour to the crown; and the sovereign and magistrates, those guardians of the public security, were interested in the violation of the laws. Crimes were tried, at that time, in a court of exchequer, and the cause became a civil suit between the person accused and the crown. The magistrate then had other powers than were necessary for the public welfare, and the criminal suffered other punishments than the necessity of example required. The judge was rather a collector for the crown, an agent for the treasury, than a protector and minister of the laws. But according to this system, for a man to confess himself guilty was to acknowledge himself a debtor to the crown; which was, and is at present (the effects continuing after the causes have ceased) the intent of all criminal causes. Thus, the criminal who refuses to confess his crime, though convicted by the most undoubted proofs, will suffer a less punishment than if he had confessed; and he will not be put to the torture to oblige him to confess other crimes which he might have committed, as he has not confessed the principal. But the confession being once obtained, the judge becomes master of his body, and torments him with a studied formality, in order to squeeze out of him all the profit possible. Confession, then, is allowed to be a convincing proof, especially when obtained by the force of torture; at the same time that an extrajudicial confession, when a man is at ease and under no apprehension, is not sufficient for his condemnation.

All inquiries which may serve to clear up the fact, but which may weaken the pretensions of the crown, are excluded. It was not from compassion to the criminal, or from considerations of humanity, that torments were sometimes spared, but out of fear of losing those rights which at present appear chimerical and inconceivable. The judge becomes an enemy to the accused, to a wretch a prey to the horrors of a dungeon, to torture, to death, and an uncertain futurity, more terrible than all; he inquires not into the truth of the fact, but the nature of the crime; he lays snares to make him convict himself; he fears lest he should not succeed in finding him guilty, and lest that infallibility which every man arrogates to himself should be called in question. It is in the power of the magistrate to determine what evidence is sufficient to send a man to prison; that he may be proved innocent, he must first be supposed guilty. This is what is called an *offensive* prosecution; and such are all criminal proceedings in the eighteenth century, in all parts of our polished Europe. The true prosecution, *for information,* that is, an impartial inquiry into the fact, that which reason prescribes, which military laws adopt, and which Asiatic despotism allows in suits of one subject against another, is very little practised in any courts of justice. What a labyrinth of absurdities! Absurdities which will appear incredible to happier posterity. The philosopher only will be able to read, in the nature of man, the possibility of there ever having been such a system.

## XVIII   Of oaths

There is a palpable contradiction between the laws and the natural sentiments of mankind in the case of *oaths,* which are administered to a criminal to make him speak the truth, when the contrary is his greatest interest; as if a man could think himself obliged to contribute to his own destruction, and as if, when interest speaks, religion was not generally silent, religion, which in all ages hath, of all other things, been most commonly abused: and indeed, upon what motive should it be respected by the wicked, when it has been thus violated by those who were esteemed the wisest of men? The motives which religion opposes to the fear of impending evil and the love of life are too weak, as they are too distant, to make any impression on the senses. The affairs of the other world are regulated by laws entirely different from those by which human affairs

are directed; why then should you endeavour to compromise matters between them? Why should a man be reduced to the terrible alternative, either of offending God, or of contributing to his own immediate destruction? The laws which require an oath in such a case leave him only the choice of becoming a bad Christian or a martyr. For this reason, oaths become, by degrees, a mere formality, and all sentiments of religion, perhaps the only motive of honesty in the greatest part of mankind, are destroyed. Experience proves their inutility: I appeal to every judge, whether he has ever known that an oath alone has brought truth from the lips of a criminal; and reason tells us, it must be so; for all laws are useless, and in consequence destructive, which contradict the natural feelings of mankind. Such laws are like a dike, opposed directly to the course of a torrent; it is either immediately overwhelmed, or, by a whirlpool formed by itself, it is gradually undermined and destroyed.

## XIX   Of the advantage
## of immediate punishment

The more immediately after the commission of a crime a punishment is inflicted, the more just and useful it will be. It will be more just, because it spares the criminal the cruel and superfluous torment of uncertainty, which increases in proportion to the strength of his imagination and the sense of his weakness; and because the privation of liberty, being a punishment, ought to be inflicted before condemnation but for as short a time as possible. Imprisonment, I say, being only the means of securing the person of the accused until he be tried, condemned, or acquitted, ought not only to be of as short duration, but attended with as little severity as possible. The time should be determined by the necessary preparation for the trial, and the right of priority in the oldest prisoners. The confinement ought not be closer than is requisite to prevent his flight, or his concealing the proofs of the crime; and the trial should be conducted with all possible expedition. Can there be a more cruel contrast than that between the indolence of a judge and the painful anxiety of the accused; the comforts and pleasures of an insensible magistrate, and the filth and misery of the prisoner? In general, as I have before observed, *The degree of the punishment, and the consequences of a crime, ought to be so contrived as to have the greatest possible effect on others, with the least possible pain to the delinquent.* If there be any society in which this is not a fundamental principle, it is an unlawful society; for mankind, by their union, originally intended to subject themselves to the least evils possible.

An immediate punishment is more useful; because the smaller the interval of time between the punishment and the crime, the stronger and more lasting will be the association of the two ideas of *crime* and *punishment;* so that they may be considered, one as the cause, and the other as the unavoidable and necessary effect. It is demonstrated, that the association of ideas is the cement which unites the fabric of the human intellect, without which pleasure and pain would be simple and ineffectual sensations. The vulgar, that is, all men who have no general ideas or universal principles, act in consequence of the most immediate and familiar associations; but the more remote and complex only present themselves to the minds of those who are passionately attached to a single object, or to those of greater understanding, who have acquired an habit of rapidly comparing together a number of objects, and of forming a conclusion; and the result, that is, the action in consequence, by these means becomes less dangerous and uncertain.

It is, then, of the greatest importance that the punishment should succeed the crime as immediately as possible, if we intend that, in the rude minds of the multitude, the seducing picture of the advantage arising from the crime should instantly awake the attendant idea of punishment. Delaying the punishment serves only to separate these two ideas, and thus affects the minds of the spectators rather as being a terrible sight than the necessary consequence of a crime, the horror of which should contribute to heighten the idea of the punishment.

There is another excellent method of strengthening this important connection between the ideas of crime and punishment; that is, to make the punishment as analogous as possible to the nature of the crime, in order that the punishment may lead the mind to consider the crime in a different point of view from that in which it was placed by the flattering idea of promised advantages.

Crimes of less importance are commonly punished either in the obscurity of a prison, or the criminal is *transported,* to give by his slavery an example to societies which he never offended; an example absolutely useless, because distant from the place where the crime was committed. Men do not, in general, commit great crimes deliberately, but rather in a sudden gust of passion; and they commonly look on the punishment due to a great crime as remote and improbable. The public punishment, therefore, of small crimes will make a greater impression, and, by deterring men from the smaller, will effectually prevent the greater.

## XX  Of acts of violence

Some crimes relate to *person,* others to *property.* The first ought to be punished corporally. The great and rich should by no means have it in their power to set a price on the security of the weak and indigent; for then riches, which, under the protection of the laws, are the reward of industry, would become the aliment of tyranny. Liberty is at an end whenever the laws permit that, in certain cases, a man may cease to be *a person,* and become *a thing.* Then will the powerful employ their address to select from the various combinations of civil society all

Torture was used in the courtroom to extract evidence and confessions, "as if truth resided in the muscles and fibres" of the accused. In this 16th-century courtroom, the prisoner is suspended by his arms and legs while water is poured into his mouth through a piece of cloth

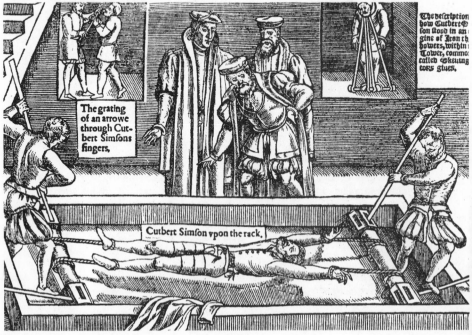

The grating of an arrowe through Cutbert Simsons fingers,

The description how Cutbert Simson stood in an engine of Iron the Towers, within the Tower, commonly called Skeuingtors gives.

Cutbert Simson vpon the rack.

Judicial torture was adapted from the Roman Code and practiced in both civil and ecclesiastical courts. The prisoner was interrogated, and if he refused to testify or admit guilt he was subjected to the pulley, the rack, *peine forte et dure* (pressing by weights), or fire

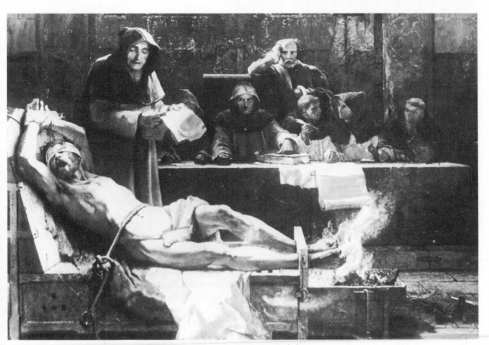

Torture on the rack is shown in the background of this 15th-century French tapestry (above). Methods of capital punishment included crushing the prisoner with a wheel (or tying the prisoner to a flat wheel and beating him), boiling in oil, and burning or "roasting" alive (opposite, top left). Agonizing death as a punishment for religious "crimes" such as heresy was recorded as late as the 18th century in Europe

Torture often preceded the execution of condemned men. François Robert Damiens, who had tried to assassinate Louis XV of France, was tormented in the "boots" before being drawn and quartered

Minor offenders were often punished by means that exposed them to public humiliation. These included forced labor such as street cleaning, and confinement to the pillory. In 1732 an English robber, locked in a pillory, was stoned to death by a crowd

Methods of torture were continually refined in Europe. Some of the most excruciating were the slicing off of fingers and toes, one at a time (opposite top), the flaying of bound prisoners, sawing prisoners in half, or enclosing them in the ''Iron Maiden,'' a coffinlike device, the interior of which was studded with knives

that is in their own favour. This is that magic art which transforms subjects into beasts of burden, and which, in the hands of the strong, is the chain that binds the weak and incautious. Thus it is that in some governments, where there is all the appearance of Liberty, tyranny lies concealed, and insinuates itself into some neglected corner of the constitution, where it gathers strength insensibly. Mankind generally oppose, with resolution, the assaults of barefaced and open tyranny, but disregard the little insect that gnaws through the dike, and opens a sure though secret passage to inundation.

## XXI   Of the punishment of the nobles

What punishments shall be ordained for the nobles, whose privileges make so great a part of the laws of nations? I do not mean to inquire whether the hereditary distinction between nobles and commoners be useful in any government, or necessary in a monarchy; or whether it be true that they form an intermediate power, of use in moderating the excess of both extremes; or whether they be not rather slaves to their own body, and to others, confining within a very small circle the natural effects and hopes of industry, like those little fruitful spots scattered here and there in the sandy deserts of Arabia; or whether it be true that a subordination of rank and condition is inevitable or useful in society; and, if so, whether this subordination should not rather subsist between individuals than particular bodies, whether it should not rather circulate through the whole body politic than be confined to one part, and, rather than be perpetual, should it not be incessantly produced and destroyed. Be these as they may, I assert that the punishment of a nobleman should in no wise differ from that of the lowest member of society.

Every lawful distinction, either in honours or riches, supposes previous equality, founded on the laws, on which all the members of society are considered as being equally dependent. We should suppose that men, in renouncing their natural despotism, said, *The wisest and most industrious among us should obtain the greatest honours, and his dignity shall descend to his posterity. The fortunate and happy may hope for greater honours, but let him not therefore be less afraid than others of violating those conditions on which he is exalted.* It is true indeed that no such degrees were ever made in a general diet of mankind, but they exist in the invariable relations of things; nor do they destroy the advantages which are supposed to be produced by the class of nobles, but prevent the inconveniences; and they make the laws respectable, by destroying all hopes of impunity.

It may be objected, that the same punishment inflicted on a nobleman and a plebeian becomes really different from the difference of their education, and from the infamy it reflects on an illustrious family: but I answer, that punishments are to be estimated, not by the sensibility of the criminal, but by the injury done to society, which injury is augmented by the high rank of the offender. The precise equality of a punishment can never be more than external, as it is in proportion to the degree of sensibility which differs in every individual. The infamy of an innocent family may be easily obliterated by some public demonstration of favour from the sovereign, and forms have always more influence than reason on the gazing multitude.

## XXII   Of robbery

The punishment of robbery, not accompanied with violence, should be pecuniary. He who endeavours to enrich himself with the property of another should be deprived of part of his own. But this crime, alas! is commonly the effect of misery and despair; the crime of that unhappy part of mankind to whom the right of exclusive property, a terrible and perhaps unnecessary right, has left but a bare existence. Besides, as pecuniary punishments may increase the number of robbers, by increasing the number of poor, and may deprive an innocent family of subsistence, the most proper punishment will be that kind of slavery which alone can be called just; that is, which makes the society, for a time, absolute master of the person and labour of the criminal, in order to oblige him to repair, by this dependence, the unjust despotism he usurped over the property of another, and his violation of the social compact.

When robbery is attended with violence, corporal punishment should be added to slavery. Many writers have shewn the evident disorder which must arise from not distinguishing the punishment due to robbery with violence, and that due to theft or robbery committed with dexterity, absurdly making a sum of money equivalent to a man's life. But it can never be superfluous to repeat, again and again, those truths of which mankind have not profited; for political machines preserve their motion much longer than others, and receive a new impulse with more difficulty. These crimes are in their nature absolutely different, and this axiom is as certain in politics as in mathematics, that between qualities of different natures there can be no similitude.

## XXIII  Of infamy, considered as a punishment

Those injuries which affect the honour, that is, that just portion of esteem which every citizen has a right to expect from others, should be punished with infamy. Infamy is a mark of the public disapprobation, which deprives the object of all consideration in the eyes of his fellow-citizens, of the confidence of his country, and of that fraternity which exists between members of the same society. This is not always in the power of the laws. It is necessary that the infamy inflicted by the laws should be the same with

that which results from the relations of things, from universal morality, or from that particular system, adopted by the nation and the laws, which governs the opinion of the vulgar. If, on the contrary, one be different from the other, either the laws will no longer be respected, or the received notions of morality and probity will vanish, in spite of the declamations of moralists, which are always too weak to resist the force of example. If we declare those actions infamous which are in themselves indifferent, we lessen the infamy of those which are really infamous.

The punishment of infamy should not be too frequent, for the power of opinion grows weaker by repetition; nor should it be inflicted on a number of persons at the same time, for the infamy of many resolves itself into the infamy of none.

Painful and corporal punishments should never be applied to fanaticism; for, being founded on pride, it glories in persecution. Infamy and ridicule only should be employed against fanatics: if the first, their pride will be overbalanced by the pride of the people; and we may judge of the power of the second, if we consider that even truth is obliged to summon all her force when attacked by error armed with ridicule. Thus, by opposing one passion to another, and opinion to opinion, a wise legislator puts an end to the admiration of the populace occasioned by a false principle, the original absurdity of which is veiled by some well deduced consequences.

This is the method to avoid confounding the immutable relations of things, or opposing nature, whose actions, not being limited by time, but operating incessantly, overturn and destroy all those vain regulations which contradict her laws. It is not only in the fine arts that the imitation of nature is the fundamental principle; it is the same in sound policy, which is no other than the art of uniting and directing to the same end the natural and immutable sentiments of mankind.

## XXIV   Of idleness

A wise government will not suffer in the midst of labour and industry, that kind of political idleness which is confounded by rigid declaimers with the leisure attending riches acquired by industry, which is of use to an increasing society when confined within proper limits. I call those politically idle, who neither contribute to the good of society by their labour nor their riches; who continually accumulate, but never spend; who are reverenced by the vulgar with stupid admiration, and regarded by the wise with disdain; who, being victims to a monastic life, and deprived of all incitement to that activity which is necessary to preserve or increase its comforts, devote all their vigour to passions of the strongest kind, the passions of opinion. I call not him idle who enjoys the fruits of the virtues or vices of his ancestors, and, in exchange for his pleasures, supports the industrious poor. It is not then the narrow virtue of austere moralists, but the laws, that should determine what species of idleness deserves punishment.

## XXV   Of banishment and confiscation

He who disturbs the public tranquillity, who does not obey the laws, who violates the conditions on which men mutually support and defend each other, ought to be excluded from society, that is, banished.

It seems as if banishment should be the punishment of those who, being accused of an atrocious crime, are probably, but not certainly, guilty. For this purpose would be required a law the least arbitrary and the most precise possible; which should condemn to banishment those who have reduced the community to the fatal alternative either of fearing or punishing them unjustly, still, however, leaving them the sacred right of proving their innocence. The reasons ought to be stronger for banishing a citizen than a stranger, and for the first accusation than for one who hath been often accused.

Should the person who is excluded for ever from society be deprived of his property? This question may be considered in different lights. The confiscation of effects, added to banishment is a greater punishment than banishment alone; there ought then to be some cases, in which, according to the crime, either the whole fortune should be confiscated, or part only, or none at all. The whole should be forfeited, when the law which ordains banishment declares, at the same time, that all connections or relations between the society and the criminal are annihilated. In this case the citizen dies; the man only remains, and, with respect to a political body, the death of the *citizen* should have the same consequences with the death of the *man*. It seems to follow then, that in this case, the effects of the criminal should devolve to his lawful heirs. But it is not on account of this refinement that I disapprove of confiscations. If some have insisted, that they were a restraint to vengeance and the violence of particulars, they have not reflected, that, though punishments be productive of good, they are not, on that account, more just; to be just, they must be necessary. Even an useful injustice can never be allowed by a legislator, who means to guard against watchful tyranny, which, under the flattering pretext of momentary advantages, would establish permanent principles of destruction, and, to procure the ease of a few in a high station, would draw tears from thousands of the poor.

The law which ordains confiscations sets a price on the head of the subject, with the guilty punishes the innocent, and, by reducing them to indigence and despair, tempts them to become criminal. Can there be a more melancholy spectacle than a whole family overwhelmed with infamy and misery from the crime of their chief? a crime, which, if it had been possible, they were restrained from preventing, by that submission which the laws themselves have ordained.

## XXVI   Of the spirit of family in states

It is remarkable, that many fatal acts of injustice have been authorised and approved, even by the wisest and most experienced men, in the freest republics. This has been owing to their having considered the state rather as a society of *families* than of *men*. Let us suppose a nation composed of an hundred thousand men, divided into twenty thousand families of five persons each, including the head or master of the family, its representative. If it be an association of *families,* there will be twenty thousand men, and eighty thousand slaves; or if of *men,* there will be an hundred thousand citizens, and not one slave. In the first case we behold a republic, and twenty thousand little monarchies, of which the heads are the sovereigns: in the second the spirit of liberty will not only breathe in every public place of the city, and in the assemblies of the nation, but in private houses, where men find the greatest part of their happiness or misery. As laws and customs are always the effect of the habitual sentiments of the members of a republic, if the society be an association of the heads of families, the spirit of monarchy will gradually make its way into the republic itself, as its effects will only be restrained by the opposite interests of each, and not by an universal spirit of liberty and equality. The private spirit of family is a spirit of minuteness, and confined to little concerns. Public spirit, on the contrary, is influenced by general principles, and from facts deduces general rules of utility to the greatest number.

In a republic of families, the children remain under the authority of the father as long as he lives, and are obliged to wait until his death for an existence dependent on the laws alone. Accustomed to kneel and tremble in their tender years, when their natural sentiments were less restrained by that caution, obtained by experience, which is called moderation, how should they resist those obstacles which vice always opposes to virtue in the languor and decline of age, when the despair of reaping the fruits is alone sufficient to damp the vigour of their resolutions?

In a republic, where every man is a citizen, family-subordination is not the effect of compulsion, but of contract; and the sons, disengaged from the natural dependence which the weakness of infancy and the necessity of education required, become free members of society, but remain subject to the head of the family for their own advantage, as in the great society.

In a republic of families, the young people, that is, the most numerous and most useful part of the nation, are at the discretion of their fathers: in a republic of men, they are attached to their parents by no other obligation than that sacred and inviolable one of mutual assistance, and of gratitude for the benefits they have received; a sentiment destroyed not so much by the wickedness of the human heart, as by a mistaken subjection prescribed by the laws.

These contradictions between the laws of families and the fundamental laws of a state are the source of many others between public and private morality, which produce a perpetual conflict in the mind. Domestic morality inspires submission and fear; the other courage and liberty. That instructs a man to confine his beneficence to a small number of persons, not of his own choice; this to extend it to all mankind. That commands a continual sacrifice of himself to a vain idol called the *good of the family,* which is often no real good to any one of those who compose it; this teaches him to consider his own advantage, without offending the laws, or excites him to sacrifice himself for the good of his country, by rewarding him beforehand with the fanaticism it inspires. Such contradictions are the reason that men neglect the pursuit of virtue, which they can hardly distinguish amidst the obscurity and confusion of natural and moral objects. How frequently are men, upon a retrospection of their actions, astonished to find themselves dishonest?

In proportion to the increase of society each member becomes a smaller part of the whole; and the republican spirit diminishes in the same proportion, if neglected by the laws. Political societies, like the human body, have their limits circumscribed, which they cannot exceed, without disturbing their economy. It seems as if the greatness of a state ought to be inversely as the sensibility and activity of the individuals; if, on the contrary, population and activity increase in the same proportion, the laws will with difficulty prevent the crimes arising from the good they have produced. An overgrown republic can only be saved from despotism by subdividing it into a number of confederate republics. But how is this practicable? By a despotic dictator, who, with the courage of *Sylla,* has as much genius for building up as that Roman had for pulling down. If he be an ambitious man, his reward will be immortal glory? if a philosopher, the blessings of his fellow-citizens will sufficiently console him for the loss of authority, though he should not be insensible to their ingratitude.

In proportion as the sentiments which unite us to the state grow weaker, those which attach us to the objects which more immediately surround us grow stronger; therefore, in the most despotic government, friendships are more durable, and domestic virtues (which are always of the lowest class) are the most common, or the only virtues existing. Hence it appears how confined have been the views of the greatest number of legislators.

## XXVII Of the mildness of punishments

The course of my ideas has carried me away from my subject, to the elucidation of which I now return. Crimes are more effectually prevented by the *certainty* than the *severity* of punishment. Hence in a magistrate the necessity of vigilance, and in a judge of implacability, which, that it may become an useful virtue, should be joined to a mild leg-

islation. The certainty of a small punishment will make a stronger impression than the fear of one more severe, if attended with the hopes of escaping; for it is the nature of mankind to be terrified at the approach of the smallest inevitable evil, whilst hope, the best gift of Heaven, hath the power of dispelling the apprehension of a greater, especially if supported by examples of impunity, which weakness or avarice too frequently afford.

If punishments be very severe, men are naturally led to the perpetration of other crimes, to avoid the punishment due to the first. The countries and times most notorious for severity of punishments were always those in which the most bloody and inhuman actions and the most atrocious crimes were committed; for the hand of the legislator and the assassin were directed by the same spirit of ferocity, which on the throne dictated laws of iron to slaves and savages, and in private instigated the subject to sacrifice one tyrant to make room for another.

In proportion as punishments become more cruel, the minds of men, as a fluid rises to the same height with that which surrounds it, grow hardened and insensible; and the force of the passions still continuing, in the space of an hundred years the *wheel* terrifies no more than formerly the *prison.* That a punishment may produce the effect required, it is sufficient that the *evil* it occasions should exceed the *good* expected from the crime, including in the calculation the certainty of the punishment, and the privation of the expected advantage. All severity beyond this is superfluous, and therefore tyrannical.

Men regulate their conduct by the repeated impression of evils they know, and not by those with which they are unacquainted. Let us, for example, suppose two nations, in one of which the greatest punishment is *perpetual slavery,* and in the other *the wheel.* I say, that both will inspire the same degree of terror, and that there can be no reasons for increasing the punishments of the first, which are not equally valid for augmenting those of the second to more lasting and more ingenious modes of tormenting, and so on to the most exquisite refinements of a science too well known to tyrants.

There are yet two other consequences of cruel punishments, which counteract the purpose of their institution, which was, to prevent crimes. The *first* arises from the impossibility of establishing an exact proportion between the crime and punishment; for though ingenious cruelty hath greatly multiplied the variety of torments, yet the human frame can suffer only to a certain degree, beyond which it is impossible to proceed, be the enormity of the crime ever so great. The *second* consequence is impunity. Human nature is limited no less in evil than in good. Excessive barbarity can never be more than temporary, it being impossible that it should be supported by a permanent system of legislation; for if the laws be too cruel, they must be altered, or anarchy and impunity will succeed.

Is it possible without shuddering with horror, to read in history of the barbarous and useless torments that were cooly invented and executed by men who were called sages? Who does not tremble at the thoughts of thousands of wretches, whom their misery, either caused or tolerated by the laws, which favoured the few and outraged the many, had forced in despair to return to a state of nature, or accused of impossible crimes, the fabric of ignorance and superstition, or guilty only of having been faithful to their own principles; who, I say, can, without horror, think of their being torn to pieces, with slow and studied barbarity, by men endowed with the same passions and the same feelings? A delightful spectacle to a fanatic multitude!

## XXVIII   Of the punishment of death

The useless profusion of punishments, which has never made men better, induces me to inquire, whether the punishment of *death* be really just or useful in a well governed state? What *right*, I ask, have men to cut the throats of their fellow-creatures? Certainly not that on which the sovereignty and laws are founded. The laws, as I have said before, are only the sum of the smallest portions of the private liberty of each individual, and represent the general will, which is the aggregate of that of each individual. Did any one ever give to others the right of taking away his life? Is it possible that, in the smallest portions of the liberty of each, sacrificed to the good of the public, can be contained the greatest of all good, life? If it were so, how shall it be reconciled to the maxim which tells us, that a man has no right to kill himself, which he certainly must have, if he could give it away to another?

But the punishment of death is not authorised by any right; for I have demonstrated that no such right exists. It is therefore a war of a whole nation against a citizen, whose destruction they consider as necessary or useful to the general good. But if I can further demonstrate that it is neither necessary nor useful, I shall have gained the cause of humanity.

The death of a citizen cannot be necessary but in one case: when, though deprived of his liberty, he has such power and connections as may endanger the security of the nation; when his existence may produce a dangerous revolution in the established form of government. But, even in this case, it can only be necessary when a nation is on the verge of recovering or losing its liberty, or in times of absolute anarchy, when the disorders themselves hold the place of laws: but in a reign of tranquillity, in a form of government approved by the united wishes of the nation, in a state well fortified from enemies without and supported by strength within, and opinion, perhaps more efficacious, where all power is lodged in the hands of a true sovereign, where riches can purchase pleasures and not authority, there can be no necessity for taking away the life of a subject.

If the experience of all ages be not sufficient to prove, that the punishment of death has never prevented determined men from injuring society, if the example of the Romans, if twenty years' reign of Elizabeth, empress of Russia, in which she gave the fathers of their country an example more illustrious than many conquests bought with blood; if, I say, all this be not sufficient to persuade mankind, who always suspect the voice of reason, and who choose rather to be led by authority, let us consult human nature in proof of my assertion.

It is not the intenseness of the pain that has the greatest effect on the mind, but its continuance; for our sensibility is more easily and more powerfully affected by weak but repeated impressions, than by a violent but momentary impulse. The power of habit is universal over every sensible being. As it is by that we learn to speak, to walk, and to satisfy our necessities, so the ideas of morality are stamped on our minds by repeated impressions. The death of a criminal is a terrible but momentary spectacle, and therefore a less efficacious method of deterring others than the continued example of a man deprived of his liberty, condemned, as a beast of burden, to repair, by his labour, the injury he has done to society. *If I commit such a crime,* says the spectator to himself, *I shall be reduced to that miserable condition for the rest of my life.* A much more powerful preventive than the fear of death which men always behold in distant obscurity.

The terrors of death make so slight an impression, that it has not force enough to withstand the forgetfulness natural to mankind, even in the most essential things, especially when assisted by the passions. Violent impressions surprise us, but their effect is momentary; they are fit to produce those revolutions which instantly transform a common man into a Lacedæmonian or a Persian; but in a free and quiet government they ought to be rather frequent than strong.

The execution of a criminal is to the multitude a spectacle which in some excites compassion mixed with indignation. These sentiments occupy the mind much more than that salutary terror which the laws endeavour to inspire; but, in the contemplation of continued suffering, terror is the only, or at least predominant sensation. The severity of a punishment should be just sufficient to excite compassion in the spectators, as it is intended more for them than for the criminal.

A punishment, to be just, should have only that degree of severity which is sufficient to deter others. Now there is no man who, upon the least reflection, would put in competition the total and perpetual loss of his liberty, with the greatest advantages he could possibly obtain in consequence of a crime. Perpetual slavery, then, has in it all that is necessary to deter the most hardened and determined, as much as the punishment of death. I say it has more. There are many who can look upon death with intrepidity and firmness, some through fanaticism, and others through vanity, which attends us even to the grave; others from a desperate resolution, either to get rid of their misery, or cease to live: but fanaticism and vanity forsake the criminal in slavery, in chains and fetters, in an iron cage, and despair seems rather the beginning than the end of their misery. The mind, by collecting itself and uniting all its force, can, for a moment, repel assailing grief; but its most vigorous efforts are insufficient to resist perpetual wretchedness.

In all nations, where death is used as a punishment, every example supposes a new crime committed; whereas, in perpetual slavery, every criminal affords a frequent and lasting example; and if it be necessary that men should often be witnesses of the power of the laws, criminals should often be put to death: but this supposes a frequency of crimes; and from hence this punishment will cease to have its effect, so that it must be useful and useless at the same time.

I shall be told that perpetual slavery is as painful a punishment as death, and therefore as cruel. I answer, that if all the miserable moments in the life of a slave were collected into one point, it would be a more cruel punishment than any other; but these are scattered through his whole life, whilst the pain of death exerts all its force in a moment. There is also another advantage in the punishment of slavery, which is, that it is more terrible to the spectator than to the sufferer himself; for the spectator considers the sum of all his wretched moments whilst the sufferer, by the misery of the present, is prevented from thinking of the future. All evils are increased by the imagination, and the sufferer finds resources and consolations of which the spectators are ignorant, who judge by their own sensibility of what passes in a mind by habit grown callous to misfortune.

Let us, for a moment, attend to the reasoning of a robber or assassin, who is deterred from violating the laws by the gibbet or the wheel. I am sensible, that to develop the sentiments of one's own heart is an art which education only can teach; but although a villain may not be able to give a clear account of his principles, they nevertheless influence his conduct. He reasons thus: "What are these laws that I am bound to respect, which make so great a difference between me and the rich man? He refuses me the farthing I ask of him, and excuses himself by bidding me have recourse to labour, with which he is unacquainted. Who made these laws? The rich and the great, who never deigned to visit the miserable hut of the poor, who have never seen him dividing a piece of mouldy bread, amidst the cries of his famished children and the tears of his wife. Let us break those ties, fatal to the greatest part of mankind, and only useful to a few indolent tyrants. Let us attack injustice at its source. I will return to my natural state of independence. I shall live free and happy on the fruits of my courage and industry. A day of pain and repentance may come, but it will be short; and for an hour of grief I shall enjoy years of pleasure and liberty. King of a small number as determined as myself, I will correct the mis-

takes of fortune, and I shall see those tyrants grow pale and tremble at the sight of him, whom, with insulting pride, they would not suffer to rank with their dogs and horses."

Religion then presents itself to the mind of this lawless villain, and, promising him almost a certainty of eternal happiness upon the easy terms of repentance, contributes much to lessen the horror of the last scene of the tragedy.

But he who foresees that he must pass a great number of years, even his whole life, in pain and slavery, a slave to those laws by which he was protected, in sight of his fellow-citizens, with whom he lives in freedom and society, makes an useful comparison between those evils, the uncertainty of his success, and the shortness of the time in which he shall enjoy the fruits of his transgression. The example of those wretches, continually before his eyes, makes a much greater impression on him than a punishment, which instead of correcting, makes him more obdurate.

The punishment of death is pernicious to society, from the example of barbarity it affords. If the passions, or the necessity of war, have taught men to shed the blood of their fellow creatures, the laws, which are intended to moderate the ferocity of mankind, should not increase it by examples of barbarity, the more horrible as this punishment is usually attended with formal pageantry. Is it not absurd, that the laws, which detest and punish homicide, should, in order to prevent murder, publicly commit murder themselves? What are the true and most useful laws? Those compacts and conditions which all would propose and observe in those moments when private interest is silent, or combined with that of the public. What are the natural sentiments of every person concerning the punishment of death? We may read them in the contempt and indignation with which every one looks on the executioner, who is nevertheless an innocent executor of the public will, a good citizen, who contributes to the advantage of society, the instrument of the general security within, as good soldiers are without. What then is the origin of this contradiction? Why is this sentiment of mankind indelible to the scandal of reason? It is, that, in a secret corner of the mind, in which the original impressions of nature are still preserved, men discover a sentiment which tells them, that their lives are not lawfully in the power of any one, but of that necessity only which with its iron sceptre rules the universe.

What must men think, when they see wise magistrates and grave ministers of justice, with indifference and tranquillity, dragging a criminal to death, and whilst a wretch trembles with agony, expecting the fatal stroke, the judge, who has condemned him, with the coldest insensibility, and perhaps with no small gratification from the exertion of his authority, quits his tribunal, to enjoy the comforts and pleasures of life? They will say, "Ah! those cruel formalities of justice are a cloak to tyranny, they are a secret language, a solemn veil, intended to conceal the sword by which we are sacrificed to the insatiable idol of despotism. Murder, which they would represent to us an horrible crime, we see practised by them without repugnance or remorse. Let us follow their example. A violent death appeared terrible in their descriptions, but we see that it is the affair of a moment. It will be still less terrible to him who, not expecting it, escapes almost all the pain." Such is the fatal though absurd reasonings of men who are disposed to commit crimes, on whom the abuse of religion has more influence than religion itself.

If it be objected, that almost all nations in all ages have punished certain crimes with death, I answer, that the force of these examples vanishes when opposed to truth, against which prescription is urged in vain. The history of mankind is an immense sea of errors, in which a few obscure truths may here and there be found.

But human sacrifices have also been common in almost all nations. That some societies only, either few in number, or for a very short time, abstained from the punishment of death, is rather favourable to my argument; for such is the fate of great truths, that their duration is only as a flash of lightning in the long and dark night of error. The happy time is not yet arrived, when truth, as falsehood has been hitherto, shall be the portion of the greatest number.

I am sensible that the voice of one philosopher is too weak to be heard amidst the clamours of a multitude, blindly influenced by custom; but there is a small number of sages scattered on the face of the earth, who will echo to me from the bottom of their hearts; and if these truths should happily force their way to the thrones of princes be it known to them, that they come attended with the secret wishes of all mankind; and tell the sovereign who deigns them a gracious reception, that his fame shall outshine the glory of conquerors, and that equitable posterity will exalt his peaceful trophies above those of a Titus, an Antoninus, or a Trajan.

How happy were mankind if laws were now to be first formed! now that we see on the thrones of Europe benevolent monarchs, friends to the virtues of peace, to the arts and sciences, fathers of their people, though crowned, yet citizens; the increase of whose authority augments the happiness of their subjects, by destroying that intermediate despotism which intercepts the prayers of the people to the throne. If these humane princes have suffered the old laws to subsist, it is doubtless because they are deterred by the numberless obstacles which oppose the subversion of errors established by the sanction of many ages; and therefore every wise citizen will wish for the increase of their authority.

## XXIX   Of imprisonment

That a magistrate, the executor of the laws, should have a power to imprison a citizen, to deprive the man he hates of his liberty, upon frivolous pretences, and to leave his friend unpunished, notwithstanding the strongest proofs of his guilt, is an error as common as it is contrary to the end of society, which is personal security.

Imprisonment is a punishment which differs from all others in this particular, that it necessarily precedes conviction; but this difference does not destroy a circumstance which is essential and common to it with all other punishments, viz. that it should never be inflicted but when ordained by the law. The law should therefore determine the crime, the presumption, and the evidence sufficient to subject the accused to imprisonment and examination. Public report, his flight, his extrajudicial confession, that of an accomplice, menaces, and his constant enmity with the person injured, the circumstances of the crime, and such other evidence, may be sufficient to justify the imprisonment of a citizen. But the nature of this evidence should be determined by the laws, and not by the magistrates, whose decrees are always contrary to political liberty, when they are not particular applications of a general maxim of the public code. When punishments become less severe, and prisons less horrible, when compassion and humanity shall penetrate the iron gates of dungeons, and direct the obdurate and inexorable ministers of justice, the laws may then be satisfied with weaker evidence for imprisonment.

A person accused, imprisoned, tried, and acquitted, ought not to be branded with any degree of infamy. Among the Romans we see that many accused of very great crimes, and afterwards declared innocent, were respected by the people, and honoured with employments in the state. But why is the fate of an innocent person so different in this age? It is because the present system of penal laws presents to our minds an idea of power rather than of justice: it is because the accused and convicted are thrown indiscriminately into the same prison; because imprisonment is rather a punishment than a means of securing the person of the accused; and because the interior power, which defends the laws, and the exterior, which defends the throne and kingdom, are separate, when they should be united. If the first were (under the common authority of the laws) combined with the right of judging, but not however immediately dependent on the magistrate, the pomp that attends a military corps would take off the infamy, which, like all popular opinions, is more attached to the manner and form than to the thing itself, as may be seen in military imprisonment, which, in the common opinion, is not so disgraceful as the civil. But the barbarity and ferocity of our ancestors, the hunters of the north, still subsist among the people in our customs and our laws, which are always several ages behind the actual refinements of a nation.

## XXX    Of prosecution and prescription

The proofs of the crime being obtained, and the certainty of it determined, it is necessary to allow the criminal time and means for his justification; but a time so short as not to diminish that promptitude of punishment, which, as we have shewn, is one of the most powerful means of preventing crimes. A mistaken humanity may object to the shortness of the time, but the force of the objection will vanish if we consider that the danger of the innocent increases with the defects of the legislation.

The time for inquiry and for justification should be fixed by the laws, and not by the judge, who, in that case, would become legislator. With regard to atrocious crimes, which are long remembered, when they are once proved, if the criminal have fled, no time should be allowed; but in less considerable and more obscure crimes, a time should be fixed, after which the delinquent should be no longer uncertain of his fate:

for, in the latter case, the length of time, in which the crime is almost forgotten, prevents the example of impunity, and allows the criminal to amend, and become a better member of society.

General principles will here be sufficient, it being impossible to fix precisely the limits of time for any given legislation, or for any society in any particular circumstance. I shall only add, that, in a nation willing to prove the utility of moderate punishment, laws which, according to the nature of the crime, increase or diminish the time of inquiry and justification, considering the imprisonment or the voluntary exile of the criminal as a part of the punishment, will form an easy division of a small number of mild punishments for a great number of crimes.

But it must be observed, the time for inquiry and justification should not increase in direct proportion to the atrociousness of crimes; for the probability of such crimes having been committed is inversely as their atrociousness. Therefore the time for inquiring ought, in some cases, to be diminished, and that for justification increased, *et vice versa*. This may appear to contradict what I have said above, namely, that equal punishments may be decreed by unequal crimes, by considering the time allowed the criminal or the prison as a punishment.

In order to explain this idea, I shall divide crimes into two classes. The first comprehends homicide, and all greater crimes; the second crimes of an inferior degree. This distinction is founded in human nature. The preservation of life is a natural right; the preservation of property is a right of society. The motives that induce men to shake off the natural sentiment of compassion, which must be destroyed before great crimes can be committed, are much less in number than those by which, from the natural desire of being happy, they are instigated to violate a right which is not founded in the heart of man, but is the work of society. The different degrees of probability

in these two classes, require that they should be regulated on different principles. In the greatest crimes, as they are less frequent, and the probability of the innocence of the accused being greater, the time allowed him for his justification should be greater, and the time of inquiry less. For, by hastening the definitive sentence, the flattering hopes of impunity are destroyed, which are more dangerous as the crime is more atrocious. On the contrary, in crimes of less importance, the probability of the innocence being less, the time of inquiry should be greater, and that of justification less, as impunity is not so dangerous.

But this division of crimes into two classes should not be admitted, if the consequences of impunity were in proportion to the probability of the crime. It should be considered, that a person accused, whose guilt or innocence is not determined for want of proofs, may be again imprisoned for the same crime, and be subject to a new trial, if fresh evidence arises within the time fixed.

This is, in my opinion, the best method of providing at the same time for the security and liberty of the subject, without favouring one at the expense of the other; which may easily happen, since both these blessings, the unalienable and equal patrimony of every citizen, are liable to be invaded, the one by open or disguised despotism, and the other by tumultuous and popular anarchy.

## XXXI   Of crimes of difficult proof

With the forgoing principles in view, it will appear astonishing, that reason hardly ever presided at the formation of the laws of nations; that the weakest and most equivocal evidence, and even conjectures, have been thought sufficient proof for crimes the most atrocious (and therefore most improbable), the most obscure and chimerical; as if it were the interest of the laws and the judge not to enquire into the truth, but to prove the crime; as if there were not a greater risk of condemning an innocent person, when the probability of his guilt is less.

The generality of men want that vigour of mind and resolution which are as necessary for great crimes as for great virtues, and which at the same time produce both the one and the other in those nations which are supported by the activity of their government, and a passion for the public good. For in those which subsist by their greatness or power, or by the goodness of their laws, the passions, being in a weaker degree, seem calculated rather to maintain than to improve the form of government. This naturally leads us to an important conclusion, viz. that great crimes do not always produce the destruction of a nation.

There are some crimes which, though frequent in society, are of difficult proof, a circumstance admitted as equal to the probability of the innocence of the accused. But as the frequency of these crimes is not owing to their impunity so much as to other causes, the danger of their passing unpunished is of less importance, and therefore the time of examination and prescription may be equally diminished. These principles are different from those commonly received; for it is in crimes which are proved with the greatest difficulty, such as adultery and sodomy, that presumptions, half proofs, etc. are admitted; as if a man could be half innocent, and half guilty, that is, half punishable and half absolvable. It is in these cases that torture should exercise its cruel power on the person of the accused, the witnesses, and even his whole family, as, with unfeeling indifference, some civilians have taught, who pretend to dictate laws to nations.

Adultery is a crime which, politically considered, owes its existence to two causes, viz. pernicious laws, and the powerful attraction between the sexes. This attraction is similar in many circumstances to gravity, the spring of motion in the universe. Like this, it is diminished by distance; one regulates the motions of the body, the other of the soul.

But they differ in one respect; the force of gravity decreases in proportion to the obstacles that oppose it, the other gathers strength and vigour as the obstacles increase.

If I were speaking to nations guided only by the laws of nature, I would tell them, that there is a considerable difference between adultery and all other crimes. Adultery proceeds from an abuse of that necessity which is constant and universal in human nature; a necessity anterior to the formation of society, and indeed the founder of society itself; whereas all other crimes tend to the destruction of society, and arise from momentary passions, and not from a natural necessity. It is the opinion of those who have studied history and mankind, that this necessity is constantly in the same degree in the same climate. If this be true, useless, or rather pernicious, must all laws and customs be which tend to diminish the sum total of the effects of this passion. Such laws would only burden one part of society with the additional necessities of the other; but, on the contrary, wise are the laws which, following the natural course of the river, divide the stream into a number of equal branches, preventing thus both sterility and inundation.

Conjugal fidelity is always greater in proportion as marriages are more numerous and less difficult. But, when the interest or pride of families, or paternal authority, not the inclination of the parties, unites the sexes, gallantry soon breaks the slender ties, in spite of common moralists, who exclaim against the effect, whilst they pardon the cause. But these reflections are useless to those who, living in the true religion, act from sublimer motives, which correct the eternal laws of nature.

The act of adultery is a crime so instantaneous, so mysterious, and so concealed by the veil which the laws themselves have woven, a veil necessary indeed, but so transparent as to heighten rather than conceal the charms of the object, the opportunities are so frequent, and the danger of discovery so easily avoided, that it were much easier for the laws to prevent this crime, than to punish it when committed.

To every crime which, from its nature, must frequently remain unpunished, the punishment is an incentive. Such is the nature of the human mind, that difficulties, if not unsurmountable, nor too great for our natural indolence, embellish the object, and spur us on to the pursuit. They are so many barriers that confine the imagination to the object, and oblige us to consider it in every point of view. In this agitation, the mind naturally inclines and fixes itself to the most agreeable part, studiously avoiding every idea that might create disgust.

The crime of sodomy, so severely punished by the laws, and for the proof of which are employed tortures, which often triumph over innocence itself, has its source much less in the passions of man in a free and independent state than in society and a slave. It is much less the effect of a satiety in pleasures, than of that education which in order to make men useful to others, begins by making them useless to themselves. In those public seminaries, where ardent youth are carefully excluded from all commerce with the other sex, as the vigour of nature blooms, it is consumed in a manner not only useless to mankind, but which accelerates the approach of old age.

The murder of bastard children is, in like manner, the effect of a cruel dilemma, in which a woman finds herself, who has been seduced through weakness, or overcome by force. The alternative is, either her own infamy, or the death of a being who is incapable of feeling the loss of life. How can she avoid preferring the last to the inevitable misery of herself and her unhappy infant! The best method of preventing this crime would be effectually to protect the weak woman from that tyranny which exaggerates all vices that cannot be concealed under the cloak of virtue.

I do not pretend to lessen that just abhorrence which these crimes deserve, but to discover the sources from whence they spring; and I think I may draw the following conclusion: *That the punishment of a crime cannot be just (that is, necessary) if the laws have not endeavoured to prevent that crime by the best means which times and circumstances would allow.*

## XXXII   Of suicide

Suicide is a crime which seems not to admit of punishment, properly speaking; for it cannot be inflicted but on the innocent, or upon an insensible dead body. In the first case, it is unjust and tyrannical, for political liberty supposes all punishments entirely personal; in the second, it has the same effect, by way of example, as the scourging of a statue. Mankind love life too well; the objects that surround them, the seducing phantom of pleasure, and hope, that sweetest error of mortals, which makes men swallow such large draughts of evil, mingled with a very few drops of good, allure them too strongly, to apprehend that this crime will ever be common from its unavoidable impunity. The laws are obeyed through fear of punishment, but death destroys all sensibility. What motive then can restrain the desperate hand of suicide?

He who kills himself does a less injury to society than he who quits his country for ever; for the other leaves his property behind him, but this carries with him at least a part of his substance. Besides, as the strength of society consists in the number of citizens, he who quits one nation to reside in another, becomes a double loss. This then is the question: whether it be advantageous to society that its members should enjoy the unlimited privilege of migration?

Every law that is not armed with force, or which, from circumstances, must be ineffectual, should not be promulgated. Opinion, which reigns over the minds of men, obeys the slow and indirect impressions of the legislator, but resists them when violently and directly applied; and useless laws communicate their insignificance to the most salutary, which are regarded more as obstacles to be surmounted than as safeguards of the public good. But further, our preceptions being limited, by enforcing the observance of laws which are evidently useless, we destroy the influence of the most salutary.

From this principle a wise dispenser of public happiness may draw some useful consequences, the explanation of which would carry me too far from my subject, which is to prove the inutility of making the nation a prison. Such a law is vain; because, unless inaccessible rocks or impassible seas divide the country from all others, how will it be possible to secure every point of the circumference, or how will you guard the guards themselves? Besides, this crime once committed cannot be punished; and to punish it before hand would be to punish the intention and not the action, the will, which is entirely out of the power of human laws. To punish the absent by confiscating his effects, besides the facility of collusion, which would inevitably be the case, and which, without tyranny, could not be prevented, would put a stop to all commerce with other nations. To punish the criminal when he returns, would be to prevent him from repairing the evil he had already done to society, by making his absence perpetual. Besides, any prohibition would increase the desire of removing, and would infallibly prevent strangers from settling in the country.

What must we think of a government which has no means but fear to keep its subjects in their own country, to which, by the first impressions of their infancy, they are so strongly attached. The most certain method of keeping men at home is to make them happy; and it is the interest of every state to turn the balance, not only of commerce, but of felicity, in favour of its subjects. The pleasures of luxury are not the principle sources of this happiness, though, by preventing the too great accumulation of wealth in a few hands, they become a necessary remedy against the too great inequality of individuals, which always increases with the progress of society.

When the populousness of a country does not increase in proportion to its extent, luxury favours despotism, for where men are most dispersed there is least industry, and where there is least industry the dependence of the poor upon the luxury of the rich is greatest, and the union of the oppressed against the oppressors is least to be feared. In such circumstances, rich and powerful men more easily command distinction, respect, and service, by which they are raised to a greater height above the poor; for men are more independent the less they are observed, and are least observed when most numerous. On the contrary, when the number of people is too great in proportion to the extent of a country, luxury is a check to despotism; because it is a spur to industry, and because the labour of the poor affords so many pleasures to the rich, that they disregard the luxury of ostentation, which would remind the people of their dependence. Hence we see, that, in vast and depopulated states, the luxury of ostentation prevails over that of convenience; but in countries more populous, the luxury of convenience tends constantly to diminish the luxury of ostentation.

The pleasures of luxury have this inconvenience, that though they employ a great number of hands, yet they are only enjoyed by a few, whilst the rest who do not partake of them, feel the want more sensibly on comparing their state with that of others. Security and liberty, restrained by the laws, are the basis of happiness, and when attended by these, the pleasures of luxury favour population, without which they become the instruments of tyranny. As the most noble and generous animals fly to solitude and inaccessible deserts, and abandon the fertile plains to man, their greatest enemy, so men reject pleasure itself when offered by the hand of tyranny.

But, to return: If it be demonstrated that the laws which imprison men in their own country are vain and unjust, it will be equally true of those which punish suicide;

for that can only be punished after death, which is in the power of God alone; but it is no crime with regard to man, because the punishment falls on an innocent family. If it be objected, that the consideration of such a punishment may prevent the crime, I answer, that he who can calmly renounce the pleasure of existence, who is so weary of life as to brave the idea of eternal misery, will never be influenced by the more distant and less powerful considerations of family and children.

## XXXIII   Of smuggling

Smuggling is a real offence against the sovereign and the nation; but the punishment should not brand the offender with infamy, because this crime is not infamous in the public opinion. By inflicting infamous punishments for crimes that are not reputed so, we destroy that idea where it may be useful. If the same punishment be decreed for killing a pheasant as for killing a man, or for forgery, all difference between those crimes will shortly vanish. It is thus that moral sentiments are destroyed in the heart of man; sentiments, the work of many ages and of much bloodshed; sentiments that are so slowly and with so much difficulty produced, and for the establishment of which such sublime motives and such an apparatus of ceremonies were thought necessary.

This crime is owing to the laws themselves; for the higher the duties the greater is the advantage, and consequently the temptation; which temptation is increased by the facility of perpetration, when the circumference that is guarded is of great extent, and the merchandise prohibited is small in bulk. The seizure and loss of the goods attempted to be smuggled, together with those that are found along with them, is just, but it would be better to lessen the duty, because men risk only in proportion to the advantage expected.

This crime being a theft of what belongs to the prince, and consequently to the nation, why is it not attended with infamy? I answer, that crimes which men consider as productive of no bad consequences to themselves, do not interest them sufficiently to excite their indignation. The generality of mankind, upon whom remote consequences make no impression, do not see the evil that may result from the practice of smuggling, especially if they reap from it any present advantage. They only perceive the loss sustained by the prince. They are not then interested in refusing their esteem to the smuggler, as to one who has committed a theft or a forgery, or other crimes, by which they themselves may suffer, from this evident principle, that a sensible being only interests himself in those evils with which he is acquainted.

Shall this crime then, committed by one who has nothing to lose, go unpunished? No. There are certain species of smuggling, which so particularly affect the revenue, a part of government so essential, and managed with so much difficulty, that they deserve imprisonment, or even slavery; but yet of such a nature as to be proportioned to the crime. For example, it would be highly unjust, that a smuggler of tobacco should suffer the same punishment with a robber or assassin; but it would be most conformable to the nature of the offence, that the produce of his labour should be applied to the use of the crown, which he intended to defraud.

## XXXIV   Of bankrupts

The necessity of good faith in contracts, and the support of commerce, oblige the legislator to secure for the creditors the persons of bankrupts. It is, however, necessary to distinguish between the fraudulent and the honest bankrupt. The fraudulent bankrupt should be punished in the same manner with him who adulterates the coin; for, to falsify a piece of coin, which is a pledge of the mutual obligations between citizens, is not a greater crime than to violate the obligations themselves. But the bankrupt who, after a strict examination, has proved before proper judges, that either the fraud or losses of others, or misfortunes unavoidable by human prudence, have stripped him of his substance, upon what barbarous pretence is he thrown into prison, and thus deprived of the only remaining good, the melancholy enjoyment of mere liberty? Why is he ranked with criminals, and in despair compelled to repent of his honesty? Conscious of his innocence, he lived easy and happy under the protection of those laws which, it is true, he violated, but not intentionally; laws dictated by the avarice of the rich, and accepted by the poor, seduced by that universal and flattering hope, which makes men believe that all unlucky accidents are the lot of others, and the most fortunate only their share. Mankind, when influenced by the first impressions, love cruel laws, although, being subject to them themselves, it is the interest of every person that they should be as mild as possible; but the fear of being injured is always more prevalent than the intention of injuring others.

But, to return to the honest bankrupt: let his debt, if you will, not be considered as cancelled, till the payment of the whole; let him be refused the liberty of leaving the country without leave of his creditors, or of carrying into another nation that industry which, under a penalty, should be obliged to employ for their benefit; but what pretence can justify the depriving an innocent though unfortunate man of his liberty, without the least utility to his creditors?

But, say they, the hardships of confinement will induce him to discover his fraudulent transactions; an event that can hardly be supposed, after a rigorous examination of his conduct and affairs. But if they are not discovered, he will escape unpunished. It is, I think, a maxim of government, that the importance of the political inconveniences arising from the impunity of a crime, are directly as the injury to the public, and inversely as the difficulty of proof.

It will be necessary to distinguish fraud, attended with aggravating circumstances, from simple fraud, and that from perfect innocence. For the first, let there be ordained the same punishment as for forgery; for the second a less punishment, but with the loss of liberty; and if perfectly honest, let the bankrupt himself choose the method of re-establishing himself, and of satisfying his creditors; or, if he should appear not to have been strictly honest, let that be determined by his creditors: but these distinctions should be fixed by the laws, which alone are impartial, and not by the arbitrary and dangerous prudence of judges.[2]

With what ease might a sagacious legislator prevent the greatest part of fraudulent bankruptcies, and remedy the misfortunes that befall the honest and industrious! A public register of all contracts, with the liberty of consulting it allowed to every citizen: a public fund, formed by a contribution of the opulent merchants, for the timely assistance of unfortunate industry, were establishments that could produce no

---

[2] It may be alleged that the interest of commerce and property should be secured; but commerce and property are not the end of the social compact, but the means of obtaining that end; and to expose all the members of society to cruel laws, to preserve them from evils necessarily occasioned by the infinite combinations which result from the actual state of political societies, would be to make the end subservient to the means, a paralogism in all sciences, and particularly in politics. In the former editions of this work I myself fell into this error, when I said that the honest bankrupt should be kept in custody, as a pledge for his debts, or employed as a slave to work for his creditors. I am ashamed of having adopted so cruel an opinion. I have been accused of impiety; I did not deserve it. I have been accused of sedition; I deserved it as little. But I insulted all the rights of humanity, and was never reproached.

real inconveniences, and many advantages. But, unhappily, the most simple, the easiest, yet the wisest laws, that wait only for the nod of the legislator, to diffuse through nations wealth, power, and felicity, laws which would be regarded by future generations with eternal gratitude, are either unknown or rejected. A restless and trifling spirit, the timid prudence of the present moment, a distrust and aversion to the most useful novelties, possess the minds of those who are empowered to regulate the actions of mankind.

## XXXV Of sanctuaries

Are sanctuaries just? Is a convention between nations mutually to give up their criminals useful?

In the whole extent of a political state there should be no place independent of the laws. Their power should follow every subject, as the shadow follows the body. Sanctuaries and impunity differ only in degree, and as the effect of punishments depends more on their certainty than their greatness, men are more strongly invited to crimes by sanctuaries than they are deterred by punishment. To increase the number of sanctuaries is to erect so many little sovereignties; for where the laws have no power, new bodies will be formed in opposition to the public good, and a spirit established contrary to that of the state. History informs us, that from the use of sanctuaries have arisen the greatest revolutions in kingdoms and in opinions.

Some have pretended, that in whatever country a crime, that is, an action contrary to the laws of society, be committed, the criminal may be justly punished for it in any other; as if the character of subject were indelible, or synonymous with or worse than that of slave; as if a man could live in one country and be subject to the laws of another, or be accountable for his actions to two sovereigns, or two codes of laws often contradictory. There are also those who

think, that an act of cruelty committed, for example, at Constantinople may be punished at Paris, for this abstracted reason, that he who offends humanity should have enemies in all mankind, and be the object of universal execration; as if judges were to be the knights-errant of human nature in general, rather than guardians of particular conventions between men. The place of punishment can certainly be no other than that where the crime was committed; for the necessity of punishing an individual for the general good, subsists there, and there only. A villain, if he has not broke through the conventions of a society, of which, by my supposition, he was not a member, may be feared, and by force banished and excluded from that society, but ought not be formally punished by the laws, which were only intended to maintain the social compact, and not to punish the intrinsic malignity of actions.

Whether it be useful that nations should mutually deliver up their criminals? Although the certainty of there being no part of the earth where crimes are not punished, may be a means of preventing them, I shall not pretend to determine this question, until laws more conformable to the necessities, and rights of humanity, and until milder punishments, and the abolition of the arbitrary power of opinion, shall afford security to virtue and innocence when oppressed; and until tyranny shall be confined to the plains of Asia, and Europe acknowledge the universal empire of reason by which the interests of sovereigns and subjects are best united.

## XXXVI Of rewards for apprehending or killing criminals

Let us now inquire, whether it be advantageous to society, to set a price on the head of a criminal, and so to make of every citizen an executioner? If the offender hath taken refuge in another state, the sovereign encourages his subjects to commit a crime, and to expose themselves to a just punishment; he insults that nation, and authorises the subjects to commit on their neighbours similar usurpations. If the criminal still remain in his own country, to set a price upon his head is the strongest proof of the weakness of the government. He who has strength to defend himself will not purchase the assistance of another. Besides, such an edict confounds all the ideas of virtue and morality, already too wavering in the mind of man. At one time treachery is punished by the laws, at another encouraged. With one hand the legislator strengthens the ties of kindred and friendship, and with the other rewards the violation of both. Always in contradiction with himself, now he invites the suspecting minds of men to mutual confidence, and now he plants distrust in every heart. To prevent one crime he gives birth to a thousand. Such are the expedients of weak nations, whose laws are like temporary repairs to a tottering fabric. On the contrary, as a nation becomes more enlightened, honesty and mutual confidence become more necessary, and are daily tending to unite with sound policy. Artifice, cabal, and obscure and indirect actions are more easily discovered, and the interest of the whole is better secured against the passions of the individual.

Even the times of ignorance, when private virtue was encouraged by public morality, may afford instruction and example to more enlightened ages. But laws which reward treason excite clandestine war and mutual distrust, and oppose that necessary union of morality and policy which is the foundation of happiness and universal peace.

## XXXVII  Of attempts, accomplices, and pardon

The laws do not punish the intention; nevertheless, an attempt, which manifests the intention of committing a crime, deserves a punishment, though less, perhaps, than if the crime were actually perpetrated. The importance of preventing even attempts to commit a crime sufficiently authorises a punishment; but, as there may be an interval of time between the attempt and the execution, it is proper to reserve the greater punishment for the actual commission, that even after the attempt there may be a motive for desisting.

In like manner, with regard to the accomplices, they ought not to suffer so severe a punishment as the immediate perpetrator of the crime: but this for a different reason. When a number of men unite, and run a common risk, the greater the danger, the more they endeavour to distribute it equally. Now, if the principals be punished more severely than the accessaries, it will prevent the danger from being equally divided, and will increase the difficulty of finding a person to execute the crime, as his danger is greater by the difference of the punishment. There can be but one exception to this rule, and that is, when the principal receives a reward from the accomplices. In that case, as the difference of the danger is compensated, the punishment should be equal. These reflections may appear too refined to those who do not consider, that it is of great importance that the laws should leave the associates as few means as possible of agreeing among themselves.

In some tribunals a pardon is offered to an accomplice in a great crime, if he discover his associates. This expedient has its advantages and disadvantages. The disadvantages are, that the law authorises treachery, which is detested even by the villains themselves, and introduces crimes of cowardice, which are much more pernicious to a nation than crimes of courage. Courage is not common, and only wants a benevolent power to direct it to the public good. Cowardice, on the contrary, is a frequent, self-interested, and contagious evil, which can never be improved into a virtue. Besides, the tribunal which has recourse to this method, betrays its fallibility, and the laws their weakness, by imploring the assistance of those by whom they are violated.

The advantages are, that it prevents great crimes, the effects of which being public, and the perpetrators concealed, terrify the people. It also contributes to prove, that he who violates the laws, which are public conventions, will also violate private compacts. It appears to me that a general law, promising a reward to every accomplice who discovers his associates, would be better than a special declaration in every particular case; because it would prevent the union of those villains, as it would inspire a mutual distrust, and each would be afraid of exposing himself alone to danger. The accomplice, however, should be pardoned, on condition of transportation.——But it is in vain that I torment myself with endeavouring to extinguish the remorse I feel in attempting to induce the sacred laws, the monument of public confidence, the foundation of human morality, to authorise dissimulation and perfidy. But what an example does it offer to a nation to see the interpreters of the laws break their promise of pardon, and on the strength of learned subtleties, and to the scandal of public faith, drag him to punishment who hath accepted of their invitation! Such examples are not uncommon, and this is the reason that political society is regarded as a complex machine, the springs of which are moved at pleasure by the most dexterous or most powerful.

## XXXVIII   Of suggestive interrogations

The laws forbid *suggestive interrogations;* that is, according to the civilians, questions which, with regard to the circumstances of the crime, are *special* when they should be *general;* or, in other words, those questions which, having an immediate reference to the crime, suggests to the criminal an immediate answer. Interrogations, according to the law, ought to lead to the fact indirectly and obliquely, but never directly or immediately. The intent of this injunction is, either that they should not suggest to the accused an immediate answer that might acquit him,

or that they think it contrary to nature that a man should accuse himself. But whatever be the motive, the laws have fallen into a palpable contradiction, in condemning suggestive interrogations, whilst they authorise torture. Can there be an interrogation more suggestive than pain? Torture will suggest to a robust villain an obstinate silence, that he may exchange a greater punishment for a less; and to a feeble man confession, to relieve him from the present pain, which affects him more than the apprehension of the future. If a special interrogation be contrary to the right of nature, as it obliges a man to accuse himself, torture will certainly do it more effectually. But men are influenced more by the names than the nature of things.

He who obstinately refuses to answer the interrogatories deserves a punishment, which should be fixed by the laws, and that of the severest kind; the criminals should not, by their silence, evade the example which they owe the public. But this punishment is not necessary when the guilt of the criminal is indisputable; because in that case interrogation is useless, as is likewise his confession, when there are, without it, proofs sufficient. This last case is most common, for experience shews, that in the greatest number of criminal prosecutions the culprit pleads not guilty.

## XXXIX   Of a particular kind of crimes

The reader will perceive that I have omitted speaking of a certain class of crimes which has covered Europe with blood, and raised up those horrid piles, from whence, amidst clouds of whirling smoke, the groans of human victims, the crackling of their bones, and the frying of their still panting bowels, were a pleasing spectacle and agreeable harmony to the fanatic multitude. But men of understanding will perceive, that the age and country in which I live, will not permit me to inquire into the nature of this crime. It were too tedious and foreign to my subject to prove the necessity of a perfect uniformity of opinions in a state, contrary to the examples of many nations; to prove that opinions, which differ from one another only in some subtle and obscure distinctions, beyond the reach of human capacity, may nevertheless disturb the public tranquillity, unless one only religion be established by authority; and that some opinions, by being contrasted and opposed to each other, in their collision strike out the truth; whilst others, feeble in themselves, require the support of power and authority. It would, I say, carry me too far, were I to prove, that, how odious soever is the empire of force over the opinions of mankind, from whom it only obtains dissimulation followed by contempt, and although it may seem contrary to the spirit of humanity and brotherly love, commanded us by reason, and authority, which we more respect, it is nevertheless necessary and indispensable. We are to believe, that all these paradoxes are solved beyond a doubt, and are conformable to the true interest of mankind, if practised by a lawful authority. I write only of *crimes* which violate the laws of nature and the social contract, and not of *sins*, even the temporal punishments of which must be determined from other principles than those of limited human philosophy.

## XL  Of false ideas of utility

A principal source of errors and injustice are false ideas of utility. For example: that legislator has false ideas of utility who considers particular more than general conveniences, who had rather command the sentiments of mankind than excite them, and dares say to reason, "Be thou a slave"; who would sacrifice a thousand real advantages to the fear of an imaginary or trifling inconvenience; who would deprive men of the use of fire for fear of their being burnt, and of water for fear of their being drowned; and who knows of no means of preventing evil but by destroying it.

The laws of this nature are those which forbid to wear arms, disarming those only who are not disposed to commit the crime which the laws mean to prevent. Can it be supposed, that those who have the courage to violate the most sacred laws of humanity, and the most important of the code, will respect the less considerable and arbitrary injunctions, the violation of which is so easy, and of so little comparative importance? Does not the execution of this law deprive the subject of that personal liberty, so dear to mankind and to the wise legislator? and does it not subject the innocent to all the disagreeable circumstances that should only fall on the guilty? It certainly makes the situation of the assaulted worse, and of the assailants better, and rather encourages than prevents murder, as it requires less courage to attack unarmed than armed persons.

It is a false idea of utility that would give to a multitude of sensible beings that symmetry and order which inanimate matter is alone capable of receiving; to neglect the present, which are the only motives that act with force and constancy on the multitude, for the more distant, whose impressions are weak and transitory, unless increased by that strength of imagination so very uncommon among mankind. Finally, that is a false idea of utility which, sacrificing things to names, separates the public good from that of individuals.

There is this difference between a state of society and a state of nature, that a savage does no more mischief to another than is necessary to procure some benefit to himself: but a man in society is sometimes tempted, from a fault in the laws, to injure another without any prospect of advantage. The tyrant inspires his vassals with fear and servility, which rebound upon him with double force, and are the cause of his torment. Fear, the more private and domestic it is, the less dangerous is it to him who makes it the instrument of his happiness; but the more it is public, and the greater number of people it affects, the greater is the probability that some mad, desperate, or designing person will seduce others to his party by flattering expectations; and this will be the more easily accomplished as the danger of the enterprise will be divided amongst a greater number, because the value the unhappy set upon their existence is less, as their misery is greater.

## XLI  Of the means of preventing crimes

It is better to prevent crimes than to punish them. This is the fundamental principle of good legislation, which is the art of conducting men to the *maximum* of happiness, and to the *minimum* of misery, if we may apply this mathematical expression to the good and evil of life. But the means hitherto employed for that purpose are generally inadequate, or contrary to the end proposed. It is impossible to reduce the tumultuous activity of mankind to absolute regularity; for, amidst the various and opposite attractions of pleasure and pain, human laws are not sufficient entirely to prevent disorders in society. Such, however is the chimera of weak men, when invested with authority. To prohibit a number of indifferent actions is not to prevent the crimes which they may produce, but to create new ones; it is to change at will the ideas of virtue and vice, which, at other times, we are told, are eternal and immutable. To what a situation should we be reduced if every thing were to be forbidden that might possibly lead to a crime? We must be deprived of the use of our senses: for one motive that induces a man to commit a real crime, there are a thousand which excite him to those indifferent actions which are called crimes by bad laws. If then the probability that a crime will be committed be in proportion to the number of motives, to extend the sphere of crimes will be to increase that probability. The generality of laws are only exclusive privileges, the tribute of all to the advantages of a few.

Would you prevent crimes? Let the laws be clear and simple, let the entire force of the nation be united in their defence, let them be intended rather to favour every individual than any particular classes of men, let the laws be feared, and the laws only. The fear of the laws is salutary, but the fear of men is a fruitful and fatal source of crimes. Men enslaved are more voluptuous, more debauched, and more cruel than those who are in a state of freedom. These study the sciences, the interest of nations, have great objects before their eyes, and imitate them; but those, whose views are confined to the present moment, endeavour, amidst the distraction of riot and debauchery, to forget their situation; accustomed to the uncertainty of all events, for the laws determine none, the consequences of their crimes become problematical, which gives an additional force to the strength of their passions.

In a nation indolent from the nature of the climate, the uncertainty of the laws confirms and increases men's indolence and stupidity. In a voluptuous but active nation, this uncertainty occasions a multiplicity of cabals and intrigues, which spread distrust and diffidence through the hearts of all, and dissimulation and treachery are the foundation of their prudence. In a brave and powerful nation, this uncertainty of the laws is at last destroyed, after many oscillations from liberty to slavery, and from slavery to liberty again.

## XLII  Of the sciences

Would you prevent crimes? Let liberty be attended with knowledge. As knowledge extends, the disadvantages which attend it diminish and the advantages increase. A daring impostor, who is always a man of some genius, is adored by the ignorant populace, and despised by men of understanding. Knowledge facilitates the comparison of objects, by shewing them in different points of view. When the clouds of ignorance are dispelled by the radiance of knowledge, authority trembles, but the force of the laws remains immoveable. Men of enlightened understanding must necessarily approve those useful conventions which are the foundation of public safety; they compare with the highest satisfaction, the inconsiderable portion of liberty of which they are deprived with the sum total sacrificed by others for their security; observing that they have only given up the pernicious liberty of injuring their fellow-creatures, they bless the throne, and the laws upon which it is established.

It is false that the sciences have always been prejudicial to mankind. When they were so, the evil was inevitable. The multiplication of the human species on the face of the earth introduced war, the rudiments of arts, and the first laws, which were temporary compacts, arising from necessity, and perishing with it. This was the first philosophy, and its few elements were just, as indolence and want of sagacity in the early inhabitants of the world preserved them from error.

But necessities increasing with the number of mankind, stronger and more lasting impressions were necessary to prevent their frequent relapses into a state of barbarity, which became every day more fatal. The first religious errors, which peopled the earth with false divinities, and created a world of invisible beings to govern the visible creation, were of the utmost service to mankind. The greatest benefactors to humanity were those who dared to deceive, and lead pliant ignorance to the foot of the altar. By presenting to the minds of the vulgar things out of the reach of their senses, which fled as they pursued, and always eluded their grasp which as they never comprehended, they never despised, their different passions were united, and attached to a single object. This was the first transition of all nations from their savage state. Such was the necessary, and perhaps the only bond of all societies at their first formation. I speak not of the chosen people of God, to whom the most extraordinary miracles and the most signal favours supplied the place of human policy. But as it is the nature of error to subdivide itself *ad infinitum,* so the pretended knowledge which sprung from it, transformed mankind into a blind fanatic multitude, jarring and destroying each other in the labyrinth in which they were inclosed: hence it is not wonderful that some sensible and philosophic minds should regret the ancient state of barbarity. This was the first epocha, in which knowledge, or rather opinions, were fatal.

The second may be found in the difficult and terrible passage from error to truth, from darkness to light. The violent shock between a mass of errors useful to the few and powerful, and the truths so important to the many and the weak, with the fermentation of passions excited on that occasion, were productive of infinite evils to unhappy mortals. In the study of history, whose principal periods, after certain intervals, much resemble each other, we frequently find in the necessary passage from the obscurity of ignorance to the light of philosophy, and from tyranny to liberty, its natural consequence, one generation sacrificed to the happiness of the next. But when this flame is extinguished, and the world delivered from its evils, truth, after a very slow progress, sits down with monarchs on the throne, and is worshipped in the assemblies of nations. Shall we then believe, that light diffused among the people is more destructive than darkness, and that the knowledge of the relation of things can ever be fatal to mankind?

Ignorance may indeed be less fatal than a small degree of knowledge, because this adds to the evils of ignorance, the inevitable errors of a confined view of things on this side the bounds of truth; but a man of enlightened understanding, appointed guardian of the laws, is the greatest blessing that a sovereign can bestow on a nation. Such a man is accustomed to behold truth, and not to fear it; unacquainted with the greatest part of those imaginary and insatiable necessities which so often put virtue to the proof, and accustomed to contemplate mankind from the most elevated point of view, he considers the nation as his family, and his fellow-citizens as brothers; the distance between the great and the vulgar appears to him the less as the number of mankind he has in view is greater.

The philosopher has necessities and interests unknown to the vulgar, and the chief of these is not to belie in public the principles he taught in obscurity, and the habit of loving virtue for its own sake. A few such philosophers would constitute the happiness of a nation; which however would be but of short duration, unless by good laws the number were so increased as to lessen the probability of an improper choice.

## XLIII  Of magistrates

Another method of preventing crimes is, to make the observance of the laws, and not their violation, the interest of the magistrate.

The greater the number of those who constitute the tribunal, the less is the danger of corruption; because the attempt will be more difficult, and the power and temptation of each individual will be proportionably less. If the sovereign, by pomp and the austerity of edicts, and by refusing to hear the complaints of the oppressed, accustom his subjects to respect the magistrates more than the laws, the magistrates will gain indeed, but it will be at the expense of public and private security.

## XLIV  Of rewards

Yet another method of preventing crimes is, to reward virtue. Upon this subject the laws of all nations are silent. If the rewards proposed by academies for the discovery of useful truths have increased our knowledge, and multiplied good books, is it not probable, that rewards, distributed by the beneficent hand of a sovereign, would also multiply virtuous actions. The coin of honour is inexhaustible, and is abundantly fruitful in the hands of a prince who distributes it wisely.

## XLV  Of education

Finally, the most certain method of preventing crimes is, to perfect the system of education. But this is an object too vast, and exceeds my plan; an object, if I may venture to declare it, which is so intimately connected with the nature of government, that it will always remain a barren spot, cultivated only by a few wise men.

A great man, who is persecuted by that world he hath enlightened, and to whom we are indebted for many important truths, hath most amply detailed the principal maxims of useful education. This chiefly consists in presenting to the mind a small number of select objects, in substituting the originals for the copies both of physical and moral phenomena, in leading the pupil to virtue by the easy road of sentiment, and in withholding him from evil by the infallible power of necessary inconveniences, rather than by command, which only obtains a counterfeit and momentary obedience.

## XLVI  Of pardons

As punishments become more mild, clemency and pardon are less necessary. Happy the nation in which they will be considered as dangerous! Clemency, which has often been deemed a sufficient substitute for every other virtue in sovereigns, should be excluded in a perfect legislation, where punishments are mild, and the proceedings in criminal cases regular and expeditious. This truth will seem cruel to those who live in countries where, from the absurdity of the laws and the severity of punishments, pardons and the clemency of the prince are necessary. It is indeed one of the noblest prerogatives of the throne, but, at the same time, a tacit disapprobation of the laws.

Clemency is a virtue which belongs to the legislator, and not to the executor of the laws; a virtue which ought to shine in the code, and not in private judgment. To shew mankind that crimes are sometimes pardoned, and that punishment is not the necessary consequence, is to nourish the flattering hope of impunity, and is the cause of their considering every punishment inflicted as an act of injustice and oppression. The prince in pardoning gives up the public security in favour of an individual, and, by his ill-judged benevolence, proclaims a public act of impunity. Let, then, the executors of the laws be inexorable, but let the legislator be tender, indulgent, and humane. He is a wise architect who erects his edifice on the foundation of self-love, and contrives that the interest of the public shall be the interest of each individual, who is not obliged, by particular laws and irregular proceedings, to separate the public good from that of individuals, and erect the image of public felicity on the basis of fear and distrust; but, like a wise philosopher, he will permit his brethren to enjoy in quiet that small portion of happiness, which the immense system, established by the first cause, permits them to taste on this earth, which is but a point in the universe.

A small crime is sometimes pardoned if the person offended chooses to forgive the offender. This may be an act of good nature and humanity, but it is contrary to the good of the public: for although a private citizen may dispense with satisfaction for the injury he has received, he cannot remove the necessity of example. The right of punishing belongs not to any individual in particular, but to society in general, or the sovereign. He may renounce his own portion of this right, but cannot give up that of others.

## XLVII Conclusion

I conclude with this reflection, that the severity of punishments ought to be in proportion to the state of the nation. Among a people hardly yet emerged from barbarity, they should be most severe, as strong impressions are required; but, in proportion as the minds of men become softened by their intercourse in society, the severity of punishments should be diminished, if it be intended that the necessary relation between the object and the sensation should be maintained.

From what I have written results the following general theorem, of considerable utility, though not conformable to custom, the common legislator of nations:

*That a punishment may not be an act of violence, of one, or of many, against a private member of society, it should be public, immediate, and necessary, the least possible in the case given, proportioned to the crime, and determined by the laws.*

NOTE TO THE READER

Two of the chapters of the *Syntopicon* deal directly with the subjects of Beccaria's concern. Chapter 74 is devoted to the idea of PUNISHMENT, and Topic 4 is on crime and punishment. Under its various sub-topics the reader will find the references to many passages in *GBWW* discussing the problems that Beccaria raises, especially 4b(1): The death penalty: its justification, and 4b(4): Torture: cruel and unusual punishments. In Chapter 46, on LAW, the reader will find discussions on criminal law in the citations listed under Topic 6e: The breach of law: crime and punishment.

# Poetry and Mathematics

Scott Buchanan

## Editor's Introduction

It is a curious feature of our specifically human powers, and of the way in which we regard them, that while we think they are peculiar to us among the creatures of the earth and thus definitive of our kind, we often seem to doubt that they are compatible with each other, or at least we find difficulties in their combination. In particular, we find it hard to reconcile the faculties of intellect and imagination, which we see, or the products of which we see, as in some way opposed. The perception of this was already old with Plato, who notes in *The Republic* that "there is an ancient quarrel between philosophy and poetry" as to which has the greater claim to men's allegiance. A related conflict was that which seemed to the medieval schoolmen to lie between philosophy and theology. During the Renaissance we find much discussion, as in Hobbes, of the difference between the works of judgment and the works of fancy. And in modern times we have declared a gulf between science and literature, the extent of which was recognized not long ago by Sir Charles Snow in his widely read book *The Two Cultures*. So great has this gulf come to seem that some writers, among them William James, have argued that there are really two kinds of human intellect—one of which James calls "the splendid," the other, "the analytic,"—which are seldom if ever found in conjunction. We are reminded of Darwin, who discovered that after the age of thirty he could no longer read poetry, look at pictures, or listen to music with any pleasure, and who concluded that the part of his brain given to "the higher aesthetic tastes" had atrophied.

There are notable exceptions, of course, in the tradition of the great books to this intellectual bifurcation, and to the acceptance of it. Plato himself was a poet before he became a philosopher, and was a master, too, of mathematics. Aristotle, whose finished writings, which do not survive, were said by the ancients to have a "golden eloquence," was in any case a profound critic of poetry and drama, besides being the scientist for all time. Dante showed himself to be learned in the mathematics and astronomy of his age when he wrote the *Divine Comedy*, as, on the other hand, Isaac Newton studied the writings of the church fathers and manifested, in the third book of *Principia Mathematica*, a capacity for religious vision. And still other figures—Gilbert, for one, and for another, Goethe—might be cited as combining the different intellectual tendencies to which James refers.

How this can be is suggested by Scott Buchanan's *Poetry and Mathematics*, which undertakes to show that these tendencies, far from indicating that two kinds of mind exist, as James believed, are merely signs of the way any mind works when it is truly thinking. For when it is truly thinking, Buchanan argues, it is making use of both the arts of language and the arts of number, which it employs to deal with the ideas it has or has been given about itself and about the world. Of course these arts can be practiced and refined to an unequal degree, and men may be more proficient in some of them than they are in others. But none of the arts can really be dispensed with (we use them unconsciously, by habit, a good deal of the time), as none can be wholly mastered without a perception of how others are implied and complemented by it. Together such arts allow us to proceed from abstractions to particulars (the mathematical arts) and from particulars to abstractions (the verbal arts), and so comprehend the basic movements of our thought.

Buchanan's classic essay was the outgrowth of some experience with the People's Institute of Cooper Union in New York City during the 1920s. Buchanan was assistant director of the Institute, and as such was responsible for certain aspects of its program of adult education. This program was designed for and largely attended by first and second generation immigrants to the United States, who were anxious to keep in touch with intellectual and educational traditions from which they had been uprooted. In the course of a series of guest lectures he arranged on psychology, economics, history, natural science, medicine, philosophy, and literature, Buchanan, himself a philosopher by training, became aware that his unacademic but intellectually sophisticated audience was deficient both in mathematics and in what he called poetry or poetics, by which he meant the free use of the imagination in dealing with doctrines and ideas. Accordingly, he undertook to give a series of lectures on both subjects, the parallelism of which gradually impressed itself upon him, and which he explored in *Poetry and Mathematics*.

Among the guest lecturers at the institute in these years were Mortimer Adler and Richard McKeon, both of whom were teaching at Columbia University. McKeon maintained that what Buchanan had rediscovered were the liberal arts, by which he meant, on the one hand, the trivium of grammar, rhetoric, and logic, which are concerned with words, and on the other hand, the quadrivium of arithmetic, geometry, music, and astronomy, which deal with number, measure, ratios, and what mathematicians call functions. It would be a good thing, McKeon argued, if he and Adler and Buchanan were to attempt the task of revising the traditional forms in which these arts have come down to us, and to reconstruct them for the sake of the order and purpose they could bring to the curriculum of contemporary colleges and universities.

This is what all three men proceeded to do, Adler and McKeon at the University of Chicago and Buchanan at St. John's College, Annapolis, Maryland. In 1937 St. John's adopted a liberal arts program that, with its balance of required readings in both the sciences and the humanities, reflected the insights that had been developed earlier at the People's Institute and in *Poetry and Mathematics*. Buchanan remained at St. John's as dean and tutor for ten years. Subsequently, he came to feel that the revival of liberal learning to which he was committed would require a revival of politics and political institutions, to the study of which he devoted the last years of his life. He wrote a book on this subject and many papers, the latter at the Center for the Study of Democratic Institutions at Santa Barbara, California, of which he was a consultant and a fellow at his death in 1968.

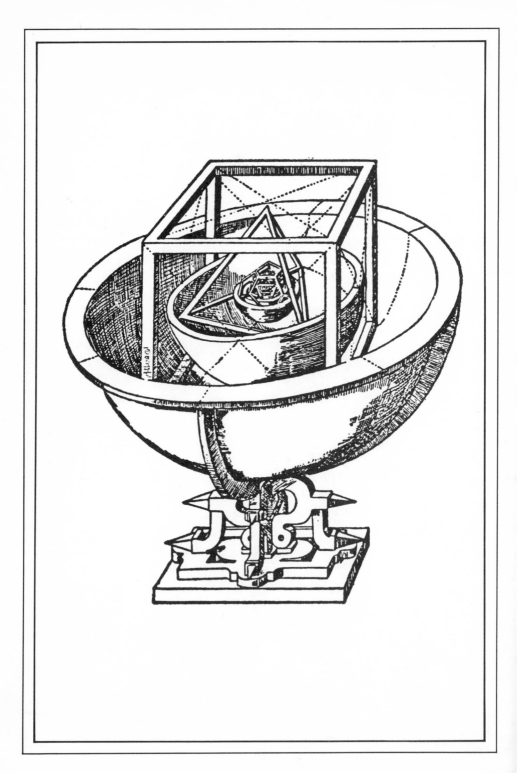

# Poetry and Mathematics

## Author's Note

This book might be dedicated to the proposition that each human being is both a poet and a mathematician, but perhaps it might better be dedicated to two human beings who were superb masters of poetry and mathematics, Dante and Kepler. Dante constructed the *Divine Comedy* on a framework of Aristotelian and Ptolemaic astronomy. Kepler transformed this framework into the modern solar system. Both were guided by the poetic considerations of theological, psychological, and moral analogies. (See the chapter on Proportions.)

The illustration on the facing page is from the original edition of Kepler's *Mysterium Cosmographicum*. It is a diagram of the solar system or cosmos constructed with six concentric spheres spaced and held apart by five regular solids. The outer sphere is the sphere of Saturn, the next the sphere of Jupiter, the next the sphere of Mars, the next the sphere of Earth, the next the sphere of Venus, and the next the sphere of Mercury. (Only the first four spheres are visible in the diagram; the others can be imagined.) The five regular solids are (reading from outside to inside):

 The cube, consisting of six squares
 The tetrahedron or pyramid, consisting of four equilateral triangles
 The dodecahedron, consisting of twelve regular pentagons
 The icosahedron, consisting of twenty equilateral triangles
 The octahedron, consisting of eight equilateral triangles

For Kepler the mystery arose from the following considerations: (1) that only these five regular solids were possible; (2) that there were six planets; (3) that thus successively inscribed in spheres the regular solids determined the correct diameters of the spheres to contain the orbits of the planets as observed by Tycho Brahe and calculated by Kepler.

The mysterious diagram was first constructed and explained in the *Mysterium Cosmographicum* in 1596, then repeated in the *Harmonies of the World* in 1616 after all the corrections and revisions in the orbits had been worked out in the *Epitome of Copernican Astronomy*. It had been the guiding vision throughout.

## CONTENTS

## I Poetry and mathematics

Our immediate intellectual ancestors were accustomed to speak of their neat and stuffy world as if it were an island of light in a sea of darkness. The figure of speech, together with the fact that they felt keenly what it expresses, conveys to us something of the origin of most of our predicaments. They were really describing a ghost, one of many which we have in our present intellectual twilight. We would rather speak, more literally, as we think, about the defects in our vision. We call our half-sight confusion, which I suppose means that we have many ghosts that we cannot tell apart.

Two of them who now walk most frequently, probably because of some peculiar odor rising from the witch's pot of industry and advertising, are inescapable for most people. They manifest a dignified agitation which is most contagious and upsetting. They seem to demand credulity and devotion, and when that is granted, run into the most whimsical and sometimes insane fits, exchanging and re-exchanging their disguises, and leaving their victims in hypnotic postures, or weak and disillusioned lethargies.

When they are entertained in the best society, they are known as mathematics and poetry. That they are often so entertained is evidence of a long record of certified and revered activities. They have founded secret societies, they have revealed the truths of religion, they have trained physicians and

magicians. Their more sober and at present most respected occupations are engineering and democratic government. For a few they are always capped and gowned educators and edifiers.

However much their appearances and activities may vary, they are always found together, one of them talking while the other works, and it is always difficult to find out whether it is the talk or the work that produces the results. Sometimes it is quite clear that the talk is in truth necessary to the work, but its value lies in its irrelevance and prestidigitatory finesse. It is no wonder that we are confused.

I am going to try to expose these ghosts. In the main I shall try to do it by analysis and illustration that shall educe from the reader an immediate realization of what they are. But before I proceed, I think it will be well to introduce the characters by saying what they are not, but are often supposed to be.

Mathematics suffers much, but most of all from its teachers. As a result of bad pedagogy—and I mean the kind often judged best by administrative pedagogues—the appearance of an algebraic formula, a geometrical figure, or an innocent set of symbols reduces the reader to an unbecoming attitude of hypocritical humility. A great many sometime students of mathematics try to persuade themselves that they haven't mathematical minds, when as a matter of fact they have only had nonmathematical teachers. Mathematics is not what most teachers of mathematics teach. They, with the good intention of conveying what they themselves have only as a skill of manipulation, have unconsciously worked hocus-pocus on their pupils. They have repeated and illustrated opaque formulae, sometimes to the admiration, but almost always to the bewilderment, of their students. The honest-minded individual has in the end, however, been resilient and recovered from such maltreatment. The textbook makers and the psychologists of education have often found the ritual ineffective; on such occasions they have rearranged the words and introduced illustrations in what is known as the psychological order. The illustrations, precisely because they were already known, remained, as they were, "facts," and the formula that comes at the end remained also, as it always had been, a matter for summarizing memory, or "outside the scope of this book." Later the student, falling by chance into some mathematical mode of thought, is shocked to discover that he has been doing mathematics with his nonmathematical mind.

In general the teacher of mathematics has been the high priest of an occult ritual, the keeper in many senses of an esoteric doctrine which only his superiors or predecessors have understood. It is no wonder that Croce, the philosophical observer of a very fruitful period of Italian mathematics and education, should have given as his final dictum on mathematics that it is a mnemonic device, like Pelmanism, merely mimicking the intellectual activities of the human mind. He is rightly describing the exoteric student of mathematics, within which classification he himself falls.

Mathematics is not a compendium of memorizable formula and magically manipulated figures. Sometimes it uses formulae and manipulates figures, but it does this because it is concerned with ideas already familiar to the ordinary mind, but needing special sets of words or symbols for the sake of precise expression and efficient communication. Further, the abstraction thus signalized, which most people from bad emotional habits fear, is actually much more familiar to the untrained mind than any observed facts could possibly be. Abstract ideas are of the very tissue of the human mind. For this reason and for many others, illustration of mathematics by concrete event, fact, or object is never as effective as illustration by equally abstract analogous ideas. But here I am dangerously near giving away the secret of the title and we are not ready for it yet.

"Proof" is another word to conjure with. This word also has been spoiled by teachers of mathematics, but perhaps even more by the emphasis laid on the conventions of mathematical exposition by certain kinds of mathematical writers. It has come to be believed that the professional mathematician is a prover of propositions. From that belief it follows that mathematics is concerned with rigid structures, chains, and networks of propositions which are related as premises and conclusions of scholastic argument. For one who has not found it necessary to argue as a lawyer in a courtroom, this makes mathematics tedious and empty. It clips the wings of the human spirit.

For a philosopher perhaps this is the saddest of all the misconceptions of mathematics, for with it goes another misconception and hatred—that which is directed at logic and speculative thought in general. It is therefore easy and pleasant to criticize, even though many mathematicians will not agree.

It is true that mathematics sometimes deals with rigid structures, chains, and networks, but they are not made of propositions, and long and elaborate arguments are most often bad mathematics. The structures with which mathematics deals are more like lace, the leaves of trees, and the play of light and shadow on a meadow or a human face, than they are like buildings and machines, the least of their representatives. The best proofs in mathematics are short and crisp like epigrams, and the longest have swings and rhythms that are like music. The structures of mathematics and the propositions about them are ways for the imagination to travel and the wings, or legs, or vehicles to take you where you want to go. The solemn sound of demonstrated mathematical truths is a professional way of announcing an arrival at some point on the journey fantastic. Let it be added for good measure that some of the greatest mathematical discoveries by the greatest mathematical minds have been theorems that they could not prove; some have never been proved. The fact of the matter is that anything worth discovering in mathematics does not need proof; it needs only to be seen or understood. I hope this will become clear as I proceed. I also hope that the uses and relevance of proofs as aids to understanding and mathematical sight will appear in their proper places.

Symbols, formulae and proofs have another hypnotic effect. Because they are not immediately understood, they, like certain jokes, are suspected of holding in some sort of magic embrace the secret of the universe, or at least some of its more hidden parts. First, it may be noted that a few numbers or counters record the contents of a wallet or a treasure chest. They will also balance against debts owed by the owner. Further, by proper manipulation numbers on slips of paper produce the same practical effects as weighed units of gold or silver—they pay bills. Finally the man who sits at his desk and inscribes numbers and code messages on bits of paper controls the markets of the world. By faith in the checking code we move ourselves, our possessions, and finally mountains. The scientist tries a similar trick on what he sees and what he would like to see in the laboratory; he decodes nature and translates his and nature's secret into a formula. The doctor of occult science sees wisdom in all that the banker and physicist have recorded and stamps it with the seal of divine knowledge. Mathematics then becomes the ladder by which we all may climb into the heaven of perfect insight and eternal satisfaction, and the solution of arithmetic and algebraic problems is connected with the salvation of our souls.

The prestige of the engineer is another accretion to the tradition of mathematics. This more than any other one thing accounts for our present mathematical complex. The engineer is fast taking the position of authority, superseding the priest, the scholar, and the statesman in our organized thought and action. We ask and take his word, not only in practical matters where the question is how to do something, but also in theoretical matters where the question is what a thing is. Therefore, when the engineer says that his specialty is mathematics, we are doubly confident that his answer and practice are correct in this field.

Unfortunately the question, what is mathematics? is one question he has never asked. It is true he has learned to use it, especially those parts of it that deal with margins of safety and error, but like good workmen in other fields, his attention is on his skill and results rather than on his tools. Consequently his mathematics is intellectually patchy, a set of rules and facts good only for approximate measurement and plan-making. Like the computations in navigation it tells one more about sailing a ship than it does about the sun, moon, and stars. We shall find it difficult, if not impossible, to distinguish between applied mathematics and astrology, alchemy, and the occult arts. As these have fogged many minds in the past, so does the whole field of applied science based on mathematics today. It makes our industry possible and makes us worry about the future of our civilization. Watch the engineer and you will learn many things, but do not ask him about mathematics, unless you want to see quite another thing, how technology and folklore get invented and broadcast. A good part of the prestige of mathematics as a science is due to the contagion of such superstition. Let not your piety mislead your understanding.

Perhaps this is the place to introduce poetry, the other and perhaps better part of engineering. Every art has its mythology and ritual. So mathematics, when it becomes an art, fuses rhythmic language and gesture

417

with intoxicating action and fact. The engineer sings as he works—often he only whistles—and in that singing there is the magic of poetry. The engineer's science, like the sailor's chanty, is good literature.

Professional poets are very often, more frequently than mathematicians, bad critics of themselves and their work. The wisest of them refuse to talk about poetry, leaving analysis and description to their more voluble companions, the critics. The critics, in turn, see so many different things reflected in poetry that they get confused and talk about many other things, among which poetry itself only incidentally gets attention. Thus it comes about that most of us only accidentally recognize poetry when we see it, and at the same time we follow the critics in using a verbal blunderbuss in our "literary conversations." The result is an intellectual confusion not only about poetry but also about many other things with which poetry is concerned.

Unfortunately, both the poet and the critic are right, the former in his silence, and the latter in his necessary loquacity. They show by their respective behaviors that they know that about which they do not talk. For poetry, at least that aspect of it about which I wish to talk, is an essential activity of human beings. It is essential in the sense that no matter what human beings may be doing they are at least poets; as in the case of so many arts, what distinguishes poetry as a fine art is an added and somewhat arbitrary differentiation. Therefore to talk about it is in a peculiar sense redundant, for talking is essentially a poetic activity, and when its subject is poetry, it is an attempt to make poetry devour and digest itself. One has the choice of refraining from such cannibalism and paying a tribute of silence, or of talking so fast and about so many things that the subject comes in of itself as a by-product.

I shall add then to the stream of words more or less poetic, choosing that part of poetry which is most often compared and contrasted with mathematics, hoping by treating poetry mathematically and mathematics poetically, to show the mutual reflections and common illuminations that they afford.

Poetry is one of the finer arts and therefore, like mathematics and the other higher studies, has specialized and refined techniques. It deals with selected language devices and aspires to the purity of form achieved only by music. It is an esoteric art. Let no one enter here who is ignorant of versification or prosody. Beware of profaning the sanctuary with sentimentality or flippant facilities. Discipline is the only road to achievement. This is the talk of the poetry workshop, the literary correlate of the Academy for painting and sculpture. It is the sage advice of professional and laureate poets. Unfortunately many great poets have not had the advantages of this higher education.

The answer comes from the poetry circle and the salon where poetry is read—with appreciation. Discriminating judgment is here scaled to the thermometer of inspiration. The poet is the seer of strange visions and polite purveyor of his insights to the vibrant few who have lived or desire to live and therefore understand. For the devotees the material of their enthusiasm is emotion recollected in intense tranquillity and released under properly controlled atmospheric conditions to drive the moral engines. Edification is the process induced and the ascent attains the plane of the higher life.

This aspect of poetry is an incident in the histories of religion and attests a character in poetry which is always subject to religious development. There are always those who will worship at the shrines of unknown gods, and it is not an unknown miracle that they often thus discover the god upon whom they wait.

Thus in the course of time the psychological critic is called in for consultation on the case. He first appears as Pan to prove the heretical nature of the poet and his cult. Then he uncovers the sins out of which the heresy grew. The worshipers justify the sins and absolve the sinner, whereupon the critic renames his victims after some fashionable neurosis, outlaws the poet, and at the same time encourages him to wander fancy-free in the Elysian fields of the abnormal. Inspiration is madness, and romance is release or compensation for early thwartings.

Psychoanalysis for art's sake is not a modern discovery. It has always been an adjunct to the temple, and the psychopathology of the poet is always a powerful, though sometimes a suppressed, interest of readers of poetry. The question, what does poetry express, is most satisfactorily answered in diagnostic and therapeutic terms. A more learned person than I might write a companion essay to this on Medicine and Poetry, laboriously making explicit the theory lying back of such collections of verse as are often called "The Poetry Cure" and "Heart Throbs," and at the same time indirectly commenting on the true subject matter of such books as *The Poetic Mind* and *The Road to Xanadu*.

Such exploitation of poetry for hygienic purposes cannot be condemned, but its quality as poetry, or poetic talk about poetry, can be noted and the naïveté of the school of psychological criticism made a matter of historical record.

The economist and sociologist will then find it and make their no less naïve case more compelling. The poet with his peculiar social heritage and delicately sensitive recording apparatus then becomes a member of the lowest rank of researchers, giving the first fumbling formulation of social conditions or *Zeitgeist*. But the poet has his revenge, for with the sociologist's reverence and hunger for recorded fact, the written word containing all the dream and madness of the writer has been accepted and gobbled up as historical evidence and is only rediscovered at some later time as the somewhat eerie and woolly conclusion of a social science. Inspiration has thus been transfigured into the spirit of the age or the progress of humanity.

The outcome of all this is the hard-head-ed conclusion of some scientific philosopher that poetry is not true. This for a hard head means that it is false. Since falsity is deception, and deception is immoral, and one ought to be moral, one must eschew poetry. The reasoning here is bad enough, but the poetry is good, at least, in its expression of human moral intent. The actual point made is a vigorous preference for one as against another kind of poetry, namely that which has a literal interpretive reference to personally collected fact. In this light, science becomes the most modern and authentic technique of poetry. The scientist is the contemporary monk copyist, writing over old literature on the palimpsest of experience, triumphantly announcing his faithfulness and accuracy in transferring the copy. *Hypotheses non fingo*. He only selects according to the canons of his school.

It will be noticed here that mathematics and poetry move together between two extremes of mysticism, the mysticism of the commonplace where ideas illuminate and create facts, and the mysticism of the extraordinary where God, the Infinite, the Real, poses the riddles of desire and disappointment, sin and salvation, effort and failure, question and paradoxical answer. It is commonly supposed that science and common sense avoid these mysteries and futilities. The tradition of experimental science has strengthened our confidence in the unaided senses and intellect. But latterly things and ideas in these regions have been behaving peculiarly. The ghosts so confidently laid by Francis Bacon and his followers are again walking in the laboratory as well as beside the man in the street. There is something persistent in what the whimsical and uncontrollable universe of ideas does to our experience, something with which Pythagoras, Plato, Plotinus, St. Augustine, Nicolas of Cusa, Galileo, Kant, and probably Einstein would be more familiar than the modern prophets who preach the control of nature. They would have called it by different names, each appropriate to the several historical occasions on which crises similar to our own have occurred. Some would have speculated about the foundations of the universe, some about the origin of the laws of nature, some about the Incarnation, some about the spontaneity of the human imagination, others about a possible transformation formula for Euclidean and non-Euclidean geometries.

Without intending to beg any metaphysical questions, I shall be referring to that sort of thing when I speak of poetry and mathematics and treating them as of equal importance and parallel developments in human culture. The nicest term to describe it is *logos*, which in Greek means equally "word" and "reason." I shall not burden the reader with further words of reverence for its historical dignity.

Very simply, poetry and mathematics are two very successful attempts to deal with ideas. In this respect they are genuine. Both employ sets of symbols and systems of notation. In this respect they have very interesting and illuminating comparisons and contrasts. As they revolve through their life cycles of fantasy, utility, culture, truth, and falsity, they reveal what I shall call aspects of the mathematical and poetic object. These accidental aspects merge and separate, giving their objects a very puzzling Protean character. They exchange disguises so that mathematics, commonly accepted for its hard-headedness, rigor and accuracy, is often poetry creating a realm of fancy; and poetry, commonly loved for its playful spontaneity and utter ineffectualness, becomes the mathematical demiurge joining words and images into a world of hard persuasive fact.

It is good fun, if not a task of paramount importance, to disentangle these aspects and trace their origins back to the mathematical and poetic objects—and thus learn to live with what are now ghosts behaving like somewhat mad Siamese twins.

The clarification of any idea, however simple or complex it may be, begins with its location on that translucent phosphorescent surface of man's thought that Plato called opinion or belief. Whether thought is like some distant gaseous star announcing its presence by a spot of light in the heavens, or like a witches' pot of potent herbs, fiery liquids and smelly vapors, boiling at the center of the human psyche, first examination always discloses this scum of amorphous cloudy opinion that represents and at the same time obscures the interior essences. The presumption is that everything inside sends up and out some ambiguous efflux of itself which is then held in suspension by the inner pressures and attractions. The astrophysicist makes telescopic and spectroscopic observations, and infers the nature of the inner fire and commotion. The psychoanalyst listens to words and watches gestures, and infers the chemistry of the soul. The dialectician by critical questioning intellectualizes and progressively eliminates the confusions of opinion until the idea stands clear and immediate to direct intuition.

Eddington and Freud are astrophysicist and psychoanalyst at present; Plato is the dialectician for all time. All three are good to mention in connection with the present undertaking, because they have been concerned, to be sure from different angles, with what I mean by poetry and mathematics. But Plato is especially relevant, not only because I too wish to be a dialectician, but also because he dealt most successfully with a crisis in the life of reason very similar to that which I wish to point out in the present.

The method and style of thought known as Pythagoreanism had achieved marked success in combining poetry and mathematics, and opinion among the Greeks showed all the vagaries and caricatures that one can imagine it possible to attach to the esoteric doctrine. Plato, the dialectician, had more than any other one man to do with the clarification of this opinion which finally issued in the science of Aristotle and the geometry of Euclid. Contemporary science shows the unmistakable symptoms of Pythagoreanism, and ordinary opinion and our rather extraordinary beliefs play with the vagaries and caricatures that are its typical companions.

Plato's method, as I have intimated, was to start with such opinion and by the continuous alternation of tentative hypothesis and criticism to make ever finer and more just distinctions until, in the language of the *Sophist*, the sameness and difference, the one and the many, the being and the non-being of the subject matter were obvious.

The literary style into which such philosophic criticism falls should be, as in Plato's model, the dialogue. Dialogue and dialectic show their affinities even in their names. But the dialogue is always a difficult form to construct, and at present it is a weak and patience-taxing vehicle of communication. Therefore, I propose to put this dialectical attempt into the less happy and adequate, but more economical, form of the essay.

By way of introducing the chief characters of the essay, I have referred them, poetry and mathematics, to the last pair of Plato's categories, their being and non-being, what they are and what they are supposed to be but are not. This ought to prepare the ground for the chapters immediately following which discuss their one and many aspects. The last two chapters deal more specifically with their similarities and differences.

To any popularizer of knowledge, let this be an invitation to suspend his labors of enlightenment until he has considered the following points in the analysis of his subject matter. I can assure him that the analysis has been made for the sake of his subject matter as much as in criticism of the aim and method of his treatment of it. His sin is usually called the inaccurate statement of half-truths. This is the burden of the criticism of all literature. Its opposing virtue, comprehensiveness and precision, is usually monopolized by the mathematician and is called *elegance*. He boasts of the economy of his style. But it is also an essential, though

old-fashioned, virtue in literature. It usually requires a fundamental rethinking of a subject matter. I hope this essay will at least in an indirect way contribute to the wider achievement of this virtue.

## II Figures

Each symbol used in mathematics, whether it be a diagram, a numeral, a letter, a sign, or a conventional hieroglyph, may be understood as a vehicle which someone has used on a journey of discovery. Many have ridden all their lives on one or another set of these symbols without finding what they were looking for, namely, the meaning of the symbol. Sometimes the riding has been so enjoyable and fruitful in by-products that the original quest has been forgotten and the question has gone unanswered until some second rider has pushed on to the end. This is the extraordinary feature of mathematical study and perhaps one of the causes of bewilderment in its students. It gives perhaps a deeper meaning than is usually assigned to Euclid's famous remark that "there is no royal road to geometry."

However, as I have intimated in the preceding chapter, the vehicles are not mathematics, and too much attention can easily be given to unessentials. Fortunately it is the privilege of anyone at this period of history to forget the ride and the vehicles used and grasp immediately the discovered object of many of the journeys. At any rate, many of the roads can be telescoped or leaped over. Furthermore it is very important to do some of this reconnoitering at the beginning, in order to keep direction and thus maintain the proper proportion between effort and interest. This is true even for the professional mathematician. It is a necessity for the amateur. It may be added that the intuitive method is the basic procedure even for the rigorous step-by-step construction of elaborate mathematical systems.

Each journey then ends in some aspect of

the mathematical object for which we search, and the next few chapters, beginning with this, will be telescoped flights from the bare symbol to some essential character of this object.

The first and perhaps the most illuminating question in mathematics is, what is a geometrical figure? I shall answer it in very general terms and then proceed to uncover their meanings. A figure in geometry is the sort of thing that retains an identical character throughout a series of possible transformations.

Lewis Carroll's Alice is obviously a geometrical figure on many occasions in Wonderland. In fact many of the characters in Lewis Carroll's writings conform to the preliminary definition I have given, and Lewis Carroll is not the only mathematician who has been able to present the mathematical object in alternative languages.

The Caterpillar in Chapter V of *Alice in Wonderland* is a typical teacher of mathematics, and Alice is a typical pupil, in this case doubly surprised and bewildered because she is at the same time the figure to be understood. Incidentally, she was also learning some first lessons in modern relativity.

*The Caterpillar and Alice looked at each other for some time in silence: at last the Caterpillar took the hookah out of its mouth, and addressed her in a languid, sleepy voice.*

*"Who are you?" said the Caterpillar.*

*This was not an encouraging opening for a conversation. Alice replied, rather shyly, "I—I hardly know, sir, just at present—at least I know who I was when I got up this morning, but I think I must have been changed several times since then."*

*"What do you mean by that?" said the Caterpillar sternly. "Explain yourself!"*

*"I can't explain myself, I'm afraid, sir," said Alice, "because I'm not myself, you see."*

*"I don't see," said the Caterpillar.*

*"I'm afraid I can't put it more clearly," Alice replied very politely, "for I can't understand it myself, to begin with; and being so many different sizes in a day is very confusing."*

*"It isn't," said the Caterpillar.*

*"Well, perhaps you haven't found it so yet," said Alice, "but when you have to turn into a chrysalis—you will some day, you know—and then after that into a butterfly, I should think you'll feel it a little queer, won't you?"*

*"Not a bit," said the Caterpillar.*

*"Well, perhaps your feelings may be different," said Alice; "all I know is, it would feel very queer to me."*

*"You!" said the Caterpillar contemptuously. "Who are you?"*

*Which brought them back again to the beginning of the conversation. Alice felt a little irritated at the Caterpillar's making such very short remarks, and she drew herself up and said very gravely, "I think you ought to tell me who you are, first."*

*"Why?" said the Caterpillar.*

*Here was another puzzling question; and as Alice could not think of any good reason, and as the Caterpillar seemed to be in a very unpleasant state of mind, she turned away.*

*"Come back!" the Caterpillar called after her. "I've something important to say!"*

*This sounded promising, certainly. Alice turned and came back again.*

*"Keep your temper," said the Caterpillar.*

*"Is that all?" said Alice, swallowing down her anger as well as she could.*

*"No," said the Caterpillar.*

*Alice thought she might as well wait, as she had nothing else to do, and perhaps after all it might tell her something worth hearing. For some minutes it puffed away without speaking; but at last it unfolded its arms, took the hookah out of its mouth again, and said, "So you think you're changed, do you?"*

*"I'm afraid I am, sir," said Alice; "I can't remember things as I used—and I don't keep the same size for ten minutes together!"*

*"Can't remember what things?" said the Caterpillar.*

*"Well, I've tried to say 'How doth the little busy bee,' but it all came different!" Alice replied in a very melancholy voice.*

*"Repeat 'You are old, Father William,' " said the Caterpillar.*

*Alice folded her hands, and began:*

*" 'You are old, Father William,' the young man said,*

'And your hair has become very white,
And yet you incessantly stand on your head—
Do you think, at your age, it is right?' "

. . . . . . . . . . . . . . . . . . . .

"That is not said right," said the Caterpillar.

"Not quite right, I'm afraid," said Alice timidly; "some of the words have got altered."

"It is wrong from beginning to end," said the Caterpillar decidedly, and there was silence for some minutes.

The Caterpillar was the first to speak.

"What size do you want to be?" it asked.

"Oh, I'm not particular as to size," Alice hastily replied; "only one doesn't like changing so often, you know."

"I don't know," said the Caterpillar.

Alice said nothing; she had never been so much contradicted in all her life before, and she felt that she was losing her temper.

"Are you content now?" said the Caterpillar.

"Well, I should like to be a little larger, sir, if you wouldn't mind," said Alice; "three inches is such a wretched height to be."

"It is a very good height indeed!" said the Caterpillar angrily, rearing itself upright as it spoke (it was exactly three inches high).

"But I'm not used to it!" pleaded poor Alice in a piteous tone. And she thought to herself, "I wish the creature wouldn't be so easily offended!"

"You'll get used to it in time," said the Caterpillar, and it put the hookah into its mouth and began smoking again.

This time Alice waited patiently until it chose to speak again. In a minute or two the Caterpillar took the hookah out of its mouth, and yawned once or twice, and shook itself. Then it got down off the mushroom, and crawled away into the grass, merely remarking as it went, "One side will make you grow taller, and the other side will make you grow shorter."

"One side of what? The other side of what?" thought Alice to herself.

"Of the mushroom," said the Caterpillar, just as if she had asked it aloud; and in another moment it was out of sight.

Alice remained looking thoughtfully at the mushroom for a minute, trying to make out which were the two sides of it; and, as it was perfectly round,

she found this a very difficult question. However, at last she stretched her arms round it as far as they would go, and broke off a bit of the edge with each hand.

"And now which is which?" she said to herself, and nibbled a little of the right-hand bit to try the effect: the next moment she felt a violent blow underneath her chin; it had struck her foot.

She was a good deal frightened by this very sudden change, but she felt that there was no time to be lost, as she was shrinking rapidly; so she set to work at once to eat some of the other bit. Her chin was pressed so closely against her foot that there was hardly room to open her mouth; but she did it at last, and managed to swallow a morsel of the left-hand bit. . . .

"Come, my head's free at last!" said Alice in a tone of delight, which changed into alarm in another moment, when she found that her shoulders were nowhere to be found; all she could see, when she looked down, was an immense length of neck, which seemed to rise like a stalk out of a sea of green leaves that lay far below her.

"What can all that green stuff be?" said Alice. "And where have my shoulders got to? And oh, my poor hands, how is it I can't see you?" She was moving them about as she spoke, but no result seemed to follow, except a little shaking among the distant green leaves.

As there seemed to be no chance of getting her hands up to her head, she tried to get her head down to them, and was delighted to find that her neck would bend about easily in any direction, like a serpent. She had just succeeded in curving it down into a graceful zigzag, and was going to dive in among the leaves, which she found to be nothing but the tops of the trees under which she had been wandering, when a sharp hiss made her draw back in a hurry; a large pigeon had flown into her face, and was beating her violently with its wings.

. . . . . . . . . . . . . . . . . . . . . . . . . . .

Alice crouched down among the trees as well as she could, for her neck kept getting entangled among the branches, and every now and then she had to stop and untwist it. After a while she remembered that she still had the pieces of mushroom in her hands, and she set to work very carefully, nibbling first at one and then at the other, growing sometimes taller and sometimes shorter, until she *had succeeded in bringing herself down to her usual height.*

*It was so long since she had been anything near the right size, that it felt quite strange at first, but she got used to it in a few minutes, and began talking to herself as usual. "Come, there's half my plan done now! I'm never sure what I'm going to be, from one minute to another! However, I've got back to my right size; the next thing is to get into that beautiful garden—how is that to be done, I wonder?" As she said this she came suddenly upon an open place, with a little house in it about four feet high. "Whoever lives there," thought Alice, "it'll never do to come upon them this size; why, I should frighten them out of their wits!" So she began nibbling at the right-hand bit again, and did not venture to go near the house till she had brought herself down to nine inches high.*

This is a highly generalized form of geometry. It is often called positional or projective geometry. Another case of it will be demanded by the conventional mathematician; I take the suggestion for it from an early work of Euclid on optics.

Suppose you are looking at some ordinary object, say a cup and saucer or a tree, and you begin speculating on the rays of light which are passing somehow from the many points of the cup and saucer or the tree. They are said to converge at some point of your eye, say between the lens and the retina. They pass through a common point. Now travel back along the bundle of rays. Stop at any point and pass a plane perpendicular to your line of vision so that it will cut all the rays from the object. You will then have on the plane a two-dimensional picture of the object. Each point in the visible object will have a corresponding point on the plane of projection. As you move the plane nearer you, you have a smaller picture, and as you move it toward the object, you have a larger picture. You will indeed have a series of possible pictures each corresponding to some possible position of the plane.

Suppose you move the plane away from you through the object, extending the rays as far as the plane. Move the plane ten feet back from the object, then one mile, then a thousand miles, as far as you please. The picture increases by definite degrees of magnification to any size you please. Bring the plane back to your eye, through the point of convergence where the picture seems to disappear in one point, and back through your head indefinitely. The picture again grows and, in a manner of speaking, grows infinitely large.

You have here a beautifully simple case of conic sections. For if you simplify the object to a sphere or a disc held perpendicular to your line of vision, the planes of projection in their various positions cut a cone of light rays whose apex is in your eye. Each section will be a circle. Change the angle of the plane to your line of vision and you can get ellipses, parabolas, and hyperbolas of any size. Each is a geometrical figure which has a long story about it in the history of mathematics. Around each of the operations with the cutting plane and the cone there has grown up a branch of mathematical study.

Projective geometry is interested in the transformations themselves: how a figure retains certain properties such as proportionality of lines and angles throughout given transformations; whether following a given set of these transformations will reproduce a given figure or always produce new ones; and the most general laws governing such properties.

Certain of these laws taken together will give you metric geometry. The application of these laws determines rigid lines and angles and these figures so produced have certain properties with which most students become familiar in courses on plane and solid geometry. It is geometry of this sort that has often clipped the wings of a young mathematical imagination. Metric geometry appears so obviously applicable that the intrinsic properties of its objects lose their charm and one becomes an inventor or engineer, and geometrical thought gets its first suppression. Then too, rigidity of line and angle has a mechanical aspect that at once frightens and hypnotizes the uninitiated into a frozen stare at what seem prison bars and mazes. This is one of the occasions when the two ghosts, mathematics and poetry, have contrived to be especially diabolical. The teacher of mathematics has introduced a bugaboo with regrettable results both in understanding and in discipline.

Rigidity is really there, but how different it is from its reputed character! The rigid figures of metric geometry are like the points of rest in the path of Zeno's famous arrow. They are the arbitrary termini of intervals, paradoxical if taken by themselves, but intelligible enough if understood as stages in a projective development or as materials to be transformed.

We have tried the variations in a single conic projective field. We accomplished that development by shifting a projective plane. Suppose now we hold the plane fixed and shift the apex of the cone. We are looking at a circle. When the line of vision is perpendicular to the plane of the circle, we see a circle. Moving away from the plane in the same line of vision makes the circle grow smaller. This shows the simple principle of painter's perspective. Now suppose we begin to move around the circle. We see a series of ellipses each a little flatter than the preceding one until, when our line of vision is in the plane of the circle, the ellipse becomes a straight line indistinguishable in length and position from the vertical diameter of the circle. Continuing our revolution around the circle, we again see the ellipses becoming fatter and finally achieving circularity. Varying the orbit of our point of vision, we can travel ideally to any point in space, and for each station on the way there will be a corresponding geometric figure discernible. Certain philosophers have proposed this set of figures as a solution of the problem of perception in the theory of knowledge. A coin is the series of aspects possible to realize by this method in all the points of space. These philosophers have been hypnotized by a field of projection whose "rigidity" they have taken for substance. But they are right

about the "rigidity" of these fields of projection. Although it would take a super-aviator, a very whimsical old lady on a broom, a disembodied fairy, or a relativity physicist to realize even a small part of the field of projection of any given object, the conditions of the transformations, the sequence of the "aspects" and the relations between the aspects would follow a rule or principle of the sort which mathematicians and some philosophers would call eternal truths; they mean that something very much like the soul of the projective field remains constant throughout an indefinite number of variations. This field is itself a geometric figure and each variation is again such a figure. Mathematical philosophers whose imaginations are touched with poetry, such as Leibniz and Bruno, see in this an account of the whole universe. It is constituted of points or monads each mirroring the whole. In other words, the universe is a very complex but unified projective field constituted of projective fields. But Leibniz, at any rate, saw that such a universe was not material; its rigidity was not a physical rigidity. Its rigidity is the rigidity of a speculative imagination.

It is not difficult to see how this sort of rigor is invoked by the poet along with the inspiration of his particular muse. Even a short poem that gives words to a mood discovers and reveals a structure, at once simple and very complex. It makes very little difference whether it is a means to the end of communicating an emotion or whether it is the very final end of the creative activity; it comes with the inspiration of the muse, and is negligible only because it will be there even when not explicitly invited.

Also even in a short poem, this structure undergoes transformation. The poet may select only the crucial changes and never note the principle, but if the poem is successful it records the intellectual rhythm along with the verbal choreography. In longer poems and in semipoetic literature, such as the drama and the novel, there is always an element, often called character, leitmotiv, or idea, undergoing a develop-

425

ment. Amid this change, it stands or becomes increasingly rigid and, for some readers and writers, substantial and real. The development may be a temporal affair, like a life or series of incidents, or it may be merely the process of revelation and clarification in the writing, but it is development by transformation in both cases. This variation according to rule is what Aristotle meant by "action" in the *Poetics*. "Poetry is the imitation of an action," the generation of a form, the adumbration of an essence. I think the comparison of mathematics and poetry is illuminating on this point, for this is one of the places where a poem and a geometrical demonstration meet. A demonstration, as we shall see, uncovers a figure in transformation just as a poem reveals a character in action. The demonstration tries to be literal; this quality is sometimes called accuracy and exactness. The poem tries to be adequate; its quality is sometimes called imagination and associative eloquence. I shall not ask the question here how far each succeeds.

The mathematical technique will clarify both. The triangle is an obsession to geometers and the rest of the world may be grateful to the geometer for cultivating such a neurosis. For most of the successful solutions of problems have been due to knowledge of triangles and their application in triangulation. It has been suggested that the Greeks had an overdeveloped Oedipus complex issuing in a fixation on the eternal triangle, and the rationalization of it ended in Euclid's *Elements*. Literary critics of the psychological school do not like this exploitation of their methods, but they should know the abundance of evidence for such an hypothesis. It is what they would call overwhelming. Plato has collected much of the evidence from the Pythagorean writings and the *Timaeus* is his account of the paranoid mechanisms of defense. It is there said that the world is constructed of triangular atoms, the chief of which is an earth atom—poor Mother Earth and the Oedipean Greeks!

Be that as it may, triangles are truly won-derful, and have enough poetry of their own without the adulteration provided by the psychologist. Chief among their various kinds is the right triangle and the most important knowledge we have of it is contained in the Pythagorean theorem. It will serve many purposes of this chapter to recount the demonstration of this theorem with enough said about triangles in general to make that possible. Not least of these purposes is a certain piety due to the geometrical tradition.

Let us start then with some preliminary play with the triangle in general. Take a straight line of a given length as a base and from one end draw another line of any length you please. Leave it attached to the base line at one end and bring it down to a position that will leave a very small angle between. Connect the two free ends by a third line. You now have a very acute-angled triangle. Now swing the second line so as to increase the acute angle and allow the third line to expand and change its direction in any way so as to keep the triangle closed. By steadily increasing the angle between the base and second line, the triangle will undergo successive transformations, revealing one after another the precious properties of the triangle. For instance, by a moment's reflection, you will realize that by certain stipulations about the length of the base and second line and the angle between them, you will be determining the size of all the other lines and angles in the triangle. Similarly, if you fix the length of the base as we have done, and in addition the size of the angles at either end of it, you will have fixed the size of the other parts of the triangle. This property is usually recorded in textbooks by two theorems about the equality of triangles. From our point of view they are important properties of the triangle in general.

Now continue the revolution of the second line until you have a right angle between it and the base line. This is a right triangle whose properties we are looking for. But before we go into that, let us find some more peculiarities of the general triangle. Continue the revolution of the second line and you have a series of obtuse triangles corresponding to stations of the second line in its revolution. It will be noticed that as the angle increases between the base line and the second line, the angle at the other end of the base line and the angle at the third vertex decrease in size. This kind of covariation is the sort of thing that a statistician thinks very significant. He would doubtless make a table of correlation in this case. We can accept what he says and go on to a further observation, namely, that as the second line continues to revolve and approach the direction of the base line, the other angles tend to disappear, and as it becomes an extension of the base line, the triangle disappears. The geometer here would be tempted to make a guess. He would reverse the revolution of the second line to some direction where it made a triangle possible. He would then draw a line from the vertex of revolution parallel to the third side of the triangle. He would also extend the base through the vertex. There would then be three angles at the vertex, one interior to the triangle and two exterior to it. Now by revolution of the second line, and by allowing the parallel to the third side to revolve so as to remain parallel, he would note the similarity of the changes in the two exterior angles and the opposite interior angles. They seem to remain equal, the opposite interior base angle to the exterior angle on the base, and the interior angle at the top vertex to the exterior angle on the second line. This is a clue worth following.

Upon investigation of parallel lines with lines running through them, it is found that the situation in our triangle exactly fulfills the conditions for two cases when the angles involved are always equal. In general, $x=w=a=d$, and $y=z=b=c$. Upon this discovery, it is easy to jump to a conclusion about the sum of the interior angles of any triangle. Their sum is always constant and equal to all the angles that can be drawn on one side of a line at a given point, or one hundred and eighty degrees. This then is a

necessary condition of being a plane Euclidean triangle, one of those intangible rigidities with which geometry deals.

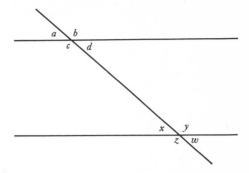

But the same figure is interesting for another reason. Draw a line from the top vertex parallel to the base letting it cut the parallel to the third line. We now have a parallelogram which is twice the original triangle. If you wish to convince yourself of this, apply the test for equal triangles and

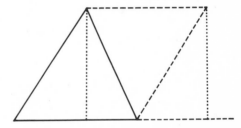

see that the second triangle is equal to the first. This may be stated formally in the theorem that the area of a parallelogram is equal to twice the area of one of the triangles formed by its diagonal. Further we can see that this area is the same as a rectangle having an equal base and altitude (the distance between the parallels along a perpendicular). Draw the altitude and see for yourself. So the area of a triangle is one half the product of its base and altitude.

Surprisingly enough, we have here enough information to allow us to put on the august robes of the Pythagorean initiate and enter the sanctum for the ritual of a rigorous geometrical proof. Here follows the

Pythagorean theorem and the proof of it preferred by Euclid.

*EUCLID, BOOK I, PROPOSITION 47*

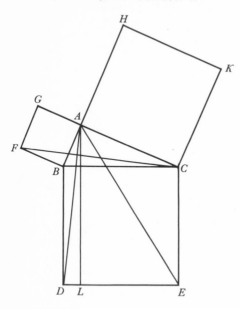

In right-angled triangles the square on the side subtending the right angle is equal to the squares on the sides containing the right angle.

*Let ABC be a right-angled triangle having the angle BAC right; I say that the square on BC is equal to the squares on BA, AC.*

*For let there be described on BC the square BDEC, and on the BA, AC the squares GB, HC; through A let AL be drawn parallel to either BD or CE, and let AD, FC be joined.*

*Then, since each of the angles BAC, BAG is right, it follows that with a straight line BA, and at the point A on it, the two straight lines AC, AG not lying on the same side make adjacent angles equal to two right angles; therefore CA is in a straight line with AG.*

*For the same reason BA is also in a straight line with AH.*

*And, since the angle DBC is equal to the angle FBA: for each is right: let the angle ABC be added to each; therefore the whole angle DBA is equal to the whole angle FBC.*

*And, since DB is equal to BC, and FB to BA,*

*the two sides AB, BD are equal to the two sides FB, BC respectively; and the angle ABD is equal to the angle FBC; therefore the base AD is equal to the base FC, and the triangle ABD is equal to the triangle FBC.*

*Now the parallelogram BL is double of the triangle ABD, for they have the same base BD and are in the same parallels BD, AL.*

*And the square GB is double of the triangle FBC, for they again have the same base FB and are in the same parallels FB, GC.*

*(But the doubles of equals are equal to one another.)*

*Therefore the parallelogram BL is also equal to the square GB.*

*Similarly if AE, BK be joined, the parallelogram CL can also be proved equal to the square HC; therefore the whole square BDEC is equal to the two squares GB, HC.*

*And the square BDEC is described on BC, and the squares GB, HC on BA, AC.*

*Therefore the square on the side BC is equal to the squares on the sides BA, AC.*

*Therefore in right-angled triangles the square on the side subtending the right angle is equal to the squares on the sides containing the right angle.*

*Quod erat demonstrandum.*

This balances the quotation from Lewis Carroll above. There we become acquainted with Alice in a most intimate and exact way, and can easily understand the rest of Wonderland. Here we become familiar with the essence of the right triangle, and will have no difficulty in going on to trigonometry, navigation, surveying, and astronomy, in short, to the triangulation of the universe from atoms to stars. In both cases an abstract idea has been presented, defined, and clarified; so it is with the geometrical and poetical treatment of ideas in general. The subtleties of geometry and imaginative literature are all of this sort, intangible but intelligible things undergoing significant variation and finding themselves in the process.

Geometry has here been introduced without the usual emphasis on demonstration or proof. This has been intentional, but an apology to pedagogical geometry will not be out of place; it will serve two purposes. First, it will distinguish the essentials from the nonessentials of geometry, as it is taught; second, it will again make explicit the relation between mathematics and poetry.

It is said that the function of geometry is to prove propositions, and by proof, it is often claimed, it establishes the truth of what it says. The thought process involved is called deduction, and by this process it is supposed we infer from the truth of first principles or axioms, which are self-evidently true, the truth of everything that follows from them, including the proposition under discussion. This would undoubtedly be a good employment of geometrical thinking if it were ever possible to be sure of the first principles. Unfortunately, we never have such certainty, as has become increasingly evident since the discovery of non-Euclidean geometries which base themselves on axioms, or postulates as they are now called, which are not compatible with Euclid's assumptions. The truth of axioms is no more evident than the truth of any other propositions in geometry, and axioms hold preferred positions only in minds that can think of no alternatives.

It further appears that deduction is only one way of linking together mathematical insights that are acquired by nondeductive means, and that any one of these insights is as good as any other, provided it is actually seen intellectually. Deduction then becomes a secondary process, systematic and integrative for separate but prior intuitions, leading to and uncovering some unsuspected aspect of the mathematical object, or aiding in the fusing of separate parts of what finally becomes a geometric system. Thus the proof of the Pythagorean theorem brings together the subject matter of the first forty-six theorems of Euclid in one grand vision of geometric relations. The recent advance of Einstein in mathematical physics is a similar integration involving non-Euclidean systems of geometry and also insights which have previously been considered physical and nongeometrical.

Demonstration is a far better term to apply to the process, especially when it is taken to mean "a pointing out" of its subject matter. It then becomes the vehicle by which we travel over the mathematical territory and gain vantage points for seeing this or that field of connections.

The truth which is claimed for mathematics is the truth of clear vision where ideas are concerned. It is related to the truth of poetic vision by a close similarity. A poem is also the vehicle for the survey of an ideal territory and its destination is equally an integration of separate insights. All good demonstration should end in the unambiguous definition of its object; and each good poem can be seen as a definitive presentation of some poetic object.

But mathematical and poetic objects are subject to other treatments and manifest themselves in other guises. For instance, the transformations of geometry occur according to definite rules which determine the order of the elements. This order, which has been taken for granted in this chapter, is the subject of a special mathematical science, the science of numbers. It is the purpose of the next chapter to present this phase of mathematical and poetic thought.

## III Numbers

There is no more impressive form of literature than the narrative epic poem. That combination of depth and breadth of conception which some have called sublimity has here found a natural and adequate expression. The theory of number is the epic poem of mathematics. The mutual reflection of the two arts will supply a sort of explanation in the intellectual dimension of the epic quality in both. It will also show how it is that the number has made some of the discoveries in physical science possible; it is to be remarked that these physical discoveries themselves have an epic quality probably due to the part numbers have played in their technical development.

But the question, what is a number? is an invitation to analyze counting and to find out what sort of thing makes counting possible. In poetry I suppose the corresponding question would be, what makes recounting possible? The answer, if it were to be complete, would take us into the most abstract and subtle mathematical thought. But the key to the problem is the simplest sort of insight. The same peculiar combination of simplicity and subtlety is involved in the theory of narrative, but as everyone knows, insight here belongs to the most common of common-sense conceptions.

Very briefly, a number is an element in a field of variation. Its specific numerical property consists in its relations with other elements in the same field, which relations are expressed in rules of order. One can see immediately how a significant event or incident in a story conforms to this definition in the general form I have given it. In geometry, the emphasis is on the constancy of elements that undergo transformation; the emphasis in arithmetic is on the order and connection of the elements in the transformation itself. Arithmetic adds the "how" to geometry's "what." Numbers reveal another aspect of the mathematical object.

The structures that make counting possible are chains and networks of relations. The understanding of a selected few of these relations will be the suggestive key to the whole realm. There are two ways of approaching these relations. One has the advantage of being itself a kind of narrative that gathers up the main turning points in the history of arithmetic. This is the theory of operations. The other is postulate theory in which collections of elements are assumed and one relation after another is introduced until a mere aggregate becomes as if by magic a number system. I shall begin with the theory of operations. It is merely a careful account of counting with special attention paid to the difficulties met and solved or circumvented.

A point of beginning is assumed, usually the number one. This is the fulcrum demanded by Archimedes when he said he would move the world by means of levers. An operator, so called, is also taken—one of Archimedes' levers. This operator is called $+1$. Then there follows a rapid process of intellectual knitting starting with $1 + 1 = 2$, $2 + 1 = 3$, $3 + 1 = 4$, . . . and ending (?) with $n + 1$, and you have the series of positive numbers to infinity. Of course infinity is not a number in this series but "to infinity" describes a property of the series, namely, that it has only the arbitrary end you wish to assign it if you want a finite series; or it has no end, that is, no last term.

Then you take another operator, $-1$, and starting with any one of the positive numbers, you can travel backwards along this series until you arrive at 1. Here you encounter a difficulty, the solution of which once bothered the mathematical consciences of many men, as much as warped space does now. What can $1 - 1$ mean? The answer is another symbol, unknown before, and, in a sense, unknown still. It is one of those vehicles which one can ride without looking under the hood. Of course we know it is 0. Once you learn to ride, it is easy enough. But still other vehicles had to be discovered or invented. For what does $0 - 1$ mean? Again consciences strained over answers obvious to us. Of course, $-1$. Then by more rapid knitting, another infinite series of negative numbers became known.

But this is not the end of the chain stitch. The operator ( $\times$ ) or ($\cdot$) was applied and rapid jumps were made back and forth over the two series which were now combined into one, containing both positive and negative numbers. $3 \times 4 = 12$, $-3 \times +4 = -12$, and $-3 \times -4 = 12$. For every multiplicative combination of numbers, whether positive or negative, there is some corresponding number of the original series. Of course this is generalized to cover 1 and 0 by special convention and it is also true for additive and subtractive combinations.

By this time the mathematical conscience had taken on great versatility and inventiveness. The moral conscience has had similar awakenings, but more regressions to somnolence. Another operator was taken up with most amazing results. $12 \div 4$ is an easy jump, apparently the converse of $3 \times 4$, but what can $12 \div 5$ mean? If you answer $2\frac{2}{5}$, you have accepted a new convention with most revolutionary consequences. For then you can also write $\frac{2}{5}$ alone, meaning $2 \div 5$, and nothing more can be done about it. It just stands there immovable and indissoluble, unless you put it with another rather improper fraction, and $\frac{2}{5} \times \frac{5}{2} = 1$ or $\frac{2}{5} \times 5 = 2$. This however undermines all you have admitted before. 5 and 2 are really no different from $\frac{5}{1}$ and $\frac{2}{1}$, and the original series is only a few selected numbers from a still "more infinite" series of fractional numbers. This series is profoundly different from the first. For between any two numbers in it, it is possible to find a third, no matter how many you have introduced in that way before. It has no beginning and no end, and in a peculiar way Zeno's paradox about passing over an infinite number of points in finite time is given further exemplification even without points and time. You can never pass from one number to another by any thoroughly step-by-step procedure. It is now a riddle not only how bodies move, but also a much worse one, how anybody counts. Incidentally, in showing how we count, we have shown how counting is impossible.

It would seem that the people with mathematical consciences were wise in sticking to the positive integers and that these riders of newfangled vehicles have gone too far. On another occasion very much like this Bishop Berkeley accused mathematicians of dealing in symbols more vicious and unintelligible than those of theology, and others went on to show that if mathematicians could prove eternal truths by such obviously questionable methods, how much more right had mystics and preachers to use questionable arguments for which they made no such ambitious claims.

Obviously here is a tangle, but it is easy to unravel. Counting is not covering ground,

any more than measuring a distance or telling a story is covering ground. It is a little more subtle. Counting has always to do with at least two sets of numbers, what have been called the numbering numbers and the numbered numbers, and the process is called one-oneing or correlation, that is, finding in one of two series a corresponding number for each number in the other. It is very easy to find a series of numbered numbers for the series of fractional or rational numbers. Euclidean space is such a series and in addition contains some extra numbers called irrationals. I shall have more to say about those when we come to the puzzles in the infinitesimal calculus. It is enough here to remark that the paradox of counting by means of an infinite series is only the occasion for new discoveries about the network of numbers. Operations merely outran analysis for a time, but like the tortoise, analysis catches up, and when it does, one sees that the conditions of the whole race are revised. Counting is a different thing because mathematicians played with unintelligible operations for a time.

But we must shift our ground of explanation of numbers to see just what this amounts to. The shift is like a certain one in narrative literature that happened long ago. At some time or other, it was supposed that a story was only a story. This has repeatedly returned as a very sophisticated dogma of criticism. Novelists are just storytellers; to claim more for them is moralism, sociologism, psychologism, or something worse, intellectualism. But at some time between this revival and its previous vogue the story was more than a story. It bore a burden, sometimes an insight, and sometimes even a moral. Epic literature has often become sacred scripture and, even more often, the repository of a people's history and civilization. When it has done this, it has not been merely a record of events and gossip about them. It has been interpretive, as we used to say. It has had a certain generality or universality, to use a higher-sounding name. In still older lingo, it had a touch of eternity about it, transcending the flow of human affairs. Its people were heroes and often were mistaken for gods. All this may have been a mistake—certainly it has worked woe as well as weal for human affairs—but the fact remains that there is something in any good story which is capable of this exploitation. I suggest that that something is the relations holding between the events or incidents. In other words, the plot of a story is an intellectual as well as an aesthetic pattern and it is this that gives the incidental elements that float in it a significance. These patterns are very abstract, very general, and capable of infinite variation, so that they may be revised and reapplied without violating their essential forms. The speculative historian can attach them to a period and name them the form spirit—Magian, Apollian, or Faustian—but they are actually more general and if they must be attached, are more discriminating. The Cinderella story is in most primitive folklore, is exploited in the cult of mariolatry, and is now in the current American magazine story, just as it is the pattern running like a phrase of music in the head of the tired stenographer or shopgirl. Is it a story, or is it a metaphysic of morals?

I prefer to compare it with number, that age-old story recounted at one time on fingers and toes, at another in the knots of a rug, at another in the constellations, the letters of the alphabet, the beads of wampum, and the modern cash register of a ten-cent store. The affinity of stories and numbers is always latent, bursting forth in magic formulae, sacred numbers, astrology, alchemy, the Cabala, and the wisdom of the Rosicrucians, and periodically hypostasized into the supreme dogma of a universal religion, as in the Trinity or the infinitude of deities in Eastern religions. Numbers are not just counters; they are elements in a system. It is this aspect of numbers with which the story of postulate theory concerns itself. It is in the findings of such studies that the necessary conditions of counting are stated.

These results have come from a peculiar sort of study. The modern mathematician has been sitting down like an Epicurean god, far from space and time, calling for chaos to play with. He gives a few brief orders and watches universes grow. He varies the orders and universes give place to still others. Sometimes he creates one very much like that in which we are accustomed to think we live, and sometimes they are unusual and bizarre like a universe that we may become accustomed to living in if we change our minds. Sometimes a system comes out of such play that sets an old system in a new light. Such is the work on number postulates.

The technique is to assume entities, elements, what-not and carefully assign certain relations to hold between them. In the case of numbers, the relations are first left unnamed and unspecified except for very general properties usually called irreflexive, asymmetric, and transitive. A relation is irreflexive when it does not hold between identical terms. For instance, an ordinal number cannot be to the right of itself; "to the right of" is an irreflexive relation, where "same as" is reflexive. A relation is asymmetric when it holds only one way between two terms; an ordinal number cannot be to the right of another given number and yet have that number to the right of itself. "Same as" would also be symmetric. A transitive relation is one that allows the inference: if A is to the right of B, and B is to the right of C, then A is to the right of C. "To the right of" is transitive. Any relation that satisfies these three requirements can be made the generating relation for what is known as a progression, variations and restrictions of which lead to the various kinds of series which we call ordinal numbers. Some of these numbers are discrete, where each number has a next successor as in the series of whole numbers. Some are not discrete but compact, when no number has a next successor as in the series of fractions. Finally there are continuous series where, in addition to compactness, it is possible to discover numbers between those in the series of fractions, the so-called irrationals. There are still other numbers which are combinations of those previously described, curious results of operations of taking the square or even-numbered roots of −1. These are called imaginary numbers and belong in series. The subtleties of these conceptions can be reduced to the obvious simplicities of the properties of relations and the order they bring to a set of entities. This holds for ordinal numbers.

The account of cardinal numbers is a subject of some controversy, but the issue can also be reduced to simple enough notions. There are two ways of introducing the persons of a story. In one of these, a person is allowed to recall his past and thus reveal what sort of person he is, or his history is told in a casual way by another character or by the author. Sometimes court procedure is followed; a collection of opinions is entered from certified witnesses and the reader is allowed to act as jury to make a summary decision. The characters of the witnesses have to be known in some stereotyped manner to make this method effective. Around these two methods there are many possible variations, but the secret is the same as the secret of ordinal numbers. Each character is to be known by the external relations it has with other members of an array of similar or relevant characters. Fielding's Tom Jones is an example of such a character.

The other method leads to cardinal characters and numbers. The identity or individuality of a person is allowed to epitomize itself in a crucial incident. This event or incident might have no antecedents or consequences, and yet it should set forth in some unforgettable and inimitable way the soul of a man. It is our impressions of actual people coming to us in this way that give us the strongest and most irrefutable convictions that man is immortal. They have their roots in fiction through which we see our friends. Specific cardinal numbers are said to have similar indifference to other numbers and an independence that results from

this indifference. They are the souls of things, both immanent and efficient causes of their being. It is on some such basis that we come to have lucky or unlucky numbers, perfect numbers, and sacred numbers. Dostoevski's Idiot and the sacred number seven are examples of such cardinality. In some sense they are internally substantiated and radiant of their own essences.

The senses in which this is true are not hard to ascertain, and their explication may on that account be disappointing. There are two main modern doctrines, revivals of ancient Greek theories, to account for this magic. I shall give them separately and briefly and then offer a combination that seems to me adequate to the theme here developed.

The first one is based on the notion of a class which has other classes for its members, in short, a class of classes. This conception has beautiful subtleties which recommend it to a certain type of mathematical philosopher who wishes to see numbers applied. It is like one of those ingenious tools which has a handle and any number of attachments to be added or dropped as the operator wishes or as the use dictates. Application and practice subtilize ideas. As morals led medieval theology into what for us is irrecoverable subtlety, so industry and applied science lead our mathematics into fantasy. I shall make use of the machinery here only to facilitate the approach to the mathematical object.

A cardinal number is the class of all those classes that have a given form. Suppose A is a class which has subclasses a, b, c, . . . as its members. Each of these classes may have members. A is a cardinal number if the subclasses a, b, c, . . . have the same form, and that form is a monad, dyad, triad, or a tetrad. That a class has one of these forms means that its members will be respectively singles, couples, or trios. For instance, the cardinal number one is the class of all those classes whose members are singles; the number two is the class of all those classes whose members are couples; and so forth.

This definition has been criticized for its circularity: it uses numbers to define numbers, since the monad means one, the dyad two, and so forth. There are two answers to this criticism. First the circularity is admitted but justified on the ground that the notions are ultimate and well enough understood in themselves to warrant circular or merely verbal definition. The other answer goes on to define the forms in terms of the relational structures of the ordinal series. The ordinal series can be broken into segments, and the relation within a given segment will define the form of a corresponding cardinal number. For instance, the relations in the segment from ordinal 0 to ordinal 2 yield the dyad, the relations in the segment from 0 to 3 yield the triad. Such parts of the ordinal series provide the forms for the subclasses of the corresponding cardinal numbers. Therefore, for every ordinal number there will be a cardinal number whose form is derived from a segment of the ordinal series beginning with 0 and ending in the given ordinal number. In terms of operations, the cardinal number represents an operation constituted of all the operations that developed the ordinal series up to a given term. The cardinal number five is the set of relations which generate the ordinal segment (1, 2, 3, 4, 5), or is the result of the combined operation $\{[(1 + 1) + 1] + 1\} + 1$.

But I suggested above that this complicated business of classes of classes was due to the engineer's love of applied mathematics. For him it is a very efficient device for subsuming things under numerical forms, since the lowest members of the subclasses are assumed to be things counted. I shall describe other devices for applying numbers in the next chapter. If we sweep away this scaffolding of classes, we can see that the essential cardinal form is nothing but a special selection from the chain of relations that constitute the ordinal series and their combination in a form. In ordinary practice such selection is always restricted to a set of relations anchored at one end in the term zero and extending to some later term in the se-

ries. This is an arbitrary restriction. The cardinal form may bind together any terms in the series, and a cardinal number is any set of ordinal numbers properly related and taken together as a whole.

So far ordinal numbers have been taken as fundamental. If cardinal numbers are taken as fundamental, the ordinal numbers can be derived from them by analysis. An ordinal number can then be defined by its relations to other ordinal numbers within the structure of a given cardinal number. Either approach to the theory of numbers is good, but the latter seems to do the mathematical object greater justice.

So it is with the ordinal and cardinal elements in a story. The storyteller operates on a set of elements, the incidents, which arrange themselves usually in some temporal order. Then characters begin to take shape. Still the author who sees himself as a craftsman only claims he has presented only a story. If he is more sophisticated and critical, he will recognize his characters and watch them remake the story. Finally, they will take the work completely out of his hands and create their own situations. His characters have then become cardinal and their action dictates the ordinal structure of the story.

The same thing happens in less narrative forms of literature. A sonnet starts out to be a pattern of words, but it ends in a couplet that confers its significance on the whole poem. An essay starts as an exposition of facts and turns into a structure of ideas interpreting a problem. In Mr. Bertrand Russell's philosophical writings there is a persistent attempt to keep to the ordinal level; this is a large part of the secret of his clarity. But at some point interpretation, usually some bad metaphysics, threatens to come in, and we catch him protesting too vehemently that he is not a system-builder. Mr. George Santayana, on the other hand, almost never condescends to the ordinal level of detailed exposition. He moves among cardinal ideas and loads his words with complex, even moral, interpretation.

As it happens, recent discussions of form in the novel approximate this theory of numbers. It seems that there are two ways of analyzing a story corresponding to the two methods I have noted of introducing characters. In one the story is a series of events that happen to a character or group of characters. Such series may be very complicated and each situation may have many elements, but the characters are to be understood as having flat mirrorlike reflecting surfaces accurately recording the incidents and their relations. Action for such a character consists in the particular quality his reflection confers on the incident. We see through his eyes and it is in his vision that the material of the story takes form. The character itself is only a reflecting background. Such characters have been called "flat"; they are at their best in the satirical or comic novel.

In the other analysis of the novel the character is cumulative. It is as if each incident or episode had changed the quality of the reflection by giving the mirror an increasingly complex texture. Actually the events seem to come from the character. The internal structure of the character at any stage of its development consists of a set of habits, virtues, sensitivities, and powers that not only record but continually transfigure the preceding course of events. All of these are brought to bear on the immediate situation, and action consists in an internal drama merely conditioned by external affairs. The relations within are like the relations in the whole story, but transformed by projection on a smaller and more complex background. Such characters have been called "round"; their function is tragic.

But flat and round characters in comic and tragic plots do not throw much light on the contemporary problems in the criticism of fiction. They give an interesting classification to classic novels of the past, but even there the classes are not mutually exclusive, and many novels can fall outside of both. One can very well describe the spirit of contemporary fiction by saying that the novelist has the choice of producing the comic effect by tragic devices or producing the tragic effect by comic devices. The fact is that the novel is at present attempting to be that ideal combination of tragedy and comedy about which Socrates spoke that morning after the Symposium at the house of Agathon, the Athenian playwright. "Aristodemus was half awake and he did not hear the beginning of the discourse; but the substance of it was that Socrates was driving them to the admission that the same man could have the knowledge required for writing comedy and tragedy, that the fully skilled tragedian could be a comedian as well."

I should like to suggest that the solution might come from an insight into the nature of the ordinal and the cardinal elements and their respective functions in the novel. The suggestion is that the ordinal character should serve as the thread or ordering principle for the materials of the story, while the cardinal character is the weaver of the plot catching the parts of the events as they pass, transforming and organizing them into an internal dramatic pattern which mirrors the whole. At present it is the fashion to take the order of events from some social science, and then attempt to superpose a personality pattern taken from the psychological laboratory or clinic. The novel is a curious combination of sociological essay and clinical report. Tom Jones has become a sentimental idiot and Prince Mishkin an epileptic buffoon. The advice of the mathematician would be to take some arbitrary but interesting order of events, and then build the cardinal characters out of the elements selected and recombined as dictated by the author's genius for distortion and projection of human beings. Lewis Carroll's Alice is a model. Perhaps such advice would be more tactfully offered to a critic, suggesting to him what might be looked for in the more successful novels of, say, a Dostoevski or a Marcel Proust. Cardinality of characters is an excellence proper to fiction.

Perhaps a reference to geometry will integrate the two perspectives of the mathematical object so far attained. Geometry tends to

435

emphasize the constancy in the mathematical object. Each new variation reestablishes this constancy by disclosing a new feature in it. Arithmetic starts with these special features and weaves a network of relations between them. The transformations and developments in projective fields proceed by definite steps in a sequence fixed by rules based on these relations. Constancy is thus reincarnated in the relations and in the order and structure they confer upon the variations. The special devices of each mathematical discipline are fitted to pass from one emphasis to another in clearly marked successive steps of the analysis. Poetry often grasps the patterns of these steps, and consequently the structures so discovered, and presents them, as in the case of cardinal characters, integrated in crystalline insights.

The fact that mathematical formulae and poetic insights are believed to contain hidden meanings is a natural result. That one can tell long coherent stories is at first an amazing discovery. That these flights of imagination and logic lead to unsuspected existences does not long go unnoticed. It leads immediately to the breathtaking generalization that the secret of nature, the universe, all possible experience, is in these stories, and that numbers, figures, ideas, or words are always effluxes from things. This in turn means that the as yet unknown is making itself known in hieroglyphs. The universe is not only a system of perspectives, but also a book of mathematical formulae or a realm of poetic insights.

Perhaps one of the most amusing of these faiths is numerology. Correlating the letters of the alphabet and the digits from 1 to 9, repeating the numbers until the alphabet is exhausted, one has a table of translation. Any name can be transliterated to numbers. Then, adding the numbers and manipulating them according to rules, one can extract the "essential number" from the name. This number expresses the essence of the person who possesses it. Then by another table describing the characteristics of the numbers,

the person will also be described. Thus it is learned that you, John Brown, are a number 2, and that 2 is practical, energetic, healthy. This tells you that you ought to be in business which is more suited to your character than your present occupation, say, teaching English literature in a high school. If you are having difficulties with your superiors or are a bad disciplinarian, this will sound inspired or scientific, as the case may be. You change your occupation and tell your friends how happy you are. They buy a book on numerology, and the cult arises whose gospel is a distant and weak caricature of Pythagoreanism.

More serious examples are found in modern developments of humanistic science. Economics and psychology are the best known repositories of this sort of wisdom. A society is translated into index numbers, or a personality into the terms of psychoanalysis. The retranslation is made into terms of applied morals and one becomes a Republican or Socialist, a married man or a divorcé, to the glory of mathematics and poetry.

Modern physical science is another case, whose forebears are astrology and alchemy. The story of how they came to be will need some more careful analysis. The next chapter is concerned with that.

## IV Proportions

I have tried to present two aspects of the mathematical object, the constancy of figures throughout regular transformations, and the rules of order governing the variations under such constants. These two aspects are often taken to be the subject matter of mathematics and are called, respectively, space and number. Recently it has become fashionable to recognize their common nature and call it the continuum. The rest of mathematics is then treated as if it were a set of puzzles, presented in this subject matter, and solved by a corresponding set of tricks. This is a professional view of the matter and is justified by the demands of technical education. It trains people to solve problems and get results.

There is another point of view—most eloquently put in Plato's *Republic*. Beginning with the principles for the deployment of troops and the building of bridges and fortifications, or the weighing and selling of goods and keeping accounts, the student of mathematics ascends from the sensory world to the questions of what figures and numbers are, by way of a hierarchy of mathematical disciplines, each of which is a little nearer than the former to the pure things of mathematics. Each level is related to the next higher as the world of sense objects is to the whole field of abstract mathematics. Anyone who has studied mathematics to understand rather than to use, will know what Plato is driving at, but not all will follow the theological trend that early Christians saw in it and developed. I do not think Plato himself would have viewed such a development with complaisance. Mathematics has more in it than such ascetic edification. It is more like poetry, I again suggest. Added words in good poetry effect more adequate revelations of the poetical object. So in mathematics, added theory and calculation effect new manifestations of the mathematical object. This may, by chance, involve greater abstraction and bring about a more comprehensive integration, but it need not, and often does not. The method of the next two chapters is prompted by an attitude between the extreme Platonist and the professional mathematician.

The symbolic key to many mathematical treasures is the ratio. Like many of the elements in Plato's lower mathematical disciplines, ratios are useful and hence familiar in mechanics, but they also have liberal functions, leading to elegant and abstract discourse in its own right.

At this point there is a fortunate linguistic bridge between poetry and mathematics. It was built in antiquity by the Greeks and Romans and apparently was overlooked and forgotten for many centuries. Just when its disuse became general, I do not know. I would like to know because I believe it a very important, perhaps unfortunate, crisis in human thought. I believe it tells us something about modern thought.

What we call reason was often referred to by the Greeks as λόγος and by the Romans as *ratio*. We refresh our classical memory by associating "logical" and "rational" in English. Lying back of these words are distinct but related *Weltanschauungen*. The search for the meaning of *logos* among the Greeks led to a scientific and speculative habit of mind ending in scientific observation and speculative thought. The following of reason among the Romans led to the ethical and religious theory under which we still live. *Logos* is still commemorated in the names of most of our sciences; *ratio* goes with our popular and practical argumentation. We rationalize.

The Greek *logos* also means "word" and in general "discourse." The Latin *ratio* means "cause" as well as "reason." These are the linguistic hinterlands. They meet on the frontier on a bridge built by mathematics. The Greeks contributed ἀνὰ λόγον signifying a technical conception thus defined by Euclid: "Magnitudes are said to be ἀνὰ λόγον to one another which are capable, when multiplied, of exceeding one another." The Romans called the same thing *ratio* and took over the word *analogia* to cover the corresponding figure of speech. It will in some sense be a restoration of the bridge if we name it "analogy" and show its mathematical and poetic constitution.

Analogical thought is so common that we are surprised, like M. Jourdain, to learn that at any given time we are speaking analogy. It has many disguised appearances, some guarded by habit and convention, and some very obvious and open to exposure. I shall have to limit the catalogue to some well-known figures of speech, namely the metaphor, the simile, and the allegory. There are many other forms starting with the Homeric epithet and the Aeschylean adjective and

437

ending with impressionistic and contemporary nonsense verse. If I did not have too many literal-minded friends, I should say that any proposition or significant sentence contained an analogy in some form or other. To escape the wrath of these, and also the more aesthetic of the poets, I will confine myself to a type of analogy midway between its two extreme forms. This type is at present called scientific language. To show it in its more extreme form, I shall take examples from the so-called humanistic sciences.

Here are seven metaphors:

> Man is a system of electrons.
> Man is a machine.
> Man is an animal.
> Man is a bundle of habits.
> Man is a soul.
> Man is an angel.
> Man is divine.

You can measure your progress in the school of modernism or hard-headedness by putting the word "dead" opposite any of these that you think are literal, and the word "alive" opposite those you think figurative or only partially true. You score one hundred per cent if you mark only the first "dead," and you approach 0 as you include more in this category. If you, as I, think they are all metaphors, you are just philosophical and a little mad.

It is a commonplace in logic that the copula "is" is a weasel word, and therefore it must be rendered unambiguous before the proposition in which it occurs is dealt with. I shall not go into the doctrine of categories here except to make an application of it. In all these metaphorical sentences "is like" ought to be substituted for "is." Each metaphor will then become a simile, and my meaning will be clear if I say that metaphors are suppressed or elliptical similes.

This leads to further scrutiny. The other words in the sentences need expansion. A "system of electrons" is a very short formula for the account a biophysicist would give of

a human body. His account can be briefly formulated as "a collection of unit charges of electricity holding those relations to each other that are described in physical chemistry." "Man" will then mean a "physical body of certain size and shape," and the whole metaphor ought to read thus: "The parts of the physical body ordinarily known as man are to the whole body as the unit charges of electricity are to the electrical field which contains them." The metaphor, previously shown to be a suppressed simile, is now a suppressed analogy. The search for greater explicitness in the formula would lead to more elaborate expansions which would stop only when the present stage of physical science has been exhausted.

Likewise, the other metaphors could be analyzed and expanded by referring the right-hand side to one of the fields of knowledge which has had due attention from human beings at some time in the past. "Man is a machine" would refer to the science of mechanics. "Man is an animal" to biology. "Man is a bundle of habits" to one or more of the current psychologies. "Man is a soul" to ancient and medieval psychology and theology. "Man is an angel" to angelology, and "Man is divine" to one of the theologies or sociologies. Your judgment of the literalness or the figurativeness would depend upon which of the sciences has dictated a metaphysics to you. If you are not careful, you will find yourself mixing metaphors and believing something like the Irish Member of Parliament who said very persuasively, "I smell a rat, I feel it in the air, and I will nip it in the bud." Such is the result of ignoring metaphysical difficulties for the sake of facts and practical affairs.

This is analogy. Before it runs away with our thoughts, it may be well to give it a definition. It is the statement of the identity or similarity of at least two relations. It says, in symbols, that the relation of A to B is the same as the relation of C to D. Of course these relations may be of any degree of complexity, provided the identity or similarity is not violated. The complexity may be increased or diminished, apparently without limit. I shall call this property of analogies their expansiveness.

Such expansion seems to have no limit, but on the other hand, analogies get stretched. They sometimes break. But since they are very elastic, they usually do not break until they have become extremely tenuous and elaborate networks, so that the fragments are often very finely wrought products of human art.

The most obvious of these expansions is the allegory. The analogy has been expanded and stretched until finally the left-hand side has been torn away and the other remains, fantastic, enigmatical, fascinating, by itself. Stories from the ancient epics and their nourishing legends and sagas down to the modern novel and its nourishing morals and sciences are allegorical. It is the worry of the individual and the task of the critic to find the other halves of these figments of analogical lore. The orphan fragments may lose their hereditary distinguishing marks, and as a consequence mixed allegories are as common for most of us as mixed metaphors for Irishmen or Greeks.

In European thought Greek tragedy set a fashion, and Christian theology from the early church fathers to the contemporary modernist has kept it going in spite of many lapses into literal-minded interpretation of the texts and commentaries. The portrayal of an heroic figure who takes on himself the sins of his ancestors and carries out the consequences to a divine dénouement can be taken from the Greek stage and seen in the legends and myths of a whole people. An historic figure may be the hero and the events in his life transfigured by analogical expansion into a cosmic drama in which each character is a tragic hero and every event a purgation. The late middle ages saw an extraordinary inflation of this analogy. St. Thomas, starting with the names of God, had extended analogical knowledge to include nature, and his followers and opponents conspired to make the extension thoroughgoing and exact. Even outside the stream of strictly Christian thought every realm of discourse became phosphorescent, impregnated with floating idea. Everything meant not only itself, but something else ad infinitum and to the glory of God. In the course of this exploration, the old bridge between imagination and mathematics was sure to be rediscovered. So it was. The Cabalistic and the Rosicrucian studies, together with alchemy and astrology, were midway of the bridge, and in one grand rush the whole realm of figure and number was taken over. This addition acted like a precipitant on an unstable chemical solution. Out of it came our modern science. The rest has steadily fallen into forgetfulness, disrepute, or opaque ritual. An analogy was stretched and broken, and we now have a mathematical-physical allegory on our hands and in our heads, and we are hunting for the rest of it, the lost symbol.

It is a little mysterious how all this happened. Man had been connected with the universe not by one but by an infinite set of ascending allegories, which had been understood and loved with subtlety and a discriminating skepticism. Suddenly, in a century, the whole structure collapsed; the clouds of glory condensed to numbers and measurements. We may be able to see how and why this happened if we analyze what is left.

"Magnitudes are said to have a ratio to one another," says Euclid, "which are capable when multiplied of exceeding one another." This definition has a subtlety at which modern mathematicians have wondered. In the first place "magnitude" may denote both numbers and figures or parts of figures. As we shall see it is itself a condensed mathematical analogy, and may refer not only to numbers and parts of figures, but also, when expanded, to apparently nonquantitative things. It anticipates analytic geometry and science as well. It thus may not exclude the lost poetry from which it came.

But a finer subtlety lies in the phrase, "capable, when multiplied, of exceeding one another." The uncriticized use of analogies had resulted in intellectual tangles before, and this phrase had been the means of disentangling ancient mathematicians from a mathematical scandal. This phrase allows for the rational treatment of the so-called irrational numbers. It brings these numbers under the control of rigorous symbols. It might have said "capable of equaling one another" and then the irrationals would have been excluded, and consequently great generality sacrificed in the conception. The definition will be clearer if the latter expression is included with the former. It will then read "capable when multiplied of equaling or exceeding one another." As it now stands, it is elegantly simple. It means that two numbers, lengths, areas, volumes, et cetera are in ratio when there is some multiplier or factor which applied to one of the magnitudes makes the resulting product equal to or greater than the other. The great power in this notion is due to a property of the operations of multiplication and division that I noted in the chapter on numbers. From the point of view of the theory of operations, multiplication and division are simple integrations or summations of complex combinations of elementary operations such as that represented by $+1$. From the point of view of postulate theory, multiplication and division are accurate and delicately discriminating selections of complex relations between elements. The ratio abstracts and fixes these relations and manipulates them without actually carrying out the operations which they make possible. It abstracts the bare relations. The irrationals are amenable to manipulation by ratios simply because of this abstraction which does not demand a completed operation. $1 : \sqrt{2}$ thus has a meaning as a ratio, that is, the relation between 1 and $\sqrt{2}$ is definite even though $\sqrt{2}$ is indeterminate as a rational number.

This abstractive property of ratios is further brought out in the proportion which,

very simply defined, is the statement of identity or similarity between two relations each of which holds between two or more magnitudes. Here no relation of identity or similarity is stated between the elementary magnitudes, that is, the terms of the proportions, but the relations between these terms are said to be identical or similar. Thus A, B, C, and D may range over the whole field of numbers, and yet it may remain true that

$$A : B :: C : D.$$

This is the strict mathematical form of the analogy, but even this strict form is capable of great versatility without losing its accuracy or elegance. For instance, once the relations in the proportion are grasped, it is immediately seen that one can take it by alternation: $A : B :: C : D$ is not violated if we say $A : C :: B : D$. Inversion produces another variation $B : A :: D : C$ and by combined alternation and inversion $C : A :: D : B$. Also $A + B : A$ or $B :: C \pm D : C$ or D. This is by composition and division. Further we may have a continued proportion of many ratios such as $A : B : C : D :: E : F : G : H$ or $A : B :: C : D :: E : F$ and these can run through the poses of alternation and division and their combinations. Add to this the possibility of substituting numbers, lengths, or any suitable magnitude, for the terms in the proportions, and the loss of allegories seems quite compensated in its mathematical offspring. In fact, close scrutiny of science shows unmistakable family resemblances between it and its theological and literary forebears.

But the greatest historical exploitations of analogy are in the field of mechanics. Archimedes and his study of the lever, following the literary exploits of the Greeks, and Galileo's and Kepler's study of nature in its larger dimensions following the theological exploits of the middle ages, throw an interesting light on the region of poetry and mathematics that is often called exact measurement. Its importance in contemporary thought merits rather special attention.

Archimedes laid the foundation of a very permanent, at least a recurring, form of intellectual equilibrium by studying equilibrium in its physical forms. The problem is epitomized in the lever, and the principle of the lever is a proportion.

It is a well-known principle to the child who has teetered on a seesaw and to the merchant who has weighed small quantities of material goods in a balance that the heavier of the two weights must be nearer the fulcrum. That such a practical maxim is the shadow of a proportion was known by many of Archimedes' predecessors. It is such a commonplace with us that I hardly know how to convey the import of its theoretical basis. Perhaps it will be best to point out that it is the result of two apparently unjustified leaps of imagination. How far the leap was encouraged by the use of such things as scales and cranks I do not know. But a double leap it is, and the reader can supply whatever theory of revelation, reincarnation, or conventional fiction he prefers, to account for it.

To say that $W_1 : W_2 :: D_2 : D_1$ is by itself ambiguous. Perhaps it only means that certain numbers stand to each other this way:

$$2 : 4 :: 3 : 6.$$

In that case it is merely a happy discovery in arithmetic. But W stands for weight and D stands for distance. It may therefore mean that the relation between two weights is the same as the relation between two distances. But this is not true for many relations; for instance, "heavier than" is a relation between two weights, but not between two distances. The only relation that works is a hybrid combination of these two.

The combination is evidently derived from two previous proportions, namely:

$$W_1 : W_2 :: 2 : 4$$

and

$$D_2 : D_1 :: 3 : 6.$$

Then because we already know in arithmetic that $2 : 4 :: 3 : 6$ we can finally see how it is that $W_1 : W_2 :: D_2 : D_1$. But why weights and distances are like numbers, to use the simile, has still to be explained. The only answer that I know is that some poet of the commonplace was playing with words, and somebody took him literally. That "somebody" was an engineer and became famous for what he could do with wonder-working machines. Archimedes was a later follower who saw levers in everything, just as poets sometimes see people in the sky. The modern folk who see vitamins in food, and vibrations in personalities belong to minor schools of this sort of poetry.

The most spectacular and convincing school is, however, that of the more natural sciences which now names Galileo, Kepler, Newton, and others of the Renaissance as its originators. They saw other proportions in things and like Archimedes generalized boldly. Their style has greater subtlety and the accompanying mathematics finally gets very complicated.

Being accustomed to think of celestial beings without body or visible form, yet present at places and times, they had a somewhat wider field for speculation and experiment. Aristotle had said that the time of a body's fall is proportional to its weight— a fairly corporeal notion. Galileo saw a different factor involved, not a mere velocity such as Aristotle saw, but a more ephemeral property which he called acceleration. This is really a ratio between two velocities and he found that for any given interval this ratio is equal to the ratio between the squares of the distances covered. The formula $V_1 : V_2 :: D_1^2 : D_2^2$ was the visible sign to convince men of the real presence of forces causing the acceleration. That forces were *verae causae* thus became a dogma believed by every scientific man till fairly recently. Not only was this true of falling bodies, but of all moving bodies. There was the force of inertia keeping bodies at constant velocities, and other more active forces, among them gravitation, changing their velocities and directions as they were able, in proportion to themselves. Galileo said he read these secrets in the book of Nature. Mathematics was only the code in which they were written. It is difficult to know whether he was a poet or a mathematician. He was like a modern engineer watching and making things act in certain ways and at the same time seeing schemes and meanings in things. The fact that he saw these in the scales and dials of his instruments hardly substantiates his reputation for skeptical experimentalism. There is a conflict here between mathematics and poetry that should after all these years be familiar. In fact it is so familiar that we ignore its metaphysical sins and call it the scientific spirit.

Another man before the time of Galileo had the same combination of traits, with the conflict even better concealed. Tycho Brahe had been looking at the stars across the sights of his instruments and writing down the numbers that appeared on the scales. He said the numbers represented the positions of the stars. Such procedure is a curious medley of ratios between lines and angles of observation, points on charts and places in the sky. He had written one of those finely wrought medieval allegories of the sky in the numbers of arithmetic. But it had been done in the finest "scientific spirit."

Johann Kepler had worked with and after him on this allegory, having in mind the less scientific, but more mathematically elegant model of the solar system fashioned by Copernicus. Kepler added the lore of conic sections that had come down from the Greeks and a touch of sun-worship from Zarathustra. With their aid he translated and condensed Tycho's allegory into three mathematical analogies:

(1) The orbit of a planet is to the sun as the circumference of an ellipse is to one of its foci.

(2) The areas swept by the radius vector (the line from the planet to the sun) are proportional to the times of revolution.

(3) The cubes of the mean distances of the planets from the sun are proportional to the times of their revolution.

It is perhaps surprising that Kepler substituted angels for the forces which Galileo had seen in the motions of more terrestrial bodies, but the reasoning from the evidence is the same. The only difference is that Galileo took an engineer's liberty with the tradition for which Kepler had a poet's love and piety. In other words Kepler was a less self-conscious poet.

It is often said that Newton saw the force of gravity in an apple. Byron assigns the origin of this insight to the piety of Newton and his preoccupation with the Biblical account of the fall of man. I shall not be so Byronic. Newton's poetic and mathematical heritage came from his more immediate past. His preoccupation with ratios is more relevant, although it may be admitted that Biblical literature and numbers have often been fine intellectual companions and emotional auxiliaries to each other. It is certainly true that he connected falling apples, cannonballs, and space in general with celestial bodies, both astronomical and divine.

Nevertheless, it was his extraordinary ability to disentangle the chain of abstract relations from the more exotic and wayward speculations of his predecessors in the school of natural analogy that led to his summary and perfection of their work. He made the analogical jump that astrophysicists are now making daily, from Galileo's art of physical experiment to Kepler's astronomical inferences. He did it by careful consideration of their ratios and a judicious sorting of their literary allusions. He finally kept all their mathematics, Galileo's forces, and Kepler's conic sections. Consequently the law of gravitation is an extraordinarily condensed version of the allegory of nature. We are still searching for the lost symbol that goes with Newtonian mechanics.

It is not the aim of this book to show that mathematics is identical with poetry, but it will do the reader no harm to read mathematics as if it were poetry. The following are some propositions from Newton's *Principia*. Mechanics is here set forth as a poem to be read, I maintain, as a litany.

*From the* Mathematical Principles of Natural Philosophy*

## Book I

### Definitions

**Definition I.** *The quantity of matter is the measure of the same, arising from its density and bulk conjunctly.*

**Definition II.** *The quantity of motion is the measure of the same, arising from the velocity and quantity of matter conjunctly.*

**Definition III.** *The* vis insita, *or innate force of matter, is the power of resisting, by which every body, as much as in it lies, endeavors to persevere in its present state, whether it be of rest, or of moving uniformly forward in a right line.*

**Definition IV.** *An impressed force is an action exerted upon a body, in order to change its state, either of rest, or of moving uniformly forward in a right line.*

**Definition V.** *A centripetal force is that by which bodies are drawn or impelled, or any way tend, towards a point as to a center.*

**Definition VI.** *The absolute quantity of a centripetal force is the measure of the same, proportional to the efficacy of the cause that propagates it from the center, through the spaces round about.*

**Definition VII.** *The accelerative quantity of a centripetal force is the measure of the same, proportional to the velocity which it generates in a given time.*

**Definition VIII.** *The motive quantity of a centripetal force is the measure of the same, proportional to the motion which it generates in a given time.*

### Axioms, or Laws of Motion

**Law I.** *Every body perseveres in its state of rest, or of uniform motion in a right line, unless it is compelled to change that state by forces impressed thereon.*

**Law II.** *The alteration of motion is ever proportional to the motive force impressed; and is made*

in the direction of the right line in which that force is impressed.

**Law III.** *To every action there is always opposed an equal reaction: or the mutual actions of two bodies upon each other are always equal, and directed to contrary parts.*

. . . . . . . . . . . . . . . . . . . . . . . . . . . . . .

## Book III

### Propositions

**Proposition I.** *That the forces by which the circumjovial planets are continually drawn off from rectilinear motions, and retained in their proper orbits, tend to Jupiter's center; and are reciprocally as the squares of the distances of the places of these planets from that center.*

**Proposition II.** *That the forces by which the primary planets are continually drawn off from rectilinear motions, and retained in their proper orbits, tend to the sun; and are reciprocally as the squares of the distances of the places of those planets from the sun's center.*

**Proposition III.** *That the force by which the moon is retained in its orbit tends to the earth; and is reciprocally as the square of the distance of its place from the earth's center.*

**Proposition IV.** *That the moon gravitates towards the earth, and by the force of gravity is continually drawn off from rectilinear motion and retained in its orbit.*

**Proposition V.** *That the circumjovial planets gravitate towards Jupiter; the circumsaturnal towards Saturn; the circumsolar towards the sun; and by the forces of their gravity are drawn off from rectilinear motions, and retained in curvilinear orbits.*

**Proposition VI.** *That all bodies gravitate towards every planet; and that the weights of bodies towards any same planet, at equal distances from the center of the planet, are proportional to the quantities of matter which they severally contain.*

**Proposition VII.** *That there is a power of gravity tending to all bodies, proportional to the several quantities of matter which they contain.*

**Proposition VIII.** *In two spheres mutually gravitating each towards the other, if the matter in*

---

* Cf. *GBWW*, Vol. 34, pp. 5–7, 14, 276–87.

*places on all sides round about and equidistant
from the centers is similar, the weight of either
sphere towards the other will be reciprocally as the
square of the distance between their centers.*

PROPOSITION IX. *That the force of gravity,
considered downward from the surface of the planets, decreases nearly in the proportion of the distances from their centers.*

PROPOSITION X. *That the motions of the planets in the heavens may subsist an exceedingly long
time.*

HYPOTHESIS I. *That the center of the system of
the world is immovable.*

PROPOSITION XI. *That the common center of
gravity of the earth, the sun, and all the planets, is
immovable.*

PROPOSITION XII. *That the sun is agitated by
a perpetual motion, but never recedes far from the
common center of gravity of all the planets.*

PROPOSITION XIII. *The planets move in ellipses which have their common focus in the center
of the sun; and, by radii drawn to that center, they
describe areas proportional to the times of description.*

PROPOSITION XIV. *The aphelions and nodes
of the planets are fixed.*

Certain more prosaic things are to be
noted in this sketch from the history of mechanics. First, motion is the quarry for which
a net is being fashioned. Certain philosophers beginning with Zeno have always said
that no net could catch the quarry. The answer has been persistently given that, as a
matter of fact and practice, mechanics does
catch it. According to the present account
the secret of the answer lies in the ratio and
proportion which constitute the soul of mechanics. They bring some of the speculative
boldness of poetry into measurement. Depending on the sweep and fineness of mesh
in the net of proportions, enough of the
whimsicality and infinite detail of nature is
caught to make an impressive display. If we
do not catch motion itself, we catch its path,
and if we do not follow the path step by step,
we follow it in leaps and bounds; if at the
end it is no longer motion that we have, but
rather its ghost, that is good mathematics

and good poetry. What really happens is a
puzzling translation of concrete event, fact
or experience into a set of abstract relations
which are symbolized and expressed in the
sciences that claim to describe our universe.
The symbols which effect this translation are
ratios in proportions. The only evidence
there could be, that the translations are accurate and the results true, would have to
be formulated in still other proportions. By
ratio and proportion our knowledge of the
universe stands or falls.

This point can be more emphatically
stated as follows. Quantity or magnitude as a
property of things is a condensed result of
analogical reasoning. When we ask, how
much? the answer we expect and are satisfied with is a mathematical metaphor. Five
pounds means that some physical object is to
some other physical object (the standard
weight) as five is to one. When we ask for the
certification of the standard, we go with
John Quincy Adams and his associates to
the stars and the proportions that describe
them.

But the importance of quantity and measurement in mathematics is habitually over-
estimated by the scientist and the engineer.
Ratios and proportions are by no means all
of mathematics. Just as poetry would be
poor indeed if it spoke only in analogies, so
mathematics would be even more clumsy
and platitudinous than poets think it is if it
calculated only in proportions. The conclusion is that if mathematics is more than proportions, quantity is not all of the mathematical object, but rather only one part.

I imagine that the reader's patience has
been tried by the general tone and manner
of this chapter. If so, he is sharing the writer's feeling about the subject matter. There
is something very puzzling and disconcerting in it all. I suspect it is very near to what is
often called the magic of poetry and at the
same time the riddle of the universe. I even
suspect that the two are one, and that Kant's
famous remark that two things he viewed

"with ever increasing awe, the starry heavens above and the moral law within," is also concerned with the same thing. It is the old Platonic problem of the relation between things and ideas. We seem to build castles in the air and recognize their fantastic unearthly character. We then turn to nature to find a local habitation and a name for them and ourselves. But we find nature and experience allegorical. Whatever direction we search to find literal truth, it always leads to the same eerie destination.

I should like to postpone facing this problem indefinitely, since it lies beyond the "scope of this book"; but to do so would be to lose the force of the argument in this chapter, and in a sense to miss the point of the whole book. I shall therefore try to answer the question that inevitably arises at this point: What is a literal statement? The only answer that is possible within the limits of the present subject matter must come by stripping rational discourse of its apparently figurative accretions and saving what is left —if indeed it is anything at all.

To begin with it seems that many important things can be defined in terms of analogies. For instance, from what has been said thus far we may derive the following definitions:

(1) Measurement is an analogy that asserts the similarity of two relations, one between things and the other between numbers. Example: Distance A is to distance B as 1 is to 10.

(2) Quantity is the condensation of an analogy of measurement into a numerical metaphor. Example: Distance B is 10. The inverse of this expresses an occult property: 10 is distance B, or 10 is perfection.

(3) A machine is a body the motions of whose parts are reciprocally proportional, or a machine is a body the relations between whose parts are similar to the relations between numbers in a proportion. Example: The lever.

(4) A scientific instrument is a machine whose parts vary from their states of rest or uniform motion in proportion to forces impressed from outside. Example: The chemist's balance.

(5) A scientific law is an analogy, or system of analogies (allegory), which asserts that the relations between things is similar to the relations between numbers. Example: A lever is in equilibrium when $W_1 : W_2 :: D_2 : D_1$.

(6) Science is an allegory that asserts that the relations between the parts of reality are similar to the relations between terms of discourse.

(7) The natural universe is the things and their relations that enter into the allegories of science.

In these seven definitions it can be seen that poetry and mathematics are constituent parts of those analogies and systems of analogies that we call scientific knowledge. Scientific objects are poetic objects whose relations are said to be similar to the relations between mathematical objects. This means that reality, in so far as it enters rational science, corresponds to the terms and relations in an analogy.

This leads to the serious proposal of a logistic that would provide a basis for scientific method. The first postulate of such a logistic system would state that any proposition in the old logic would be a metaphor subject to expansion into similes, analogies, and allegories. Such expansion would provide terms for the expression of any universe of discourse as an allegory whose atomic elements would be ratios. If there is objection to generalizing the term, ratio, in this fashion, we might speak of *logoi* as the constituents of allegories. It should be noted that such logical atoms are merely unit elements, not absolute simples which cannot be analyzed. They are atomic only relatively, that is, with respect to any given allegory.

The advantages of this terminology would be many. Let me note a few of them. First, it has long been noted that analogies play a large part in scientific thought, but, due to the loose terminology used in many arguments by analogy, it has been supposed that analogies themselves are untrustworthy. The fact that mathematics has achieved such remarkable advances in rigor and accuracy by means of ratios and proportions, as will appear in the following chapters, should quiet such fears. The admission of poetic analogies to intellectual respectability would confer similar intellectual responsibilities on the darker side of scientific thought. There seems to be no reason to suppose that they would not be fulfilled.

Second, the problems involved in measurement, use of instruments, observation, and verification in scientific method could be more clearly seen in terms of analogies. The definitions I have given of some of the constituents of scientific technique are capable of refinement, but even in them some usually unnoticed presuppositions of science are manifest in a rather startling way.

Third, the recent attempt to popularize scientific knowledge and the scientific attitude of mind has paralleled a revival of interest in the critical methodology of science. It now seems that the popular educational movement has had a rather unpleasant recoil in the mind of the technical scientist. The difficulties in translating mathematics into expository literature have uncovered terminological confusions in the laboratory itself. These difficulties have been seen first in the loose analogies of the popular version, but it is admitted that analogies are also used as scaffolding for the construction of the hypotheses to be tested by experiment and are apt to come out with the conclusions that result from the experiment. The passing of the classical analogy of the engineer's model is compensated for by elaborate imaginative pictures, or the purely operational interpretation expounded in Bridgman's *Logic of Modern Physics*. All of these are more or less poetic analogues for mathematical notions. The problem of "physical interpretation" of mathematical formulae is an integral part of scientific method, and could be clarified and ordered by a properly formulated calculus of analogies. Such a calculus might lead to a more fruitful and systematic exploitation of the historical notions in science which now return to the laboratory almost by accident and by the back door.

The obscurantism of occult and pure mathematics has been continually purified by formalization. A similar purification of scientific thought is badly needed at present.

This leads back to the question that I promised to face: What is a literal statement? Curiously enough, literalness is to be found in the more elaborate expansions of figurative statements. The literal interpretation of a proposition is to be found in the allegory. Early in this chapter it became clear that the peculiar function of the ratio was to isolate and abstract relations from their geometric and numerical contexts. The expansion of metaphors to allegories fulfills the same function in a poetic subject matter. Expanding analogies progressively reveal relations; argument by analogy is the fundamental technique in the process of abstraction. This should be clear from a former illustration. The proposition, "man is a machine," if it is taken as a statement of fact, is obscure and ambiguous. It is an allegory condensed and badly crushed. Properly expanded it is the explicit detailed analysis of a man's body, an allegory stating that the temporal and spatial parts of the human body are related and articulated according to the laws of motion. On one side of the allegory we have a diagram of the body and on the other side we have the abstract formulae that describe its motions. The farther the expansion is carried out the higher the degree of abstractness and explicitness achieved. If the allegory could be completely expanded and one side separated from the other, either side would be a literal statement. But curiously enough, the expansion can take place only when the two sides are allowed to interact symbolically; a *logos* or *ratio* in one must suggest and lead to the discernment of its analogue in the other. There seems to be no end to this process and therefore no end to the expansion. A purely formal and therefore literal statement is never possible. Pure poetry and pure mathematics, like pure music, are never expressed. The extreme case would be symbols expressing themselves, but even there the distinction would have to be made between symbols as things and symbols as ideas. Discourse is allegorical or nonsensical.

For the poet facts, like words, are symbols, and knowledge consists in the insight into the symbolic relation. For him the world is a poem to be read. Its laws are the laws that govern his words. For the mathematician and the scientist facts are to be referred to principles and causes. The allegorical correspondence of his ideas with the facts is the truth. The world is a network of relations which his formulae reflect.

Perhaps the question about literal statements should not have been answered here. At any rate now that it is answered after a fashion, it will be well for us to go on to further complications of mathematical and poetic analogies. We shall find that the proportion and the analogy are fundamental in what follows, and that even what has gone before is picked up and reorganized in an allegorical medium. An algebraic equation is a complex pattern of ratios, and the corresponding poetic forms are expanded metaphors. Mathematical and poetic objects wear that sort of clothes.

## V Equations

The statement that ratios are fundamental in mathematics was not intended to be a promise of what is to come in the following chapters. It would certainly not be agreeable to the professional mathematician who knows how cumbersome and awkward the more advanced parts of mathematics would be if they were treated with the calculus of ratios. Still it is surprising and important to realize that very many of the fundamental conceptions in the "higher" mathematics were first defined as special combinations of ratios. In many cases the original meaning is lost, but this is merely another way of saying

that the new terms and conceptions have absorbed and reinterpreted the old.

For example, the science of trigonometry, or the measurement of things by triangulation, is founded on three simple ratios. In any right triangle each of the acute angles can be measured by the *sine* which is defined as the ratio of the opposite side to the hypotenuse; or it can be measured by the *cosine* which is defined by the ratio of the adjacent side to the hypotenuse; or finally, it is measured by the *tangent* which is defined by the ratio of the opposite side to the adjacent side. Each of these measurements of an angle by lines involves a proportion, and the constituent ratios can be extracted and rearranged in new formulae. If the hypotenuse is arbitrarily given the value one, then, by the Pythagorean theorem, the square of the sine plus the square of the cosine is equal to the square of the hypotenuse which is one. This is the fundamental law in trigonometry; by suitable manipulations it can be expanded into the other laws by means of which any part of the intelligible universe can be reduced to numbers. Plato's prophecy in the *Timaeus* that the world could be made intelligible by transcription to a system of right triangles is fulfilled in this science.

But this use of ratios goes considerably beyond the rules for proportions that one would find in any textbook of arithmetic or geometry. In the first place, the laws of trigonometry are formulae that combine ratios as numbers are combined in arithmetic. This means that ratios have been substituted for numbers and come under the control of the arithmetic operations, addition, subtraction, multiplication and division. Trigonometric calculation has absorbed more notions from arithmetic than proportions could use. The resulting formulae themselves are much more like allegories than they are like simple analogies.

Further, the ratios are treated as if they were fractions according to the special rules for reduction to lowest terms and similar transformations. Both ratios and fractions gain in significance and power by this combination, and with it another mathematical notion, variation, has crept in unnoticed from geometry. Figures vary in geometry and because of their variation can undergo transformation. Numbers were brought in to formulate the order of their transformations, but variation itself was left unformulated. It is involved in these trigonometric formulae and as a matter of fact is fundamental in any complete account of proportions. The proportion really states the principle of such variation. It says that one ratio is substitutible for another. Thus, $1 : 3 :: 4 : 12$ means in terms of fractions that $\frac{1}{3} = \frac{4}{12}$ and we might go on indefinitely equating equivalent fractions. In some sense geometrical figures in the same field of projection or group are alternative expressions for one thing which is equally manifest in each, just as these fractions are representative of some generalized quantity. This one thing that the proportion indirectly symbolizes is called a variable and may have a special symbol, such as x, y, etc. Special classes of numerical expressions are said to represent its possible values. A variable is said to have an unlimited number of values which together constitute its field of variability. The values may be other variables, but are usually understood to be numbers, or expressions containing numbers. Numerical values are called constants in contrast to the variables whose field they constitute.

Thus, when ratios become terms in arithmetical or algebraic formulae, they exhibit new properties in addition to those recognized explicitly by Euclid. They still retain the properties they had in proportions, but they are also variables subject to the more general rules of algebra and arithmetic. This increased generality is the first property to be noted in the terms of mathematical allegories. It is nicely exemplified in the theoretic power of trigonometry.

Descartes begins his *Geometry* with considerations like these. From the time of the Greeks the more complicated parts of mathematics had been handled by ratios and proportions only. Euclid had written two separate books of the *Elements* on proportions, one dealing with numerical ratios, and the other with geometric ratios. He had seen the possibility of applying one to the other, but had kept them apart to insure more thorough treatment. He had expanded the metaphors of measurement, but had kept their constituents distinct. On the other hand Archimedes and Galileo had learned much both in arithmetic and geometry by combining them with a third analogue, nature. They had proceeded back and forth between numbers, figures, and natural objects, discovering and tracing down relations in a triple allegory. Descartes resolved to restrict himself to arithmetic and geometry to discover the secret of the allegory.

He began with an old problem of Apollonius: To find the position of a given point relative to a given set of straight lines. It was for Descartes a problem in proportions. Instead of measuring each distance and tabulating the result, he extended the lines until they intersected and made triangles. He could then state the distances from the lines to the point in ratios and proportions. The result was a collection of interrelated proportions which he simplified by the rules of arithmetic into a single formula consisting "of terms, some known and some unknown, some of which were equal to the rest; or rather all of which taken together are equal to nothing; for this is often the best form to consider." He called such formulae equations.

In this manipulation he had performed a peculiar, though mathematically familiar, trick. He had expressed the relations between distances without knowing or trying to discover their specific numerical values. It will be recalled that ratios allow this since they indicate arithmetical operations without requiring that they be actually completed. In this case the trick has peculiar consequences. The formula actually gave him the solution of his problem, namely the relative position of the given point with respect to the set of lines, but it also gave him the position of an "infinity of points" which satisfied the same conditions. The formula was too general; it selected a whole class of points instead of only one. He suspected that the unknown terms had something to do with the superfluous generality. This suspicion led to a discovery that had greater importance than the original problem. Formulae could be made to select and describe specific classes, or infinities, of points that constitute well-known geometric figures. As it happened, he had before him an old friend, a conic section. He tried the trick on several other sets of lines, and found that he could derive the equations not only for the other conic sections, but also for more complicated curves. There were evidently equations for every geometric figure.

Further analysis uncovered just what was involved in this discovery. It had long been known that a line could be defined as the path of a moving point; that a plane is the path of a moving line; and that a volume is the path of a moving plane. Lines, planes and volumes, so defined, are called loci. The infinity of points might then be understood as the positions occupied successively by a point moving under specified conditions. Geometrical instruments, such as compasses, parallel rulers, and other devices that had previously interested Descartes embodied such conditions for the construction of figures. Descartes happily recalled that these instruments also embodied ratios and proportions like those he had combined to solve the problem of Apollonius. Following this clue he assumed that the equations expressed the conditions governing the generation of loci; loci and equations were the two analogues constituting the geometrico-algebraic allegory.

For instance, he found that a parabola is a locus of a point such that its distance from a fixed point, called the focus, is always equal to its distance from a fixed line, called the directrix; the corresponding equation is $y^2 = apx$. The ellipse is the locus of a point such that the sum of its distances from two fixed points is constant; its equation, $\frac{x^2}{a^2} + \frac{y^2}{b^2} = 1$. The circle is an ellipse whose two fixed points, its foci, are identical: $x^2 + y^2 = r^2$. The hyperbola is the locus of a point such that the differences of its distances from two fixed points is constant: $\frac{x^2}{a^2} - \frac{y^2}{b^2} = 1$. These definitions, like the equations, summarize very complicated analogical reasoning. Almost every term is a metaphorical expression for a proportion. We shall see that the theory of conic sections in analytic geometry expands these statements and integrates them in an allegory of still higher degree of complexity.

It remained for the analyst to show the specific correspondences between the separate elementary terms in each side of the allegory. There were knowns, or constants, and unknowns, or variables, in the equations. This distinction had been found important in measurements. But measurements involved a scale. So Descartes set up an artificial scale for the measurement of his curves. He chose two fixed lines perpendicular to one another, and marked off unit distances on each. By means of triangulation he measured a locus. In this way the constants became known in terms of the unit distances on the scales, and they turned out to be the numerical conditions governing the generation of the locus. Further, the roots of the equation, that is, the values for the variables, measured the distances of the points on the locus from the axes. The infinity of values corresponded to the infinity of points. The variables under the control of the constants allegorically represented the locus.

One further point in the allegory must be noted. Descartes said that the best way to understand the equation was to think all the terms together as equal to nothing. This does not mean that the equation disappears, but rather that in this way the form of the equation was more adequately seen. Descartes was interested in the forms of these equations; such an interest should accompany the allegorical method. In this case the allegory that Descartes discovered shows that the equation and the locus have the same form, a principle of great importance but not easily observable. Stating the equation in some standard fashion, with all the terms together and with the distinction made between variables and constants, facilitates the necessary abstraction. Then it can be seen that the principle governing the variation of the variables is the same as the principle that governs the generation of the locus. Finally, the form of the equation itself emerges and can be compared or contrasted with the forms of other equations, term for term. In fact, the form turns out to be itself a variable whose values are special equations that are equivalent to each other in certain respects, just as equivalent ratios are values for a variable. The class of similar equations taken together constitute a manifold allegory. This leads into the second and perhaps more important part of analytic geometry where equations are distinguished and classified systematically. Before we go on to that, it may be well to record some points in literary criticism, the algebra of poetry.

The origins of mathematical and literary forms always make interesting and controversial theory. Mathematics is on the one hand said to have been revealed to priests and on the other to have been derived from surveying and commerce. Descartes worked in natural science, and the project for an analytic geometry was proposed to him by an angel in a vision. Likewise the drama was a religious ritual demanded by the gods, and yet it pictured the social and economic conditions of its devotees. In both cases the activity of an allegorical mind is discernible, whatever the conclusions about origin are, and the allegories come into the genetic theories as the original logical insights which are arranged by the historical mind in a temporal order, so that the first allegory contains the original form from which the others grow. If we reverse the argument, the conclusion is that at least form is present and can be isolated and analyzed.

As far back in the history of drama as we wish to go, dramatic form is found reflected in things and reflecting them in turn, and its constituents are abstract terms more or less easily recognizable even in the presentation on the stage. Aristotle says that characters in Greek tragedy are a little better than ordinary men, and the characters in comedy are a little worse. They are types, I suppose this means. On the stage the actors wore masks containing megaphones to insure a formal aspect and a dignified manner. Comedies use corresponding devices to sharpen the formal presentation.

Further, the persons of the drama are usually limited in number, and are embedded in a set of conventionally determined relations. Each character has a definite capacity for a certain set of motives and acts which fill in the pattern of the play. A role is defined within its range of possible events by constant relations between characters and between characters and circumstances. A dramatic character is a variable in a dramatic equation acting with other characters under constant conditions to determine the plot of the play. This applies to both modern and classic drama as well as to the marionette stage or the Punch-and-Judy show. A game of chess with its pieces and their possible moves and the sequence of their plays is a limiting case which illustrates the breadth of the principle. The items in the "dramatis personae" and the "argument" or "preface" are the usual ways of acquainting the audience with the formal demands that the playwright, the producer and the actors satisfy as their abilities permit. The dramatic critic discusses many other things, but the degree to which form has been grasped and realized decides. As algebra is to arithmetic and geometry, so is the drama to narrative forms of literature. Algebra marks the discovery of variables and forms; the drama isolates and emphasizes character and plot.

The notion lying back of "the persons of the drama" contributes to the theory of the novel that we discussed in Chapter IV. It introduces the notion of a variable character or dramatic type, that aspect of a character that remains identical and establishes continuity throughout the narrative development. The ordinal and cardinal aspects of character emerge from the story like figures in the projective field of geometry. They register and epitomize the passage of events, but at the same time they are manifestations of more general characters that run through the development, just as points fall within a locus and numbers are substituted for variables in equations.

The ordinal character is passive to events; the cardinal character achieves a certain independence and power of initiating action; but it is the variable character that achieves the independence of generality and informs the whole story. It is the interplay of variable characters that constitutes the plot, or form of the drama. Furthermore a variable character can step out of one story and into another, or out into the familiar world of human experience, where it recreates itself whenever human material and circumstance give it content. Thus we understand our friends and ourselves *sub specie aeternitatis* in terms of dramatic types and the world is populated with Oedipuses, Don Quixotes, Fausts, Falstaffs, Hamlets, and Bovaries. They are dramatic ideas which, once embodied, never die.

Any character may on analysis show three aspects: the ordinal which merely reflects the passage of events; the cardinal which works them over and transforms them into action; and finally the variable which informs the action with ideas. They are rather like the vegetative, animal, and rational souls discovered by Aristotle.

One is tempted to speculate on the possible consequences if Descartes had carried out his project of applying his analytic method to human morals. He could have found his material in the theater and the literature of the stage, and gone on to develop an analytic geometry of the soul. He himself might have become a great dramatic critic or a Jungian psychoanalyst defining the orders and types of human character. Perhaps it is just as well that he went on with metaphysics.

One of the more important results of the discovery of form and the isolation of variables in equations has been a greater freedom in mathematical styles. The ratio and the proportion achieved a certain freedom by substituting numbers for numbers, ratios for ratios, and geometric magnitudes for geometric magnitudes. The success of ancient mathematics and early science was due in part to that freedom. But the equation provided new machinery for the interchange of terms. The emphasis on the unknown terms as variables tempted the adventurer with symbols. If a variable can be manipulated as a blank term, restricted only by the rules for algebraic operations, all sorts of tentative substitutions can be made and the consequences watched. Descartes and his successors found that a given equation could pass from one form to another by suitable substitutions. Substitutions may be divided into two classes: those which do not violate the form of the equation; and those which do change its form. The former might be called regular and the latter irregular.

Transformations of both sorts have occurred in literature. For instance, the history of European literature shows a continual interchange of values in the pattern of Greek tragedy and comedy. I have already pointed out in the last chapter how the form of tragedy is expanded and binds medieval theology together. Similar transfigurations have come to special characters in the plays of Aeschylus, Sophocles, and Euripides. They are not only immortal; they have had many reincarnations. In Aeschylus' *Furies*, Orestes is caught in the dilemma of vengeance and comes increasingly under the influence of otherworldly creatures to his mental discomfiture, his practical undoing, and final judgment. The elements in the situation are simple, the complication obvious, and the dénouement necessary. It is the formula of the Greek tragedy which is so powerful in its extreme simplicity. By the time of Dante the motif has reached its greatest allegorical expansion and it blossoms into the infinitely complex expression of the *Divine Comedy.* Each variable in the original formula is still present, the original sin, the fall of man, the struggle for redemption amid the horror of hell and purgatory, the thwarted love of woman and deity, and the graduated blessedness of a just heaven. Dante expanded the formula by substituting mankind for Orestes and the whole cosmos for the ancient Greek world. The change in physical dimensions suggests the change in poetic depth.

The actual distance from this to *Don Quixote* is in terms of atmospheres very slight, as it is in time, but the change is crucial. Lucian in his *True History* had tried a similar change, but it was trivial in comparison with Cervantes' achievement. Their method was to make irregular substitutions. Lucian's *True History* and Cervantes' *Don Quixote* revel in the irrelevance of irregular substitution. In place of the moral problem and the need of redemption we have the crushed paper flower of knighthood, and ennui. In place of Electra and Beatrice we have the far-off loves of medieval romance embodied in a lady of doubtful reputation and in serving maids. In place of the hierarchy of furies, demons, and angels we have the mistaken identities of the countryside. In place of the way of sorrow and repentance we have the series of mad adventures encountered by the valiant knight, Don Quixote de la Mancha. In spite of the tone of burlesque there is the high seriousness demanded by Aristotle in great tragedy.

I shall not burden the reader with the details of the later transformations of the Orestes formula. As Descartes says very often in his *Geometry,* the reader will understand better and enjoy more if he makes his own discoveries and applications. I suggest Shakespeare's *Hamlet,* Flaubert's *Madame Bovary,* and Dostoevski's *The Idiot* as relevant exercises. Sinclair Lewis's *Main Street* and almost any play of Ibsen are easy to begin with.

It is in the more extreme types of irregular substitution that we find the secret of poetic humor. In recent years there have been many serious books written on this subject. They have been concerned chiefly with a psychological explanation of laughter. The logic of humor has been neglected. It would run somewhat as follows. Some formal pattern is invented, such as Greek tragedy, and a great deal of imagination and thought is poured into the mold. It becomes classic. Then a substitution is made which explosively breaks through the form. The Greek satyr play and comedy illustrate the result. New wine is poured into old bottles and there is laughter when the bottles break. Cervantes, Boccaccio, and Rabelais produce more subtle transformations. Their substitutions mix the tragic and comic forms and result in the marvelously fertile forms of the modern novel.

Descartes made another use of irregular substitution. His substitutions broke through the old forms and established new forms of higher generality and greater inclusiveness. In his hands irregular substitutions became the means of discovering the higher genera for the species of equations already discovered. It is now evident that Descartes' chief work was the second part of his analysis; it has led to a complete classification of equations. The method is called the "discussion of equations."

He first made the distinction between the variables and constants in the formulae resulting from his combinations of ratios. He then noted that the variables occurred in multiplicative relations with themselves. In his *Geometry* he wrote such terms as products thus: $x \cdot x \cdot x$. We now write such terms with exponential numbers, thus $x^3$, and call the exponential number the power of the variable. It designates the number of times that the given variable is to be taken as a factor in the product. When no number is given it is to be understood that the power of the variable is one. Equations can then be divided into *orders* according to the highest exponential numbers occurring in them. An equation containing a third-powered variable is of the third order. It is interesting to know that the order of the equation corresponds to the number of lines used in the original geometric derivation of the equation.

Having ordered equations according to the powers of their variables, Descartes went on to subdivide the orders into *types* which correspond to the manner in which the constants contribute to the form of the equation. For this purpose he distinguished between two kinds of constants. Some of these resembled variables in that they could be generalized for purposes of discussion and consequently might take on more than one value, but they also resembled constants in that they were assumed to be single-valued for any formal manipulation of the equation. These he called arbitrary constants. The other constants were numbers; these he called absolute constants. Constants of both kinds entered equations as factors in products with variables or as separate terms. In using constants to distinguish types it is sometimes necessary to assume that a term is missing because it has zero as a factor; it is then formally present though notationally absent. Constants occurring as factors are in general called coefficients.

By means of these distinctions and the appropriate symbolic conventions it was possible to state what are now called general equations which represent the form that an indefinite number of similar equations may embody. For instance

$$Ax^2 + Bxy + Cy^2 + Dx + Ey + F = 0$$

is the general equation for all conic sections. It is an equation of the second order according to the highest exponential number it contains. A, B, C, D, E, and F are here arbitrary constants; for purposes of discussion they represent substitutible numerical values. If numbers or absolute constants are substituted for them, the various specific equations for the conic sections will result. Thus if zero is substituted for A, B, E, and F and some numerical values other than zero are substituted for the remaining coefficients, we have the equation for a parabola. For instance let C = 1 and D = −8 and we have the parabola, y = 8x. Other substitutions produce other conics.

These arbitrary constants and the numbers which may be substituted for them are vestigial remains of the ratios which determine the locus of the equation. Descartes knew this and succeeded in formulating general rules in terms of them for abstracting from any equation the differentiae of the types of equation of any given order. For the conic sections these rules are as follows:

If in an equation of the second degree

$B^2 − 4\,AC = 0$, then the equation is a parabola;

$B^2 − 4\,AC < 0$, then the equation is an ellipse;

$B^2 − 4\,AC > 0$, then the equation is a hyperbola.

$B^2 − 4\,AC$ is therefore called the "characteristic" for conic sections.

The method which applies such rules to general equations is adequate for the classification of any equation that may occur. It is the basis for a great deal of the work that has been done on equations. Some such scheme is a necessary adjunct to any use of analogy or allegory to prevent errors and misuse of formulae. It is also true, but often ignored, that some insight into form is necessary for the solution of even the simplest problem in applied algebra, mathematical or poetic.

It seems that a rigorous "discussion" of the forms of literature might aid in literary criticism, where there is so much confusion about standards of classification. Now some sociological, historical, psychological, or naturalistic criterion is applied before it is analyzed and understood. No doubt these criteria contain rigorous formulae in terms of which discrimination is possible, but who knows what a literary "characteristic" is?

Aristotle defined in fairly rigorous terms, which have often been misused, the forms of Greek tragedy. There have been attempts to go on where he left off. These attempts have approximated a parallel with the analytic methods of Descartes. The dramatist has used analogies to abstract his forms from his materials, and the critic has isolated and formulated general formulae in terms of types of character and constant conditions, the conventions and limitations of writing and production. All this might be pushed further if the method itself were better understood.

For instance, within the general form of Greek tragedy, Aeschylus' Orestes might be defined as a variable character whose acts are equally determined by practical and imaginary or theoretic considerations. Antigone is a variable character whose acts are determined more by imaginary or theoretic than by practical considerations. Clytemnestra is a variable character whose acts are determined more by practical than by imaginary or theoretic considerations. Then one might go on to the content of such formulae in terms of cardinal and ordinal elements in each type of character. Whether the results of such analysis would be useful or not I do not know. The analysis itself, I do know, has the same fascination that mathematics has. Perhaps some committee of censors would lobby a bill through a state legislature requiring that all publications have their formulae printed on their jackets—a pure literature law. Publishers' salesmen could psychoanalyze their clients and prescribe the proper literary purchases. A worried critic might even be able to decide whether a novel or a play is art or not.

Descartes did not know what utility was hidden in analytic geometry, but this is what he said he had done; he is giving the geometric statement of the allegory:

"But it is not my purpose to write a large book. I am trying rather to include much in a few words, as will perhaps be inferred from what I have done, if it is considered that, while reducing to a single construction all the problems of one class, I have at the same time given a method of transforming them into an infinity of others, and thus of solving each in an infinite number of ways: that furthermore, having constructed all plane problems by the cutting of a circle by a straight line, and all solid problems by the cutting of a circle by a parabola; and finally all that are but one degree more complex by cutting a circle by a curve but one degree higher than the parabola, it is only necessary to follow the general method to construct all problems, more and more complex, ad infinitum; for in the case of a mathematical progression, whenever the first two or three terms are given, it is easy to find the rest.

"I hope that posterity will judge me kindly not only as to things which I have explained, but also as to those which I have intentionally omitted so as to leave to others the pleasures of discovery."

There is prophecy in this last paragraph, but the events are more wonderful than the prophecy. As usual the analogical applications of the pure mathematical theory have been myriad. As it happens, the orbits of planets and comets, not to mention the paths of other less spectacular material bodies, are conic sections. Descartes himself went on to construct his own physics and astronomy, in which the properties of matter are essentially exemplifications of equations. Physicists still pay tribute to Descartes by referring all their discoveries in the laboratory to his realm of equations. There is now said to be a general equation for the motion of any particle of matter anywhere in the universe.

But there is also in this quotation an atmosphere that would be called foreshadowing in the drama. There was a prophecy that analytic geometry itself would go far, and the suggestion that it would provide the map for still greater explorations in the territory of pure mathematics. So it has done. The classification of equations might be compared to Linnaeus' classification of plants and the map it provided for the biological explorations of Darwin and Wallace. Descartes' work was to be accepted and reinterpreted in terms of the calculuses of Newton and Leibniz and the modern developments in the theory of functions. The species of equations were still to find their places in an hereditary series. The next chapter discusses mathematical heredity.

## VI Functions

The reader with strictly literary interests will have wondered for some time how long the writer of these pages would go on talking of the poetry in literature in nonliterary terms; in other words, where discussion of style is to find a place in this logomachy. For, after all, words are the elementary units of the poet's craft, and the light from mathematical theory is weak if it cannot lift the mystery from this dark corner in literary criticism.

It may surprise the reader to learn that it is just here that the problem of poetry and mathematics started up in the writer's mind, and that it has taken the roundabout road I have been traveling to come to anything like a solution. I approached the subject from logic and mathematics. In the attempt to find out what they were talking about I found the literary analogy most illuminating. Impressed and a little puzzled by that discovery, I was tempted to push the analysis of literature to the end. The result has been only to arrive at the beginning, but even there the reward is the discovery of what is at least for me a new dimension in literature, amenable to logical treatment and yet rich in what are known as literary or critical overtones. These overtones are usually discounted by the logician and credited to the deceitful ambiguities of words. It is thus that logicians and mathematicians are wont in their youth to escape from the siren of literature. Later in life they usually fall before her enticements and call the results of their delayed romance scientific philosophy. Words have in truth been their undoing.

Some verbal Satan has come in the guise of the second person of the Trinity, Logos, and another intellectual sin has been committed by a garrulous old man. The current doctrine of emergent evolution is a case of this.

I have decided to deal with the verbal enchantress now. I am reassured by the appearance at this point of an important distinction and corresponding relation between poetry and mathematics. What is most abstract in poetry is most concrete in mathematics, and what is most abstract in mathematics is most concrete in poetry. Specifically, ideal character, its structure and its development, is abstract in poetry and corresponds to figure and number which are as near as mathematics ever comes to concrete elements and data. I am about to show that words and style which are concrete in poetry correspond to functions, the typical abstractions of mathematics. Further, it appears that what is most essential in each, the poetic and mathematical object, is most adequately expressed in words and functions respectively. I believe the end of our wandering is in sight in this thesis.

If I were to adduce evidence for it, I would have to draw it from several studies that "fall outside the scope of this book." I refer to that family of genetic studies that goes by the name of philology, in which the interplay of geography, physiology, psychology, sociology, and anthropology weaves scientific myths and legends around our words and what they mean. A study of the part played by scientific instruments in the choice of mathematical symbolism is most needed in this field at present. But I am always dissatisfied with the inconclusive conclusions of these studies. They are themselves mathematical and poetic stories and therefore beg my question. I shall therefore state the thesis as if there were no evidence for it and let the reader use his own good sense in judgment.

The problem of style, as it actually faces a writer, is the difficulty in finding words to fit a subject matter. There is a rightness and a wrongness about words that is inescapable, yet in the end ineffable. Essays on style often speak of word-values, emotional connotations, sense of language, tones of voice, experience with the classics, even verbal inspiration, and refer the inevitabilities of style to these creative factors. Which or how many of these are involved, I do not know, but I am convinced that the ever present and crucial factor is a subject matter which is the dictator of practice, and the standard of judgment. The problem of style is the fitful faithfulness of symbols to an ideal subject matter. The mathematician and the poet have had long experience with it, and their products are the facts to be considered.

On the side of theory, I propose to turn two traditional doctrines, one philosophical and one mathematical, to the end of educing the basic principles of a science of style. Such a science might be called, by analogy with music, linguistic harmony. It would contain the dialectical conclusion of this argument about poetry and mathematics. The doctrines that I propose are to be found in idealistic logic and infinitesimal calculus, respectively. I might derive both of them from the philosophy of Leibniz, but for purposes of exposition other sources are more useful.

The incidental suggestion for using idealistic logic comes from a criticism that is usually accepted as its refutation. It is said that idealism is a philosophy founded on grammar, and that its metaphysics contains the fallacy of imputing grammatical conventions and rhetorical forms to reality in general. Suppose we accept the point as regards logic and let the metaphysics go. Idealistic logic should then show us at least the structure and ideal function of language, and in the end we should discover what are the significant connections between words and their meanings.

The criticism with which we start was first directed by the idealists themselves against what they took to be Aristotelian logic. Aristotle in one of his definitions of substance had said that a substance is that which cannot be predicated of anything else, but of which other things are predicated. By this

he is supposed to have identified substance with the grammatical subject of a sentence, and to have vitiated the rest of his logical theory. Supposing he did do that, what follows?

John Locke, a reformer of medical theory and practice, a critic of Christianity, a social theorist, and a generalizer of what he took to be Newtonian scientific method, showed to his own satisfaction that any substance of the sort that carried attributes or qualities could not be known, but only inferred, and that anything known immediately in experience would be a quality only. He then proceeded to divide qualities into different kinds. There were primary qualities, those talked about in physical science and therefore independent of our experience though capable of appearing there; and there were secondary qualities which always depended on our sense organs as well as physical objects for even their existence. Locke further divided primary qualities into classes which he called solidity, size, shape, and motion; and secondary qualities into classes whose names were taken from the various senses which gave them their existence. These distinctions were not original with Locke, rather with Galileo, but they became the foundation of idealistic logic in his writings.

After Locke, Bishop Berkeley and David Hume successively broke down these neat conventional divisions and left the qualities in a near-chaos whose only remnant of order came from the rather weak laws of association. Our experience contains objects only because we are in the habit of associating ideas by their similarities, differences and their succession in time and space. Substance which had been an unknown $x$ in Locke's critique is now only the ghost of primitive mental habits of such association.

All this, if it is the logic of grammar, means that all words are adjectives whose behavior and company are determined only by accidental associations. If style is at all relevant, it means that it is a matter of chance. At best style can be no better than experience in its order and excellences.

What is skepticism in the theory of knowledge is nihilism as regards literature.

But skepticism and nihilism clear ground for new building. As in the textbook history of philosophy, Kant comes next. That he also follows Leibniz may not be wholly irrelevant in a discussion of the logic of grammar. Kant showed how Hume's skepticism was somewhat sentimental and melodramatic, that, with a little closer analysis, the laws of association were enough to give us back our real objects, or at least permanent substrata to which qualities and attributes could belong in our minds. In the course of the demonstration he also listed the meanings of the word "is," to which I referred in the chapter on analogy, and believed he had found a limited number of possible ways for combining substances with qualities, and qualities with qualities. These were his categories, and together they revise Aristotle's grammar so that it becomes the canon of style for Newtonian physics.

But Kant's substance was a bit ghostly and his categories were too neat. Later logicians found more meanings for "is" until finally Hegel realized that there were an infinite number of them; also that Kant's substance was itself adjectival. He organized a method for dealing with these infinite qualities and categories. They would now come in threes, a positive, a negative, and a synthesis of the two. He used the resulting style to write a history of the human spirit, a fine demonstration of what a style can do to transform a subject matter.

However, Hegel's architecture was too heavy for the quick changes that literature and logic have to make. F. H. Bradley saw the problem. He accepted the merely adjectival function of all words and discourse, but proceeded with more caution and subtlety than his predecessors to invent some general but still versatile method for discovering the delicate organization of words into propositions, propositions into systems, and systems into universes of discourse. He worked with three criteria in mind, coherence, inclusiveness, and concreteness. It

should be remarked that his own style admirably fulfills these criteria, but for him they were properties of thought, to which discourse must be faithful. Adjectives must not contradict each other, any adjectival unit must include as many sub-adjectives as possible, and the generality must not violate the distinctions in the detail of the subject matter. It might well be said that F. H. Bradley wrote logic like a literary critic and his brother, A. C. Bradley, wrote literary criticism like a logician. The implied comparison with William and Henry James is not unjust.

The result of these studies in the logic of adjectives may best be stated in terms of a recent theory by W. E. Johnson, who himself is not an idealist, but has availed himself and logicians in general of some of the insights of the idealists.

If we say something is red, we speak accurately only if the something is also colored. The applicability of the adjective "red" depends upon the applicability of the adjective "colored." "Colored" is more inclusive than "red," and is therefore said to be a determinable and "red" is its determinate. Further, if a thing is red, it must also have some determinate shade or tint of red. Such a shade or tint would then be a determinate of "red" and a subdeterminate of "colored." "Green" is also a determinate of "colored" and might be called a codeterminate of "red." The distinction between "determinable" and "determinate" is of course only relative. That is, "colored" may also be a determinate, say, of the determinable, "visible." Similarly, a given shade of "red" may be a determinable for still lower determinates. It is important to notice that there seem to be no upper or lower limits to the adjectival hierarchy.

On the other hand there are distinct limits in the horizontal dimension. For instance, "sweet" does not belong to "colored," and "invisible" is wholly excluded from the hierarchy under consideration. In other words, the line between contradictories and the line between opposites mark outer boundaries and inner divisions respectively in any given family of adjectives. Adjectives thus have harmonies and discords similar to those in music.

It may seem foolhardy to try to apply any such wooden machinery to the subtleties of style, but such an objection would be based on a misconception of the nature and function of logic. Logic does not dictate rules even to argument. It follows both argument and lyric as fast as it can, and records, analyzes and criticizes. Logic would be disgraced in its own home if it could not handle literary criticism. This theory, cumbersome and pedantic as it may sound, takes care of the most radical innovations in style, as well as the more plodding discourse of science.

Certain modern writers of verse delight in the mixture of sense departments, as in "echoing light." The problem that this raises for the logician is to locate the determinable under which these adjectival words will live in harmony. This example is rather like Dante. It may refer to a neo-Platonic universe where all ideas are antiphonal, or, depending on its context, it may invoke elements from the world of modern physics. The Homeric epithet, though conventionally accepted as commonplace, transports one to a special sector of the ideal sphere where dawns are necessarily connected with rosy-fingered goddesses. The more surprising and unique the combination of words, the higher and more delicate the abstraction achieved with no consequent loss of what are called concrete values. Thus poetic license and poetic justice play complementary guiding roles in the exploration of the realm of intellectual imagination.

Contemporary science which might be supposed to be conservative in such matters has just recently been outdoing the poets in its usages. "Warped space" and "motion without matter" are dictated by logical necessities of a subject matter which has outgrown the analogies of straight-line rulers and marbles. It is logic, not drugs or dreams, that justifies men in strange fantastic ways.

The school of idealism in philosophy met a crisis in the rise of the romantic school in literature. Newton's fluxional calculus and Leibniz' infinitesimal calculus mark the crisis in a similar game of mathematical tradition and innovation. These mathematicians practiced a license that roused the conventional mathematician and philosopher to protests comparable with classicist attacks on romantic experiments. It was in fact a romantic movement in mathematics, and its application in science and industry laid the conditions for romantic literature and gave a hint even for its style and atmosphere. But again it was not essentially a revolt against convention, but rather a fresh attempt to render symbols faithful to an ideal subject matter. Almost as an accidental consequence, it has revolutionized the whole of mathematics, logic, and philosophy, to say nothing of the physical sciences.

Newton was chiefly concerned with the analogy between the paths of projectiles and the orbits of the moon and planets. In order to work it out, he required some general method for expressing the rates of change in their velocities and directions; in short, their accelerations at any given instant and point. Galileo had used ratios to express such accelerations over given intervals. Newton's task was to get a ratio which could be applied at any point in the motion. For this he hit upon the notion that intervals might approximate points if they were allowed to grow smaller and smaller. If the ratio of acceleration for an interval could be caught just as the interval disappeared into a point, it would express the acceleration for that point without further consideration of the interval. Starting with the ratio for a given interval, he would allow it to vary with the decreasing interval, and watch its behavior until the interval disappeared. The ratio at the beginning was called a prime ratio, and at the disappearance of the interval, an ultimate ratio. Since it expressed the ratio of acceleration for a moving point, and was itself a variable quantity, he called it a "fluxion."

As on former occasions in the history of

mathematics, what was needed was new symbolic means for handling ratios, and the solution was reached by indulging in mathematical license. New symbols were to come by the misuse of old symbols. The mathematician's technique in such a crisis is to close the eyes of his mind and follow his nose for symbols wherever it may lead; he can explain later what happened. In technical language an expression containing some irregularity is used as an operator on a known formula, just as $+1$ and $-1$ were used without question as operators to develop numbers. When some important transformation is made by this means, as in the case of the negative numbers, it is hailed as an invention, and becomes an established part of mathematical technique. Later someone explains what the operation actually does to the mathematical object and the result is then called a discovery.

The trick this time was to allow the denominator of a fraction, the second term in the ratio, to disappear. According to the rules of algebra such a misused fraction retaliates by becoming paradoxical or indeterminate. But in this case, if the sin were ignored, a very valuable expression would remain.

Thus the ratio, $\Delta y/\Delta x$, is an operator applied to an algebraic expression. As $\Delta y$ and $\Delta x$ grow smaller and smaller, "as small as you please," there emerges from the operation the desired expression. The sin is overlooked and the result is accepted and called a fluxion or differential, $dy/dx$ for short. This operation was very successful in extracting the precious ratios from all sorts of algebraic equations, and was the foundation for a new branch of mathematics. Its success sent many minds in search of its theoretical justification in terms of an underlying relational structure.

But both the verbal and the algebraic accounts are paradoxical. Intervals after all are not points, no matter how small they become, and $dy/dx$ actually contains an indeterminate expression, $0/0$. The mathematical classicists made fun of this "ghost of

a departed magnitude," this quantity that was zero and infinity at the same time and yet had the appearance of an honest finite quantity. The theologians like Bishop Berkeley saw a fine opportunity for a *tu quoque* against their scientific critics who boasted of consistency and precision. Newton called his invention a fluxion while Leibniz, with a more efficient notation, called his a differential. Neither gave a respectable mathematical account and a long controversy was started and continued for more than a hundred years. It was further complicated by a professional attempt to assign credit for the invention to one of two people, neither of whom had a clear idea of what he had done.

The settlement of the main controversy had to wait until Dedekind and Weierstrass in the nineteenth century generalized the problem to include the scandal of the irrational numbers and the incommensurable magnitudes, such for instance as the ratio between the radius and circumference of a circle, or the ratio between the diagonal and a side of a square.

These bothersome numbers and magnitudes were first discovered by the Pythagoreans. They also had started such a controversy that the members of the mathematical cult made a secret of them. One man who divulged the secret was drowned on a prearranged sea voyage, it is said. By the Pythagorean theorem the diagonal of a square with sides, say, one inch long, has a length expressible only as $\sqrt{2}$, the square root of the sum of the squares of two sides. But $\sqrt{2}$ is neither a whole number nor a fraction. It is apparently no number at all. The simple and almost sacred square contains a mystery not open to Pythagorean treatment by numbers.

Euclid had a method of handling these numbers in proportions. I have noted this in remarking on the subtlety of his definition of a ratio. "Two numbers are in ratio which when multiplied are capable of exceeding each other." Although they do not become rational numbers, they could be handled in ratios and proportions. Dedekind took advantage of this notion of ratio and generalized it so as to redefine numbers both rational and irrational. He did it by means of a conception which he called a "cut" (*Schnitt*). This conception is necessary to make the Euclidean definition explicit.

He defines a cut as follows: If an ordered class C is divided into two non-empty subclasses $C_1$, $C_2$, such that every element of C is an element either of $C_1$ or of $C_2$, and such that every element of $C_1$ precedes every element of $C_2$, then there exists an element x which affects this division. Such a division of C into $C_1$ and $C_2$ is a cut. This means that any irrational number, say $\sqrt{2}$, corresponds to a cut of the class of numbers into two subclasses, the first of which contains all those numbers whose squares are less than two, the second of which contains all those numbers whose squares are greater than 2. ($\sqrt{2}$ can belong to either one but not both of these subclasses.) Obviously a whole or fractional number corresponds to a similar cut, and it is essential that it should.

The irrational numbers had been excluded because they were unending decimals whose exact value could not be ascertained. But if the essential properties of numbers do not require countability, but mere position, and the irrationals have the other properties that are essential, there remains no reason for excluding them. A further question remains as to where they belong in the series that we know. Dedekind's answer is that they go between the fractions, after those less than themselves and before those greater than themselves. No other objection of serious nature has yet been raised.

But there are more consequences. If you feel your feet leaving the solid ground of countable numbers, you have understood the point of Dedekind's definition, but you must also realize that you are merely shifting the whole number system to more solid ground. You will see that the essential nature of numbers, from the point of view of the theory of functions, is to be found in such relations as "greater than," "less than,"

"before," and "after." By means of these relations you have discovered a class of numbers that come between the members of the compact series of fractional numbers, and render the number series as continuous, as free from jumps, as we understand space to be.

It is not too difficult to transfer the rule from numbers to fluxions and infinitesimals; that is what Dedekind and Weierstrass did. Instead of trying to find some unique member of the number series corresponding to the differential, they redefined the differential in terms of relations. As in the case of numbers, this shift in definition gave the whole realm of mathematics a jolt and a reorientation. It revealed new properties of the mathematical object, and these new properties were soon seen to be fundamental.

The differential, or the fluxion, is the result of an algebraic operation on equations. Its unconventional and apparently illegitimate character comes from the old story of the mathematician following symbols in search of a new style and his return with intellectual trophies. When $\Delta y/\Delta x$ becomes $dy/dx$, it means that algebraic rules have given way to analysis of a new aspect of the equation, not hitherto isolated. This is the pure relational structure within which variables are merely obedient elements. An equation in stating the equality of sets of symbols expresses the relations that hold between classes of values. The numbers and points of analytic geometry emphasize these values. Although Descartes' attention was called to the relational aspects, his work ended in techniques of substitution and manipulation of values. It was in terms of these techniques that he passed from one type of equation to another. The effect of applying the notion of the "cut" to the differential was to throw the emphasis on the purely relational aspect of equations.

It is as if the philologist had been interested only in the meanings and derivations of single words, and had given his account of grammar and usage in terms of such atomic elements as phrases, sentences, and paragraphs. He would then be an etymologist. Suppose the grammarian suggested that the relations between words were the more important properties for linguistics. The philologist might then see that even the meanings of single words come from the structures in which they occur in discourse. The words are merely the points of reference in the context, each dependent on its companions for its own character. This would be an exaggeration, like saying that characters in a novel are nothing but the intersection of forces and lines of action in the plot. We are familiar with the fallacy in political science that says the individual is nothing but a creation of the political state. But it is nevertheless an important aspect of numbers, novels, states, and equations. It marks an advance in the direction of subtlety and precision of thought.

This new aspect of the mathematical object is called functionality. As soon as it is seen in the differential, it is applied to any equation, and as soon as it is seen there, it is extended to cover all statements or exemplifications of mathematical conceptions. The reader of these pages should not be wholly unfamiliar with it, for my exposition of the various aspects of the mathematical object has consisted in selecting perspectives on it which would show the functional characters in each case. The new definition of the mathematical object that comes to light has application to all that has gone before. x, y, etc., are said to be in functional relation when there is a law or form by which the variation of one or more variables determines the variation of the others. We now can write the formula for any mathematical element in terms of a function of one or more variables thus: $F(x)$, $F(x, y)$, $F(x, y, z)$. Thus we say $F(x) = x^2$ and $F'(x) = 2x$ where $F(x)$ means the original function and $F'(x)$ means the differential or, as we now call it, the derivative function.

Before we pass on to further developments of this in the calculus, it may be well to point out the various properties of single functions. First, they exhibit a constant or invariant form or pattern of relations. Second, they contain variables between which the relations hold. Third, on account of the constancy and variability in the pattern, the change of value in any subsumed variable brings about a corresponding change in the value of the other variables. It is rather too bad that Newton's term *fluxion* has fallen into disuse. It is a more descriptive term for the properties of functions. "Flowing magnitudes" catches an essential property not conveyed by "function."

Among many consequences of this interpretation is the much-discussed notion of relativity. The value of any variable is relative to the value of any other variable by virtue of the constant relations holding between them. We have not only equational functions, but also complicated system functions, and finally transformation functions for systems. Relativity is the most spectacular functional property noted in such systems as modern mathematical physics.

The calculus goes on to further consequences. Since derivatives are themselves functions, new or second derivatives can be found for first derivatives. Theoretically, there is an infinite number of such derivatives for any given function. Each derivative selects and isolates properties from the original function and the limits of such analysis are only those of ingenuity. At present such analysis ends, in practice, with numbers, which are considered constant in an arbitrarily absolute sense. But the series of derivative functions is ideally infinite.

Of course this series suggests its reverse. Any given function may be considered a derivative function, and there will be at least one function from which it is derived. Thus if $F(x) = 5x^2$, $F'(x) = 10x$, and $F''(x) = 10$, $F'(x)$ and $F''(x)$ are first and second derivatives. The reverse of differentiation is called integration. Starting with $F(x) = 10$, $\int 10 = 10x$, $\int 10x = 5x^2$, and $\int 5x^2 = \frac{5}{3}x^3$, by introducing arbitrary constants we may develop an indefinite number of variants on each of the integral functions. Thus functions belong in families having a vertical order constituted by integral and differential relations, each level of which has a horizontal order consisting of variants generated by the substitutions of arbitrary constants. The project stated by Descartes at the end of the last chapter is thus fulfilled in more elegant fashion than he had imagined.

The English mathematician Taylor contrived a formula for expressing these connections. The formula now goes by his name, Taylor's Series:

$$f(x) = f(x_0) + f'(x_0)\ (x - x_0)$$

$$+ f''(x_0)\ \frac{(x - x_0)^2}{2!}$$

$$+ f'''(x_0)\ \frac{(x - x_0)^3}{3!} + \ \cdot\ \cdot\ \cdot\ \cdot\ \cdot$$

In this series functions are treated as variables and substitutions can be made by which any function can be expanded and its properties revealed and marshaled for observation, as chemical compounds and biological functions are studied in the laboratory—perhaps with greater precision. Newton's Binomial Series is a case of this.

Of course there are literally myriads of applications of the calculus and the functions which it studies. Newton's success with physics promised much and the calculus has borne out the expectation. Most of modern physics depends upon the use of derivative and integral functions in differential equations. Here functions themselves are taken on as variables and the solutions found by a combination of algebraic and differential operations. The analogical inferences that can thus be drawn are truly miraculous.

Successful application of the calculus in the natural sciences led to many ambitious projects in other fields. Economists and sociologists found happy illustrations of functional relations in the statistical records of their observations. They have spent much time and energy in matching such records with conic sections and other functional symbols, and in hunting for more data to correct discrepancies. But perhaps the hap-

piest thought found root in logic. Logicians for a long time had found fault with the propositions and classes of Aristotle's logic. Boole, the Irish mathematician, conceived the possibility of working out the parallel between algebra and logic. In this project Taylor's Series came in for attention and a variation on it was found most powerful in rendering the import of propositions explicit. There immediately appeared the term "propositional function." $f(x)$ or $\phi(x)$ now would represent a proposition whose form could be considered without reference to its content or values. Now it is possible to abstract such forms for any discursive statement and propositional functions have become the subject matter of logic. Logic and much philosophy have been rendered responsible to a more refined type of rigor. The revolution that this signifies has incidentally made even more clear what the subject matter of mathematics itself is. Mathematics is the science of relations as such.

These extensions suggest another application more nearly relevant to the present purpose. At least the intellectual basis of style in literature can now be made explicit. Style is an unconscious witness to the presence of a system of abstract relations among adjectives. Perhaps it is better not to tell the poet this, but it might be whispered to a critic.

There is a theory in metaphysics that ideas are floating singly; they are wandering adjectives. This most certainly is not true if the styles of the derivative and the poem are admissible evidence. Adjectives, and by adjectives I mean words in general, come together, or they are not significant, and therefore not words. They are selections from vast systems, the clouds of glory from the intellectual heaven which is our artistic home.

I do not mean by such expressions to drag in any super-Platonic metaphysics. The walk of a friend, the line of a melody, the healthy vibration of a motor are known when they are seen or heard. To most things of this sort we respond by a feeling or action. If we are poets, we speak and in some sense are possessed by these things. To put it crudely, we dance to their rhythms. But we are not these things. We are acting out an analogy and it is only their forms that possess us, maybe in body only, but sometimes in soul as well. When it is the latter we have discerned a function, and if we speak, we speak literature. In this way words and symbols are only the carriers and for the most part they are not very willing servants, not found at the proper time, or manipulated in harmony with what they symbolize. Here lies the problem of style. Few of us are poets or mathematicians; we do not think or speak poetry and mathematics most of the time. But when we and they are engaged in such happy activity, we are catching relations and realizing values, and our symbols in word or act are faithful to their subject matter.

This is where psychology, sociology, prosody, mathematical logic, and a thousand other unclassified studies throw light. They are concerned with the controlling constants of mathematics and poetry. They attempt to show the "how" of expression. They should not be condemned for not telling what gets expressed, nor should they claim that they do tell that.

This opens the way and demands attention to the metaphysics of this essay. For the most part it will be postponed to the next chapters, but a preliminary distinction can be made.

What is the difference between mathematics and poetry? I have been at pains to describe their meeting points, but have in no way intended to assert their identity. Briefly, the difference is this. The mathematician sees and deals with relations; the poet sees and deals with qualities. Functions and adjectives respectively are the symbols through which they see and with which they operate. Mathematics is analytic, seeing wholes as systems of relations; poetry is synthetic, seeing wholes as simple qualities. The qualities that the poet sees are due to relations, says the mathematician. They need

purgation. The relations that the mathematician sees are concrete and factual, says the poet. They need appreciation and love.

The difference is possible because of the way experience comes, qualities in relation, substances with attributes, wholes and parts. Both poet and mathematician select and abstract what they see and in that they are free minds. Sometimes they, and almost always we, get confused, taking relations for qualities and qualities for relations. The result is belief.

Belief is the natural attitude of a thwarted mind. It arises from fatigue and confusion. The psychologist may tell us about fatigue, but the critic must point out the confusion. For the most part confusion is of two sorts, one involving symbols, and the other metaphysical nostalgia, the tendency of thought toward the absolute. The next two chapters view these regions from a distance.

## VII Symbols

In the first chapter the field of these critical excursions was roughly defined as the various attempts to deal with ideas by means of symbols. It was then postulated and it has been taken for granted throughout that the relation between symbols and ideas is such that poetry and mathematics are possible. It is now time to show what such a possibility involves.

The answer to the question requires a brief discussion of the aesthetics of poetry and mathematics. It is a truism that poetry has aesthetic properties, and it is true, though less often noted, that mathematics for a mathematician also has aesthetic properties. I have been at pains to show their intellectual properties, but I hope it has not obscured their more obvious and immediate aspects.

As a matter of fact aesthetic properties have appeared in the course of expounding the intellectual properties. In the discussion of geometric figures as projective fields, cones of light rays were cut by planes and the results were pictures. If the base of the cone was a disc, then the various pictures were specific circles, ellipses, parabolas, hyperbolas or pairs of straight lines. Working under geometric rules, analysis immediately follows the fixing of such static pictures and the pictures are dissolved into sets of relations; the emphasis is on intellectual properties. From the point of view of the artist or seeker for aesthetic objects these static pictures are destinations rather than points in progressive analysis. They are designs and forms to be reproduced in chosen media.

A recent critic of painting has shown how all the designs in pictures can be derived from the projective field developed from the spiral. By proper transformations within this field seven basic designs, each with infinite variations, are produced. More specialized bases such as the logarithmic spiral give rise to the designs of Greek vases and temples as well as many objects of nature. These aesthetic objects can be extracted from apparently strict mathematical considerations. They can be analyzed into mathematical relations and generalized, but their strictly aesthetic character as they stand is exhibited in their uniqueness and concreteness.

Literature is occupied with such objects and is concerned to present them as vividly and efficiently as possible. The literary realization, as in *Alice in Wonderland*, of any segment of the intellectual realm involves the provision of such suitable aesthetic objects. The art of poetry is primarily directed to this end.

I should like to call this immediate aspect of poetry and mathematics the aesthetic object. Its relation to the intellectual object or idea I shall call its symbolic function. Geometrical figures and sets of words, as unique objects of contemplation, are thus symbols in so far as they realize and exhibit corresponding intellectual forms.

The symbolic relation is often understood to hold between three instead of two terms. There is said to be (1) a conventional or artificial sign standing for (2) an idea, which points to (3) one or more real objects. It is hard to see the justification for the assumption in this statement that man-made things, such as signs, are different in any fundamental way from real objects. My contention is that sign and real object are equally symbolic. They both give rise to pictures, or other aesthetic objects, which show forth in their forms the intellectual object. It is not only in formulae, figures, and poems that the elements are symbols, but anything perceived suggests and exhibits ideas.

It is true that perceived things are ambiguous, that is, any one such thing suggests and exhibits many alternative ideas, but that is only because we jump from one to another symbol without noting the change in projective reference. If we held one element fixed, it would not be ambiguous in its ideal references.

Perhaps an old-fashioned theory of knowledge is relevant here. In the Continental philosophical tradition from Descartes to Kant there was a general agreement about three stages of knowledge. There were confused ideas, clear and distinct ideas, and insight or intellectual intuition. Below these three there was also recognized a chaos of feeling or sensation. Baumgarten identified the confused ideas as aesthetic objects, and the clear and distinct ideas as intellectual objects. Baumgarten's terms were dictated by the analogy with vision. The mathematical analogy with fields of projection would be appropriate and more explicit. Objects are vaguely perceived in sensation or feeling. They are partially clarified in the process of picture-making by projection or some other appropriate transformation and the resulting pictures are confused ideas, or aesthetic objects, in which distortion and design are present. When they take on the ideal reference, which I have called the symbolic function, they exhibit also the clear and distinct ideas which I have called intellectual objects. Ambiguity marks the difficulty of the first clarification. Ordered projection overcomes this by differentiating and ordering the pictures until they become focused on their respective ideas.

All this is well exemplified in the various ways of reading poetry. There is the emotional school whose devotees recollect emotions and imagery on the occasion of following the lines of a poem. They go in for feeling and sensation. Then there is the aesthetic school, whose members select merely some aspect of rhythm, verbal music, or even the spacing of words, lines and capital letters. They can read the list of stations on a Continental railway with pure appreciation of its poetry, or the *Odyssey* for its roar and thunder. Finally there is the intellectual school who go from science to morals by way of metaphysics on the occasion of seeing a "flower in the crannied wall." The more dogmatic members of the school believe they can read poetry without emotion or imagery.

This is all quite obvious in the case of poetry, but it is a shock to find oneself reading mathematics from such points of view. Leibniz said he began by tasting the pleasant bits scattered here and there in mathematical treatises, and began composing his own differential calculus before he had studied either Euclid or Descartes thoroughly and analytically. He was ashamed when he met Huyghens because he had missed some simple points on the disciplinary side. Mathematics does contain many "pleasant bits." For the properly tuned eye there are many aesthetic objects even apart from geometrical figures. In the transformation of the equations of analytic geometry there is a free play of the imagination in perhaps an unrecognized harmony with the concepts of the understanding. It is true that $x$, $y$, $=$, $+$, et cetera, by themselves are opaque and uninteresting aesthetically, but the visual-intellectual aspect of an equation has significant form even for the person who has no analytical training. There is a "purposiveness without a purpose," a "disinterested interest," the two properties of the aesthetic object according to Kant, in $a^2 + b^2 = c^2$ even for one who does not know that it is

the fundamental equation in trigonometry. Proportions are fascinating even to a small child. Nine-tenths of the skill with number and formulae in professional mathematical technique is due to an aesthetic appreciation of symbolic form. It is achieved in the same manner that the appreciation of sculpture and music is attained. The position of words in a poem, the network of lines in a figure, the flow of terms in a formula, present qualities and values as truly as the flight of birds, the frost figures on the windowpane, or the march of moon and stars across the sky.

It is this fitness of things, both artificial and natural, to express ideas that gives plausibility to the mysteries of ritual and the universe. Religious ritual and natural process imitate the manipulations of things by which the playwright and actor create the illusion of the stage. Science is an apt pupil in this school of natural dramaturgy whose most familiar precursors were alchemy and astrology. The aesthetic properties of ceremony, formula, natural processes are intimations of complex and profound intellectual objects, but the difficulties in intellectual clarification and discrimination leave the mind in various attitudes of belief. For every intellectual object, half-comprehended, there is an aesthetic object before which we bow in more or less deep reverence. Pure aesthetic contemplation and complete intellectual clarity are seldom found in human beings, and any middle ground is touched with credulity and idolatry.

Ultimately the difficulty of clarification becomes impossibility. For the only method we have of isolating the symbol and articulating it with the idea is transformation by analogy, of which projection in geometry is a special case. We can take the word, or the thing, and break it up into parts and say that the relation of one part of the symbol to another is the same as the relation of one part of the idea to another. Thus we isolate and identify one relation in each, but the rest of the symbol remains confused. Further, the analogy by which this is done is itself another symbol with its own confusions and mysteries. Mathematics is as much a case of this as poetry. In despair of explanation we are driven to new analogies or new symbolic statements and a molehill becomes a mountain of significance.

As a matter of fact no explanation is needed. The coincidence of symbol and idea is an insight, a happy outcome for any intellectual process. In place of explanation there is continuous criticism of symbols. Symbols are metaphors or condensed analogies. They may be expanded into allegorical networks in which the relations may be distinguished and abstracted. Then more adequate symbols for these relations may be introduced by poet or mathematician. A critic again expands the resulting formula and new relations are discovered and again symbolized. So goes the life of reason from aesthetic object to intellectual object, gathering precious treasures of insight for the empirical scientist and man of action to use and enjoy.

The extraordinary position and power of proportions in mathematics and the essential metaphorical character of poetry are thus not mere accidents of history, but the key to an inward dialectic of thought. It is by expansion of metaphor that fact becomes intelligible, the world measured, and the complexities of experience described in language. Any history of thought might begin and end with the statement that man is an analogical animal.

## VIII Tragedy and comedy

The shift of attention in mathematics from ratios and proportions to functions has had many important consequences, or if you like, there have been corresponding shifts of attention in other fields. It has become increasingly obvious in the last few years that science is abandoning its single-minded devotion to mechanics and its appropriate methods of investigation for a new and apparently more flexible set of ideas. Some see in this an emancipation from the dogmatic

determinism of physics, and jump to the analogy of the biological organism. Others fear that it is a return to the pre-mechanistic theological attitude of mind and a consequent loss of skeptical rigor. Still others think of it as an impressionistic movement in science catching up with similar movements in art. As I see it, it is another case of the Pythagorean exploitation of mathematical forms. It is the latest betrothal of mathematics and poetry.

The mathematician has again been lured to an adventure with a symbolic hobbyhorse and has discovered new routes to the absolute or infinite. After a trial journey he has come back to earth and sets a new fashion in intellectual locomotion. The new vehicle feels like an airplane supported only by thin air, but the view from the rider's seat is familiar even though it involves distortions of the old perspective. Newly discovered abstractions always have an exotic manner.

Pythagoras and his disciples discovered certain numerical relations. Before they knew what they were doing, they had duplicated these relations and imputed them to geometry, calling the result magnitude. They again duplicated them and imputed them to musical instruments and sounds and called the result harmony. The accumulation was projected on the starry sky and the result was the harmony of the spheres. The process was so swift that they condensed their language and said that the world was a realm of numbers.

They had confused numbering numbers and numbered numbers. As we have seen, counting involves at least two similar series. Pythagoras saw not only two, but many more, and then said that they were all identical with the first. This was real and the rest of the world was confused experience, or prime matter. He might have done otherwise. Geometrical Pythagoreans saw the multiplication of triangles and said the world was a realm of triangles. It is an easy trick. Take any formula, find a similar form or some material that is plastic, select a suitable analogy, condense the analogy to a metaphor, take the metaphor literally, and you have a scientific philosophy. It has been done with less rigorous formulae than those of arithmetic and geometry. Thus mechanism came from the proportion, the Daltonian atom from weights and measures of the laboratory, the solar system from conic sections, Bohr's atom from the solar system, Marxian theory of history from mechanics and Christian theology.

Quite recently we have been invited to imagine movement without forces and mass, and qualities without substances. For some time the psychologist had been doing without soul and mind, and the political scientist without the sovereign state. The shock of all this is somewhat like the state of mind produced by Laplace's famous remark that he did not need God in physics. This is what happens when the mathematical physicist changes his mind, that is, his analogies.

In the present case he has been keeping company with the modern Pythagoreans. They have been analogizing with functions and the physicist has been giving us his account of their sayings. In describing functions they have been saying that for any value of the variable there is a corresponding value of the function. The physicist has asked the traditional question: What varies? and the Pythagorean has answered laconically: Everything, even the function is a variable. The so-called constants are only relations governing the variations, and even these so-called constants are only arbitrarily fixed by reference to still other merely arbitrary constants. Even the numbers are thus relative.

This would have been bad news in the seventeenth century, but since that time the physicist has been watching electrical phenomena and trying to keep his accounts straight in the old terms of proportions and equations where constants were constant. But latterly the ratios have slipped and the accounts have got tangled up. The numbers seem to be elastic. Forces, masses, and weights won't stay put. The elements begin to move about on the Mendeleeff chart. The old method of calculating errors of measurement seems to signify more than human and material imperfection. It is therefore good news now that mathematics has an analogous, but clearer notion to offer to the scientist. So the physicist has translated the language of the mathematician into his own terms and has had some terms such as mass, substance, force, or cause, left over. These he threw overboard and the accounts begin to come out straight again. The mathematics is now verified by observation. The new analogies work.

The result sounds like the biologist's description of organisms. They too are forms undergoing apparently significant variation in every part. Life is an equilibrium of changes. Aminals were for a time compared with machines, but with very meager results. Now the whole physical universe is compared to an organism with apparently great results. The physical universe is an organism of organisms. Or not to throw over the old tradition too quickly, the world is an organic mechanism. Biological function and mathematical function are the same. The analogy has been condensed, and the resulting metaphor is metaphysical truth. It spreads to psychology which needed it badly and, with suitable revisions, we have *Gestalten* or forms devouring the faculties of the soul, the complexes of the psyche, and the reflexes of the nervous system. It becomes a philosophy of life in emergent evolution. Pythagoras has another reincarnation in which the former rooster has become the superman.

Mathematics and poetry, as forms of thought, have a peculiar property which I have called expansiveness. They are always restless and hungry for more. Sometimes this has the aspect of the search for an absolute. In mathematics the appearance of this aspect is the sign of the completion of a symbolic episode, and the imminence of a new extension in the direction of greater generality. In poetry it is the sign of a religious and mystical peace and acquiescence. At other times expansiveness wears an air of piety to a tradition and devotes itself to the task of refinement and assimilation of detail. Both of these in terms of logic are the play of ultimate categories such as sameness and difference, one and many, and the being and not-being of negation and affirmation. A dialectical investigation of these, such as Plato made, would show that the play and consequently the expansion of ideas is unlimited except by the energy and inclination of thinking beings. Some have found in this a metaphysical secret.

There is a recurrent aphorism in philosophy that summarizes this feature of thought. It says that reality is a sphere having an infinite radius and a center at every point. I mentioned this in connection with the generalization of the notion of projective fields made by Bruno and Leibniz, and I might have added some of the dark remarks of Einstein about the shape of the universe. The saying is not wholly nonsensical; its principle of order can be stated.

The infinite sphere denotes a series of spheres each of which represents a stage of mathematical discovery. A set of assumptions is laid down and developed by deductive and intuitive methods into a system. The system so generated is a finite sphere. As soon as it is sufficiently developed, there is discovered an underlying set of assumptions with a larger system than the former as its consequence. When this is developed, it is a sphere including the former as one of its dependent parts. Modern multidimensional geometry thus includes Euclidean geometry. This latter sphere is in turn a subdivision of a still more inclusive sphere, and the expansive process apparently never ends. The study of comparative literature shows similarly ordered sets of allegories.

This is the cultural macrocosm. The microcosm of the individual mind is similar, and the corresponding series of spheres is an intellectual biography, a mind in the making.

We can be more explicit. The infinity of these spheres is suggestive of the number system with its densities, compactnesses, and continuities. The paradoxes of counting are solved by correlating the members of one series with those of another. We can bring a similar analogical calculus to bear on the series of mathematical and poetical spheres.

Mathematics deals with relations, and poetry deals with qualities. A sphere results when we can see the *relations* holding between *qualities*. Then the two series can be correlated. Mathematical functions find elementary values in qualities. Qualities find their relations in the functions of mathematics. Whenever this happens, a system is recognized, and it takes on a quasi-independence and reality. Often the effect in the thinker is a conviction. Belief attaches itself only to such systems. The further expansions and the wider assumptions are ignored and there is a resting point for thought in a mathematico-poetic allegory.

This is the secret of the drama which at its best undercuts the scientific and religious attitude of mind. Consequently the best metaphysical criticism of mathematics and poetry is to be found in the drama and the novel. Tragedy and comedy are the classic modes of treatment of this theme. Their analysis will exhibit it further.

The fundamental notions in tragedy are called *hybris* and *nemesis*. The first is the attitude of arrogance or insolence that arises from blindness in human nature. The second is the eventual consequence of that blindness and arrogance, the vengeance that the ignored factor in a situation takes on man and his virtues. These are moralistic terms but the intellectualistic transformation is easy. It can be performed on the terms of Aristotle's analysis of tragedy.

A tragic character must have besides hybris, the virtue of irony. This quality is the exercise of the capacity to discover and systematize clear ideas. It appears at first as a naïve idealism that makes it impossible to take circumstances at their face value, and expresses itself in a kind of satirical questioning, such as that of Socrates. Accompanying it is a sense of humor which condenses and dispels intervening fogs. At bottom it is a faith that there are ideas to be discovered and a conviction that the task is not easy. St. Francis and Don Quixote are additional good examples in literature. Dramatic tragedy usually discloses such a character in some advanced stage when the idea is in sight, so that action is understood as aiming to achieve its clarification. This is the situation presented in the prologue.

Action moves on exemplifying and expanding the idea. Even at this point there are at least two possible interpretations of the events. One is held by the audience who usually know the outcome already. The other is that held by the hero who is possessed of the idea to such an extent that he builds up a separate story or interpretation for himself in conformity with his ideal. Events pile up and are turned to his account by the alchemy of his own rationality. The situation becomes complicated and each event is charged with dramatic foreshadowing. The hero sees dilemmas in everything and sticks to his course in spite of the oppositions. His determination finally reaches desperation. This is the complication of the situation and the advent of hybris.

At length he is faced with some crucial and unavoidable predicament. He must decide. Using all his intellectual powers he makes the only decision possible on his interpretation of the situation. This is the crisis. In terms of mathematics and poetry, he has developed a system of relations, his idea; and the events have supplied a corresponding set of qualities. The situation is a full-rounded sphere.

Events come faster and pile themselves high on either side of his chosen path. They now have a threatening aspect for him, but there is no turning back. There is a dull inevitability about them. Finally they break and all is ruin with no compensating circumstance. This is the reversal of circumstance and catastrophe. The rounded sphere of apparent success is in a thousand pieces.

Then if he has the true quality of irony there is a recognition of what he had ignored. There comes the still small voice in the calm following the thunder and the earthquake, the voice of a god speaking not words of pity or revenge, but the decrees of necessity on his situation and his idea. Both are thrown upon a vaster background than he had envisaged, the doings of fate. In these decrees there is light and the hero recognizes himself, his idea, and his plight in terms of laws that are not for yesterday, today or tomorrow, but for always. This is the purgation.

But this may be only one episode, the first of a trilogy. The same hero, or another implicated character goes on into the new sphere with the new version of the eternal verities. No man should be judged happy until he is dead.

This pattern is the Greek view of life. It is the method of their and our science, history, and philosophy. In it poetry becomes criticism of life. It is, I believe, the final metaphysical conclusion of Greek philosophy in Plato and Aristotle.

The Greek employment of it had been humanistic in the main. The Greek tragic hero was a typical man isolated and projected on a background of fate. The late middle ages and the Renaissance substituted natural objects for the heroes of vicarious tragedies, the experiments in the laboratory. They put such objects under controlled conditions, introduced artificial complications, and waited for the answering pronouncement of fate. The crucial experiment is the crisis of an attempt to rationalize experience, that is, to force it into our analogies. Purgation and recognition are now called elimination of false hypotheses and verification. The shift is significant, but the essential tragic pattern of tragedy is still there. The popularizer of science is inviting us to reverse the change and rehumanize tragedy. There is some doubt whether he knows what he is proposing.

Tragedy proceeds by analogy and homogeneous substitution in the rationalizing thought of the hero. Events are prepared, "controlled," willed, interpreted, so as to be consistent with the idea or hypothesis. The direction of expansion is integration and generality. It ends in a cumulative catastrophe and a general purgation. Comedy seems to provide another method. It proceeds by wide variation and heterogeneous substitution. Every turn in the action marks an inconsistency discovered, a plan gone wrong, a platitude rendered paradoxical, a principle disproved, a fact caught in duplicity. There is expansion here also, but in the phase of discrimination and distinction-making. The hero of a comedy must see the point of every joke or of none, so that all the ideas may have equal opportunity for conflict and continual purgation. In a good comedy every idea must be deflated and purged by the ordeal of laughter. One laughs with or at the hero who exposes them and himself to the comic purgation.

Of course, there are many kinds of comedy, each type depending on some one of the types of heterogeneous substitution. There is the pun based on verbal substitution, the practical joke ranging from slapstick to farcical humor based on substitutions of actions for words or ideas. Finally, there is the comedy of manners based on the substitution of ideas. This can be illustrated in mathematics.

In the study of functions and their properties it is customary to substitute trial values for one variable at a time and watch the result in the values taken on by the other variables and the whole function in consequence. By a series of such trials the limiting values are found. This is the Greek method of solving equations and was revived in analytic geometry for the purpose of isolating the general properties of equations. It is also used in the calculus and the theory of functions. McClaurin substituted zero for x in Taylor's Series and discovered the method for expanding any function by using derivative functions. The study of maxima and minima, or the greatest and least values of functions, is another application. In general the unusual or unique values are substituted. Sometimes the result is an indeterminate or nonsensical expression, and some-

times it is a transformation into another class of functions whose unsuspected relations to the original class are thus discovered. The mathematical result is, as in the comedy of literature, a clarification and definition of the properties of the ideas involved.

The main points in the comparison of the forms of tragedy and comedy, and their modern descendants in drama and fiction, also the operation of the principles of substitution and expansion that relate them, may be seen in three versions of the Oedipus story.

The first is the Sophoclean argument:

The god, Apollo, has made it known through the Oracle at Delphi that the son of Laius, King of Thebes, will kill his father and marry Jocasta, his mother. In accordance with the Greek practice with regard to the pronouncements of the Oracle Laius plans to circumvent the divine decree by having his son Oedipus exposed. A shepherd is given the commission to dispose of the child. But he is touched by pity and hands him over to the care of another shepherd, who in turn passes him on to Polybus, King of Corinth, in whose house Oedipus is reared as heir to the Corinthian throne. As a grown man he hears a rumor that he is not the son of his apparent parents. He starts to Delphi to find out his true origin. On the way he meets a royal chariot, and is pushed off the narrow road by its attendants. He attacks the occupant, kills him, and the attendants also, except one who escapes.

Proceeding on his way, in due time he nears Thebes, which is mourning the death of its king. He who can answer the riddle of the Sphinx will be made king. Oedipus answers the riddle, is made king, and becomes famous for his just rule. Soon there are reports of a plague in the city of Thebes, and King Oedipus sends to the Delphic Oracle to learn its cause. The answer comes that the plague is punishment for a crime committed in the city. As soon as the offender is found and punished, the plague will disappear. The King imposes a penalty, exile, and curses the guilty. The investigation proceeds without result. Oedipus intensifies the search, and a rumor starts that he himself is the offender. He accuses his brother-in-law, Creon, of plotting to seize the throne for himself. The blind seer Teiresias is called in to arbitrate. He confirms the rumor against Oedipus and is accused of a lying conspiracy with Creon.

Finally, the escaped attendant on Laius' chariot is called in to describe the murderer of the former king. It is still uncertain, and the shepherds are sought. They convince Oedipus that he is guilty of incest and murdering his father. He puts out his own eyes, and Jocasta hangs herself. Blind Oedipus and his daughter, Antigone, go into exile to free the city of the plague.

The comic version might go as follows:

A shepherd has come to Thebes to celebrate a short vacation from sheep-watching. He is making merry with wine and old friends. They tell him about the death of the king and encourage him to answer the riddle of the Sphinx. In his state of inebriation and spiritual ecstasy he accidentally hits upon the right answer. He is taken to the court and made king of Thebes, by this time sober and embarrassed. He marries Jocasta.

In the course of time the ceremonies and royal duties begin to bore him. He plans to escape. The plague comes to Thebes. He sends an old shepherd friend as messenger to Delphi, instructing him before he leaves what his report is to be. The shepherd returns and says that the King is Oedipus, Laius' son, who escaped exposure, and has fulfilled the prophecy that he would kill his father and marry his mother. There is danger that the King and Queen will be stoned by the people.

Meanwhile Jocasta has fallen in love with the shepherd and is also bored with court life. The herald reports that she has hanged herself, and as they carry out a dummy corpse to show the people, the King and Queen escape by another route to the hills where they tend sheep in peace.

A modern novel:

King Laius of Thebes is loved by his people for his strong and just administration of the laws, but he has a bad temper. In a fit of temper brought on by some insubordination of his own six-year-old son, Oedipus, he bursts a blood vessel and dies. A regency is declared until Oedipus is old enough to take on his father's duties. Creon, the brother of Jocasta, the queen, becomes regent. Oedipus is sent to be educated at the Persian court.

At the age of twenty-one he returns, a man of the world, but in ill health. He is loved by the people because they think his ill health is due to his grief for his father, also because he reminds them of his father in his passion for justice. He marries the Princess of the house of Corinth, who also wins the hearts of the people because she resembles Jocasta, their former queen.

Some years later there is a plague in Thebes. The people are going blind. Oedipus' wife is a victim and dies. The Oracle is consulted and its answer is that the cause of the blindness is a mysterious Persian disease that has spread from the palace itself to the town. Oedipus hands over the throne to Haemon, the son of Creon, with whom Antigone, Oedipus' daughter, is in love. Antigone will not marry him for fear of continuing the plague. Oedipus grows blind, and Antigone devotes the rest of her life to caring for her father in a country home near Thebes. Haemon comes often to see her.

Oedipus dies calling for his mother and the sun.

Critical philosophy is the highest type of intellectual comedy, and Plato is the best comic poet of philosophy. It is said that Plato as a youth wrote comedies for the Olympic prizes. The plays are lost, but the marks of the comic poet are to be found in his dialogues. For in them we find all the types of humor bent to the somewhat tragic purpose of a moral philosophy. He is a master of heterogeneous substitution, and in the mouth of Socrates such substitutions get the sparkling expression that comedy should provide.

All the persons of the drama speak in character. In the early dialogues Socrates is talking with Sophists of one sort or another. He catches them making comic substitutions without a smile, usually aping a tragic *deus ex machina* in their manner and matter. He takes up the game and carries it to the extremes where the pun or witticism can be seen. These first dialogues should be read with one eye on the comic poet George Bernard Shaw, in whom the same Platonic blend of comedy and tragedy is articulate.

In the *Republic* Plato is exposing the Pythagorean secrets of the Delphic Oracle, which is the Greek analogue of our modern research foundations. It expounded the mathematical and poetic secrets of the universe in moral precepts for the people. In the later dialogues the theory of ideas, a common doctrine of the day and the pet device of Socrates to confound his opponents, undergoes the ordeal by laughter. The humor becomes more intellectual and abstract, and the sparkle becomes the play of philosophic insights. Poetry and mathematics meet and part in perfect freedom and lack of mutual embarrassment. Most of the dialogues end with an epilogue, the first part of which is mathematics, and the second part of which a poetic myth. Many have misunderstood these endings and taken the myth as the final interpretation of the mathematics. They do Plato a great injustice. His only conclusions are the clear and distinct ideas that his comic treatment reveals in unsuspected turns of the dialogues.

But comedy plays with the ideas to which tragedy has given birth. It is never the discoverer or creator. Plato's philosophy never quite frees its doctrines from their traditional origins, although it does give them an ideal dimension. The play of ideas is always hedged about with the darkness and mystery of tragic issues. This is inevitable. There probably never was a pure comedy or tragedy. The drama is often spoiled by a bad mixture of the two. Ibsen tried to fill comic situations with fate. Comic characters strut across the stage inflating the comedy, the play of local customs and popular science, with a pseudo-seriousness. This is the tragicomedy of the melodrama and contains a sentimental faith and a preaching hero. It is an unconscious parody on tragic purgation.

Ibsen on the other hand is an authentic historian, and the times he describes are not remote from the present. Most of us live with the mixture of poetry and mathematics in our heads which makes our understanding melodramatic. Our romanticism and our realism are seldom purged. One reason for this is that science is being preached to us before it is understood by the preachers. We apply it without irony and study it without humor. The consequence is sentimentalism in our action and mystification at the dénouement.

It is this situation that has aroused the present controversy over the popularization of science. It is a typical crisis in the life of reason. Reason oscillates between tragic pain and comic disillusionment. The popularizer is speaking seriously for the method of the laboratory. He is the stage manager for the world and wishes people to act and speak by the book of science. If his management were successful there would be the crisis in civilization which he foretells and fears. Whether there are enough tragic heroes to give it a high seriousness, nobody knows. But it seems at present that the actors have missed the spirit of the play. Most of them are melodramatic heroes and villains who now and then suffer comic relief. There are here and there signs of the play of clear and distinct ideas that go with comedy. There are a few individuals with insight and love of ideas, who understand without believing. But on the whole science is not yet a tradition within which one can play. The result is a confusion of mathematics and poetry in experience that I pointed out at the beginning.

It would be a pleasant prospect if this essay were an introduction to a *De Rerum Natura* or a *Divine Comedy.* When such a work is worthily done it will be clear what the difference between tragedy and comedy is. It will then be possible to decide what to do with modern scientific opinion. It is said that the function of theology has always been to spiritualize the sacraments, that is, to discover and formulate their symbolic function and to reduce popular belief in their causal efficacy to its proper status. The function of philosophical criticism is to intellectualize scientific method, that is, to discover and formulate its symbolic significance and to reduce popular belief in its causal efficacy to its proper status. With regard to the symbolic function of science and its conclusions, at present it can only be said that they are wavering shadows of those clear and distinct ideas without which experience is neither good nor true. Their present mathematical and poetic embodiments are intimations of some such immortality.

## NOTE TO THE READER

POETRY is the subject of Chapter 69 and MATHEMATICS that of Chapter 52 in the *Syntopicon.* Among the many references to the first, which are listed following the discussion of it, those at Topic 4 concerned with the major kinds of poetry, at Topics 7*a* and 7*b* dealing with plot and character, and at Topic 8 devoted to poetics are the most relevant. In the Chapter on MATHEMATICS, Topics 3 and 4, which deal with mathematical methods and techniques, indicate the readings that would be most useful to follow up.

Other *Syntopicon* chapters also contain readings that bear on these two subjects. Among such readings are those listed in Chapter 45, LANGUAGE, at Topic 9, which is concerned with the language of poetry; in Chapter 49, LOGIC, at Topic 4*a*, dealing with mathematical analysis and reasoning; in Chapter 76, on QUANTITY, at Topic 6*b*, concerned with mathematical procedures in measurement, such as ratio and proportions, and parameters and coordinates; and in Chapter 85, SIGN AND SYMBOL, where all of the readings listed at Topic 3, devoted to the patterns of meaning in human discourse, are in point.

There are several items in Volume 5 of *GGB* that deal with POETRY in various aspects and from various points of view. Among them are Matthew Arnold's essay "The Study of Poetry," pp. 19–41; Thomas de Quincey, "Literature of Knowledge and Literature of Power" and "On the Knocking at the Gate in Macbeth," pp. 358–66; Dr. Johnson's "Preface to Shakespeare," pp. 316–53; Shelley's "A Defense of Poetry," pp. 216–42; Schiller, "On Simple and Sentimental Poetry," pp. 155–211; and Whitman's "Preface" to *Leaves of Grass,* pp. 247–59.

There is an even larger selection of writings on MATHEMATICS in *GGB,* Vol. 9. See Norman R. Campbell, "Measurement" and "Numerical Laws and the Use of Mathematics," pp. 204–38; Andrew Russell Forsyth, "Mathematics, in Life and Thought," pp. 26–46; Lancelot Hogben, "Mathematics, the Mirror of Civilization," pp. 3–23; Henri Poincaré's "Mathematical Creation," pp. 294–304; three essays by Bertrand Russell—"The Study of Mathematics," "Mathematics and the Metaphysicians," and "Definition of Number"—pp. 84–117; and two more by Alfred North Whitehead—"On Mathematical Method," from *An Introduction to Mathematics,* and "On the Nature of a Calculus"—pp. 51–78.

# PICTURE CREDITS

*Key to abbreviations used to indicate location of pictures on page: r.—right; l.—left; t.—top; b.—bottom; c.—center; *—courtesy. Abbreviations are combined to indicate unusual placement.*

# Authors

*in Great Books of the Western World*

| | |
|---|---|
| Homer | Nicomachus |
| Aeschylus | Ptolemy |
| Sophocles | Marcus Aurelius |
| Herodotus | Galen |
| Euripides | Plotinus |
| Thucydides | Augustine |
| Hippocrates | Thomas Aquinas |
| Aristophanes | Dante |
| Plato | Chaucer |
| Aristotle | Machiavelli |
| Euclid | Copernicus |
| Archimedes | Rabelais |
| Apollonius | Montaigne |
| Lucretius | Gilbert |
| Virgil | Cervantes |
| Plutarch | Francis Bacon |
| Tacitus | Galileo |
| Epictetus | Shakespeare |
| | Kepler |